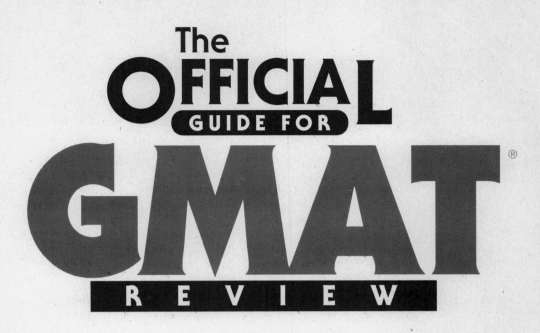

The OFFICIAL GUIDE FOR GMAT® REVIEW

Prepared for the
Graduate Management Admission Council
by Educational Testing Service

Inquiries concerning this publication should be directed to GMAT Program Direction Office,
Educational Testing Service, P.O. Box 6106, Princeton, NJ 08541-6106.

USA: 0-446-39207-3
CAN: 0-446-39208-1

In association with Warner Books, Inc., a Warner Communications Company

Contents

Contents *continued*

Graduate Management Admission Council

The Graduate Management Admission Council (GMAC) is an organization of graduate business and management schools sharing a common interest in professional management education. The Council provides information to schools and prospective students to help both make reasoned choices in the admission process. It also provides a forum for the exchange of information through research, educational programs, and other services among the broad constituency of individuals and institutions concerned with management education.

The Council has three basic service objectives:

1. to enhance the management education admission process by:

   ■ developing and administering appropriate assessment instruments;

   ■ developing other services and materials related to the selection process;

   ■ informing schools and students about the appropriate use of such instruments and materials;

   ■ providing opportunities for the exchange of information between students and schools.

2. to broaden knowledge about management education by:

   ■ conducting educational research;

   ■ disseminating information about relevant research;

   ■ encouraging the development and exchange of information by professionals in the field.

3. to promote the highest standards of professional practice in the administration of management education programs and related activities by:

   ■ developing appropriate standards of practice;

   ■ offering educational programs and publications to provide essential knowledge, skills, and values;

   ■ providing other opportunities for professional development.

The Council currently contracts with Educational Testing Service (ETS) for development of GMAT test material, administration of the GMAT test, and preparation and distribution of GMAT score reports. The Council also determines policies and procedures for research and development of the GMAT; for publication of materials for students, guidance counselors, and admissions officers; and for nontesting services offered to management schools and applicants.

Member Schools

Arizona State University
College of Business

Babson College
Graduate School of Business

Baruch College
School of Business and Public Administration

Baylor University
Hankamer School of Business

Boston College
The Wallace E. Carroll Graduate School of Management

Boston University
School of Management

Bowling Green State University
College of Business Administration

Brigham Young University
Marriott School of Management

California State University, Los Angeles
School of Business and Economics

Carnegie Mellon University
Graduate School of Industrial Administration

Case Western Reserve University
Weatherhead School of Management

Clark Atlanta University
Graduate School of Business Administration

College of William and Mary
Graduate School of Business Administration

Columbia University
Columbia Business School

Cornell University
Johnson Graduate School of Management

Dartmouth College
Amos Tuck School of Business Administration

Duke University
Fuqua School of Business

East Carolina University
School of Business

Emory University
Emory Business School

Florida State University
College of Business

George Mason University
School of Business Administration

Georgetown University
School of Business Administration

Georgia Institute of Technology
College of Management

Georgia State University
College of Business Administration

Hofstra University
School of Business

Howard University
School of Business

Indiana University (Bloomington)
Graduate School of Business

Kent State University
Graduate School of Management

Lehigh University
College of Business and Economics

Marquette University
College of Business Administration

Massachusetts Institute of Technology
Sloan School of Management

Michigan State University
Graduate School of Business Administration

New York University
Leonard N. Stern School of Business

Northeastern University
Graduate School of Business Administration

Northwestern University
J. L. Kellogg Graduate School of Management

The Ohio State University
College of Business

Penn State University Park Campus
College of Business Administration

Purdue University (West Lafayette)
Krannert Graduate School of Management

Rollins College
Roy E. Crummer Graduate School of Business

Rutgers, The State University of New Jersey
Graduate School of Management

San Francisco State University
School of Business

Seton Hall University
W. Paul Stillman School of Business

Southern Methodist University
Edwin L. Cox School of Business

Stanford University
Graduate School of Business

Syracuse University
School of Management

Temple University
School of Business and Management

Texas A&M University
College of Business Administration

Texas Christian University
M. J. Neeley School of Business

Tulane University
A. B. Freeman School of Business

The University of Alabama
Manderson Graduate School of Business

University of Arizona
Karl Eller Graduate School of Management

University at Buffalo (State University of New York)
School of Management

University of California at Berkeley
Walter A. Haas School of Business

University of California, Irvine
Graduate School of Management

University of California, Los Angeles
John E. Anderson Graduate School of Management

The University of Chicago
Graduate School of Business

University of Cincinnati
College of Business Administration

University of Colorado (Boulder)
Graduate School of Business Administration

University of Connecticut (Storrs)
School of Business Administration

University of Denver
Graduate School of Business

University of Florida
Graduate School of Business

University of Georgia
Graduate School of Business Administration

University of Hawaii at Manoa
College of Business Administration

University of Houston
College of Business Administration

University of Illinois at Chicago
College of Business Administration

University of Illinois at Urbana-Champaign
College of Commerce and Business Administration

University of Iowa
College of Business Administration

The University of Kansas
School of Business

University of Kentucky
College of Business and Economics

University of Maryland
College of Business and Management

University of Miami
Graduate Business Programs

The University of Michigan (Ann Arbor)
The Michigan Business School

University of Minnesota
Curtis L. Carlson School of Management

University of Missouri—Columbia
College of Business and Public Administration

University of Missouri—St. Louis
School of Business Administration

University of North Carolina at Chapel Hill
CUNC Business School at Chapel Hill

University of Notre Dame
College of Business Administration

University of Oklahoma
College of Business Administration

University of Pennsylvania
The Wharton School (Graduate Division)

University of Pittsburgh
Joseph M. Katz Graduate School of Business

University of Rhode Island
College of Business Administration

University of Richmond
Richard S. Reynolds Graduate School

University of Rochester
William E. Simon Graduate School of
    Business Administration

University of San Francisco
McLaren College of Business

University of South Carolina
College of Business Administration

University of South Florida
College of Business Administration

University of Southern California
Graduate School of Business Administration

The University of Tennessee, Knoxville
College of Business Administration

University of Texas at Austin
Graduate School of Business

The University of Tulsa
College of Business Administration

University of Utah
Graduate School of Business

University of Virginia
The Colgate Darden Graduate School of
    Business Administration

University of Washington
Graduate School of Business Administration

University of Wisconsin—Milwaukee
School of Business Administration

Vanderbilt University
Owen Graduate School of Management

Virginia Commonwealth University
School of Business

Virginia Polytechnic Institute and State University
R. B. Pamplin College of Business

Washington State University
College of Business and Economics

Washington University (St. Louis)
John M. Olin School of Business

Introduction

The Official Guide for GMAT Review has been designed and written by the staff of Educational Testing Service, which prepares the Graduate Management Admission Test used by many graduate schools of business and management as one criterion in considering applications for admission to their graduate programs. This book is intended to be a general guide to the kinds of verbal and mathematical questions likely to appear in the GMAT. All questions used to illustrate the various types of questions are taken from actual editions of the GMAT administered between June 1982 and June 1989.*

The GMAT is not a test of knowledge in specific subjects—for example, it does not test knowledge specifically or uniquely acquired in accounting or economics courses. Rather, it is a test of certain skills and abilities that have been found to contribute to success in graduate programs in business and management. For this reason, it is useful to familiarize yourself with the general types of questions likely to be found in editions of the GMAT and the reasoning skills and problem-solving strategies that these types of questions demand. This book illustrates various types of questions that appear in the GMAT and explains in detail some of the most effective strategies for mastering these questions.

The most efficient and productive way to use this book is to read first through Chapter 1. Each type of question is briefly described, the directions are given, one or two examples are presented, and the skills each question type measures are outlined. You should pay particular attention to the directions for each question type. This is especially important for the Data Sufficiency questions, which have lengthy and complex directions.

Chapters 3-7 provide detailed illustrations and explanations of individual question types. After you read Chapter 1, you will find the most advantageous way to use the book is to choose a chapter on a particular question type, read carefully the introductory material, and then do the sample test sections in that chapter. As you take the sample test sections, follow the directions and time specifications given. When you complete a sample test section, use the answer key that follows it to check your responses. Then review the sample test section carefully, spending as much time as is necessary to familiarize yourself with the range of questions or problems presented in the sample test section.

You may find it useful to read through all of Chapter 2, Math Review, before working through Chapters 3, Problem Solving, and 4, Data Sufficiency, or you may wish to use Chapter 2 as a reference, noting—in Chapters 3 and 4—the suggested sections at the end of each explanation following the first sample test sections as you go along. However, since Chapter 2 is intended to provide you with a comprehensive review of the basic mathematical concepts used in the quantitative sections of the GMAT, you may find it valuable to read through the chapter as a whole.

The introductory material, sample test sections, and answer keys to the sample test sections in Chapter 5, Reading Comprehension, Chapter 6, Critical Reasoning, and Chapter 7, Sentence Correction, should be approached in the way suggested above. The explanatory materials for Reading Comprehension and Critical Reasoning have been written as thorough explanations of the reasoning and problem-solving challenges each question type presents. Demonstrating strategies for successfully meeting these challenges, regardless of the particular content of the questions or problems that appear in a specific edition of the GMAT, is the objective of these explanations.

After you complete the review and practice built in to each chapter you should turn to Chapter 8, which includes an authentic GMAT test. It will be most helpful in preparing yourself to take the GMAT if you regard the test in Chapter 8 as a facsimile of the test you will take for scoring. Time yourself on each section, and follow the directions exactly as given.

Following the test reprinted in Chapter 8 is an answer key, information about scoring and score interpretation, and an explanation for every question on that test. Guidelines for the use of GMAT scores are also given.

---

*The material in *The Official Guide for GMAT Review* is intended to familiarize you with the types of questions found on the GMAT. Although the questions on the sample test sections in Chapters 3-7 represent the general nature of the questions on the test, it is possible that a type of question not illustrated by and explained in the *Guide* may appear on the GMAT. It is also possible that material illustrated by and explained in the *Guide* may not appear on the test.

1 Description of the Graduate Management Admission Test

The Graduate Management Admission Test is designed to help graduate schools assess the qualifications of applicants for advanced study in business and management. The test can be used by both schools and students in evaluating verbal and mathematical skills as well as general knowledge and preparation for graduate study. Note, however, that GMAT scores should be considered as only one of several indicators of ability.

Format

The current GMAT consists entirely of multiple-choice questions, which are divided among seven separately timed sections; the total testing time is about three and a half hours. Each question offers five choices from which the examinee is to select the best answer.

Every form of the test contains one section of trial questions that are needed for pretesting and equating purposes. These questions, however, are not identified, and you should do your best on all questions. The answers to trial questions are not counted in your test score.

Both the Graduate Management Admission Council and Educational Testing Service are aware of the limits of the multiple-choice format, particularly in measuring an applicant's ability to formulate general concepts or to develop detailed supportive or opposing arguments. However, in a national testing program designed for a wide variety of people with different backgrounds, the use of a large number of short, multiple-choice questions has proved to be an effective and reliable way of providing a fair and valid evaluation of specific skills.

Content

It is important to recognize that the GMAT evaluates skills and abilities that develop over relatively long periods of time. Although the sections are basically verbal or mathematical, the complete test provides one method of measuring overall ability. The GMAT does not test specific knowledge obtained in college course work, and it does not seek to measure achievements in any specific areas of study.

The Graduate Management Admission Council recognizes that questions arise concerning techniques for taking standardized examinations such as the GMAT, and it is hoped that the descriptions, sample test sections, and explanations given here, along with the authentic test, will give you a practical familiarity with both the concepts and techniques required by GMAT questions.

The material on the following pages provides a general description and brief discussion of the objectives and techniques for each question type.

Following this general description of the GMAT are a math review designed to help you review basic mathematical skills useful in the Problem Solving and Data Sufficiency sections of the GMAT and five chapters, one for each question type, that present sample test sections with answer keys and detailed explanations of the specific question types and of all questions and answers from the sample test sections. (The sample test sections are made up of questions that have appeared in the actual GMAT.) Methods of determining the best answer to a particular kind of question as well as explanations of the different kinds of questions appearing in any one section are also presented in these chapters. Chapter 8 contains an authentic GMAT test. This is followed by an answer key, explanations for each question, and scoring information, which explains how GMAT scores are calculated and how they are interpreted.

Problem Solving Questions

This section of the GMAT is designed to test (1) basic mathematical skills, (2) understanding of elementary mathematical concepts, and (3) the ability to reason quantitatively and to solve quantitative problems. Approximately half the problems in the test are in a mathematical setting; the remainder are based on "real life" situations.

WHAT IS MEASURED

Problem Solving questions test your ability to understand verbal descriptions of situations and to solve problems using arithmetic, elementary algebra, or commonly known concepts of geometry.

The directions for Problem Solving questions read as follows:

Directions: In this section solve each problem, using any available space on the page for scratchwork. Then indicate the best of the answer choices given.

Numbers: All numbers used are real numbers.

Figures: Figures that accompany problems in this section are intended to provide information useful in solving the problems. They are drawn as accurately as possible EXCEPT when it is stated in a specific problem that its figure is not drawn to scale. All figures lie in a plane unless otherwise indicated.

Data Sufficiency Questions

Each of the problems in the Data Sufficiency section of the GMAT consists of a question, often accompanied by some initial information, and two statements, labeled (1) and (2), containing additional information. You must decide whether sufficient information to answer the question is given by either (1) or (2) individually or—if not—by both combined.

These are the directions that you will find for the Data Sufficiency section of the GMAT. Read them carefully.

Directions: Each of the data sufficiency problems below consists of a question and two statements, labeled (1) and (2), in which certain data are given. You have to decide whether the data given in the statements are *sufficient* for answering the question. Using the data given in the statements *plus* your knowledge of mathematics and everyday facts (such as the number of days in July or the meaning of *counterclockwise*), you are to fill in oval

A if statement (1) ALONE is sufficient, but statement (2) alone is not sufficient to answer the question asked;

B if statement (2) ALONE is sufficient, but statement (1) alone is not sufficient to answer the question asked;

C if BOTH statements (1) and (2) TOGETHER are sufficient to answer the question asked, but NEITHER statement ALONE is sufficient;

D if EACH statement ALONE is sufficient to answer the question asked;

E if statements (1) and (2) TOGETHER are NOT sufficient to answer the question asked, and additional data specific to the problem are needed.

Numbers: All numbers used are real numbers.

Figures: A figure in a data sufficiency problem will conform to the information given in the question, but will not necessarily conform to the additional information given in statements (1) and (2).

You may assume that lines shown as straight are straight and that angle measures are greater than zero.

You may assume that the positions of points, angles, regions, etc., exist in the order shown.

All figures lie in a plane unless otherwise indicated.

Example:

In $\triangle PQR$, what is the value of x?

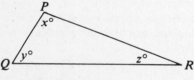

(1) $PQ = PR$
(2) $y = 40$

Explanation: According to statement (1), $PQ = PR$; therefore, $\triangle PQR$ is isosceles and $y = z$. Since $x + y + z = 180$, $x + 2y = 180$. Since statement (1) does not give a value for y, you cannot answer the question using statement (1) by itself. According to statement (2), $y = 40$; therefore, $x + z = 140$. Since statement (2) does not give a value for z, you cannot answer the question using statement (2) by itself. Using both statements together you can find y and z; therefore, you can find x, and the answer to the problem is C.

WHAT IS MEASURED

Data Sufficiency questions are designed to measure your ability to analyze a quantitative problem, to recognize which information is relevant, and to determine at what point there is sufficient information to solve the problem.

Reading Comprehension Questions

The Reading Comprehension section is made up of several reading passages about which you will be asked interpretive, applicative, and inferential questions. The passages are up to 450 words long, and they discuss topics from the social sciences, the physical or biological sciences, and business-related fields such as marketing, economics, and human resource management. Because every Reading Comprehension section includes passages from several different content areas, you will probably be generally familiar with some of the material; however, neither the passages nor the questions assume detailed knowledge of the topics discussed.

WHAT IS MEASURED

Reading Comprehension questions measure your ability to understand, analyze, and apply information and concepts presented in written form. All questions are to be answered on the basis of what is stated or implied in the reading material, and no specific knowledge of the material is required. Reading Comprehension therefore, evaluates your ability to

- understand words and statements in the reading passages (Questions of this type are not vocabulary questions. These questions test your understanding of and ability to use specialized terms as well as your understanding of the English language. You may also find that questions of this type ask about the overall meaning of a passage);

- understand the logical relationships between significant points and concepts in the reading passages (For example, such questions may ask you to determine the strong and weak points of an argument or to evaluate the importance of arguments and ideas in a passage);

- draw inferences from facts and statements in the reading passages (The inference questions will ask you to consider factual statements or information and, on the basis of that information, reach a general conclusion);

- understand and follow the development of quantitative concepts as they are presented in verbal material (This may involve the interpretation of numerical data or the use of simple arithmetic to reach conclusions about material in a passage).

The directions for Reading Comprehension questions read as follows:

Directions: Each passage in this group is followed by questions based on its content. After reading a passage, choose the best answer to each question and fill in the corresponding oval on the answer sheet. Answer all questions following a passage on the basis of what is *stated* or *implied* in that passage.

Critical Reasoning Questions

The Critical Reasoning section of the GMAT is designed to test the reasoning skills involved (1) in making arguments, (2) in evaluating arguments, and (3) in formulating or evaluating a plan of action. Most of the questions are based on a separate argument or set of statements; occasionally, two or three questions are based on the same argument or set of statements. The materials on which questions are based are drawn from a variety of sources. No familiarity with the subject matter of those materials is presupposed.

WHAT IS MEASURED

Critical Reasoning questions are designed to provide one measure of your ability to reason effectively in the areas of

- argument construction (Questions in this category may ask you to recognize such things as the basic structure of an argument; properly drawn conclusions; underlying assumptions; well-supported explanatory hypotheses; parallels between structurally similar arguments);

- argument evaluation (Questions in this category may ask you to analyze a given argument and to recognize such things as factors that would strengthen, or weaken, the given argument; reasoning errors committed in making that argument; aspects of the method by which the argument proceeds);

- formulating and evaluating a plan of action (Questions in this category may ask you to recognize such things as the relative appropriateness, effectiveness, or efficiency of different plans of action; factors that would strengthen, or weaken, the prospects of success for a proposed plan of action; assumptions underlying a proposed plan of action).

The directions for Critical Reasoning questions read as follows:

Directions: For each question in this section, select the best of the answer choices given.

Sentence Correction Questions

Sentence Correction questions ask you which of the five choices best expresses an idea or relationship. The questions will require you to be familiar with the stylistic conventions and grammatical rules of standard written English and to demonstrate your ability to improve incorrect or ineffective expressions.

WHAT IS MEASURED

Sentence Correction questions test two broad aspects of language proficiency:

1. *Correct expression.* A correct sentence is grammatically and structurally sound. It conforms to all the rules of standard written English (for example: noun-verb agreement, noun-pronoun agreement, pronoun consistency, pronoun case, and verb tense sequence). Further, a correct sentence will not have dangling, misplaced, or improperly formed modifiers, will not have unidiomatic or inconsistent expressions, and will not have faults in parallel construction.

2. *Effective expression.* An effective sentence expresses an idea or relationship clearly and concisely as well as grammatically. This does not mean that the choice with the fewest and simplest words is necessarily the best answer. It means that there are no superfluous words or needlessly complicated expressions in the best choice.

In addition, an effective sentence uses proper diction. (Diction refers to the standard dictionary meaning of words and the appropriateness of words in context.) In evaluating the diction of a sentence, you must be able to recognize whether the words are well chosen, accurate, and suitable for the context.

The directions for Sentence Correction questions read as follows:

Directions: In each of the following sentences, some part of the sentence or the entire sentence is underlined. Beneath each sentence you will find five ways of phrasing the underlined part. The first of these repeats the original; the other four are different. If you think the original is better than any of the alternatives, choose answer A; otherwise choose one of the others. Select the best version and fill in the corresponding oval on your answer sheet.

This is a test of correctness and effectiveness of expression. In choosing answers, follow the requirements of standard written English; that is, pay attention to grammar, choice of words, and sentence construction.

Choose the answer that expresses most effectively what is presented in the original sentence; this answer should be clear and exact, without awkwardness, ambiguity, or redundancy.

Examples:
A thunderclap is a complex acoustic signal <u>as a result of</u> rapid expansion of heated air in the path of a lightning flash.

(A) as a result of
(B) caused as a result of
(C) resulting because of the
(D) resulting from the
(E) that results because there is

In choice A, *is a . . . . signal as a result of* is incorrect. It is the thunderclap that results from the expansion; its being a signal is irrelevant. In choice B, it is superfluous to use both *caused* and *result,* and it is also superfluous to use both *result* and *because* in choices C and E. In choice C, *because of* is not the correct preposition to use after *resulting; from* is correct and is used in the best answer, D.

<u>Ever since the Civil War, the status of women was</u> a live social issue in this country.

(A) Ever since the Civil War, the status of women was
(B) Since the Civil War, women's status was
(C) Ever since the Civil War, the status of women has been
(D) Even at the time of the Civil War, the status of women has been
(E) From the times of the Civil War, the status of women has been

In choice A, the verb following *women* should be *has been,* not *was,* because *ever since* denotes a period of time continuing from the past into the present. For the same reason, *was* is inappropriately used with *since* in choice B. In choice D, *even at* changes the meaning of the original sentence substantially and does not fit with *has been; was* is correct with *even at.* In choice E, *times* is incorrect; the standard phrase is *from the time of.* C is the best answer.

General Test-Taking Suggestions

1. Although the GMAT stresses accuracy more than speed, it is important to use the allotted time wisely. You will be able to do so if you are familiar with the mechanics of the test and the kinds of materials, questions, and directions in the test. Therefore, become familiar with the formats and requirements of each section of the test.

2. After you become generally familiar with all question types, use the individual chapters on each question type in this book (Chapters 3-7), which include sample test sections and detailed explanations, to prepare yourself for the actual GMAT test in Chapter 8. When taking the test, try to follow all the requirements specified in the directions and keep within the time limits.

While this test is useful for familiarization, it cannot be used to predict your performance on the actual test.

3. Read all test directions carefully. Since many answer sheets give indications that the examinees do not follow directions, this suggestion is particularly important. The directions explain exactly what each section requires in order to answer each question type. If you read hastily, you may miss important instructions and seriously jeopardize your scores.

4. Answer as many questions as possible, but avoid random guessing. Your GMAT scores will be based on the number of questions you answer correctly minus a fraction of the number you answer incorrectly. Therefore, it is unlikely that mere guessing will improve your scores significantly, and it does take time. However, if you have some knowledge of a question and can eliminate at least one of the answer choices as wrong, your chance of getting the best answer is improved, and it will be to your advantage to answer the question. If you know nothing at all about a particular question, it is probably better to skip it. The number of omitted questions will not be subtracted.

5. Take a watch to the examination and be sure to note the time limit for each section. Since each question has the same weight, it is not wise to spend too much time on one question if that causes you to neglect other questions.

6. Make every effort to pace yourself. Work steadily and as rapidly as possible without being careless.

7. A wise practice is to answer the questions you are sure of first. Then, if time permits, go back and attempt the more difficult questions.

8. Read each question carefully and thoroughly. Before answering a question, determine exactly what is being asked. Never skim a question or the possible answers. Skimming may cause you to miss important information or nuances in the question.

9. Do not become upset if you cannot answer a question. A person can do very well without answering every question or finishing every section. No one is expected to get a perfect score.

10. When you take the test, you will mark your answers on a separate answer sheet. As you go through the test, be sure that the number of each answer on the answer sheet matches the corresponding question number in the test book. Your answer sheet may contain space for more answers or questions than there are in the test book. Do not be concerned, but be careful. Indicate each of your answers with a dark mark that completely fills the response position on the answer sheet. Light or partial marks may not be properly read by the scoring machine. Indicate only one response to each question, and erase all unintended marks completely.

GMAT: Test Specifications

All editions of the GMAT are constructed to measure the same skills and meet the same specifications. Thus, each section of the test is constructed according to the same specifications for every edition of the GMAT. These specifications include definite requirements for the number of questions, the points tested by each question, the kinds of questions, and the difficulty of each question.

Because the various editions of the test inevitably differ somewhat in difficulty, they are made equivalent to each other by statistical methods. This equating process makes it possible to assure that all reported scores of a given value denote approximately the same level of ability regardless of the edition being used or of the particular group taking the test at a given time.

Test Development Process

Educational Testing Service professional staff responsible for developing the verbal measures of the GMAT have backgrounds and advanced degrees in the humanities or in measurement. Those responsible for the quantitative portion have advanced degrees in mathematics or related fields.

Standardized procedures have been developed to guide the test-generation process, to assure high-quality test material, to avoid idiosyncratic questions, and to encourage development of test material that is widely appropriate.

An important part of the development of test material is the review process. Each question, as well as any stimulus material on which questions are based, must be reviewed by several independent critics. In appropriate cases, questions are also reviewed by experts outside ETS who can bring fresh perspectives to bear on the questions in terms of actual content or in terms of sensitivity to minority and women's concerns.

After the questions have been reviewed and revised as appropriate, they are assembled into clusters suitable for trial during actual administrations of the GMAT. In this manner, new questions are tried out, under standard testing conditions, by representative samples of GMAT examinees. Questions being tried out do not affect examinees' scores but are themselves evaluated: they are analyzed statistically for usefulness and weaknesses. The questions that perform satisfactorily become part of a pool of questions from which future editions of the GMAT can be assembled; those that do not are rewritten to correct the flaws and tried out again—or discarded.

In preparing those sections of the GMAT that will contribute to the scoring process, the test assembler uses only questions that have been successfully tried out. The test assembler considers not only each question's characteristics but also the relationship of the question to the entire group of questions with respect to the test specifications discussed above. When the test has been assembled, it is reviewed by a second test specialist and by the test development coordinator for the GMAT.

After satisfactory resolution of any points raised in these reviews, the test goes to a test editor. The test editor's review is likely to result in further suggestions for change, and the test assembler must decide how these suggested changes will be handled. If a suggested change yields an editorial improvement, without jeopardizing content integrity, the change is adopted; otherwise, new wording is sought that will meet the dual concerns of content integrity and editorial style. The review process is continued at each stage of test assembly and copy preparation, down to careful scrutiny of the final proof immediately prior to printing.

All reviewers except the editor and proofreader must attempt to answer each question without the help of the answer key. Thus, each reviewer "takes the test," uninfluenced by knowledge of what the question writer or test assembler believed each answer should be. The answer key is certified as official only after at least three reviewers have agreed independently on the best answer for each question.

The extensive, careful procedure described here has been developed over the years to assure that every question in any new edition of the GMAT is appropriate and useful and that the combination of questions that make up the new edition is satisfactory. Nevertheless, the appraisal is not complete until after the new edition has been administered during a national test administration and subjected to a rigorous process of analysis to see whether each question yields the expected result. This further appraisal sometimes reveals that a question is not satisfactory after all; it may prove to be ambiguous, or require information beyond the scope of the test, or be otherwise unsuitable. Answers to such questions are not used in computing scores.

2 Math Review

Although this chapter provides a review of some of the mathematical concepts of arithmetic, algebra, and geometry, it is not intended to be a textbook. You should use this chapter to familiarize yourself with the kinds of topics that are tested in the GMAT. You may wish to consult an arithmetic, algebra, or geometry book for a more detailed discussion of some of the topics.

The topics that are covered in Section A, arithmetic, include:

1. Properties of integers
2. Fractions
3. Decimals
4. Real numbers
5. Positive and negative numbers
6. Ratio and proportion
7. Percents
8. Equivalent forms of a number
9. Powers and roots of numbers
10. Mean
11. Median
12. Mode

The content of Section B, algebra, does not extend beyond what is covered in a first-year high school course. The topics included are:

1. Simplifying algebraic expressions
2. Equations
3. Solving linear equations with one unknown
4. Solving two linear equations with two unknowns
5. Solving factorable quadratic equations
6. Exponents
7. Absolute value
8. Inequalities

Section C, geometry, is limited primarily to measurement and intuitive geometry or spatial visualization. Extensive knowledge of theorems and the ability to construct proofs, skills that are usually developed in a formal geometry course, are not tested. The topics included in this section are:

1. Lines
2. Intersecting lines and angles
3. Perpendicular lines
4. Parallel lines
5. Polygons (convex)
6. Triangles
7. Quadrilaterals
8. Circles
9. Solids
10. Rectangular solids
11. Cylinders
12. Pyramids
13. Coordinate geometry

Section D, word problems, presents examples of and solutions to the following types of word problems:

1. Rate
2. Work
3. Mixture
4. Interest
5. Discount
6. Profit
7. Sets
8. Geometry
9. Measurement
10. Data interpretation

A. Arithmetic

1. INTEGERS

An *integer* is any number in the set $\{\ldots, -3, -2, -1, 0, 1, 2, 3, \ldots\}$. If x and y are integers and $x \neq 0$, x is a *divisor* (*factor*) of y provided that $y = xn$ for some integer n. In this case y is also said to be *divisible* by x or to be a *multiple* of x. For example, 7 is a divisor or factor of 28 since $28 = 7 \cdot 4$, but 6 is not a divisor of 28 since there is no integer n such that $28 = 6n$.

Any integer that is divisible by 2 is an *even integer*; the set of even integers is $\{\ldots -4, -2, 0, 2, 4, 6, 8, \ldots\}$. Integers that are not divisible by 2 are *odd integers*; $\{\ldots -3, -1, 1, 3, 5, \ldots\}$ is the set of odd integers.

If at least one factor of a product of integers is even, then the product is even; otherwise the product is odd. If two integers are both even or both odd, then their sum and their difference are even. Otherwise, their sum and their difference are odd.

A *prime* number is an integer that has exactly two different positive divisors, 1 and itself. For example, 2, 3, 5, 7, 11, and 13 are prime numbers, but 15 is not, since 15 has four different positive divisors, 1, 3, 5, and 15. The number 1 is not a prime number, since it has only one positive divisor.

The numbers -2, -1, 0, 1, 2, 3, 4, 5 are *consecutive integers*. Consecutive integers can be represented by n, n + 1, n + 2, n + 3, . . ., where n is an integer. The numbers 0, 2, 4, 6, 8 are *consecutive even integers*, and 1, 3, 5, 7, 9 are *consecutive odd integers*. Consecutive even integers can be represented by 2n, 2n + 2, 2n + 4, . . ., and consecutive odd integers can be represented by 2n + 1, 2n + 3, 2n + 5, . . ., where n is an integer.

Properties of the integer 1. If n is any number, then $1 \cdot n = n$, and for any number $n \neq 0$, $n \cdot \frac{1}{n} = 1$. The number 1 can be expressed in many ways, e.g., $\frac{n}{n} = 1$ for any number $n \neq 0$. Multiplying or dividing an expression by 1, in any form, does not change the value of that expression.

Properties of the integer zero. The integer zero is neither positive nor negative. If n is any number, then $n + 0 = n$ and $n \cdot 0 = 0$. Division by zero is not defined.

2. FRACTIONS

In a fraction $\frac{n}{d}$, n is the *numerator* and d is the *denominator*. The denominator of a fraction can never be zero, because division by zero is not defined.

Two fractions are said to be *equivalent* if they represent the same number. For example, $\frac{4}{8}$, $\frac{3}{6}$, and $\frac{1}{2}$ are equivalent since all three represent the number $\frac{1}{2}$.

Addition and subtraction of fractions. To add or subtract two fractions with the same denominator, simply perform the required operation with the numerators, leaving the denominators the same. For example, $\frac{3}{5} + \frac{4}{5} = \frac{3+4}{5} = \frac{7}{5}$, and $\frac{5}{7} - \frac{2}{7} = \frac{5-2}{7} = \frac{3}{7}$. If two fractions do not have the same denominator, express them as equivalent fractions with the same denominator. For example, to add $\frac{3}{5}$ and $\frac{4}{7}$, multiply the numerator and denominator of the first fraction by 7 and the numerator and denominator of the second fraction by 5, obtaining $\frac{21}{35}$ and $\frac{20}{35}$, respectively;

$$\frac{21}{35} + \frac{20}{35} = \frac{41}{35}.$$

Also,

$$\frac{2}{3} + \frac{1}{6} = \frac{2}{3} \cdot \frac{2}{2} + \frac{1}{6} = \frac{4}{6} + \frac{1}{6} = \frac{5}{6}.$$

Multiplication and division of fractions. To multiply two fractions, simply multiply the two numerators and multiply the two denominators. For example, $\frac{2}{3} \times \frac{4}{7} = \frac{2 \times 4}{3 \times 7} = \frac{8}{21}$.

To divide by a fraction, invert the divisor (i.e., find its *reciprocal*) and multiply. For example, $\frac{2}{3} \div \frac{4}{7} = \frac{2}{3} \times \frac{7}{4} = \frac{14}{12} = \frac{7}{6}$.

In the problem above, the reciprocal of $\frac{4}{7}$ is $\frac{7}{4}$. In general, the reciprocal of a fraction $\frac{n}{d}$ is $\frac{d}{n}$, where n and d are not zero.

Mixed numbers. A number that consists of a whole number and a fraction, e.g., $7\frac{2}{3}$, is a mixed number. $7\frac{2}{3}$ means $7 + \frac{2}{3}$.

To change a mixed number into a fraction, multiply the whole number by the denominator of the fraction and add this number to the numerator of the fraction; then put the result over the denominator of the fraction. For example,

$$7\frac{2}{3} = \frac{(3 \times 7) + 2}{3} = \frac{23}{3}.$$

3. DECIMALS

In the decimal system, the position of the period or *decimal point* determines the place value of the digits. For example, the digits in the number 7,654.321 have the following place values:

Thousands	Hundreds	Tens	Ones or units	Tenths	Hundredths	Thousandths
7 ,	6	5	4 .	3	2	1

Some examples of decimals follow.

$$0.321 = \frac{3}{10} + \frac{2}{100} + \frac{1}{1,000} = \frac{321}{1,000}$$

$$0.0321 = \frac{0}{10} + \frac{3}{100} + \frac{2}{1,000} + \frac{1}{10,000} = \frac{321}{10,000}$$

$$1.56 = 1 + \frac{5}{10} + \frac{6}{100} = \frac{156}{100}$$

Sometimes decimals are expressed as the product of a number with only one digit to the left of the decimal point and a power of 10. For example, 231 may be written as 2.31×10^2 and 0.0231 may be written as 2.31×10^{-2}. The exponent on the 10 indicates the number of places that the decimal point is to be moved in the number that is to be multiplied by a power of 10 in order to obtain the product. The decimal point is moved to the right if the exponent is positive and to the left if the exponent is negative. For example, 20.13×10^3 is equal to 20,130 and 1.91×10^{-4} is equal to 0.000191.

Addition and subtraction of decimals. To add or subtract two decimals, the decimal points of both numbers should be lined up. If one of the numbers has fewer digits to the right of the decimal point than the other, zeros may be inserted to the right of the last digit. For example, to add 17.6512 and 653.27, set up the numbers in a column and add:

$$\begin{array}{r} 17.6512 \\ + 653.2700 \\ \hline 670.9212 \end{array}$$

Likewise, 653.27 minus 17.6512 =

$$\begin{array}{r} 653.2700 \\ - 17.6512 \\ \hline 635.6188 \end{array}$$

Multiplication of decimals. To multiply decimals, multiply the numbers as if they were whole numbers and then insert the decimal point in the product so that the number of digits to the right of the decimal point is equal to the sum of the numbers of digits to the right of the decimal points in the numbers being multiplied. For example:

$$
\begin{array}{r}
2.09 \quad \text{(2 digits to the right)} \\
\times\ 1.3 \quad \text{(1 digit to the right)} \\
\hline
627 \\
209 \\
\hline
2.717 \quad \text{(2 + 1 = 3 digits to the right)}
\end{array}
$$

Division of decimals. To divide a number (the dividend) by a decimal (the divisor), move the decimal point of the divisor to the right until the divisor is a whole number. Then move the decimal point of the dividend the same number of places to the right, and divide as you would by a whole number. The decimal point in the quotient will be directly above the decimal point in the new dividend. For example, to divide 698.12 by 12.4:

$$12.4\,\overline{)698.12}$$

will be replaced by

$$124\,\overline{)6981.2}$$

and the division would proceed as follows:

$$
\begin{array}{r}
56.3 \\
124\,\overline{)6981.2} \\
\underline{620} \\
781 \\
\underline{744} \\
372 \\
\underline{372}
\end{array}
$$

4. REAL NUMBERS

All *real* numbers correspond to points on the number line and all points on the number line correspond to real numbers. All real numbers except zero are either positive or negative.

On a number line, numbers corresponding to points to the left of zero are negative and numbers corresponding to points to the right of zero are positive. For any two numbers on the number line, the number to the left is less than the number to the right; for example,

$-4 < -3, \frac{1}{2} < \frac{3}{4}$, and $0.05 < 0.12$.

To say that the number n is between 1 and 4 on the number line means that $n > 1$ and $n < 4$; i.e., $1 < n < 4$.

The distance between a number and zero on the number line is called the *absolute value* (magnitude) of the number. Thus 3 and -3 have the same absolute value, 3, since they are both three units from zero. The absolute value of 3 is denoted $|3|$. Examples of absolute values of numbers are

$$|-5| = |5| = 5, \left|-\frac{7}{2}\right| = \frac{7}{2}, \text{ and } |0| = 0.$$

Note that the absolute value of any nonzero number is positive.

5. POSITIVE AND NEGATIVE NUMBERS

Addition and subtraction. To add two numbers that have the same sign, add the absolute values of the numbers and insert the common sign. For example:

$$(-7) + (-9) = -16$$

because

$$(-7) + (-9) = -(|-7| + |-9|) = -(7 + 9) = -16.$$

To add two numbers with different signs, find the positive difference between their absolute values and insert the sign of the number with the greater absolute value. For example,

$$(-13) + 19 = 6$$

because

$$(-13) + 19 = +(|19| - |-13|) = +(19 - 13) = 6.$$

Similarly,

$$-16 + 8 = -8$$

because

$$-16 + 8 = -(|-16| - |8|) = -(16 - 8) = -8.$$

To subtract one number from another, express the difference as a sum and add as indicated above. That is, $a - b = a + (-b)$. For example:

$$(-7) - (5) = -7 + (-5) = -12$$

$$6 - (-4) = 6 + [-(-4] = 6 + 4 = 10$$

$$-54 - (-23) = -54 + [-(-23)] = -54 + 23$$

$$= -(54 - 23) = -31$$

(Note that for any number n, $-(-n) = n$.)

Multiplication and division. To multiply or divide two numbers with the same sign, multiply or divide their absolute values; thus, the product and quotient are positive. For example:

$$(-13)(-3) = (13)(3) = 39$$

$$(-14) \div (-2) = 14 \div 2 = 7$$

To multiply or divide two numbers with different signs, multiply or divide their absolute values and insert a negative sign; thus, the product and quotient are negative. For example:

$$(13)(-3) = -(13)(3) = -39$$

$$(-14) \div 2 = -(14 \div 2) = -7$$

Some properties of real numbers that are used frequently follow. If x, y, and z are real numbers, then

(1) $x + y = y + x$ and $xy = yx$.

For example, $8 + 3 = 3 + 8 = 11$, and $17 \cdot 5 = 5 \cdot 17 = 85$.

(2) $(x + y) + z = x + (y + z)$ and $(x \cdot y)z = x(y \cdot z)$.

For example, $(7 + 5) + 2 = 7 + (5 + 2) = 7 + (7) = 14$,
and $(5 \cdot \sqrt{3})(\sqrt{3}) = 5(\sqrt{3} \cdot \sqrt{3}) = 5 \cdot 3 = 15$.

(3) $x(y + z) = xy + xz$.

For example, $718(36) + 718(64) = 718(36 + 64) = 718(100) = 71,800$.

6. RATIO AND PROPORTION

The *ratio* of the number a to the number b (b $\neq$ 0) is $\frac{a}{b}$.

A ratio may be expressed or represented in several ways. For example, the ratio of the number 2 to the number 3 can be written 2 to 3, 2:3, and $\frac{2}{3}$. The order of the terms of a ratio is important. For example, the ratio of the number of months with exactly 30 days to the number with exactly 31 days is $\frac{4}{7}$, not $\frac{7}{4}$.

A *proportion* is a statement that two ratios are equal; for example, $\frac{2}{3} = \frac{8}{12}$ is a proportion. One way to solve a proportion involving an unknown is to cross multiply, obtaining a new equality. For example, to solve for n in the proportion $\frac{2}{3} = \frac{n}{12}$, cross multiply, obtaining $24 = 3n$; then divide both sides by 3, to get $n = 8$.

7. PERCENTS

Percent means per hundred or number out of 100. A percent can be represented as a fraction with a denominator of 100, or as a decimal. For example,

$37\% = \frac{37}{100} = 0.37$.

To find a certain percent of a number, multiply the number by the percent expressed as a decimal or fraction. For example:

$$20\% \text{ of } 90 = 0.20 \times 90 = 18$$

or

$$20\% \text{ of } 90 = \frac{20}{100} \times 90 = \frac{1}{5} \times 90 = 18.$$

Percents greater than 100. Percents greater than 100 are represented by numbers greater than 1. For example:

$$300\% = \frac{300}{100} = 3$$

$$250\% \text{ of } 80 = 2.5 \times 80 = 200$$

Percents less than 1. The percent 0.5% means $\frac{1}{2}$ of 1 percent. For example, 0.5% of 12 is equal to $0.005 \times 12 = 0.06$.

Percent change. Often a problem will ask for the percent increase or decrease from one quantity to another quantity. For example, "If the price of an item increases from \$24 to \$30, what is the percent increase in price?" To find the percent increase, first find the amount of the increase; then divide this increase by the original amount, and express this quotient as a percent. In the example above, the percent increase would be found in the following way: the amount of the increase is $(30 - 24) = 6$.

Therefore, the percent increase is $\frac{6}{24} = 0.25 = 25\%$.

Likewise, to find the percent decrease (e.g., the price of an item is reduced from $30 to $24), first find the amount of the decrease; then divide this decrease by the original amount, and express this quotient as a percent. In the example above, the amount of decrease is $(30 - 24) = 6$. Therefore, the percent decrease is

$\frac{6}{30} = 0.20 = 20\%$.

Note that the percent increase from 24 to 30 is not the same as the percent decrease from 30 to 24.

In the following example, the increase is greater than 100 percent: If the cost of a certain house in 1983 was 300 percent of its cost in 1970, by what percent did the cost increase?

If n is the cost in 1970, then the percent increase is equal to $\frac{3n - n}{n} = \frac{2n}{n} = 2$, or 200 percent.

8. EQUIVALENT FORMS OF A NUMBER

In solving a particular problem, it may be helpful to convert the given form of a number to a more convenient form.

To convert a fraction to a decimal, divide the numerator by the denominator, e.g., $\frac{3}{4} = 0.75$.

$$
\begin{array}{r}
0.75 \\
4\overline{)3.00} \\
28 \\
\hline
20 \\
20 \\
\hline
\end{array}
$$

To convert a number to a percent, multiply by 100. For example, $0.75 = (0.75 \times 100)\% = 75\%$.

The decimal 0.625 means $\frac{625}{1,000}$ (see page 17). This fraction may be simplified by dividing the numerator and denominator by common factors. For example:

$\frac{625}{1,000} = \frac{5 \cdot \cancel{5} \cdot \cancel{5} \cdot \cancel{5}}{2 \cdot 2 \cdot 2 \cdot \cancel{5} \cdot \cancel{5} \cdot \cancel{5}} = \frac{5}{8}$.

To convert a percent to a decimal, divide by 100; e.g.:

$24\% = \frac{24}{100} = 0.24$.

In the following examples, it is helpful to convert from one form of a number to another form.

Of the following, which is LEAST?

(A) 35% (B) $\frac{9}{20}$ (C) 0.42 (D) $\frac{(0.9)(4)}{10}$ (E) $\frac{3}{13}$

These numbers can be compared more easily if they are all converted to decimals:

$$35\% = 0.35$$

$$\frac{9}{20} = 0.45$$

$$0.42 = 0.42$$

$$\frac{(0.9)(4)}{10} = 0.36$$

$$\frac{3}{13} = 0.23 \text{ (to 2 decimal places)}$$

Thus, $\frac{3}{13}$ is the least of the numbers.

9. POWERS AND ROOTS OF NUMBERS

When a number k is to be used n times as a factor in a product, it can be expressed as k^n, which means the nth power of k. For example, $2^2 = 2 \times 2 = 4$ and $2^3 = 2 \times 2 \times 2 = 8$ are powers of 2.

Squaring a number that is greater than 1, or raising it to a higher power, results in a larger number; squaring a number between 0 and 1 results in a smaller number. For example:

$$3^2 = 9 \qquad\qquad (9 > 3)$$

$$\left(\frac{1}{3}\right)^2 = \frac{1}{9} \qquad\qquad \left(\frac{1}{9} < \frac{1}{3}\right)$$

$$(0.1)^2 = 0.01 \qquad\qquad (0.01 < 0.1)$$

A *square root* of a non-negative number n is a number that when squared is equal to n. Every positive number n has two square roots, one positive and the other negative, but $\sqrt{n}$ denotes the positive number whose square is n. For example, $\sqrt{9}$ denotes 3. The two square roots of 9 are $\sqrt{9} = 3$ and $-\sqrt{9} = -3$.

Every real number r has exactly one real *cube root*, which is the number s such that $s^3 = r$. The real cube root of r is denoted by $\sqrt[3]{r}$. Since $2^3 = 8$, $\sqrt[3]{8} = 2$. Similarly, $\sqrt[3]{-8} = -2$, because $(-2)^3 = -8$.

10. MEAN

The *average (arithmetic mean)* of n values is equal to the sum of the n values divided by n. For example, the average (arithmetic mean) of 9, 6, 5, and 12 is $\frac{9 + 6 + 5 + 12}{4} = 8$.

11. MEDIAN

When an odd number of values are ordered from least to greatest or from greatest to least, the value in the middle is the *median;* i.e., there are equal numbers of values above and below the median. For example, the median of 4, 7, 3, 10, and 8 is 7, since, when ordered from least to greatest (3,4,7,8,10), 7 is the middle value. When there is an even number of values, the median is the average of the two middle values. For example, the median of 5,3,2,10,7, and 8 is $\frac{5 + 7}{2} = 6$.

12. MODE

The *mode* of a list of values is the value that occurs most frequently. For example, the mode of 1, 3, 6, 4, 3, and 5 is 3. A list of values may have more than one mode. For example, the list of values 1,2,3,3,3,5,7,10,10,10,20 has two modes, 3 and 10.

B. Algebra

In algebra, a letter such as x or n is used to represent an unknown quantity. For example, suppose Pam has 5 more pencils than Fred. If you let f represent the number of pencils that Fred has, then the number of pencils that Pam has is f + 5.

A combination of letters and mathematical operations, such as f + 5, $\dfrac{3x^3}{2x - 5}$, and 19x² + 6x + 3, is called an *algebraic expression*.

In the expression 9x − 6, 9x and −6 are *terms* of the expression; 9 is called the *coefficient* of x.

1. SIMPLIFYING ALGEBRAIC EXPRESSIONS

Often when working with algebraic expressions, it is necessary to simplify them by factoring or combining *like* terms. For example, the expression 6x + 5x is equivalent to (6 + 5)x or 11x. In the expression 9x − 3y, 3 is a factor common to both terms: 9x − 3y = 3(3x − y). In the expression 5x² + 6y, there are no like terms and no common factors.

If there are common factors in the numerator and denominator of an expression, they can be divided out, provided that they are not equal to zero.

For example, if x ≠ 3, $\dfrac{3xy - 9y}{x - 3}$ is equal to $\dfrac{3y(x - 3)}{x - 3}$; since

$\dfrac{x - 3}{x - 3}$ is equal to 1, $\dfrac{3y(x - 3)}{x - 3}$ = 3y · 1 = 3y.

To multiply two algebraic expressions, each term of one expression is multiplied by each term of the other expression. For example:

$$(3x - 4)(9y + x) \text{ is equal to } 3x(9y + x) - 4(9y + x) =$$
$$(3x)(9y) + (3x)(x) + (-4)(9y) + (-4)(x) =$$
$$27xy + 3x^2 - 36y - 4x$$

An algebraic expression can be evaluated by substituting values of the unknowns in the expression. For example, if x = 3 and y = −2, 3xy − x² + y can be evaluated as

$$3(3)(-2) - (3)^2 + (-2) = -18 - 9 - 2 = -29.$$

2. EQUATIONS

A statement that two algebraic expressions are equal is an *equation*. Some examples of equations are

$$5x - 2 = 9$$

and

$$3x + 1 = y - 2.$$

Two equations having the same solution(s) are *equivalent*. For example,

$$2 + x = 3$$

and

$$4 + 2x = 6$$

are equivalent equations, as are

$$3x - y = 6$$

and

$$6x = 2y + 12.$$

3. SOLVING LINEAR EQUATIONS WITH ONE UNKNOWN

To solve a linear equation (i.e., to find the value of the unknown that satisfies the equation) you need to isolate the unknown on one side of the equation. This can be done by performing the same mathematical operations on both sides of the equation.

Remember that if the same number is added to or subtracted from both sides of the equation, this does not change the equality; likewise, multiplying or dividing both sides by the same nonzero number does not change the equality. For example, to solve the equation $\frac{5x - 6}{3} = 4$ for x, you can isolate x using the following steps:

$$\frac{5x - 6}{3} = 4$$
$$5x - 6 = 12 \quad \text{(multiplying by 3)}$$
$$5x = 12 + 6 = 18 \quad \text{(adding 6)}$$
$$x = \frac{18}{5} \quad \text{(dividing by 5)}$$

The solution, $\frac{18}{5}$, can be checked by substituting it in the original equation for x to determine whether it satisfies that equation. For example:

$$\frac{5\left(\frac{18}{5}\right) - 6}{3} = \frac{18 - 6}{3} = \frac{12}{3} = 4$$

Therefore, the value of x obtained above is the solution.

4. SOLVING TWO LINEAR EQUATIONS WITH TWO UNKNOWNS

If you have two linear equations that are not equivalent, you can find any values for the two unknowns that satisfy both equations. One way to solve for the two unknowns is to express one of the unknowns in terms of the other using one of the equations, and then substitute it into the remaining equation to obtain an equation with one unknown. This equation can be solved and the value substituted in one of the equations to find the value of the other unknown. For example, the following two equations can be solved for x and y.

$$(1) \quad 3x + 2y = 11$$
$$(2) \quad x - y = 2$$

In equation (2), $x = 2 + y$. Substitute $2 + y$ in equation (1) for x:

$$3(2 + y) + 2y = 11$$
$$6 + 3y + 2y = 11$$
$$6 + 5y = 11$$
$$5y = 5$$
$$y = 1$$

If $y = 1$, then $x = 2 + 1 = 3$.

Another way to solve for x and y is to solve the two equations simultaneously. The purpose is to eliminate one of the unknowns. This can be done by making the coefficients of one of the unknowns the same (disregarding the sign) in both equations and either adding the equations or subtracting one equation from the other. For example, to solve the equations below simultaneously

$$(1) \quad 6x + 5y = 29$$
$$(2) \quad 4x - 3y = -6$$

multiply equation (1) by 3 and equation (2) by 5 to get

$$18x + 15y = 87$$
$$20x - 15y = -30$$

By adding the two equations you can eliminate y and get $38x = 57$ or $x = \frac{3}{2}$. Then substitute $\frac{3}{2}$ for x in one of the equations to find $y = 4$. These answers can be checked by substituting both values into both of the original equations.

5. SOLVING FACTORABLE QUADRATIC EQUATIONS

An equation that can be put in the standard form

$$ax^2 + bx + c = 0,$$

where a, b, and c are real numbers and $a \neq 0$, is a *quadratic* equation. For example,

$$x^2 + 6x + 5 = 0,$$
$$x^2 - 2x = 0,$$

and

$$x^2 - 4 = 5$$

are quadratic equations. Some quadratic equations can be solved by factoring. For example:

(1) $x^2 + 6x + 5 = 0$
$(x + 5)(x + 1) = 0$
$x + 5 = 0$ or $x + 1 = 0$
$x = -5$ or $x = -1$

(2) $x^2 - 2x = 0$
$x(x - 2) = 0$
$x = 0$ or $x = 2$

(3) $3x^2 - 3 = 8x$
$3x^2 - 8x - 3 = 0$
$(3x + 1)(x - 3) = 0$
$3x + 1 = 0$ or $x - 3 = 0$
$x = -\frac{1}{3}$ or $x = 3$

In general, first put the quadratic equation into the standard form $ax^2 + bx + c = 0$, then factor the left-hand side of the equation, i.e., find two linear expressions whose product is the given quadratic expression. Since the product of the factors is equal to zero, at least one of the factors must be equal to zero. The values found by setting the factors equal to zero are called the *roots* of the equation. These roots can be checked by substituting them into the original equation to determine whether they satisfy the equation.

A quadratic equation has at most two real roots and may have just one or even no real root. For example, the equation $x^2 - 6x + 9 = 0$ can be expressed as $(x - 3)^2 = 0$ or $(x - 3)(x - 3) = 0$; thus the only root is 3.

The equation $x^2 + 1 = 0$ has no real root. Since the square of any real number is greater than or equal to zero, $x^2 + 1$ must be greater than zero.

An expression in the form $a^2 - b^2$ is equal to

$$(a - b)(a + b).$$

For example, if

$$9x^2 - 25 = 0,$$

then

$$(3x - 5)(3x + 5) = 0;$$
$$3x - 5 = 0 \text{ or } 3x + 5 = 0;$$
$$x = \frac{5}{3} \text{ or } x = -\frac{5}{3}.$$

Therefore, the roots are $\frac{5}{3}$ and $-\frac{5}{3}$.

6. EXPONENTS

A positive integer exponent on a number indicates the number of times that number is to be a factor in the product. For example, x^5 means $x \cdot x \cdot x \cdot x \cdot x$; i.e., x is a factor in the product 5 times.

Some rules about exponents are:

Let r, s, x, and y be positive integers.

(1) $(x^r)(x^s) = x^{(r+s)}$; for example $2^2 \cdot 2^3 = 2^{(2+3)} = 2^5 = 32$.

(2) $(x^r)(y^r) = (xy)^r$; for example, $3^3 \cdot 4^3 = 12^3 = 1{,}728$.

(3) $\left(\dfrac{x}{y}\right)^r = \dfrac{x^r}{y^r}$; for example, $\left(\dfrac{2}{3}\right)^3 = \dfrac{2^3}{3^3} = \dfrac{8}{27}$.

(4) $\dfrac{x^r}{x^s} = x^{r-s}$; for example, $\dfrac{4^5}{4^2} = 4^{5-2} = 4^3 = 64$.

(5) $(x^r)^s = x^{rs} = (x^s)^r$; for example, $(x^3)^4 = x^{12} = (x^4)^3$.

(6) $x^{\frac{r}{s}} = \left(x^{\frac{1}{s}}\right)^r = \left(x^r\right)^{\frac{1}{s}} = \sqrt[s]{x^r}$; for example, $8^{\frac{2}{3}} = \left(8^{\frac{1}{3}}\right)^2 = \left(8^2\right)^{\frac{1}{3}} = \sqrt[3]{8^2} = \sqrt[3]{64} = 4$ and $9^{\frac{1}{2}} = \sqrt{9} = 3$.

(7) $x^{-r} = \dfrac{1}{x^r}$; for example, $3^{-2} = \dfrac{1}{3^2} = \dfrac{1}{9}$.

(8) $x^0 = 1$; for example $6^0 = 1$; 0^0 is undefined.

The rules above also apply when r, s, x and y are not integers. Furthermore, the rules also apply when the numbers are negative, except for (5) and (6), which hold in some cases but not others.

7. ABSOLUTE VALUE

The absolute value of x, denoted $|x|$, is defined to be x if $x \geq 0$ and $-x$ if $x < 0$. Note that $\sqrt{x^2}$ denotes the non-negative square root of x^2, that is $\sqrt{x^2} = |x|$.

8. INEQUALITIES

An *inequality* is a statement that uses one of the following symbols:

$\neq$ not equal to

$>$ greater than

$\geq$ greater than or equal to

$<$ less than

$\leq$ less than or equal to

Some examples of inequalities are $5x - 3 < 9$, $6x \geq y$, and $\dfrac{1}{2} < \dfrac{3}{4}$. Solving an inequality is similar to solving an equation; the unknown is isolated on one side of the inequality. Like an equation, the same number can be added to or subtracted from both sides of the inequality or both sides of an inequality can be multiplied or divided by a positive number without changing the truth of the inequality. However, multiplying or dividing an inequality by a negative number reverses the order of the inequality. For example, $6 > 2$, but $(-1)(6) < (-1)(2)$.

To solve the inequality $3x - 2 > 5$ for x, isolate x by using the following steps:

$$3x - 2 > 5$$
$$3x > 7 \text{ (adding 2 to both sides)}$$
$$x > \frac{7}{3} \text{ (dividing both sides by 3)}$$

To solve the inequality $\dfrac{5x-1}{-2} < 3$ for x, isolate x by using the following steps:

$$\frac{5x-1}{-2} < 3$$

$$5x - 1 > -6 \text{ (multiplying both sides by } -2)$$

$$5x > -5 \text{ (adding 1 to both sides)}$$

$$x > -1 \text{ (dividing both sides by 5)}$$

C. Geometry

1. LINES

In geometry, the word "line" refers to a straight line.

The line above can be referred to as line PQ or line ℓ. The part of the line from P to Q is called a *line segment*. P and Q are the *endpoints* of the segment. The notation PQ is used to denote both the segment and the length of the segment. The intention of the notation can be determined from the context.

2. INTERSECTING LINES AND ANGLES

If two lines intersect, the opposite angles are vertical angles and have the same measure. In the figure

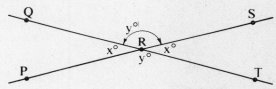

$\angle$PRQ and $\angle$SRT are vertical angles and $\angle$QRS and $\angle$PRT are vertical angles.

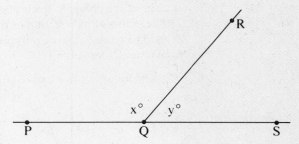

In the figure above, PQS is a straight line, or straight angle, and $x + y = 180$. $\angle$PQR and $\angle$RQS are adjacent angles since they share a common side.

An angle that has a measure of 90° is a *right* angle.

Two angles whose measures sum to 90° are *complementary* angles, and two angles whose measures sum to 180° are *supplementary* angles.

3. PERPENDICULAR LINES

If two lines intersect at right angles, the lines are *perpendicular*. For example:

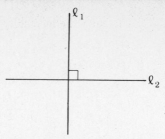

ℓ_1 and ℓ_2 are perpendicular, denoted by $\ell_1 \perp \ell_2$. A right angle symbol in an angle of intersection indicates that the lines are perpendicular.

4. PARALLEL LINES

If two lines that are in the same plane do not intersect, the two lines are *parallel*. In the figure

lines ℓ_1 and ℓ_2 are parallel, denoted by $\ell_1 \parallel \ell_2$. If two parallel lines are intersected by a third line, as shown below, the angle measures are related in the following ways, where $x + y = 180$.

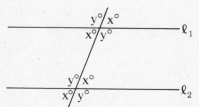

5. POLYGONS (CONVEX)

A *polygon* is a closed plane figure formed by three or more line segments, called the *sides* of the polygon. Each side intersects exactly two other sides at their endpoints. The points of intersection of the sides are *vertices*. The term "polygon" will be used to mean a convex polygon, i.e., a polygon in which each interior angle has a measure of less than 180°.

The following figures are polygons:

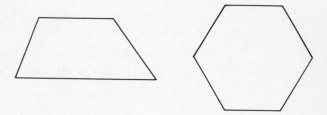

The following figures are not polygons:

A polygon with three sides is a *triangle*; with four sides, a *quadrilateral*; with five sides, a *pentagon*; and with six sides, a *hexagon*.

The sum of the angle measures of a triangle is 180°. In general, the sum of the angle measures of a polygon with n sides is equal to $(n - 2)180°$. For example, a pentagon has $(5 - 2)180 = (3)180 = 540$ degrees.

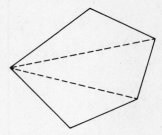

Note that a pentagon can be partitioned into three triangles and therefore the sum of the angle measures can be found by adding the sum of the angle measures of three triangles.

The *perimeter* of a polygon is the sum of the lengths of its sides.

The commonly used phrase ''area of a polygon (or any other plane figure)'' will be used to mean the area of the region enclosed by that figure.

6. TRIANGLES

An *equilateral* triangle has all sides of equal length. All angles of an equilateral triangle have equal measure. An *isosceles* triangle has at least two sides of the same length. If two sides of a triangle have the same length, then the two angles opposite those sides have the same measure. Conversely, if two angles of a triangle have the same measure, then the sides opposite those angles have the same length. In isosceles triangle PQR,

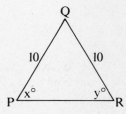

$x = y$ since $PQ = QR$.

A triangle that has a right angle is a *right* triangle. In a right triangle, the side opposite the right angle is the *hypotenuse,* and the other two sides are the *legs.* An important theorem concerning right triangles is the *Pythagorean Theorem*, which states: In a right triangle, the square of the length of the hypotenuse is equal to the sum of the squares of the lengths of the legs.

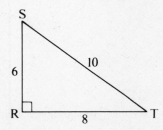

In right $\triangle RST$, $(RS)^2 + (RT)^2 = (ST)^2$. For example, if RS = 6 and RT = 8, then ST = 10, since $6^2 + 8^2 = 36 + 64 = 100 = (ST)^2$ and ST = $\sqrt{100}$. Any triangle in which the lengths of the sides are in the ratio 3:4:5 is a right triangle. In general, if a, b, and c are the lengths of the sides of a triangle and $a^2 + b^2 = c^2$, then the triangle is a right triangle.

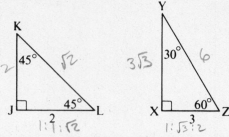

In 45°-45°-90° triangles, the lengths of the sides are in the ratio 1:1:$\sqrt{2}$. For example, in $\triangle JKL$, if JL = 2, then JK = 2, and KL = $2\sqrt{2}$. In 30°-60°-90° triangles, the lengths of the sides are in the ratio 1:$\sqrt{3}$:2. For example, in $\triangle XYZ$, if XZ = 3, then XY = $3\sqrt{3}$, and YZ = 6.

Area. The area of a triangle is equal to:

$$\frac{\text{(the length of the altitude)} \times \text{(the length of the base)}}{2}$$

The *altitude* of a triangle is the segment drawn from a vertex perpendicular to the side opposite that vertex. Relative to that vertex and altitude, the opposite side is called the *base*.

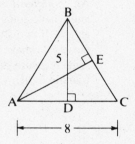

In $\triangle ABC$, BD is the altitude to base AC and AE is the altitude to base BC. The area of $\triangle ABC$ is equal to

$$\frac{BD \times AC}{2} = \frac{5 \times 8}{2} = 20.$$

The area is also equal to $\frac{AE \times BC}{2}$. If $\triangle ABC$ above is isosceles and AB = BC, then altitude BD bisects the base; i.e., AD = DC = 4. Similarly, any altitude of an equilateral triangle bisects the side to which it is drawn.

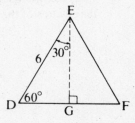

In equilateral triangle DEF, if DE = 6, then DG = 3, and EG = $3\sqrt{3}$. The area of $\triangle DEF$ is equal to $\frac{3\sqrt{3} \times 6}{2} = 9\sqrt{3}$.

7. QUADRILATERALS

A polygon with four sides is a *quadrilateral.* A quadrilateral in which both pairs of opposite sides are parallel is a *parallelogram.* The opposite sides of a parallelogram also have equal length.

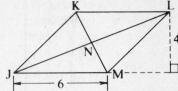

In parallelogram JKLM, JK ∥ LM and JK = LM; KL ∥ JM and KL = JM.

The diagonals of a parallelogram bisect each other (i.e., KN = NM and JN = NL).

The area of a parallelogram is equal to

(the length of the altitude) × (the length of the base).

The area of JKLM is equal to $4 \times 6 = 24$.

A parallelogram with right angles is a *rectangle,* and a rectangle with all sides of equal length is a *square.*

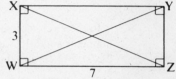

The perimeter of WXYZ = $2(3) + 2(7) = 20$ and the area of WXYZ is equal to $3 \times 7 = 21$. The diagonals of a rectangle are equal; therefore WY = XZ = $\sqrt{9 + 49} = \sqrt{58}$.

Note that a quadrilateral can have two right angles and not be a rectangle. For example, the figures

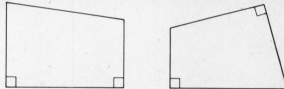

are not rectangles. But, if a quadrilateral has at least three right angles, then it must be a rectangle.

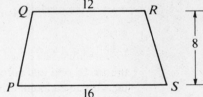

A quadrilateral with two sides that are parallel, as shown above, is a *trapezoid.* The area of trapezoid PQRS may be calculated as follows:

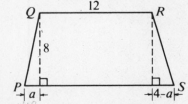

$$\text{Area} = 12 \times 8 + \frac{1}{2}(8a) + \frac{1}{2}(8)(4 - a) = 96 + 16 = 112$$

The area of the trapezoid is also equal to

$$\frac{1}{2}(\text{sum of bases})(\text{height}) = \frac{1}{2}(QR + PS)(8) = \frac{1}{2}(28 \times 8) = 112.$$

8. CIRCLES

A *circle* is a set of points in a plane that are all located the same distance from a fixed point (the *center* of the circle).

A *chord* of a circle is a line segment that has its endpoints on the circle. A chord that passes through the center of the circle is a *diameter* of the circle. A *radius* of a circle is a segment from the center of the circle to a point on the circle. The words ''diameter'' and ''radius'' are also used to refer to the lengths of these segments.

The *circumference* of a circle is the distance around the circle. If r is the radius of the circle, then the circumference is equal to $2\pi r$, where π is approximately $\frac{22}{7}$ or 3.14. The area of a circle of radius r is equal to πr^2.

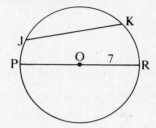

In the circle above, O is the center of the circle and JK and PR are chords. PR is a diameter and OR is a radius. If OR = 7, then the circumference of the circle is $2\pi(7) = 14\pi$ and the area of the circle is $\pi(7)^2 = 49\pi$.

The number of degrees of arc in a circle (or the number of degrees in a complete revolution) is 360.

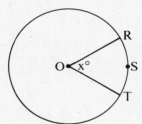

In the circle with center O above, the length of arc RST is $\frac{x}{360}$ of the circumfer-

ence of the circle; e.g., if x = 60, arc RST has length $\frac{1}{6}$ of the circumference of the circle.

A line that has exactly one point in common with the circle is said to be *tangent* to the circle, and that common point is called the *point of tangency*. A radius or diameter with an endpoint at the point of tangency is perpendicular to the tangent line, and, conversely, a line that is perpendicular to a diameter at one of its endpoints is tangent to the circle at that endpoint.

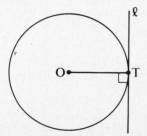

The line ℓ above is tangent to the circle and radius OT is perpendicular to ℓ.

Two different circles that have the same center, as shown below, are *concentric* circles.

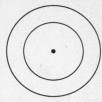

If each vertex of a polygon lies on a circle, then the polygon is *inscribed* in the circle and the circle is *circumscribed* about the polygon. If each side of a polygon is tangent to a circle, then the polygon is *circumscribed* about the circle and the circle is *inscribed* in the polygon.

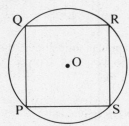 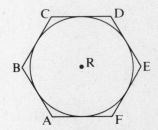

Quadrilateral PQRS is inscribed in circle O and hexagon ABCDEF is circumscribed about circle R.

If a triangle is inscribed in a circle so that one of its sides is a diameter of the circle, then the triangle is a right triangle.

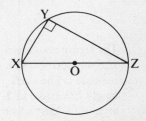

In the circle above, XZ is a diameter and the measure of $\angle XYZ = 90°$.

9. SOLIDS

The following are examples of three-dimensional figures called *solids:*

Rectangular   Cylinder   Pyramid   Sphere   Cone
Solid

10. RECTANGULAR SOLIDS

The *rectangular solid* shown above is formed by six rectangular surfaces. Each rectangular surface is a *face.* Each solid or dotted line segment is an *edge,* and each point at which the edges meet is a *vertex.* A rectangular solid has six faces, twelve edges, and eight vertices. Opposite faces are parallel rectangles that have the same dimensions. A rectangular solid in which all edges are of equal length is a *cube.*

The *surface area* of a rectangular solid is equal to the sum of the areas of all the faces. The *volume* is equal to

$$(\text{length}) \times (\text{width}) \times (\text{height});$$
in other words, $(\text{area of base}) \times (\text{height}).$

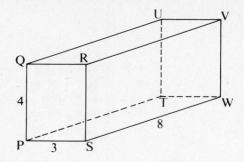

In the rectangular solid above, the dimensions are 3, 4, and 8. The surface area is equal to $2(3 \times 4) + 2(3 \times 8) + 2(4 \times 8) = 136$. The volume is equal to $3 \times 4 \times 8 = 96$.

11. CYLINDERS

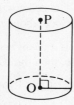

The figure above is a right circular *cylinder*. The two bases are circles of the same size with centers O and P, respectively, and altitude (height) OP is perpendicular to the bases. The surface area of a right circular cylinder with a base of radius r and height h is equal to $2(\pi r^2) + 2\pi rh$ (the sum of the areas of the two bases plus the area of the curved surface).

The volume of a cylinder is equal to $\pi r^2 h$, i.e.:

$$(\text{area of base}) \times (\text{height}).$$

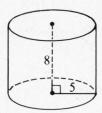

In the cylinder above, the surface area is equal to

$$2(25\pi) + 2\pi(5)(8) = 130\pi,$$

and the volume is equal to

$$25\pi(8) = 200\pi.$$

12. PYRAMIDS

Another solid with plane surfaces as faces is a *pyramid*. One of the faces (called the base) can be a polygon with any number of edges; the remaining faces are triangles. The figures below are pyramids. The shaded faces are the bases.

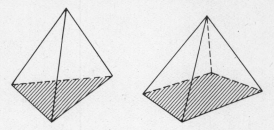

In the pyramid below, PQRS is a square, and the four triangles are the same size. V, the lower endpoint of altitude TV, is the center of the square.

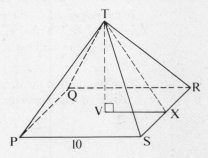

If altitude TV = 12 and VX = $\frac{1}{2}$ PS = 5, then, by the Pythagorean Theorem,

TX = $\sqrt{5^2 + 12^2}$ = 13. Since TX = 13, and SX = $\frac{1}{2}$ RS = 5, therefore

TS = $\sqrt{13^2 + 5^2}$ = $\sqrt{194}$.

13. COORDINATE GEOMETRY

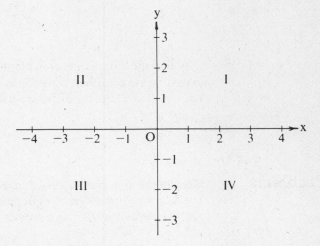

The figure above shows the (rectangular) *coordinate plane*. The horizontal line is called the *x-axis* and the perpendicular vertical line is called the *y-axis*. The point at which these two axes intersect, designated O, is called the *origin*. The axes divide the plane into four quadrants, I, II, III, and IV, as shown.

Each point in the plane has an *x-coordinate* and a *y-coordinate*. A point is identified by an ordered pair (x,y) of numbers in which the x-coordinate is the first number and the y-coordinate is the second number.

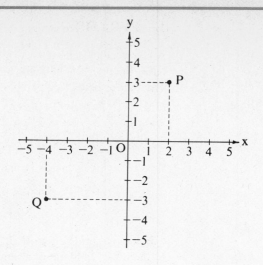

In the graph above, the (x,y) coordinates of point P are (2,3) since P is 2 units to the right of the y-axis (i.e., x = 2) and 3 units above the x-axis (i.e., y = 3). Similarly, the (x,y) coordinates of point Q are (−4, −3). The origin O has coordinates (0,0).

One way to find the distance between two points in the coordinate plane is to use the Pythagorean Theorem.

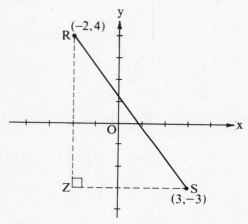

To find the distance between points R and S using the Pythagorean Theorem, draw in the triangle as shown. Note that Z has (x,y) coordinates (−2, −3), RZ = 7, and ZS = 5. Therefore, the distance between R and S is equal to:

$$\sqrt{7^2 + 5^2} = \sqrt{74}.$$

D. Word Problems

Many of the principles discussed in this chapter are used to solve word problems. The following discussion of word problems illustrates some of the techniques and concepts used in solving such problems.

1. RATE PROBLEMS

The distance that an object travels is equal to the product of the average speed at which it travels and the amount of time it takes to travel that distance; i.e.,

$$\text{Rate} \times \text{Time} = \text{Distance}.$$

Example 1: If a car travels at an average speed of 70 kilometers per hour for 4 hours, how many kilometers does it travel?

Solution: Since rate × time = distance, simply multiply 70 km/hour × 4 hours. Thus, the car travels 280 kilometers in 4 hours.

To determine the average rate at which an object travels, divide the total distance traveled by the total amount of time.

Example 2: On a 400-mile trip car X traveled half the distance at 40 miles per hour and the other half at 50 miles per hour. What was the average speed of car X?

Solution: First it is necessary to determine the amount of traveling time. During the first 200 miles the car traveled at 40 mph; therefore, it took $\frac{200}{40} = 5$ hours to travel the first 200 miles. During the second 200 miles the car traveled at 50 mph; therefore, it took $\frac{200}{50} = 4$ hours to travel the second 200 miles. Thus, the average speed of car X was $\frac{400}{9} = 44\frac{4}{9}$ mph. Note that the average speed is *not* $\frac{40 + 50}{2} = 45$.

Some of the problems can be solved by using ratios.

Example 3: If 5 shirts cost $44, then, at this rate, what is the cost of 8 shirts?

Solution: If c is the cost of the 8 shirts, then $\frac{5}{44} = \frac{8}{c}$. Cross multiplication results in the equation

$$5c = 8 \times 44 = 352$$

$$c = \frac{352}{5} = 70.40$$

The 8 shirts cost $70.40.

2. WORK PROBLEMS

In a work problem, the rates at which certain persons or machines work alone are usually given, and it is necessary to compute the rate at which they work together (or vice versa).

The basic formula for solving work problems is: $\frac{1}{r} + \frac{1}{s} = \frac{1}{h}$, where r and s are, for example, the number of hours it takes Rae and Sam, respectively, to complete a job when working alone and h is the number of hours it takes Rae and Sam to do the job when working together. The reasoning is that in 1 hour Rae does $\frac{1}{r}$ of the job, Sam does $\frac{1}{s}$ of the job, and Rae and Sam together do $\frac{1}{h}$ of the job.

Example 1: If machine X can produce 1,000 bolts in 4 hours and machine Y can produce 1,000 bolts in 5 hours, in how many hours can machines X and Y, working together at these constant rates, produce 1,000 bolts?

Solution: $\quad \frac{1}{4} + \frac{1}{5} = \frac{1}{h}$

$$\frac{5}{20} + \frac{4}{20} = \frac{1}{h}$$

$$\frac{9}{20} = \frac{1}{h}$$

$$9h = 20$$

$$h = \frac{20}{9} = 2\frac{2}{9} \text{ hours}$$

Working together, machines X and Y can produce 1,000 bolts in $2\frac{2}{9}$ hours.

Example 2: If Art and Rita can do a job in 4 hours when working together at their respective rates and Art can do the job alone in 6 hours, in how many hours can Rita do the job alone?

Solution: $\frac{1}{6} + \frac{1}{R} = \frac{1}{4}$

$$\frac{R + 6}{6R} = \frac{1}{4}$$

$$4R + 24 = 6R$$
$$24 = 2R$$
$$12 = R$$

Working alone, Rita can do the job in 12 hours.

3. MIXTURE PROBLEMS

In mixture problems, substances with different characteristics are combined, and it is necessary to determine the characteristics of the resulting mixture.

Example 1: If 6 pounds of nuts that cost $1.20 per pound are mixed with 2 pounds of nuts that cost $1.60 per pound, what is the cost per pound of the mixture?

Solution: The total cost of the 8 pounds of nuts is

$$6(\$1.20) + 2(\$1.60) = \$10.40.$$

The cost per pound is $\frac{\$10.40}{8}$ = $1.30.

Example 2: How many liters of a solution that is 15 percent salt must be added to 5 liters of a solution that is 8 percent salt so that the resulting solution is 10 percent salt?

Solution: Let n represent the number of liters of the 15% solution. The amount of salt in the 15% solution [0.15n] plus the amount of salt in the 8% solution [(0.08)(5)] must be equal to the amount of salt in the 10% mixture [0.10 (n+5)]. Therefore,

$$0.15n + 0.08(5) = 0.10 (n + 5)$$
$$15n + 40 = 10n + 50$$
$$5n = 10$$
$$n = 2 \text{ liters}$$

Two liters of the 15% salt solution must be added to the 8% solution to obtain the 10% solution.

4. INTEREST PROBLEMS

Interest can be computed in two basic ways. With simple annual interest, the interest is computed on the principal only. If interest is compounded, then interest is computed on the principal as well as on any interest already earned.

Example 1: If $8,000 is invested at 6 percent simple annual interest, how much interest is earned after 3 months?

Solution: Since the annual interest rate is 6%, the interest for 1 year is

(0.06) (8,000) = $480. The interest earned in 3 months is $\frac{3}{12}$(480) = $120.

Example 2: If $10,000 is invested at 10 percent annual interest, compounded semiannually, what is the balance after 1 year?

Solution: The balance after the first 6 months would be
$10,000 + (10,000)(0.05) = 10,500$. The balance after one year would be
$10,500 + (10,500)(0.05) = \$11,025$.

5. DISCOUNT

If a price is discounted by n percent, then the price becomes $(100 - n)$ percent of the original price.

Example 1: A certain customer paid $24 for a dress. If that price represented a 25 percent discount on the original price of the dress, what was the original price of the dress?

Solution: If p is the original price of the dress, then 0.75p is the discounted price and $0.75p = \$24$ or $p = \$32$. The original price of the dress was $32.

Example 2: The price of an item is discounted by 20 percent and then this reduced price is discounted by an additional 30 percent. These two discounts are equal to an overall discount of what percent?

Solution: If p is the original price of the item, then 0.8p is the price after the first discount. The price after the second discount is $(0.7)(0.8)p = 0.56p$. This represents an overall discount of 44 percent $(100 - 56)$.

6. PROFIT

Profit is equal to revenues minus expenses, i.e., selling price minus cost.

Example 1: A certain appliance costs a merchant $30. At what price should the merchant sell the appliance in order to make a gross profit of 50 percent of the cost of the appliance?

Solution: If s is the selling price of the appliance, then $s - 30 = (0.5)(30)$ or $s = \$45$. The merchant should sell the appliance for $45.

7. SETS

If S is the set of numbers 1, 2, 3, and 4, you can write $S = \{1,2,3,4\}$. Sets can also be represented by Venn diagrams. That is, the relationship among the members of sets can be represented by circles.

Example 1: Each of 25 people is enrolled in history, mathematics, or both. If 20 are enrolled in history and 18 are enrolled in mathematics, how many are enrolled in both history and mathematics?

Solution: The 25 people can be divided into three sets: those who study history only, those who study mathematics only, and those who study history and mathematics. Thus a diagram may be drawn as follows where n is the number of people enrolled in both courses, 20-n is the number enrolled in history only, and 18-n is the number enrolled in mathematics only.

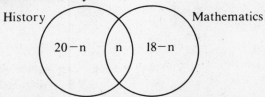

Since there is a total of 25 people, $(20 - n) + n + (18 - n) = 25$, or $n = 13$. Thirteen people are enrolled in both history and mathematics. Note that $20 + 18 - 13 = 25$.

Example 2: In a certain production lot, 40 percent of the toys are red and the remaining toys are green. Half of the toys are small and half are large. If 10 percent of the toys are red and small, and 40 toys are green and large, how many of the toys are red and large?

Solution: For this kind of problem, it is helpful to organize the information in a table:

	red	green	
small	10%		50%
large			50%
	40%	60%	100%

The numbers in the table are the percents given. The following percents can be computed on the basis of what is given:

	red	green	
small	10%	40%	50%
large	30%	20%	50%
	40%	60%	100%

Since 20% of the number of toys (n) are green and large, $0.20n = 40$ (40 toys are green and large), or $n = 200$. Therefore, 30% of the 200 toys, or $(0.3)(200) = 60$, are red and large.

8. GEOMETRY PROBLEMS

The following is an example of a word problem involving geometry.

Example 1:

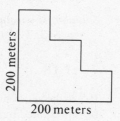

The figure above shows a piece of land. If all angles shown are right angles, what is the perimeter of the piece of land?

Solution: For reference, label the figure as

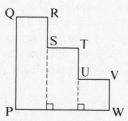

If all the angles are right angles, then QR + ST + UV = PW, and RS + TU + VW = PQ. Hence, the perimeter of the land is $2PW + 2PQ = 2 \times 200 + 2 \times 200 = 800$ meters.

9. MEASUREMENT PROBLEMS

Some questions on the GMAT involve metric units of measure, whereas others involve English units of measure. However, except for units of time, if a question requires conversion from one unit of measure to another, the relationship between those units will be given.

Example 1: A train travels at a constant rate of 25 meters per second. How many kilometers does it travel in 5 minutes? (1 kilometer = 1,000 meters)

Solution: In 1 minute the train travels $(25) \cdot (60) = 1,500$ meters, so in 5 minutes it travels 7,500 meters. Since 1 kilometer = 1,000 meters, 7,500 meters equals $\frac{7,500}{1,000}$ or 7.5 kilometers.

10. DATA INTERPRETATION

Occasionally a question or set of questions will be based on data provided in a table or graph. Some examples of tables and graphs are given below.

Example 1:

UNITED STATES POPULATION—BY AGE GROUP
(in thousands)

Age	Population
17 years and under	63,376
18-44 years	86,738
45-64 years	43,845
65 years and over	24,054

How many people are 44 years old or younger?

Solution: The figures in the table are given in thousands. The answer in thousands can be obtained by adding 63,376 thousand and 86,738 thousand. The result is 150,114 thousand, which is 150,114,000.

Example 2:

AVERAGE TEMPERATURE AND PRECIPITATION IN CITY X

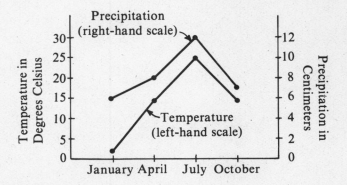

What are the average temperature and precipitation in city X during April?

Solution: Note that the scale on the left applies to the temperature line graph and the one on the right applies to the precipitation line graph.

According to the graph, during April the average temperature is approximately 14° Celsius and the average precipitation is 8 centimenters.

Example 3:

DISTRIBUTION OF AL'S WEEKLY NET SALARY

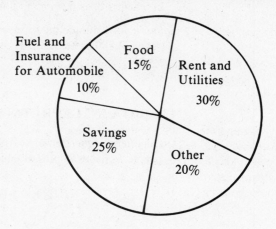

Weekly Net Salary = $350

To how many of the categories listed was at least $80 of Al's weekly net salary allocated?

Solution: In the circle graph the relative sizes of the sectors are proportional to their corresponding values and the sum of the percents given is 100%. $\frac{80}{350}$ is approximately 23%, so at least $80 was allocated to each of 2 categories—Rent and Utilities, and Savings—since their allocations are each greater than 23%.

3 Problem Solving

In these questions you are to solve each problem and select the best of the five answer choices given. The mathematics required to answer the questions does not extend beyond that assumed to be common to the mathematics background of all examinees.

The following pages include test-taking strategies, eight sample test sections (with answer keys), and detailed explanations of every problem on the sample test sections. These explanations present possible problem-solving strategies for the problems.

Test-Taking Strategies for Problem Solving

1. Pacing yourself is very important. Take a watch with you and consult it from time to time. Work as carefully as possible, but do not spend valuable time checking answers or pondering over problems that you find difficult. Make a check mark in your test book next to the troublesome problems or those problems you feel you should double-check. When you have completed the section, go back and spend the remaining time on those difficult problems. Remember, each question has the same weight.

2. Space is available in the test book for scratchwork. Working a problem out in writing may help you avoid errors in solving the problem. If diagrams or figures are not presented, it may help if you draw your own.

3. Read each question carefully to determine what information is given and what is being asked. For word problems, take one step at a time, reading each sentence carefully and translating the information into equations.

4. Before attempting to answer a question, scan the answer choices; otherwise you may waste time putting answers in a form that is not given (for example, putting an answer in the form $\frac{\sqrt{2}}{2}$ when the options are given in the form $\frac{1}{\sqrt{2}}$ or finding the answer in decimal form, such as 0.25, when the choices are given in fractional form, such as $\frac{1}{4}$).

5. For questions that require approximations, scan the options to get some idea of the required closeness of approximation; otherwise, you may waste time on long computations where a short mental process would serve as well (for example, taking 48 percent of a number instead of half the number).

6. If you cannot solve a problem but you can eliminate some of the options as being unlikely, you should guess. If the options are equally plausible, you should not guess. Remember, a percentage of the wrong answers will be subtracted from the number of right answers to compensate for guessing, but the number of omitted questions will not be subtracted.

When you take the sample test sections, use the answer spaces on pages 45 and 46 to mark your answers.

Answer Spaces for Problem Solving Sample Test Sections

Sample Test Section 1

1 Ⓐ Ⓑ Ⓒ Ⓓ Ⓔ	6 Ⓐ Ⓑ Ⓒ Ⓓ Ⓔ	11 Ⓐ Ⓑ Ⓒ Ⓓ Ⓔ	16 Ⓐ Ⓑ Ⓒ Ⓓ Ⓔ
2 Ⓐ Ⓑ Ⓒ Ⓓ Ⓔ	7 Ⓐ Ⓑ Ⓒ Ⓓ Ⓔ	12 Ⓐ Ⓑ Ⓒ Ⓓ Ⓔ	17 Ⓐ Ⓑ Ⓒ Ⓓ Ⓔ
3 Ⓐ Ⓑ Ⓒ Ⓓ Ⓔ	8 Ⓐ Ⓑ Ⓒ Ⓓ Ⓔ	13 Ⓐ Ⓑ Ⓒ Ⓓ Ⓔ	18 Ⓐ Ⓑ Ⓒ Ⓓ Ⓔ
4 Ⓐ Ⓑ Ⓒ Ⓓ Ⓔ	9 Ⓐ Ⓑ Ⓒ Ⓓ Ⓔ	14 Ⓐ Ⓑ Ⓒ Ⓓ Ⓔ	19 Ⓐ Ⓑ Ⓒ Ⓓ Ⓔ
5 Ⓐ Ⓑ Ⓒ Ⓓ Ⓔ	10 Ⓐ Ⓑ Ⓒ Ⓓ Ⓔ	15 Ⓐ Ⓑ Ⓒ Ⓓ Ⓔ	20 Ⓐ Ⓑ Ⓒ Ⓓ Ⓔ

Sample Test Section 2

1 Ⓐ Ⓑ Ⓒ Ⓓ Ⓔ	6 Ⓐ Ⓑ Ⓒ Ⓓ Ⓔ	11 Ⓐ Ⓑ Ⓒ Ⓓ Ⓔ	16 Ⓐ Ⓑ Ⓒ Ⓓ Ⓔ
2 Ⓐ Ⓑ Ⓒ Ⓓ Ⓔ	7 Ⓐ Ⓑ Ⓒ Ⓓ Ⓔ	12 Ⓐ Ⓑ Ⓒ Ⓓ Ⓔ	17 Ⓐ Ⓑ Ⓒ Ⓓ Ⓔ
3 Ⓐ Ⓑ Ⓒ Ⓓ Ⓔ	8 Ⓐ Ⓑ Ⓒ Ⓓ Ⓔ	13 Ⓐ Ⓑ Ⓒ Ⓓ Ⓔ	18 Ⓐ Ⓑ Ⓒ Ⓓ Ⓔ
4 Ⓐ Ⓑ Ⓒ Ⓓ Ⓔ	9 Ⓐ Ⓑ Ⓒ Ⓓ Ⓔ	14 Ⓐ Ⓑ Ⓒ Ⓓ Ⓔ	19 Ⓐ Ⓑ Ⓒ Ⓓ Ⓔ
5 Ⓐ Ⓑ Ⓒ Ⓓ Ⓔ	10 Ⓐ Ⓑ Ⓒ Ⓓ Ⓔ	15 Ⓐ Ⓑ Ⓒ Ⓓ Ⓔ	20 Ⓐ Ⓑ Ⓒ Ⓓ Ⓔ

Sample Test Section 3

1 Ⓐ Ⓑ Ⓒ Ⓓ Ⓔ	6 Ⓐ Ⓑ Ⓒ Ⓓ Ⓔ	11 Ⓐ Ⓑ Ⓒ Ⓓ Ⓔ	16 Ⓐ Ⓑ Ⓒ Ⓓ Ⓔ
2 Ⓐ Ⓑ Ⓒ Ⓓ Ⓔ	7 Ⓐ Ⓑ Ⓒ Ⓓ Ⓔ	12 Ⓐ Ⓑ Ⓒ Ⓓ Ⓔ	17 Ⓐ Ⓑ Ⓒ Ⓓ Ⓔ
3 Ⓐ Ⓑ Ⓒ Ⓓ Ⓔ	8 Ⓐ Ⓑ Ⓒ Ⓓ Ⓔ	13 Ⓐ Ⓑ Ⓒ Ⓓ Ⓔ	18 Ⓐ Ⓑ Ⓒ Ⓓ Ⓔ
4 Ⓐ Ⓑ Ⓒ Ⓓ Ⓔ	9 Ⓐ Ⓑ Ⓒ Ⓓ Ⓔ	14 Ⓐ Ⓑ Ⓒ Ⓓ Ⓔ	19 Ⓐ Ⓑ Ⓒ Ⓓ Ⓔ
5 Ⓐ Ⓑ Ⓒ Ⓓ Ⓔ	10 Ⓐ Ⓑ Ⓒ Ⓓ Ⓔ	15 Ⓐ Ⓑ Ⓒ Ⓓ Ⓔ	20 Ⓐ Ⓑ Ⓒ Ⓓ Ⓔ

Sample Test Section 4

1 Ⓐ Ⓑ Ⓒ Ⓓ Ⓔ	6 Ⓐ Ⓑ Ⓒ Ⓓ Ⓔ	11 Ⓐ Ⓑ Ⓒ Ⓓ Ⓔ	16 Ⓐ Ⓑ Ⓒ Ⓓ Ⓔ
2 Ⓐ Ⓑ Ⓒ Ⓓ Ⓔ	7 Ⓐ Ⓑ Ⓒ Ⓓ Ⓔ	12 Ⓐ Ⓑ Ⓒ Ⓓ Ⓔ	17 Ⓐ Ⓑ Ⓒ Ⓓ Ⓔ
3 Ⓐ Ⓑ Ⓒ Ⓓ Ⓔ	8 Ⓐ Ⓑ Ⓒ Ⓓ Ⓔ	13 Ⓐ Ⓑ Ⓒ Ⓓ Ⓔ	18 Ⓐ Ⓑ Ⓒ Ⓓ Ⓔ
4 Ⓐ Ⓑ Ⓒ Ⓓ Ⓔ	9 Ⓐ Ⓑ Ⓒ Ⓓ Ⓔ	14 Ⓐ Ⓑ Ⓒ Ⓓ Ⓔ	19 Ⓐ Ⓑ Ⓒ Ⓓ Ⓔ
5 Ⓐ Ⓑ Ⓒ Ⓓ Ⓔ	10 Ⓐ Ⓑ Ⓒ Ⓓ Ⓔ	15 Ⓐ Ⓑ Ⓒ Ⓓ Ⓔ	20 Ⓐ Ⓑ Ⓒ Ⓓ Ⓔ

Sample Test Section 5

1 Ⓐ Ⓑ Ⓒ Ⓓ Ⓔ		6 Ⓐ Ⓑ Ⓒ Ⓓ Ⓔ		11 Ⓐ Ⓑ Ⓒ Ⓓ Ⓔ		16 Ⓐ Ⓑ Ⓒ Ⓓ Ⓔ
2 Ⓐ Ⓑ Ⓒ Ⓓ Ⓔ		7 Ⓐ Ⓑ Ⓒ Ⓓ Ⓔ		12 Ⓐ Ⓑ Ⓒ Ⓓ Ⓔ		17 Ⓐ Ⓑ Ⓒ Ⓓ Ⓔ
3 Ⓐ Ⓑ Ⓒ Ⓓ Ⓔ		8 Ⓐ Ⓑ Ⓒ Ⓓ Ⓔ		13 Ⓐ Ⓑ Ⓒ Ⓓ Ⓔ		18 Ⓐ Ⓑ Ⓒ Ⓓ Ⓔ
4 Ⓐ Ⓑ Ⓒ Ⓓ Ⓔ		9 Ⓐ Ⓑ Ⓒ Ⓓ Ⓔ		14 Ⓐ Ⓑ Ⓒ Ⓓ Ⓔ		19 Ⓐ Ⓑ Ⓒ Ⓓ Ⓔ
5 Ⓐ Ⓑ Ⓒ Ⓓ Ⓔ		10 Ⓐ Ⓑ Ⓒ Ⓓ Ⓔ		15 Ⓐ Ⓑ Ⓒ Ⓓ Ⓔ		20 Ⓐ Ⓑ Ⓒ Ⓓ Ⓔ

Sample Test Section 6

1 Ⓐ Ⓑ Ⓒ Ⓓ Ⓔ		6 Ⓐ Ⓑ Ⓒ Ⓓ Ⓔ		11 Ⓐ Ⓑ Ⓒ Ⓓ Ⓔ		16 Ⓐ Ⓑ Ⓒ Ⓓ Ⓔ
2 Ⓐ Ⓑ Ⓒ Ⓓ Ⓔ		7 Ⓐ Ⓑ Ⓒ Ⓓ Ⓔ		12 Ⓐ Ⓑ Ⓒ Ⓓ Ⓔ		17 Ⓐ Ⓑ Ⓒ Ⓓ Ⓔ
3 Ⓐ Ⓑ Ⓒ Ⓓ Ⓔ		8 Ⓐ Ⓑ Ⓒ Ⓓ Ⓔ		13 Ⓐ Ⓑ Ⓒ Ⓓ Ⓔ		18 Ⓐ Ⓑ Ⓒ Ⓓ Ⓔ
4 Ⓐ Ⓑ Ⓒ Ⓓ Ⓔ		9 Ⓐ Ⓑ Ⓒ Ⓓ Ⓔ		14 Ⓐ Ⓑ Ⓒ Ⓓ Ⓔ		19 Ⓐ Ⓑ Ⓒ Ⓓ Ⓔ
5 Ⓐ Ⓑ Ⓒ Ⓓ Ⓔ		10 Ⓐ Ⓑ Ⓒ Ⓓ Ⓔ		15 Ⓐ Ⓑ Ⓒ Ⓓ Ⓔ		20 Ⓐ Ⓑ Ⓒ Ⓓ Ⓔ

Sample Test Section 7

1 Ⓐ Ⓑ Ⓒ Ⓓ Ⓔ		6 Ⓐ Ⓑ Ⓒ Ⓓ Ⓔ		11 Ⓐ Ⓑ Ⓒ Ⓓ Ⓔ		16 Ⓐ Ⓑ Ⓒ Ⓓ Ⓔ
2 Ⓐ Ⓑ Ⓒ Ⓓ Ⓔ		7 Ⓐ Ⓑ Ⓒ Ⓓ Ⓔ		12 Ⓐ Ⓑ Ⓒ Ⓓ Ⓔ		17 Ⓐ Ⓑ Ⓒ Ⓓ Ⓔ
3 Ⓐ Ⓑ Ⓒ Ⓓ Ⓔ		8 Ⓐ Ⓑ Ⓒ Ⓓ Ⓔ		13 Ⓐ Ⓑ Ⓒ Ⓓ Ⓔ		18 Ⓐ Ⓑ Ⓒ Ⓓ Ⓔ
4 Ⓐ Ⓑ Ⓒ Ⓓ Ⓔ		9 Ⓐ Ⓑ Ⓒ Ⓓ Ⓔ		14 Ⓐ Ⓑ Ⓒ Ⓓ Ⓔ		19 Ⓐ Ⓑ Ⓒ Ⓓ Ⓔ
5 Ⓐ Ⓑ Ⓒ Ⓓ Ⓔ		10 Ⓐ Ⓑ Ⓒ Ⓓ Ⓔ		15 Ⓐ Ⓑ Ⓒ Ⓓ Ⓔ		20 Ⓐ Ⓑ Ⓒ Ⓓ Ⓔ

Sample Test Section 8

1 Ⓐ Ⓑ Ⓒ Ⓓ Ⓔ		6 Ⓐ Ⓑ Ⓒ Ⓓ Ⓔ		11 Ⓐ Ⓑ Ⓒ Ⓓ Ⓔ		16 Ⓐ Ⓑ Ⓒ Ⓓ Ⓔ
2 Ⓐ Ⓑ Ⓒ Ⓓ Ⓔ		7 Ⓐ Ⓑ Ⓒ Ⓓ Ⓔ		12 Ⓐ Ⓑ Ⓒ Ⓓ Ⓔ		17 Ⓐ Ⓑ Ⓒ Ⓓ Ⓔ
3 Ⓐ Ⓑ Ⓒ Ⓓ Ⓔ		8 Ⓐ Ⓑ Ⓒ Ⓓ Ⓔ		13 Ⓐ Ⓑ Ⓒ Ⓓ Ⓔ		18 Ⓐ Ⓑ Ⓒ Ⓓ Ⓔ
4 Ⓐ Ⓑ Ⓒ Ⓓ Ⓔ		9 Ⓐ Ⓑ Ⓒ Ⓓ Ⓔ		14 Ⓐ Ⓑ Ⓒ Ⓓ Ⓔ		19 Ⓐ Ⓑ Ⓒ Ⓓ Ⓔ
5 Ⓐ Ⓑ Ⓒ Ⓓ Ⓔ		10 Ⓐ Ⓑ Ⓒ Ⓓ Ⓔ		15 Ⓐ Ⓑ Ⓒ Ⓓ Ⓔ		20 Ⓐ Ⓑ Ⓒ Ⓓ Ⓔ

PROBLEM SOLVING SAMPLE TEST SECTION 1

30 Minutes
20 Questions

Directions: In this section solve each problem, using any available space on the page for scratchwork. Then indicate the best of the answer choices given.

Numbers: All numbers used are real numbers.

Figures: Figures that accompany problems in this section are intended to provide information useful in solving the problems. They are drawn as accurately as possible EXCEPT when it is stated in a specific problem that its figure is not drawn to scale. All figures lie in a plane unless otherwise indicated.

1. A national travel survey in 1977 found that Americans took 382.6 million trips within the United States. California was the destination of 38 million trips. Approximately what percent of the trips had California as the destination?

   (A) 0.01%   (B) 0.1%   (C) 1%
   (D) 3.8%   (E) 10%

2. How many of the integers between 25 and 45 are even?

   (A) 21   (B) 20   (C) 11   (D) 10   (E) 9

3. If taxi fares were $1.00 for the first $\frac{1}{5}$ mile and $0.20 for each $\frac{1}{5}$ mile thereafter, then the taxi fare for a 3-mile ride was

   (A) $1.56
   (B) $2.40
   (C) $3.00
   (D) $3.80
   (E) $4.20

4. A computer routine was developed to generate two numbers, (x, y), the first being a random number between 0 and 100 inclusive, and the second being less than or equal to the square root of the first. Each of the following pairs satisfies this routine EXCEPT

   (A) (99, 10)
   (B) (85, 9)
   (C) (50, 7)
   (D) (1, 1)
   (E) (1, 0)

GO ON TO THE NEXT PAGE.

5. A warehouse had a square floor with area 10,000 square meters. A rectangular addition was built along one entire side of the warehouse that increased the floor area by one-half as much as the original floor area. How many meters did the addition extend beyond the original building?

(A) 10   (B) 20   (C) 50   (D) 200   (E) 500

6. A digital wristwatch was set accurately at 8:30 a.m. and then lost 2 seconds every 5 minutes. What time was indicated on the watch at 6:30 p.m. of the same day if the watch operated continuously until that time?

(A) 5:56
(B) 5:58
(C) 6:00
(D) 6:23
(E) 6:26

7. If x and y are integers and $xy = 5$, then $(x + y)^2 =$

(A) 13   (B) 16   (C) 25   (D) 26   (E) 36

GO ON TO THE NEXT PAGE.

Questions 8-9 refer to the following graphs.

REVENUE FOR STORE X DURING WEEK 1

Distribution of Total Revenue

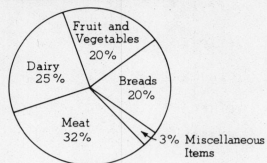

Amount of Revenue from Dairy Products

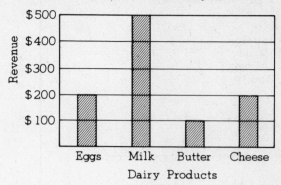

8. During week 1, revenue from eggs provided what percent of the total revenue for Store X ?

    (A) 4%
    (B) 5%
    (C) 8%
    (D) 20%
    (E) 25%

9. If the revenue from the sale of apples was equal to the revenue from the sale of miscellaneous items, what percent of the revenue from the sale of fruit and vegetables was accounted for by apples?

    (A) 60%
    (B) 15%
    (C) 12%
    (D) 6%
    (E) 3%

GO ON TO THE NEXT PAGE.

10. The (x, y) pair (−1, 1) satisfies which of the following equations?

   I. $2x^3 - y^2 = -3$

   II. $2x^2 - y^3 = 1$

   III. $x^2 - 2y^3 = -1$

(A) I only
(B) I and II only
(C) I and III only
(D) II and III only
(E) I, II, and III

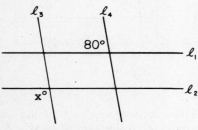

Note: Figure not drawn to scale.

11. If $\ell_1 \parallel \ell_2$ in the figure above, what is the value of x ?

(A) 80
(B) 90
(C) 100
(D) 120
(E) It cannot be determined from the information given.

12. A 5-liter jug contains 4 liters of a saltwater solution that is 15 percent salt. If 1.5 liters of the solution spills out of the jug, and the jug is then filled to capacity with water, approximately what percent of the resulting solution in the jug is salt?

(A) $7\frac{1}{2}\%$

(B) $9\frac{3}{8}\%$

(C) $10\frac{1}{2}\%$

(D) 12%

(E) 15%

13. The average (arithmetic mean) of 3 different positive integers is 100 and the largest of these 3 integers is 120. What is the least possible value of the smallest of these 3 integers?

(A) 1   (B) 10   (C) 61   (D) 71   (E) 80

GO ON TO THE NEXT PAGE.

-50-

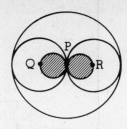

14. In the figure above, the five circles have points in common as shown. P is the center of the largest circle, Q and R are centers of the medium-sized circles, and Q, P, and R are points on a straight line. What fraction of the largest circular region is shaded?

(A) $\frac{1}{16}$ (B) $\frac{1}{8}$ (C) $\frac{3}{16}$ (D) $\frac{1}{4}$ (E) $\frac{1}{2}$

15. If $xyz \neq 0$ and x percent of y percent of z is t, then z =

(A) $\frac{100t}{xy}$

(B) $\frac{1,000t}{xy}$

(C) $\frac{10,000t}{xy}$

(D) $\frac{xy}{10,000t}$

(E) $\frac{10,000xy}{t}$

16. A plane traveled k miles in the first 96 minutes of flight time. If it completed the remaining 300 miles of the trip in t minutes, what was its average speed, in miles per hour, for the entire trip?

(A) $\frac{60(k + 300)}{96 + t}$

(B) $\frac{kt + 96(300)}{96t}$

(C) $\frac{k + 300}{60(96 + t)}$

(D) $\frac{5k}{8} + \frac{60(300)}{t}$

(E) $\frac{5k}{8} + 5t$

GO ON TO THE NEXT PAGE.

-51-

17. A merchant sells an item at a 20 percent discount, but still makes a gross profit of 20 percent of the cost. What percent of the cost would the gross profit on the item have been if it had been sold without the discount?

(A) 20%
(B) 40%
(C) 50%
(D) 60%
(E) 75%

18. A milliner bought a job lot of hats, $\frac{1}{4}$ of which were brown. The milliner sold $\frac{2}{3}$ of the hats including $\frac{4}{5}$ of the brown hats. What fraction of the unsold hats were brown?

(A) $\frac{1}{60}$ (B) $\frac{2}{15}$ (C) $\frac{3}{20}$ (D) $\frac{3}{5}$ (E) $\frac{3}{4}$

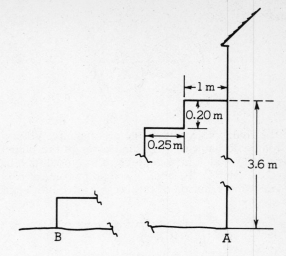

Note: Figure not drawn to scale.

19. Each step of a staircase is 0.25 meter wide and 0.20 meter high, as shown in the figure above. All angles shown in the figure are right angles. If the height of the staircase is 3.6 meters and the landing at the top of the staircase is 1 meter wide, how long, in meters, is AB ?

(A) 3.0
(B) 4.25
(C) 4.5
(D) 5.25
(E) 5.5

20. How many integers n greater than 10 and less than 100 are there such that, if the digits of n are reversed, the resulting integer is n + 9 ?

(A) 5   (B) 6   (C) 7   (D) 8   (E) 9

S T O P

**IF YOU FINISH BEFORE TIME IS CALLED, YOU MAY CHECK YOUR WORK ON THIS SECTION ONLY.
DO NOT TURN TO ANY OTHER SECTION IN THE TEST.**

Answer Key for Sample Test Section 1
PROBLEM SOLVING

1. E	11. E
2. D	12. A
3. D	13. C
4. A	14. B
5. C	15. C
6. E	16. A
7. E	17. C
8. B	18. C
9. B	19. D
10. E	20. D

Explanatory Material:
Problem Solving Sample Test Section 1

1. A national travel survey in 1977 found that Americans took 382.6 million trips within the United States. California was the destination of 38 million trips. Approximately what percent of the trips had California as the destination?

   (A) 0.01%   (B) 0.1%   (C) 1%
   (D) 3.8%   (E) 10%

By rounding 382.6 to 380, it can readily be seen that 38 million is approximately 1/10 or 10 percent of 382.6 million. Thus, the best answer is E.

2. How many of the integers between 25 and 45 are even?

   (A) 21   (B) 20   (C) 11   (D) 10   (E) 9

The even integers between 25 and 45 are 2(13), 2(14), . . ., 2(22). Thus, there are as many even integers between 25 and 45 as there are consecutive integers between 12 and 23. It may be faster to jot them down and count, or to think: 22 integers minus the first 12 integers is 10 integers. Thus, the best answer is D.

3. If taxi fares were \$1.00 for the first $\frac{1}{5}$ mile and \$0.20 for each $\frac{1}{5}$ mile thereafter, then the taxi fare for a 3-mile ride was

   (A) \$1.56
   (B) \$2.40
   (C) \$3.00
   (D) \$3.80
   (E) \$4.20

The 3-mile trip can be thought of as fifteen $\frac{1}{5}$-mile segments.

Then the fare would be \$1.00 for the first segment plus \$0.20(14) for the remaining fourteen segments of the trip, or \$1.00 + \$2.80 = \$3.80. Thus, the best answer is D.

4. A computer routine was developed to generate two numbers, (x, y), the first being a random number between 0 and 100 inclusive, and the second being less than or equal to the square root of the first. Each of the following pairs satisfies this routine EXCEPT

   (A) (99, 10)
   (B) (85, 9)
   (C) (50, 7)
   (D) (1, 1)
   (E) (1, 0)

On examination of each of the choices, it is noted that $10 > \sqrt{99}$, $9 < \sqrt{85}$, $7 < \sqrt{50}$, $1 = \sqrt{1}$, and $0 < \sqrt{1}$. A is the only option containing a second number that is NOT less than or equal to the square root of the first number. Thus, the best answer is A.

5. A warehouse had a square floor with area 10,000 square meters. A rectangular addition was built along one entire side of the warehouse that increased the floor area by one-half as much as the original floor area. How many meters did the addition extend beyond the original building?

   (A) 10   (B) 20   (C) 50   (D) 200   (E) 500

Since the floor was square, the sides of the floor were $\sqrt{10,000}$ or 100 meters. Since the rectangular addition was made on one entire side of the square, its width can be found by using the area formula A = lw: $\frac{10,000}{2} = 100w$ and w = 50. Thus, the best answer is C.

6. A digital wristwatch was set accurately at 8:30 a.m., and then lost 2 seconds every 5 minutes. What time was indicated on the watch at 6:30 p.m. of the same day if the watch operated continuously until that time?

   (A) 5:56
   (B) 5:58
   (C) 6:00
   (D) 6:23
   (E) 6:26

If the watch lost 2 seconds every 5 minutes, it lost $2\left(\frac{60 \text{ min}}{5 \text{ min}}\right)$ or 24 seconds every hour. From 8:30 a.m. until 6:30 p.m., a total of 10 hours elapsed and the watch lost a total of (24 sec/hr)(10 hrs) or 240 seconds. Therefore, the watch lost $\frac{240 \text{ sec}}{60 \text{ sec/min}}$ or 4 minutes in all. At 6:30 p.m., the watch showed 6:26. Thus, the best answer is E.

7. If x and y are integers and xy = 5, then $(x + y)^2 =$

(A) 13 (B) 16 (C) 25 (D) 26 (E) 36

Since x and y are integers and the product xy equals 5, a positive prime number, x and y must be either -1 and -5 or 1 and 5. Regardless of which pair of values x and y have, $(x + y)^2 = 36$. Thus, the best answer is E.

Questions 8-9 refer to the following graphs.

REVENUE FOR STORE X DURING WEEK 1

Distribution of Total Revenue

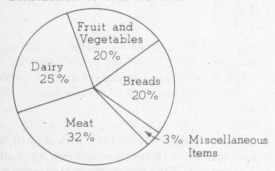

Amount of Revenue from Dairy Products

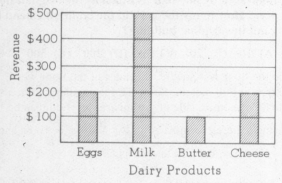

8. During week 1, revenue from eggs provided what percent of the total revenue for Store X?

(A) 4%
(B) 5%
(C) 8%
(D) 20%
(E) 25%

From the bar graph, it can be determined that total revenue from dairy products was \$200 + \$500 + \$100 + \$200 = \$1,000, and the revenue from eggs was $\frac{200}{1,000}$ or $\frac{1}{5}$ of the total for dairy products. The circle graph shows that 25 percent of the store's revenue was from dairy products. Therefore, revenue from eggs provided $\frac{1}{5}$ of 25 percent or 5 percent of the total revenues for store X. Thus, the best answer is B.

9. If the revenue from the sale of apples was equal to the revenue from the sale of miscellaneous items, what percent of the revenue from the sale of fruit and vegetables was accounted for by apples?

(A) 60%
(B) 15%
(C) 12%
(D)   6%
(E)   3%

Let t represent the total revenue. The circle graph shows that revenue from the sale of miscellaneous items (or apples) was 0.03t and revenue from fruits and vegetables was 0.20t. Therefore, revenue from the sale of apples as a percent of revenues from the sale of fruits and vegetables was $\frac{0.03t}{0.20t} = \frac{3}{20} = 15\%$. Thus, the best answer is B.

10. The (x, y) pair $(-1, 1)$ satisfies which of the following equations?

I. $2x^3 - y^2 = -3$
II. $2x^2 - y^3 = 1$
III. $x^2 - 2y^3 = -1$

(A) I only
(B) I and II only
(C) I and III only
(D) II and III only
(E) I, II, and III

By substituting -1 for x and 1 for y in each of the equations, it can be verified that $(-1,1)$ satisfies all three equations:

I. $2(-1)^3 - 1^2 = -2 - 1 = -3$
II. $2(-1)^2 - (1)^3 = 2 - 1 = 1$
III. $(-1)^2 - 2(1)^3 = 1 - 2 = -1$

Thus, the best answer is E.

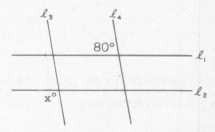

Note: Figure not drawn to scale.

11. If $\ell_1 \parallel \ell_2$ in the figure above, what is the value of x?

(A) 80
(B) 90
(C) 100
(D) 120
(E) It cannot be determined from the information given.

Since the problem states that ℓ_1 is parallel to ℓ_2 and the figure shows that ℓ_4 intersects these parallel lines at an 80-degree angle, all of the angles associated with lines ℓ_1, ℓ_2, and ℓ_4 measure either 80 degrees or 100 degrees. However, since no information is given about the slope of line ℓ_3, the value of x could be any number between 0 and 180. Thus, the best answer is E.

12. A 5-liter jug contains 4 liters of a saltwater solution that is 15 percent salt. If 1.5 liters of the solution spills out of the jug, and the jug is then filled to capacity with water, approximately what percent of the resulting solution in the jug is salt?

(A) $7\frac{1}{2}\%$

(B) $9\frac{3}{8}\%$

(C) $10\frac{1}{2}\%$

(D) 12%
(E) 15%

At the outset the jug contains 4 liters of the solution, but 1.5 liters are spilled, leaving only 2.5 liters. If 15 percent of the solution is salt, the jug contains $0.15(2.5) = 0.375$ liters of salt. When water is added to fill the jug to capacity, the jug will contain 5 liters of a weaker solution. Since no salt was added, there is still 0.375 liters of salt in the weaker solution.

Therefore, the resulting solution contains $\frac{0.375}{5} = 7.5\%$ salt.

Thus, the best answer is A.

13. The average (arithmetic mean) of 3 different positive integers is 100 and the largest of these 3 integers is 120. What is the least possible value of the smallest of these 3 integers?

(A) 1 (B) 10 (C) 61 (D) 71 (E) 80

If the average of three integers is 100, then the sum of the three integers is 3(100) or 300. If the largest of the three is 120, then the sum of the other two must be $300 - 120 = 180$. Suppose that x is the smaller of the two integers and y is the larger. Now x will assume its least value when y assumes its greatest value since $x + y = 180$. Since 120 is the greatest of the three integers, y can assume a maximum value of 119, and the least possible value of x is $180 - 119 = 61$. Thus, the best answer is C.

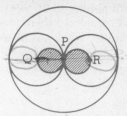

14. In the figure above, the five circles have points in common as shown. P is the center of the largest circle, Q and R are centers of the medium-sized circles, and Q, P, and R are points on a straight line. What fraction of the largest circular region is shaded?

(A) $\frac{1}{16}$ (B) $\frac{1}{8}$ (C) $\frac{3}{16}$ (D) $\frac{1}{4}$ (E) $\frac{1}{2}$

Since points Q, P, and R are points on a line and P is the center of the largest circle, Q, P, and R lie on the diameter of the largest circle and also on the diameters of the four smaller circles. Thus, it becomes obvious that the diameter of the largest circle is 4 times the diameter of one of the smallest circles; similarly the radius of the largest circle is 4 times the radius of the smallest circle. Therefore, if the radius of the smallest circle is r, the radius of the largest circle is 4r and the ratio of the area of the shaded region to the area of the largest circle is

$$\frac{2(\pi r^2)}{\pi(4r)^2} = \frac{2\pi r^2}{16\pi r^2} = \frac{1}{8}.$$

Thus, the best answer is B.

15. If $xyz \neq 0$ and x percent of y percent of z is t, then z =

(A) $\frac{100t}{xy}$

(B) $\frac{1,000t}{xy}$

(C) $\frac{10,000t}{xy}$

(D) $\frac{xy}{10,000t}$

(E) $\frac{10,000xy}{t}$

x percent of y percent of z is equivalent to $\left(\frac{x}{100}\right)\left(\frac{y}{100}\right)z$, which is equal to t. If $\frac{xyz}{10,000} = t$, then $xyz = 10,000t$ and $z = \frac{10,000t}{xy}$. Thus, the best answer is C.

-55-

16. A plane traveled k miles in the first 96 minutes of flight time. If it completed the remaining 300 miles of the trip in t minutes, what was its average speed, in miles per hour, for the entire trip?

(A) $\dfrac{60(k + 300)}{96 + t}$

(B) $\dfrac{kt + 96(300)}{96t}$

(C) $\dfrac{k + 300}{60(96 + t)}$

(D) $\dfrac{5k}{8} + \dfrac{60(300)}{t}$

(E) $\dfrac{5k}{8} + 5t$

The average speed, in miles per hour, for the entire trip is equal to the total distance in miles (k + 300) divided by the total time in hours, $\left(\dfrac{96 + t}{60}\right)$ or $\dfrac{k + 300}{\dfrac{96 + t}{60}}$. The division can be simplified by multiplying both the numerator and denominator by 60 and obtaining $\dfrac{60(k + 300)}{96 + t}$. Thus, the best answer is A.

17. A merchant sells an item at a 20 percent discount, but still makes a gross profit of 20 percent of the cost. What percent of the cost would the gross profit on the item have been if it had been sold without the discount?

(A) 20%
(B) 40%
(C) 50%
(D) 60%
(E) 75%

Let x represent the price before the 20 percent discount and let c represent the cost. Then the merchant sold the item for 0.8x, which was equal to 120% of the cost c. Algebraically, the relationship is 0.8x = 1.2c and x = 1.5c = cost plus 50% profit. Thus, had the item been sold at the original price, the gross profit would have been 50 percent of the cost. Thus, the best answer is C.

18. A milliner bought a job lot of hats, $\frac{1}{4}$ of which were brown. The milliner sold $\frac{2}{3}$ of the hats including $\frac{4}{5}$ of the brown hats. What fraction of the unsold hats were brown?

(A) $\dfrac{1}{60}$ (B) $\dfrac{2}{15}$ (C) $\dfrac{3}{20}$ (D) $\dfrac{3}{5}$ (E) $\dfrac{3}{4}$

Let t be the total number of hats in the lot. Then, from the information in the problem, the following table of values can be assembled:

Hats sold: $\frac{2t}{3}$	Brown hats: $\frac{1}{4}t$
Hats unsold: $\left(t - \dfrac{2t}{3}\right) = \dfrac{t}{3}$	Brown hats sold: $\dfrac{4}{5}\left(\dfrac{t}{4}\right) = \dfrac{t}{5}$
	Brown hats unsold: $\dfrac{1}{5}\left(\dfrac{t}{4}\right) = \dfrac{t}{20}$

To find the fraction of the unsold hats that were brown, it is necessary to take the ratio of brown hats unsold $\left(\dfrac{t}{20}\right)$ to total unsold hats $\left(\dfrac{t}{3}\right)$. The ratio $\dfrac{t}{20} : \dfrac{t}{3} = \dfrac{3}{20}$. Thus, the best answer is C.

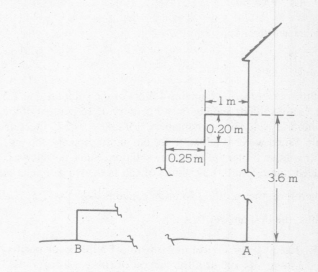

Note: Figure not drawn to scale.

19. Each step of a staircase is 0.25 meter wide and 0.20 meter high, as shown in the figure above. All angles shown in the figure are right angles. If the height of the staircase is 3.6 meters and the landing at the top of the staircase is 1 meter wide, how long, in meters, is AB?

(A) 3.0
(B) 4.25
(C) 4.5
(D) 5.25
(E) 5.5

The sum of the widths of the steps, including the landing, is equal to the length of AB. This can be seen by projecting the width of each step onto segment AB. Therefore, to find the length of AB, it is sufficient to find the number of steps, each 0.25 meters wide, and then to add on the 1-meter width of the landing at the top. Since the rise (total height) up to the last step before the landing is 3.6 − 0.20 or 3.4 meters, you can find the number of steps by dividing this total height by the height of each step. Thus, $3.4 \div 0.20 = 17$ steps, and length AB is $17(0.25) + 1 = 5.25$ meters. Thus, the best answer is D.

20. **How many integers n greater than 10 and less than 100 are there such that, if the digits of n are reversed, the resulting integer is n + 9?**

 (A) 5 (B) 6 (C) 7 (D) 8 (E) 9

To solve a problem that involves the digits of a number, it is convenient to let t represent the tens' digit and u represent the units' digit. Since n is between 10 and 100, n is a two-digit number that has the value $10t + u$ and $n + 9$ can be represented by the expression $(10t + u) + 9$. If the digits of n are reversed, the value of the resulting integer will be $10u + t$. According to the problem, $10u + t = n + 9$ or $10u + t = (10t + u) + 9$, which simplifies to $u = t + 1$. In other words, n must be a two-digit number in which the units' digit is one more than the tens' digit. The eight numbers that have this property are 12, 23, 34, 45, 56, 67, 78, and 89. Thus, the best answer is D.

PROBLEM SOLVING SAMPLE TEST SECTION 2

30 Minutes
20 Questions

Directions: In this section solve each problem, using any available space on the page for scratchwork. Then indicate the best of the answer choices given.

Numbers: All numbers used are real numbers.

Figures: Figures that accompany problems in this section are intended to provide information useful in solving the problems. They are drawn as accurately as possible EXCEPT when it is stated in a specific problem that its figure is not drawn to scale. All figures lie in a plane unless otherwise indicated.

1. An investor purchased x shares of stock at a certain price. If the stock then increased in price $0.25 per share and the total increase for the x shares was $12.50, how many shares of stock had been purchased?

   (A) 25   (B) 50   (C) 75   (D) 100   (E) 125

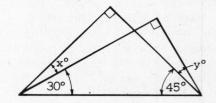

2. If $x > 0$ and $x^2 = 161$, what is the best whole number approximation of x ?

   (A) 13   (B) 18   (C) 41   (D) 80   (E) 2,560

3. In the figure above, what is the value of $2x - y$?

   (A) 0   (B) 15   (C) 30   (D) 45   (E) 60

GO ON TO THE NEXT PAGE.

-58-

4. $\dfrac{\dfrac{1}{2}\left(\dfrac{\frac{3}{4}}{\frac{2}{3}}\right)}{\dfrac{2}{9}} =$

(A) $\dfrac{81}{32}$ (B) $\dfrac{9}{4}$ (C) $\dfrac{9}{8}$ (D) $\dfrac{1}{8}$ (E) $\dfrac{1}{18}$

5. At a special sale, 5 tickets can be purchased for the price of 3 tickets. If 5 tickets are purchased at this sale, the amount saved will be what percent of the original price of the 5 tickets?

(A)   20%

(B) $33\dfrac{1}{3}\%$

(C)   40%

(D)   60%

(E) $66\dfrac{2}{3}\%$

6. Which of the following is equal to $\dfrac{3}{8}$ of 1.28 ?

(A) $\dfrac{24}{5}$

(B) $\dfrac{12}{25}$

(C) $\dfrac{13}{50}$

(D) $\dfrac{6}{25}$

(E) $\dfrac{4}{25}$

GO ON TO THE NEXT PAGE.

7. Working independently, Tina can do a certain job in 12 hours. Working independently, Ann can do the same job in 9 hours. If Tina works independently at the job for 8 hours and then Ann works independently, how many hours will it take Ann to complete the remainder of the job?

(A) $\frac{2}{3}$ (B) $\frac{3}{4}$ (C) 1   (D) 2   (E) 3

8. A factory normally produces x units per working day. In a month with 22 working days, no units are produced in the first y working days because of a strike. How many units must be produced per day on each of the rest of the working days of the month in order to have an average of x units per working day for the entire month?

(A) 11x

(B) 22x

(C) $\frac{22x}{y}$

(D) $\frac{22x}{22-y}$

(E) $\frac{22x}{22xy-y}$

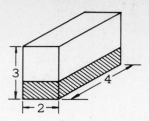

9. An enclosed rectangular tank with dimensions 2 meters by 3 meters by 4 meters is filled with water to a depth of 1 meter as shown by the shaded region in the figure above. If the tank is turned so that it rests on one of its smallest faces, the depth, in meters, of the water will be

(A) $\frac{2}{3}$ (B) 1   (C) $\frac{4}{3}$ (D) $\frac{5}{3}$ (E) 2

GO ON TO THE NEXT PAGE.

10. A person bought a ticket to a ball game for $15 and later sold the ticket for $60. What was the percent increase in the price of the ticket?

(A)　25%

(B)　$33\frac{1}{3}\%$

(C)　75%

(D)　300%

(E)　400%

11. A decorator bought a bolt of defective cloth that he judged to be $\frac{3}{4}$ usable, in which case the cost would be $0.80 per usable yard. If it was later found that only $\frac{2}{3}$ of the bolt could be used, what was the actual cost per usable yard?

(A) $0.60
(B) $0.90
(C) $1.00
(D) $1.20
(E) $1.70

Week	Number of Tickets Sold
1	1,000,000
2	1,000,000
3	750,000
4	250,000

12. The table above shows the number of tickets sold during each of the first 4 weeks after a movie was released. The producer of the movie received 10 percent of the revenue from every ticket sold with a guaranteed minimum of $200,000 per week for the first 4 weeks. If tickets sold for $4 each, how much did the producer receive for the first 4 weeks?

(A)　$800,000
(B)　$900,000
(C)　$1,000,000
(D)　$1,200,000
(E)　$1,300,000

13. If x, y, and z are single-digit integers and $100(x) + 1,000(y) + 10(z) = N$, what is the units' digit of the number N ?

(A) 0　(B) 1　(C) x　(D) y　(E) z

GO ON TO THE NEXT PAGE.

14. Three stacks containing equal numbers of chips are to be made from 9 red chips, 7 blue chips, and 5 green chips. If all of these chips are used and each stack contains at least 1 chip of each color, what is the maximum number of red chips in any one stack?

(A) 7
(B) 6
(C) 5
(D) 4
(E) 3

15. Three automobiles travel distances that are in the ratios of $1:2:3$. If the ratios of the traveling times over these distances for these automobiles are $3:2:1$ in the same respective order, what are the ratios of their respective average speeds?

(A) $1:1:1$
(B) $1:2:3$
(C) $1:3:9$
(D) $3:2:1$
(E) $3:4:3$

16. Over the last three years a scientist had an average (arithmetic mean) yearly income of $45,000. The scientist earned $1\frac{1}{2}$ times as much the second year as the first year and $2\frac{1}{2}$ times as much the third year as the first year. What was the scientist's income the second year?

(A) $9,000
(B) $13,500
(C) $27,000
(D) $40,500
(E) $45,000

17. How many two-digit whole numbers yield a remainder of 1 when divided by 10 and also yield a remainder of 1 when divided by 6?

(A) None   (B) One   (C) Two
(D) Three   (E) Four

GO ON TO THE NEXT PAGE.

18. If $x \neq 3$ and $\dfrac{x^2 - 9}{2y} = \dfrac{x - 3}{4}$, then, in terms of y, x =

(A) $\dfrac{y - 6}{2}$

(B) $\dfrac{y - 3}{2}$

(C) $y - 3$

(D) $y - 6$

(E) $\dfrac{y + 6}{2}$

19. The figure above shows the shape of a sign to be placed in front of a flower store. The sign has a semicircle on each side of the square. If the sign is 3 centimeters thick and if each side of the square is 50 centimeters long, what is the volume, in cubic centimeters, of the sign?

(A) $1,250\pi + 2,500$
(B) $3,750\pi$
(C) $3,750\pi + 7,500$
(D) $5,000\pi + 7,500$
(E) $11,250\pi$

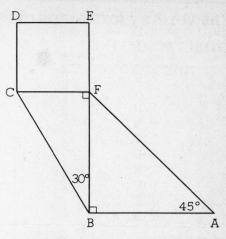

20. In the figure above, square CDEF has area 4. What is the area of $\triangle ABF$?

(A) $2\sqrt{2}$ (B) $2\sqrt{3}$ (C) 4   (D) $3\sqrt{3}$ (E) 6

S T O P

IF YOU FINISH BEFORE TIME IS CALLED, YOU MAY CHECK YOUR WORK ON THIS SECTION ONLY.
DO NOT TURN TO ANY OTHER SECTION IN THE TEST.

Answer Key for Sample Test Section 2

PROBLEM SOLVING

1. B	11. B
2. A	12. E
3. B	13. A
4. A	14. C
5. C	15. C
6. B	16. D
7. E	17. D
8. D	18. A
9. C	19. C
10. D	20. E

Explanatory Material: Problem Solving Sample Test Section 2

1. An investor purchased x shares of stock at a certain price. If the stock then increased in price $0.25 per share and the total increase for the x shares was $12.50, how many shares of stock had been purchased?

   (A) 25   (B) 50   (C) 75   (D) 100   (E) 125

If each of the x shares of stock increased by $0.25, and the total increase was $12.50, then $0.25x = 12.50$ and $x = 12.50/0.25 = 50$. Thus, the best answer is B.

2. If $x > 0$ and $x^2 = 161$, what is the best whole number approximation of x?

   (A) 13   (B) 18   (C) 41   (D) 80   (E) 2,560

Since $x^2 = 161$ and x is positive, $x = \sqrt{161}$. Since $12^2 = 144$ and $13^2 = 169$, $12 < \sqrt{161} < 13$. Therefore, 13 is the best whole number approximation of x among the options given, and the best answer is A.

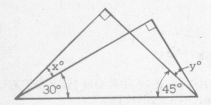

3. In the figure above, what is the value of $2x - y$?

   (A) 0   (B) 15   (C) 30   (D) 45   (E) 60

In both right triangles, the sum of the measures of the two acute angles must equal 90°. Therefore, $x + 30 + 45 = 90$, $x = 15$; and $y + 45 + 30 = 90$, $y = 15$. Thus, $2x - y = 2(15) - 15 = 15$, and the best answer is B.

4. $\dfrac{\dfrac{1}{2}\left(\dfrac{\frac{3}{4}}{\frac{2}{3}}\right)}{\frac{2}{9}} =$

   (A) $\frac{81}{32}$ (B) $\frac{9}{4}$ (C) $\frac{9}{8}$ (D) $\frac{1}{8}$ (E) $\frac{1}{18}$

To simplify, $\dfrac{\dfrac{1}{2}\left(\dfrac{\frac{3}{4}}{\frac{2}{3}}\right)}{\frac{2}{9}} = \dfrac{\frac{1}{2}\left(\frac{3}{4} \cdot \frac{3}{2}\right)}{\frac{2}{9}} = \dfrac{\frac{9}{16}}{\frac{2}{9}} = \frac{9}{16} \cdot \frac{9}{2} = \frac{81}{32}.$

Thus, the best answer is A.

5. At a special sale, 5 tickets can be purchased for the price of 3 tickets. If 5 tickets are purchased at this sale, the amount saved will be what percent of the original price of the 5 tickets?

   (A) 20%

   (B) $33\frac{1}{3}\%$

   (C) 40%

   (D) 60%

   (E) $66\frac{2}{3}\%$

If 5 tickets at sale price s cost the same as 3 tickets at the regular price p, then $5s = 3p$ and $s = \frac{3}{5}p$. Since the sale price is $\frac{3}{5}$ or 60 percent of the original price, $\frac{2}{5}$ or 40 percent is saved. Thus, the best answer is C.

6. Which of the following is equal to $\frac{3}{8}$ of 1.28?

   (A) $\frac{24}{5}$

   (B) $\frac{12}{25}$

   (C) $\frac{13}{50}$

   (D) $\frac{6}{25}$

   (E) $\frac{4}{25}$

$\frac{3}{8}$ of $1.28 = \left(\frac{3}{8}\right)\left(\frac{\overset{32}{\cancel{128}}}{\underset{25}{\cancel{100}}}\right) = \left(\frac{3}{\cancel{8}}\right)\left(\frac{\overset{4}{\cancel{32}}}{\underset{1}{25}}\right) = \frac{12}{25}.$

Thus, the best answer is B.

7. Working independently, Tina can do a certain job in 12 hours. Working independently, Ann can do the same job in 9 hours. If Tina works independently at the job for 8 hours and then Ann works independently, how many hours will it take Ann to complete the remainder of the job?

(A) $\frac{2}{3}$ (B) $\frac{3}{4}$ (C) 1 (D) 2 (E) 3

Since Tina can do the job in 12 hours, in 8 hours she can do 8/12, or 2/3, of the job. This leaves 1/3 of the job for Ann to complete. Since Ann can do the job in 9 hours, she can do 1/3 of the job in 3 hours. Thus, the best answer is E.

8. A factory normally produces x units per working day. In a month with 22 working days, no units are produced in the first y working days because of a strike. How many units must be produced per day on each of the rest of the working days of the month in order to have an average of x units per working day for the entire month?

(A) 11x

(B) 22x

(C) $\frac{22x}{y}$

(D) $\frac{22x}{22-y}$

(E) $\frac{22x}{22xy-y}$

To have an average of x units per day for the 22 days, a total of 22x units must be produced in the shorter period, 22 − y days. The number to be produced per day =

$\frac{\text{total production}}{\text{number of production days}} = \frac{22x}{22-y}$. Thus, the best answer is D.

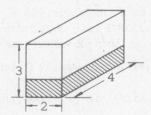

9. An enclosed rectangular tank with dimensions 2 meters by 3 meters by 4 meters is filled with water to a depth of 1 meter as shown by the shaded region in the figure above. If the tank is turned so that it rests on one of its smallest faces, the depth, in meters, of the water will be

(A) $\frac{2}{3}$ (B) 1 (C) $\frac{4}{3}$ (D) $\frac{5}{3}$ (E) 2

The total volume of water in the tank is 2·4·1 = 8 cubic meters. If the tank were placed on one of its 2-meter by 3-meter faces, the total volume of water could be expressed as 2·3·d = 6d cubic meters, where d is the depth of the water.

Since the volume of the water is the same regardless of the face on which the tank rests,

6d = 8, or d = $\frac{4}{3}$ meters. Thus, the best answer is C.

10. A person bought a ticket to a ball game for $15 and later sold the ticket for $60. What was the percent increase in the price of the ticket?

(A)   25%

(B) $33\frac{1}{3}$%

(C)   75%

(D)   300%

(E)   400%

The increase in the price was $60 − $15 = $45. Therefore, the percent increase was $\frac{\$45}{\$15}$ = 3 = 300%. Thus, the best answer is D.

11. A decorator bought a bolt of defective cloth that he judged to be $\frac{3}{4}$ usable, in which case the cost would be $0.80 per usable yard. If it was later found that only $\frac{2}{3}$ of the bolt could be used, what was the actual cost per usable yard?

(A) $0.60
(B) $0.90
(C) $1.00
(D) $1.20
(E) $1.70

Of the N original yards of cloth, $\frac{3N}{4}$ were judged to be usable. Therefore, the total cost for the usable yards can be represented by $0.80\left(\frac{3N}{4}\right)$. If, in fact, only 2/3 of N are usable, and c is the cost per usable yard, the total cost for the usable yards would be $c\left(\frac{2N}{3}\right)$. Therefore,

$c\left(\frac{2N}{3}\right) = 0.80\left(\frac{3N}{4}\right)$.

When both sides of the equation are multiplied by 12, the result is c(8N) = 0.80 (9N), 8c = 7.20, and c = $0.90. Thus, the best answer is B.

Week	Number of Tickets Sold
1	1,000,000
2	1,000,000
3	750,000
4	250,000

12. The table above shows the number of tickets sold during each of the first 4 weeks after a movie was released. The producer of the movie received 10 percent of the revenue from every ticket sold with a guaranteed minimum of $200,000 each week for the first 4 weeks. If tickets sold for $4 each, how much did the producer receive for the first 4 weeks?

(A) $800,000
(B) $900,000
(C) $1,000,000
(D) $1,200,000
(E) $1,300,000

Since the producer received 10 percent of the revenue and each ticket sold for $4, the producer received $0.40 per ticket sold. Therefore, the producer's income each week was:

Week 1 : 1,000,000(0.40) = $400,000
Week 2 : 1,000,000(0.40) = $400,000
Week 3 :   750,000(0.40) = $300,000
Week 4 :   250,000(0.40) = $100,000 + $100,000*

Total = $1,300,000

*There was a guaranteed minimum of $200,000 each week.

Thus, the best answer is E.

13. If x, y, and z are single-digit integers and $100(x) + 1,000(y) + 10(z) = N$, what is the units' digit of the number N?

(A) 0   (B) 1   (C) x   (D) y   (E) z

Since each of the three terms of N is a multiple of 10, N is a multiple of 10. Thus, the units' digit of N must be zero, and the best answer is A.

14. Three stacks containing equal numbers of chips are to be made from 9 red chips, 7 blue chips, and 5 green chips. If all of these chips are used and each stack contains at least 1 chip of each color, what is the maximum number of red chips in any one stack?

(A) 7
(B) 6
(C) 5
(D) 4
(E) 3

Since there is a total of 21 chips, each of the three stacks must contain 7 chips and at least one chip of each color. If one blue and one green chip are part of the stack, the maximum number of red chips in any one stack is 5. Thus, the best answer is C.

15. Three automobiles travel distances that are in the ratios of 1:2:3. If the ratios of the traveling times over these distances for these automobiles are 3:2:1 in the same respective order, what are the ratios of their respective average speeds?

(A) 1:1:1
(B) 1:3:3
(C) 1:3:9
(D) 3:2:1
(E) 3:4:3

Since speed $= \dfrac{\text{distance}}{\text{time}}$, the ratios of the speeds for the three automobiles must be $\frac{1}{3} : \frac{2}{2} : \frac{3}{1}$, which is equivalent to $3\left(\frac{1}{3}\right) : 3\left(\frac{2}{2}\right) : 3\left(\frac{3}{1}\right)$ or $1 : 3 : 9$. Thus, the best answer is C.

16. Over the last three years a scientist had an average (arithmetic mean) yearly income of $45,000. The scientist earned $1\frac{1}{2}$ times as much the second year as the first year and $2\frac{1}{2}$ times as much the third year as the first year. What was the scientist's income the second year?

(A) $9,000
(B) $13,500
(C) $27,000
(D) $40,500
(E) $45,000

The total income for the three years was $(3)(45,000) = \$135,000$. Let x represent the scientist's income the first year. Then the second-year income was $\frac{3}{2}x$ and the third-year income was $\frac{5}{2}x$. Therefore,

$x + \frac{3}{2}x + \frac{5}{2}x = 135,000$, $5x = 135,000$, and $x = 27,000$.

Thus the second-year income was $\frac{3}{2}(27,000) = \$40,500$.

Thus, the best answer is D.

17. How many two-digit whole numbers yield a remainder of 1 when divided by 10 and also yield a remainder of 1 when divided by 6?

(A) None   (B) One   (C) Two
   (D) Three   (E) Four

For a whole number n to have a remainder of 1 when divided by both 10 and 6, n − 1 must be divisible by both 10 and 6, or by the least common multiple of 10 and 6, which is 30. Therefore, the two-digit whole numbers that yield a remainder of 1 when divided by both 6 and 10 are 31, 61, and 91. There are only three such numbers, and the best answer is D.

18. If $x \neq 3$ and $\frac{x^2 - 9}{2y} = \frac{x - 3}{4}$, then, in terms

of y, x =

(A) $\frac{y - 6}{2}$

(B) $\frac{y - 3}{2}$

(C) $y - 3$

(D) $y - 6$

(E) $\frac{y + 6}{2}$

First, multiply both sides of the equation by the least

common denominator, 4y: $4y\left(\frac{x^2 - 9}{2y}\right) = 4y\left(\frac{x - 3}{4}\right)$,

and $2(x^2 - 9) = y(x - 3)$.

Then, express $x^2 - 9$ as $(x + 3)(x - 3)$ and divide both sides by x − 3:

$$\frac{2(x + 3)(x - 3)}{x - 3} = \frac{y(x - 3)}{x - 3}$$

$$2(x + 3) = y$$
$$2x + 6 = y$$
$$2x = y - 6$$
$$x = \frac{y - 6}{2}$$

Thus, the best answer is A.

19. The figure above shows the shape of a sign to be placed in front of a flower store. The sign has a semicircle on each side of the square. If the sign is 3 centimeters thick and if each side of the square is 50 centimeters long, what is the volume, in cubic centimeters, of the sign?

(A) $1,250\pi + 2,500$
(B) $3,750\pi$
(C) $3,750\pi + 7,500$
(D) $5,000\pi + 7,500$
(E) $11,250\pi$

The volume of the sign is equal to the surface area times the depth. The surface consists of a square and four semicircles (two whole circles). The area of the square is $(50)^2$ or 2,500. Each of the two circles has diameter 50 and radius 25; therefore, the area of each of the two circles is $\pi(25)^2 = 625\pi$. The total surface area equals $2,500 + (2 \times 625\pi)$, or $2,500 + 1,250\pi$. The volume is $3(2,500 + 1,250\pi)$, or $7,500 + 3,750\pi$. Thus, the best answer is C.

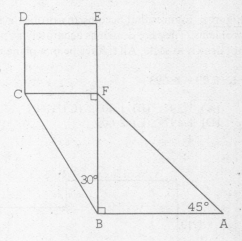

20. In the figure above, square CDEF has area 4. What is the area of △ABF?

(A) $2\sqrt{2}$ (B) $2\sqrt{3}$ (C) 4 (D) $3\sqrt{3}$ (E) 6

Since the square has area 4, CF = 2. Triangle BCF is a 30-60-90 right triangle; therefore, CB = 2(CF) = 2(2) = 4. Applying the Pythagorean Theorem to

△BCF: $(BF)^2 = (CB)^2 − (CF)^2 = 4^2 − 2^2 = 12$,

and $BF = \sqrt{12}$. BF = BA, since they are both opposite 45° angles. Therefore, $BA = \sqrt{12}$ and the area of

$\triangle ABF = \frac{(BA)(BF)}{2} = \frac{(\sqrt{12})\sqrt{12}}{2} = 6$. Thus, the best

answer is E.

PROBLEM SOLVING SAMPLE TEST SECTION 3

30 Minutes
20 Questions

Directions: In this section solve each problem, using any available space on the page for scratchwork. Then indicate the best of the answer choices given.

Numbers: All numbers used are real numbers.

Figures: Figures that accompany problems in this section are intended to provide information useful in solving the problems. They are drawn as accurately as possible EXCEPT when it is stated in a specific problem that its figure is not drawn to scale. All figures lie in a plane unless otherwise indicated.

1. $6.09 - 4.693 =$

(A) 1.397 (B) 1.403 (C) 1.407
(D) 1.497 (E) 2.603

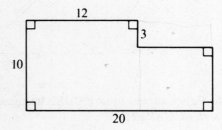

2. What is the area of the region enclosed by the figure above?

(A) 116 (B) 144 (C) 176
(D) 179 (E) 284

3. If $p = 0.2$ and $n = 100$, then $\sqrt{\dfrac{p(1-p)}{n}} =$

(A) $-\sqrt{0.002}$
(B) $\sqrt{0.02} - 0.02$
(C) 0
(D) 0.04
(E) 0.4

4. If each of 4 subsidiaries of Corporation R has been granted a line of credit of $700,000 and each of the other 3 subsidiaries of Corporation R has been granted a line of credit of $112,000, what is the average (arithmetic mean) line of credit granted to a subsidiary of Corporation R?

(A) $1,568,000
(B) $448,000
(C) $406,000
(D) $313,600
(E) $116,000

GO ON TO THE NEXT PAGE.

-68-

5. If x is a number such that $x^2 - 3x + 2 = 0$ and $x^2 - x - 2 = 0$, what is the value of x?

   (A) -2
   (B) -1
   (C)   0
   (D)   1
   (E)   2

6. In traveling from a dormitory to a certain city, a student went $\frac{1}{5}$ of the way by foot, $\frac{2}{3}$ of the way by bus, and the remaining 8 kilometers by car. What is the distance, in kilometers, from the dormitory to the city?

   (A) 30 (B) 45 (C) 60 (D) 90 (E) 120

7. A certain elevator has a safe weight limit of 2,000 pounds. What is the greatest possible number of people who can safely ride on the elevator at one time with the average (arithmetic mean) weight of half the riders being 180 pounds and the average weight of the others being 215 pounds?

   (A) 7
   (B) 8
   (C) 9
   (D) 10
   (E) 11

8. After paying a 10 percent tax on all income over $3,000, a person had a net income of $12,000. What was the income before taxes?

   (A) $13,300
   (B) $13,000
   (C) $12,900
   (D) $10,000
   (E) $9,000

GO ON TO THE NEXT PAGE.

9. $1 - [2 - (3 - [4 - 5] + 6) + 7] =$

   (A) -2 (B) 0 (C) 1 (D) 2 (E) 16

10. The price of a model M camera is $209 and the price of a special lens is $69. When the camera and lens are purchased together, the price is $239. The amount saved by purchasing the camera and lens together is approximately what percent of the total price of the camera and lens when purchased separately?

    (A) 14%
    (B) 16%
    (C) 29%
    (D) 33%
    (E) 86%

11. If 0.497 mark has the value of one dollar, what is the value to the nearest dollar of 350 marks?

    (A) $174 (B) $176 (C) $524
    (D) $696 (E) $704

12. A right cylindrical container with radius 2 meters and height 1 meter is filled to capacity with oil. How many empty right cylindrical cans, each with radius $\frac{1}{2}$ meter and height 4 meters, can be filled to capacity with the oil in this container?

    (A) 1
    (B) 2
    (C) 4
    (D) 8
    (E) 16

13. If a sequence of 8 consecutive odd integers with increasing values has 9 as its 7th term, what is the sum of the terms of the sequence?

    (A) 22
    (B) 32
    (C) 36
    (D) 40
    (E) 44

GO ON TO THE NEXT PAGE.

14. A rectangular floor is covered by a rug except for a strip p meters wide along each of the four edges. If the floor is m meters by n meters, what is the area of the rug, in square meters?

(A) $mn - p(m + n)$
(B) $mn - 2p(m + n)$
(C) $mn - p^2$
(D) $(m - p)(n - p)$
(E) $(m - 2p)(n - 2p)$

15. Working alone, R can complete a certain kind of job in 9 hours. R and S, working together at their respective rates, can complete one of these jobs in 6 hours. In how many hours can S, working alone, complete one of these jobs?

(A) 18
(B) 12
(C) 9
(D) 6
(E) 3

16. A family made a down payment of $75 and borrowed the balance on a set of encyclopedias that cost $400. The balance with interest was paid in 23 monthly payments of $16 each and a final payment of $9. The amount of interest paid was what percent of the amount borrowed?

(A) 6%
(B) 12%
(C) 14%
(D) 16%
(E) 20%

17. If $x \neq 0$ and $x = \sqrt{4xy - 4y^2}$, then, in terms of y, $x =$

(A) $2y$
(B) y
(C) $\dfrac{y}{2}$
(D) $\dfrac{-4y^2}{1 - 4y}$
(E) $-2y$

GO ON TO THE NEXT PAGE.

18. Solution Y is 30 percent liquid X and 70 percent water. If 2 kilograms of water evaporate from 8 kilograms of solution Y and 2 kilograms of solution Y are added to the remaining 6 kilograms of liquid, what percent of this new solution is liquid X?

(A) 30%

(B) $33\frac{1}{3}$%

(C) $37\frac{1}{2}$%

(D) 40%

(E) 50%

19. $\dfrac{1}{\dfrac{1}{0.03}+\dfrac{1}{0.37}}=$

(A) 0.004
(B) 0.02775
(C) 2.775
(D) 3.6036
(E) 36.036

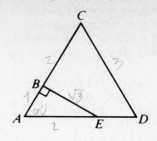

20. If each side of $\triangle ACD$ above has length 3 and if AB has length 1, what is the area of region $BCDE$?

(A) $\dfrac{9}{4}$ (B) $\dfrac{7}{4}\sqrt{3}$ (C) $\dfrac{9}{4}\sqrt{3}$

(D) $\dfrac{7}{2}\sqrt{3}$ (E) $6+\sqrt{3}$

S T O P

IF YOU FINISH BEFORE TIME IS CALLED, YOU MAY CHECK YOUR WORK ON THIS SECTION ONLY.
DO NOT TURN TO ANY OTHER SECTION IN THE TEST.

Answer Key for Sample Test Section 3

PROBLEM SOLVING

1.	A	11.	E
2.	C	12.	C
3.	D	13.	B
4.	B	14.	E
5.	E	15.	A
6.	C	16.	D
7.	D	17.	A
8.	B	18.	C
9.	D	19.	B
10.	A	20.	B

Explanatory Material: Problem Solving Sample Test Section 3

1. $6.09 - 4.693 =$

   (A) 1.397   (B) 1.403   (C) 1.407
   (D) 1.497   (E) 2.603

$$\begin{array}{r} 6.090 \\ -4.693 \\ \hline 1.397 \end{array}$$

Thus, the best answer is A.

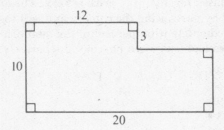

2. **What is the area of the region enclosed by the figure above?**

   (A) 116   (B) 144   (C) 176
   (D) 179   (E) 284

If a line is drawn dividing the figure into two rectangles, the length of the horizontal segment is $20 - 12 = 8$ and the length of the vertical segment of the smaller rectangle is $10 - 3 = 7$. (See below.)

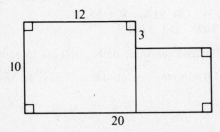

Thus, the area of the region is $(10 \times 12) + (8 \times 7) = 176$. Therefore, the best answer is C.

3. If $p = 0.2$ and $n = 100$, then $\sqrt{\dfrac{p(1 - p)}{n}} =$

   (A) $-\sqrt{0.002}$
   (B) $\sqrt{0.0002} - 0.02$
   (C) 0
   (D) 0.04
   (E) 0.4

Substituting for p and n in the radical expression yields:

$$\sqrt{\frac{(0.2)(1 - 0.2)}{100}} = \sqrt{\frac{(0.2)(0.8)}{100}} = \sqrt{\frac{0.16}{100}} = \frac{0.4}{10} = 0.04$$

Thus, the best answer is D.

4. **If each of 4 subsidiaries of Corporation R has been granted a line of credit of \$700,000 and each of the other 3 subsidiaries of Corporation R has been granted a line of credit of \$112,000, what is the average (arithmetic mean) line of credit granted to a subsidiary of Corporation R?**

   (A) \$1,568,000
   (B) \$ 448,000
   (C) \$ 406,000
   (D) \$ 313,600
   (E) \$ 116,000

The total amount of credit for the 7 subsidiaries is:

$4(\$700,000) + 3(\$112,000) = \$3,136,000$.

Therefore, the average per subsidiary is $\dfrac{\$3,136,000}{7} =$ \$448,000, and the best answer is B.

5. **If x is a number such that $x^2 - 3x + 2 = 0$ and $x^2 - x - 2 = 0$, what is the value of x?**

   (A) -2
   (B) -1
   (C) 0
   (D) 1
   (E) 2

Since both polynomials are equal to 0, they are equal to each other. Thus, $x^2 - 3x + 2 = x^2 - x - 2$, $-2x = -4$ and $x = 2$. Therefore, the best answer is E.

6. In traveling from a dormitory to a certain city, a student went $\frac{1}{5}$ of the way by foot, $\frac{2}{3}$ of the way by bus, and the remaining 8 kilometers by car. What is the distance, in kilometers, from the dormitory to the city?

   (A) 30　(B) 45　(C) 60　(D) 90　(E) 120

The student went on foot and by bus $\frac{1}{5} + \frac{2}{3}$ of the way, which is $\frac{3}{15} + \frac{10}{15} = \frac{13}{15}$. Therefore, the student went $1 - \frac{13}{15}$ of the way by car. Since $\frac{2}{15}$ of the distance from the dormitory to the city equals 8 kilometers, the distance equals $\frac{15}{2} \cdot 8 = 60$ kilometers. Thus, the best answer is C.

7. A certain elevator has a safe weight limit of 2,000 pounds. What is the greatest possible number of people who can safely ride on the elevator at one time with the average (arithmetic mean) weight of half the riders being 180 pounds and the average weight of the others being 215 pounds?

   (A)　7
   (B)　8
   (C)　9
   (D)　10
   (E)　11

If n is the greatest number of people who safely ride on the elevator at one time,

$\frac{n}{2}(180)$ is the total weight of half the group

and $\frac{n}{2}(215)$ is the total weight of the other half.

Therefore, $\frac{n}{2}(180) + \frac{n}{2}(215) \leq 2,000$

$$180n + 215n \leq 4,000$$
$$395n \leq 4,000$$
$$n \leq 10.2$$

Since n must be an integer, n = 10. Therefore, the best answer is D.

8. After paying a 10 percent tax on all income over $3,000, a person had a net income of $12,000. What was the income before taxes?

   (A) $13,300
   (B) $13,000
   (C) $12,900
   (D) $10,000
   (E) $ 9,000

If x dollars is the income before taxes, then the net income of $12,000 is equal to $3,000 plus the amount left over after the remaining (x − 3,000) dollars is taxed 10 percent, or (0.9)(x − 3,000) dollars. Therefore,

$$3,000 + (0.9)(x - 3,000) = 12,000$$
$$(0.9)(x - 3,000) = 9,000$$
$$0.9x - 2,700 = 9,000$$
$$0.9x = 11,700$$
$$x = \frac{11,700}{0.9} = 13,000$$

Thus, the best answer is B.

9. $1 - [2 - (3 - [4 - 5] + 6) + 7]$

   (A) −2　(B) 0　(C) 1　(D) 2　(E) 16

When removing parentheses and brackets, always remove the innermost parentheses first.

$1 - [2 - (3 - [4 - 5] + 6) + 7] =$
$1 - [2 - (3 - [-1] + 6) + 7] =$
$1 - [2 - (3 + 1 + 6) + 7] =$
$1 - [2 - 10 + 7] =$
$1 - [-1] = 1 + 1 = 2$

Thus, the best answer is D.

10. The price of a model *M* camera is $209 and the price of a special lens is $69. When the camera and lens are purchased together, the price is $239. The amount saved by purchasing the camera and lens together is approximately what percent of the total price of the camera and lens when purchased separately?

    (A) 14%
    (B) 16%
    (C) 29%
    (D) 33%
    (E) 86%

The total price of the camera and lens purchased separately is $209 + $69 = $278. The amount saved by purchasing the two together is $278 − $239 = $39. Therefore, the percent saving is $\frac{\$39}{\$278}$ or approximately 14%. Thus, the best answer is A.

11. If 0.497 mark has the value of one dollar, what is the value to the nearest dollar of 350 marks?

    (A) $174　(B) $176　(C) $524
    (D) $696　(E) $704

Since 0.497 mark equals one dollar, 350 marks equal $\frac{350}{0.497}$ dollars, or $704, to the nearest dollar. Thus, the best answer is E.

12. A right cylindrical container with radius 2 meters and height 1 meter is filled to capacity with oil. How many empty right cylindrical cans, each with radius $\frac{1}{2}$ meter and height 4 meters, can be filled to capacity with the oil in this container?

(A) 1
(B) 2
(C) 4
(D) 8
(E) 16

The total capacity of the right cylindrical container is $\pi r^2 h = \pi(2)^2(1) = 4\pi$ cubic meters. Each right cylindrical can has a total capacity of $\pi\left(\frac{1}{2}\right)^2(4) = \pi$ cubic meters. Therefore, the container can fill up $\frac{4\pi}{\pi}$, or 4, cans. Thus, the best answer is C.

13. If a sequence of 8 consecutive odd integers with increasing values has 9 as its 7th term, what is the sum of the terms of the sequence?

(A) 22
(B) 32
(C) 36
(D) 40
(E) 44

To derive the terms in the sequences, it is only necessary to write 9 and the six consecutive odd integers less than 9 and the next one greater than 9.

The sequence is: $-3, -1, 1, 3, 5, 7, 9, 11$, and the sum of the terms in the sequence is 32. Thus, the best answer is B.

14. A rectangular floor is covered by a rug except for a strip p meters wide along each of the four edges. If the floor is m meters by n meters, what is the area of the rug, in square meters?

(A) $mn - p(m + n)$
(B) $mn - 2p(m + n)$
(C) $mn - p^2$
(D) $(m - p)(n - p)$
(E) $(m - 2p)(n - 2p)$

It may be helpful to draw a diagram:

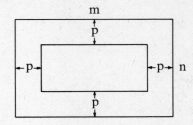

The rug is represented by the inside rectangle with dimensions $m - 2p$ and $n - 2p$. Therefore, its area is $(m - 2p)(n - 2p)$. Thus, the best answer is E.

15. Working alone, R can complete a certain kind of job in 9 hours. R and S, working together at their respective rates, can complete one of these jobs in 6 hours. In how many hours can S, working alone, complete one of these jobs?

(A) 18
(B) 12
(C) 9
(D) 6
(E) 3

If x is the number of hours S needs to complete the job alone, then S can do $\frac{1}{x}$ of the job in one hour. Similarly, R can do $\frac{1}{9}$ of the job in one hour, and R and S, working together, can do $\frac{1}{6}$ of the job in one hour. Therefore, $\frac{1}{x} + \frac{1}{9} = \frac{1}{6}$, and x = 18 hours. Thus, the best answer is A.

16. A family made a down payment of $75 and borrowed the balance on a set of encyclopedias that cost $400. The balance with interest was paid in 23 monthly payments of $16 each and a final payment of $9. The amount of interest paid was what percent of the amount borrowed?

(A) 6%
(B) 12%
(C) 14%
(D) 16%
(E) 20%

The family had to borrow $400 − $75 = $325. They paid back 23(16) + $9 = $377. Therefore, they paid $377 − $325 = $52 in interest, which was $\frac{52}{325} = 16\%$ of the amount borrowed. Thus, the best answer is D.

17. If $x \neq 0$ and $x = \sqrt{4xy - 4y^2}$, then in terms of y, $x =$

(A) $2y$

(B) y

(C) $\dfrac{y}{2}$

(D) $\dfrac{-4y^2}{1 - 4y}$

(E) $-2y$

The value of x can be expressed in terms of y as follows:

$$x = \sqrt{4xy - 4y^2}$$
$$x^2 = 4xy - 4y^2$$
$$x^2 - 4xy + 4y^2 = 0$$
$$(x - 2y)^2 = 0$$
$$x - 2y = 0$$
$$x = 2y$$

Therefore, the best answer is A.

18. Solution Y is 30 percent liquid X and 70 percent water. If 2 kilograms of water evaporate from 8 kilograms of solution Y and 2 kilograms of solution Y are added to the remaining 6 kilograms of liquid, what percent of this new solution is liquid X?

(A) 30%

(B) $33\frac{1}{3}$%

(C) $37\frac{1}{2}$%

(D) 40%

(E) 50%

The original 8 kilograms (kg) of solution Y contains 30%, or 2.4 kg, of liquid X. If 2 kg of water evaporate from the 8 kg, that would leave 6 kg, of which 2.4 kg is liquid X. If 2 kg of solution Y is added to the remaining 6 kg of solution, the resulting 8 kg-solution would contain 2.4 + 0.3(2) kg of liquid X. Therefore, the percent of liquid X in the new solution would be

$$\frac{2.4 + 0.6}{8} = \frac{3}{8} = 37\frac{1}{2}\%.$$

Thus, the best answer is C.

19. $\dfrac{1}{\dfrac{1}{0.03} + \dfrac{1}{0.37}} =$

(A) 0.004

(B) 0.02775

(C) 2.775

(D) 3.6036

(E) 36.036

The value of the expression can be found as follows:

$$\frac{1}{\dfrac{1}{0.03} + \dfrac{1}{0.37}} = \frac{1}{\dfrac{0.37 + 0.03}{(0.03)(0.37)}} = \frac{(0.03)(0.37)}{0.37 + 0.03} = \frac{0.0111}{0.4} = 0.02775$$

Therefore, the best answer is B.

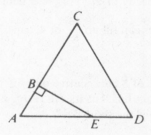

20. If each side of $\triangle ACD$ above has length 3 and if AB has length 1, what is the area of region $BCDE$?

(A) $\dfrac{9}{4}$ (B) $\dfrac{7}{4}\sqrt{3}$ (C) $\dfrac{9}{4}\sqrt{3}$

(D) $\dfrac{7}{2}\sqrt{3}$ (E) $6 + \sqrt{3}$

The area of region BCDE can be found by subtracting the area of $\triangle$ABE from the area of $\triangle$ACD. Since ACD is equilateral, an altitude to its base divides the triangle into two identical right triangles with acute angles of 30 and 60 degrees. Since the hypotenuse of each right triangle is 3 and the base is $\frac{3}{2}$, the altitude must be $\sqrt{3^2 - \left(\frac{3}{2}\right)^2}$ or $\frac{3\sqrt{3}}{2}$, which is also the altitude of $\triangle$ACD. Therefore, the area of $\triangle$ACD is $\frac{1}{2}(3)\left(\frac{3\sqrt{3}}{2}\right) = \frac{9}{4}\sqrt{3}$. Since right $\triangle$ABE also has acute angles of 30 and 60 degrees and AB = 1, then AE = 2(1) and BE = $\sqrt{2^2 - 1^2} = \sqrt{3}$. The area of $\triangle$ABE is $\frac{1}{2}(1)(\sqrt{3}) = \frac{\sqrt{3}}{2}$. Therefore, the area of region BCDE is $\frac{9}{4}\sqrt{3} - \frac{1}{2}(\sqrt{3}) = \frac{7}{4}\sqrt{3}$, and the best answer is B.

PROBLEM SOLVING SAMPLE TEST SECTION 4

30 Minutes
20 Questions

Directions: In this section solve each problem, using any available space on the page for scratchwork. Then indicate the best of the answer choices given.

Numbers: All numbers used are real numbers.

Figures: Figures that accompany problems in this section are intended to provide information useful in solving the problems. They are drawn as accurately as possible EXCEPT when it is stated in a specific problem that its figure is not drawn to scale. All figures lie in a plane unless otherwise indicated.

1. Which of the following is equal to 85 percent of 160?

   (A) 1.88 (B) 13.6 (C) 136
   (D) 188 (E) 13,600

2. The regular hourly wage for an employee of a certain factory is $5.60. If the employee worked 8 hours overtime and earned $1\frac{1}{2}$ times this regular hourly wage for overtime, how much overtime money was earned?

   (A) $67.20
   (B) $55.40
   (C) $50.00
   (D) $44.80
   (E) $12.00

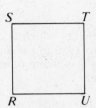

3. Square *RSTU* shown above is rotated in a plane about its center in a clockwise direction the minimum number of degrees necessary for *T* to be in the position where *S* is now shown. The number of degrees through which *RSTU* is rotated is

   (A) 135° (B) 180° (C) 225°
   (D) 270° (E) 315°

GO ON TO THE NEXT PAGE.

BREAKDOWN OF COST TO CONSUMER FOR THE PRODUCTION OF 6 OUNCES OF FROZEN ORANGE JUICE

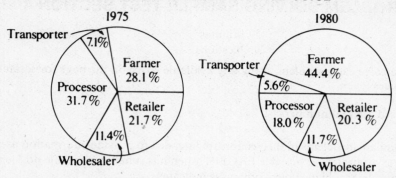

Cost to Consumer: $0.30   Cost to Consumer: $0.70

4. Of the following, which is closest to the increase from 1975 to 1980 in the amount received by the processor in producing 6 ounces of frozen orange juice?

(A) $0.03   (B) $0.05   (C) $0.06
(D) $0.08   (E) $0.13

5. In 1980, approximately what fraction of the cost to the consumer for the production of 6 ounces of frozen orange juice went to the farmer?

(A) $\frac{3}{11}$ (B) $\frac{1}{3}$ (C) $\frac{4}{9}$ (D) $\frac{5}{9}$ (E) $\frac{3}{5}$

GO ON TO THE NEXT PAGE.

6. $\sqrt[4]{496}$ is between

(A) 3 and 4
(B) 4 and 5
(C) 5 and 6
(D) 6 and 7
(E) 7 and 8

7. If $x \neq 0$, $2x = 5y$, and $3z = 7x$, what is the ratio of z to y?

(A) 2 to 21   (B) 3 to 5   (C) 14 to 15
(D) 6 to 5   (E) 35 to 6

8. A grocer purchased a quantity of bananas at 3 pounds for $0.50 and sold the entire quantity at 4 pounds for $1.00. How many pounds did the grocer purchase if the profit from selling the bananas was $10.00?

(A)   40
(B)   60
(C)   90
(D) 120
(E) 240

9. There are between 100 and 110 cards in a collection of cards. If they are counted out 3 at a time, there are 2 left over, but if they are counted out 4 at a time, there is 1 left over. How many cards are in the collection?

(A) 101   (B) 103   (C) 106   (D) 107   (E) 109

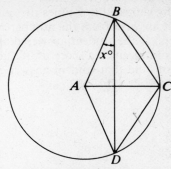

Note: Figure not drawn to scale.

10. If A is the center of the circle shown above and $AB = BC = CD$, what is the value of x?

(A) 15   (B) 30   (C) 45   (D) 60   (E) 75

11. Out of a total of 1,000 employees at a certain corporation, 52 percent are female and 40 percent of these females work in research. If 60 percent of the total number of employees work in research, how many male employees do NOT work in research?

(A) 520
(B) 480
(C) 392
(D) 208
(E)   88

GO ON TO THE NEXT PAGE.

12. An instructor scored a student's test of 50 questions by subtracting 2 times the number of incorrect answers from the number of correct answers. If the student answered all of the questions and received a score of 38, how many questions did that student answer correctly?

(A) 19
(B) 38
(C) 41
(D) 44
(E) 46

13. Which of the following integers does NOT have a divisor greater than 1 that is the square of an integer?

(A) 75
(B) 42
(C) 32
(D) 25
(E) 12

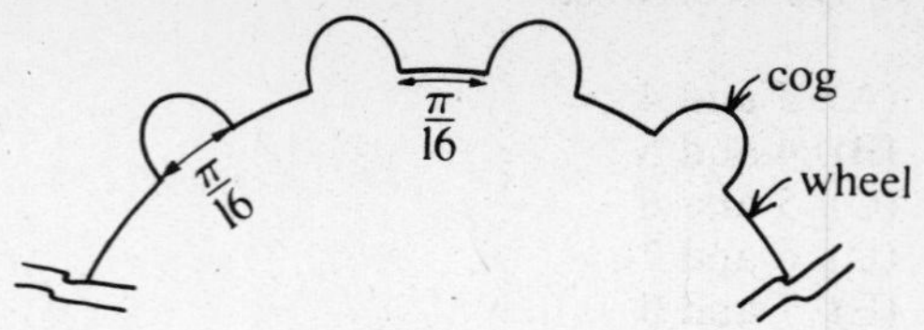

14. There are cogs around the circumference of a wheel and each cog is $\frac{\pi}{16}$ centimeter wide with a space of $\frac{\pi}{16}$ centimeter between consecutive cogs, as shown above. How many cogs of this size, with the same space between any two consecutive cogs, fit on a wheel with diameter 6 centimeters?

(A) 96
(B) 64
(C) 48
(D) 32
(E) 24

GO ON TO THE NEXT PAGE.

15. If $r \odot s = rs + r + s,$ then for what value of s is $r \odot s$ equal to r for all values of r?

(A) -1 (B) 0 (C) 1 (D) $\dfrac{1}{r+1}$ (E) r

16. In each production lot for a certain toy, 25 percent of the toys are red and 75 percent of the toys are blue. Half the toys are size A and half are size B. If 10 out of a lot of 100 toys are red and size A, how many of the toys are blue and size B?

(A) 15
(B) 25
(C) 30
(D) 35
(E) 40

17. If $2x + 5y = 8$ and $3x = 2y,$ what is the value of $2x + y$?

(A) 4

(B) $\dfrac{70}{19}$

(C) $\dfrac{64}{19}$

(D) $\dfrac{56}{19}$

(E) $\dfrac{40}{19}$

18. A ladder 25 feet long is leaning against a wall that is perpendicular to level ground. The bottom of the ladder is 7 feet from the base of the wall. If the top of the ladder slips down 4 feet, how many feet will the bottom of the ladder slip?

(A) 4
(B) 5
(C) 8
(D) 9
(E) 15

19. What is the least possible product of 4 different integers, each of which has a value between -5 and 10, inclusive?

(A) -5040 (B) -3600 (C) -720
(D) -600 (E) -120

20. If a motorist had driven 1 hour longer on a certain day and at an average rate of 5 miles per hour faster, he would have covered 70 more miles than he actually did. How many more miles would he have covered than he actually did if he had driven 2 hours longer and at an average rate of 10 miles per hour faster on that day?

(A) 100
(B) 120
(C) 140
(D) 150
(E) 160

S T O P

**IF YOU FINISH BEFORE TIME IS CALLED, YOU MAY CHECK YOUR WORK ON THIS SECTION ONLY.
DO NOT TURN TO ANY OTHER SECTION IN THE TEST.**

Answer Key for Sample Test Section 4

PROBLEM SOLVING

1. C	11. E
2. A	12. E
3. D	13. B
4. A	14. C
5. C	15. B
6. B	16. D
7. E	17. D
8. D	18. C
9. A	19. B
10. B	20. D

Explanatory Material: Problem Solving Sample Test Section 4

1. Which of the following is equal to 85 percent of 160?

   (A) 1.88   (B) 13.6   (C) 136
   (D) 188   (E) 13,600

The number equal to 85 percent of 160 can be found by multiplying $160 \times .85 = 136$. Therefore, the best answer is C.

2. The regular hourly wage for an employee of a certain factory is $5.60. If the employee worked 8 hours overtime and earned $1\frac{1}{2}$ times this regular hourly wage for overtime, how much overtime money was earned?

   (A) $67.20
   (B) $55.40
   (C) $50.00
   (D) $44.80
   (E) $12.00

The employee would have earned $8 \times \$5.60 = \$44.80$ at the regular rate. For overtime he receives an additional amount equal to half the regular rate, or $22.40. The total overtime earnings are therefore $\$44.80 + \$22.40 = \$67.20$, so the best answer is A.

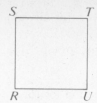

3. Square *RSTU* shown above is rotated in a plane about its center in a clockwise direction the minimum number of degrees necessary for *T* to be in the position where *S* is now shown. The number of degrees through which *RSTU* is rotated is

   (A) 135°   (B) 180°   (C) 225°
   (D) 270°   (E) 315°

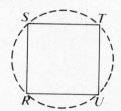

The figure above shows the circle traced by point T as square RSTU rotates about its center. If the square made one complete rotation so that T returned to its original position, the square would have rotated 360 degrees. Since the square rotates clockwise only until point T moves to position S, which is $\frac{3}{4}$ of the way around the circle, the square rotates $\frac{3}{4}$ of 360 or 270 degrees. Thus, the best answer is D.

BREAKDOWN OF COST TO CONSUMER
FOR THE PRODUCTION OF
6 OUNCES OF FROZEN ORANGE JUICE

1975

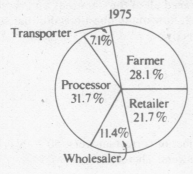

Cost to Consumer: $0.30

1980

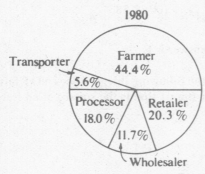

Cost to Consumer: $0.70

4. **Of the following, which is closest to the increase from 1975 to 1980 in the amount received by the processor in producing 6 ounces of frozen orange juice?**

   (A) $0.03 (B) $0.05 (C) $0.06
   (D) $0.08 (E) $0.13

In 1975 the processor received 31.7% of the total $0.30 cost, or approximately $0.10. In 1980 the processor received 18% of the total $0.70 cost, or approximately $0.13. The increase is therefore approximately $0.03. The best answer is therefore A.

5. **In 1980, approximately what fraction of the cost to the consumer for the production of 6 ounces of frozen orange juice went to the farmer?**

   (A) $\frac{3}{11}$ (B) $\frac{1}{3}$ (C) $\frac{4}{9}$ (D) $\frac{5}{9}$ (E) $\frac{3}{5}$

The farmer received 44.4% of the total, which is somewhat less than half. Answers D and E can be eliminated because each exceeds $\frac{1}{2}$. A and B can be eliminated because they are too small: $\frac{3}{11}$ is less than 30% and $\frac{1}{3}$ is about 33%. That C is the best answer can be confirmed by finding the decimal equivalent of $\frac{4}{9}$, which is approximately 0.44.

6. $\sqrt[4]{496}$ is between

   (A) 3 and 4
   (B) 4 and 5
   (C) 5 and 6
   (D) 6 and 7
   (E) 7 and 8

If $x = \sqrt[4]{496}$, then $x^4 = 496$. Since $4^4 = 256$ and $5^4 = 625$, x must be between 4 and 5. Thus, the best answer is B.

7. **If $x \neq 0$, $2x = 5y$, and $3z = 7x$, what is the ratio of z to y?**

   (A) 2 to 21   (B) 3 to 5   (C) 14 to 15
   (D) 6 to 5   (E) 35 to 6

To find the ratio of z to y, it is convenient to express both z and y in terms of x. Thus $z = \frac{7}{3}x$ and $y = \frac{2}{5}x$. Then the ratio of z to y is $\frac{7}{3}x : \frac{2}{5}x = \left(\frac{7}{3}\right)\left(\frac{5}{2}\right) = \frac{35}{6}$. Thus, the best answer is E.

8. **A grocer purchased a quantity of bananas at 3 pounds for $0.50 and sold the entire quantity at 4 pounds for $1.00. How many pounds did the grocer purchase if the profit from selling the bananas was $10.00?**

   (A)   40
   (B)   60
   (C)   90
   (D)   120
   (E)   240

Let P represent the number of pounds purchased. Then the grocer's cost is $\left(\frac{0.50}{3}\right)P$ and his revenue is $\left(\frac{1.00}{4}\right)P$. Profit is revenue minus cost, so

$$10 = \left(\frac{1.00}{4}\right)P - \left(\frac{0.50}{3}\right)P$$

$$120 = 3P - 2P = P$$

Thus, the best answer is D.

9. **There are between 100 and 110 cards in a collection of cards. If they are counted out 3 at a time, there are 2 left over, but if they are counted out 4 at a time, there is 1 left over. How many cards are in the collection?**

   (A) 101   (B) 103   (C) 106   (D) 107   (E) 109

If the cards are counted three at a time with two left over, the possible totals are 101, 104, or 107. If they are counted four at a time with one left over, the total must be 101, 105, or 109. The only answer that satisfied both conditions is 101, so the best answer is A.

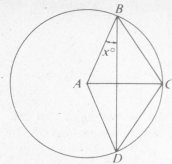

Note: Figure not drawn to scale.

10. If A is the center of the circle shown above and $AB = BC = CD$, what is the value of x?

(A) 15 (B) 30 (C) 45 (D) 60 (E) 75

$AC = AB = AD$, since all are radii of the same circle. Therefore, $AB = BC = CD = AC = AD$, and the triangles ABC and ACD are both equilateral and their angles are all equal to 60°. Because $AB = AD$, $\triangle ABD$ is an isosceles triangle and its base angles are therefore equal. Thus, the measure of $\angle ADB$ is x°. The sum of the degree measures of the angles of triangle ABD is $2x + 60 + 60 = 180$, so $x = 30$. The best answer is therefore B.

11. Out of a total of 1,000 employees at a certain corporation, 52 percent are female and 40 percent of these females work in research. If 60 percent of the total number of employees work in research, how many male employees do NOT work in research?

(A) 520
(B) 480
(C) 392
(D) 208
(E) 88

	Total Employees	Research Workers
Female	520	208
Male	480	392
TOTAL	1,000	600

The information presented in the problem is summarized in the table above. Of the 520 females (.52 × 1,000), 208 work in research (.40 × 520 = 208). The number of research workers who are male is 392, since 208 of the 600 (.60 × 1,000) research workers are female. Thus, there are $480 - 392 = 88$ males who do not work in research. Therefore, the best answer is E.

12. An instructor scored a student's test of 50 questions by subtracting 2 times the number of incorrect answers from the number of correct answers. If the student answered all of the questions and received a score of 38, how many questions did that student answer correctly?

(A) 19
(B) 38
(C) 41
(D) 44
(E) 46

If N is the number of correct answers, $50 - N$ is the number of incorrect answers. Therefore,

$$N - 2(50 - N) = 38$$
$$3N - 100 = 38$$
$$N = \frac{100 + 38}{3} = 46$$

Thus, the best answer is E.

13. Which of the following integers does NOT have a divisor greater than 1 that is the square of an integer?

(A) 75
(B) 42
(C) 32
(D) 25
(E) 12

Note that $75 = 3 \times 5^2$, $32 = 2 \times 4^2$, $25 = 1 \times 5^2$ and $12 = 3 \times 2^2$. Since $42 = 2 \times 3 \times 7$ and so does not have a divisor greater than 1 that is the square of an integer, the best answer is B.

14. There are cogs around the circumference of a wheel and each cog is $\frac{\pi}{16}$ centimeter wide with a space of $\frac{\pi}{16}$ centimeter between consecutive cogs, as shown above. How many cogs of this size, with the same space between any two consecutive cogs, fit on a wheel with diameter 6 centimeters?

(A) 96
(B) 64
(C) 48
(D) 32
(E) 24

The circumference of a circle equals π times the diameter. If the diameter is 6 cm, the circumference is 6π. Each cog, together with a space separating it from the next one, uses

$2 \times \frac{\pi}{16} = \frac{\pi}{8}$ cm. The total number of cogs that would fit is therefore $6\pi \div \left(\frac{\pi}{8}\right) = 6\pi \times \frac{8}{\pi} = 48$. Thus, the best answer is C.

15. If $r \odot s = rs + r + s$, then for what value of s is $r \odot s$ equal to r for all values of r?

(A) −1 (B) 0 (C) 1 (D) $\frac{1}{r+1}$ (E) r

For $r \odot s$ to equal r,
$$rs + r + s = r$$
$$rs + s = 0$$
$$s(r + 1) = 0$$

If $s = 0$, than $s(r + 1) = 0$ is true for all values of r. If $s \neq 0$, than $s(r + 1) = 0$ is true only if $r = -1$. Thus, the best answer is B.

16. In each production lot for a certain toy, 25 percent of the toys are red and 75 percent of the toys are blue. Half the toys are size A and half are size B. If 10 out of a lot of 100 toys are red and size A, how many of the toys are blue and size B?

(A) 15
(B) 25
(C) 30
(D) 35
(E) 40

	Total	Size A	Size B
Red	25	10	15
Blue	75	40	35
Total	100	50	50

The information presented in the problem is summarized in the table above. If 50 of the toys are size A, and 10 are red, then 40 of the size A toys are blue. If 75 toys are blue, and 40 of these are size A, then $75 - 40 = 35$ toys are size B and blue. The best answer is therefore D.

17. If $2x + 5y = 8$ and $3x = 2y$, what is the value of $2x + y$?

(A) 4
(B) $\frac{70}{19}$
(C) $\frac{64}{19}$
(D) $\frac{56}{19}$
(E) $\frac{40}{19}$

Since $3x = 2y$, $x = \frac{2y}{3}$. Substituting into the other equation for x yields

$$2\left(\frac{2y}{3}\right) + 5y = 8$$
$$4y + 15y = 24$$
$$19y = 24$$
$$y = \frac{24}{19}$$

Then
$$x = \left(\frac{2}{3}\right)\left(\frac{24}{19}\right) = \frac{16}{19}, \text{ and } 2x + y = 2\left(\frac{16}{19}\right) + \frac{24}{19} = \frac{56}{19}.$$

Thus, the best answer is D.

18. A ladder 25 feet long is leaning against a wall that is perpendicular to level ground. The bottom of the ladder is 7 feet from the base of the wall. If the top of the ladder slips down 4 feet, how many feet will the bottom of the ladder slip?

(A) 4
(B) 5
(C) 8
(D) 9
(E) 15

It may be helpful to draw a figure showing the information given:

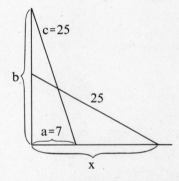

The original height of the top of the ladder can be obtained by the equation $a^2 + b^2 = c^2$ from the Pythagorean Theorem. In this case, $7^2 + b^2 = 25^2$, so $b^2 = 625 - 49 = 576$, or $b = 24$.

After the ladder slips, the hypotenuse of the new triangle is still 25, but the vertical side is now 4 feet shorter, or 20 feet. The new base, x, can be obtained using the same procedure: $20^2 + x^2 = 25^2$, so $x = \sqrt{625 - 400} = 15$.

Since the bottom of the ladder was originally 7 feet from the wall and is now 15 feet from the wall, it has slipped 8 feet. Therefore, the best answer is C.

19. What is the least possible product of 4 different integers, each of which has a value between -5 and 10, inclusive?

(A) -5040 (B) -3600 (C) -720
(D) -600 (E) -120

The least possible product in this case is the negative product having greatest absolute value, which can be obtained by multiplying $(-5) \times 10 \times 9 \times 8 = -3,600$. Thus, the best answer is B.

20. If a motorist had driven 1 hour longer on a certain day and at an average rate of 5 miles per hour faster, he would have covered 70 more miles than he actually did. How many more miles would he have covered than he actually did if he had driven 2 hours longer and at an average rate of 10 miles per hour faster on that day?

(A) 100
(B) 120
(C) 140
(D) 150
(E) 160

Since distance equals rate times time, $D = rt$, where D, r, and t are the actual distance, rate, and time traveled. If the motorist drives 1 hour longer and at a rate 5 mph faster, the new distance

$$D' = (r + 5)(t + 1) = rt + 70$$
$$rt + 5t + r + 5 = rt + 70$$
$$5t + r = 65$$

If instead he drives 2 hours longer, and at a rate 10 mph faster, the new distance

$$D'' = (r + 10)(t + 2) = rt + 10t + 2r + 20$$
$$= rt + 2(5t + r) + 20.$$

Then

$$D'' - D = rt + 2(5t + r) + 20 - rt$$
$$= 2(65) + 20 = 150.$$

The best answer is therefore D.

PROBLEM SOLVING SAMPLE TEST SECTION 5

30 Minutes
20 Questions

Directions: In this section solve each problem, using any available space on the page for scratchwork. Then indicate the best of the answer choices given.

Numbers: All numbers used are real numbers.

Figures: Figures that accompany problems in this section are intended to provide information useful in solving the problems. They are drawn as accurately as possible EXCEPT when it is stated in a specific problem that its figure is not drawn to scale. All figures lie in a plane unless otherwise indicated.

1. What is the average (arithmetic mean) of the numbers 15, 16, 17, 17, 18, and 19 ?

   (A) 14.2   (B) 16.5   (C) 17   (D) 17.5   (E) 18

2. Kathy bought 4 times as many shares in Company X as Carl, and Carl bought 3 times as many shares in the same company as Tom. Which of the following is the ratio of the number of shares bought by Kathy to the number of shares bought by Tom?

   (A) $\frac{3}{4}$

   (B) $\frac{4}{3}$

   (C) $\frac{3}{1}$

   (D) $\frac{4}{1}$

   (E) $\frac{12}{1}$

3. Of the following, which is closest to $\dfrac{0.15 \times 495}{9.97}$?

   (A) 7.5   (B) 15   (C) 75   (D) 150   (E) 750

4. A manager has $6,000 budgeted for raises for 4 full-time and 2 part-time employees. Each of the full-time employees receives the same raise, which is twice the raise that each of the part-time employees receives. What is the amount of the raise that each full-time employee receives?

   (A) $750
   (B) $1,000
   (C) $1,200
   (D) $1,500
   (E) $3,000

GO ON TO THE NEXT PAGE.

5. $x^2 - \left(\dfrac{x}{2}\right)^2 =$

    (A) $x^2 - x$

    (B) $\dfrac{x^2}{4}$

    (C) $\dfrac{x^2}{2}$

    (D) $\dfrac{3x^2}{4}$

    (E) $\dfrac{3x^2}{2}$

6. A hospital pharmacy charges $0.40 per fluidram of a certain medicine but allows a discount of 15 percent to Medicare patients. How much should the pharmacy charge a Medicare patient for 3 fluidounces of the medicine? (128 fluidrams = 16 fluidounces)

    (A) $9.60
    (B) $8.16
    (C) $3.20
    (D) $2.72
    (E) $1.02

7. $(-1)^2 - (-1)^3 =$

    (A) -2 (B) -1 (C) 0 (D) 1 (E) 2

8. At a certain bowling alley, it costs $0.50 to rent bowling shoes for the day and $1.25 to bowl 1 game. If a person has $12.80 and must rent shoes, what is the greatest number of complete games that person can bowl in one day?

    (A) 7
    (B) 8
    (C) 9
    (D) 10
    (E) 11

GO ON TO THE NEXT PAGE.

9. If $\frac{x}{y} = 2$, then $\frac{x - y}{x} =$

(A) -1

(B) $-\frac{1}{2}$

(C) $\frac{1}{2}$

(D) 1

(E) 2

10. If each photocopy of a manuscript costs 4 cents per page, what is the cost, in cents, to reproduce x copies of an x-page manuscript?

(A) $4x$ (B) $16x$ (C) x^2

(D) $4x^2$ (E) $16x^2$

11. Ken left a job paying $75,000 per year to accept a sales job paying $45,000 per year plus 15 percent commission. If each of his sales is for $750, what is the least number of sales he must make per year if he is not to lose money because of the change?

(A) 40
(B) 200
(C) 266
(D) 267
(E) 600

GO ON TO THE NEXT PAGE.

MONTHLY KILOWATT-HOURS

	500	1,000	1,500	2,000
Present	$24.00	$41.00	$57.00	$73.00
Proposed	$26.00	$45.00	$62.00	$79.00

12. The table above shows present rates and proposed rates for electricity for residential customers. For which of the monthly kilowatt-hours shown would the proposed rate be the greatest percent increase over the present rate?

(A) 500
(B) 1,000
(C) 1,500
(D) 2,000
(E) Each of the percent increases is the same.

13. If a, b, and c are three consecutive odd integers such that $10 < a < b < c < 20$ and if b and c are prime numbers, what is the value of $a + b$?

(A) 24
(B) 28
(C) 30
(D) 32
(E) 36

14. Of a group of people surveyed in a political poll, 60 percent said that they would vote for candidate R. Of those who said they would vote for R, 90 percent actually voted for R, and of those who did not say that they would vote for R, 5 percent actually voted for R. What percent of the group voted for R?

(A) 56%
(B) 59%
(C) 62%
(D) 65%
(E) 74%

15. If $r = 1 + \dfrac{1}{3} + \dfrac{1}{9} + \dfrac{1}{27}$ and $s = 1 + \dfrac{1}{3}r$, then s exceeds r by

(A) $\dfrac{1}{3}$ (B) $\dfrac{1}{6}$ (C) $\dfrac{1}{9}$ (D) $\dfrac{1}{27}$ (E) $\dfrac{1}{81}$

GO ON TO THE NEXT PAGE.

16. $\dfrac{0.025 \times \frac{15}{2} \times 48}{5 \times 0.0024 \times \frac{3}{4}} =$

    (A)   0.1
    (B)   0.2
    (C)   100
    (D)   200
    (E) 1,000

17. A student responded to all of the 22 questions on a test and received a score of 63.5. If the scores were derived by adding 3.5 points for each correct answer and deducting 1 point for each incorrect answer, how many questions did the student answer <u>incorrectly</u>?

    (A) 3   (B) 4   (C) 15   (D) 18   (E) 20

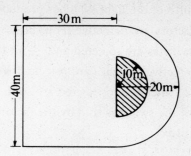

18. The figure above represents a rectangular parking lot that is 30 meters by 40 meters and an attached semicircular driveway that has an outer radius of 20 meters and an inner radius of 10 meters. If the shaded region is <u>not</u> included, what is the area, in square meters, of the lot and driveway?

    (A) $1,350\pi$
    (B) $1,200 + 400\pi$
    (C) $1,200 + 300\pi$
    (D) $1,200 + 200\pi$
    (E) $1,200 + 150\pi$

GO ON TO THE NEXT PAGE.

19. One-fifth of the light switches produced by a certain factory are defective. Four-fifths of the defective switches are rejected and $\frac{1}{20}$ of the nondefective switches are rejected by mistake. If all the switches not rejected are sold, what percent of the switches sold by the factory are defective?

(A) 4%
(B) 5%
(C) 6.25%
(D) 11%
(E) 16%

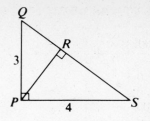

20. In $\triangle PQS$ above, if $PQ = 3$ and $PS = 4$, then $PR =$

(A) $\frac{9}{4}$ (B) $\frac{12}{5}$ (C) $\frac{16}{5}$ (D) $\frac{15}{4}$ (E) $\frac{20}{3}$

S T O P

IF YOU FINISH BEFORE TIME IS CALLED, YOU MAY CHECK YOUR WORK ON THIS SECTION ONLY. DO NOT TURN TO ANY OTHER SECTION IN THE TEST.

Answer Key for Sample Test Section 5

PROBLEM SOLVING

1. C	11. D
2. E	12. B
3. A	13. D
4. C	14. A
5. D	15. E
6. B	16. E
7. E	17. A
8. C	18. E
9. C	19. B
10. D	20. B

Explanatory Material: Problem Solving Sample Test Section 5

1. **What is the average (arithmetic mean) of the numbers 15, 16, 17, 17, 18, and 19?**

   (A) 14.2   (B) 16.5   (C) 17   (D) 17.5   (E) 18

The "brute force" method of solving this problem is to add the six numbers and divide the sum by 6. However, the same answer can be obtained by inspection, by observing that the mean of the first three numbers is 16 and the mean of the last three numbers is 18. The mean of the original six numbers is equal to the mean of 16 and 18, or 17. Thus, the best answer is C.

2. **Kathy bought 4 times as many shares in Company X as Carl, and Carl bought 3 times as many shares in the same company as Tom. Which of the following is the ratio of the number of shares bought by Kathy to the number of shares bought by Tom?**

   (A) $\frac{3}{4}$

   (B) $\frac{4}{3}$

   (C) $\frac{3}{1}$

   (D) $\frac{4}{1}$

   (E) $\frac{12}{1}$

Let K = Kathy's shares, C = Carl's shares, and T = Tom's shares. Then

K = 4C
C = 3T
K = 4(3T) = 12T
$\frac{K}{T} = \frac{12}{1}$

Therefore, E is the best answer.

3. **Of the following, which is closest to $\frac{0.15 \times 495}{9.97}$?**

   (A) 7.5   (B) 15   (C) 75   (D) 150   (E) 750

The value of the expression can be estimated by calculating

$$\frac{0.15 \times 500}{10} = 7.5.$$

Thus, the best answer is A.

4. **A manager has $6,000 budgeted for raises for 4 full-time and 2 part-time employees. Each of the full-time employees receives the same raise, which is twice the raise that each of the part-time employees receives. What is the amount of the raise that each full-time employee receives?**

   (A) $ 750
   (B) $1,000
   (C) $1,200
   (D) $1,500
   (E) $3,000

If P is the raise a part-time employee receives, each full-time employee receives 2P. Then the total for the 2 part-time and 4 full-time employees is 2P + 4(2P) = 6,000; so 10P = 6,000 and P = 600. Then each full-time employee receives $1,200, and C is the best answer.

5. $x^2 - \left(\frac{x}{2}\right)^2 =$

   (A) $x^2 - x$

   (B) $\frac{x^2}{4}$

   (C) $\frac{x^2}{2}$

   (D) $\frac{3x^2}{4}$

   (E) $\frac{3x^2}{2}$

$$x^2 - \left(\frac{x}{2}\right)^2 = x^2 - \frac{x^2}{4} = \frac{4x^2 - x^2}{4} = \frac{3x^2}{4}.$$

Therefore, D is the best answer.

6. A hospital pharmacy charges $0.40 per fluidram of a certain medicine but allows a discount of 15 percent to Medicare patients. How much should the pharmacy charge a Medicare patient for 3 fluidounces of the medicine? (128 fluidrams = 16 fluidounces)

(A) $9.60
(B) $8.16
(C) $3.20
(D) $2.72
(E) $1.02

One fluidounce equals $\frac{128}{16}$ or 8 fluidrams, so 3 fluidounces equal 24 fluidrams. The regular cost would be $0.40 \times 24 = \$9.60$, and a 15 percent discount ($1.44) would yield a cost to the Medicare patient of $9.60 − $1.44 = $8.16. Thus, the best answer is B.

7. $(-1)^2 - (-1)^3 =$

(A) -2 (B) -1 (C) 0 (D) 1 (E) 2

$(-1)^2 - (-1)^3 = (1) - (-1) = 2$. Thus, the best answer is E.

8. At a certain bowling alley, it costs $0.50 to rent bowling shoes for the day and $1.25 to bowl 1 game. If a person has $12.80 and must rent shoes, what is the greatest number of complete games that person can bowl in one day?

(A) 7
(B) 8
(C) 9
(D) 10
(E) 11

The amount the bowler has to spend on games is $12.30 after subtracting the $0.50 to rent shoes. The quotient $\frac{12.30}{1.25}$ is greater than 9 but less than 10, so he can bowl at most 9 games. Thus, the best answer is C.

9. If $\frac{x}{y} = 2$, then $\frac{x - y}{x} =$

(A) -1

(B) $-\frac{1}{2}$

(C) $\frac{1}{2}$

(D) 1

(E) 2

If $\frac{x}{y} = 2$, $x = 2y$. Then $\frac{x - y}{x} = \frac{2y - y}{2y} = \frac{y}{2y} = \frac{1}{2}$. Thus, the best answer is C.

10. If each photocopy of a manuscript costs 4 cents per page, what is the cost, in cents, to reproduce x copies of an x-page manuscript?

(A) $4x$ (B) $16x$ (C) x^2
(D) $4x^2$ (E) $16x^2$

The total cost is the cost per page times the number of pages per copy times the number of copies, or $4 \cdot x \cdot x = 4x^2$. Thus, the best answer is D.

11. Ken left a job paying $75,000 per year to accept a sales job paying $45,000 per year plus 15 percent commission. If each of his sales is for $750, what is the least number of sales he must make per year if he is not to lose money because of the change?

(A) 40
(B) 200
(C) 266
(D) 267
(E) 600

The difference between Ken's base salary and his previous salary is $30,000. To make up the difference in 15 percent commissions on $750 sales, the number of sales he must make is at least $\frac{30,000}{0.15 \times 750} = 266.67$. Thus, the least (integer) number of sales he must make to avoid losing money is 267, and the best answer is therefore D.

MONTHLY KILOWATT-HOURS

	500	1,000	1,500	2,000
Present	$24.00	$41.00	$57.00	$73.00
Proposed	$26.00	$45.00	$62.00	$79.00

12. The table above shows present rates and proposed rates for electricity for residential customers. For which of the monthly kilowatt-hours shown would the proposed rate be the greatest percent increase over the present rate?

(A) 500
(B) 1,000
(C) 1,500
(D) 2,000
(E) Each of the percent increases is the same.

	500	1,000	1,500	2,000
Percent Change	$\frac{2}{24}$	$\frac{4}{41}$	$\frac{5}{57}$	$\frac{6}{73}$

In order to compare the percent increases for the four rates, it is only necessary to compare the four ratios shown in the table, since they correspond to the percent increases. Since

$$\frac{2}{24} = \frac{1}{12}, \; \frac{4}{41} > \frac{4}{44} \left(= \frac{1}{11} \right), \; \frac{5}{57} < \frac{5}{55} \left(= \frac{1}{11} \right), \text{ and}$$

$$\frac{6}{73} < \frac{6}{72} \left(= \frac{1}{12} \right), \text{ the best answer is B.}$$

13. If a, b, and c are three consecutive odd integers such that $10 < a < b < c < 20$ and if b and c are prime numbers, what is the value of $a + b$?

(A) 24
(B) 28
(C) 30
(D) 32
(E) 36

The only sets of consecutive odd integers for which $10 < a < b < c < 20$ are $\{11,13,15\}$, $\{13,15,17\}$, and $\{15,17,19\}$. The first two sets are eliminated because b and c must be prime and 15 is not a prime. Therefore, $\{15,17,19\}$ is the only set that meets all the conditions, so a = 15 and b = 17. Then a + b = 32, and the best answer is D.

14. Of a group of people surveyed in a political poll, 60 percent said that they would vote for candidate R. Of those who said they would vote for R, 90 percent actually voted for R, and of those who did not say that they would vote for R, 5 percent actually voted for R. What percent of the group voted for R?

(A) 56%
(B) 59%
(C) 62%
(D) 65%
(E) 74%

Of the 60 percent who said they would vote for R, 90 percent (54 percent of the total group) actually did. Of the 40 percent who did not say they would vote for R, 5 percent (2 percent of the total group) actually did. Thus, $54 + 2 = 56$ percent of the total group voted for R. The best answer is therefore A.

15. If $r = 1 + \frac{1}{3} + \frac{1}{9} + \frac{1}{27}$ and $s = 1 + \frac{1}{3}r$, then s exceeds r by

(A) $\frac{1}{3}$ (B) $\frac{1}{6}$ (C) $\frac{1}{9}$ (D) $\frac{1}{27}$ (E) $\frac{1}{81}$

One way to solve this problem is first to compute r by adding the four terms. However, note that each successive term of r is $\frac{1}{3}$ the previous term. Thus,

$$s = 1 + \frac{1}{3}r = 1 + \frac{1}{3} + \frac{1}{9} + \frac{1}{27} + \frac{1}{81} = r + \frac{1}{81},$$

and s exceeds r by $\frac{1}{81}$. Therefore, the best answer is E.

16. $\dfrac{0.025 \times \frac{15}{2} \times 48}{5 \times 0.0024 \times \frac{3}{4}} =$

(A)   0.1
(B)   0.2
(C)   100
(D)   200
(E)   1,000

Multiplying both the numerator and denominator by 10,000 yields

$$\frac{250 \times \frac{15}{2} \times 48}{5 \times 24 \times \frac{3}{4}}.$$

Simplifying the numerator and denominator further yields

$$\frac{250 \times 15 \times 24}{5 \times 6 \times 3} = 1,000.$$

Thus, the best answer is E.

17. A student responded to all of the 22 questions on a test and received a score of 63.5. If the scores were derived by adding 3.5 points for each correct answer and deducting 1 point for each incorrect answer, how many questions did the student answer <u>incorrectly</u>?

(A) 3 (B) 4 (C) 15 (D) 18 (E) 20

If c is the number of correct answers, the number of incorrect answers is $(22 - c)$ and

$$3.5c - 1(22 - c) = 63.5$$
$$3.5c - 22 + c = 63.5$$
$$4.5c = 85.5$$
$$c = 19$$
$$22 - c = 3$$

Thus, the number of incorrect answers is 3 and the best answer is A.

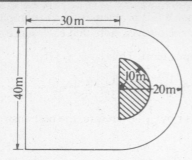

18. The figure above represents a rectangular parking lot that is 30 meters by 40 meters and an attached semi-circular driveway that has an outer radius of 20 meters and an inner radius of 10 meters. If the shaded region is <u>not</u> included, what is the area, in square meters, of the lot and driveway?

(A) $1,350\pi$
(B) $1,200 + 400\pi$
(C) $1,200 + 300\pi$
(D) $1,200 + 200\pi$
(E) $1,200 + 150\pi$

The area of the rectangular section is $30 \times 40 = 1,200$. Since the area of a semicircle is $\frac{1}{2}\pi r^2$, the large semicircular area is $\frac{1}{2} \times \pi \times 20^2 = 200\pi$. The shaded area, also semicircular, is $\frac{1}{2} \times \pi \times 10^2 = 50\pi$. Thus, the total area of the lot, excluding the shaded part, is
$$1,200 + 200\pi - 50\pi = 1,200 + 150\pi.$$
The best answer is therefore E.

19. One-fifth of the light switches produced by a certain factory are defective. Four-fifths of the defective switches are rejected and $\frac{1}{20}$ of the nondefective switches are rejected by mistake. If all the switches not rejected are sold, what percent of the switches sold by the factory are defective?

(A) 4%
(B) 5%
(C) 6.25%
(D) 11%
(E) 16%

The following table describes the condition of each hundred switches the firm makes:

	Rejected	Sold	Total
Nondefective	4	76	80
Defective	16	4	20
Total	20	80	100

If $\frac{4}{5}$ of the defective switches are rejected, 16 are rejected and 4 are sold. If $\frac{1}{20}$ of the 80 nondefective switches are rejected, 4 are rejected and 76 are sold. Thus, a total of 80 switches are sold, of which 4 are defective, or $\frac{4}{80} = 5\%$. Therefore, the best answer is B.

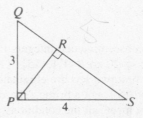

20. In $\triangle PQS$ above, if $PQ = 3$ and $PS = 4$, then $PR =$
(A) $\frac{9}{4}$ (B) $\frac{12}{5}$ (C) $\frac{16}{5}$ (D) $\frac{15}{4}$ (E) $\frac{20}{3}$

By the Pythagorean Theorem, $QS = \sqrt{3^2 + 4^2} = 5$. The tedious, but perhaps the most apparent, way to find PR would be to apply the Pythagorean Theorem again and solve the equation $3^2 - (QR)^2 = 4^2 - (5 - QR)^2$. A much simpler approach to the problem would be to recognize that, for any triangle with sides of lengths a_1, a_2, and a_3 and corresponding altitudes to those sides with lengths h_1, h_2, and h_3, the area can be expressed as half the product of any side and the altitude to that side. Thus, $a_1 h_1 = a_2 h_2 = a_3 h_3$, and in this particular problem $(PR)(QS) = (3)(4)$, $(PR)5 = 12$, and $PR = \frac{12}{5}$. Therefore, the best answer is B.

PROBLEM SOLVING SAMPLE TEST SECTION 6

30 Minutes
20 Questions

Directions: In this section solve each problem, using any available space on the page for scratchwork. Then indicate the best of the answer choices given.

Numbers: All numbers used are real numbers.

Figures: Figures that accompany problems in this section are intended to provide information useful in solving the problems. They are drawn as accurately as possible EXCEPT when it is stated in a specific problem that its figure is not drawn to scale. All figures lie in a plane unless otherwise indicated.

1. If x is an even integer, which of the following is an odd integer?

(A) $3x + 2$

(B) $7x$

(C) $8x + 5$

(D) x^2

(E) x^3

2. On a purchase of $120, a store offered a payment plan consisting of a $20 down payment and 12 monthly payments of $10 each. What percent of the purchase price, to the nearest tenth of a percent, did the customer pay in interest by using this plan?

(A) 16.7%

(B) 30%

(C) 75.8%

(D) 106.7%

(E) 107.5%

3. $\dfrac{5}{4}\left(42 \div \dfrac{3}{16}\right) =$

(A) 6.3   (B) 9.8   (C) 179.2

(D) 224   (E) 280

4. When magnified 1,000 times by an electron microscope, the image of a certain circular piece of tissue has a diameter of 0.5 centimeter. The actual diameter of the tissue, in centimeters, is

(A) 0.005

(B) 0.002

(C) 0.001

(D) 0.0005

(E) 0.0002

GO ON TO THE NEXT PAGE.

5. In 1970 there were 8,902 women stockbrokers in the United States. By 1978 the number had increased to 19,947. Approximately what was the percent increase?

(A) 45%

(B) 125%

(C) 145%

(D) 150%

(E) 225%

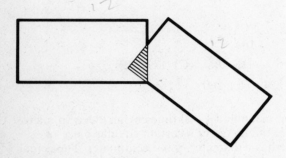

6. In the figure above, two rectangles with the same dimensions overlap to form the shaded region. If each rectangle has perimeter 12 and the shaded region has perimeter 3, what is the total length of the heavy line segments?

(A) 15   (B) 18   (C) 21   (D) 22   (E) 23

7. If one root of the equation $2x^2 + 3x - k = 0$ is 6, what is the value of k?

(A)   90

(B)   42

(C)   18

(D)   10

(E) -10

8. Bottle R contains 250 capsules and costs $6.25. Bottle T contains 130 capsules and costs $2.99. What is the difference between the cost per capsule for bottle R and the cost per capsule for bottle T?

(A) $0.25

(B) $0.12

(C) $0.05

(D) $0.03

(E) $0.002

GO ON TO THE NEXT PAGE.

9. Trucking transportation rates are x dollars per metric ton per kilometer. How much does it cost, in dollars, to transport one dozen cars, which weigh two metric tons each, n kilometers by truck?

(A) $\frac{x}{12n}$ (B) $\frac{x}{24n}$ (C) $\frac{xn}{24}$

(D) $12xn$ (E) $24xn$

10. For a positive integer n, the number $n!$ is defined to be $n(n-1)(n-2)\ldots(1)$. For example, $4! = 4(3)(2)(1)$. What is the value of $5! - 3!$?

(A) 120

(B) 114

(C) 20

(D) 15

(E)   2

11. A man who died left an estate valued at $111,000. His will stipulated that his estate was to be distributed so that each of his three children received from the estate and his previous gifts, combined, the same total amount. If he had previously given his oldest child $15,000, his middle child $10,000, and his youngest $2,000, how much did the youngest child receive from the estate?

(A) $50,000

(B) $48,000

(C) $46,000

(D) $44,000

(E) $39,000

GO ON TO THE NEXT PAGE.

12. If $y > 0$, which of the following is equal to $\sqrt{48y^3}$?

(A) $4y\sqrt{3y}$

(B) $3y\sqrt{4y}$

(C) $2\sqrt{12y}$

(D) $3\sqrt{8y}$

(E) $16y\sqrt{3y}$

13. The volume of a box with a square base is 54 cubic centimeters. If the height of the box is twice the width of the base, what is the height, in centimeters?

(A) 2

(B) 3

(C) 4

(D) 6

(E) 9

$$q = 3\sqrt{3}$$
$$r = 1 + 2\sqrt{3}$$
$$s = 3 + \sqrt{3}$$

14. If q, r, and s are the numbers shown above, which of the following shows their order from greatest to least?

(A) q, r, s (B) q, s, r (C) r, q, s

(D) s, q, r (E) s, r, q

15. The sum of the interior angles of any polygon with n sides is $180(n - 2)$ degrees. If the sum of the interior angles of polygon P is three times the sum of the interior angles of quadrilateral Q, how many sides does P have?

(A) 6 (B) 8 (C) 10 (D) 12 (E) 14

16. In Company X, 30 percent of the employees live over ten miles from work and 60 percent of the employees who live over ten miles from work are in car pools. If 40 percent of the employees of Company X are in car pools, what percent of the employees of Company X live ten miles or less from work and are in car pools?

(A) 12%

(B) 20%

(C) 22%

(D) 28%

(E) 32%

GO ON TO THE NEXT PAGE.

17. If an organization were to sell n tickets for a theater production, the total revenue from ticket sales would be 20 percent greater than the total costs of the production. If the organization actually sold all but 5 percent of the n tickets, the total revenue from ticket sales was what percent greater than the total costs of the production?

    (A) 4%

    (B) 10%

    (C) 14%

    (D) 15%

    (E) 18%

18. When the integer n is divided by 6, the remainder is 3. Which of the following is NOT a multiple of 6?

    (A) $n - 3$ (B) $n + 3$ (C) $2n$

    (D) $3n$ (E) $4n$

19. How many liters of pure alcohol must be added to a 100-liter solution that is 20 percent alcohol in order to produce a solution that is 25 percent alcohol?

    (A) $\frac{7}{2}$

    (B) 5

    (C) $\frac{20}{3}$

    (D) 8

    (E) $\frac{39}{4}$

20. If 10 persons meet at a reunion and each person shakes hands exactly once with each of the others, what is the total number of handshakes?

    (A) $10 \cdot 9 \cdot 8 \cdot 7 \cdot 6 \cdot 5 \cdot 4 \cdot 3 \cdot 2 \cdot 1$

    (B) $10 \cdot 10$

    (C) $10 \cdot 9$

    (D) 45

    (E) 36

S T O P

IF YOU FINISH BEFORE TIME IS CALLED, YOU MAY CHECK YOUR WORK ON THIS SECTION ONLY.
DO NOT TURN TO ANY OTHER SECTION IN THE TEST.

Answer Key for Sample Test Section 6

PROBLEM SOLVING

1. C	11. D
2. A	12. A
3. E	13. D
4. D	14. B
5. B	15. B
6. C	16. C
7. A	17. C
8. E	18. D
9. E	19. C
10. B	20. D

Explanatory Material:
Problem Solving Sample Test Section 6

1. If x is an even integer, which of the following is an odd integer?

   (A) $3x + 2$
   (B) $7x$
   (C) $8x + 5$
   (D) x^2
   (E) x^3

Since x is an even integer, it contains the factor 2 and any multiple (or power) of x contains the factor 2. Therefore, choices B, D, and E list expressions that must be even. The expression 3x + 2 is even because it is the sum of two even integers. Since 8x + 5 is the sum of an even integer and an odd integer, it must be odd, so the best answer is C.

2. On a purchase of $120, a store offered a payment plan consisting of a $20 down payment and 12 monthly payments of $10 each. What percent of the purchase price, to the nearest tenth of a percent, did the customer pay in interest by using this plan?

   (A) 16.7%
   (B) 30%
   (C) 75.8%
   (D) 106.7%
   (E) 107.5%

The purchase price was $120, but the customer actually paid a total of $20 + 12($10) = $140. Thus, the interest is equal to the difference $140 − $120 = $20, and the interest as a percent of the purchase price is $\frac{20}{120} = \frac{1}{6} = 16\frac{2}{3}\%$. The best answer is therefore A.

3. $\frac{5}{4}\left(42 \div \frac{3}{16}\right) =$

   (A) 6.3   (B) 9.8   (C) 179.2
   (D) 224   (E) 280

This computation can be done in a number of ways. Perhaps the easiest is: $\frac{5}{4}\left(42 \div \frac{3}{16}\right) = \frac{5}{4}\left(42 \times \frac{16}{3}\right) = \frac{5}{4}(14 \times 16) = 5 \times 14 \times 4 = 20(14) = 280$.
Thus, the best answer is E.

4. When magnified 1,000 times by an electron microscope, the image of a certain circular piece of tissue has a diameter of 0.5 centimeter. The actual diameter of the tissue, in centimeters, is

   (A) 0.005
   (B) 0.002
   (C) 0.001
   (D) 0.0005
   (E) 0.0002

Let d be the diameter, in centimeters, of the piece of tissue. Then 1,000d = 0.5, and $d = \frac{0.5}{1000} = \frac{5}{10,000} = 0.0005$ cm. Thus, the best answer is D.

5. In 1970 there were 8,902 women stockbrokers in the United States. By 1978 the number had increased to 19,947. Approximately what was the percent increase?

   (A) 45%
   (B) 125%
   (C) 145%
   (D) 150%
   (E) 225%

From 1970 to 1978, the number of women stockbrokers increased from approximately 8,900 to 19,900, an increase of a little more than 11,000. Thus, the percent increase is a little more than $\frac{11,000}{8,900}$, which is approximately $\frac{11}{9}$ or 122.2%. The best answer therefore is B.

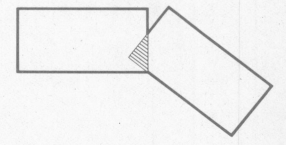

6. In the figure above, two rectangles with the same dimensions overlap to form the shaded region. If each rectangle has perimeter 12 and the shaded region has perimeter 3, what is the total length of the heavy line segments?

   (A) 15   (B) 18   (C) 21   (D) 22   (E) 23

The total length of the heavy line segments is equal to the sum of the perimeters of the two rectangles (24) minus the total length of the light line segments forming the shaded region. Since the total length of the light line segments is equal to the perimeter of the shaded region, the heavy line segments have total length $24 - 3 = 21$. The best answer is C.

7. If one root of the equation $2x^2 + 3x - k = 0$ is 6, what is the value of k?

   (A)   90
   (B)   42
   (C)   18
   (D)   10
   (E) -10

If 6 is a root of the equation, then $x = 6$ must satisfy the equation. Thus, $2(6)^2 + 3(6) - k = 0$, and $k = 2(36) + 18 = 90$. The best answer is A.

8. Bottle R contains 250 capsules and costs \$6.25. Bottle T contains 130 capsules and costs \$2.99. What is the difference between the cost per capsule for bottle R and the cost per capsule for bottle T?

   (A) \$0.25
   (B) \$0.12
   (C) \$0.05
   (D) \$0.03
   (E) \$0.002

The cost per capsule in bottle R is $\frac{625}{250} = 2.5$ cents. The cost per capsule in bottle T is $\frac{299}{130} = 2.3$ cents. The difference is $2.5 - 2.3 = 0.2$ cents, or \$0.002, so the best answer is E.

9. Trucking transportation rates are x dollars per metric ton per kilometer. How much does it cost, in dollars, to transport one dozen cars, which weigh two metric tons each, n kilometers by truck?

   (A) $\frac{x}{12n}$ (B) $\frac{x}{24n}$ (C) $\frac{xn}{24}$

   (D) $12xn$ (E) $24xn$

The total weight of the 12 cars to be transported is $12(2) = 24$ metric tons. Since the cost per kilometer for 1 metric ton is x dollars, the cost per kilometer for 24 metric tons is 24x dollars. If the cost to transport the entire shipment is 24x dollars per kilometer, the cost is 24xn dollars for a distance of n kilometers. The best answer is E.

10. For a positive integer n, the number $n!$ is defined to be $n(n - 1)(n - 2) \ldots (1)$. For example, $4! = 4(3)(2)(1)$. What is the value of $5! - 3!$?

   (A) 120   (B) 114   (C) 20
   (D) 15   (E) 2

$5! - 3! = 5(4)(3)(2)(1) - (3)(2)(1) = 120 - 6 = 114$. Thus, the best answer is B.

11. A man who died left an estate valued at \$111,000. His will stipulated that his estate was to be distributed so that each of his three children received from the estate and his previous gifts, combined, the same total amount. If he had previously given his oldest child \$15,000, his middle child \$10,000, and his youngest \$2,000, how much did the youngest child receive from the estate?

   (A) \$50,000
   (B) \$48,000
   (C) \$46,000
   (D) \$44,000
   (E) \$39,000

The total value of the estate and the three previous gifts was $\$111,000 + \$15,000 + \$10,000 + \$2,000 = \$138,000$. Since each child was to receive an equal share of this total, each was to receive $\frac{\$138,000}{3}$, or a total of \$46,000. Therefore, the youngest child, who had previously received only \$2,000 of the \$46,000 share, received $\$46,000 - \$2,000 = \$44,000$ from the estate, and the best answer is D.

12. If $y > 0$, which of the following is equal to $\sqrt{48y^3}$?

   (A) $4y\sqrt{3y}$
   (B) $3y\sqrt{4y}$
   (C) $2\sqrt{12y}$
   (D) $3\sqrt{8y}$
   (E) $16y\sqrt{3y}$

To simplify, $\sqrt{48y^3} = (\sqrt{16y^2})(\sqrt{3y}) = 4y\sqrt{3y}$. Thus, the best answer is A.

13. The volume of a box with a square base is 54 cubic centimeters. If the height of the box is twice the width of the base, what is the height, in centimeters?

   (A) 2
   (B) 3
   (C) 4
   (D) 6
   (E) 9

The volume of the box is $x^2y = 54$, where x is the length of a side of the square base and y is the height of the box. Since $y = 2x$, it follows that $x^2(2x) = 54$, or $x = 3$. Therefore, $y = 2x = 2(3) = 6$ centimeters, and the best answer is D.

$$q = 3\sqrt{3}$$
$$r = 1 + 2\sqrt{3}$$
$$s = 3 + \sqrt{3}$$

14. If q, r, and s are the numbers shown above, which of the following shows their order from greatest to least?

(A) q, r, s (B) q, s, r (C) r, q, s
(D) s, q, r (E) s, r, q

In comparing q, r, and s, it is convenient to subtract $\sqrt{3}$ from each of the numbers and then to compare only the residues Q, R, and S; the order of q, r, and s will be the same as the order of Q, R, and S. Now $Q = 2\sqrt{3}$, $R = 1 + \sqrt{3}$, and $S = 3$. Clearly $Q > R$ since $\sqrt{3} > 1$. Also note that $Q^2 = 12$ and $S^2 = 9$; therefore, $Q > S$. Since Q is greater than either R or S, the answer must be A or B. If 1 is subtracted from both R and S, it can be seen that $S > R$ since $2 > \sqrt{3}$. Therefore $Q > S > R$, and the best answer is B.

15. The sum of the interior angles of any polygon with n sides is $180(n - 2)$ degrees. If the sum of the interior angles of polygon P is three times the sum of the interior angles of quadrilateral Q, how many sides does P have?

(A) 6   (B) 8   (C) 10   (D) 12   (E) 14

The sum of the interior angles of quadrilateral Q is 360 degrees, since Q has 4 sides and $180(4 - 2) = 360$. The sum of the interior angles of polygon P is $3(360) = 1,080$ degrees. Now $1,080 = 180(n - 2)$ where n is the number of sides polygon P has. When each side of the equation is divided by 180, $6 = n - 2$ and $n = 8$. Thus, the best answer is B.

16. In Company X, 30 percent of the employees live over ten miles from work and 60 percent of the employees who live over ten miles from work are in car pools. If 40 percent of the employees of Company X are in car pools, what percent of the employees of Company X live ten miles or less from work and are in car pools?

(A) 12%
(B) 20%
(C) 22%
(D) 28%
(E) 32%

To solve problems of this type, where the categories are mutually exclusive, it is most convenient to organize the information in a two-dimensional table as shown below:

	10 Miles or Less from Work	More Than 10 Miles from Work	Total
Car Pool		18% (60% of 30%)	40%
No Car Pool			
Total		30%	100%

It is very easy to complete the table by finding the necessary percents to make the totals in each row or column. In this case, since a total of 40 percent of the employees are in car pools and 18 percent live more than 10 miles from work, $40 - 18 = 22\%$ live 10 miles or less from work and are in car pools. Thus, the best answer is C.

17. If an organization were to sell n tickets for a theater production, the total revenue from ticket sales would be 20 percent greater than the total costs of the production. If the organization actually sold all but 5 percent of the n tickets, the total revenue from ticket sales was what percent greater than the total costs of the production?

(A) 4%
(B) 10%
(C) 14%
(D) 15%
(E) 18%

Let p be the price per ticket. Then if n tickets were sold, total revenues would be np. Let c be the total cost of the production. Then, if np is 20 percent greater than c, $np = 1.2c$. Since only 95 percent of the n tickets were sold, $0.95(np) = 0.95(1.2c) = 1.14c$. Therefore, the total revenue from ticket sales was 14 percent greater than the total cost of production. Therefore, the best answer is C.

18. When the integer n is divided by 6, the remainder is 3. Which of the following is NOT a multiple of 6?

(A) $n - 3$ (B) $n + 3$ (C) $2n$
(D) $3n$ (E) $4n$

If the integer n has a remainder of 3 when it is divided by 6, then n is a number of the form $6q + 3$, where q is an integer. Therefore, $6q + 3$ can be substituted for n in each of the expressions listed until an expression is found that is not a multiple of 6 (does not have 6 as a factor). For example:
$n - 3 = (6q + 3) - 3 = 6q$;
$n + 3 = (6q + 3) + 3 = 6q + 6 = 6(q + 1)$;
$2n = 2(6q + 3) = 12q + 6 = 6(2q + 1)$;
$3n = 3(6q + 3) = 18q + 9 = 6(3q + 1) + 3$.
Since the expression given for choice D has a remainder of 3 when divided by 6, it is not a multiple of 6. Therefore, the best answer is D.

19. How many liters of pure alcohol must be added to a 100-liter solution that is 20 percent alcohol in order to produce a solution that is 25 percent alcohol?

(A) $\frac{7}{2}$

(B) 5

(C) $\frac{20}{3}$

(D) 8

(E) $\frac{39}{4}$

If x is the number of liters of alcohol that must be added to a solution that already contains 20 liters of alcohol (20% of 100 liters), then $20 + x$ liters must be 25 percent of the total number of liters in the new solution, which will consist of $100 + x$ liters. Therefore, the equation to be solved is $20 + x = 0.25(100 + x)$. This reduces to $20 + x = 25 + 0.25x$, and $0.75x = 5$. The value of $x = \frac{5}{0.75} = \frac{20}{3}$, and the best answer is C.

20. If 10 persons meet at a reunion and each person shakes hands exactly once with each of the others, what is the total number of handshakes?

(A) $10 \cdot 9 \cdot 8 \cdot 7 \cdot 6 \cdot 5 \cdot 4 \cdot 3 \cdot 2 \cdot 1$
(B) $10 \cdot 10$
(C) $10 \cdot 9$
(D) 45
(E) 36

Each of the 10 persons shakes hands 9 times, once with each of the other 9 people at the reunion. Since there are 10 people, each of whom shakes hands with the other 9 people, it would seem at first that there are 10(9) or 90 handshakes. However, since each handshake was counted twice, once for each of the two people involved, the correct number of handshakes is $\frac{90}{2}$, or 45. Thus, the best answer is D.

PROBLEM SOLVING SAMPLE TEST SECTION 7

30 Minutes
20 Questions

Directions: In this section solve each problem, using any available space on the page for scratchwork. Then indicate the best of the answer choices given.

Numbers: All numbers used are real numbers.

Figures: Figures that accompany problems in this section are intended to provide information useful in solving the problems. They are drawn as accurately as possible EXCEPT when it is stated in a specific problem that its figure is not drawn to scale. All figures lie in a plane unless otherwise indicated.

1. At the rate of $7.50 per hour, how many hours must a person work to earn $232.50 ?

   (A) 25   (B) 27   (C) 29   (D) 30   (E) 31

2. Each month for 6 months the amount of money in a benefit fund is doubled. At the end of the 6 months there is a total of $640 in the fund. How much money was in the fund at the end of 3 months?

   (A) $80   (B) $100   (C) $120
   (D) $160   (E) $320

3. $6[-2(6-9)+11-23] =$

   (A) -224 (B) -108 (C) -36
   (D) 24   (E) 79

4. If $\frac{2}{3} \times \frac{3}{5} \times \frac{5}{8} \times \frac{8}{n} = \frac{2}{10}$, then $n =$

   (A) $\frac{1}{10}$ (B) $\frac{1}{5}$ (C) 5   (D) 10   (E) 100

5. If $d = 3.0641$ and $\bar{d}$ is the number obtained by rounding d to the nearest hundredth, then $d - \bar{d} =$

   (A) 0.0001
   (B) 0.0041
   (C) 0.0059
   (D) 0.0141
   (E) 0.0410

GO ON TO THE NEXT PAGE.

6. Mr. Jones drove from Town A to Town B in x hours. On the return trip over the same route, his average speed was twice as fast. Which of the following expresses the total number of driving hours for the round trip?

(A) $\frac{2}{3}x$

(B) $\frac{3}{2}x$

(C) $\frac{5}{3}x$

(D) $2x$

(E) $3x$

7. If 3 is the greatest common divisor of positive integers r and s, what is the greatest common divisor of $2r$ and $2s$?

(A) 2   (B) 3   (C) 4   (D) 6   (E) 12

8. If $x + y = 5$ and $xy = 6$, then $\frac{1}{x} + \frac{1}{y} =$

(A) $\frac{1}{6}$ (B) $\frac{1}{5}$ (C) $\frac{5}{6}$ (D) $\frac{6}{5}$ (E) 5

9. After 5 games, a rugby team had an average of 28 points per game. In order to increase the average by n points, how many points must be scored in a 6th game?

(A) n
(B) $6n$
(C) $28n$
(D) $28 + n$
(E) $28 + 6n$

10. On July 1, 1982, Ms. Fox deposited $10,000 in a new account at the annual interest rate of 12 percent compounded monthly. If no additional deposits or withdrawals were made and if interest was credited on the last day of each month, what was the amount of money in the account on September 1, 1982?

(A) $10,200
(B) $10,201
(C) $11,100
(D) $12,100
(E) $12,544

GO ON TO THE NEXT PAGE.

11. How many prime numbers are less than 25 and greater than 10 ?

    (A) Three   (B) Four   (C) Five
    (D) Six   (E) Seven

12. Erica has $460 in 5- and 10-dollar bills only. If she has fewer 10- than 5-dollar bills, what is the least possible number of 5-dollar bills she could have?

    (A) 32
    (B) 30
    (C) 29
    (D) 28
    (E) 27

13. Which of the following is equivalent to the statement that 0.5 is between $\frac{2}{n}$ and $\frac{3}{n}$?

    (A) $1 < n < 6$
    (B) $2 < n < 3$
    (C) $2 < n < 5$
    (D) $4 < n < 6$
    (E) $n > 10$

14. A corporation with 5,000,000 shares of publicly listed stock reported total earnings of $7.20 per share for the first 9 months of operation. During the final quarter the number of publicly listed shares was increased to 10,000,000 shares, and fourth quarter earnings were reported as $1.25 per share. What are the average annual earnings per share based on the number of shares at the end of the year?

    (A) $1.83
    (B) $2.43
    (C) $4.85
    (D) $8.45
    (E) $9.70

15. In 1980 the government spent $12 billion for direct cash payments to single parents with dependent children. If this was 2,000 percent of the amount spent in 1956, what was the amount spent in 1956 ? (1 billion = 1,000,000,000)

    (A) $6 million
    (B) $24 million
    (C) $60 million
    (D) $240 million
    (E) $600 million

GO ON TO THE NEXT PAGE.

16. The triangles in the figure above are equilateral and the ratio of the length of a side of the larger triangle to the length of a side of the smaller triangle is $\frac{2}{1}$. If the area of the larger triangular region is K, what is the area of the shaded region in terms of K?

(A) $\frac{3}{4}K$ (B) $\frac{2}{3}K$ (C) $\frac{1}{2}K$

(D) $\frac{1}{3}K$ (E) $\frac{1}{4}K$

17. Four cups of milk are to be poured into a 2-cup bottle and a 4-cup bottle. If each bottle is to be filled to the same fraction of its capacity, how many cups of milk should be poured into the 4-cup bottle?

(A) $\frac{2}{3}$

(B) $\frac{7}{3}$

(C) $\frac{5}{2}$

(D) $\frac{8}{3}$

(E) 3

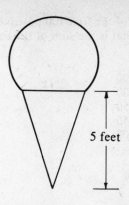

5 feet

18. The outline of a sign for an ice-cream store is made by placing $\frac{3}{4}$ of the circumference of a circle with radius 2 feet on top of an isosceles triangle with height 5 feet, as shown above. What is the perimeter, in feet, of the sign?

(A) $3\pi + 3\sqrt{3}$
(B) $3\pi + 6\sqrt{3}$
(C) $3\pi + 2\sqrt{33}$
(D) $4\pi + 3\sqrt{3}$
(E) $4\pi + 6\sqrt{3}$

GO ON TO THE NEXT PAGE.

19. The sum of the first 100 positive integers is 5,050. What is the sum of the first 200 positive integers?

(A) 10,100
(B) 10,200
(C) 15,050
(D) 20,050
(E) 20,100

20. A merchant purchased a jacket for $60 and then determined a selling price that equalled the purchase price of the jacket plus a markup that was 25 percent of the selling price. During a sale, the merchant discounted the selling price by 20 percent and sold the jacket. What was the merchant's gross profit on this sale?

(A) $0   (B) $3   (C) $4
(D) $12   (E) $15

S T O P

IF YOU FINISH BEFORE TIME IS CALLED, YOU MAY CHECK YOUR WORK ON THIS SECTION ONLY.
DO NOT TURN TO ANY OTHER SECTION IN THE TEST.

Answer Key for Sample Test Section 7

PROBLEM SOLVING

1. E	11. C
2. A	12. A
3. C	13. D
4. D	14. C
5. B	15. E
6. B	16. A
7. D	17. D
8. C	18. B
9. E	19. E
10. B	20. C

Explanatory Material: Problem Solving Sample Test Section 7

1. At the rate of $7.50 per hour, how many hours must a person work to earn $232.50?

   (A) 25   (B) 27   (C) 29   (D) 30   (E) 31

If a person earned $232.50 working h hours at $7.50 per hour, then $7.50h = 232.50$, or $h = 232.50/7.50 = 31$. Therefore, the best answer is E.

2. Each month for 6 months the amount of money in a benefit fund is doubled. At the end of the 6 months there is a total of $640 in the fund. How much money was in the fund at the end of 3 months?

   (A) $80   (B) $100   (C) $120   (D) $160   (E) $320

Since the fund doubled each of the 6 months, the amount in the fund at the end of month 3 can be found by starting with $640 and successively dividing by 2: month 5 − $320, month 4 − $160, month 3 − $80. Thus, the best answer is A.

3. $6[-2(6 - 9) + 11 - 23] =$

   (A) −224   (B) −108   (C) −36
   (D) 24   (E) 79

$$6[-2(6 - 9) + 11 - 23] = 6[-2(-3) + 11 - 23]$$
$$= 6[6 + 11 - 23]$$
$$= 6[-6]$$
$$= -36.$$

The best answer is C.

4. If $\frac{2}{3} \times \frac{3}{5} \times \frac{5}{8} \times \frac{8}{n} = \frac{2}{10}$, then $n =$

   (A) $\frac{1}{10}$ (B) $\frac{1}{5}$ (C) 5   (D) 10   (E) 100

By cancellation of the common factors 3, 5, and 8 in numerator and denominator, the equation reduces to $2/n = 2/10$. Therefore, $n = 10$. The best answer is D.

5. If $d = 3.0641$ and $\bar{d}$ is the number obtained by rounding d to the nearest hundredth, then $d - \bar{d} =$

   (A) 0.0001
   (B) 0.0041
   (C) 0.0059
   (D) 0.0141
   (E) 0.0410

Rounding d to the nearest hundredth gives $\bar{d} = 3.06$; thus, $d - \bar{d} = 3.0641 - 3.06 = 0.0041$, and B is the best answer.

6. Mr. Jones drove from Town A to Town B in x hours. On the return trip over the same route, his average speed was twice as fast. Which of the following expresses the total number of driving hours for the round trip?

   (A) $\frac{2}{3}x$

   (B) $\frac{3}{2}x$

   (C) $\frac{5}{3}x$

   (D) $2x$

   (E) $3x$

Since the distance traveled equals the product of the average speed and the time traveled, doubling the speed results in halving the time. Therefore, the total number of driving hours for the round trip is $x + x/2 = 3x/2$, and the best answer is B.

7. If 3 is the greatest common divisor of positive integers r and s, what is the greatest common divisor of $2r$ and $2s$?

   (A) 2   (B) 3   (C) 4   (D) 6   (E) 12

Since 2 is a factor of both $2r$ and $2s$, it is a common divisor of $2r$ and $2s$. Since the greatest common divisor of r and s is 3, it follows that the greatest common divisor of $2r$ and $2s$ is $(2)(3)$, or 6. Thus, the best answer is D.

8. If $x + y = 5$ and $xy = 6$, then $\dfrac{1}{x} + \dfrac{1}{y} =$

(A) $\dfrac{1}{6}$ (B) $\dfrac{1}{5}$ (C) $\dfrac{5}{6}$ (D) $\dfrac{6}{5}$ (E) 5

Because it is given that $x + y = 5$ and $xy = 6$,
$\dfrac{1}{x} + \dfrac{1}{y} = \dfrac{y}{xy} + \dfrac{x}{xy} = \dfrac{y + x}{xy} = \dfrac{5}{6}$. Therefore, the best answer is C.

9. After 5 games, a rugby team had an average of 28 points per game. In order to increase the average by n points, how many points must be scored in a 6th game?

(A) n
(B) $6n$
(C) $28n$
(D) $28 + n$
(E) $28 + 6n$

The average number of points for 5 games is 28, so the total number of points for the 5 games is $5(28) = 140$. If the team were to score x points in the 6th game, the average for 6 games would be $\dfrac{140 + x}{6}$. We want this average to be n greater than 28. Therefore,
$$\dfrac{140 + x}{6} = 28 + n$$
$$140 + x = 168 + 6n$$
$$x = 28 + 6n.$$
Choice E is the best answer.

10. On July 1, 1982, Ms. Fox deposited $10,000 in a new account at the annual interest rate of 12 percent compounded monthly. If no additional deposits or withdrawals were made and if interest was credited on the last day of each month, what was the amount of money in the account on September 1, 1982?

(A) $10,200
(B) $10,201
(C) $11,100
(D) $12,100
(E) $12,544

Since the annual interest rate is 12 percent, the monthly rate is 1 percent. On August 1, 1982, the total amount in the account would be $(1.01)(10,000) = \$10,100$. On September 1, 1982, the total would be $(1.01)(10,100) = \$10,201$, so B is the best answer.

11. How many prime numbers are less than 25 and greater than 10?

(A) Three (B) Four (C) Five
(D) Six (E) Seven

A prime number n cannot have any positive factors other than 1 and n. Therefore, the prime numbers between 10 and 25 are 11, 13, 17, 19, and 23. Since there are five, the best answer is C.

12. Erica has $460 in 5- and 10-dollar bills only. If she has fewer 10- than 5-dollar bills, what is the least possible number of 5-dollar bills she could have?

(A) 32
(B) 30
(C) 29
(D) 28
(E) 27

If Erica has f 5-dollar bills and t 10-dollar bills totaling $460, then $5f + 10t = 460$, or, dividing by 5, $f + 2t = 92$. This equation has many solutions (e.g., $f = 2, t = 45$). We want the solution that makes f as small as possible but larger than t (i.e., $f > t$). Since $f > t$, $2f > 2t$ and it follows from the equation that $f + 2f > 92$ or $3f > 92$; and, since f must be even, the least possible value of f is 32. (This solution might also be found through trial and error, using the equation $f + 2t = 92$.) The best answer, therefore, is A.

13. Which of the following is equivalent to the statement that 0.5 is between $\dfrac{2}{n}$ and $\dfrac{3}{n}$?

(A) $1 < n < 6$
(B) $2 < n < 3$
(C) $2 < n < 5$
(D) $4 < n < 6$
(E) $n > 10$

The statement "0.5 is between $\dfrac{2}{n}$ and $\dfrac{3}{n}$" can be written:
$$\dfrac{2}{n} < 0.5 < \dfrac{3}{n}.$$
Since n must be positive, multiplying through the inequality by $2n$ gives
$$(2n)\left(\dfrac{2}{n}\right) < (2n)(0.5) < (2n)\left(\dfrac{3}{n}\right), \text{ or } 4 < n < 6.$$
The best answer is D.

14. A corporation with 5,000,000 shares of publicly listed stock reported total earnings of $7.20 per share for the first 9 months of operation. During the final quarter the number of publicly listed shares was increased to 10,000,000 shares, and fourth quarter earnings were reported as $1.25 per share. What are the average annual earnings per share based on the number of shares at the end of the year?

(A) $1.83
(B) $2.43
(C) $4.85
(D) $8.45
(E) $9.70

The total earnings for the year were
$$(5,000,000)(7.20) + (10,000,000)(1.25) = \$48,500,000.$$

The per-share earnings based on the number of shares at the end of the year are
$$48,500,000/10,000,000 = \$4.85.$$

Therefore, the best answer is C.

15. In 1980 the government spent $12 billion for direct cash payments to single parents with dependent children. If this was 2,000 percent of the amount spent in 1956, what was the amount spent in 1956? (1 billion = 1,000,000,000)

(A) $6 million
(B) $24 million
(C) $60 million
(D) $240 million
(E) $600 million

If x is the amount spent in 1956, then
$$(2,000\%)x = 12,000,000,000$$
$$20x = 12,000,000,000$$
$$x = \$600,000,000.$$
Therefore, E is the best answer.

16. The triangles in the figure above are equilateral and the ratio of the length of a side of the larger triangle to the length of a side of the smaller triangle is $\frac{2}{1}$. If the area of the larger triangular region is K, what is the area of the shaded region in terms of K?

(A) $\frac{3}{4}K$ (B) $\frac{2}{3}K$ (C) $\frac{1}{2}K$

   (D) $\frac{1}{3}K$ (E) $\frac{1}{4}K$

The area of any triangle is 1/2 the product of the base and the corresponding altitude. Since each dimension of the smaller triangle is 1/2 the corresponding dimension of the larger triangle, the area of the smaller triangle is 1/4 the area of the larger triangle, or $K/4$. Thus, the area of the shaded region is

$$K - \frac{K}{4} = \frac{3K}{4}.$$

The best answer is A.

17. Four cups of milk are to be poured into a 2-cup bottle and a 4-cup bottle. If each bottle is to be filled to the same fraction of its capacity, how many cups of milk should be poured into the 4-cup bottle?

(A) $\frac{2}{3}$

(B) $\frac{7}{3}$

(C) $\frac{5}{2}$

(D) $\frac{8}{3}$

(E) 3

Since each bottle is to be filled to the same fraction of its capacity, and since the 4-cup bottle has 2/3 of the total capacity of the two bottles, the 4-cup bottle will get 2/3 of the 4 cups of milk, or

$$\left(\frac{2}{3}\right)(4) = \frac{8}{3}.$$

Or, to use algebraic terms, if x is the number of cups of milk that should be poured into the 4-cup bottle, then $4 - x$ is the number of cups left to be poured into the 2-cup bottle. Because the fraction of milk in a bottle must be the same for both bottles, it follows that

$$\frac{x}{4} = \frac{4-x}{2}.$$

Thus, $$2x = 16 - 4x$$
$$6x = 16$$
$$x = \frac{16}{6} = \frac{8}{3} \text{ cups.}$$

The best answer is D.

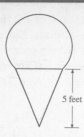

18. The outline of a sign for an ice-cream store is made by placing $\frac{3}{4}$ of the circumference of a circle with radius 2 feet on top of an isosceles triangle with height 5 feet, as shown above. What is the perimeter, in feet, of the sign?

(A) $3\pi + 3\sqrt{3}$
(B) $3\pi + 6\sqrt{3}$
(C) $3\pi + 2\sqrt{33}$
(D) $4\pi + 3\sqrt{3}$
(E) $4\pi + 6\sqrt{3}$

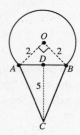

In the figure, O is the center of the partial circle. The measure of $\angle AOB$ is 90° because it cuts off an arc that is 1/4 of the circumference. So, in right $\triangle AOB$,

$$AB = \sqrt{2^2 + 2^2} = \sqrt{8} = 2\sqrt{2}.$$

Therefore, $AD = DB = \frac{1}{2}(AB) = \frac{1}{2}(2\sqrt{2}) = \sqrt{2}$. In right $\triangle CDB$, $BC = \sqrt{5^2 + (\sqrt{2})^2} = \sqrt{27} = 3\sqrt{3}$. Similarly, $AC = 3\sqrt{3}$. The length of the curved line is

$$3/4 \text{ (circumference)} = (3/4)(2\pi r)$$
$$= (3/4)(2\pi)(2)$$
$$= 3\pi.$$

Thus, the perimeter of the sign is

$$3\pi + AC + BC = 3\pi + 3\sqrt{3} + 3\sqrt{3} = 3\pi + 6\sqrt{3},$$
and the best answer is B.

19. The sum of the first 100 positive integers is 5,050. What is the sum of the first 200 positive integers?

(A) 10,100
(B) 10,200
(C) 15,050
(D) 20,050
(E) 20,100

Each number in the sequence
$$101, 102, 103, \ldots, 200$$
is 100 larger than the corresponding number in the sequence
$$1, 2, 3, \ldots, 100.$$
Since the sum of the numbers in the latter sequence is 5,050, the sum of the former sequence must be
$$5,050 + 100(100) = 15,050.$$
The sum of the first 200 positive integers is
$$(1+2+3+\ldots+100) + (101+102+103+\ldots+200)$$
$$= 5,050 + 15,050$$
$$= 20,100.$$
Thus, the best answer is E.

20. A merchant purchased a jacket for $60 and then determined a selling price that equalled the purchase price of the jacket plus a markup that was 25 percent of the selling price. During a sale, the merchant discounted the selling price by 20 percent and sold the jacket. What was the merchant's gross profit on this sale?

(A) $0   (B) $3   (C) $4
(D) $12   (E) $15

If the selling price is x dollars, then
$$60 + 0.25x = x$$
$$60 = 0.75x$$
$$80 = x.$$
The merchant sold the jacket for 80 percent of the selling price (due to the 20 percent discount), or
$$(0.8)(\$80) = \$64.$$
Therefore, the merchant's gross profit on the sale was $64 − $60 = $4. The best answer is C.

PROBLEM SOLVING SAMPLE TEST SECTION 8

30 Minutes
20 Questions

Directions: In this section solve each problem, using any available space on the page for scratchwork. Then indicate the best of the answer choices given.

Numbers: All numbers used are real numbers.

Figures: Figures that accompany problems in this section are intended to provide information useful in solving the problems. They are drawn as accurately as possible EXCEPT when it is stated in a specific problem that its figure is not drawn to scale. All figures lie in a plane unless otherwise indicated.

1. A certain club has 237 local branches, one national office, and one social service office. If each local branch has 2 officers, and each of the two other offices has 4 officers, how many officers does the club have altogether?

    (A) 482
    (B) 476
    (C) 474
    (D) 239
    (E) 235

2. An employee is paid a salary of $300 per month and earns a 6 percent commission on all her sales. What must her annual sales be in order for her to have a gross annual salary of exactly $21,600 ?

    (A) $22,896   (B) $26,712   (C) $300,000

    (D) $330,000   (E) $360,000

3. Of the 1,000 students who entered College X as freshmen in September 1979, 112 did not graduate in May 1983. If 962 students graduated in May 1983, how many of the graduates did not enter College X as freshmen in September 1979 ?

    (A)   38
    (B)   74
    (C)   112
    (D)   150
    (E)   188

GO ON TO THE NEXT PAGE.

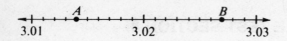

3.01   3.02   3.03

4. On the number line above, what is the length of segment AB?

(A) 13   (B) 1.4   (C) 1.3

(D) 0.13   (E) 0.013

5. Which of the following has a value greater than 1 ?

(A) $\dfrac{2}{\sqrt{3}}$ (B) $\dfrac{\sqrt{2}}{2}$ (C) $\left(\dfrac{3}{4}\right)^2$

(D) $\left(\dfrac{7}{8}\right)^3$ (E) $2\left(\dfrac{3}{7}\right)$

6. If $\dfrac{m^2 + m - 3}{3} = 1$, then m could equal

(A) -1
(B) 0
(C) 1
(D) 2
(E) 3

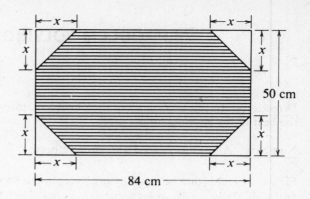

7. The figure above represents a rectangular desk blotter in a holder with dimensions shown. If $x = 8$ centimeters, what is the area, in square centimeters, of the shaded portion of the blotter?

(A) 4,200
(B) 4,184
(C) 4,124
(D) 4,072
(E) 3,944

GO ON TO THE NEXT PAGE.

8. The number 25 is 2.5 percent of which of the following?

(A)   10
(B)   62.5
(C)   100
(D)   625
(E)   1,000

9. Cottages at a resort are rented for half the summer price in each of the 3 spring months and one-third the summer price in each of the 6 fall and winter months. If each cottage brings in a total of $3,861 when rented for each of the 12 months of the year, what is the monthly rent for each of the 3 summer months?

(A) $297
(B) $594
(C) $702
(D) $858
(E) $1,782

10. In 1980 John's salary was $15,000 a year and Don's salary was $20,000 a year. If every year thereafter, John receives a raise of $2,450 and Don receives a raise of $2,000, the first year in which John's salary will be more than Don's salary is

(A)   1987
(B)   1988
(C)   1991
(D)   1992
(E)   2000

11. Which of the following is equal to $\frac{351}{558}$?

(A) $\frac{7}{11}$ (B) $\frac{39}{62}$ (C) $\frac{19}{31}$

(D) $\frac{117}{196}$ (E) $\frac{107}{186}$

GO ON TO THE NEXT PAGE.

12. On a certain airline, the price of a ticket is directly proportional to the number of miles to be traveled. If the ticket for a 900-mile trip on this airline costs $120, which of the following gives the number of dollars charged for a k-mile trip on this airline?

(A) $\frac{2k}{15}$　(B) $\frac{2}{15k}$　(C) $\frac{15}{2k}$

(D) $\frac{15k}{2}$　(E) $\frac{40k}{3}$

13. If $\frac{n}{41}$ is 1 more than $\frac{m}{41}$, then $n =$

(A) $m - 41$　(B) $m + 1$　(C) $m + 41$

(D) $m + 42$　(E) $41m$

14. A discount of 20 percent on an order of goods followed by a discount of 10 percent amounts to

(A) less than one 15 percent discount
(B) the same as one 15 percent discount
(C) the same as one 30 percent discount
(D) less than a discount of 10 percent followed by a discount of 20 percent
(E) the same as a discount of 10 percent followed by a discount of 20 percent

15. If k is an even integer and p and r are odd integers, which of the following CANNOT be an integer?

(A) $\frac{r}{k}$　(B) $\frac{k}{p}$　(C) $\frac{p}{r}$　(D) $\frac{kp}{r}$　(E) $\frac{kr}{p}$

16. Today Al is 3 times as old as Pat. In 13 years, Al will be one year less than twice as old as Pat will be then. How many years old is Al today?

(A) 12
(B) 33
(C) 36
(D) 42
(E) 49

17. When the integer n is divided by 17, the quotient is x and the remainder is 5. When n is divided by 23, the quotient is y and the remainder is 14. Which of the following is true?

(A) $23x + 17y = 19$
(B) $17x - 23y = 9$
(C) $17x + 23y = 19$
(D) $14x + 5y = 6$
(E) $5x - 14y = -6$

GO ON TO THE NEXT PAGE.

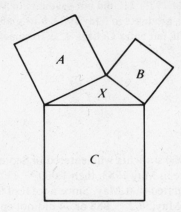

Note: Figure not drawn to scale.

18. In the figure above, three squares and a triangle have areas of A, B, C, and X as shown. If $A = 144$, $B = 81$, and $C = 225$, then $X =$

(A) 150   (B) 144   (C) 80
(D) 54   (E) 36

19. Three types of pencils, J, K, and L, cost 0.05, 0.10, and 0.25 each, respectively. If a box of 32 of these pencils costs a total of 3.40 and if there are twice as many K pencils as L pencils in the box, how many J pencils are in the box?

(A) 6
(B) 12
(C) 14
(D) 18
(E) 20

20. Forty percent of the rats included in an experiment were male rats. If some of the rats died during the experiment and 30 percent of the rats that died were male rats, what was the ratio of the death rate among the male rats to the death rate among the female rats?

(A) $\frac{9}{14}$ (B) $\frac{3}{4}$ (C) $\frac{9}{11}$ (D) $\frac{6}{7}$ (E) $\frac{7}{8}$

S T O P

IF YOU FINISH BEFORE TIME IS CALLED, YOU MAY CHECK YOUR WORK ON THIS SECTION ONLY.
DO NOT TURN TO ANY OTHER SECTION IN THE TEST.

Answer Key for Sample Test Section 8

PROBLEM SOLVING

1. A	11. B
2. C	12. A
3. B	13. C
4. E	14. E
5. A	15. A
6. D	16. C
7. D	17. B
8. E	18. D
9. B	19. C
10. D	20. A

Explanatory Material: Problem Solving Sample Test Section 8

1. A certain club has 237 local branches, one national office, and one social service office. If each local branch has 2 officers, and each of the two other offices has 4 officers, how many officers does the club have altogether?

   (A) 482
   (B) 476
   (C) 474
   (D) 239
   (E) 235

There are 237(2) officers at local branches and 2(4) officers at the other offices, or $474 + 8 = 482$ officers altogether. The best answer is A.

2. An employee is paid a salary of $300 per month and earns a 6 percent commission on all her sales. What must her annual sales be in order for her to have a gross annual salary of exactly $21,600?

   (A) $22,896   (B) $26,712   (C) $300,000
   (D) $330,000   (E) $360,000

The gross annual salary of $21,600 includes 300(12), or $3,600, plus 6 percent commission on all sales. Therefore, $21,600 = 3,600 + 0.06s$, where s is the amount of sales; $0.06s = 18,000$ and $s = \$300,000$. The best answer is C.

3. Of the 1,000 students who entered College X as freshmen in September 1979, 112 did not graduate in May 1983. If 962 students graduate in May 1983, how many of the graduates did not enter College X as freshmen in September 1979?

   (A) 38
   (B) 74
   (C) 112
   (D) 150
   (E) 188

If 112 of the 1,000 students who entered in September 1979 did not graduate in May 1983, then $1,000 - 112$ or 888 must have graduated that May. Since a total of 962 students graduated that May, $962 - 888$ or 74 did not enter as freshmen in September 1979. The best answer is B.

4. On the number line above, what is the length of segment AB?

   (A) 13   (B) 1.4   (C) 1.3
   (D) 0.13   (E) 0.013

Each small interval between consecutive gradations on the segment has length $\frac{0.01}{10} = 0.001$. Therefore, since segment AB consists of 13 small intervals, it has length $13(0.001) = 0.013$. The best answer is E.

5. Which of the following has a value greater than 1?

   (A) $\dfrac{2}{\sqrt{3}}$ (B) $\dfrac{\sqrt{2}}{2}$ (C) $\left(\dfrac{3}{4}\right)^2$

   (D) $\left(\dfrac{7}{8}\right)^3$ (E) $2\left(\dfrac{3}{7}\right)$

For a ratio to have a value greater than 1, the numerator of the ratio must be greater than the denominator. Since $2 > \sqrt{3}$, choice A gives a number greater than 1 and is, thus, the best answer.

6. If $\dfrac{m^2 + m - 3}{3} = 1$, then m could equal

(A) -1
(B) 0
(C) 1
(D) 2
(E) 3

To solve this equation, it is convenient to multiply both sides of the equation by 3. Then $m^2 + m - 3 = 3$, $m^2 + m - 6 = 0$, and $(m + 3)(m - 2) = 0$. Since one of the factors must be equal to 0, $m = -3$ or $m = 2$. Therefore, the best answer is D.

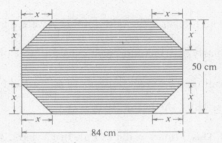

7. The figure above represents a rectangular desk blotter in a holder with dimensions shown. If $x = 8$ centimeters, what is the area, in square centimeters, of the shaded portion of the blotter?

(A) 4,200
(B) 4,184
(C) 4,124
(D) 4,072
(E) 3,944

The area of the entire blotter is $50(84) = 4,200$ square centimeters. The area of each corner is $\dfrac{x^2}{2} = \dfrac{8^2}{2} = 32$. Therefore, the area of the shaded portion is 4,200 minus the areas of the four corners or $4,200 - 4(32) = 4,200 - 128 = 4,072$. The best answer is D.

8. The number 25 is 2.5 percent of which of the following?

(A) 10
(B) 62.5
(C) 100
(D) 625
(E) 1,000

If 25 is 2.5 percent of a number, then 250 is 25 percent of the number, and $4(250) = 1,000$ is $4(25\%)$ or 100 percent of the number. Another approach is to solve the equation $25 = 0.025n$, where n represents the number. The best answer is E.

9. Cottages at a resort are rented for half the summer price in each of the 3 spring months and one-third the summer price in each of the 6 fall and winter months. If each cottage brings in a total of $3,861 when rented for each of the 12 months of the year, what is the monthly rent for each of the 3 summer months?

(A) $297
(B) $594
(C) $702
(D) $858
(E) $1,782

Let s be the monthly rent for each of the 3 summer months. Then $\dfrac{s}{2}$ is the rent for each of the 3 spring months, and $\dfrac{s}{3}$ is the rent for each of the 6 fall and winter months. Since the total rent for all 12 months is $3,861, the total can be expressed as $3s + 3(\dfrac{s}{2}) + 6(\dfrac{s}{3}) = 3,861$, or $3s + 1.5s + 2s = 3,861$; $6.5s = 3,861$, and $s = \$594$. The best answer is B.

10. In 1980 John's salary was $15,000 a year and Don's salary was $20,000 a year. If every year thereafter, John receives a raise of $2,450 and Don receives a raise of $2,000, the first year in which John's salary will be more than Don's salary is

(A) 1987
(B) 1988
(C) 1991
(D) 1992
(E) 2000

Let n represent the number of years after 1980 until John's salary first exceeds Don's salary. Then $15,000 + 2,450n > 20,000 + 2,000n$, and $n > 11$. Thus, John's salary will first exceed Don's in the twelfth year after 1980, or $1980 + 12 = 1992$. The best answer is D.

11. Which of the following is equal to $\dfrac{351}{558}$?

(A) $\dfrac{7}{11}$ (B) $\dfrac{39}{62}$ (C) $\dfrac{19}{31}$

(D) $\dfrac{117}{196}$ (E) $\dfrac{107}{186}$

One method of reducing a fraction such as $\dfrac{351}{558}$, where the greatest common factor of the terms may not be apparent, is to test whether any of the first few odd prime numbers, 3, 5, 7, etc., are common factors of the two terms. Since a number is divisible by 3 if the sum of its digits is divisible by 3, 3 is a common factor. Thus, $\dfrac{351}{558} = \dfrac{3 \times 117}{3 \times 186}$. The fraction $\dfrac{117}{186}$ is not one of the options; however, 3 is a common factor of 117 and 186, and so $\dfrac{117}{186} = \dfrac{3 \times 39}{3 \times 62}$. The best answer is B.

12. On a certain airline, the price of a ticket is directly proportional to the number of miles to be traveled. If the ticket for a 900-mile trip on this airline costs $120, which of the following gives the number of dollars charged for a k-mile trip on this airline?

(A) $\dfrac{2k}{15}$ (B) $\dfrac{2}{15k}$ (C) $\dfrac{15}{2k}$

(D) $\dfrac{15k}{2}$ (E) $\dfrac{40k}{3}$

Since the price is directly proportional to the distance and the price of a 900-mile trip is $120, the price per mile is $\dfrac{120}{900}$ or $\dfrac{2}{15}$ dollars, and the price of a k-mile trip is $\dfrac{2k}{15}$ dollars. The best answer is A.

13. If $\dfrac{n}{41}$ is 1 more than $\dfrac{m}{41}$, then $n =$

(A) $m - 41$ (B) $m + 1$ (C) $m + 41$
(D) $m + 42$ (E) $41m$

The statement in the problem is equivalent to the equation $\dfrac{n}{41} = \dfrac{m}{41} + 1$. To solve for n, it is convenient to multiply both sides of the equation by 41, which yields $n = m + 41$. The best answer is C.

14. A discount of 20 percent on an order of goods followed by a discount of 10 percent amounts to

(A) less than one 15 percent discount
(B) the same as one 15 percent discount
(C) the same as one 30 percent discount
(D) less than a discount of 10 percent followed by a discount of 20 percent
(E) the same as a discount of 10 percent followed by a discount of 20 percent

To see the precise effect of successive discounts, let p be the original price of the goods, and then express the price after each successive discount in terms of p. After a 20 percent discount on p, the new price will be $0.8p$. If a second discount, of 10 percent, is taken on $0.8p$, the new price will be $0.9(0.8p) = 0.72p$, which means that the successive discounts are equivalent to a single discount of $(100 - 72)$ or 28 percent. Since $0.9(0.8p) = 0.8(0.9p)$, the total discount is the same regardless of the order in which the two discounts are taken. The best answer is E.

15. If k is an even integer and p and r are odd integers, which of the following CANNOT be an integer?

(A) $\dfrac{r}{k}$ (B) $\dfrac{k}{p}$ (C) $\dfrac{p}{r}$ (D) $\dfrac{kp}{r}$ (E) $\dfrac{kr}{p}$

For a rational number to be equal to an integer, each factor of the denominator must be a factor of the numerator. Since k is an even integer, 2 is a factor of k; 2 is not a factor of any odd number. Thus, choice A cannot be an integer since 2 is a factor of k but not of r. Since the ratio given in A cannot be an integer, it is not necessary to examine the other options. Note, however, that each of the other ratios could be an integer: $\dfrac{k}{p}$ could be an integer if k were an even multiple of p; $\dfrac{p}{r}$ could be an integer if the odd number p were a multiple of r, and similarly, $k(\dfrac{p}{r})$ would be an even multiple of $\dfrac{p}{r}$. By the same reasoning, if r were a multiple of p, $\dfrac{r}{p}$ and $k(\dfrac{r}{p})$ would be integers. Thus, the best answer is A.

16. Today Al is 3 times as old as Pat. In 13 years, Al will be one year less than twice as old as Pat will be then. How many years old is Al today?

(A) 12
(B) 33
(C) 36
(D) 42
(E) 49

If Pat is x years old today, then Al is $3x$ years old. In 13 years, Pat will be $x + 13$ and Al will be $3x + 13$ years old. If these expressions and the information in the problem are used, it follows that $3x + 13 = 2(x + 13) - 1$, and Pat's age is 12. Therefore, Al's age is $3x = 3(12) = 36$. The best answer is C.

17. When the integer n is divided by 17, the quotient is x and the remainder is 5. When n is divided by 23, the quotient is y and the remainder is 14. Which of the following is true?

(A) $23x + 17y = 19$
(B) $17x - 23y = 9$
(C) $17x + 23y = 19$
(D) $14x + 5y = 6$
(E) $5x - 14y = -6$

According to the first sentence, $n = 17x + 5$; similarly, from the second sentence, $n = 23y + 14$. If both expressions are equal to n, then the two expressions are equal to each other, which is to say $17x + 5 = 23y + 14$, or $17x - 23y = 9$. The best answer is B.

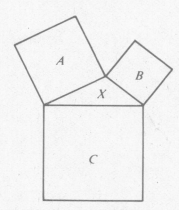

Note: Figure not drawn to scale.

18. In the figure above, three squares and a triangle have areas of A, B, C, and X as shown. If $A = 144$, $B = 81$, and $C = 225$, then $X =$

(A) 150   (B) 144   (C) 80
   (D) 54   (E) 36

Since the sum of the squares of two sides of the triangle is equal to the square of the third side, the triangle must be a right triangle. The sides of the triangle are 12, 9, and 15 (the square roots of the areas of the three squares). The area of the triangle, X, is half the product of the lengths of the two legs, or $(9 \times 12) \div 2 = 54$. The best answer is D.

19. Three types of pencils, J, K, and L, cost $0.05, $0.10, and $0.25 each, respectively. If a box of 32 of these pencils costs a total of $3.40 and if there are twice as many K pencils as L pencils in the box, how many J pencils are in the box?

(A) 6
(B) 12
(C) 14
(D) 18
(E) 20

Let n be the number of type L pencils in the box. Then the number of type K pencils can be denoted by $2n$ and the number of type J pencils can be denoted by $32 - (2n + n)$ or $32 - 3n$. Applying the unit prices, in cents, to these respective quantities yields the equation $25n + 10(2n) + 5(32 - 3n) = 340$; $30n + 160 = 340$, and $n = 6$. Since the number of type J pencils is $32 - 3n$ and $n = 6$, the number is $32 - 3(6) = 14$. The best answer is C.

20. Forty percent of the rats included in an experiment were male rats. If some of the rats died during the experiment and 30 percent of the rats that died were male rats, what was the ratio of the death rate among the male rats to the death rate among the female rats?

(A) $\dfrac{9}{14}$ (B) $\dfrac{3}{4}$ (C) $\dfrac{9}{11}$ (D) $\dfrac{6}{7}$ (E) $\dfrac{7}{8}$

If t represents the total number of rats, then $0.4t$ is the number of male rats and $0.6t$ is the number of female rats. If d represents the total number of rats that died, then $0.3d$ is the number of male rats that died and $0.7d$ is the number of female rats that died. The death rate in each of the groups is the ratio of the number in the group that died to the total number in the group. Thus, the death rate among the male rats was $\dfrac{0.3d}{0.4t}$ and among the female rats was $\dfrac{0.7d}{0.6t}$, and the ratio of the two death rates was $\dfrac{\dfrac{0.3d}{0.4t}}{\dfrac{0.7d}{0.6t}} = \dfrac{9}{14}$. The best answer is A.

4 Data Sufficiency

In this section of the GMAT, you are to classify each problem according to the five fixed answer choices, rather than find a solution to the problem. Each problem consists of a question and two statements. You are to decide whether the information in each statement alone is sufficient to answer the question or, if neither is, whether the information in the two statements together is sufficient.

The following pages include test-taking strategies, sample test sections (with answer keys), and detailed explanations of every problem from the sample test sections. These explanations present possible problem-solving strategies for the examples. At the end of each explanation following the first sample test section is a reference to the particular section(s) of Chapter 2, Math Review, that you may find helpful in reviewing the mathematical concepts on which the problem is based.

Test-Taking Strategies for Data Sufficiency

1. Do not waste valuable time solving a problem; you are only to determine whether sufficient information is given to solve the problem. After you have considered statement (1), make a check mark next to (1) if you can determine the answer and a cross mark if you cannot. Be sure to disregard all the information learned from statement (1) while considering statement (2). This is very difficult to do and often results in erroneously choosing answer C when the answer should be B or choosing B when the answer should be C. Suppose statement (2) alone is sufficient. Then a check mark next to (1) indicates that D is the correct answer; a cross mark next to (1) indicates that B is correct. Suppose statement (2) alone is not sufficient. A check mark next to (1) indicates that A is the correct answer; a cross mark next to (1) indicates that you must now consider whether the two statements taken together give sufficient information; if they do, the answer is C; if not, the answer is E.

2. If you determine that the information in statement (1) is sufficient to answer the question, the answer is necessarily either A or D. If you are not sure about statement (1) but you know that statement (2) alone is sufficient, the answer is necessarily either B or D. If neither statement taken alone is sufficient, the answer is either C or E. Thus, if you have doubts about certain portions of the information given but are relatively sure about other portions, you can logically eliminate two or three options and more than double your chances of guessing correctly.

3. Remember that when you are determining whether there is sufficient information to answer a question of the form, "What is the value of y?" the information given must be sufficient to find one and only one value for y. Being able to determine minimum or maximum values or an answer of the form $y = x + 2$ is not sufficient, because such answers constitute a range of values rather than "the value of y."

4. When geometric figures are involved, be very careful not to make unwarranted assumptions based on the figures. A triangle may appear to be isosceles, but can you detect the difference in the lengths of segments 1.8 inches long and 1.85 inches long? Furthermore, the figures are not necessarily drawn to scale; they are generalized figures showing little more than intersecting line segments and the betweenness of points, angles, and regions.

When you take the sample test sections, use the answer spaces on pages 127 and 128 to mark your answers.

Answer Spaces for Data Sufficiency Sample Test Sections

Sample Test Section 1

1 (A) (B) (C) (D) (E)	8 (A) (B) (C) (D) (E)	15 (A) (B) (C) (D) (E)	22 (A) (B) (C) (D) (E)
2 (A) (B) (C) (D) (E)	9 (A) (B) (C) (D) (E)	16 (A) (B) (C) (D) (E)	23 (A) (B) (C) (D) (E)
3 (A) (B) (C) (D) (E)	10 (A) (B) (C) (D) (E)	17 (A) (B) (C) (D) (E)	24 (A) (B) (C) (D) (E)
4 (A) (B) (C) (D) (E)	11 (A) (B) (C) (D) (E)	18 (A) (B) (C) (D) (E)	25 (A) (B) (C) (D) (E)
5 (A) (B) (C) (D) (E)	12 (A) (B) (C) (D) (E)	19 (A) (B) (C) (D) (E)	
6 (A) (B) (C) (D) (E)	13 (A) (B) (C) (D) (E)	20 (A) (B) (C) (D) (E)	
7 (A) (B) (C) (D) (E)	14 (A) (B) (C) (D) (E)	21 (A) (B) (C) (D) (E)	

Sample Test Section 2

1 (A) (B) (C) (D) (E)	8 (A) (B) (C) (D) (E)	15 (A) (B) (C) (D) (E)	22 (A) (B) (C) (D) (E)
2 (A) (B) (C) (D) (E)	9 (A) (B) (C) (D) (E)	16 (A) (B) (C) (D) (E)	23 (A) (B) (C) (D) (E)
3 (A) (B) (C) (D) (E)	10 (A) (B) (C) (D) (E)	17 (A) (B) (C) (D) (E)	24 (A) (B) (C) (D) (E)
4 (A) (B) (C) (D) (E)	11 (A) (B) (C) (D) (E)	18 (A) (B) (C) (D) (E)	25 (A) (B) (C) (D) (E)
5 (A) (B) (C) (D) (E)	12 (A) (B) (C) (D) (E)	19 (A) (B) (C) (D) (E)	
6 (A) (B) (C) (D) (E)	13 (A) (B) (C) (D) (E)	20 (A) (B) (C) (D) (E)	
7 (A) (B) (C) (D) (E)	14 (A) (B) (C) (D) (E)	21 (A) (B) (C) (D) (E)	

Sample Test Section 3

1 (A) (B) (C) (D) (E)	8 (A) (B) (C) (D) (E)	15 (A) (B) (C) (D) (E)	22 (A) (B) (C) (D) (E)
2 (A) (B) (C) (D) (E)	9 (A) (B) (C) (D) (E)	16 (A) (B) (C) (D) (E)	23 (A) (B) (C) (D) (E)
3 (A) (B) (C) (D) (E)	10 (A) (B) (C) (D) (E)	17 (A) (B) (C) (D) (E)	24 (A) (B) (C) (D) (E)
4 (A) (B) (C) (D) (E)	11 (A) (B) (C) (D) (E)	18 (A) (B) (C) (D) (E)	25 (A) (B) (C) (D) (E)
5 (A) (B) (C) (D) (E)	12 (A) (B) (C) (D) (E)	19 (A) (B) (C) (D) (E)	
6 (A) (B) (C) (D) (E)	13 (A) (B) (C) (D) (E)	20 (A) (B) (C) (D) (E)	
7 (A) (B) (C) (D) (E)	14 (A) (B) (C) (D) (E)	21 (A) (B) (C) (D) (E)	

Sample Test Section 4

1 (A) (B) (C) (D) (E)	8 (A) (B) (C) (D) (E)	15 (A) (B) (C) (D) (E)	22 (A) (B) (C) (D) (E)
2 (A) (B) (C) (D) (E)	9 (A) (B) (C) (D) (E)	16 (A) (B) (C) (D) (E)	23 (A) (B) (C) (D) (E)
3 (A) (B) (C) (D) (E)	10 (A) (B) (C) (D) (E)	17 (A) (B) (C) (D) (E)	24 (A) (B) (C) (D) (E)
4 (A) (B) (C) (D) (E)	11 (A) (B) (C) (D) (E)	18 (A) (B) (C) (D) (E)	25 (A) (B) (C) (D) (E)
5 (A) (B) (C) (D) (E)	12 (A) (B) (C) (D) (E)	19 (A) (B) (C) (D) (E)	
6 (A) (B) (C) (D) (E)	13 (A) (B) (C) (D) (E)	20 (A) (B) (C) (D) (E)	
7 (A) (B) (C) (D) (E)	14 (A) (B) (C) (D) (E)	21 (A) (B) (C) (D) (E)	

Sample Test Section 5

```
1  Ⓐ Ⓑ Ⓒ Ⓓ Ⓔ      8  Ⓐ Ⓑ Ⓒ Ⓓ Ⓔ     15  Ⓐ Ⓑ Ⓒ Ⓓ Ⓔ     22  Ⓐ Ⓑ Ⓒ Ⓓ Ⓔ
2  Ⓐ Ⓑ Ⓒ Ⓓ Ⓔ      9  Ⓐ Ⓑ Ⓒ Ⓓ Ⓔ     16  Ⓐ Ⓑ Ⓒ Ⓓ Ⓔ     23  Ⓐ Ⓑ Ⓒ Ⓓ Ⓔ
3  Ⓐ Ⓑ Ⓒ Ⓓ Ⓔ     10  Ⓐ Ⓑ Ⓒ Ⓓ Ⓔ     17  Ⓐ Ⓑ Ⓒ Ⓓ Ⓔ     24  Ⓐ Ⓑ Ⓒ Ⓓ Ⓔ
4  Ⓐ Ⓑ Ⓒ Ⓓ Ⓔ     11  Ⓐ Ⓑ Ⓒ Ⓓ Ⓔ     18  Ⓐ Ⓑ Ⓒ Ⓓ Ⓔ     25  Ⓐ Ⓑ Ⓒ Ⓓ Ⓔ
5  Ⓐ Ⓑ Ⓒ Ⓓ Ⓔ     12  Ⓐ Ⓑ Ⓒ Ⓓ Ⓔ     19  Ⓐ Ⓑ Ⓒ Ⓓ Ⓔ
6  Ⓐ Ⓑ Ⓒ Ⓓ Ⓔ     13  Ⓐ Ⓑ Ⓒ Ⓓ Ⓔ     20  Ⓐ Ⓑ Ⓒ Ⓓ Ⓔ
7  Ⓐ Ⓑ Ⓒ Ⓓ Ⓔ     14  Ⓐ Ⓑ Ⓒ Ⓓ Ⓔ     21  Ⓐ Ⓑ Ⓒ Ⓓ Ⓔ
```

DATA SUFFICIENCY SAMPLE TEST SECTION 1

30 Minutes
25 Questions

<u>Directions:</u> Each of the data sufficiency problems below consists of a question and two statements, labeled (1) and (2), in which certain data are given. You have to decide whether the data given in the statements are <u>sufficient</u> for answering the question. Using the data given in the statements <u>plus</u> your knowledge of mathematics and everyday facts (such as the number of days in July or the meaning of <u>counterclockwise</u>), you are to fill in oval

    A   if statement (1) ALONE is sufficient, but statement (2) alone is not sufficient to answer the question asked;

    B   if statement (2) ALONE is sufficient, but statement (1) alone is not sufficient to answer the question asked;

    C   if BOTH statements (1) and (2) TOGETHER are sufficient to answer the question asked, but NEITHER statement ALONE is sufficient;

    D   if EACH statement ALONE is sufficient to answer the question asked;

    E   if statements (1) and (2) TOGETHER are NOT sufficient to answer the question asked, and additional data specific to the problem are needed.

<u>Numbers:</u> All numbers used are real numbers.

<u>Figures:</u>   A figure in a data sufficiency problem will conform to the information given in the question, but will not necessarily conform to the additional information given in statements (1) and (2).

    You may assume that lines shown as straight are straight and that angle measures are greater than zero.

    You may assume that the positions of points, angles, regions, etc., exist in the order shown.

    All figures lie in a plane unless otherwise indicated.

<u>Example:</u>

    In $\triangle PQR$, what is the value of x?

    (1) $PQ = PR$

    (2) $y = 40$

<u>Explanation:</u> According to statement (1), $PQ = PR$; therefore, $\triangle PQR$ is isosceles and $y = z$. Since $x + y + z = 180$, $x + 2y = 180$. Since statement (1) does not give a value for y, you cannot answer the question using statement (1) by itself. According to statement (2), $y = 40$; therefore, $x + z = 140$. Since statement (2) does not give a value for z, you cannot answer the question using statement (2) by itself. Using both statements together, you can find y and z; therefore, you can find x, and the answer to the problem is C.

GO ON TO THE NEXT PAGE.

A Statement (1) ALONE is sufficient, but statement (2) alone is not sufficient.
B Statement (2) ALONE is sufficient, but statement (1) alone is not sufficient.
C BOTH statements TOGETHER are sufficient, but NEITHER statement ALONE is sufficient.
D EACH statement ALONE is sufficient.
E Statements (1) and (2) TOGETHER are NOT sufficient.

1. What is the 1st term in sequence S ?

   (1) The 3rd term in S is 2.

   (2) The 2nd term in S is twice the 1st, and the 3rd term is three times the 2nd.

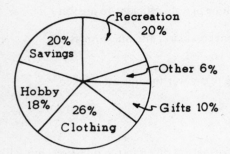

2. The chart above shows how Jeff spent his earnings for one year. How much did Jeff spend for clothing?

   (1) He spent $18 during the year on tennis balls.

   (2) He spent $190 during the year on recreation.

3. Is $x > y$?

   (1) $0 < x < 0.75$

   (2) $0.25 < y < 1.0$

4. Car X and car Y ran a 500-kilometer race. What was the average speed of car X ?

   (1) Car X completed the race in 6 hours and 40 minutes.

   (2) Car Y, at an average speed of 100 kilometers per hour, completed the race 1 hour and 40 minutes before car X crossed the finish line.

5. In a refinery, the capacity of oil tank A is 70 per cent of the capacity of oil tank B. How many more gallons of oil are in tank A than in tank B ?

   (1) Tank A is 90 per cent full; tank B is 50 per cent full.

   (2) When full, tank A contains 50,000 gallons of oil.

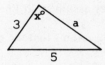

6. What is the area of the triangle above?

   (1) $a^2 + 9 = 25$

   (2) $x = 90$

GO ON TO THE NEXT PAGE.

A Statement (1) ALONE is sufficient, but statement (2) alone is not sufficient.
B Statement (2) ALONE is sufficient, but statement (1) alone is not sufficient.
C BOTH statements TOGETHER are sufficient, but NEITHER statement ALONE is sufficient.
D EACH statement ALONE is sufficient.
E Statements (1) and (2) TOGETHER are NOT sufficient.

7. What is the remainder when the positive integer x is divided by 2 ?

   (1) x is an odd integer.

   (2) x is a multiple of 3.

8. Is $x > y$?

   (1) $x^2 > y^2$

   (2) $x - y > 0$

9. If the ratio of men to women employed by Company S in 1975 was $\frac{1}{2}$, what is the ratio of men to women employed by Company S in 1976 ?

   (1) Company S employed 20 more women in 1976 than in 1975.

   (2) Company S employed 20 more men in 1976 than in 1975.

10. Exactly how many bonds does Bob have?

    (1) Of Bob's bonds, exactly 21 are worth at leas. $5,000 each.

    (2) Of Bob's bonds, exactly 65 per cent are worth less than $5,000 each.

11. What is the volume of rectangular box R ?

    (1) The total surface area of R is 12 square meters.

    (2) The height of R is 50 centimeters.

12. What is the value of the two-digit number x ?

    (1) The sum of the two digits is 4.

    (2) The difference between the two digits is 2.

13. A rectangle is defined to be "silver" if and only if the ratio of its length to its width is 2 to 1. If rectangle S is silver, is rectangle R silver?

    (1) R has the same area as S.

    (2) The ratio of one side of R to one side of S is 2 to 1.

14. Is $xy < 0$?

    (1) $x^2 y^3 < 0$

    (2) $xy^2 > 0$

GO ON TO THE NEXT PAGE.

A Statement (1) ALONE is sufficient, but statement (2) alone is not sufficient.
B Statement (2) ALONE is sufficient, but statement (1) alone is not sufficient.
C BOTH statements TOGETHER are sufficient, but NEITHER statement ALONE is sufficient.
D EACH statement ALONE is sufficient.
E Statements (1) and (2) TOGETHER are NOT sufficient.

15. If x is an integer, is $\frac{x}{2}$ an <u>even</u> integer?

   (1) x is a multiple of 2.
   (2) x is a multiple of 4.

16. What is the value of x − y ?

   (1) x − y = y − x
   (2) x − y = x² − y²

17. If x = y², what is the value of y − x ?

   (1) x = 4
   (2) x + y = 2

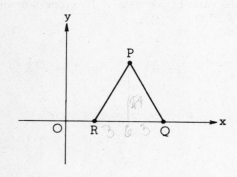

18. In the figure above, R and Q are points on the x-axis. What is the area of equilateral △PQR ?

   (1) The coordinates of point P are (6, 2√3).
   (2) The coordinates of point Q are (8, 0).

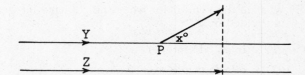

19. Cars Y and Z travel side by side at the same rate of speed along parallel roads as shown above. When car Y reaches point P, it forks to the left at angle x°, changes speed, and continues to stay even with car Z as shown by the dotted line. The speed of car Y beyond point P is what per cent of the speed of car Z ?

   (1) The speed of car Z is 50 miles per hour.
   (2) x = 45

20. If each of the 20 bolts of fabric on a shelf is either 100 percent cotton, 100 percent wool, or a mixture of cotton and wool, how many bolts are cotton and wool mixtures?

   (1) Of the 20 bolts, 18 contain some wool and 14 contain some cotton.
   (2) Of the 20 bolts, 6 are 100 percent wool.

21. If xy ≠ 0, what is the value of $\frac{x^4y^2 - (xy)^2}{x^3y^2}$?

   (1) x = 2
   (2) y = 8

GO ON TO THE NEXT PAGE.

-132-

A Statement (1) ALONE is sufficient, but statement (2) alone is not sufficient.
B Statement (2) ALONE is sufficient, but statement (1) alone is not sufficient.
C BOTH statements TOGETHER are sufficient, but NEITHER statement ALONE is sufficient.
D EACH statement ALONE is sufficient.
E Statements (1) and (2) TOGETHER are NOT sufficient.

22. Are there exactly 3 distinct symbols used to create the code words in language Q ?

   (1) The set of all code words in language Q is the set of all possible distinct horizontal arrangements of one or more symbols, with no repetition.

   (2) There are exactly 15 code words in language Q.

23. If x, y, and z are the lengths of the three sides of a triangle, is y > 4 ?

   (1) z = x + 4

   (2) x = 3 and z = 7

24. How many minutes long is time period X ?

   (1) Time period X is 3 hours long.

   (2) Time period X starts at 11 p.m. and ends at 2 a.m.

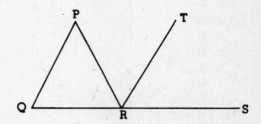

25. In the figure above, QRS is a straight line and line TR bisects ∠PRS. Is it true that lines TR and PQ are parallel?

   (1) PQ = PR

   (2) QR = PR

S T O P

**IF YOU FINISH BEFORE TIME IS CALLED, YOU MAY CHECK YOUR WORK ON THIS SECTION ONLY.
DO NOT TURN TO ANY OTHER SECTION IN THE TEST.**

Answer Key for Sample Test Section 1

DATA SUFFICIENCY

1. C	14. C
2. B	15. B
3. E	16. A
4. D	17. C
5. C	18. A
6. D	19. B
7. A	20. A
8. B	21. A
9. E	22. C
10. C	23. D
11. E	24. A
12. E	25. B
13. E	

Explanatory Material: Data Sufficiency

The following discussion of Data Sufficiency is intended to familiarize you with the most efficient and effective approaches to the kinds of problems common to Data Suffi ciency. The problems on the sample test sections in this chapter are generally representative of the kinds of question you will encounter in this section of the GMAT. Remember that it is the problem-solving strategy that is important, not the specific details of a particular question.

Sample Test Section 1

1. What is the 1st term in sequence S ?

   (1) The 3rd term in S is 2.
   (2) The 2nd term in S is twice the 1st, and the 3rd term is three times the 2nd.

It is clear that (1) offers no help in determining the first term in S. Thus, the answer is B, C, or E. Although (2) gives the relationships among the first three terms in S, it is not suffi cient to answer the question asked, and the answer must be C or E. From (1) and (2) together it can be determined that the 2nd term is $\frac{1}{3}$ the 3rd term $\left(\frac{1}{3}(2) = \frac{2}{3}\right)$ and the 1st term is $\frac{1}{2}$ the 2nd term $\left(\frac{1}{2}\left(\frac{2}{3}\right) = \frac{1}{3}\right)$. Therefore, the best answer is C.

(See Chapter 2, Math Review, Section B.2.)

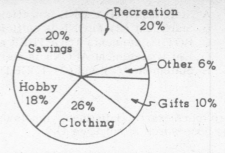

2. The chart above shows how Jeff spent his earnings for one year. How much did Jeff spend for clothing?

   (1) He spent $18 during the year on tennis balls.
   (2) He spent $190 during the year on recreation.

From (1) you know that Jeff spent at least $18 on "recrea tion" expenses. Since you do not know what additional ex penses are included in that 20 percent recreation expense, (1) alone is not sufficient to answer the question. Thus, the an swer must be B, C, or E. From (2), you know that $190 is equal to 20 percent of Jeff's earnings. You can compute Jeff's earnings and the amount spent on clothing. Therefore, the best answer is B. (See Chapter 2, Math Review, Section A.7.)

3. Is x > y?

   (1) $0 < x < 0.75$
   (2) $0.25 < y < 1.0$

Clearly neither (1) nor (2) alone is sufficient to determine whether x > y; thus, the answer must be C or E. Statements (1) and (2) together are also not sufficient to answer the ques tion. For example, if x = 0.6 and y = 0.5, x > y; but, if x = 0.6 and y = 0.9, x < y. Both these examples are consis tent with (1) and (2); therefore, the best answer is E. (See Chapter 2, Math Review, Section B.8.)

4. Car X and car Y ran a 500-kilometer race. What was the average speed of car X?

   (1) Car X completed the race in 6 hours and 40 minutes.
   (2) Car Y, at an average speed of 100 kilometers per hour, completed the race 1 hour and 40 minutes before car X crossed the finish line.

Statement (1) is sufficient because from statement (1) the av erage speed of car X can be determined by dividing 500 kilometers by $6\frac{2}{3}$ hours; thus, the answer is A or D.

Statement (2) implies that car Y took 5 hours to complete the race and car X took $6\frac{2}{3}$ hours. Therefore, (2) alone is also sufficient to determine the average speed of car X, and the best answer is D. (See Chapter 2, Math Review, Section D.1.)

5. In a refinery, the capacity of oil tank A is 70 percent of the capacity of oil tank B. How many more gallons of oil are in tank A than in tank B?

    (1) Tank A is 90 percent full; tank B is 50 percent full.

    (2) When full, tank A contains 50,000 gallons of oil.

Since you do not know the number of gallons in either tank A or tank B, (1) alone is not sufficient; the answer must be B, C, or E. From (2) alone, you can determine the capacities of tanks A and B, but you do not know whether the tanks are full, so the answer must be C or E. Using (1) and (2) together, you can determine the number of gallons in A and B; therefore, the best answer is C. (See Chapter 2, Math Review, Section A.7.)

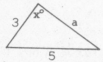

6. What is the area of the triangle above?

    (1) $a^2 + 9 = 25$

    (2) $x = 90$

Statement (1) implies that $a = 4$. Thus, the figure shows a 3-4-5 triangle, and so $x = 90$. Therefore, the area of the triangle is $\frac{(3)(4)}{2}$, and the answer is A or D. Statement (2) indicates that the triangle is a right triangle. Therefore, since $a = 4$, the area is $\frac{(3)(4)}{2}$, and the best answer is D. (See Chapter 2, Math Review, Section C.6.)

7. What is the remainder when the positive integer x is divided by 2?

    (1) x is an odd integer.

    (2) x is a multiple of 3.

Statement (1) is sufficient because from (1) you know that the remainder is 1; whenever an odd integer is divided by 2, the remainder is 1. Thus, the answer is A or D. The question cannot be answered from (2) alone because x could be odd (e.g., 3) or could be even (e.g., 6). Therefore, the best answer is A. (See Chapter 2, Math Review, Section A. 1.)

8. Is $x > y$?

    (1) $x^2 > y^2$

    (2) $x - y > 0$

Statement (1) is insufficient to determine whether $x > y$ because (1) implies nothing about the signs of x and y. For example, if $x = 3$ and $y = 2$, $x > y$, but if $x = -3$ and $y = 2$, $x < y$. Thus, the answer is B, C, or E. By adding y to both sides of (2), you get $x > y$; therefore, the best answer is B. (See Chapter 2, Math Review, Section A.9 and Section B.8.)

9. If the ratio of men to women employed by Company S in 1975 was $\frac{1}{2}$, what is the ratio of men to women employed by Company S in 1976?

    (1) Company S employed 20 more women in 1976 than in 1975.

    (2) Company S employed 20 more men in 1976 than in 1975.

Clearly, neither (1) nor (2) alone is sufficient to determine the ratio for 1976 since neither gives any information about the actual numbers of men or women employed in either 1975 or 1976. Thus, the answer must be C or E. If n is the number of men employed in 1975, then from (1) and (2) together the ratio of men to women employed in 1976 is $\frac{n + 20}{2n + 20}$. Since you do not know the value of n, you cannot determine the ratio for 1976, and the best answer is E. (See Chapter 2, Math Review, Section A.6.)

10. Exactly how many bonds does Bob have?

    (1) Of Bob's bonds, exactly 21 are worth at least $5,000 each.

    (2) Of Bob's bonds, exactly 65 percent are worth less than $5,000 each.

Statement (1) tells you the number of bonds that Bob has that are worth at least $5,000, but you do not know how many of Bob's bonds are worth less than $5,000 each; the answer must be B, C, or E. Statement (2) alone is also not sufficient, because it only gives the percent of Bob's bonds that are worth less than $5,000 each. However, (2) does tell you that 35 percent of Bob's bonds are worth at least $5,000 each. From (1) and (2) together you know that 35 percent of Bob's bonds is equal to 21, and the best answer is C. (See Chapter 2, Math Review, Section A.7.)

11. What is the volume of rectangular box R?

    (1) The total surface area of R is 12 square meters.

    (2) The height of R is 50 centimeters.

For this problem it may be helpful to draw a diagram:

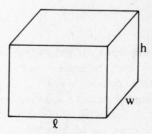

From (1) you know that $2\,(\ell w + wh + \ell h) = 12$, but since you do not know, ℓ, w, or h, (1) is not sufficient to determine the volume of the box ($\ell \times w \times h$), and the answer must be B, C, or E. Since (2) gives just one dimension of the box, it is also not sufficient to determine the volume, and the answer must be C or E. From (1) and (2) together you know that

$$\ell w + \frac{w}{2} + \frac{\ell}{2} = 6,$$

because 50 centimeters $= \frac{1}{2}$ meter, but you still need to know either the length or the width of the box to determine its volume. The best answer is E. (See Chapter 2, Math Review, Section C.10.)

12. **What is the value of the two-digit number x?**

   (1) **The sum of the two digits is 4.**
   (2) **The difference between the two digits is 2.**

Statement (1) implies that x is 13, 22, 31, or 40; thus (1) alone is insufficient, and the answer must be B, C, or E. Statement (2) implies that x could have any one of a number of values, including 13, 24, 31, 42, ... From (1) and (2) together there are still two possibilities for x, 13 and 31; therefore, the best answer is E. (See Chapter 2, Math Review, Section A.1.)

13. **A rectangle is defined to be "silver" if and only if the ratio of its length to its width is 2 to 1. If rectangle S is silver, is rectangle R silver?**

   (1) **R has the same area as S.**
   (2) **The ratio of one side of R to one side of S is 2 to 1.**

Statement (1) alone is not sufficient to answer the question because R could have the same dimensions as S (e.g., 4 × 2) and be silver, or R could have different dimensions (e.g., 8 × 1) and not be silver. Thus, the answer is B, C, or E. Statement (2) alone does not tell anything about the relationship between the other sides of R and S, and so it is not sufficient; the answer must be C or E. The logic applied to (1) can also be applied to the information given in (2); thus (1) and (2) together are not sufficient, and the best answer is E. (See Chapter 2, Math Review, Section C.7.)

14. **Is xy < 0?**

   (1) $x^2 y^3 < 0$
   (2) $xy^2 > 0$

Statement (1) implies that $x \neq 0$ and $y \neq 0$ since the product is not equal to zero. x^2 must be greater than zero because the square of any nonzero number is positive. A positive number times a negative number equals a negative number; thus $y^3 < 0$ since $x^2 y^3 < 0$. Likewise, if $y^3 < 0$, $y < 0$. However, (1) is not sufficient to determine whether $xy < 0$ because you do not know whether $x > 0$ or $x < 0$; thus, the answer is B, C, or E. Similarly, from (2) alone you know that $x > 0$ since $xy^2 > 0$ and $y^2 > 0$, but you do not know whether $y > 0$ or $y < 0$. Combining the information from (1) and (2) you know $y < 0$ and $x > 0$, and so $xy < 0$; the best answer is C. (See Chapter 2, Math Review, Section A.5.)

15. **If x is an integer, is $\frac{x}{2}$ an <u>even</u> integer?**

   (1) **x is a multiple of 2.**
   (2) **x is a multiple of 4.**

Statement (1) implies that x is an even integer, but not that $\frac{x}{2}$ is necessarily even. For example, if x = 8, $\frac{x}{2}$ is even, but if x = 6, $\frac{x}{2}$ is odd; in both cases (1) is satisfied. Thus, the answer is B, C, or E. Statement (2) implies that $x = 2 \cdot 2 \cdot n$, where n is an integer. Hence, $\frac{x}{2} = 2n$ and 2n is even. Therefore, the best answer is B. (See Chapter 2, Math Review, Section A.1.)

16. **What is the value of x − y?**

   (1) $x - y = y - x$
   (2) $x - y = x^2 - y^2$

From (1) you know that 2x = 2y or x = y, and x − y = 0; thus, the answer is A or D. Statement (2) can be expressed as $x - y = (x - y)(x + y)$, which implies that x − y = 0 or x + y = 1; however, this is not sufficient to determine the value of x − y. For example, if $x = y = \frac{1}{2}$, x − y = 0, but if x = 2 and y = −1, x − y = 3. Therefore, the best answer is A. (See Chapter 2, Math Review, Section B.1 and Section B.4.)

17. **If $x = y^2$, what is the value of y − x?**

   (1) **x = 4**
   (2) **x + y = 2**

From (1) you find that y = 2 or y = −2, but which of these values y has cannot be determined. Therefore, (1) alone is not sufficient to answer the question asked, and the answer is B, C, or E. Substituting y^2 for x in (2), you find that y = 1 or y = −2; therefore, (2) alone is not sufficient, and the answer is C or E. Using (1) and (2) together, you find that x = 4, and y = −2, so the value of y − x can be found. Therefore, the best answer is C. (See Chapter 2, Math Review, Section B.5.)

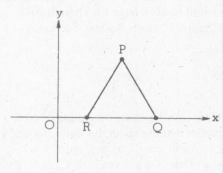

18. **In the figure above, R and Q are points on the x-axis. What is the area of equilateral △PQR?**

   (1) **The coordinates of point P are (6, $2\sqrt{3}$).**
   (2) **The coordinates of point Q are (8, 0).**

Statement (1) gives the height of triangle PQR, and, since ΔPQR is equilateral, its other dimensions can be determined:

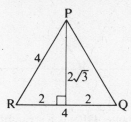

Thus, the area of ΔPQR is $\frac{(2\sqrt{3})(4)}{2}$, and the answer is A or D. Since (2) does not give any information about the coordinates of either of the other points, the length of RQ cannot be determined, and (2) is insufficient. Therefore, the best answer is A. (See Chapter 2, Math Review, Section C.6 and Section C.13.)

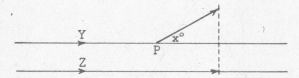

19. **Cars Y and Z travel side by side at the same rate of speed along parallel roads as shown above. When car Y reaches point P, it forks to the left at angle x°, changes speed, and continues to stay even with car Z as shown by the dotted line. The speed of car Y beyond point P is what percent of the speed of car Z?**

    (1) **The speed of car Z is 50 miles per hour.**
    (2) **x = 45**

This is a rate/distance problem; it is helpful to keep in mind that rate × time = distance (i.e., symbolically r × t = d). In this case the times for Y and Z are equal, and so you have the equation $\frac{d_y}{r_y} = \frac{d_z}{r_z}$. Since (1) does not give any information about the distances traveled, it is not sufficient, and the answer must be B, C, or E. Since the angles of the triangle formed are 45°, 45°, and 90° and d_y is the hypotenuse of the triangle, (2) implies that $d_y = \sqrt{2}\, d_z$. Therefore $\frac{\sqrt{2}\, d_z}{r_y} = \frac{d_z}{r_z}$. From this information it can be determined that $r_y = \sqrt{2}\, r_z$, and therefore the speed of car Y beyond point P is $100\sqrt{2}$ percent of the speed of car Z. Thus, the best answer is B. (See Chapter 2, Math Review, Section A.7, Section C.6, and Section D.1.)

20. **If each of the 20 bolts of fabric on a shelf is either 100 percent cotton, 100 percent wool, or a mixture of cotton and wool, how many bolts are cotton and wool mixtures?**

    (1) **Of the 20 bolts, 18 contain some wool and 14 contain some cotton.**
    (2) **Of the 20 bolts, 6 are 100 percent wool.**

One way to solve this problem is to draw a circle diagram.

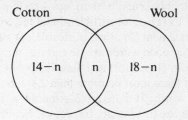

From (1), if n is the number of bolts that are cotton and wool mixtures, then $(14-n) + n + (18-n) = 20$, and $n = 12$. Therefore, (1) is sufficient to answer the question, and the answer must be A or D. From (2),

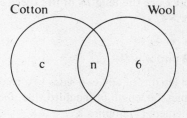

if c is the number of bolts that are 100 percent cotton, then $c + n + 6 = 20$. Since the number of bolts that are 100 percent cotton cannot be determined, the question cannot be answered from (2) alone. Therefore, the best answer is A. (See Chapter 2, Math Review, Section D.7.)

21. **If $xy \neq 0$, what is the value of $\frac{x^4y^2 - (xy)^2}{x^3y^2}$?**

    (1) **x = 2**
    (2) **y = 8**

It is helpful to simplify the expression in the question:

$$\frac{x^4y^2 - (xy)^2}{x^3y^2} = \frac{y^2\,(x^4 - x^2)}{x^3y^2} = \frac{x^4 - x^2}{x^3}$$

Since statement (1) gives the value of x, the value of the expression can be determined, and the answer is A or D. Statement (2) alone is insufficient to answer the question asked because the value of x is not given and is not deducible. Hence, the value of the expression cannot be determined from (2), and the best answer is A. (See Chapter 2, Math Review, Section B.1.)

22. **Are there exactly 3 distinct symbols used to create the code words in language Q?**

    (1) **The set of all code words in language Q is the set of all possible distinct horizontal arrangements of one or more symbols, with no repetition.**
    (2) **There are exactly 15 code words in language Q.**

Statement (1) tells you what code words are, but it does not say anything about the number of symbols. For example, if there is only one symbol, a, there is just 1 code word; but if there are 2 symbols, a and b, there are 4 code words, a, b, ab, and ba. Thus (1) is not sufficient, and the answer must be B, C, or E. Statement (2) alone is insufficient since it does not specify what code words are; therefore, the answer must be C or E. From (1) and (2) and the examples given above, you know that there must be more than 2 symbols if there are to be 15 code words. If there are 3 symbols, a, b, and c, then the code words are a, b, c, ab, ba, ac, ca, bc, cb, abc, acb, bac, bca, cab, and cba; i.e., there are 15 code words. Clearly, if there were 4 or more symbols, there would be more than 15 code words. Thus, the best answer is C. (See Chapter 2, Math Review, Section D.7.)

23. If x, y, and z are the lengths of the three sides of a triangle, is $y > 4$?

(1) $z = x + 4$

(2) $x = 3$ and $z = 7$

The sum of the lengths of any two sides of a triangle is always greater than the length of the third side; therefore, $x + y > z$. Statement (1) implies $x + y > x + 4$, and $y > 4$. Therefore, the answer must be A or D. Statement (2) implies $3 + y > 7$ and $y > 4$. Thus, the best answer is D. (See Chapter 2, Math Review, Section B.8 and Section C.6.)

24. How many minutes long is time period X?

(1) Time period X is 3 hours long.

(2) Time period X starts at 11 p.m. and ends at 2 a.m.

Statement (1) is sufficient because from (1) you can determine that time period X is 180 minutes long; thus, the answer must be A or D. Statement (2) alone is not sufficient to answer the question because you do not know whether the two times given are for consecutive days. This is a question that depends not on calculation but on your analysis of the assumptions made or not made by the statement. Therefore, the best answer is A.

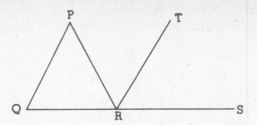

25. In the figure above, QRS is a straight line and line TR bisects ∠PRS. Is it true that lines TR and PQ are parallel?

(1) $PQ = PR$

(2) $QR = PR$

Let the angles of the figure have the following measures:

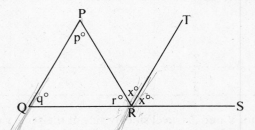

Since QRS is a straight line, $r + 2x = 180$. For PQ∥TR, x must equal p. From (1) you know that $q = r$, but there is no way to determine whether $p = x$. So the answer must be B, C, or E. From (2) you know that $q = p$ and that $r + 2p = 180 = r + 2x$ and thus $p = x$. Therefore, PQ∥TR, and the best answer is B. (See Chapter 2, Math Review, Section C.4 and Section C.5.)

DATA SUFFICIENCY SAMPLE TEST SECTION 2

30 Minutes
25 Questions

<u>Directions:</u> Each of the data sufficiency problems below consists of a question and two statements, labeled (1) and (2), in which certain data are given. You have to decide whether the data given in the statements are <u>sufficient</u> for answering the question. Using the data given in the statements <u>plus</u> your knowledge of mathematics and everyday facts (such as the number of days in July or the meaning of <u>counterclockwise</u>), you are to fill in oval

A   if statement (1) ALONE is sufficient, but statement (2) alone is not sufficient to answer the question asked;

B   if statement (2) ALONE is sufficient, but statement (1) alone is not sufficient to answer the question asked;

C   if BOTH statements (1) and (2) TOGETHER are sufficient to answer the question asked, but NEITHER statement ALONE is sufficient;

D   if EACH statement ALONE is sufficient to answer the question asked;

E   if statements (1) and (2) TOGETHER are NOT sufficient to answer the question asked, and additional data specific to the problem are needed.

<u>Numbers:</u> All numbers used are real numbers.

<u>Figures:</u> A figure in a data sufficiency problem will conform to the information given in the question, but will not necessarily conform to the additional information given in statements (1) and (2).

You may assume that lines shown as straight are straight and that angle measures are greater than zero.

You may assume that the positions of points, angles, regions, etc., exist in the order shown.

All figures lie in a plane unless otherwise indicated.

<u>Example:</u>

In $\triangle PQR$, what is the value of x ?

(1) $PQ = PR$
(2) $y = 40$

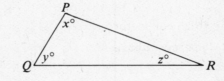

<u>Explanation:</u> According to statement (1), $PQ = PR$; therefore, $\triangle PQR$ is isosceles and $y = z$. Since $x + y + z = 180$, $x + 2y = 180$. Since statement (1) does not give a value for y, you cannot answer the question using statement (1) by itself. According to statement (2), $y = 40$; therefore, $x + z = 140$. Since statement (2) does not give a value for z, you cannot answer the question using statement (2) by itself. Using both statements together, you can find y and z; therefore, you can find x, and the answer to the problem is C.

1. What is the value of x ?

(1) 5x − 3 = 7

(2) $\dfrac{x}{10} = \dfrac{1}{5}$

2. How many students are enrolled in the Groveville Public Schools?

(1) There are 30 students per classroom in the Groveville Public Schools.

(2) The student-teacher ratio is 20 to 1 in the Groveville Public Schools.

GO ON TO THE NEXT PAGE.

A Statement (1) ALONE is sufficient, but statement (2) alone is not sufficient.
B Statement (2) ALONE is sufficient, but statement (1) alone is not sufficient.
C BOTH statements TOGETHER are sufficient, but NEITHER statement ALONE is sufficient.
D EACH statement ALONE is sufficient.
E Statements (1) and (2) TOGETHER are NOT sufficient.

3. P is a particle on the circle shown above. What is the length of the path traveled by P in one complete revolution around the circle?

   (1) The diameter of the circle is 1.5 meters.

   (2) The particle P moves in a clockwise direction at 0.5 meter per second.

4. If the price of potatoes is $0.20 per pound, what is the maximum number of potatoes that can be bought for $1.00 ?

   (1) The price of a bag of potatoes is $2.80.

   (2) There are 15 to 18 potatoes in every 5 pounds.

5. A sewing store buys fabric X by the bolt at the wholesale price. If each bolt contains 50 meters of fabric X, what is the wholesale price of a bolt of fabric X ?

   (1) The store sells fabric X for $6.25 per meter.

   (2) The store sells fabric X at 25 percent above the wholesale price.

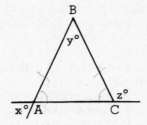

6. In △ABC above, if AB = BC, what is the value of y ?

   (1) x = 50

   (2) z = 130

7. In a sequence of numbers in which each term is 2 more than the preceding term, what is the fourth term?

   (1) The last term is 90.

   (2) The first term is 2.

GO ON TO THE NEXT PAGE.

A Statement (1) ALONE is sufficient, but statement (2) alone is not sufficient.
B Statement (2) ALONE is sufficient, but statement (1) alone is not sufficient.
C BOTH statements TOGETHER are sufficient, but NEITHER statement ALONE is sufficient.
D EACH statement ALONE is sufficient.
E Statements (1) and (2) TOGETHER are NOT sufficient.

8. How much nitrogen is needed in the mixture used by a lawn maintenance company to fertilize the grass on a certain portion of a golf course?

(1) The portion of the golf course to be fertilized is 30 meters by 50 meters.

(2) The amount of fertilizer needed is 40 kilograms, and the fertilizer must be composed of nitrogen, phosphorus, and potash in the proportions 5: 7: 4, respectively.

9. A certain alloy contains only lead, copper, and tin. How many pounds of tin are contained in 56 pounds of the alloy?

(1) By weight the alloy is $\frac{3}{7}$ lead and $\frac{5}{14}$ copper.

(2) By weight the alloy contains 6 parts lead and 5 parts copper.

10. If n is a positive integer, are n and 1 the only positive divisors of n ?

(1) n is less than 14.

(2) If n is doubled, the result is less than 27.

11. What is the perimeter of △PQR ?

(1) The measures of ∠PQR, ∠QRP, and ∠RPQ are x°, 2x°, and 3x°, respectively.

(2) The altitude of △PQR from Q to PR is 4.

12. Two accountants, Rhodes and Smith, went to a business meeting together. Rhodes drove to the meeting and Smith drove back from the meeting. If Rhodes and Smith each drove 140 kilometers, what was the average speed, in kilometers per hour, at which Rhodes drove?

(1) The average speed at which Smith drove was 70 kilometers per hour.

(2) Rhodes drove for exactly 2 hours.

13. If ϕ is an operation, is the value of b ϕ c greater than 10 ?

(1) x ϕ y = $x^2 + y^2$ for all x and y.

(2) b = 3 and c = 2

14. What percent of the employees of Company X are technicians?

(1) Exactly 40 percent of the men and 55 percent of the women employed by Company X are technicians.

(2) At Company X, the ratio of the number of technicians to the number of nontechnicians is 9 to 11.

GO ON TO THE NEXT PAGE.

A Statement (1) ALONE is sufficient, but statement (2) alone is not sufficient.
B Statement (2) ALONE is sufficient, but statement (1) alone is not sufficient.
C BOTH statements TOGETHER are sufficient, but NEITHER statement ALONE is sufficient.
D EACH statement ALONE is sufficient.
E Statements (1) and (2) TOGETHER are NOT sufficient.

15. If tank X contains only gasoline, how many kiloliters of gasoline are in tank X ?

   (1) If $\frac{1}{2}$ of the gasoline in tank X were pumped out, the tank would be filled to $\frac{1}{3}$ of its capacity.

   (2) If 0.75 kiloliter of gasoline were pumped into tank X, it would be filled to capacity.

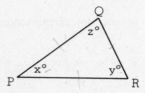

16. In △PQR above, is PQ > PR ?

   (1) x = y

   (2) y = z

17. Is the positive integer x an even number?

   (1) If x is divided by 3, the remainder is 2.

   (2) If x is divided by 5, the remainder is 2.

18. Land for a pasture is enclosed in the shape of a 6-sided figure; all sides are the same length and all angles have the same measure. What is the area of the enclosed land?

   (1) Each side is 8 meters long.

   (2) The distance from the center of the land to the midpoint of one of the sides is $4\sqrt{3}$ meters.

19. In a retail store, the average (arithmetic mean) sale for month M was d dollars. Was the average (arithmetic mean) sale for month J at least 20 percent higher than that for month M ?

   (1) For month M, total revenue from sales was $3,500.

   (2) For month J, total revenue from sales was $6,000.

20. In a certain store, item X sells for 10 percent less than item Y. What is the ratio of the store's revenue from the sales of item X to that from the sales of item Y ?

   (1) The store sells 20 percent more units of item Y than of item X.

   (2) The store's revenue from the sales of item X is $6,000 and from the sales of item Y is $8,000.

GO ON TO THE NEXT PAGE.

A Statement (1) ALONE is sufficient, but statement (2) alone is not sufficient.
B Statement (2) ALONE is sufficient, but statement (1) alone is not sufficient.
C BOTH statements TOGETHER are sufficient, but NEITHER statement ALONE is sufficient.
D EACH statement ALONE is sufficient.
E Statements (1) and (2) TOGETHER are NOT sufficient.

21. During a 3-year period, the profits of Company X changed by what percent from the second year to the third year?

 (1) The increase in profits of Company X from the first year to the second year was the same as the increase from the first year to the third year.

 (2) For Company X, the profits for the first year were $13,800 and the profits for the third year were $15,900.

22. A pyramidal-shaped box to protect a plant is constructed with 4 lateral faces and an open bottom. What is the lateral area of the box?

 (1) The base of the pyramid is a polygon with all sides of equal length, and the perimeter of the base is 1 meter.

 (2) The lateral faces are isosceles triangles that have the same size and shape.

23. What is the value of $x^2 - y^2$?

 (1) $x + y = 2x$

 (2) $x + y = 0$

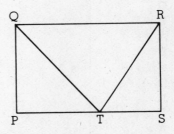

24. In rectangular region PQRS above, T is a point on side PS. If PS = 4, what is the area of region PQRS ?

 (1) $\triangle$QTR is equilateral.

 (2) Segments PT and TS have equal length.

25. Does x = 2 ?

 (1) x is a number such that $x^2 - 3x + 2 = 0$.

 (2) x is a number such that $x^2 - x - 2 = 0$.

S T O P

IF YOU FINISH BEFORE TIME IS CALLED, YOU MAY CHECK YOUR WORK ON THIS SECTION ONLY.
DO NOT TURN TO ANY OTHER SECTION IN THE TEST.

Answer Key for Sample Test Section 2

DATA SUFFICIENCY

1. D	14. B
2. E	15. C
3. A	16. B
4. B	17. E
5. C	18. D
6. D	19. E
7. B	20. D
8. B	21. A
9. A	22. E
10. E	23. D
11. C	24. A
12. B	25. C
13. C	

Explanatory Material:
Data Sufficiency Sample Test Section 2

1. What is the value of x?

(1) $5x - 3 = 7$

(2) $\frac{x}{10} = \frac{1}{5}$

Statement (1) implies that $x = 2$. Thus, the answer is A or D. Since statement (2) also implies that $x = 2$, the best answer is D.

2. **How many students are enrolled in the Groveville Public Schools?**

(1) **There are 30 students per classroom in the Groveville Public Schools.**

(2) **The student-teacher ratio is 20 to 1 in the Groveville Public Schools.**

Statement (1) alone is insufficient to answer the question asked since you do not know the number of classrooms. Thus, the answer must be B, C, or E. Statement (2) alone also is insufficient because you do not know the number of teachers. Clearly (1) and (2) together are insufficient, so the best answer is E.

P

3. **P is a particle on the circle shown above. What is the length of the path traveled by P in one complete revolution around the circle?**

(1) **The diameter of the circle is 1.5 meters.**

(2) **The particle P moves in a clockwise direction at 0.5 meter per second.**

Since the circumference of a circle is π times the diameter, statement (1) alone is sufficient. Thus, the answer must be A or D. Statement (2) alone is not sufficient because no information is given concerning the amount of time particle P takes to make one complete revolution. Therefore, the best answer is A.

4. **If the price of potatoes is $0.20 per pound, what is the maximum number of potatoes that can be bought for $1.00?**

(1) **The price of a bag of potatoes is $2.80.**

(2) **There are 15 to 18 potatoes in every 5 pounds.**

Clearly statement (1) alone is not sufficient to answer the question. Thus, the answer must be B, C, or E. Statement (2) alone is sufficient because 5 pounds of potatoes can be bought for $1.00 and the maximum number of potatoes in 5 pounds is 18. Therefore, B is the best answer.

5. **A sewing store buys fabric X by the bolt at the wholesale price. If each bolt contains 50 meters of fabric X, what is the wholesale price of a bolt of fabric X?**

(1) **The store sells fabric X for $6.25 per meter.**

(2) **The store sells fabric X at 25 percent above the wholesale price.**

Neither statement (1) alone nor statement (2) alone is sufficient to answer the question; thus, the answer must be C or E. From (1) and (2) together you know that $6.25 equals 1.25 times the wholesale price, or that the wholesale price is $5.00 per meter. Thus, the best answer is C.

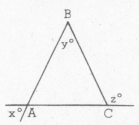

6. **In △ABC above, if AB = BC, what is the value of y?**

(1) **x = 50**

(2) **z = 130**

From statement (1) you know that the measure of ∠BAC is 50°, since vertical angles have the same measure. Since AB = BC, the measure of ∠BCA is also 50°. Therefore, $y = 180 - (50 + 50)$ or $y = 80$. Thus, the answer is A or D. From statement (2) you know that the measure of ∠BCA is 50° because ∠BCA is a supplement of the angle labeled z°; again you can determine that $y = 80°$. Therefore, the best answer is D.

7. In a sequence of numbers in which each term is 2 more than the preceding term, what is the fourth term?

  (1) The last term is 90.

  (2) The first term is 2.

Statement (1) alone is not sufficient because you do not know the first term of the sequence or the number of terms. For example, the sequence 80, 82, 84, 86, 88, 90 and the sequence 82, 84, 86, 88, 90 are both consistent with (1) and the information given in the question; however, the fourth term is different in each of these cases. Thus, the answer must be B, C, or E. From (2) you know that the first four terms are 2, 4, 6, and 8. Therefore, the best answer is B.

8. How much nitrogen is needed in the mixture used by a lawn maintenance company to fertilize the grass on a certain portion of a golf course?

  (1) The portion of the golf course to be fertilized is 30 meters by 50 meters.

  (2) The amount of fertilizer needed is 40 kilograms, and the fertilizer must be composed of nitrogen, phosphorus, and potash in the proportions 5:7:4, respectively.

Statement (1) alone is clearly insufficient to answer the question since it provides no information about the amount of nitrogen needed. Thus, the answer must be B, C, or E. Statement (2) alone is sufficient: Since the ratios of the three ingredients in the fertilizer are 5:7:4, the amount of nitrogen is 5/16 of 40, or 12.5 kilograms. Therefore, the best answer is B.

9. A certain alloy contains only lead, copper, and tin. How many pounds of tin are contained in 56 pounds of the alloy?

  (1) By weight the alloy is $\frac{3}{7}$ lead and $\frac{5}{14}$ copper.

  (2) By weight the alloy contains 6 parts lead and 5 parts copper.

From statement (1) you know that the alloy is $\frac{3}{14}$ tin by weight so that $\frac{3}{14} \cdot 56$ or 12 pounds of the alloy is tin. Thus, the answer is A or D. Since statement (2) does not tell you how many parts tin are in the alloy, you cannot answer the question from (2) alone. Therefore, the best answer is A.

10. If n is a positive integer, are n and 1 the only positive divisors of n?

  (1) n is less than 14.

  (2) If n is doubled, the result is less than 27.

From statement (1) you do not know whether or not n is a prime number, and thus whether n and 1 are the only positive divisors of n. For example, 1 and 5 are the only positive divi-

sors of 5, but 2 and 3 as well as 1 and 6 are positive divisors of 6. Thus, the answer must be B, C, or E. Since statement (2) is no more restrictive than (1), the best answer is E.

11. What is the perimeter of △PQR?

  (1) The measures of ∠PQR, ∠QRP, and ∠RPQ are x°, 2x°, and 3x°, respectively.

  (2) The altitude of △PQR from Q to PR is 4.

For this problem, drawing a figure may be helpful:

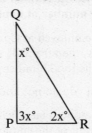

From statement (1) you know that x = 30, 2x = 60, and 3x = 90, since 6x = 180; however, you do not know the length of any side, and therefore (1) alone is not sufficient. Thus, the answer must be B, C, or E. Since the perimeter cannot be found given only the length of an altitude, statement (2) alone is insufficient, and the answer must be C or E. From (1) and (2) together, since △PQR is a 30-60-90 right triangle, the altitude from Q to PR is PQ, so PQ = 4; therefore, PR = $\frac{4\sqrt{3}}{3}$, RQ = $\frac{8\sqrt{3}}{3}$, and the best answer is C.

12. Two accountants, Rhodes and Smith, went to a business meeting together. Rhodes drove to the meeting and Smith drove back from the meeting. If Rhodes and Smith each drove 140 kilometers, what was the average speed, in kilometers per hour, at which Rhodes drove?

  (1) The average speed at which Smith drove was 70 kilometers per hour.

  (2) Rhodes drove for exactly 2 hours.

Statement (1) alone is clearly insufficient to answer the question because no relationship between the driving speeds of Rhodes and Smith is given. Thus, the answer must be B, C, or E. From statement (2) you know that Rhodes' average driving speed was 140/2 or 70 kilometers per hour. Therefore, the best answer is B.

13. If ϕ is an operation, is the value of b ϕ c greater than 10?

  (1) x ϕ y = $x^2 + y^2$ for all x and y.

  (2) b = 3 and c = 2

Statement (1) alone is not sufficient to answer the question because you do not know the value of b and c; statement (2) alone is not sufficient because you do not know what operation φ represents. Thus, the answer must be C or E. From (1) and (2) together you know that $3\phi2 = 3^2 + 2^2 = 13$; therefore, the best answer is C.

14. **What percent of the employees of Company X are technicians?**

    (1) **Exactly 40 percent of the men and 55 percent of the women employed by Company X are technicians.**

    (2) **At Company X, the ratio of the number of technicians to the number of nontechnicians is 9 to 11.**

If the number of men employed at Company X is m and the number of women is w, then from (1) the ratio of the number of technicians to the total number of employees is $\frac{0.40m + 0.55w}{m + w}$. Since you do not know any relationship between m and w, (1) alone is insufficient. For example, if m = w, then 47.5 percent of the employees are technicians; but if w = 2m, then 50 percent of the employees are technicians. Thus, the answer is B, C, or E. Statement (2) implies that $\frac{9}{20}$, or 45 percent, of the employees are technicians. Therefore, the best answer is B.

15. **If tank X contains only gasoline, how many kiloliters of gasoline are in tank X?**

    (1) **If $\frac{1}{2}$ of the gasoline in tank X were pumped out, the tank would be filled to $\frac{1}{3}$ of its capacity.**

    (2) **If 0.75 kiloliter of gasoline were pumped into tank X, it would be filled to capacity.**

From statement (1) you know that the amount of gasoline in the tank is $\frac{2}{3}$ of the tank's capacity, but you do not know the tank's capacity, and so (1) alone is insufficient. Thus, the answer is B, C, or E. From statement (2) you know only that the amount of gasoline in the tank is 0.75 kiloliter less than the tank's capacity, and so (2) alone is insufficient. Therefore, the answer is C or E. If the capacity of the tank is x kiloliters, then (1) and (2) together imply that $x - 0.75 = \frac{2}{3}x$, or x = 2.25 kiloliters. Thus, there are 1.5 kiloliters of gasoline in the tank and the best answer is C.

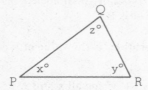

16. **In △PQR above, is PQ > RP?**

    (1) x = y

    (2) y = z

Statement (1) implies that PQ = QR; however, the base PR may or may not equal PQ, and so (1) alone is not sufficient.

Thus, the answer must be B, C, or E. Statement (2) implies that PQ = PR, or that PQ is not greater than PR. Therefore, the best answer is B.

17. **Is the positive integer x an even number?**

    (1) **If x is divided by 3, the remainder is 2.**

    (2) **If x is divided by 5, the remainder is 2.**

Statement (1) implies only that x − 2 is a multiple of 3. Since x can be odd or even (5 or 8, for example), (1) alone is not sufficient. Thus, the answer must be B, C, or E. Similarly, statement (2) implies only that x − 2 is a multiple of 5, and so (2) alone is not sufficient. Statements (1) and (2) together imply only that x − 2 is a multiple of 15. Since x can be odd or even, the best answer is E.

18. **Land for a pasture is enclosed in the shape of a 6-sided figure; all sides are the same length and all angles have the same measure. What is the area of the enclosed land?**

    (1) **Each side is 8 meters long.**
    (2) **The distance from the center of the land to the midpoint of one of the sides is $4\sqrt{3}$ meters.**

For this problem, drawing a figure may be helpful:

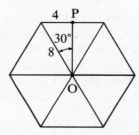

Since six sides have the same length and the six interior angles have the same measure, each of the six triangles shown above is equilateral; therefore, the area of the enclosed land is 6 times the area of any of these triangular regions. From (1) you can determine that the altitude OP shown in the figure has length $4\sqrt{3}$ m and that the area of the enclosed land is $(4\sqrt{3})(4)(6)$m², or $96\sqrt{3}$ m². Therefore, the answer must be A or D. Similarly, from (2) you can determine that the length of each side is 8 m, and thus that the total area is $96\sqrt{3}$ m². Thus, the best answer is D.

19. **In a retail store, the average (arithmetic mean) sale for month M was d dollars. Was the average (arithmetic mean) sale for month J at least 20 percent higher than that for month M?**

    (1) **For month M, total revenue from sales was $3,500.**

    (2) **For month J, total revenue from sales was $6,000.**

Note that to find the average sale for a month, you need to know the number of sales for the month as well as the total revenue from these sales. Since statements (1) and (2) give only the total revenue from sales for each of the two months, the best answer is E.

20. In a certain store, item X sells for 10 percent less than item Y. What is the ratio of the store's revenue from the sales of item X to that from the sales of item Y?

   (1) The store sells 20 percent more units of item Y than of item X.

   (2) The store's revenue from the sales of item X is $6,000 and from the sales of item Y is $8,000.

If the price that item Y sells for is y dollars, then the price that item X sells for is 0.9y dollars. If the store sells n units of item X, then from (1) you know that it sells 1.2n units of item Y. Thus, the ratio of the revenue from the sales of item X to the revenue from the sales of item Y is $\frac{(0.9y)n}{(1.2n)y}$ or $\frac{3}{4}$.

Thus, the answer must be A or D. Statement (2) alone is sufficient because $\frac{\$6,000}{\$8,000} = \frac{3}{4}$; therefore, the best answer is D.

21. During a 3-year period, the profits of Company X changed by what percent from the second year to the third year?

   (1) The increase in profits of Company X from the first year to the second year was the same as the increase from the first year to the third year.

   (2) For Company X, the profits for the first year were $13,800 and the profits for the third year were $15,900.

From statement (1) you know that the profits for the third year amounted to the same as those for the second year, so there was no percent change in profits from the second year to the third year. Thus, the answer must be A or D. Obviously (2) is insufficient, giving no information concerning profits for the second year. Therefore, the best answer is A.

22. A pyramidal-shaped box to protect a plant is constructed with 4 lateral faces and an open bottom. What is the lateral area of the box?

   (1) The base of the pyramid is a polygon with all sides of equal length, and the perimeter of the base is 1 meter.

   (2) The lateral faces are isosceles triangles that have the same size and shape.

Statement (1) alone is not sufficient since neither the exact shape of the pyramid nor its height is known. Statement (2) gives additional information about the shape of the pyramid but not enough to determine the shape, and since (2) also does not give any additional numerical data, the answer must be C or E. From (1) and (2) together you still do not know the exact shape of the pyramid nor, more importantly, its height. Therefore, the best answer is E.

23. What is the value of $x^2 - y^2$?

   (1) $x + y = 2x$

   (2) $x + y = 0$

Note that $x^2 - y^2 = (x + y)(x - y)$ will have a value of 0 if either $x + y = 0$ or $x - y = 0$. Since statement (1) implies that $x - y = 0$, statement (1) alone is sufficient to determine that the value of $x^2 - y^2$ is 0. Thus, the answer must be A or D. Since (2) also implies that $x^2 - y^2 = 0$, the best answer is D.

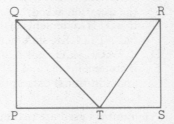

24. In rectangular region PQRS above, T is a point on side PS. If PS = 4, what is the area of region PQRS?

   (1) △QTR is equilateral.

   (2) Segments PT and TS have equal length.

Note that the area of region PQRS is twice the area of △QTR; QP equals the length of the altitude from point T to side QR, and thus the area of △QTR is (½)QP·QR. From statement (1) alone you can determine the area of △QTR and thus the area of region PQRS. Since the altitude from T to side QR is opposite ∠TQR = 60°, it has length $2\sqrt{3}$, and the area of △QTR is $4\sqrt{3}$. Thus, the answer is A or D. Since statement (2) does not imply the length of PQ, the best answer is A.

25. Does x = 2?

   (1) x is a number such that $x^2 - 3x + 2 = 0$.

   (2) x is a number such that $x^2 - x - 2 = 0$.

Since $x^2 - 3x + 2 = (x - 2)(x - 1)$, statement (1) implies that x = 2 or x = 1. Since you do not know which of these two values x is equal to, the answer must be B, C, or E. Since $x^2 - x - 2 = (x - 2)(x + 1)$, statement (2) implies that x = -1 or x = 2, so statement (2) alone also is not sufficient, and the answer must be C or E. Together (1) and (2) imply that x = 2; therefore, the best answer is C.

DATA SUFFICIENCY SAMPLE TEST SECTION 3

30 Minutes
25 Questions

Directions: Each of the data sufficiency problems below consists of a question and two statements, labeled (1) and (2), in which certain data are given. You have to decide whether the data given in the statements are <u>sufficient</u> for answering the question. Using the data given in the statements <u>plus</u> your knowledge of mathematics and everyday facts (such as the number of days in July or the meaning of <u>counterclockwise</u>), you are to fill in oval

A if statement (1) ALONE is sufficient, but statement (2) alone is not sufficient to answer the question asked;

B if statement (2) ALONE is sufficient, but statement (1) alone is not sufficient to answer the question asked;

C if BOTH statements (1) and (2) TOGETHER are sufficient to answer the question asked, but NEITHER statement ALONE is sufficient;

D if EACH statement ALONE is sufficient to answer the question asked;

E if statements (1) and (2) TOGETHER are NOT sufficient to answer the question asked, and additional data specific to the problem are needed.

Numbers: All numbers used are real numbers.

Figures: A figure in a data sufficiency problem will conform to the information given in the question, but will not necessarily conform to the additional information given in statements (1) and (2).

You may assume that lines shown as straight are straight and that angle measures are greater than zero.

You may assume that the positions of points, angles, regions, etc., exist in the order shown.

All figures lie in a plane unless otherwise indicated.

Example:

In $\triangle PQR$, what is the value of x?

(1) $PQ = PR$

(2) $y = 40$

Explanation: According to statement (1), $PQ = PR$; therefore, $\triangle PQR$ is isosceles and $y = z$. Since $x + y + z = 180$, $x + 2y = 180$. Since statement (1) does not give a value for y, you cannot answer the question using statement (1) by itself. According to statement (2), $y = 40$; therefore, $x + z = 140$. Since statement (2) does not give a value for z, you cannot answer the question using statement (2) by itself. Using both statements together, you can find y and z; therefore, you can find x, and the answer to the problem is C.

1. If today the price of an item is $3,600, what was the price of the item exactly 2 years ago?

  (1) The price of the item increased by 10 percent per year during this 2-year period.

  (2) Today the price of the item is 1.21 times its price exactly 2 years ago.

2. By what percent has the price of an overcoat been reduced?

  (1) The original price was $380.

  (2) The original price was $50 more than the reduced price.

GO ON TO THE NEXT PAGE.

A Statement (1) ALONE is sufficient, but statement (2) alone is not sufficient.
B Statement (2) ALONE is sufficient, but statement (1) alone is not sufficient.
C BOTH statements TOGETHER are sufficient, but NEITHER statement ALONE is sufficient.
D EACH statement ALONE is sufficient.
E Statements (1) and (2) TOGETHER are NOT sufficient.

3. If the Longfellow Playground is rectangular, what is its width?

   (1) The ratio of its length to its width is 7 to 2.

   (2) The perimeter of the playground is 396 meters.

4. What is the value of $x - 1$?

   (1) $x + 1 = 3$

   (2) $x - 1 < 3$

5. Is William taller than Jane?

   (1) William is taller than Anna.

   (2) Anna is not as tall as Jane.

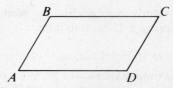

6. In parallelogram $ABCD$ above, what is the measure of $\angle ADC$?

   (1) The measure of $\angle ABC$ is greater than 90°.

   (2) The measure of $\angle BCD$ is 70°.

7. Is x^2 equal to xy?

   (1) $x^2 - y^2 = (x + 5)(y - 5)$

   (2) $x = y$

8. Was 70 the average (arithmetic mean) grade on a class test?

   (1) On the test, half of the class had grades below 70 and half of the class had grades above 70.

   (2) The lowest grade on the test was 45 and the highest grade on the test was 95.

GO ON TO THE NEXT PAGE.

A   Statement (1) ALONE is sufficient, but statement (2) alone is not sufficient.
B   Statement (2) ALONE is sufficient, but statement (1) alone is not sufficient.
C   BOTH statements TOGETHER are sufficient, but NEITHER statement ALONE is sufficient.
D   EACH statement ALONE is sufficient.
E   Statements (1) and (2) TOGETHER are NOT sufficient.

9. What was John's average driving speed in miles per hour during a 15-minute interval?

   (1) He drove 10 miles during this interval.

   (2) His maximum speed was 50 miles per hour and his minimum speed was 35 miles per hour during this interval.

10. Is $\triangle MNP$ isosceles?

   (1) Exactly two of the angles, $\angle M$ and $\angle N$, have the same measure.

   (2) $\angle N$ and $\angle P$ do not have the same measure.

11. Is n an integer greater than 4?

   (1) $3n$ is a positive integer.

   (2) $\frac{n}{3}$ is a positive integer.

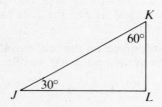

12. In $\triangle JKL$ shown above, what is the length of segment JL?

   (1) $JK = 10$
   (2) $KL = 5$

13. A coal company can choose to transport coal to one of its customers by railroad or by truck. If the railroad charges by the mile and the trucking company charges by the ton, which means of transporting the coal would cost less than the other?

   (1) The railroad charges $5,000 plus $0.01 per mile per railroad car used, and the trucking company charges $3,000 plus $85 per ton.

   (2) The customer to whom the coal is to be sent is 195 miles away from the coal company.

14. Is $x - y > r - s$?

   (1) $x > r$ and $y < s$.
   (2) $y = 2$, $s = 3$, $r = 5$, and $x = 6$.

15. On a certain day it took Bill three times as long to drive from home to work as it took Sue to drive from home to work. How many kilometers did Bill drive from home to work?

   (1) Sue drove 10 kilometers from home to work, and the ratio of
   $$\frac{\text{distance driven from home to work}}{\text{time to drive from home to work}}$$
   was the same for Bill and Sue that day.

   (2) The ratio of
   $$\frac{\text{distance driven from home to work}}{\text{time to drive from home to work}}$$
   for Sue that day was 64 kilometers per hour.

GO ON TO THE NEXT PAGE.

A Statement (1) ALONE is sufficient, but statement (2) alone is not sufficient.
B Statement (2) ALONE is sufficient, but statement (1) alone is not sufficient.
C BOTH statements TOGETHER are sufficient, but NEITHER statement ALONE is sufficient.
D EACH statement ALONE is sufficient.
E Statements (1) and (2) TOGETHER are NOT sufficient.

16. The figure above represents the floor of a square foyer with a circular rug partially covering the floor and extending to the outer edges of the floor as shown. What is the area of the foyer that is not covered by the rug?

    (1) The area of the foyer is 9 square meters.

    (2) The area of the rug is 2.25π square meters.

17. At a certain university, if 50 percent of the people who inquire about admission policies actually submit applications for admission, what percent of those who submit applications for admission enroll in classes at the university?

    (1) Fifteen percent of those who submit applications for admission are accepted at the university.

    (2) Eighty percent of those who are accepted send a deposit to the university.

18. If x and y are nonzero integers, is $\frac{x}{y}$ an integer?

    (1) x is the product of 2 and some other integer.

    (2) There is only one pair of positive integers whose product equals y.

19. If x is an integer, what is the value of x?

    (1) $\frac{1}{5} < \frac{1}{x+1} < \frac{1}{2}$

    (2) $(x-3)(x-4) = 0$

20. Is quadrilateral Q a square?

    (1) The sides of Q have the same length.

    (2) The diagonals of Q have the same length.

21. If K is a positive integer less than 10 and $N = 4{,}321 + K$, what is the value of K?

    (1) N is divisible by 3.

    (2) N is divisible by 7.

GO ON TO THE NEXT PAGE.

A   Statement (1) ALONE is sufficient, but statement (2) alone is not sufficient.
B   Statement (2) ALONE is sufficient, but statement (1) alone is not sufficient.
C   BOTH statements TOGETHER are sufficient, but NEITHER statement ALONE is sufficient.
D   EACH statement ALONE is sufficient.
E   Statements (1) and (2) TOGETHER are NOT sufficient.

22. A jewelry dealer initially offered a bracelet for sale at an asking price that would give a profit to the dealer of 40 percent of the original cost. What was the original cost of the bracelet?

(1) After reducing this asking price by 10 percent, the jewelry dealer sold the bracelet at a profit of $403.

(2) The jewelry dealer sold the bracelet for $1,953.

23. If n is an integer between 2 and 100 and if n is also the square of an integer, what is the value of n?

(1) n is the cube of an integer.

(2) n is even.

24. Is $x^2 - y^2$ a positive number?

(1) $x - y$ is a positive number.

(2) $x + y$ is a positive number.

25. The surface area of a square tabletop was changed so that one of the dimensions was reduced by 1 inch and the other dimension was increased by 2 inches. What was the surface area before these changes were made?

(1) After the changes were made, the surface area was 70 square inches.

(2) There was a 25 percent increase in one of the dimensions.

S T O P

IF YOU FINISH BEFORE TIME IS CALLED, YOU MAY CHECK YOUR WORK ON THIS SECTION ONLY.
DO NOT TURN TO ANY OTHER SECTION IN THE TEST.

Answer Key for Sample Test Section 3

DATA SUFFICIENCY

1.	D	14.	D
2.	C	15.	A
3.	C	16.	D
4.	A	17.	E
5.	E	18.	E
6.	B	19.	C
7.	B	20.	C
8.	E	21.	B
9.	A	22.	A
10.	A	23.	A
11.	E	24.	C
12.	D	25.	D
13.	E		

Explanatory Material: Data Sufficiency Sample Test Section 3

1. **If today the price of an item is $3,600, what was the price of the item exactly 2 years ago?**

   (1) The price of the item increased by 10 percent per year during this 2-year period.

   (2) Today the price of the item is 1.21 times its price exactly 2 years ago.

From (1) it can be determined that if x was the price two years ago, then 110 percent of x, or 1.1x, was the price one year ago, and $1.1(1.1x) = 1.21x$ is the price today. By solving the equation $1.21x = \$3,600$, it is possible to find x, the price 2 years ago. Therefore, (1) alone is sufficient to answer the question and the answer must be either A or D. Since (2) gives the same information derived in (1), it also is sufficient by itself to answer the question. Therefore, each statement alone is sufficient to answer the question and the best answer is D.

2. **By what percent has the price of an overcoat been reduced?**

   (1) The original price was $380.

   (2) The original price was $50 more than the reduced price.

The percent reduction is the ratio of the amount of reduction to the original price. Since (1) gives no information about the amount of reduction, (1) alone is not sufficient to answer the question, and the answer must be B, C, or E. Statement (2) alone gives $50 as the amount of the reduction but gives no information about the original price. Therefore, (2) alone is not sufficient and the answer must be either C or E. Since (1) and (2) together give both pieces of information needed, the percent reduction can be computed. Therefore, the best answer is C.

3. **If the Longfellow Playground is rectangular, what is its width?**

   (1) The ratio of its length to its width is 7 to 2.

   (2) The perimeter of the playground is 396 meters.

From (1) it can be determined that for some positive number x, the length L of the playground is 7x and the width W is 2x. Since only the ratio $\frac{L}{W} = \frac{7}{2}$ is given, (1) is not sufficient to answer the question and the answer must be B, C, or E. Statement (2) provides the information that the perimeter, or $2L + 2W$, is equal to 396, but (2) gives no information about the relationship between L and W. Therefore, (2) alone is not sufficient and the answer must be C or E. From (1) and (2) together, it can be determined that $L + W = 7x + 2x = 198$. The width can be determined by solving the equation for x. Therefore, the best answer is C.

4. **What is the value of $x - 1$?**

   (1) $x + 1 = 3$

   (2) $x - 1 < 3$

From (1) the value of x, and thus $x - 1$, can be determined, and the answer must be A or D. Since (2) gives a range rather than a specific value of x, the question cannot be answered from (2); therefore, the best answer is A.

5. **Is William taller than Jane?**

   (1) William is taller than Anna.

   (2) Anna is not as tall as Jane.

Statement (1) relates William's height to Anna's and (2) relates Jane's height to Anna's. Neither statement relates William's height to Jane's. Therefore, the answer must be either C or E. When (1) and (2) are taken together, it is possible to determine that Anna is the shortest of the three; however, Jane could be either shorter or taller than William. Since the question cannot be answered, the best answer is E.

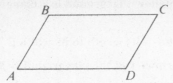

6. In parallelogram *ABCD* above, what is the measure of ∠*ADC*?

   (1) The measure of ∠*ABC* is greater than 90°.

   (2) The measure of ∠*BCD* is 70°.

From (1) it can only be determined that the measure of ∠ADC is greater than 90° since ∠ABC = ∠ADC. Since this information is not sufficient to answer the question, the answer must be B, C, or E. From (2) alone, it can be determined that the measure of ∠ADC is 110° since ∠ADC is a supplement of ∠BCD. Therefore, the best answer is B.

7. Is x^2 equal to *xy*?

   (1) $x^2 - y^2 = (x + 5)(y - 5)$

   (2) $x = y$

If x^2 is equal to xy, then either x = 0 or x = y. From (1), if x = −5 or y = 5, then (x + 5)(y − 5) = 0, so $x^2 - y^2 = 0$, and it follows that x = y or x = −y. Thus, (1) would be true whether x = y = 5 or x = −5 and y = 5. Since there are several possibilities, the question cannot be answered from (1) alone, and the answer must be B, C, or E. From (2) alone, it can be determined that $x^2 = xy$ and the best answer is B.

8. Was 70 the average (arithmetic mean) grade on a class test?

   (1) On the test, half of the class had grades below 70 and half of the class had grades above 70.

   (2) The lowest grade on the test was 45 and the highest grade on the test was 95.

Note that the average (arithmetic mean) grade depends on the distribution of the grades. Statement (1) alone is not sufficient since it does not specify how the grades are distributed with respect to 70. Therefore, the answer must be B, C, or E. Obviously (2) is also not sufficient since it only indicates the range of the grades but not their distribution. From (1) and (2) together, the distribution of the grades is not known and so the average cannot be determined. Thus, the best answer is E.

9. What was John's average driving speed in miles per hour during a 15-minute interval?

   (1) He drove 10 miles during this interval.

   (2) His maximum speed was 50 miles per hour and his minimum speed was 35 miles per hour during this interval.

From (1) alone it can be determined that John's average driving speed was 10 miles/0.25 hr = 40 miles per hour. Therefore, the answer is either A or D. Since (2) does not give enough information to determine the total distance driven from which the average driving speed could be derived, the best answer is A.

10. Is △*MNP* isosceles?

    (1) Exactly two of the angles, ∠*M* and ∠*N*, have the same measure.

    (2) ∠*N* and ∠*P* do not have the same measure.

If △MNP has two equal sides, then it is isosceles. If any triangle has two equal angles, the sides opposite the equal angles are also equal. From (1) alone it can be determined that △MNP is isosceles; therefore, the answer must be A or D. From (2) alone, it cannot be determined that △MNP has two equal angles. Therefore, the best answer is A.

11. Is *n* an integer greater than 4?

    (1) 3*n* is a positive integer.

    (2) $\frac{n}{3}$ is a positive integer.

From (1), n could be any positive integer, or even a fraction such as $\frac{1}{3}$. Since the question cannot be answered from (1) alone, the answer must be B, C, or E. From (2) it can be determined that n is a positive multiple of 3, but it cannot be determined whether it is greater or less than 4. Therefore, the answer must be C or E. Since (1) and (2) together do not give any information that precludes n from being 3, it cannot be determined whether n is greater or less than 4 and the best answer is E.

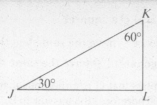

12. In △JKL shown above, what is the length of segment JL?

 (1) $JK = 10$

 (2) $KL = 5$

From the angle measures given in the figure, JKL is a right triangle and $KL = \frac{1}{2}JK$. From (1) it can be determined that $KL = 5$ and, by the Pythagorean relationship, that $JL = \sqrt{100 - 25}$. Therefore, the answer is A or D. Similarly, from (2) alone, all sides of the triangle can be found. Therefore, the best answer is D.

13. A coal company can choose to transport coal to one of its customers by railroad or by truck. If the railroad charges by the mile and the trucking company charges by the ton, which means of transporting the coal would cost <u>less</u> than the other?

 (1) The railroad charges $5,000 plus $0.01 per mile per railroad car used, and the trucking company charges $3,000 plus $85 per ton.

 (2) The customer to whom the coal is to be sent is 195 miles away from the coal company.

Although (1) gives detailed information about the rail and truck rates, it gives no information about the weights and distances to which these rates are to be applied. Therefore, the question cannot be answered and the answer must be B, C, or E. Since (2) only gives information about the distance, and (1) and (2) together do not provide information about the tonnage and the number of railroad cars needed, the best answer is E.

14. Is $x - y > r - s$?

 (1) $x > r$ and $y < s$.

 (2) $y = 2, s = 3, r = 5,$ and $x = 6$.

From (1), if $x > r$ and $y < s$, then $-y > -s$ and $x - y > r - s$. Since the answer can be determined from (1) alone, the answer must be A or D. From (2), the values of x, y, r, and s can be substituted into the inequality to answer the question. Therefore, the best answer is D.

15. On a certain day it took Bill three times as long to drive from home to work as it took Sue to drive from home to work. How many kilometers did Bill drive from home to work?

 (1) Sue drove 10 kilometers from home to work, and the ratio of

 $$\frac{\text{distance driven from home to work}}{\text{time to drive from home to work}}$$

 was the same for Bill and Sue that day.

 (2) The ratio of

 $$\frac{\text{distance driven from home to work}}{\text{time to drive from home to work}}$$

 for Sue that day was 64 kilometers per hour.

From (1) and the information given in the problem, it can be determined that $\frac{\text{Sue's distance}}{\text{Sue's time t}} = \frac{\text{Bill's distance d}}{3t}$ or $\frac{10}{t} = \frac{d}{3t}$ and $d = 30$ kilometers. Therefore, the answer must be A or D. Since (2) gives no information about Sue's time (from which we could compute Bill's time) and Bill's speed, the question cannot be answered from (2) alone and the best answer is A.

16. The figure above represents the floor of a square foyer with a circular rug partially covering the floor and extending to the outer edges of the floor as shown. What is the area of the foyer floor that is not covered by the rug?

 (1) The area of the foyer is 9 square meters.

 (2) The area of the rug is 2.25π square meters.

From (1), the diameter of the circle is equal to the side of the square, or 3 meters, and the area of the uncovered region is $9 - \pi\left(\frac{3}{2}\right)^2$. Therefore, the answer must be A or D. From (2), the radius of the circle is $\sqrt{2.25} = 1.5$ and the side of the square is $2(1.5) = 3$. Therefore, the area of the uncovered region is $3^2 - 2.25\pi$, and the best answer is D.

17. At a certain university, if 50 percent of the people who inquire about admission policies actually submit applications for admission, what percent of those who submit applications for admission enroll in classes at the university?

   (1) Fifteen percent of those who submit applications for admission are accepted at the university.

   (2) Eighty percent of those who are accepted send a deposit to the university.

From (1) and (2) taken together, it can only be determined that $(0.15)(0.8) = 12$ percent of the applicants are accepted and make a deposit. Since neither (1) nor (2) gives information as to what portion of this 12 percent actually enrolls in classes, the best answer is E.

18. If x and y are nonzero integers, is $\frac{x}{y}$ an integer?

   (1) x is the product of 2 and some other integer.

   (2) There is only one pair of positive integers whose product equals y.

From (1), it can be determined that x is an even integer. Since y may, or may not, be a divisor of x, the question cannot be answered from (1) alone and the answer must be B, C, or E. Statement (2) implies that y is a prime number but gives no information about x. Therefore, the answer must be C or E. From (1) and (2) together, x is an even number and y is a prime number. Since y could be the even number 2, in which case $\frac{x}{y}$ would be an integer, or y could be an odd integer, in which case $\frac{x}{y}$ might not be an integer, the best answer is E.

19. If x is an integer, what is the value of x?

   (1) $\frac{1}{5} < \frac{1}{x+1} < \frac{1}{2}$

   (2) $(x - 3)(x - 4) = 0$

From (1) it can be determined that x + 1 = 3 or x + 1 = 4; thus x = 2 or x = 3. From (2) it can be determined that x = 3 or x = 4. Since the precise value of x cannot be determined from either (1) or (2) taken alone, the answer must be C or E. If (1) and (2) are considered together, the only value of x that satisfies both conditions is x = 3. Therefore, the best answer is C.

20. Is quadrilateral Q a square?

   (1) The sides of Q have the same length.

   (2) The diagonals of Q have the same length.

Statement (1) implies that Q is a rhombus that may, or may not, be a square. Therefore, the answer is B, C, or E. Statement (2) alone does not imply that Q is a square since any rectangle or isosceles trapezoid has diagonals of equal length. Therefore, the answer must be C or E. If (1) and (2) are considered together, Q is a rhombus that has diagonals of equal length. Since only a square has both properties, Q is a square and the best answer is C.

21. If K is a positive integer less than 10 and $N = 4{,}321 + K$, what is the value of K?

   (1) N is divisible by 3.

   (2) N is divisible by 7.

Statement (1) implies that K is one of the integers 2, 5, or 8, since only these values of K will make N divisible by 3. Since the precise value of K cannot be determined from (1), the answer must be B, C, or E. Statement (2) implies that K = 5, since that is the only positive value of K that will make N divisible by 7. Therefore, the best answer is B.

22. A jewelry dealer initially offered a bracelet for sale at an asking price that would give a profit to the dealer of 40 percent of the original cost. What was the original cost of the bracelet?

   (1) After reducing this asking price by 10 percent, the jewelry dealer sold the bracelet at a profit of $403.

   (2) The jewelry dealer sold the bracelet for $1,953.

The problem states that the initial asking price p was equal to 140 percent of the cost c, or p = 1.4c. From (1), the equation 0.9p = c + 403 can be derived. Substituting 1.4c for p and then solving the equation 0.9(1.4c) = c + 403 will yield the cost ($1,550). Therefore, the answer must be A or D. From (2) alone, the cost cannot be related to the selling price. The use of "initially offered" suggests that there was at least one subsequent offer about which (2) gives little useful information. Therefore, the best answer is A.

23. If n is an integer between 2 and 100 and if n is also the square of an integer, what is the value of n?

(1) n is the cube of an integer.

(2) n is even.

The problem is to find which of the integers 4, 9, 16, 25, 36, 49, 64, or 81 is n. Statement (1) implies that n = 64 since 64 is the only one of these squares that is also the cube of an integer. Therefore, the answer must be A or D. From (2) alone, the integer n could be any of the integers 4, 16, 36, or 64. Therefore, the best answer is A.

24. Is $x^2 - y^2$ a positive number?

(1) $x - y$ is a positive number.

(2) $x + y$ is a positive number.

The expression $x^2 - y^2$ is a positive number if, and only if, both of its factors $x + y$ and $x - y$ are positive or both are negative. From (1) alone it cannot be determined whether $x + y$ is positive. For example, if x = −2 and y = −3, then x + y is negative, whereas if x = 3 and y = 2, then x + y is positive. Thus the answer is B, C, or E. Similarly, from (2) it cannot be determined whether x − y is positive, and the answer is C or E. Since both (1) and (2) are needed to establish that the two factors have the same sign, the best answer is C.

25. The surface area of a square tabletop was changed so that one of the dimensions was reduced by 1 inch and the other dimension was increased by 2 inches. What was the surface area before these changes were made?

(1) After the changes were made, the surface area was 70 square inches.

(2) There was a 25 percent increase in one of the dimensions.

From the information in the problem and (1), if s is the length of a side of the square tabletop, then $(s - 1)(s + 2) = 70$ or $s^2 + s - 72 = 0$. There are two values of s that satisfy this equation, 8 and −9; however, since s cannot be negative in the context of this problem, s = 8. Therefore, the answer must be A or D. From (2) it can be determined that 0.25s = 2 and s = 8. Therefore, the best answer is D.

DATA SUFFICIENCY SAMPLE TEST SECTION 4

30 Minutes
25 Questions

Directions: Each of the data sufficiency problems below consists of a question and two statements, labeled (1) and (2), in which certain data are given. You have to decide whether the data given in the statements are <u>sufficient</u> for answering the question. Using the data given in the statements <u>plus</u> your knowledge of mathematics and everyday facts (such as the number of days in July or the meaning of <u>counterclockwise</u>), you are to fill in oval

A   if statement (1) ALONE is sufficient, but statement (2) alone is not sufficient to answer the question asked;

B   if statement (2) ALONE is sufficient, but statement (1) alone is not sufficient to answer the question asked;

C   if BOTH statements (1) and (2) TOGETHER are sufficient to answer the question asked, but NEITHER statement ALONE is sufficient;

D   if EACH statement ALONE is sufficient to answer the question asked;

E   if statements (1) and (2) TOGETHER are NOT sufficient to answer the question asked, and additional data specific to the problem are needed.

Numbers: All numbers used are real numbers.

Figures: A figure in a data sufficiency problem will conform to the information given in the question, but will not necessarily conform to the additional information given in statements (1) and (2).

You may assume that lines shown as straight are straight and that angle measures are greater than zero.

You may assume that the positions of points, angles, regions, etc., exist in the order shown.

All figures lie in a plane unless otherwise indicated.

Example:

In $\triangle PQR$, what is the value of x ?

(1) $PQ = PR$
(2) $y = 40$

Explanation: According to statement (1), $PQ = PR$; therefore, $\triangle PQR$ is isosceles and $y = z$. Since $x + y + z = 180$, $x + 2y = 180$. Since statement (1) does not give a value for y, you cannot answer the question using statement (1) by itself. According to statement (2), $y = 40$; therefore, $x + z = 140$. Since statement (2) does not give a value for z, you cannot answer the question using statement (2) by itself. Using both statements together, you can find y and z; therefore, you can find x, and the answer to the problem is C.

GO ON TO THE NEXT PAGE.

A   Statement (1) ALONE is sufficient, but statement (2) alone is not sufficient.
B   Statement (2) ALONE is sufficient, but statement (1) alone is not sufficient.
C   BOTH statements TOGETHER are sufficient, but NEITHER statement ALONE is sufficient.
D   EACH statement ALONE is sufficient.
E   Statements (1) and (2) TOGETHER are NOT sufficient.

1. Who types at a faster rate, John or Bob?

   (1) The difference between their typing rates is 10 words per minute.

   (2) Bob types at a constant rate of 80 words per minute.

2. What is the average distance that automobile D travels on one full tank of gasoline?

   (1) Automobile D averages 8.5 kilometers per liter of gasoline.

   (2) The gasoline tank of automobile D holds exactly 40 liters of gasoline.

3. If l_1, l_2 and l_3 are lines in a plane, is l_1 perpendicular to l_3?

   (1) l_1 is perpendicular to l_2.
   (2) l_2 is perpendicular to l_3.

4. In a certain packinghouse, grapefruit are packed in bags and the bags are packed in cases. How many grapefruit are in each case that is packed?

   (1) The grapefruit are always packed 5 to a bag and the bags are always packed 8 to a case.

   (2) Each case is always 80 percent full.

5. What is the value of x ?
   (1) $x + y = 7$
   (2) $x - y = 3 - y$

6. A rectangular floor that is 4 meters wide is to be completely covered with nonoverlapping square tiles, each with side of length 0.25 meter, with no portion of any tile remaining. What is the least number of such tiles that will be required?

   (1) The length of the floor is three times the width.

   (2) The area of the floor is 48 square meters.

GO ON TO THE NEXT PAGE.

A Statement (1) ALONE is sufficient, but statement (2) alone is not sufficient.
B Statement (2) ALONE is sufficient, but statement (1) alone is not sufficient.
C BOTH statements TOGETHER are sufficient, but NEITHER statement ALONE is sufficient.
D EACH statement ALONE is sufficient.
E Statements (1) and (2) TOGETHER are NOT sufficient.

7. If a rope is cut into three pieces of unequal length, what is the length of the shortest of these pieces of rope?

    (1) The combined length of the longer two pieces of rope is 12 meters.

    (2) The combined length of the shorter two pieces of rope is 11 meters.

8. A certain company paid bonuses of $125 to each of its executive employees and $75 to each of its nonexecutive employees. If 100 of the employees were nonexecutives, how many were executives?

    (1) The company has a total of 120 employees.

    (2) The total amount that the company paid in bonuses to its employees was $10,000.

9. What fraction of his salary did Mr. Johnson put into savings last week?

    (1) Last week Mr. Johnson put $17 into savings.

    (2) Last week Mr. Johnson put 5% of his salary into savings.

10. For integers a, b, and c, $\dfrac{a}{b - c} = 1$. What is the value of $\dfrac{b - c}{b}$?

    (1) $\dfrac{a}{b} = \dfrac{3}{5}$

    (2) a and b have no common factors greater than 1.

11. If the price of a magazine is to be doubled, by what percent will the number of magazines sold decrease?

    (1) The current price of the magazine is $1.00.

    (2) For every $0.25 of increase in price, the number of magazines sold will decrease by 10 percent of the number sold at the current price.

12. If J, K, L, M, and N are positive integers in ascending order, what is the value of L?

    (1) The value of K is 3.

    (2) The value of M is 7.

GO ON TO THE NEXT PAGE.

A Statement (1) ALONE is sufficient, but statement (2) alone is not sufficient.
B Statement (2) ALONE is sufficient, but statement (1) alone is not sufficient.
C BOTH statements TOGETHER are sufficient, but NEITHER statement ALONE is sufficient.
D EACH statement ALONE is sufficient.
E Statements (1) and (2) TOGETHER are NOT sufficient.

13. If a, b, and c are integers, is the number $3(a + b) + c$ divisible by 3 ?

   (1) $a + b$ is divisible by 3.

   (2) c is divisible by 3.

14. Each M-type memory unit will increase the base memory capacity of a certain computer by 3 megabytes. What is the base memory capacity, in megabytes, of the computer?

   (1) 2 M-type memory units will increase the computer's base memory capacity by 300 percent.

   (2) The memory capacity of the computer after 2 M-type memory units are added to the base memory capacity is 1.6 times the memory capacity of the computer after 1 M-type memory unit is added to the base memory capacity.

15. If $xyz \neq 0$, what is the value of $\dfrac{x^5 y^4 z^2}{z^2 y^4 x^2}$?

   (1) $x = 1$

   (2) $y = 3$

16. What fractional part of the total surface area of cube C is red?

   (1) Each of 3 faces of C is exactly $\dfrac{1}{2}$ red.

   (2) Each of 3 faces of C is entirely white.

17. If positive integer x is divided by 2, the remainder is 1. What is the remainder when x is divided by 4 ?

   (1) $31 < x < 35$

   (2) x is a multiple of 3.

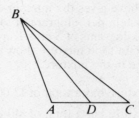

18. In the figure above, D is a point on side AC of $\triangle ABC$. Is $\triangle ABC$ isosceles?

   (1) The area of triangular region ABD is equal to the area of triangular region DBC.

   (2) $BD \perp AC$ and $AD = DC$.

19. If x is an integer, what is the value of x ?

   (1) $-2(x + 5) < -1$

   (2) $-3x > 9$

GO ON TO THE NEXT PAGE.

A   Statement (1) ALONE is sufficient, but statement (2) alone is not sufficient.
B   Statement (2) ALONE is sufficient, but statement (1) alone is not sufficient.
C   BOTH statements TOGETHER are sufficient, but NEITHER statement ALONE is sufficient.
D   EACH statement ALONE is sufficient.
E   Statements (1) and (2) TOGETHER are NOT sufficient.

Food	Number of Calories per Kilogram	Number of Grams of Protein per Kilogram
S	2,000	150
T	1,500	90

20. The table above gives the number of calories and grams of protein per kilogram of foods S and T. If a total of 7 kilograms of S and T are combined to make a certain food mixture, how many kilograms of food S are in the mixture?

    (1) The mixture has a total of 12,000 calories.

    (2) The mixture has a total of 810 grams of protein.

21. If $y \neq 0$ and $y \neq -1$, which is greater,

    $\dfrac{x}{y}$ or $\dfrac{x}{y + 1}$?

    (1) $x \neq 0$

    (2) $x > y$

22. Each person on a committee with 40 members voted for exactly one of 3 candidates, F, G, or H. Did Candidate F receive the most votes from the 40 votes cast?

    (1) Candidate F received 11 of the votes.

    (2) Candidate H received 14 of the votes.

23. S is a set of integers such that

    i) if a is in S, then $-a$ is in S, and
    ii) if each of a and b is in S, then ab is in S.

    Is -4 in S ?

    (1) 1 is in S.

    (2) 2 is in S.

24. If the area of triangular region RST is 25, what is the perimeter of RST ?

    (1) The length of one side of RST is $5\sqrt{2}$.

    (2) RST is a right isosceles triangle.

25. If x and y are consecutive odd integers, what is the sum of x and y ?

    (1) The product of x and y is negative.

    (2) One of the integers is equal to -1.

S T O P

IF YOU FINISH BEFORE TIME IS CALLED, YOU MAY CHECK YOUR WORK ON THIS SECTION ONLY.
DO NOT TURN TO ANY OTHER SECTION IN THE TEST.

Answer Key for Sample Test Section 4

DATA SUFFICIENCY

1. E	14. D
2. C	15. A
3. C	16. C
4. A	17. A
5. B	18. B
6. D	19. C
7. E	20. D
8. D	21. E
9. B	22. A
10. A	23. B
11. C	24. B
12. E	25. A
13. B	

Explanatory Material:
Data Sufficiency Sample Test Section 4

1. Who types at a faster rate, John or Bob?

(1) **The difference between their typing rates is 10 words per minute.**

(2) **Bob types at a constant rate of 80 words per minute.**

Statement (1) alone is not sufficient to answer the question since it does not identify who types at the faster rate. Thus, the answer must be B, C, or E. Clearly (2) alone is not sufficient since it provides no information about John's rate. Thus, the answer must be C or E. From (1) and (2) together it can be determined only that John's rate is 70 or 90 words per minute; therefore, the best answer is E.

2. What is the average distance that automobile D travels on one full tank of gasoline?

(1) **Automobile D averages 8.5 kilometers per liter of gasoline.**

(2) **The gasoline tank of automobile D holds exactly 40 liters of gasoline.**

Statement (1) alone is not sufficient because the capacity of the automobile's gasoline tank is not given. Thus, the answer must be B, C, or E. Statement (2) alone is not sufficient because the average mileage of the automobile is not given. Since (1) and (2) together supply both of these pieces of information, the average distance traveled per tank of gasoline can be determined; thus the best answer is C.

3. If ℓ_1, ℓ_2 and ℓ_3 are lines in a plane, is ℓ_1 perpendicular to ℓ_3?

(1) **ℓ_1 is perpendicular to ℓ_2.**

(2) **ℓ_2 is perpendicular to ℓ_3.**

Clearly (1) alone and (2) alone are not sufficient to answer the question since neither statement alone gives any information concerning the pair ℓ_1 and ℓ_3. Thus, the answer must be C or E. From (1) and (2) together it can be determined that ℓ_1 and ℓ_3 are parallel rather than perpendicular, since two coplanar lines perpendicular to the same line are parallel. Therefore, the best answer is C.

4. In a certain packinghouse, grapefruit are packed in bags and the bags are packed in cases. How many grapefruit are in each case that is packed?

(1) **The grapefruit are always packed 5 to a bag and the bags are always packed 8 to a case.**

(2) **Each case is always 80 percent full.**

Statement (1) alone is sufficient since it can be determined from (1) that the grapefruit are packed 40 to a case. Therefore, the answer must be A or D. Clearly (2) alone is not sufficient since it provides no information about how many grapefruit are packed in a case that is 80 percent full. Thus, the best answer is A.

5. What is the value of x?

(1) $x + y = 7$

(2) $x - y = 3 - y$

Statement (1) alone is not sufficient since the value of y is not known. Thus, the answer must be B, C, or E. From (2) it can be determined that $x = 3$ after y is added to both sides of the equation. Therefore, the best answer is B.

6. A rectangular floor that is 4 meters wide is to be completely covered with nonoverlapping square tiles, each with side of length 0.25 meter, with no portion of any tile remaining. What is the least number of such tiles that will be required?

(1) **The length of the floor is three times the width.**

(2) **The area of the floor is 48 square meters.**

From (1) it can be determined that the number of tiles required is $\dfrac{4(3 \cdot 4)}{(0.25)^2}$. Thus, the answer must be A or D. From (2) it can be determined that the number of tiles required is $\dfrac{48}{(0.25)^2}$. Therefore, the best answer is D.

7. If a rope is cut into three pieces of unequal length, what is the length of the shortest of these pieces of rope?

   (1) The combined length of the longer two pieces of rope is 12 meters.

   (2) The combined length of the shorter two pieces of rope is 11 meters.

Let x, y, and z be the lengths of the pieces, $x < y < z$. Statement (1) indicates that $y + z = 12$, and therefore $y < 6$ and $z > 6$. Since (1) alone provides no information about the value of x, the answer must be B, C, or E. Statement (2) indicates that $x + y = 11$, and therefore, $x < 5\frac{1}{2}$ and $y > 5\frac{1}{2}$. Thus, the answer must be C or E. From (1) and (2) together, it can only be determined that $5 < x < 5\frac{1}{2}$, which is a range of values and not a particular value. Therefore, the best answer is E.

8. A certain company paid bonuses of $125 to each of its executive employees and $75 to each of its nonexecutive employees. If 100 of the employees were nonexecutives, how many were executives?

   (1) The company has a total of 120 employees.

   (2) The total amount that the company paid in bonuses to its employees was $10,000.

Let e be the number of executives and n the number of nonexecutives. From (1) alone it can be determined that $120 = 100 + e$, or $e = 20$. Thus, the answer must be A or D. The information in (2) can be expressed by the equation $10,000 = 75 \cdot 100 + 125e$, which can also be solved for e. Therefore, the best answer is D.

9. What fraction of his salary did Mr. Johnson put into savings last week?

   (1) Last week Mr. Johnson put $17 into savings.

   (2) Last week Mr. Johnson put 5% of his salary into savings.

Clearly (1) alone is not sufficient since Mr. Johnson's salary is not given. Thus, the answer must be B, C, or E. But (2) alone is sufficient since $5\% = \frac{5}{100} = \frac{1}{20}$. Therefore, the best answer is B.

10. For integers *a*, *b*, and *c*, $\frac{a}{b - c} = 1$. What is the value of $\frac{b - c}{b}$?

    (1) $\frac{a}{b} = \frac{3}{5}$

    (2) *a* and *b* have no common factors greater than 1.

Note that $a = b - c$, since $\frac{a}{b - c} = 1$; and so $\frac{b - c}{b} = \frac{a}{b}$. Since (1) gives the value of $\frac{a}{b}$, (1) alone is sufficient. Therefore, the answer must be A or D. However, (2) alone is clearly not sufficient since the value of $\frac{a}{b}$ cannot be determined. Thus, the best answer is A.

11. If the price of a magazine is to be doubled, by what percent will the number of magazines sold decrease?

    (1) The current price of the magazine is $1.00.

    (2) For every $0.25 of increase in price, the number of magazines sold will decrease by 10 percent of the number sold at the current price.

From (1) it can be determined that the price of the magazine is to be increased by $1.00, but no information is given as to what effect this price increase will have on sales. Thus, (1) alone is not sufficient, and the answer must be B, C, or E. Statement (2) indicates how sales are affected by price increases of $0.25 increments, but it does not indicate the number of such increments equal to the total increase. Thus, (2) alone is not sufficient, and so the answer must be C or E. From (1) and (2) together, it can be determined that sales will decrease by 40 percent of current sales. Therefore, the best answer is C.

12. If *J, K, L, M,* and *N* are positive integers in ascending order, what is the value of *L*?

    (1) The value of *K* is 3.
    (2) The value of *M* is 7.

Note that $J < K < L < M < N$. From (1) it can only be determined that $L \geq 4$. Therefore, (1) alone is not sufficient, and so the answer must be B, C, or E. From (2) it can only be determined that $L \leq 6$; thus (2) alone is also not sufficient. From (1) and (2) together, $4 \leq L \leq 6$, that is $L = 4, 5,$ or 6. But since the precise value of L cannot be determined, the best answer is E.

13. If *a, b,* and *c* are integers, is the number $3(a + b) + c$ divisible by 3?

    (1) $a + b$ is divisible by 3.
    (2) *c* is divisible by 3.

Note that $3(a + b)$ is a multiple of 3 and so is divisible by 3 for any integers a and b. Thus $3(a + b) + c$ will be divisible by 3 if and only if c is divisible by 3. Statement (1) is not sufficient since it gives no information about c. Thus, the answer must be B, C, or E. However, (2) alone is sufficient, in view of the information given above. Therefore, the best answer is B.

14. Each *M*-type memory unit will increase the base memory capacity of a certain computer by 3 megabytes. What is the base memory capacity, in megabytes, of the computer?

   (1) 2 *M*-type memory units will increase the computer's base memory capacity by 300 percent.
   (2) The memory capacity of the computer after 2 *M*-type memory units are added to the base memory capacity is 1.6 times the memory capacity of the computer after 1 *M*-type memory unit is added to the base memory capacity.

Let c be the base memory capacity of the computer in megabytes. The information given in (1) can be expressed by the equation $6 = 3c$. Therefore (1) alone is sufficient, and the answer must be A or D. The information in (2) can be expressed by the equation $c + 6 = (1.6)(c + 3)$, from which the value of c can again be determined. Thus, (2) alone is also sufficient, and the best answer is D.

15. If $xyz \neq 0$, what is the value of $\frac{x^5y^4z^2}{z^2y^4x^2}$?
   (1) $x = 1$
   (2) $y = 3$

Since $xyz \neq 0$, the expression $\frac{x^5y^4z^2}{z^2y^4x^2}$ is equal to x^3. Now it is easy to see that (1) alone gives the needed information and that (2) is irrelevant. Therefore, the best answer is A.

16. What fractional part of the total surface area of cube *C* is red?
   (1) Each of 3 faces of *C* is exactly $\frac{1}{2}$ red.
   (2) Each of 3 faces of *C* is entirely white.

Neither (1) nor (2), considered separately, gives sufficient information to answer the question since each provides information about only three of the six faces. Therefore, the answer must be C or E. From (1) and (2) together, it can be determined that $\frac{1}{4}$ of the surface area of the cube is red. The best answer is C.

17. If positive integer *x* is divided by 2, the remainder is 1. What is the remainder when *x* is divided by 4?
   (1) $31 < x < 35$
   (2) *x* is a multiple of 3.

Since x has a remainder of 1 when divided by 2, x is an odd integer. From (1), it can be determined that $x = 33$, since 32 and 34 are not odd integers. Therefore, (1) alone is sufficient, and the answer must be A or D. However, (2) alone is not sufficient, since an odd multiple of 3 may have a remainder of either 1 or 3 when divided by 4. For example, $21 = 4(5) + 1$ and $27 = 4(6) + 3$. Thus, the best answer is A.

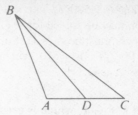

18. In the figure above, *D* is a point on side *AC* of △*ABC*. Is △*ABC* isosceles?

   (1) The area of triangular region *ABD* is equal to the area of triangular region *DBC*.
   (2) $BD \perp AC$ and $AD = DC$

From the fact in (1) that the area of region ABD is equal to the area of region DBC, and the fact that the two triangles have the same altitude from B, it can be determined that AD = DC, but not that △ABC is isosceles. Thus, (1) alone is not sufficient, and the answer must be B, C, or E. From (2) it follows that △ABD and △DBC are right triangles. Since AD = DC and BD is a common side, it follows, by the Pythagorean theorem, that AB = BC, and so △ABC is isosceles. Thus (2) alone is sufficient, and the best answer is B.

19. If *x* is an integer, what is the value of *x*?
   (1) $-2(x + 5) < -1$
   (2) $-3x > 9$

Clearly (1) alone and (2) alone are insufficient since there is a range of integers for which (1) is true and a range of integers for which (2) is true. Thus, the answer must be C or E. To determine whether the two inequalities, taken together, limit the range sufficiently to determine the value of x, one must solve each inequality. Inequality (1) is equivalent to $x > -4\frac{1}{2}$, and inequality (2) is equivalent to $x < -3$. If x is an integer and $-4\frac{1}{2} < x < -3$, then $x = -4$, and the best answer is C.

Food	Number of Calories per Kilogram	Number of Grams of Protein per Kilogram
S	2,000	150
T	1,500	90

20. The table above gives the number of calories and grams of protein per kilogram of foods *S* and *T*. If a total of 7 kilograms of *S* and *T* are combined to make a certain food mixture, how many kilograms of food *S* are in the mixture?

   (1) The mixture has a total of 12,000 calories.
   (2) The mixture has a total of 810 grams of protein.

Let s equal the number of kilograms of food S in the mixture, and (7 − s) the number of kilograms of food T in the mixture. Then (1) yields the equation

$$2,000s + 1,500(7 - s) = 12,000.$$

Since this equation may be solved for s, (1) alone is sufficient, and the answer must be A or D. Since (2) yields the equation $150s + 90(7 - s) = 810$, which can also be solved for s, the best answer is D.

21. If $y \neq 0$ and $y \neq -1$, which is greater, $\frac{x}{y}$ or $\frac{x}{y + 1}$?

    (1) $x \neq 0$
    (2) $x > y$

In approaching a question such as this, you should remember to consider the possibility of negative values of x and y. Note that $y < y + 1$ for all values of y, so that $\frac{1}{y} > \frac{1}{y + 1}$ for $y > 0$ or for $y < -1$, whereas $\frac{1}{y} < \frac{1}{y + 1}$ for $-1 < y < 0$. Thus, if $x > y > 0$, then $\frac{x}{y} > \frac{x}{y + 1}$, but if $y < x < -1$, then $\frac{x}{y} < \frac{x}{y + 1}$. Therefore, the order relation between $\frac{x}{y}$ and $\frac{x}{y + 1}$ cannot be determined from (1) and (2) together, and the best answer is E.

22. Each person on a committee with 40 members voted for exactly one of 3 candidates, *F, G,* or *H*. Did Candidate *F* receive the most votes from the 40 votes cast?

    (1) Candidate *F* received 11 of the votes.
    (2) Candidate *H* received 14 of the votes.

From (1), it can be determined that F did not receive the most votes since G and H received the remaining 29 votes, and G and H could not both have received less than 11 votes. Thus, from (1) alone it can be determined whether or not F received the most votes, and the answer must be A or D. From (2), it can only be determined that F and G received 26 votes combined; however, F may or may not have received more than 14 votes. Therefore, the best answer is A.

23. *S* is a set of integers such that

    i) if *a* is in *S*, then $-a$ is in *S*, and
    ii) if each of *a* and *b* is in *S*, then *ab* is in *S*.

    Is -4 in *S*?

    (1) 1 is in *S*.
    (2) 2 is in *S*.

From (1) and the definition of *S*, it can only be determined that 1 and -1 are in *S*. Thus, (1) alone is not sufficient, and the answer must be B, C, or E. From (2) and part (i) of the definition of *S*, it can be determined that -2 is in *S*. From (ii), if 2 and -2 are in set *S*, then $2(-2)$ or -4 is also in *S*. Thus, (2) alone is sufficient, and the best answer is B.

24. If the area of triangular region *RST* is 25, what is the perimeter of *RST*?

    (1) The length of one side of *RST* is $5\sqrt{2}$.
    (2) *RST* is a right isosceles triangle.

It may be helpful to draw a figure:

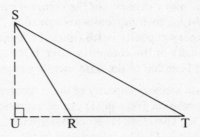

If the length of RT is $5\sqrt{2}$, then it can be determined that the altitude SU from S to side RT has length $5\sqrt{2}$, since $\frac{1}{2}(5\sqrt{2})h = 25$. If this altitude coincides with side SR, then $\triangle RST$ is a right triangle and, by the Pythagorean theorem, the length of the hypotenuse ST may be computed and the perimeter determined. However, as the figure shows, side SR need not be perpendicular to side RT, in which case the perimeter cannot be determined. Therefore, (1) alone is not sufficient and the answer must be B, C, or E. From (2) alone, two sides of the triangle are equal and are perpendicular to each other. If these two sides have length x, then $\frac{1}{2}x^2 = 25$ and $x = 5\sqrt{2}$. Now that the lengths of the legs are known, the hypotenuse can be determined using the Pythagorean theorem, and then the perimeter of the triangle can be computed. Therefore, (2) alone is sufficient, and the best answer is B.

25. If *x* and *y* are consecutive odd integers, what is the sum of *x* and *y*?

    (1) The product of *x* and *y* is negative.
    (2) One of the integers is equal to -1.

If $x < y$, it can be determined from (1) that x is negative and y is positive, since the product of two negative numbers or two positive numbers is positive, whereas the product of a negative number and a positive number is negative. Since x and y are consecutive odd integers, $y - x = 2$, so x cannot be less than -1. Hence $x = -1$ and $y = 1$, and the answer must be A or D. However, (2) alone is not sufficient since it cannot be determined whether $x = -3$ and $y = -1$ or whether $x = -1$ and $y = 1$. Therefore, the best answer is A.

DATA SUFFICIENCY SAMPLE TEST SECTION 5

30 Minutes
25 Questions

<u>Directions:</u> Each of the data sufficiency problems below consists of a question and two statements, labeled (1) and (2), in which certain data are given. You have to decide whether the data given in the statements are <u>sufficient</u> for answering the question. Using the data given in the statements <u>plus</u> your knowledge of mathematics and everyday facts (such as the number of days in July or the meaning of <u>counterclockwise</u>), you are to fill in oval

    A   if statement (1) ALONE is sufficient, but statement (2) alone is not sufficient to answer the question asked;

    B   if statement (2) ALONE is sufficient, but statement (1) alone is not sufficient to answer the question asked;

    C   if BOTH statements (1) and (2) TOGETHER are sufficient to answer the question asked, but NEITHER statement ALONE is sufficient;

    D   if EACH statement ALONE is sufficient to answer the question asked;

    E   if statements (1) and (2) TOGETHER are NOT sufficient to answer the question asked, and additional data specific to the problem are needed.

<u>Numbers:</u> All numbers used are real numbers.

<u>Figures:</u> A figure in a data sufficiency problem will conform to the information given in the question, but will not necessarily conform to the additional information given in statements (1) and (2).

    You may assume that lines shown as straight are straight and that angle measures are greater than zero.

    You may assume that the positions of points, angles, regions, etc., exist in the order shown.

    All figures lie in a plane unless otherwise indicated.

<u>Example:</u>

In $\triangle PQR$, what is the value of x?

(1) $PQ = PR$
(2) $y = 40$

<u>Explanation:</u> According to statement (1), $PQ = PR$; therefore, $\triangle PQR$ is isosceles and $y = z$. Since $x + y + z = 180$, $x + 2y = 180$. Since statement (1) does not give a value for y, you cannot answer the question using statement (1) by itself. According to statement (2), $y = 40$; therefore, $x + z = 140$. Since statement (2) does not give a value for z, you cannot answer the question using statement (2) by itself. Using both statements together, you can find y and z; therefore, you can find x, and the answer to the problem is C.

1. For a certain bottle and cork, what is the price of the cork?

  (1) The combined price of the bottle and the cork is 95 cents.

  (2) The price of the bottle is 75 cents more than the price of the cork.

2. Last year an employee received a gross annual salary of $18,000, which was paid in equal paychecks throughout the year. What was the gross salary received in each of the paychecks?

  (1) The employee received a total of 24 paychecks during the year.

  (2) The employee received a paycheck twice a month each month during the year.

GO ON TO THE NEXT PAGE.

A Statement (1) ALONE is sufficient, but statement (2) alone is not sufficient.
B Statement (2) ALONE is sufficient, but statement (1) alone is not sufficient.
C BOTH statements TOGETHER are sufficient, but NEITHER statement ALONE is sufficient.
D EACH statement ALONE is sufficient.
E Statements (1) and (2) TOGETHER are NOT sufficient.

3. What was Bill's average (arithmetic mean) grade for all of his courses?

   (1) His grade in social studies was 75, and his grade in science was 75.

   (2) His grade in mathematics was 95.

4. If $x = 2y$, what is the value of xy ?

   (1) $x > y$

   (2) $3x - 2y = 14$

5. A rectangular garden that is 10 feet long and 5 feet wide is to be covered with a layer of mulch 0.5 foot deep. At which store, K or L, will the cost of the necessary amount of mulch be less?

   (1) Store K sells mulch only in bags, each of which costs $7 and contains 6.25 cubic feet of mulch.

   (2) Store L sells mulch only in bags, each of which costs $40 and contains 25 cubic feet of mulch.

6. If $S = \{2, 3, x, y\}$, what is the value of $x + y$?

   (1) x and y are prime numbers.

   (2) 3, x, and y are consecutive odd integers in ascending order.

7. In $\triangle HGM$, what is the length of side HM ?

   (1) $HG = 5$

   (2) $GM = 8$

8. Claire paid a total of $1.60 for stamps, some of which cost $0.20 each, and the rest of which cost $0.15 each. How many 20-cent stamps did Claire buy?

   (1) Claire bought exactly 9 stamps.

   (2) The number of 20-cent stamps Claire bought was 1 more than the number of 15-cent stamps she bought.

9. If Ruth began a job and worked continuously until she finished, at what time of day did she finish the job?

   (1) She started the job at 8:15 a.m. and at noon of the same day she had worked exactly half of the time that it took her to do the whole job.

   (2) She was finished exactly $7\frac{1}{2}$ hours after she had started.

GO ON TO THE NEXT PAGE.

A   Statement (1) ALONE is sufficient, but statement (2) alone is not sufficient.
B   Statement (2) ALONE is sufficient, but statement (1) alone is not sufficient.
C   BOTH statements TOGETHER are sufficient, but NEITHER statement ALONE is sufficient.
D   EACH statement ALONE is sufficient.
E   Statements (1) and (2) TOGETHER are NOT sufficient.

10. What is the value of x ?

(1) $3 + x + y = 14$ and $2x + y = 15$
(2) $3x + 2y = 12 + 2y$

11. Is x an even integer?

(1) x is the square of an integer.
(2) x is the cube of an integer.

12. If John is exactly 4 years older than Bill, how old is John?

(1) Exactly 9 years ago John was 5 times as old as Bill was then.
(2) Bill is more than 9 years old.

13. Before play-offs, a certain team had won 80 percent of its games. After play-offs, what percent of all its games had the team won?

(1) The team competed in 4 play-off games.
(2) The team won all of its play-off games.

14. If x and y are integers, is $xy + 1$ divisible by 3 ?

(1) When x is divided by 3, the remainder is 1.
(2) When y is divided by 9, the remainder is 8.

15. If $x \neq 0$, is $|x| < 1$?

(1) $x^2 < 1$
(2) $|x| < \dfrac{1}{x}$

16. The cost to charter a certain airplane is x dollars. If the 25 members of a club chartered the plane and shared the cost equally, what was the cost per member?

(1) If there had been 5 more members and all 30 had shared the cost equally, the cost per member would have been $40 less.
(2) The cost per member was 10 percent less than the cost per person on a regularly scheduled flight.

GO ON TO THE NEXT PAGE.

A   Statement (1) ALONE is sufficient, but statement (2) alone is not sufficient.
B   Statement (2) ALONE is sufficient, but statement (1) alone is not sufficient.
C   BOTH statements TOGETHER are sufficient, but NEITHER statement ALONE is sufficient.
D   EACH statement ALONE is sufficient.
E   Statements (1) and (2) TOGETHER are NOT sufficient.

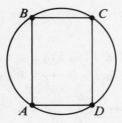

17. Rectangle $ABCD$ is inscribed in a circle as shown above. What is the radius of the circle?

   (1)   The length of the rectangle is $\sqrt{3}$ and the width of the rectangle is 1.

   (2)   The length of arc AB is $\frac{1}{3}$ of the circumference of the circle.

18. Bowls X and Y each contained exactly 2 jelly beans, each of which was either red or black. One of the jelly beans in bowl X was exchanged with one of the jelly beans in bowl Y. After the exchange, were both of the jelly beans in bowl X black?

   (1)   Before the exchange, bowl X contained 2 black jelly beans.

   (2)   After the exchange, bowl Y contained 1 jelly bean of each color.

19. Does $x + y = 0$?

   (1) $xy < 0$
   (2) $x^2 = y^2$

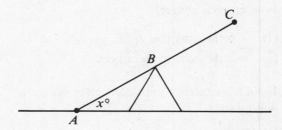

20. In the figure above, line AC represents a seesaw that is touching level ground at point A. If B is the midpoint of AC, how far above the ground is point C?

   (1) $x = 30$
   (2)   Point B is 5 feet above the ground.

GO ON TO THE NEXT PAGE.

A   Statement (1) ALONE is sufficient, but statement (2) alone is not sufficient.
B   Statement (2) ALONE is sufficient, but statement (1) alone is not sufficient.
C   BOTH statements TOGETHER are sufficient, but NEITHER statement ALONE is sufficient.
D   EACH statement ALONE is sufficient.
E   Statements (1) and (2) TOGETHER are NOT sufficient.

21. If $\square$ represents a digit in the 7-digit number 3,62$\square$,215, what is the value of $\square$?

(1)   The sum of the 7 digits is equal to 4 times an integer.

(2)   The missing digit is different from any of the other digits in the number.

22. Last Tuesday a trucker paid $155.76, including 10 percent state and federal taxes, for diesel fuel. What was the price per gallon for the fuel if the taxes are excluded?

(1)   The trucker paid $0.118 per gallon in state and federal taxes on the fuel last Tuesday.

(2)   The trucker purchased 120 gallons of the fuel last Tuesday.

23. Is x less than y ?

(1) $x - y + 1 < 0$

(2) $x - y - 1 < 0$

24. Is quadrilateral $RSTV$ a rectangle?

(1)   The measure of $\angle RST$ is $90°$.

(2)   The measure of $\angle TVR$ is $90°$.

25. If b is an integer, is $\sqrt{a^2 + b^2}$ an integer?

(1) $a^2 + b^2$ is an integer.

(2) $a^2 - 3b^2 = 0$

S T O P

IF YOU FINISH BEFORE TIME IS CALLED, YOU MAY CHECK YOUR WORK ON THIS SECTION ONLY.
DO NOT TURN TO ANY OTHER SECTION IN THE TEST.

Answer Key for Sample Test Section 5

DATA SUFFICIENCY

1. C	14. C
2. D	15. D
3. E	16. A
4. B	17. A
5. C	18. E
6. B	19. C
7. E	20. B
8. D	21. C
9. A	22. D
10. D	23. A
11. E	24. E
12. A	25. B
13. E	

Explanatory Material: Data Sufficiency Sample Test Section 5

1. **For a certain bottle and cork, what is the price of the cork?**

   (1) The combined price of the bottle and the cork is 95 cents.
   (2) The price of the bottle is 75 cents more than the price of the cork.

If b and c denote the costs of the bottle and cork, respectively, then statement (1) yields $b + c = 95$. Since the value of c cannot be determined, statement (1) alone is insufficient to answer the question. Thus, the answer must be B, C, or E. Similarly, statement (2) alone is insufficient since it yields only that $b = c + 75$. However, the value of c can be determined by solving both equations simultaneously; thus, the best answer is C.

2. **Last year an employee received a gross annual salary of $18,000, which was paid in equal paychecks throughout the year. What was the gross salary received in each of the paychecks?**

   (1) The employee received a total of 24 paychecks during the year.
   (2) The employee received a paycheck twice a month each month during the year.

To answer the question it is sufficient to know the number of paychecks received throughout the year, since the answer to the question can be obtained by dividing the gross annual salary by this number. Both statement (1) and statement (2) yield this information. Therefore, the best answer is D.

3. **What was Bill's average (arithmetic mean) grade for all his courses?**

   (1) His grade in social studies was 75, and his grade in science was 75.
   (2) His grade in mathematics was 95.

Statement (1) alone is not sufficient, since it cannot be concluded that social studies and science comprise all of Bill's courses. Therefore, the answer must be B, C, or E. Since from statement (2) it still cannot be concluded that the three courses mentioned comprise all of Bill's courses, the best answer is E.

4. **If $x = 2y$, what is the value of xy?**

   (1) $x > y$
   (2) $3x - 2y = 14$

Statement (1) alone is not sufficient, since there are many pairs of values of x and y such that $x = 2y$ and $x > y$, and these pairs yield different values of xy. Thus, the answer must be B, C, or E. From statement (2) it can be concluded that $2x = 14$ by substituting x for $2y$ in the equation $3x - 2y = 14$, and thus the value of xy can be determined. Therefore, the best answer is B.

5. **A rectangular garden that is 10 feet long and 5 feet wide is to be covered with a layer of mulch 0.5 foot deep. At which store, K or L, will the cost of the necessary amount of mulch be less?**

   (1) Store K sells mulch only in bags, each of which costs $7 and contains 6.25 cubic feet of mulch.
   (2) Store L sells mulch only in bags, each of which costs $40 and contains 25 cubic feet of mulch.

Note that $(10)(5)(0.5) = 25$ cubic feet of mulch is needed. Statement (1) implies that the cost of the necessary amount of mulch at store K will be 4 ($7) = $28, but gives no information about the cost of the mulch at store L. Therefore, the answer must be B, C, or E. Statement (2) implies that the cost of the mulch at store L will be $40, but gives no information about the cost of the mulch at store K. From (1) and (2) together it can be determined that the cost of the mulch will be less at store K than at store L. Thus, the best answer is C.

6. If $S = \{2, 3, x, y\}$, what is the value of $x + y$?

   (1) x and y are prime numbers.
   (2) 3, x, and y are consecutive odd integers in ascending order.

Statement (1) alone is not sufficient to determine the value of $x + y$, since there are many possible values of x and y that are prime numbers. Thus, the answer must be B, C, or E. Statement (2) implies that $x = 5$ and $y = 7$, and thus $x + y = 12$. Therefore, the best answer is B.

7. In $\triangle HGM$, what is the length of side HM?

   (1) $HG = 5$
   (2) $GM = 8$

Neither statement (1) alone nor statement (2) alone is sufficient to determine the length of side HM. Thus, the answer must be C or E. However, even together the two statements are not sufficient, because a triangle is not uniquely determined by two of its sides. For instance, the length of side HM will vary between 3 and 13, depending on the size of the angle formed by sides HG and GM. Therefore, the best answer is E.

8. Claire paid a total of $1.60 for stamps, some of which cost $0.20 each, and the rest of which cost $0.15 each. How many 20-cent stamps did Claire buy?

   (1) Claire bought exactly 9 stamps.
   (2) The number of 20-cent stamps Claire bought was 1 more than the number of 15-cent stamps she bought.

If x and y denote the number of 20-cent stamps and 15-cent stamps, respectively, then $20x + 15y = 160$. Since this equation has two unknowns, another equation in the unknowns is needed to find the value of x. Statement (1) implies that $x + y = 9$, or $y = 9 - x$. Now the equation becomes $20x + 15(9 - x) = 160$, which can be solved for x. Thus the answer is A or D. Statement (2) implies that $x = y + 1$, or $y = x - 1$, and thus the equation $20x + 15(x - 1) = 160$ can be solved for x. The best answer is D.

9. If Ruth began a job and worked continuously until she finished, at what time of day did she finish the job?

   (1) She started the job at 8:15 a.m. and at noon of the same day she had worked exactly half of the time that it took her to do the whole job.
   (2) She was finished exactly $7\frac{1}{2}$ hours after she had started.

Statement (1) gives the starting time and the time at which she had completed half the job; from this information, it is possible to compute the finishing time. Thus, the answer must be A or D. Statement (2) alone is not sufficient: it gives the total amount of time it took to do the job, but not the starting time. Therefore, the best answer is A.

10. What is the value of x?

    (1) $3 + x + y = 14$ and $2x + y = 15$
    (2) $3x + 2y = 12 + 2y$

Statement (1) gives two linear equations involving x and y. By inspection it can be determined that the two equations do not represent parallel lines, hence that they have a solution. Therefore, (1) is sufficient, and the answer must be A or D. Statement (2) is equivalent to $3x = 12$, or $x = 4$. Thus, (2) alone is also sufficient, and the best answer is D.

11. Is x an even integer?

    (1) x is the square of an integer.
    (2) x is the cube of an integer.

Note that any positive integer power of an even integer is even, while any positive integer power of an odd integer is odd. Since it cannot be determined whether x is odd or even by knowing that it is a square or a cube or both, statements (1) and (2), either alone or together, do not give sufficient information. Thus, the best answer is E.

12. If John is exactly 4 years older than Bill, how old is John?

    (1) Exactly 9 years ago John was 5 times as old as Bill was then.
    (2) Bill is more than 9 years old.

If j and b denote the ages, in years, of John and Bill, respectively, then $j = b + 4$. Statement (1) yields the equation $j - 9 = 5(b - 9)$; substituting $j - 4$ for b in this equation results in an equation in j alone from which the value of j can be determined. Thus, the answer must be A or D. Statement (2) implies only that John is more than 13 years old. Therefore, the best answer is A.

13. Before play-offs, a certain team had won 80 percent of its games. After play-offs, what percent of all its games had the team won?

    (1) The team competed in 4 play-off games.
    (2) The team won all of its play-off games.

If x denotes the number of games the team played before play-offs, and y and z the number of play-off wins and play-off games, respectively, then the question asks for the value of $\dfrac{(0.8)x + y}{x + z}$. Statement (1) yields only that $z = 4$. Thus, the value of the ratio cannot be determined, and the answer must be B, C, or E. Statement (2) yields only the value of y, and it is also not sufficient. Since (1) and (2) together do not give the value of x, the value of the ratio, and thus the answer to the question, cannot be determined. Thus, the best answer is E.

14. If x and y are integers, is $xy + 1$ divisible by 3?

    (1) When x is divided by 3, the remainder is 1.
    (2) When y is divided by 9, the remainder is 8.

To determine whether $xy + 1$ is divisible by 3, one must use the given information to see whether the expression $xy + 1$ can be transformed into an expression of the form $3k$, where k is an integer. It should be clear that information is needed about the remainders when both x and y are divided by 3; thus, statements (1) and (2) alone are insufficient, and the answer must be C or E. From the information in both (1) and (2), $x = 3p + 1$ and $y = 9q + 8$, for integers p and q. Substituting these expressions into $xy + 1$, one gets:
$$xy + 1 = (3p + 1)(9q + 8) + 1$$
$$= 27pq + 24p + 9q + 8 + 1,$$
which equals $3(9pq + 8p + 3q + 3)$. Thus, $xy + 1 = 3k$, where k is an integer, and the best answer is C.

15. If $x \neq 0$, is $|x| < 1$?

    (1) $x^2 < 1$
    (2) $|x| < \dfrac{1}{x}$

Note that $|x|$, which denotes the absolute value of x, equals x if $x > 0$ and equals $-x$ if $x < 0$. Thus, $|x| < 1$ if, and only if, $-1 < x < 1$. Since $x^2 < 1$ is equivalent to $-1 < x < 1$, statement (1) alone is sufficient, and the answer must be A or D. Statement (2) implies that $x > 0$, or $|x| = x$; thus, $|x| < 1/|x|$, or $|x|^2 < 1$. Therefore, (2) alone is also sufficient. The best answer is D.

16. The cost to charter a certain airplane is x dollars. If the 25 members of a club chartered the plane and shared the cost equally, what was the cost per member?

    (1) If there had been 5 more members and all 30 had shared the cost equally, the cost per member would have been $40 less.
    (2) The cost per member was 10 percent less than the cost per person on a regularly scheduled flight.

The cost per member can be expressed as $x/25$. Statement (1) yields the equation $\dfrac{x}{30} = \dfrac{x}{25} - 40$, from which the value of x can be determined. Thus, (1) alone is sufficient to determine the value of $\dfrac{x}{25}$, and the answer must be A or D. However, statement (2) alone is not sufficient, because the cost per person on a regularly scheduled flight is not given. Thus, the best answer is A.

17. Rectangle $ABCD$ is inscribed in a circle as shown above. What is the radius of the circle?

    (1) The length of the rectangle is $\sqrt{3}$ and the width of the rectangle is 1.
    (2) The length of arc AB is $\dfrac{1}{3}$ of the circumference of the circle.

Note that the diagonal AC is a diameter of the circle, since $\angle ABC$ is a right angle. From statement (1), the length of AC, which is also the hypotenuse of $\triangle ABC$, can be found by using the Pythagorean Theorem. Since AC is a diameter of the circle, the radius is half the length of AC. Therefore, (1) alone is sufficient to answer the question; the answer must be A or D. Statement (2) implies that arc AB has measure 120°, and thus that $\triangle ABC$ is a $30° - 60° - 90°$ triangle; however, it does not specify the length of any of its sides. Thus, (2) alone is not sufficient; the best answer is A.

18. Bowls X and Y each contained exactly 2 jelly beans, each of which was either red or black. One of the jelly beans in bowl X was exchanged with one of the jelly beans in bowl Y. After the exchange, were both of the jelly beans in bowl X black?

    (1) Before the exchange, bowl X contained 2 black jelly beans.
    (2) After the exchange, bowl Y contained 1 jelly bean of each color.

Statement (1) alone is insufficient to answer the question, since bowl Y may or may not have contained any black jelly beans before the exchange. Therefore, the answer must be B, C, or E. Statement (2) alone is also insufficient, since there is no information about the contents of bowl X. Thus, the answer must be C or E. Together (1) and (2) are insufficient, since there are still two possibilities for the contents of bowl X after the exchange. Thus, the best answer is E.

19. Does $x + y = 0$?

    (1) $xy < 0$
    (2) $x^2 = y^2$

To answer the question, it suffices to determine whether $x = -y$. Statement (1) implies that $x < 0$ and $y > 0$, or that $x > 0$ and $y < 0$; however, it cannot be concluded that $x = -y$. For example, $x = 2$ and $y = -3$ is consistent with statement (1). Thus, (1) alone is not sufficient; the answer must be B, C, or E. Statement (2) implies that $x = y$ or that $x = -y$. Since $y = -y$ only if $y = 0$, it cannot be concluded that $x = -y$. Thus, (2) alone is also insufficient; the answer must be C or E. However, it can be determined from (1) and (2) together that $x = -y$, and therefore the best answer is C.

20. In the figure above, line AC represents a seesaw that is touching level ground at point A. If B is the midpoint of AC, how far above the ground is point C?

(1) $x = 30$
(2) Point B is 5 feet above the ground.

It may be helpful to represent C's distance above the ground by drawing in perpendicular segment CE, and B's distance above the ground by drawing in perpendicular segment BD as shown below:

Note that $\triangle ABD$ and $\triangle ACE$ are similar right triangles, and thus their corresponding sides are in the same proportion. Statement (1) implies that $\triangle ACE$ is a $30° - 60° - 90°$ triangle, and thus the sides are in the ratio $1: \sqrt{3}: 2$. However, without the length of at least one of the sides, the scale of the drawing cannot be determined. Thus, (1) alone is not sufficient; the answer must be B, C, or E. Statement (2) alone, however, is sufficient to determine that the length of CE is 10, since the lengths of the sides of $\triangle ACE$ must be twice the lengths of the corresponding sides of $\triangle ABD$, regardless of the value of x. Thus, the best answer is B.

21. If $\square$ represents a digit in the 7-digit number $3,62\square,215$, what is the value of $\square$?

(1) The sum of the 7 digits is equal to 4 times an integer.
(2) The missing digit is different from any of the other digits in the number.

The sum of the 7 digits is $19 + \square$. Since $\square$ is one of the integers from 0 to 9, inclusive, the value of $19 + \square$ satisfies $19 \leq 19 + \square \leq 28$. From statement (1), therefore, it can be concluded that $19 + \square$ equals 20, 24, or 28, so $\square$ equals 1, 5, or 9. Thus, (1) alone is not sufficient; the answer must be B, C, or E. Statement (2) implies that $\square$ equals 0, 4, 7, 8, or 9 and, therefore, is not sufficient. However, it can be determined from (1) and (2) together that $\square$ equals 9. Thus, the best answer is C.

22. Last Tuesday a trucker paid $155.76, including 10 percent state and federal taxes, for diesel fuel. What was the price per gallon for the fuel if the taxes are excluded?

(1) The trucker paid $0.118 per gallon in state and federal taxes on the fuel last Tuesday.
(2) The trucker puchased 120 gallons of the fuel last Tuesday.

Note that 110 percent of the total price of the fuel was equal to $155.76; so the price of the fuel exclusive of the taxes was $\dfrac{155.76}{1.1}$. Hence it suffices to determine the number of gallons of fuel purchased. From statement (1), the number of gallons can be determined, since the amount of the taxes is $t = \dfrac{(0.1)(155.76)}{(1.1)}$; thus, the number of gallons is $\dfrac{t}{(0.118)}$. Therefore, (1) alone is sufficient, and the answer must be A or D. Statement (2) alone is sufficient since, as was already noted, it suffices to know the number of gallons of fuel. Thus, the best answer is D.

23. Is x less than y?

(1) $x - y + 1 < 0$
(2) $x - y - 1 < 0$

Statement (1) alone is sufficient, as can be seen by adding $y - 1$ to both sides of the inequality: $x < y - 1$. Since $y - 1 < y$ for all values of y, $x < y$. Thus, (1) alone is sufficient; the answer must be A or D. Statement (2) implies that $x < y + 1$. Since $x = y$ and $x < y$ are each consistent with (2), statement (2) alone is not sufficient; the best answer is A.

24. Is quadrilateral $RSTV$ a rectangle?

(1) The measure of $\angle RST$ is $90°$.
(2) The measure of $\angle TVR$ is $90°$.

For $RSTV$ to be a rectangle, it is necessary and sufficient that each of the four angles be right angles. Clearly, therefore, neither statement (1) alone nor statement (2) alone is sufficient to determine whether $RSTV$ is a rectangle: Given that one of the angles is a right angle does not imply that any of the other three angles are right angles. Therefore, the answer must be C or E. However, it also does not follow that $RSTV$ is a rectangle even if a pair of opposite angles are right angles. For example, $RSTV$ could look like this:

To understand why this figure is possible, it may be helpful to imagine points S and V as two points on the circumference of a circle and to draw a diameter RT between points S and V. Then angles TVR and TSR will be right angles and the shape of quadrilateral $RSTV$ has an infinite number of possibilities, many of which are nonrectangular. The best answer, therefore, is E.

25. If b is an integer, is $\sqrt{a^2 + b^2}$ an integer?

(1) $a^2 + b^2$ is an integer.
(2) $a^2 - 3b^2 = 0$

Note that for $\sqrt{a^2 + b^2}$ to be an integer, it is necessary and sufficient that $a^2 + b^2$ be the square of an integer. Statement (1) alone is not sufficient, since $a^2 + b^2$ may or may not be the square of an integer: $3^2 + 4^2 = 5^2$, but $2^2 + 3^2 = 13$, which is not the square of an integer. Thus, the answer must be B, C, or E. From statement (2) it can be concluded that $a^2 = 3b^2$ or that $a^2 + b^2 = 4b^2 = (2b)^2$. Therefore, (2) alone is sufficient; the best answer is B.

5 Reading Comprehension

There are six kinds of Reading Comprehension questions, each of which tests a different reading skill. The following pages include descriptions of the various question types, test-taking strategies, sample test sections (with answer keys), and detailed explanations of every question on the sample test sections. The explanations further illustrate the ways in which Reading Comprehension questions evaluate basic reading skills.

Reading Comprehension questions include:

1. **Questions that ask about the main idea of a passage**
   Each Reading Comprehension passage in the GMAT is a unified whole—that is, the individual sentences and paragraphs support and develop one main idea or central point. Sometimes you will be told the central point in the passage itself, and sometimes it will be necessary for you to determine the central point from the overall organization or development of the passage. You may be asked in this kind of question to recognize a correct restatement, or paraphrase, of the main idea of a passage; to identify the author's primary purpose, or objective, in writing the passage; or to assign a title that summarizes briefly and pointedly the main idea developed in the passage.

2. **Questions that ask about the supporting ideas presented in a passage**
   These questions measure your ability to comprehend the supporting ideas in a passage and to differentiate those supporting ideas from the main idea. The questions also measure your ability to differentiate ideas that are *explicitly stated* in a passage from ideas that are *implied* by the author but are not explicitly stated. You may be asked about facts cited in a passage, or about the specific content of arguments presented by the author in support of his or her views, or about descriptive details used to support or elaborate on the main idea. Whereas questions about the main idea ask you to determine the meaning of a passage *as a whole,* questions about supporting ideas ask you to determine the meanings of individual sentences and paragraphs that *contribute* to the meaning of the passage as a whole. One way to think about these questions is to see them as questions asking for the main point of *one small part* of the passage.

3. **Questions that ask for inferences based on information presented in a passage**
   These questions ask about ideas that are not explicitly stated in a passage but are *strongly implied* by the author. Unlike questions about supporting details, which ask about information that is directly stated in a passage, inference questions ask about ideas or meanings that must be inferred from information that is directly stated. Authors can make their points in indirect ways, suggesting ideas without actually stating them. These questions measure your ability to infer an author's intended meaning in parts of a passage where the meaning is only suggested. The questions do not ask about meanings or implications that are remote from the passage but about meanings that are developed indirectly or implications specifically suggested by the author. To answer these questions, you may have to carry statements made by the author one step beyond their literal meanings, or recognize the *opposite* of a statement made by the author, or identify the intended meaning of a word used figuratively in a passage. If a passage explicitly states an effect, for example, you may be asked to infer its cause. If the author compares two phenomena, you may be asked to infer the basis for the comparison. You may be asked to infer the characteristics of an old policy from an explicit description of a new one. When you read a passage, therefore, you should concentrate not only on the explicit meaning of the author's words, but also on the more subtle meaning implied by those words.

4. **Questions that ask how information given in a passage can be applied to a context outside the passage itself**

    These questions measure your ability to discern the relationships between situations or ideas presented by the author and other situations or ideas that might parallel those in the passage. In this kind of question, you may be asked to identify a hypothetical situation that is comparable to a situation presented in the passage, or to select an example that is similar to an example provided in the passage, or to apply ideas given in the passage to a situation not mentioned by the author, or to recognize ideas that the author would probably agree or disagree with on the basis of statements made in the passage. Unlike inference questions, these questions use ideas or situations *not* taken from the passage. Ideas and situations given in a question are *like* those given in the passage, and they parallel ideas and situations given in the passage. Therefore, to answer the question, you must do more than recall what you read. You must recognize the essential attributes of ideas and situations presented in the passage when they appear in different words and in an entirely new context.

5. **Questions that ask about the logical structure of a passage**

    These questions ask you to analyze and evaluate the organization and the logic of a passage. They may ask how a passage is constructed: for instance, does it define, does it compare or contrast, does it present a new idea, does it refute an idea. They may also ask how the author persuades readers to accept his or her assertions, or about the reason behind the author's use of any particular supporting detail. You may also be asked to identify assumptions that the author is making, to assess the strengths and weaknesses of the author's arguments, or to recognize appropriate counterarguments. These questions measure your ability not only to comprehend a passage but to evaluate it critically. However, it is important for you to realize that these questions do not rely on any kind of formal logic, nor do they require that you be familiar with specific terms of logic or argumentation. You can answer these questions using only the information in the passage and careful reasoning.

6. **Questions that ask about the style and tone of a passage**

    These questions ask about the language of a passage and about the ideas in a passage that may be expressed through its language. You may be asked to deduce the author's attitude toward an idea, a fact, or a situation from the words that he or she uses to describe it. You may also be asked to select a word that accurately describes the tone of a passage—for instance, ''critical,'' ''questioning,'' ''objective,'' or ''enthusiastic.'' To answer this type of question, you will have to consider the language of the passage as a whole: it takes more than one pointed critical word to make the tone of an entire passage ''critical.'' Sometimes, these questions ask what audience the passage was probably intended for or what type of publication it probably appeared in. Style and tone questions may apply to one small part of the passage or to the passage as a whole. To answer them, you must ask yourself what meanings are contained in the words of a passage beyond their literal meanings. Were such words selected because of their emotional content, or because of their suggestiveness, or because a particular audience would expect to hear them? Remember, these questions measure your ability to discern meaning expressed by the author through his or her choice of words.

Test-Taking Strategies for Reading Comprehension

1. You should not expect to be completely familiar with any of the material presented in Reading Comprehension passages. You may find some passages easier to understand than others, but all passages are designed to present a challenge. If you have some familiarity with the material being presented in a passage, do not let this knowledge influence your choice of answers to the questions. Answer all questions on the basis of what is *stated or implied* in the passage itself.

2. Since the questions require specific and detailed understanding of the material in a passage, analyze each passage carefully the first time you read it. Even if you read at a relatively slow rate, you should be able to read the passages in about 6 minutes and will have about 24 minutes left for answering the questions. You should, of course, be sure to allow sufficient time to work on each passage and its questions. There are other ways of approaching Reading Comprehension passages: some test-takers prefer to skim the passages the first time through or even to read the questions before reading the passages. You should choose the method most suitable for you.

3. Underlining parts of a passage may be helpful to you. Focus on key words and phrases and try to follow exactly the development of separate ideas. In the margins, note where each important idea, argument, or set of related facts begins. Make every effort to avoid losing the sense of what is being discussed. If you become lost, you will have to go back over the material, and that wastes time. Keep the following in mind:

   - Note how each fact relates to an idea or an argument.
   - Note where the passage moves from one idea to the next.
   - Separate main ideas from supporting ideas.
   - Determine what conclusions are reached and why.

4. Read the questions carefully, making certain that you understand what is being asked. An answer choice may be incorrect, even though it accurately restates information given in the passage, if it does not answer the question. If you need to, refer back to the passage for clarification.

5. Read all the choices carefully. Never assume that you have selected the best answer without first reading all the choices.

6. Select the choice that best answers the question in terms of the information given in the passage. Do not rely on outside knowledge of the material for answering the questions.

7. Remember that understanding, not speed, is the critical factor in reading comprehension.

When you take the sample test sections, use the answer spaces on pages 181 and 182 to mark your answers.

Answer Spaces for Reading Comprehension Sample Test Sections

Sample Test Section 1

1 A B C D E	8 A B C D E	15 A B C D E	22 A B C D E
2 A B C D E	9 A B C D E	16 A B C D E	23 A B C D E
3 A B C D E	10 A B C D E	17 A B C D E	24 A B C D E
4 A B C D E	11 A B C D E	18 A B C D E	25 A B C D E
5 A B C D E	12 A B C D E	19 A B C D E	
6 A B C D E	13 A B C D E	20 A B C D E	
7 A B C D E	14 A B C D E	21 A B C D E	

Sample Test Section 2

1 A B C D E	8 A B C D E	15 A B C D E	22 A B C D E
2 A B C D E	9 A B C D E	16 A B C D E	23 A B C D E
3 A B C D E	10 A B C D E	17 A B C D E	24 A B C D E
4 A B C D E	11 A B C D E	18 A B C D E	25 A B C D E
5 A B C D E	12 A B C D E	19 A B C D E	
6 A B C D E	13 A B C D E	20 A B C D E	
7 A B C D E	14 A B C D E	21 A B C D E	

Sample Test Section 3

1 A B C D E	8 A B C D E	15 A B C D E	22 A B C D E
2 A B C D E	9 A B C D E	16 A B C D E	23 A B C D E
3 A B C D E	10 A B C D E	17 A B C D E	24 A B C D E
4 A B C D E	11 A B C D E	18 A B C D E	25 A B C D E
5 A B C D E	12 A B C D E	19 A B C D E	
6 A B C D E	13 A B C D E	20 A B C D E	
7 A B C D E	14 A B C D E	21 A B C D E	

Sample Test Section 4

1 A B C D E	8 A B C D E	15 A B C D E	22 A B C D E
2 A B C D E	9 A B C D E	16 A B C D E	23 A B C D E
3 A B C D E	10 A B C D E	17 A B C D E	24 A B C D E
4 A B C D E	11 A B C D E	18 A B C D E	25 A B C D E
5 A B C D E	12 A B C D E	19 A B C D E	
6 A B C D E	13 A B C D E	20 A B C D E	
7 A B C D E	14 A B C D E	21 A B C D E	

Sample Test Section 5

1 Ⓐ Ⓑ Ⓒ Ⓓ Ⓔ	8 Ⓐ Ⓑ Ⓒ Ⓓ Ⓔ	15 Ⓐ Ⓑ Ⓒ Ⓓ Ⓔ	22 Ⓐ Ⓑ Ⓒ Ⓓ Ⓔ
2 Ⓐ Ⓑ Ⓒ Ⓓ Ⓔ	9 Ⓐ Ⓑ Ⓒ Ⓓ Ⓔ	16 Ⓐ Ⓑ Ⓒ Ⓓ Ⓔ	23 Ⓐ Ⓑ Ⓒ Ⓓ Ⓔ
3 Ⓐ Ⓑ Ⓒ Ⓓ Ⓔ	10 Ⓐ Ⓑ Ⓒ Ⓓ Ⓔ	17 Ⓐ Ⓑ Ⓒ Ⓓ Ⓔ	24 Ⓐ Ⓑ Ⓒ Ⓓ Ⓔ
4 Ⓐ Ⓑ Ⓒ Ⓓ Ⓔ	11 Ⓐ Ⓑ Ⓒ Ⓓ Ⓔ	18 Ⓐ Ⓑ Ⓒ Ⓓ Ⓔ	
5 Ⓐ Ⓑ Ⓒ Ⓓ Ⓔ	12 Ⓐ Ⓑ Ⓒ Ⓓ Ⓔ	19 Ⓐ Ⓑ Ⓒ Ⓓ Ⓔ	
6 Ⓐ Ⓑ Ⓒ Ⓓ Ⓔ	13 Ⓐ Ⓑ Ⓒ Ⓓ Ⓔ	20 Ⓐ Ⓑ Ⓒ Ⓓ Ⓔ	
7 Ⓐ Ⓑ Ⓒ Ⓓ Ⓔ	14 Ⓐ Ⓑ Ⓒ Ⓓ Ⓔ	21 Ⓐ Ⓑ Ⓒ Ⓓ Ⓔ	

READING COMPREHENSION SAMPLE TEST SECTION 1

30 Minutes

25 Questions

<u>Directions:</u> Each passage in this group is followed by questions based on its content. After reading a passage, choose the best answer to each question and fill in the corresponding oval on the answer sheet. Answer all questions following a passage on the basis of what is <u>stated</u> or <u>implied</u> in that passage.

Most economists in the United States seem captivated by the spell of the free market. Consequently, nothing seems good or normal that does not accord with the requirements of the free market.
(5) A price that is determined by the seller or, for that matter, established by anyone other than the aggregate of consumers seems pernicious. Accordingly, it requires a major act of will to think of price-fixing (the determination of prices by the
(10) seller) as both "normal" and having a valuable economic function. In fact, price-fixing is normal in all industrialized societies because the industrial system itself provides, as an effortless consequence of its own development, the price-fixing
(15) that it requires. Modern industrial planning requires and rewards great size. Hence, a comparatively small number of large firms will be competing for the same group of consumers. That each large firm will act with consideration of
(20) its own needs and thus avoid selling its products for more than its competitors charge is commonly recognized by advocates of free-market economic theories. But each large firm will also act with full consideration of the needs that it has in
(25) common with the other large firms competing for the same customers. Each large firm will thus avoid significant price-cutting, because price-cutting would be prejudicial to the common interest in a stable demand for products. Most economists
(30) do not see price-fixing when it occurs because they expect it to be brought about by a number of explicit agreements among large firms; it is not.
Moreover, those economists who argue that allowing the free market to operate without inter-
(35) ference is the most efficient method of establishing prices have not considered the economies of nonsocialist countries other than the United States. These economies employ intentional price-fixing, usually in an overt fashion. Formal price-fixing
(40) by cartel and informal price-fixing by agreements covering the members of an industry are commonplace. Were there something peculiarly efficient about the free market and inefficient about price-fixing, the countries that have avoided the first
(45) and used the second would have suffered drastically in their economic development. There is no indication that they have.
Socialist industry also works within a framework of controlled prices. In the early 1970's,
(50) the Soviet Union began to give firms and industries some of the flexibility in adjusting prices that a more informal evolution has accorded the capitalist system. Economists in the United States have hailed the change as a return to the free market.
(55) But Soviet firms are no more subject to prices established by a free market over which they exercise little influence than are capitalist firms; rather, Soviet firms have been given the power to fix prices.

1. The primary purpose of the passage is to

   (A) refute the theory that the free market plays a useful role in the development of industrialized societies
   (B) suggest methods by which economists and members of the government of the United States can recognize and combat price-fixing by large firms
   (C) show that in industrialized societies price-fixing and the operation of the free market are not only compatible but also mutually beneficial
   (D) explain the various ways in which industrialized societies can fix prices in order to stabilize the free market
   (E) argue that price-fixing, in one form or another, is an inevitable part of and benefit to the economy of any industrialized society

2. The passage provides information that would answer which of the following questions about price-fixing?

   I. What are some of the ways in which prices can be fixed?
   II. For what products is price-fixing likely to be more profitable than the operation of the free market?
   III. Is price-fixing more common in socialist industrialized societies or in nonsocialist industrialized societies?

   (A) I only
   (B) III only
   (C) I and II only
   (D) II and III only
   (E) I, II, and III

GO ON TO THE NEXT PAGE.

3. The author's attitude toward "Most economists in the United States" (line 1) can best be described as

(A) spiteful and envious
(B) scornful and denunciatory
(C) critical and condescending
(D) ambivalent but deferential
(E) uncertain but interested

4. It can be inferred from the author's argument that a price fixed by the seller "seems pernicious" (line 7) because

(A) people do not have confidence in large firms
(B) people do not expect the government to regulate prices
(C) most economists believe that consumers as a group should determine prices
(D) most economists associate fixed prices with communist and socialist economies
(E) most economists believe that no one group should determine prices

5. The suggestion in the passage that price-fixing in industrialized societies is normal arises from the author's statement that price-fixing is

(A) a profitable result of economic development
(B) an inevitable result of the industrial system
(C) the result of a number of carefully organized decisions
(D) a phenomenon common to industrialized and nonindustrialized societies
(E) a phenomenon best achieved cooperatively by government and industry

6. According to the author, price-fixing in nonsocialist countries is often

(A) accidental but productive
(B) illegal but useful
(C) legal and innovative
(D) traditional and rigid
(E) intentional and widespread

7. According to the author, what is the result of the Soviet Union's change in economic policy in the 1970's?

(A) Soviet firms show greater profit.
(B) Soviet firms have less control over the free market.
(C) Soviet firms are able to adjust to technological advances.
(D) Soviet firms have some authority to fix prices.
(E) Soviet firms are more responsive to the free market.

8. With which of the following statements regarding the behavior of large firms in industrialized societies would the author be most likely to agree?

(A) The directors of large firms will continue to anticipate the demand for products.
(B) The directors of large firms are less interested in achieving a predictable level of profit than in achieving a large profit.
(C) The directors of large firms will strive to reduce the costs of their products.
(D) Many directors of large firms believe that the government should establish the prices that will be charged for products.
(E) Many directors of large firms believe that the price charged for products is likely to increase annually.

9. In the passage, the author is primarily concerned with

(A) predicting the consequences of a practice
(B) criticizing a point of view
(C) calling attention to recent discoveries
(D) proposing a topic for research
(E) summarizing conflicting opinions

GO ON TO THE NEXT PAGE.

The discoveries of the white dwarf, the neutron star, and the black hole, coming well after the discovery of the red giant, are among the most exciting developments in decades because they
(5) may well present physicists with their greatest challenge since the failure of classical mechanics. In the life cycle of a star, after all of the hydrogen and helium fuel has been burned, the delicate balance between the outward nuclear radiation pres-
(10) sure and the stable gravitational force becomes disturbed and slow contraction begins. As compression increases, a very dense plasma forms. If the initial star had a mass of less than 1.4 solar masses (1.4 times the mass of our sun), the pro-
(15) cess ceases at a density of 1,000 tons per cubic inch, and the star becomes a white dwarf. However, if the star was originally more massive, the white dwarf plasma cannot resist the gravitational pressures, and, in a rapid collapse, all nuclei of
(20) the star are converted to a gas of free neutrons. Gravitational attraction compresses this neutron gas rapidly until a density of 10^9 tons per cubic inch is reached; at this point the strong nuclear force resists further contraction. If the mass of
(25) the star was between 1.4 and a few solar masses, the process stops here, and we have a neutron star.

But if the original star was more massive than a few solar masses, even the strong nuclear forces
(30) cannot resist the gravitational crunch. The neutrons are forced into one another to form heavier hadrons—and these in turn coalesce to form heavier entities, of which we as yet know nothing. At this point, a complete collapse of
(35) the stellar mass occurs; existing theories predict a collapse to infinite density and infinitely small dimensions. Well before this, however, the surface gravitational force would become so strong that no signal could ever leave the star—
(40) any photon emitted would fall back under gravitational attraction—and the star would become a black hole in space.

This gravitational collapse poses a fundamental challenge to physics. When the most widely
(45) accepted theories predict such improbable things as infinite density and infinitely small dimensions, it simply means that we are missing some vital insight. This last happened in physics in the 1930's, when we faced a fundamental paradox
(50) concerning atomic structure. At that time, it was recognized that electrons moved in stable orbits about nuclei in atoms. However, it was also recognized that if a charge is accelerated, as it

must be to remain in orbit, it radiates energy;
(55) so, theoretically, the electron would be expected eventually to spiral into the nucleus and destroy the atom. Studies centered around this paradox led to the development of quantum mechanics. It may well be that an equivalent advance awaits us in
(60) investigating the theoretical problems presented by the phenomenon of gravitational collapse.

10. The primary purpose of the passage is to

   (A) offer new explanations for the collapse of stars
   (B) explain the origins of black holes, neutron stars, and white dwarfs
   (C) compare the structure of atoms with the structure of the solar system
   (D) explain how the collapse of stars challenges accepted theories of physics
   (E) describe the imbalance between radiation pressure and gravitational force

11. According to the passage, in the final stages of its development our own sun is likely to take the form of a

   (A) white dwarf
   (B) neutron star
   (C) red giant
   (D) gas of free neutrons
   (E) black hole

12. According to the passage, an imbalance arises between nuclear radiation pressure and gravitational force in stars because

   (A) the density of a star increases as it ages
   (B) radiation pressure increases as a star increases in mass
   (C) radiation pressure decreases when a star's fuel has been consumed
   (D) the collapse of a star increases its gravitational force
   (E) a dense plasma decreases the star's gravitational force

GO ON TO THE NEXT PAGE.

13. The author asserts that the discoveries of the white dwarf, the neutron star, and the black hole are significant because these discoveries

(A) demonstrate the probability of infinite density and infinitely small dimensions
(B) pose the most comprehensive and fundamental problem faced by physicists in decades
(C) clarify the paradox suggested by the collapse of electrons into atomic nuclei
(D) establish the relationship between mass and gravitational pressure
(E) assist in establishing the age of the universe by tracing the life histories of stars

14. The passage contains information that answers which of the following questions?

I. What is the density limit of the gravitational collapse of neutron stars?
II. At what point in its life cycle does a star begin to contract?
III. What resists the gravitational collapse of a star?

(A) I only
(B) III only
(C) I and II only
(D) II and III only
(E) I, II, and III

15. The author introduces the discussion of the paradox concerning atomic structure (lines 48-58) in order to

(A) show why it was necessary to develop quantum mechanics
(B) compare the structure of an atom with the structure of a star
(C) demonstrate by analogy that a vital insight in astrophysics is missing
(D) illustrate the contention that improbable things do happen in astrophysics
(E) argue that atoms can collapse if their electrons do not remain in orbit

16. According to the passage, paradoxes are useful in scientific investigation because they

(A) point to the likelihood of impending discoveries
(B) assist scientists in making comparisons with other branches of knowledge
(C) disprove theories that have been called into question
(D) call attention to inadequacies of existing theory
(E) suggest new hypotheses that can be tested by observation

GO ON TO THE NEXT PAGE.

At the time Jane Austen's novels were published—between 1811 and 1818—English literature
was not part of any academic curriculum. In
addition, fiction was under strenuous attack.
(5) Certain religious and political groups felt novels
had the power to make so-called immoral characters so interesting that young readers would
identify with them; these groups also considered
novels to be of little practical use. Even Cole-
(10) ridge, certainly no literary reactionary, spoke for
many when he asserted that "novel-reading occa-
sions the destruction of the mind's powers."
      These attitudes toward novels help explain why
Austen received little attention from early nine-
(15) teenth-century literary critics. (In any case, a
novelist published anonymously, as Austen was,
would not be likely to receive much critical attention.) The literary response that was accorded
her, however, was often as incisive as twentieth-
(20) century criticism. In his attack in 1816 on novel-
istic portrayals "outside of ordinary experience,"
for example, Scott made an insightful remark about
the merits of Austen's fiction. Her novels, wrote
Scott, "present to the reader an accurate and exact
(25) picture of ordinary everyday people and places,
reminiscent of seventeenth-century Flemish
painting." Scott did not use the word "realism,"
but he undoubtedly used a standard of realistic
probability in judging novels. The critic Whately
(30) did not use the word realism either, but he
expressed agreement with Scott's evaluation,
and went on to suggest the possibilities for moral
instruction in what we have called Austen's realistic method. Her characters, wrote Whately,
(35) are persuasive agents for moral truth since they
are ordinary persons "so clearly evoked that we
feel an interest in their fate as if it were our own."
Moral instruction, explained Whately, is more
likely to be effective when conveyed through recog-
(40) nizably human and interesting characters than
when imparted by a sermonizing narrator. Whately
especially praised Austen's ability to create
characters who "mingle goodness and villainy,
weakness and virtue, as in life they are always
(45) mingled." Whately concluded his remarks by
comparing Austen's art of characterization to
Dickens', stating his preference for Austen's.
      Yet the response of nineteenth-century literary
critics to Austen was not always so laudatory, and
(50) often anticipated the reservations of twentieth-
century critics. An example of such a response
was Lewes' complaint in 1859 that Austen's range
of subjects and characters was too narrow. Prais-
ing her verisimilitude, Lewes added that nonethe-
(55) less her focus was too often upon only the unlofty
and the commonplace. (Twentieth-century Marxists, on the other hand, were to complain about
what they saw as her exclusive emphasis on a lofty
upper-middle class.) In any case, having been
(60) rescued by some literary critics from neglect and
indeed gradually lionized by them, Austen steadily
reached, by the mid-nineteenth century, the enviable pinnacle of being considered controversial.

17. The primary purpose of the passage is to

   (A) demonstrate the nineteenth-century preference
       for realistic novels rather than romantic ones
   (B) explain why Jane Austen's novels were not
       included in any academic curriculum in the
       early nineteenth century
   (C) urge a reassessment of Jane Austen's novels
       by twentieth-century literary critics
   (D) describe some of the responses of nineteenth-
       century critics to Jane Austen's novels as
       well as to fiction in general
   (E) argue that realistic character portrayal is the
       novelist's most difficult task as well as the
       aspect of a novel most likely to elicit critical
       response

18. The passage supplies information for answering
    which of the following questions?

   (A) Was Whately aware of Scott's remarks about
       Jane Austen's novels?
   (B) Who is an example of a twentieth-century
       Marxist critic?
   (C) Who is an example of a twentieth-century
       critic who admired Jane Austen's novels?
   (D) What is the author's judgment of Dickens?
   (E) Did Jane Austen express her opinion of those
       nineteenth-century critics who admired her
       novels?

19. The author mentions that English literature "was
    not part of any academic curriculum" (line 3)
    in the early nineteenth century in order to

   (A) emphasize the need for Jane Austen to create
       ordinary, everyday characters in her novels
   (B) give support to those religious and political
       groups that had attacked fiction
   (C) give one reason why Jane Austen's novels
       received little critical attention in the early
       nineteenth century
   (D) suggest the superiority of an informal and
       unsystematized approach to the study of
       literature
   (E) contrast nineteenth-century attitudes toward
       English literature with those toward classical
       literature

GO ON TO THE NEXT PAGE.

20. The passage supplies information to suggest that the religious and political groups mentioned in lines 5-9 and Whately might have agreed that a novel

(A) has little practical use
(B) has the ability to influence the moral values of its readers
(C) is of most interest to readers when representing ordinary human characters
(D) should not be read by young readers
(E) needs the sermonizing of a narrator in order to impart moral truths

21. The author quotes Coleridge (lines 11-12) in order to

(A) refute the literary opinions of certain religious and political groups
(B) make a case for the inferiority of novels to poetry
(C) give an example of a writer who was not a literary reactionary
(D) illustrate the early nineteenth-century belief that fiction was especially appealing to young readers
(E) indicate how widespread was the attack on novels in the early nineteenth century

22. The passage suggests that twentieth-century Marxists would have admired Jane Austen's novels more if the novels, as the Marxists understood them, had

(A) described the values of upper-middle class society
(B) avoided moral instruction and sermonizing
(C) depicted ordinary society in a more flattering light
(D) portrayed characters from more than one class of society
(E) anticipated some of the controversial social problems of the twentieth century

23. It can be inferred from the passage that Whately found Dickens' characters to be

(A) especially interesting to young readers
(B) ordinary persons in recognizably human situations
(C) less liable than Jane Austen's characters to have a realistic mixture of moral qualities
(D) more often villainous and weak than virtuous and good
(E) less susceptible than Jane Austen's characters to the moral judgments of a sermonizing narrator

24. According to the passage, the lack of critical attention paid to Jane Austen can be explained by all of the following nineteenth-century attitudes toward the novel EXCEPT the

(A) assurance felt by many people that novels weakened the mind
(B) certainty shared by many political commentators that the range of novels was too narrow
(C) lack of interest shown by some critics in novels that were published anonymously
(D) fear exhibited by some religious and political groups that novels had the power to portray immoral characters attractively
(E) belief held by some religious and political groups that novels had no practical value

25. The author would most likely agree that which of the following is the best measure of a writer's literary success?

(A) Inclusion of the writer's work in an academic curriculum
(B) Publication of the writer's work in the writer's own name
(C) Existence of debate among critics about the writer's work
(D) Praise of the writer's work by religious and political groups
(E) Ability of the writer's work to appeal to ordinary people

S T O P

IF YOU FINISH BEFORE TIME IS CALLED, YOU MAY CHECK YOUR WORK ON THIS SECTION ONLY.
DO NOT TURN TO ANY OTHER SECTION IN THE TEST.

Answer Key for Sample Test Section 1

READING COMPREHENSION

1. E	14. E
2. A	15. C
3. C	16. D
4. C	17. D
5. B	18. A
6. E	19. C
7. D	20. B
8. A	21. E
9. B	22. D
10. D	23. C
11. A	24. B
12. C	25. C
13. B	

Explanatory Material: Reading Comprehension

The following discussion of Reading Comprehension is intended to familiarize you with the most efficient and effective approaches to the kinds of problems common to Reading Comprehension. The particular questions on the sample test sections in this chapter are generally representative of the kinds of questions you will encounter in this section of the GMAT. Remember that it is the problem-solving strategy that is important, not the specific details of a particular question.

Sample Test Section 1

1. The primary purpose of the passage is to

    (A) refute the theory that the free market plays a useful role in the development of industrialized societies
    (B) suggest methods by which economists and members of the government of the United States can recognize and combat price-fixing by large firms
    (C) show that in industrialized societies price-fixing and the operation of the free market are not only compatible but also mutually beneficial
    (D) explain the various ways in which industrialized societies can fix prices in order to stabilize the free market
    (E) argue that price-fixing, in one form or another, is an inevitable part of and benefit to the economy of any industrialized society

The best answer is E. The author contends in lines 7-15 that price-fixing is normal and beneficial in industrialized societies. The author proceeds to support this assertion with descriptions of various forms of price-fixing in various kinds of industrialized societies (lines 23-29, 36-42, and 48-59).

Moreover, in lines 42-47, in the context of a discussion of nonsocialist countries other than the United States, the author indirectly restates the argument in favor of price-fixing.

2. The passage provides information that would answer which of the following questions about price-fixing?

    I. What are some of the ways in which prices can be fixed?
    II. For what products is price-fixing likely to be more profitable than the operation of the free market?
    III. Is price-fixing more common in socialist industrialized societies or in nonsocialist industrialized societies?

    (A) I only
    (B) III only
    (C) I and II only
    (D) II and III only
    (E) I, II, and III

This question asks whether one or more of the questions identified by Roman numerals can be answered on the basis of the information given in the passage. In questions of this kind, each part identified by a Roman numeral must be considered individually. Question I can be answered by information in lines 26-27, 31-32, 38-42, and 50-53 of the passage, which mention some different ways of fixing prices. Questions II and III cannot be answered from information provided by the passage. The best answer, therefore, is A (I only).

3. The author's attitude toward "Most economists in the United States" (line 1) can best be described as

    (A) spiteful and envious
    (B) scornful and denunciatory
    (C) critical and condescending
    (D) ambivalent but deferential
    (E) uncertain but interested

The best answer is C. Determining the author's attitude toward a topic requires locating all references to the topic in the passage and considering both the literal meanings and the connotations of the words used concerning the topic. Thus, the author refers to "most economists" or "economists in the United States" or "those economists" in lines 1-2, 29-32, 33-37, and 53-54. The author describes them as "captivated by the spell of the free market," as failing to see price-fixing when it occurs, as failing to consider the economies of nonsocialist countries other than the United States, and as mistakenly "hailing" price-fixing in the Soviet Union as a return to the free market. The choice that best describes these references is "critical and condescending."

4. It can be inferred from the author's argument that a price fixed by the seller "seems pernicious" (line 7) because

   (A) people do not have confidence in large firms
   (B) people do not expect the government to regulate prices
   (C) most economists believe that consumers as a group should determine prices
   (D) most economists associate fixed prices with communist and socialist economies
   (E) most economists believe that no one group should determine prices

The best answer is C. Lines 1-7 allow one to infer that it is to "Most economists" (line 1) that a price fixed by the seller "seems pernicious," and that these economists consider price-fixing pernicious because they believe that only the "aggregate of consumers" (line 7) should establish prices.

5. The suggestion in the passage that price-fixing in industrialized societies is normal arises from the author's statement that price-fixing is

   (A) a profitable result of economic development
   (B) an inevitable result of the industrial system
   (C) the result of a number of carefully organized decisions
   (D) a phenomenon common to industrialized and nonindustrialized societies
   (E) a phenomenon best achieved cooperatively by government and industry

The best answer is B, based on lines 11-15, which state that price-fixing is normal in all industrialized societies because the industrial system provides price-fixing "as an effortless consequence of its own development."

6. According to the author, price-fixing in nonsocialistic countries is often

   (A) accidental but productive
   (B) illegal but useful
   (C) legal and innovative
   (D) traditional and rigid
   (E) intentional and widespread

The best answer is E, based on lines 38 ("intentional price-fixing") and 41-42 ("commonplace").

7. According to the author, what is the result of the Soviet Union's change in economic policy in the 1970's?

   (A) Soviet firms show greater profit.
   (B) Soviet firms have less control over the free market.
   (C) Soviet firms are able to adjust to technological advances.
   (D) Soviet firms have some authority to fix prices.
   (E) Soviet firms are more responsive to the free market.

The best answer is D. In lines 49-53, the author states that, in the early 1970's, the Soviet Union gave firms some "flexibility in adjusting prices." In lines 58-59, the author states that what these firms have in fact been given is "the power to fix prices." Thus, the result of the Soviet Union's change in economic policy in the 1970's is choice D, "Soviet firms have some authority to fix prices."

8. With which of the following statements regarding the behavior of large firms in industrialized societies would the author be most likely to agree?

   (A) The directors of large firms will continue to anticipate the demand for products.
   (B) The directors of large firms are less interested in achieving a predictable level of profit than in achieving a large profit.
   (C) The directors of large firms will strive to reduce the costs of their products.
   (D) Many directors of large firms believe that the government should establish the prices that will be charged for products.
   (E) Many directors of large firms believe that the price charged for products is likely to increase annually.

The best answer is A. The author discusses the behavior of large firms in industrialized societies in lines 15-29. In lines 26-29, the author refers to the firms' "common interest in a stable demand for products." It can be inferred from these references that the author believes that the directors of large firms currently anticipate the demand for products. Since the author describes price-fixing as an ongoing phenomenon (lines 11-29), it can be inferred that the author would be likely to agree that the large firms' directors will also continue to anticipate the demand for products.

9. In the passage, the author is primarily concerned with

   (A) predicting the consequences of a practice
   (B) criticizing a point of view
   (C) calling attention to recent discoveries
   (D) proposing a topic for research
   (E) summarizing conflicting opinions

The best answer is B. Throughout the passage, the author criticizes the point of view of "most economists in the United States"—those who believe that the free market is best and that price-fixing is pernicious. Thus, the first paragraph argues that price-fixing is normal and valuable in all industrialized countries. The second paragraph argues that the experience of nonsocialist countries other than the United States provides no support for the point of view of these economists. The third paragraph argues that these economists are wrong in thinking that the Soviet Union has moved toward a free market. Thus, it can be inferred that the author's primary concern is to criticize this point of view.

10. The primary purpose of the passage is to

   (A) offer new explanations for the collapse of stars
   (B) explain the origins of black holes, neutron stars, and white dwarfs
   (C) compare the structure of atoms with the structure of the solar system
   (D) explain how the collapse of stars challenges accepted theories of physics
   (E) describe the imbalance between radiation pressure and gravitational force

The best answer is D. The central idea of the passage is that the final possible stage in the gravitational collapse of a star, a black hole, produces a state of affairs in which "widely accepted theories predict . . . improbable things" (lines 44-45). This situation, the author points out, "may well present physicists with their greatest challenge" since the failure of classical physics (lines 5-6) and "poses a fundamental challenge to physics" (lines 43-44). The idea of challenge is reinforced by the analogy drawn between this situation in physics and the atomic structure paradox of the 1930's. Thus the whole purpose of the passage is to explain the process of gravitational collapse and to suggest how this challenges accepted theories in physics.

11. According to the passage, in the final stages of its development our own sun is likely to take the form of a

   (A) white dwarf
   (B) neutron star
   (C) red giant
   (D) gas of free neutrons
   (E) black hole

The best answer is A because lines 12-16 indicate that all stars with a mass less than 1.4 times the mass of our sun will collapse into white dwarfs. As our sun fits this condition, it must eventually collapse into a white dwarf.

12. According to the passage, an imbalance arises between nuclear radiation pressure and gravitational force in stars because

   (A) the density of a star increases as it ages
   (B) radiation pressure increases as a star increases in mass
   (C) radiation pressure decreases when a star's fuel has been consumed
   (D) the collapse of a star increases its gravitational force
   (E) a dense plasma decreases the star's gravitational force

The best answer is C because lines 7-11 indicate that a disturbance in the balance between outward nuclear radiation and stable inward gravitational force occurs "after all of the hydrogen and helium fuel has been burned." Since "slow contraction begins" after the fuel is consumed, and since the gravitational force is stable, the imbalance must be caused by a lessening in the outward radiation pressure.

13. The author asserts that the discoveries of the white dwarf, the neutron star, and the black hole are significant because these discoveries

   (A) demonstrate the probability of infinite density and infinitely small dimensions
   (B) pose the most comprehensive and fundamental problem faced by physicists in decades
   (C) clarify the paradox suggested by the collapse of electrons into atomic nuclei
   (D) establish the relationship between mass and gravitational pressure
   (E) assist in establishing the age of the universe by tracing the life histories of stars

The best answer is B. Lines 1-6 state that the discoveries of the white dwarf, the neutron star, and the black hole are among the most exciting developments in recent physics and "may well present physicists with their greatest challenge since the failure of classical mechanics." This "challenge" is explained in the rest of the passage, where it is described as "fundamental" (line 43), as being of a magnitude that was last seen in physics "in the 1930's" (lines 48-49), and as conceivably leading to an advance the equivalent of the development of quantum mechanics (lines 57-61). Thus the author considers the discoveries significant because they pose problems of a magnitude that physics has not seen since the 1930's.

14. The passage contains information that answers which of the following questions?

   I. What is the density limit of the gravitational collapse of neutron stars?
   II. At what point in its life cycle does a star begin to contract?
   III. What resists the gravitational collapse of a star?

   (A) I only
   (B) III only
   (C) I and II only
   (D) II and III only
   (E) I, II, and III

The best answer is E. Question I is answered in lines 21-23, where it is stated that in the case of neutron stars, gravitational compression continues until a density of 10^9 tons per cubic inch is reached. Question II is answered in lines 7-11, where it is stated that stars begin to contract after all hydrogen and helium fuel has been burned. Question III has three answers, depending on what stage a star is in. First, outward nuclear radiation resists gravitational collapse (lines 8-10); next the white dwarf plasma resists gravitational collapse (lines 18-19); and finally the strong nuclear force resists gravitational collapse (lines 21-24). Thus all three questions are answered in the passage and E is the correct choice.

15. The author introduces the discussion of the paradox concerning atomic structure (lines 48-58) in order to

(A) show why it was necessary to develop quantum mechanics
(B) compare the structure of an atom with the structure of a star
(C) demonstrate by analogy that a vital insight in astrophysics is missing
(D) illustrate the contention that improbable things do happen in astrophysics
(E) argue that atoms can collapse if their electrons do not remain in orbit

The best answer is C. In lines 44-48 the author introduces the discussion of the atomic structure paradox by noting that when improbable things happen it means that physicists "are missing some vital insight." The author then states that "This last happened in physics in the 1930's, when we faced a fundamental paradox concerning atomic structure" (lines 48-50). The author closes the discussion by suggesting "that an equivalent advance awaits us" (line 59) in astrophysics. Together these imply that the author sees an analogy between the atomic structure paradox and the gravitational collapse problem in astrophysics, and anticipates that the second will be solved in the same way as the first, by a new vital insight.

16. According to the passage, paradoxes are useful in scientific investigation because they

(A) point to the likelihood of impending discoveries
(B) assist scientists in making comparisons with other branches of knowledge
(C) disprove theories that have been called into question
(D) call attention to inadequacies of existing theory
(E) suggest new hypotheses that can be tested by observation

The best answer is D. Two paradoxes are described in the passage, the atomic structure problem of the 1930's and the gravitational collapse problem, and both are depicted as calling attention to problems in existing scientific theories. In lines 57-58 the author notes that work in atomic structure physics focused on the inconsistencies of the existing theories, and in lines 44-48 that the discoveries of such paradoxical phenomena as infinite density and infinitely small dimensions tell physicists that "some vital insight" is missing within existing theory. Thus in both cases the paradoxes serve to point out problems with existing theories and to draw the attention of physicists toward solving them.

17. The primary purpose of the passage is to

(A) demonstrate the nineteenth-century preference for realistic novels rather than romantic ones
(B) explain why Jane Austen's novels were not included in any academic curriculum in the early nineteenth century
(C) urge a reassessment of Jane Austen's novels by twentieth-century literary critics
(D) describe some of the responses of nineteenth-century critics to Jane Austen's novels as well as to fiction in general
(E) argue that realistic character portrayal is the novelist's most difficult task as well as the aspect of a novel most likely to elicit critical response

The best answer is D. When asked to identify the primary purpose of a passage, you must select the answer choice that states what the passage, as a whole, achieves. Choice D correctly identifies the passage as descriptive and goes on to accurately state the broad categories of things described. The passage does not contrast realistic and romantic novels, as choice A suggests. Austen's absence from academic curricula is mentioned only to support a larger point; thus, choice B is incorrect. Choice C is incorrect because the passage judges twentieth-century assessments satisfactory, leaving no reason to urge reassessment. Nothing is mentioned about the relative difficulty of realistic character portrayal or its tendency to attract more criticism than other aspects of novels; thus choice E can be eliminated.

18. The passage supplies information for answering which of the following questions?

(A) Was Whately aware of Scott's remarks about Jane Austen's novels?
(B) Who is an example of a twentieth-century Marxist critic?
(C) Who is an example of a twentieth-century critic who admired Jane Austen's novels?
(D) What is the author's judgment of Dickens?
(E) Did Jane Austen express her opinion of those nineteenth-century critics who admired her novels?

The best answer is A. In order to answer this question, you should work through each of the choices, checking whether or not the passage supplies enough information to answer the question posed in the choice. Lines 30-31 tell us that Whately "expressed agreement with Scott's evaluation" of Austen's fictions; in order to agree, Whately must have been aware of Scott's remarks. Thus, an answer to the question posed in choice A is provided. Although the passage mentions Marxists, none is specifically named, thus choice B can be eliminated. The same reasoning eliminates choice C. Choice D can be eliminated because, while Whately's opinion *is* mentioned, the author's own is not. Choice E can be eliminated, because the passage nowhere indicates that Austen was even aware of criticism of her work.

19. The author mentions that English literature "was not part of any academic curriculum" (line 3) in the early nineteenth century in order to

    (A) emphasize the need for Jane Austen to create ordinary, everyday characters in her novels
    (B) give support to those religious and political groups that had attacked fiction
    (C) give one reason why Jane Austen's novels received little critical attention in the early nineteenth century
    (D) suggest the superiority of an informal and unsystematized approach to the study of literature
    (E) contrast nineteenth-century attitudes toward English literature with those toward classical literature

The best answer is C. This question asks you to identify a reason for the author's selection of a particular supporting detail in the passage. You can approach this question by first re-reading the part of the passage cited. Then, determine the reason for the author's selection and pick the answer choice that most nearly states what you consider the reason. Lines 13-15 are a straightforward indication of the author's reason for mentioning the absence of English literature in academic curricula: it is one indication of "attitudes . . . [that] help explain" why Austen was neglected by critics around the time her fiction was published. Choice C is very nearly a restatement of that idea.

20. The passage supplies information to suggest that the religious and political groups mentioned in lines 5-9 and Whately might have agreed that a novel

    (A) has little practical use
    (B) has the ability to influence the moral values of its readers
    (C) is of most interest to readers when representing ordinary human characters
    (D) should not be read by young readers
    (E) needs the sermonizing of a narrator in order to impart moral truths

The best answer is B. This question requires you to start with a proposition *not* stated in the passage, i.e., that Whately and the groups mentioned share an opinion. The answer choices present possible opinions. Using the information given in the passage, you must determine which of the possible opinions could have been held in common. The passage indicates that the religious and political groups feared that readers would identify with immoral characters. It suggests that Whately thought that novels could be vehicles of moral instruction. Although they disagree about the value of such influence, they agree that novels can influence moral behavior. The other choices contain opinions that one or the other, but not both, holds (choices A, C, D), or an opinion that can not be attributed to either (choice E).

21. The author quotes Coleridge (lines 11-12) in order to

    (A) refute the literary opinions of certain religious and political groups
    (B) make a case for the inferiority of novels to poetry
    (C) give an example of a writer who was not a literary reactionary
    (D) illustrate the early nineteenth-century belief that fiction was especially appealing to young readers
    (E) indicate how widespread was the attack on novels in the early nineteenth century

The best answer is E. This question asks you to identify a reason for the author's choice of a particular quotation in the passage. You can approach the question by first determining the reason and then selecting the answer choice that most nearly states what you consider that reason. The reference to Coleridge appears in a paragraph devoted to outlining the extent of opposition to novel-reading at the time of the publication of Austen's fiction. The phrase "Even Coleridge, certainly no literary reactionary . . ." (lines 9-10) suggests that Coleridge might be expected to differ, but the quotation demonstrates that Coleridge, too, was suspicious of novels. It illustrates the point that fiction was under strenuous, and widespread, attack. Choice E is very nearly a restatement of that idea.

22. The passage suggests that twentieth-century Marxists would have admired Jane Austen's novels more if the novels, as the Marxists understood them, had

    (A) described the values of upper-middle class society
    (B) avoided moral instruction and sermonizing
    (C) depicted ordinary society in a more flattering light
    (D) portrayed characters from more than one class of society
    (E) anticipated some of the controversial social problems of the twentieth century

The best answer is D. The question requires you to determine a quality that Marxists find admirable in fiction, but that is missing from Austen's fiction. You should first look for the specific reference to Marxists. Lines 56-59 indicate that Marxists criticize Austen's fiction for its exclusive focus on the upper-middle class. This suggests that a Marxist criterion for judging novels involves the degree to which a novel represents a variety of social classes. If Austen's novels had portrayed characters from more than one class of society, as choice D states, it can be inferred that Marxists would value them more highly. Choice A is incorrect, because it states precisely what the Marxists object to. There is no information to support any of the remaining choices.

23. It can be inferred from the passage that Whately found Dickens' characters to be

(A) especially interesting to young readers
(B) ordinary persons in recognizably human situations
(C) less liable than Jane Austen's characters to have a realistic mixture of moral qualities
(D) more often villainous and weak than virtuous and good
(E) less susceptible than Jane Austen's characters to the moral judgments of a sermonizing narrator

The best answer is C. This question requires you to infer Whately's opinion of Dickens' characters. It is important to note that Dickens' method of characterization is mentioned only in contrast to Austen's. Lines 41-45 indicate that Whately particularly admired in Austen's characters a mingling of "goodness and villainy, weakness and virtue, as in life they are always mingled." The passage then indicates that Whately preferred Austen's "art of characterization" to that of Dickens. Such a preference implies a significant difference between the two writers, suggesting that Dickens' method lacks a central characteristic of Austen's, that is, portrayal of characters with realistically mixed virtues and flaws. Choice C is very nearly a restatement of that idea.

24. According to the passage, the lack of critical attention paid to Jane Austen can be explained by all of the following nineteenth-century attitudes toward the novel EXCEPT the

(A) assurance felt by many people that novels weakened the mind
(B) certainty shared by many political commentators that the range of novels was too narrow
(C) lack of interest shown by some critics in novels that were published anonymously
(D) fear exhibited by some religious and political groups that novels had the power to portray immoral characters attractively
(E) belief held by some religious and political groups that novels had no practical value

The best answer is B. This question requires you to evaluate each of the answer choices and to judge which is not mentioned in the passage as an explanation for the critical neglect Austen suffered in the nineteenth century. Each of the answer choices *could* conceivably serve as an explanation, so it is important that you carefully consider what the passage actually mentions. The explanations offered in the first paragraph of the passage are those stated in choices A, D, and E. Lines 16-18 indicate that books published anonymously were unlikely to be reviewed; thus, choice C is also one of the explanations cited in the passage. The passage does not suggest that concerns about the narrow range of Austen's novels resulted in critical neglect; in fact, the contrary is suggested (lines 51-56). Thus, B is the best choice.

25. The author would most likely agree that which of the following is the best measure of a writer's literary success?

(A) Inclusion of the writer's work in an academic curriculum
(B) Publication of the writer's work in the writer's own name
(C) Existence of debate among critics about the writer's work
(D) Praise of the writer's work by religious and political groups
(E) Ability of the writer's work to appeal to ordinary people

The best answer is C. This question requires you to determine, on the basis of ideas presented in the passage, what the author might think of an idea *not* presented in the passage, in this case, what constitutes the best measure of literary success. Although choices A, D, and E are plausible measures of a writer's success, nothing in the passage suggests that the author considers any of them "best," while choice B is not clearly a criterion for judgment. Lines 61-63, however, indicate that Austen has reached the "enviable pinnacle of being considered controversial," that is, the highest point one can reach. Thus, from the author's point of view, the best measure of an author's success is, as paraphrased in choice C, the existence of debate about the author.

READING COMPREHENSION SAMPLE TEST SECTION 2

30 Minutes
25 Questions

<u>Directions:</u> Each passage in this group is followed by questions based on its content. After reading a passage, choose the best answer to each question and fill in the corresponding oval on the answer sheet. Answer all questions following a passage on the basis of what is <u>stated</u> or <u>implied</u> in that passage.

(This passage was written in 1978.)

Recent years have brought minority-owned businesses in the United States unprecedented opportunities—as well as new and significant risks. Civil rights activists have long argued that one of
(5) the principal reasons why Blacks, Hispanics, and other minority groups have difficulty establishing themselves in business is that they lack access to the sizable orders and subcontracts that are generated by large companies. Now Congress, in appar-
(10) ent agreement, has required by law that businesses awarded federal contracts of more than $500,000 do their best to find minority subcontractors and record their efforts to do so on forms filed with the government. Indeed, some federal and local agen-
(15) cies have gone so far as to set specific percentage goals for apportioning parts of public works contracts to minority enterprises.
Corporate response appears to have been substantial. According to figures collected in 1977,
(20) the total of corporate contracts with minority businesses rose from $77 million in 1972 to $1.1 billion in 1977. The projected total of corporate contracts with minority businesses for the early 1980's is estimated to be over $3 billion per year with no
(25) letup anticipated in the next decade.
Promising as it is for minority businesses, this increased patronage poses dangers for them, too. First, minority firms risk expanding too fast and overextending themselves financially, since most
(30) are small concerns and, unlike large businesses, they often need to make substantial investments in new plants, staff, equipment, and the like in order to perform work subcontracted to them. If, there-after, their subcontracts are for some reason
(35) reduced, such firms can face potentially crippling fixed expenses. The world of corporate purchasing can be frustrating for small entrepreneurs who get requests for elaborate formal estimates and bids. Both consume valuable time and resources, and a
(40) small company's efforts must soon result in orders, or both the morale and the financial health of the business will suffer.
A second risk is that White-owned companies may seek to cash in on the increasing apportion-
(45) ments through formation of joint ventures with minority-owned concerns. Of course, in many instances there are legitimate reasons for joint ventures; clearly, White and minority enterprises can team up to acquire business that neither could
(50) acquire alone. But civil rights groups and minority business owners have complained to Congress about minorities being set up as "fronts" with White back-

ing, rather than being accepted as full partners in legitimate joint ventures.
(55) Third, a minority enterprise that secures the business of one large corporate customer often runs the danger of becoming—and remaining—dependent. Even in the best of circumstances, fierce competition from larger, more established companies
(60) makes it difficult for small concerns to broaden their customer bases; when such firms have nearly guaranteed orders from a single corporate bene-factor, they may truly have to struggle against complacency arising from their current success.

1. The primary purpose of the passage is to

(A) present a commonplace idea and its inac-curacies
(B) describe a situation and its potential drawbacks
(C) propose a temporary solution to a problem
(D) analyze a frequent source of disagreement
(E) explore the implications of a finding

2. The passage supplies information that would answer which of the following questions?

(A) What federal agencies have set percentage goals for the use of minority-owned busi-nesses in public works contracts?
(B) To which government agencies must businesses awarded federal contracts report their efforts to find minority subcontractors?
(C) How widespread is the use of minority-owned concerns as "fronts" by White backers seek-ing to obtain subcontracts?
(D) How many more minority-owned businesses were there in 1977 than in 1972 ?
(E) What is one set of conditions under which a small business might find itself financially overextended?

GO ON TO THE NEXT PAGE.

3. According to the passage, civil rights activists maintain that one disadvantage under which minority-owned businesses have traditionally had to labor is that they have

(A) been especially vulnerable to governmental mismanagement of the economy
(B) been denied bank loans at rates comparable to those afforded larger competitors
(C) not had sufficient opportunity to secure business created by large corporations
(D) not been able to advertise in those media that reach large numbers of potential customers
(E) not had adequate representation in the centers of government power

4. The passage suggests that the failure of a large business to have its bids for subcontracts result quickly in orders might cause it to

(A) experience frustration but not serious financial harm
(B) face potentially crippling fixed expenses
(C) have to record its efforts on forms filed with the government
(D) increase its spending with minority subcontractors
(E) revise its procedure for making bids for federal contracts and subcontracts

5. The author implies that a minority-owned concern that does the greater part of its business with one large corporate customer should

(A) avoid competition with larger, more established concerns by not expanding
(B) concentrate on securing even more business from that corporation
(C) try to expand its customer base to avoid becoming dependent on the corporation
(D) pass on some of the work to be done for the corporation to other minority-owned concerns
(E) use its influence with the corporation to promote subcontracting with other minority concerns

6. It can be inferred from the passage that, compared with the requirements of law, the percentage goals set by "some federal and local agencies" (lines 14-15) are

(A) more popular with large corporations
(B) more specific
(C) less controversial
(D) less expensive to enforce
(E) easier to comply with

7. Which of the following, if true, would most weaken the author's assertion that, in the 1970's, corporate response to federal requirements (lines 18-19) was substantial?

(A) Corporate contracts with minority-owned businesses totaled $2 billion in 1979.
(B) Between 1970 and 1972, corporate contracts with minority-owned businesses declined by 25 percent.
(C) The figures collected in 1977 underrepresented the extent of corporate contracts with minority-owned businesses.
(D) The estimate of corporate spending with minority-owned businesses in 1980 is approximately $10 million too high.
(E) The $1.1 billion represented the same percentage of total corporate spending in 1977 as did $77 million in 1972.

8. The passage most likely appeared in

(A) a business magazine
(B) an encyclopedia of Black history to 1945
(C) a dictionary of financial terms
(D) a yearbook of business statistics
(E) an accounting textbook

9. The author would most likely agree with which of the following statements about corporate response to working with minority subcontractors?

(A) Annoyed by the proliferation of "front" organizations, corporations are likely to reduce their efforts to work with minority-owned subcontractors in the near future.
(B) Although corporations showed considerable interest in working with minority businesses in the 1970's, their aversion to government paperwork made them reluctant to pursue many government contracts.
(C) The significant response of corporations in the 1970's is likely to be sustained and conceivably be increased throughout the 1980's.
(D) Although corporations are eager to cooperate with minority-owned businesses, a shortage of capital in the 1970's made substantial response impossible.
(E) The enormous corporate response has all but eliminated the dangers of overexpansion that used to plague small minority-owned businesses.

GO ON TO THE NEXT PAGE.

In strongly territorial birds such as the indigo bunting, song is the main mechanism for securing, defining, and defending an adequate breeding area. When population density is high, only the strongest males can retain a suitable area. The weakest males do not breed or are forced to nest on poor or marginal territories.

During the breeding season, the male indigo bunting sings in his territory; each song lasts two or three seconds with a very short pause between songs. Melodic and rhythmic characteristics are produced by rapid changes in sound frequency and some regularity of silent periods between sounds. These modulated sounds form recognizable units, called figures, each of which is reproduced again and again with remarkable consistency. Despite the large frequency range of these sounds and the rapid frequency changes that the bird makes, the number of figures is very limited. Further, although we found some unique figures in different geographical populations, more than 90 percent of all the figures of birds from different regions are alike. Indigo bunting figures are extremely stable on a geographic basis. In our studies of isolated buntings we found that male indigo buntings are capable of singing many more types of figures than they usually do. Thus, it would seem that they copy their figures from other buntings they hear singing.

Realizing that the ability to distinguish the songs of one species from those of another could be an important factor in the evolution of the figures, we tested species recognition of a song. When we played a tape recording of a lazuli bunting or a painted bunting, male indigo buntings did not respond, even when a dummy of a male indigo bunting was placed near the tape recorder. Playing an indigo bunting song, however, usually brought an immediate response, making it clear that a male indigo bunting can readily distinguish songs of its own species from those of other species.

The role of the song figures in intraspecies recognition was then examined. We created experimental songs composed of new figures by playing a normal song backwards, which changed the detailed forms of the figures without altering frequency ranges or gross temporal features. Since the male indigos gave almost a full response to the backward song, we concluded that a wide range of figure shapes can evoke positive responses. It seems likely, therefore, that a specific configuration is not essential for intraspecies recognition, but it is clear that song figures must conform to a particular frequency range, must be within narrow limits of duration, and must be spaced at particular intervals.

There is evidence that new figures may arise within a population through a slow process of change and selection. This variety is probably a valuable adaptation for survival: if every bird sang only a few types of figures, in dense woods or underbrush a female might have difficulty recognizing her mate's song, and a male might not be able to distinguish a neighbor from a stranger. Our studies led us to conclude that there must be a balance between song stability and conservatism, which lead to clear-cut species recognition, and song variation, which leads to individual recognition.

10. The primary purpose of the passage is to

(A) raise new issues
(B) explain an enigma
(C) refute misconceptions
(D) reconcile differing theories
(E) analyze a phenomenon

11. According to the passage, which of the following is true about the number and general nature of figures sung by the indigo bunting?

(A) They are established at birth.
(B) They evolve slowly as the bird learns.
(C) They are learned from other indigo buntings.
(D) They develop after the bird has been forced onto marginal breeding areas.
(E) They gradually develop through contact with prospective mates.

12. It can be inferred that the investigation that determined the similarity among more than 90 percent of all the figures produced by birds living in different regions was undertaken to answer which of the following questions?

  I. How much variation, if any, is there in the figure types produced by indigo buntings in different locales?
 II. Do local populations of indigo buntings develop their own dialects of figure types?
III. Do figure similarities among indigo buntings decline with increasing geographic separation?

(A) II only
(B) III only
(C) I and II only
(D) II and III only
(E) I, II, and III

GO ON TO THE NEXT PAGE.

13. It can be inferred from the passage that the existence of only a limited number of indigo bunting figures serves primarily to

    (A) ensure species survival by increasing competition among the fittest males for the females
    (B) increase population density by eliminating ambiguity in the figures to which the females must respond
    (C) maintain the integrity of the species by restricting the degree of figure variation and change
    (D) enhance species recognition by decreasing the number of figure patterns to which the bird must respond
    (E) avoid confusion between species by clearly demarcating the figure patterns of each species

14. It can be inferred that a dummy of a male indigo bunting was placed near the tape recorder that played the songs of different species in order to try to

    (A) simulate the conditions in nature
    (B) rule out visual cues as a factor in species recognition
    (C) supply an additional clue to species recognition for the indigo bunting
    (D) provide data on the habits of bunting species other than the indigo bunting
    (E) confound the indigo buntings in the experiment

15. According to the passage, the authors played a normal indigo bunting song backwards in order to determine which of the following?

    (A) What are the limits of the frequency range that will provide recognition by the indigo bunting?
    (B) What is the time duration necessary for recognition by the indigo bunting?
    (C) How specific must a figure shape be for it to be recognized by the indigo bunting?
    (D) How does variation in the pacing of song figures affect the indigo bunting's recognition of the figures?
    (E) Is the indigo bunting responding to cues other than those in the song figures?

16. According to the passage, the indigo buntings' songs function in which of the following ways?

    I. To delineate a breeding area
    II. To defend a breeding area
    III. To identify the birds to their mates

    (A) I only
    (B) II only
    (C) I and III only
    (D) II and III only
    (E) I, II, and III

GO ON TO THE NEXT PAGE.

Despite their many differences of temperament and of literary perspective, Emerson, Thoreau, Hawthorne, Melville, and Whitman share certain beliefs. Common to all these writers is their
(5) humanistic perspective. Its basic premises are that humans are the spiritual center of the universe and that in them alone is the clue to nature, history, and ultimately the cosmos itself. Without denying outright the existence either of a deity or of brute
(10) matter, this perspective nevertheless rejects them as exclusive principles of interpretation and prefers to explain humans and the world in terms of humanity itself. This preference is expressed most clearly in the Transcendentalist principle
(15) that the structure of the universe literally duplicates the structure of the individual self; therefore, all knowledge begins with self-knowledge.

This common perspective is almost always universalized. Its emphasis is not upon the
(20) individual as a particular European or American, but upon the human as universal, freed from the accidents of time, space, birth, and talent. Thus, for Emerson, the "American Scholar" turns out to be simply "Man Thinking"; while, for Whitman,
(25) the "Song of Myself" merges imperceptibly into a song of all the "children of Adam," where "every atom belonging to me as good belongs to you."

Also common to all five writers is the belief that individual virtue and happiness depend upon
(30) self-realization, which, in turn, depends upon the harmonious reconciliation of two universal psychological tendencies: first, the self-asserting impulse of the individual to withdraw, to remain unique and separate, and to be responsible only to
(35) himself or herself, and second, the self-transcending impulse of the individual to embrace the whole world in the experience of a single moment and to know and become one with that world. These conflicting impulses can be seen in the
(40) democratic ethic. Democracy advocates individualism, the preservation of the individual's freedom and self-expression. But the democratic self is torn between the duty to self, which is implied by the concept of liberty, and the duty to society,
(45) which is implied by the concepts of equality and fraternity.

A third assumption common to the five writers is that intuition and imagination offer a surer road to truth than does abstract logic or scientific
(50) method. It is illustrated by their emphasis upon introspection—their belief that the clue to external nature is to be found in the inner world of individual psychology—and by their interpretation of experience as, in essence, symbolic. Both these stresses
(55) presume an organic relationship between the self and the cosmos of which only intuition and imagination can properly take account. These writers' faith in the imagination and in themselves as practitioners of imagination led them to conceive
(60) of the writer as a seer and enabled them to achieve supreme confidence in their own moral and metaphysical insights.

17. The author's discussion of Emerson, Thoreau, Hawthorne, Melville, and Whitman is primarily concerned with explaining

(A) some of their beliefs about the difficulties involved in self-realization
(B) some of their beliefs concerning the world and the place that humanity occupies in the universal order
(C) some of their beliefs concerning the relationship between humanism and democracy
(D) the way some of their beliefs are shaped by differences in temperament and literary outlook
(E) the effects of some of their beliefs on their writings

18. According to the passage, the humanistic perspective of the five writers presupposes which of the following?

I. The structure of the universe can be discovered through self-knowledge.
II. The world can be explained in terms of humanity.
III. The spiritual and the material worlds are incompatible.

(A) I only
(B) II only
(C) I and II only
(D) II and III only
(E) I, II, and III

19. The author quotes Whitman primarily in order to

(A) show that the poet does not agree with Emerson
(B) indicate the way the poet uses the humanist ideal to praise himself
(C) suggest that the poet adapts the basic premises of humanism to his own individual outlook on the world
(D) illustrate a way the poet expresses the relationship of the individual to the humanistic universe
(E) demonstrate that the poet is concerned with the well-being of all humans

GO ON TO THE NEXT PAGE.

20. According to the passage, the five writers object to the scientific method primarily because they think it

(A) is not the best way to obtain an understanding of the relationship between the individual and the cosmos
(B) is so specialized that it leads to an understanding of separate parts of the universe but not of the relationships among those parts
(C) cannot provide an adequate explanation of intuition and imagination
(D) misleads people into believing they have an understanding of truth, when they do not
(E) prevents people from recognizing the symbolic nature of experience

21. Which of the following statements would be compatible with the beliefs of the five writers as described in the passage?

   I. Democracy works as a form of government because every individual is unique.
   II. Nature alone exists, and each person is nothing more than a shadow of that substance which is the world.
   III. The human mind is capable of discovering the meaning of life and understanding the order in the universe.

(A) I only
(B) III only
(C) I and II only
(D) I and III only
(E) I, II, and III

22. It can be inferred that intuition is important to the five writers primarily because it provides them with

(A) information useful for understanding abstract logic and scientific method
(B) the discipline needed in the search for truth
(C) inspiration for their best writing
(D) clues to the interpretation of symbolic experience
(E) the means of resolving conflicts between the self and the world

23. The author discusses "the democratic ethic" (lines 39-46) in order to

(A) explain the relationship between external experience and inner imagination
(B) support the notion that the self contains two conflicting and irreconcilable factions
(C) illustrate the relationship between the self's desire to be individual and its desire to merge with all other selves
(D) elaborate on the concept that the self constantly desires to realize its potential
(E) give an example of the idea that, in order to be happy, the self must reconcile its desires with external reality

24. It can be inferred that the idea of "an organic relationship between the self and the cosmos" (lines 55-56) is necessary to the thinking of the five writers because such a relationship

(A) enables them to assert the importance of the democratic ethic
(B) justifies their concept of the freedom of the individual
(C) sustains their faith in the existence of a deity
(D) is the foundation of their humanistic view of existence
(E) is the basis for their claim that the writer is a seer

25. The passage is most relevant to which of the following areas of study?

(A) Aesthetics and logic
(B) History and literature
(C) Theology and sociology
(D) Anthropology and political science
(E) Linguistics and art

S T O P

**IF YOU FINISH BEFORE TIME IS CALLED, YOU MAY CHECK YOUR WORK ON THIS SECTION ONLY.
DO NOT TURN TO ANY OTHER SECTION IN THE TEST.**

Answer Key for Sample Test Section 2

READING COMPREHENSION

1. B	14. B
2. E	15. C
3. C	16. E
4. A	17. B
5. C	18. C
6. B	19. D
7. E	20. A
8. A	21. B
9. C	22. D
10. E	23. C
11. C	24. D
12. E	25. B
13. D	

Explanatory Material: Reading Comprehension Sample Test Section 2

1. **The primary purpose of the passage is to**

   (A) present a commonplace idea and its inaccuracies
   (B) describe a situation and its potential drawbacks
   (C) propose a temporary solution to a problem
   (D) analyze a frequent source of disagreement
   (E) explore the implications of a finding

The best answer is B. The author begins by describing in the first two paragraphs the new opportunities for minority-owned businesses in the United States engendered by changes in federal law. The author then goes on in the last three paragraphs to point out three specific risks for minority-owned businesses posed by the new federal laws. Thus a situation is described and the drawbacks that it might entail are suggested.

2. **The passage supplies information that would answer which of the following questions?**

   (A) What federal agencies have set percentage goals for the use of minority-owned businesses in public works contracts?
   (B) To which government agencies must businesses awarded federal contracts report their efforts to find minority subcontractors?
   (C) How widespread is the use of minority-owned concerns as "fronts" by White backers seeking to obtain subcontracts?
   (D) How many more minority-owned businesses were there in 1977 than in 1972?
   (E) What is one set of conditions under which a small business might find itself financially overextended?

The best answer is E. Choices A and B can be eliminated because the passage mentions only "some federal and local agencies" (lines 14-15), not any specific ones. C and D can be eliminated because no specific data are provided about minority-owned firms except in the area of the value of their corporate contracts. Only E is clearly answered by the passage; the author describes in lines 33-36 the possibility of a reduction in subcontracts leaving a small business that had just expanded (lines 28-33) financially overextended.

3. **According to the passage, civil rights activists maintain that one disadvantage under which minority-owned businesses have traditionally had to labor is that they have**

   (A) been especially vulnerable to governmental mismanagement of the economy
   (B) been denied bank loans at rates comparable to those afforded larger competitors
   (C) not had sufficient opportunity to secure business created by large corporations
   (D) not been able to advertise in those media that reach large numbers of potential customers
   (E) not had adequate representation in the centers of government power

The best answer is C because lines 4-9 state that civil rights activists have long argued that a problem for members of minority groups who are attempting to establish businesses has been that minority groups "lack access to the sizable orders and subcontracts that are generated by large companies."

4. **The passage suggests that the failure of a large business to have its bids for subcontracts result quickly in orders might cause it to**

   (A) experience frustration but not serious financial harm
   (B) face potentially crippling fixed expenses
   (C) have to record its efforts on forms filed with the government
   (D) increase its spending with minority subcontractors
   (E) revise its procedure for making bids for federal contracts and subcontracts

The best answer is A. In lines 28-36 the author points out that small businesses might have to make substantial new investments to meet the demands of a large subcontract, and that small businesses could thus "face potentially crippling fixed expenses." Large businesses, the author suggests in line 30, would not have to make such investments, and therefore would not face serious financial consequences. In lines 39-42 the author notes that if a company is small, it must get orders quickly, or "the financial health of the business will suffer." Thus, although any firm would suffer if it did not receive orders for subcontracts quickly, only small firms facing large fixed expenses would experience serious financial harm. Large firms do not face or can handle these expenses.

5. The author implies that a minority-owned concern that does the greater part of its business with one large corporate customer should

   (A) avoid competition with larger, more established concerns by not expanding
   (B) concentrate on securing even more business from that corporation
   (C) try to expand its customer base to avoid becoming dependent on the corporation
   (D) pass on some of the work to be done for the corporation to other minority-owned concerns
   (E) use its influence with the corporation to promote subcontracting with other minority concerns

The best answer is C. The passage states in lines 55-57 that becoming dependent on one large corporate customer constitutes a "danger" for a minority enterprise. It is then noted in lines 58-64 that it is "difficult for small concerns to broaden their customer bases" even at the best of times, but that it is important that they "struggle against complacency." Thus, the author implies that a minority firm should attempt to escape the danger of dependency on a single corporate customer, and that in order to do so such a firm must try to expand its customer base.

6. It can be inferred from the passage that, compared with the requirements of law, the percentage goals set by "some federal and local agencies" (lines 14-15) are

   (A) more popular with large corporations
   (B) more specific
   (C) less controversial
   (D) less expensive to enforce
   (E) easier to comply with

The best answer is B. Lines 9-14 state that the law mandates that businesses simply "do their best" to use minority subcontractors and report their efforts to the federal government. In contrast, the author notes in lines 14-17 that some federal and local agencies have gone much further, "so far as to set specific percentage goals." Thus, it can be inferred that the author considers the percentage goals of the federal and local agencies to be more specific than the more general requirements of federal law.

7. Which of the following, if true, would most weaken the author's assertion that, in the 1970's, corporate response to federal requirements (lines 18-19) was substantial?

   (A) Corporate contracts with minority-owned businesses totaled $2 billion in 1979.
   (B) Between 1970 and 1972, corporate contracts with minority-owned businesses declined by 25 percent.
   (C) The figures collected in 1977 underrepresented the extent of corporate contracts with minority-owned businesses.
   (D) The estimate of corporate spending with minority-owned businesses in 1980 is approximately $10 million too high.
   (E) The $1.1 billion represented the same percentage of total corporate spending in 1977 as did $77 million in 1972.

The best answer is E. The author's assertion that, in the 1970's, the corporate response to federal requirements was substantial rests on the fact that "corporate contracts with minority businesses rose from $77 million in 1972 to $1.1 billion in 1977" (lines 20-22). The author's claim that such a rise indicates a substantial corporate response to federal requirements would be weakened if other factors were at work. Such a condition is presented only in choice E, where it is stated that the percentage of corporate spending remained constant; this implies that the increased dollar amount allocated to minority businesses was due simply to general economic growth, and that minority businesses proportionally gained nothing during those years.

8. The passage most likely appeared in

   (A) a business magazine
   (B) an encyclopedia of Black history to 1945
   (C) a dictionary of financial terms
   (D) a yearbook of business statistics
   (E) an accounting textbook

The best answer is A. The passage presents general information about a business topic in a manner accessible to the interested reading public. The language is not technical, the statistics are few, and yet the focus is resolutely on a contemporary business phenomenon. This style suggests a publication oriented toward presenting general news and analysis of the business world to the interested public. Of the five choices only A does this. B focuses on the wrong time period, C on a task—definition of financial terms—not performed by the passage, and D and E on information not present to any significant degree in the passage.

9. The author would most likely agree with which of the following statements about corporate response to working with minority subcontractors?

   (A) Annoyed by the proliferation of "front" organizations, corporations are likely to reduce their efforts to work with minority-owned subcontractors in the near future.
   (B) Although corporations showed considerable interest in working with minority businesses in the 1970's, their aversion to government paperwork made them reluctant to pursue many government contracts.
   (C) The significant response of corporations in the 1970's is likely to be sustained and conceivably be increased throughout the 1980's.
   (D) Although corporations are eager to cooperate with minority-owned businesses, a shortage of capital in the 1970's made substantial response impossible.
   (E) The enormous corporate response has all but eliminated the dangers of overexpansion that used to plague small minority-owned businesses.

The best answer is C, because the author states in lines 22-25 that "no letup [is] anticipated" in the projected total of corporate contracts with minority businesses throughout the next decade. There is no support in the passage for any of the other choices.

10. The primary purpose of the passage is to

    (A) raise new issues
    (B) explain an enigma
    (C) refute misconceptions
    (D) reconcile differing theories
    (E) analyze a phenomenon

The best answer is E. When asked to identify the primary purpose of a passage, you should select the answer choice that states what the passage as a whole achieves. The passage is primarily a discussion of a natural phenomenon, the song of the male indigo bunting. This discussion focuses on the components, form, and function of the song. Such a discussion can correctly be called an analysis, and E presents such a choice. There is no evidence in the passage that suggests that the issues presented are new (choice A), or that any of the matters discussed are enigmas or misconceptions (choices B and C). The discussion is not primarily a presentation of theory but of empirical evidence and observed phenomena; thus, choice D is not correct.

11. According to the passage, which of the following is true about the number and general nature of figures sung by the indigo bunting?

    (A) They are established at birth.
    (B) They evolve slowly as the bird learns.
    (C) They are learned from other indigo buntings.
    (D) They develop after the bird has been forced onto marginal breeding areas.
    (E) They gradually develop through contact with prospective mates.

The best answer is C. To answer this question, you should examine each of the choices to determine which makes an accurate statement, based on evidence in the passage, about the number and general nature of the figures sung by the indigo bunting. In the second paragraph, the author concludes that male indigo buntings in a natural environment copy figures from other buntings, a fact that explains why the number and general nature of figures remain limited. Thus, choice C is true and is the intended answer. The other choices are plausible statements, but they are not asserted in the passage.

12. It can be inferred that the investigation that determined the similarity among more than 90 percent of all the figures produced by birds living in different regions was undertaken to answer which of the following questions?

    I. How much variation, if any, is there in the figure types produced by indigo buntings in different locales?
    II. Do local populations of indigo buntings develop their own dialects of figure types?
    III. Do figure similarities among indigo buntings decline with increasing geographic separation?

    (A) II only
    (B) III only
    (C) I and II only
    (D) II and III only
    (E) I, II, and III

The best answer is E. The format of this question requires you to evaluate each of the questions designated with Roman numerals separately and carefully. In this question, you must infer from the passage what information the investigation discussed in the second paragraph was designed to obtain. According to the passage, the investigation yielded information that permitted researchers to draw conclusions about variation in figure types, about unique figures among birds, and about the effects of increasing geographic separation. The second paragraph describes some of the strategies used by the investigators to obtain precisely this information. I, II, and III are all questions that the investigators set out to explore, and E is the correct answer.

13. It can be inferred from the passage that the existence of only a limited number of indigo bunting figures serves primarily to

(A) ensure species survival by increasing competition among the fittest males for the females
(B) increase population density by eliminating ambiguity in the figures to which the females must respond
(C) maintain the integrity of the species by restricting the degree of figure variation and change
(D) enhance species recognition by decreasing the number of figure patterns to which the bird must respond
(E) avoid confusion between species by clearly demarcating the figure patterns of each species

The best answer is D. This question requires you to determine why the number of indigo bunting figures is as limited as it is. In order to make this determination, it is necessary to consider several facts presented in the passage and their relationship to each other. The third paragraph indicates that the songs serve as a means of recognition for members of the same species. The fourth paragraph discusses the strict limitations on the ways in which figures are produced. The last paragraph indicates that "song stability and conservatism," that is, limits to the numbers of figures and variations, are essential for clear-cut species recognition. Choice D is a statement of that idea.

14. It can be inferred that a dummy of a male indigo bunting was placed near the tape recorder that played the songs of different species in order to try to

(A) simulate the conditions in nature
(B) rule out visual cues as a factor in species recognition
(C) supply an additional clue to species recognition for the indigo bunting
(D) provide data on the habits of bunting species other than the indigo bunting
(E) confound the indigo buntings in the experiment

The best answer is B. This question requires you to determine the reason for the researcher's use of a dummy male indigo bunting. The passage indicates that the sight of the dummy was not enough to cause subject male indigo buntings to react to songs of lazuli and painted buntings. This result suggests that the indigo bunting identifies others of the species on the basis of song rather than sight. The fact that the researchers performed an additional check in which an indigo bunting song, did, in fact, provoke responses from the subject indigos further rules out visual clues.

15. According to the passage, the authors played a normal indigo bunting song backwards in order to determine which of the following?

(A) What are the limits of the frequency range that will provide recognition by the indigo bunting?
(B) What is the time duration necessary for recognition by the indigo bunting?
(C) How specific must a figure shape be for it to be recognized by the indigo bunting?
(D) How does variation in the pacing of song figures affect the indigo bunting's recognition of the figures?
(E) Is the indigo bunting responding to cues other than those in the song figures?

The best answer is C. The fourth paragraph states that the researchers played songs backwards, a technique that changed the forms of the figures without changing frequency ranges or gross temporal features. Since figure shape, therefore, is the only element to be altered, the results of the experiment would give information about the role of figure shape in species recognition. Choice C is the only choice that addresses the question of figure shapes, and, in fact, the fourth paragraph indicates that the experiment was designed to determine what changes in detail would fail to elicit responses from the subject buntings.

16. According to the passage, the indigo buntings' songs function in which of the following ways?

   I. To delineate a breeding area
  II. To defend a breeding area
 III. To identify the birds to their mates

(A) I only
(B) II only
(C) I and III only
(D) II and III only
(E) I, II, and III

The best answer is E. The format of this question requires you to evaluate each of the phrases designated with Roman numerals separately and carefully. The question requires you to look up information explicitly stated in the passage. The first sentence in the first paragraph states that in birds such as the indigo bunting, "song is the main mechanism for securing, defining, and defending an adequate breeding area." I and II are restatements of parts of this idea. The last paragraph indicates that songs serve the function of identification within the species and that females can differentiate the songs of their mates from those of other males, thus indicating that III is also correct; therefore, E (I, II, and III) is the best choice.

17. The author's discussion of Emerson, Thoreau, Hawthorne, Melville, and Whitman is primarily concerned with explaining

   (A) some of their beliefs about the difficulties involved in self-realization
   (B) some of their beliefs concerning the world and the place that humanity occupies in the universal order
   (C) some of their beliefs concerning the relationship between humanism and democracy
   (D) the way some of their beliefs are shaped by differences in temperament and literary outlook
   (E) the effects of some of their beliefs on their writings

The best answer is B. This question asks you to identify the choice that best states the primary concern, or central topic, of the author's discussion. Thus, the best answer must be comprehensive enough to include all aspects of the author's discussion. Choice A mentions one aspect of the author's discussion, which appears in the third paragraph along with the topic mentioned in choice C. Neither of these choices includes the matters under discussion in paragraphs one, two, and four. Choices D and E mention topics not discussed in the passage. Choice B presents a broad topic that includes the matters discussed in all four paragraphs of the passage.

18. According to the passage, the humanistic perspective of the five writers presupposes which of the following?

   I. The structure of the universe can be discovered through self-knowledge.
   II. The world can be explained in terms of humanity.
   III. The spiritual and the material worlds are incompatible.

   (A) I only
   (B) II only
   (C) I and II only
   (D) II and III only
   (E) I, II, and III

The best answer is C. This question asks you to evaluate the three statements designated with Roman numerals in terms of "the humanistic perspective of the five writers." Paragraph one discusses the "humanistic perspective" (line 5) and explains its "basic premises" (lines 5-8). After looking back at paragraph one, you can decide whether or not the "humanistic perspective" presupposes statements I, II, and/or III. The last sentence of paragraph one says that ". . . all knowledge begins with self-knowledge"; thus, statement I is a presupposition of the "humanistic perspective." Lines 5-13 explain in some detail the point briefly stated in statement II. The point made in statement III is neither stated nor implied in the passage.

19. The author quotes Whitman primarily in order to

   (A) show that the poet does not agree with Emerson
   (B) indicate the way the poet uses the humanist ideal to praise himself
   (C) suggest that the poet adapts the basic premises of humanism to his own individual outlook on the world
   (D) illustrate a way the poet expresses the relationship of the individual to the humanistic universe
   (E) demonstrate that the poet is concerned with the well-being of all humans

The best answer is D. This question asks you to identify the function of a quotation in the author's discussion. First, locate the quotation from Whitman in lines 24-27. The first two sentences of the paragraph make the point that the five writers under discussion emphasize not the individual, but the "human as universal" (line 21). The author of the passage then says, "Thus, for Emerson . . . while, for Whitman" (lines 22-24). The use of the word "Thus" indicates that the author is giving a specific instance or example of the point. The only choice that states a purpose for the quotation compatible with the author's point in this paragraph is D.

20. According to the passage, the five writers object to the scientific method primarily because they think it

   (A) is not the best way to obtain an understanding of the relationship between the individual and the cosmos
   (B) is so specialized that it leads to an understanding of separate parts of the universe but not of the relationships among those parts
   (C) cannot provide an adequate explanation of intuition and imagination
   (D) misleads people into believing they have an understanding of truth, when they do not
   (E) prevents people from recognizing the symbolic nature of experience

The best answer is A. The author of the passage, in the first sentence of the fourth paragraph, says that the five writers assumed "that intuition and imagination offer a surer road to truth" than the scientific method, and that they presumed "an organic relationship between the self and the cosmos of which only intuition and imagination can properly take account" (lines 55-57). Choice A restates this point by saying that the scientific method "is not the best way to obtain an understanding of the relationship between the individual and the cosmos." Choices B, C, D, and E mention plausible possible objections to the use of the scientific method, but none of these are mentioned in the passage.

21. Which of the following statements would be compatible with the beliefs of the five writers as described in the passage?

    I. Democracy works as a form of government because every individual is unique.
    II. Nature alone exists, and each person is nothing more than a shadow of that substance which is the world.
    III. The human mind is capable of discovering the meaning of life and understanding the order in the universe.

    (A) I only
    (B) III only
    (C) I and II only
    (D) I and III only
    (E) I, II, and III

The best answer is B. This question asks you to evaluate statements I, II, and III and decide whether each of the three statements is compatible with the beliefs of the authors as they are presented in the passage. Statement I concerns democracy, which is discussed in the passage in lines 39-46. It is clear from these lines that I is not compatible with the authors' beliefs as they are presented in the passage. Statement II begins "Nature alone exists. . ."; this part of the statement directly contradicts the discussion of the humanistic perspective in the first paragraph of the passage. Statement III summarizes the basic points made about the humanistic perspective in the first paragraph.

22. It can be inferred that intuition is important to the five writers primarily because it provides them with

    (A) information useful for understanding abstract logic and scientific method
    (B) the discipline needed in the search for truth
    (C) inspiration for their best writing
    (D) clues to the interpretation of symbolic experience
    (E) the means of resolving conflicts between the self and the world

The best answer is D. In the fourth paragraph of the passage, the author says that the five writers assume that intuition and imagination "offer a surer road to truth" (lines 48-49). The author of the passage then gives two illustrations of this assumption, one of which is the writers' emphasis on "interpretation of experience as, in essence, symbolic." Choice A can be eliminated because the fourth paragraph states that intuition and imagination are alternatives to logic and scientific method. The material in choices B and C is not implied in the fourth paragraph. Choice E suggests, correctly, that intuition and imagination connect the self to the world, but the resolution of conflicts between the self and world mentioned in E is not discussed in the passage.

23. The author discusses "the democratic ethic" (lines 39-46) in order to

    (A) explain the relationship between external experience and inner imagination
    (B) support the notion that the self contains two conflicting and irreconcilable factions
    (C) illustrate the relationship between the self's desire to be individual and its desire to merge with all other selves
    (D) elaborate on the concept that the self constantly desires to realize its potential
    (E) give an example of the idea that, in order to be happy, the self must reconcile its desires with external reality

The best answer is C. First, reread the lines cited in the question. They appear at the end of the third paragraph, which begins with a statement of the five writers' belief in the necessity for "harmonious reconciliation of two universal psychological tendencies. . ." (lines 31-32), tendencies of withdrawal, on the one hand, and outreach, on the other (lines 32-38). The next sentence introduces the "democratic ethic" as an illustration of such reconciliation. Thus, choice C is the only choice that expresses the connection between the first part of the paragraph and the example of the democratic ethic.

24. It can be inferred that the idea of "an organic relationship between the self and the cosmos" (lines 55-56) is necessary to the thinking of the five writers because such a relationship

(A) enables them to assert the importance of the democratic ethic
(B) justifies their concept of the freedom of the individual
(C) sustains their faith in the existence of a deity
(D) is the foundation of their humanistic view of existence
(E) is the basis for their claim that the writer is a seer

The best answer is D. This question asks you to connect the quoted phrase to "the thinking of the five writers." Choice A is inadequate because nothing in the passage suggests that the five writers asserted the importance of the democratic ethic. Choice B mentions the concept of the freedom of the individual, which is certainly implicit in the five writers' beliefs, but the relationship cited in the quoted phrase cannot be said to justify their concept. Choice C makes a statement unsupported by the passage. Choice E is related to the quoted phrase, in that the writers' faith in the imagination, which is the mental pathway to understanding the relationship cited in the quoted phrase, led them to see the writer as a seer. The necessary connection between the quoted phrase and the writers' beliefs, however, comes from their shared humanistic perspective, explained in detail in the first and fourth paragraphs, a perspective that is grounded in the idea contained in the quoted phrase.

25. The passage is most relevant to which of the following areas of study?

(A) Aesthetics and logic
(B) History and literature
(C) Theology and sociology
(D) Anthropology and political science
(E) Linguistics and art

The best answer is B. Choices A and E mention areas of study not relevant to the subject of the passage, the common beliefs of five writers. Choices C and D each mention one area, theology and political science, respectively, that could be seen as connected to the discussion presented in the passage. However, the principal concerns of sociology and anthropology are not connected with the subject of the passage. The central concerns of the passage, presenting the ideas and beliefs of significant thinkers, are the principal concerns of the fields of history and literature.

30 Minutes
25 Questions

Directions: Each passage in this group is followed by questions based on its content. After reading a passage, choose the best answer to each question and fill in the corresponding oval on the answer sheet. Answer all questions following a passage on the basis of what is stated or implied in that passage.

In the eighteenth century, Japan's feudal overlords, from the shogun to the humblest samurai, found themselves under financial stress. In part, this stress can be attributed to
(5) the overlords' failure to adjust to a rapidly expanding economy, but the stress was also due to factors beyond the overlords' control. Concentration of the samurai in castle-towns had acted as a stimulus to trade. Commercial efficiency, in
(10) turn, had put temptations in the way of buyers. Since most samurai had been reduced to idleness by years of peace, encouraged to engage in scholarship and martial exercises or to perform administrative tasks that took little time, it is
(15) not surprising that their tastes and habits grew expensive. Overlords' income, despite the increase in rice production among their tenant farmers, failed to keep pace with their expenses. Although shortfalls in overlords' income re-
(20) sulted almost as much from laxity among their tax collectors (the nearly inevitable outcome of hereditary officeholding) as from their higher standards of living, a misfortune like a fire or flood, bringing an increase in expenses or a drop
(25) in revenue, could put a domain in debt to the city rice-brokers who handled its finances. Once in debt, neither the individual samurai nor the shogun himself found it easy to recover.
It was difficult for individual samurai over-
(30) lords to increase their income because the amount of rice that farmers could be made to pay in taxes was not unlimited, and since the income of Japan's central government consisted in part of taxes collected by the shogun from his
(35) huge domain, the government too was constrained. Therefore, the Tokugawa shoguns began to look to other sources for revenue. Cash profits from government-owned mines were already on the decline because the most
(40) easily worked deposits of silver and gold had been exhausted, although debasement of the coinage had compensated for the loss. Opening up new farmland was a possibility, but most of what was suitable had already been exploited
(45) and further reclamation was technically unfeasible. Direct taxation of the samurai themselves would be politically dangerous. This left the shoguns only commerce as a potential source of government income.
(50) Most of the country's wealth, or so it seemed, was finding its way into the hands of city mer-

chants. It appeared reasonable that they should contribute part of that revenue to ease the shogun's burden of financing the state. A means
(55) of obtaining such revenue was soon found by levying forced loans, known as goyo-kin; although these were not taxes in the strict sense, since they were irregular in timing and arbitrary in amount, they were high in yield. Unfortunate-
(60) ly, they pushed up prices. Thus, regrettably, the Tokugawa shoguns' search for solvency for the government made it increasingly difficult for individual Japanese who lived on fixed stipends to make ends meet.

1. The passage is most probably an excerpt from

   (A) an economic history of Japan
   (B) the memoirs of a samurai warrior
   (C) a modern novel about eighteenth-century Japan
   (D) an essay contrasting Japanese feudalism with its Western counterpart
   (E) an introduction to a collection of Japanese folktales

2. Which of the following financial situations is most analogous to the financial situation in which Japan's Tokugawa shoguns found themselves in the eighteenth century?

   (A) A small business borrows heavily to invest in new equipment, but is able to pay off its debt early when it is awarded a lucrative government contract.
   (B) Fire destroys a small business, but insurance covers the cost of rebuilding.
   (C) A small business is turned down for a loan at a local bank because the owners have no credit history.
   (D) A small business has to struggle to meet operating expenses when its profits decrease.
   (E) A small business is able to cut back sharply on spending through greater commercial efficiency and thereby compensate for a loss of revenue.

GO ON TO THE NEXT PAGE.

3. Which of the following best describes the attitude of the author toward the samurai discussed in lines 11-16?

(A) Warmly approving
(B) Mildly sympathetic
(C) Bitterly disappointed
(D) Harshly disdainful
(E) Profoundly shocked

4. According to the passage, the major reason for the financial problems experienced by Japan's feudal overlords in the eighteenth century was that

(A) spending had outdistanced income
(B) trade had fallen off
(C) profits from mining had declined
(D) the coinage had been sharply debased
(E) the samurai had concentrated in castle-towns

5. The passage implies that individual samurai did not find it easy to recover from debt for which of the following reasons?

(A) Agricultural production had increased.
(B) Taxes were irregular in timing and arbitrary in amount.
(C) The Japanese government had failed to adjust to the needs of a changing economy.
(D) The domains of samurai overlords were becoming smaller and poorer as government revenues increased.
(E) There was a limit to the amount in taxes that farmers could be made to pay.

6. The passage suggests that, in eighteenth-century Japan, the office of tax collector

(A) was a source of personal profit to the officeholder
(B) was regarded with derision by many Japanese
(C) remained within families
(D) existed only in castle-towns
(E) took up most of the officeholder's time

7. Which of the following could best be substituted for the word "This" in line 47 without changing the meaning of the passage?

(A) The search of Japan's Tokugawa shoguns for solvency
(B) The importance of commerce in feudal Japan
(C) The unfairness of the tax structure in eighteenth-century Japan
(D) The difficulty of increasing government income by other means
(E) The difficulty experienced by both individual samurai and the shogun himself in extricating themselves from debt

8. The passage implies that which of the following was the primary reason why the Tokugawa shoguns turned to city merchants for help in financing the state?

(A) A series of costly wars had depleted the national treasury.
(B) Most of the country's wealth appeared to be in city merchants' hands.
(C) Japan had suffered a series of economic reversals due to natural disasters such as floods.
(D) The merchants were already heavily indebted to the shoguns.
(E) Further reclamation of land would not have been economically advantageous.

9. According to the passage, the actions of the Tokugawa shoguns in their search for solvency for the government were regrettable because those actions

(A) raised the cost of living by pushing up prices
(B) resulted in the exhaustion of the most easily worked deposits of silver and gold
(C) were far lower in yield than had originally been anticipated
(D) did not succeed in reducing government spending
(E) acted as a deterrent to trade

GO ON TO THE NEXT PAGE.

This history of responses to the work of the artist Sandro Botticelli (1444?-1510) suggests that widespread appreciation by critics is a relatively recent phenomenon. Writing in 1550,
(5) Vasari expressed an unease with Botticelli's work, admitting that the artist fitted awkwardly into his (Vasari's) evolutionary scheme of the history of art. Over the next two centuries, academic art historians denigrated Botticelli in
(10) favor of his fellow Florentine, Michelangelo. Even when antiacademic art historians of the early nineteenth century rejected many of the standards of evaluation espoused by their predecessors, Botticelli's work remained outside of ac-
(15) cepted taste, pleasing neither amateur observers nor connoisseurs. (Many of his best paintings, however, remained hidden away in obscure churches and private homes.)

The primary reason for Botticelli's unpopu-
(20) larity is not difficult to understand: most observers, up until the mid-nineteenth century, did not consider him to be noteworthy because his work, for the most part, did not seem to these observers to exhibit the traditional characteris-
(25) tics of fifteenth-century Florentine art. For example, Botticelli rarely employed the technique of strict perspective and, unlike Michelangelo, never used chiaroscuro. Another reason for Botticelli's unpopularity may have been that his at-
(30) titude toward the style of classical art was very different from that of his contemporaries. Although he was thoroughly exposed to classical art, he showed little interest in borrowing from the classical style. Indeed, it is paradoxical that
(35) a painter of large-scale classical subjects adopted a style that was only slightly similar to that of classical art.

In any case, when viewers began to examine more closely the relationship of Botticelli's work
(40) to the tradition of fifteenth-century Florentine art, his reputation began to grow. Analyses and assessments of Botticelli made between 1850 and 1870 by the artists of the Pre-Raphaelite movement, as well as by the writer Pater (although
(45) he, unfortunately, based his assessment on an incorrect analysis of Botticelli's personality), inspired a new appreciation of Botticelli throughout the English-speaking world. Yet Botticelli's work, especially the Sistine frescoes, did not
(50) generate worldwide attention until it was finally subjected to a comprehensive and scrupulous analysis by Horne in 1908. Horne rightly demonstrated that the frescoes shared important features with paintings by other fifteenth-century
(55) Florentines—features such as skillful representation of anatomical proportions, and of the human figure in motion. However, Horne argued that Botticelli did not treat these qualities as ends in themselves—rather, that he empha-

(60) sized clear depiction of a story, a unique achievement and one that made the traditional Florentine qualities less central. Because of Horne's emphasis on the way a talented artist reflects a tradition yet moves beyond that tradi-
(65) tion, an emphasis crucial to any study of art, the twentieth century has come to appreciate Botticelli's achievements.

10. Which of the following would be the most appropriate title for the passage?

(A) Botticelli's Contribution to Florentine Art
(B) Botticelli and the Traditions of Classical Art
(C) Sandro Botticelli: From Denigration to Appreciation
(D) Botticelli and Michelangelo: A Study in Contrasts
(E) Standards of Taste: Botticelli's Critical Reputation up to the Nineteenth Century

11. It can be inferred that the author of the passage would be likely to find most beneficial a study of an artist that

(A) avoided placing the artist in an evolutionary scheme of the history of art
(B) analyzed the artist's work in relation to the artist's personality
(C) analyzed the artist's relationship to the style and subject matter of classical art
(D) analyzed the artist's work in terms of both traditional characteristics and unique achievement
(E) sanctioned and extended the evaluation of the artist's work made by the artist's contemporaries

12. The passage suggests that Vasari would most probably have been more enthusiastic about Botticelli's work if that artist's work

(A) had not revealed Botticelli's inability to depict a story clearly
(B) had not evolved so straightforwardly from the Florentine art of the fourteenth century
(C) had not seemed to Vasari to be so similar to classical art
(D) could have been appreciated by amateur viewers as well as by connoisseurs
(E) could have been included more easily in Vasari's discussion of art history

GO ON TO THE NEXT PAGE.

13. The author most likely mentions the fact that many of Botticelli's best paintings were "hidden away in obscure churches and private homes" (lines 17-18) in order to

(A) indicate the difficulty of trying to determine what an artist's best work is
(B) persuade the reader that an artist's work should be available for general public viewing
(C) prove that academic art historians had succeeded in keeping Botticelli's work from general public view
(D) call into question the assertion that antiacademic art historians disagreed with their predecessors
(E) suggest a reason why, for a period of time, Botticelli's work was not generally appreciated

14. The passage suggests that most seventeenth- and eighteenth-century academic art historians and most early-nineteenth-century antiacademic art historians would have disagreed significantly about which of the following?

I. The artistic value of Botticelli's work
II. The criteria by which art should be judged
III. The features that characterized fifteenth-century Florentine art

(A) I only
(B) II only
(C) III only
(D) II and III only
(E) I, II, and III

15. According to the passage, which of the following is an accurate statement about Botticelli's relation to classical art?

(A) Botticelli more often made use of classical subject matter than classical style.
(B) Botticelli's interest in perspective led him to study classical art.
(C) Botticelli's style does not share any similarities with the style of classical art.
(D) Because he saw little classical art, Botticelli did not exhibit much interest in imitating such art.
(E) Although Botticelli sometimes borrowed his subject matter from classical art, he did not create large-scale paintings of these subjects.

16. According to the passage, Horne believed which of the following about the relation of the Sistine frescoes to the tradition of fifteenth-century Florentine art?

(A) The frescoes do not exhibit characteristics of such art.
(B) The frescoes exhibit more characteristics of such art than do the paintings of Michelangelo.
(C) The frescoes exhibit some characteristics of such art, but these qualities are not the dominant features of the frescoes.
(D) Some of the frescoes exhibit characteristics of such art, but most do not.
(E) More of the frescoes exhibit skillful representation of anatomical proportions than skillful representation of the human figure in motion.

17. The passage suggests that, before Horne began to study Botticelli's work in 1908, there had been

(A) little appreciation of Botticelli in the English-speaking world
(B) an overemphasis on Botticelli's transformation, in the Sistine frescoes, of the principles of classical art
(C) no attempt to compare Botticelli's work to that of Michelangelo
(D) no thorough investigation of Botticelli's Sistine frescoes
(E) little agreement among connoisseurs and amateurs about the merits of Botticelli's work

GO ON TO THE NEXT PAGE.

The antigen-antibody immunological reaction used to be regarded as typical of immunological responses. Antibodies are proteins synthesized by specialized cells called plasma cells, which are
(5) formed by lymphocytes (cells from the lymph system) when an antigen, a substance foreign to the organism's body, comes in contact with lymphocytes. Two important manifestations of antigen-antibody immunity are lysis, the rapid
(10) physical rupture of antigenic cells and the liberation of their contents into the surrounding medium, and phagocytosis, a process in which antigenic particles are engulfed by and very often digested by macrophages and polymorphs.
(15) The process of lysis is executed by a complex and unstable blood constituent known as *complement,* which will not work unless it is activated by a specific antibody; the process of phagocytosis is greatly facilitated when the par-
(20) ticles to be engulfed are coated by a specific antibody directed against them.

The reluctance to abandon this hypothesis, however well it explains specific processes, impeded new research, and for many years anti-
(25) gens and antibodies dominated the thoughts of immunologists so completely that those immunologists overlooked certain difficulties. Perhaps the primary difficulty with the antigen-antibody explanation is the informational problem of how
(30) an antigen is recognized and how a structure exactly complementary to it is then synthesized. When molecular biologists discovered, moreover, that such information cannot flow from protein to protein, but only from nucleic acid to
(35) protein, the theory that an antigen itself provided the mold that directed the synthesis of an antibody had to be seriously qualified. The attempts at qualification and the information provided by research in molecular biology led
(40) scientists to realize that a second immunological reaction is mediated through the lymphocytes that are hostile to and bring about the destruction of the antigen. This type of immunological response is called cell-mediated immunity.
(45) Recent research in cell-mediated immunity has been concerned not only with the development of new and better vaccines, but also with the problem of transplanting tissues and organs from one organism to another, for although cir-
(50) culating antibodies play a part in the rejection of transplanted tissues, the primary role is played by cell-mediated reactions. During cell-mediated responses, receptor sites on specific lymphocytes and surface antigens on the foreign
(55) tissue cells form a complex that binds the lymphocytes to the tissue. Such lymphocytes do not give rise to antibody-producing plasma cells but themselves bring about the death of the foreign-tissue cells, probably by secreting a variety of

(60) substances, some of which are toxic to the tissue cells and some of which stimulate increased phagocytic activity by white blood cells of the macrophage type. Cell-mediated immunity also accounts for the destruction of intracellular parasites.

18. The author is primarily concerned with

   (A) proving that immunological reactions do not involve antibodies
   (B) establishing that most immunological reactions involve antigens
   (C) criticizing scientists who will not change their theories regarding immunology
   (D) analyzing the importance of cells in fighting disease
   (E) explaining two different kinds of immunological reactions

19. The author argues that the antigen-antibody explanation of immunity "had to be seriously qualified" (line 37) because

   (A) antibodies were found to activate unstable components in the blood
   (B) antigens are not exactly complementary to antibodies
   (C) lymphocytes have the ability to bind to the surface of antigens
   (D) antibodies are synthesized from protein whereas antigens are made from nucleic acid
   (E) antigens have no apparent mechanism to direct the formation of an antibody

20. The author most probably believes that the antigen-antibody theory of immunological reaction

   (A) is wrong
   (B) was accepted without evidence
   (C) is unverifiable
   (D) is a partial explanation
   (E) has been a divisive issue among scientists

21. The author mentions all of the following as being involved in antigen-antibody immunological reactions EXCEPT the

   (A) synthesis of a protein
   (B) activation of *complement* in the bloodstream
   (C) destruction of antibodies
   (D) entrapment of antigens by macrophages
   (E) formation of a substance with a structure complementary to that of an antigen

GO ON TO THE NEXT PAGE.

22. The passage contains information that would answer which of the following questions about cell-mediated immunological reactions?

    I. Do lymphocytes form antibodies during cell-mediated immunological reactions?
    II. Why are lymphocytes more hostile to antigens during cell-mediated immunological reactions than are other cell groups?
    III. Are cell-mediated reactions more pronounced after transplants than they are after parasites have invaded the organism?

(A) I only
(B) I and II only
(C) I and III only
(D) II and III only
(E) I, II, and III

23. The passage suggests that scientists might not have developed the theory of cell-mediated immunological reactions if

(A) proteins existed in specific group types
(B) proteins could have been shown to direct the synthesis of other proteins
(C) antigens were always destroyed by proteins
(D) antibodies were composed only of protein
(E) antibodies were the body's primary means of resisting disease

24. According to the passage, antibody-antigen and cell-mediated immunological reactions both involve which of the following processes?

    I. The destruction of antigens
    II. The creation of antibodies
    III. The destruction of intracellular parasites

(A) I only
(B) II only
(C) III only
(D) I and II only
(E) II and III only

25. The author supports the theory of cell-mediated reactions primarily by

(A) pointing out a contradiction in the assumption leading to the antigen-antibody theory
(B) explaining how cell mediation accounts for phenomena that the antigen-antibody theory cannot account for
(C) revealing new data that scientists arguing for the antigen-antibody theory have continued to ignore
(D) showing that the antigen-antibody theory fails to account for the breakup of antigens
(E) demonstrating that cell mediation explains lysis and phagocytosis more fully than the antigen-antibody theory does

S T O P

IF YOU FINISH BEFORE TIME IS CALLED, YOU MAY CHECK YOUR WORK ON THIS SECTION ONLY.
DO NOT TURN TO ANY OTHER SECTION IN THE TEST.

Answer Key for Sample Test Section 3

READING COMPREHENSION

1. A	14. B
2. D	15. A
3. B	16. C
4. A	17. D
5. E	18. E
6. C	19. E
7. D	20. D
8. B	21. C
9. A	22. A
10. C	23. B
11. D	24. A
12. E	25. B
13. E	

Explanatory Material: Reading Comprehension Sample Test Section 3

1. The passage is most probably an excerpt from

   (A) an economic history of Japan
   (B) the memoirs of a samurai warrior
   (C) a modern novel about eighteenth-century Japan
   (D) an essay contrasting Japanese feudalism with its Western counterpart
   (E) an introduction to a collection of Japanese folktales

The best answer is A. This question requires you to make two judgments: what is the general nature of the style and content of the passage and in what kind of publication would a passage of that nature appear? The passage is a somewhat technical discussion of the economic situation of a certain class of eighteenth-century Japanese, focusing on an analysis of then prevalent economic practices and trends. Thus, an economic history of Japan (choice A) is certainly a probable source for such material. Although any of the works in the other choices could conceivably contain such material, it is not probable, and there is no internal evidence to suggest that this excerpt could be appropriately placed in the types of works listed in choices B, C, D, or E.

2. Which of the following financial situations is most analogous to the financial situation in which Japan's Tokugawa shoguns found themselves in the eighteenth century?

   (A) A small business borrows heavily to invest in new equipment, but is able to pay off its debt early when it is awarded a lucrative government contract.
   (B) Fire destroys a small business, but insurance covers the cost of rebuilding.
   (C) A small business is turned down for a loan at a local bank because the owners have no credit history.
   (D) A small business has to struggle to meet operating expenses when its profits decrease.
   (E) A small business is able to cut back sharply on spending through greater commercial efficiency and thereby compensate for a loss of revenue.

The best answer is D. In order to answer this question you must first determine what were the essential elements of the shoguns' financial situation and then decide which of the choices presents a situation with the same basic elements. Lines 16-18 indicate that the overlords' income failed to keep pace with their expenses. Lines 19-26 describe some of the reasons expenses rose while income declined. Choice D is the only choice that contains these two critical elements. With the exception of E, the other choices describe situations in which one of the elements is analogous to critical elements in the shoguns' situation, but the other is not. Choice E is not analogous in either of its elements.

3. Which of the following best describes the attitude of the author toward the samurai discussed in lines 11-16?

   (A) Warmly approving
   (B) Mildly sympathetic
   (C) Bitterly disappointed
   (D) Harshly disdainful
   (E) Profoundly shocked

The best answer is B. This question asks about the attitude of the author toward a particular group as that attitude is revealed in the language of the passage. To answer this question, you should first re-examine the lines cited. The samurai are described as idle and given to expensive pursuits. The author, however, does not dismiss them; rather, it is implied that their idleness is not totally a matter of choice: they were "reduced to idleness," (line 11) and their response seems to the author "not surprising." Thus, the author's attitude can be described as "mildly sympathetic."

4. According to the passage, the major reason for the financial problems experienced by Japan's feudal overlords in the eighteenth century was that

   (A) spending had outdistanced income
   (B) trade had fallen off
   (C) profits from mining had declined
   (D) the coinage had been sharply debased
   (E) the samurai had concentrated in castle-towns

The best answer is A. This question requires you to identify the major reason stated in the passage for the problems of the feudal overlords. To answer the question, it is necessary to distinguish between the major reason and the factors that contributed to, but alone do not completely account for, the problem. Lines 16-18 state that the overlords' income "failed to keep pace with their expenses." The rest of the paragraph goes on to explain the various factors that contributed to the problem. Notice that choices C, D, and E are discussed in the passage as factors influencing the economic situation; they are not, however, the major reason for the problems of the overlords.

5. The passage implies that individual samurai did not find it easy to recover from debt for which of the following reasons?

   (A) Agricultural production had increased.
   (B) Taxes were irregular in timing and arbitrary in amount.
   (C) The Japanese government had failed to adjust to the needs of a changing economy.
   (D) The domains of samurai overlords were becoming smaller and poorer as government revenues increased.
   (E) There was a limit to the amount in taxes that farmers could be made to pay.

The best answer is E. This question asks you to identify the reason that individual samurai, once they had become indebted, could not extricate themselves from debt. Lines 16-18 suggest that individual samurai drew their income from rice production among tenant farmers, and lines 30-32 indicate that this income could not be increased indefinitely. Thus, it can be concluded that the samurai could not raise enough money to recover from debt because they could not increase the income derived from tenant farms. Choice E is a statement of this idea.

6. The passage suggests that, in eighteenth-century Japan, the office of tax collector

   (A) was a source of personal profit to the officeholder
   (B) was regarded with derision by many Japanese
   (C) remained within families
   (D) existed only in castle-towns
   (E) took up most of the officeholder's time

The best answer is C. This question asks for a specific supporting detail presented in the passage. To answer the question, it is necessary to locate the reference in the passage to the office of tax collector. Lines 21-22 contain a parenthetical reference to the office of tax collector. It is indicated there that the office of tax collector is hereditary. Choice C presents a paraphrase of this idea: the office "remained within families." There is no evidence to support any of the statements made in the other choices.

7. Which of the following could best be substituted for the word "This" in line 47 without changing the meaning of the passage?

   (A) The search of Japan's Tokugawa shoguns for solvency
   (B) The importance of commerce in feudal Japan
   (C) The unfairness of the tax structure in eighteenth-century Japan
   (D) The difficulty of increasing government income by other means
   (E) The difficulty experienced by both individual samurai and the shogun himself in extricating themselves from debt

The best answer is D. This question requires you to determine the referent of the pronoun "This" in line 47. You should first reread the paragraph containing the sentence, and decide what "This" refers to. The paragraph discusses ways in which the Tokugawa shogun and the government attempted to increase revenues and explains why each of the attempts fell short of solving the problem. The pronoun "This" in line 47 introduces a sentence that draws a conclusion based on the fact that most means of increasing government revenue had been exhausted; "This" can only refer to the difficulty they experienced. Choice D contains a phrase that conveys this idea and that can be substituted for the pronoun "This" without altering the meaning of the sentence.

8. The passage implies that which of the following was the primary reason why the Tokugawa shoguns turned to city merchants for help in financing the state?

   (A) A series of costly wars had depleted the national treasury.
   (B) Most of the country's wealth appeared to be in city merchants' hands.
   (C) Japan had suffered a series of economic reversals due to natural disasters such as floods.
   (D) The merchants were already heavily indebted to the shoguns.
   (E) Further reclamation of land would not have been economically advantageous.

The best answer is B. This question requires you to identify the major reason why the Tokugawa shoguns began to require city merchants to contribute to the state revenues. The second paragraph indicates that the shoguns had exhausted most sources of revenue for the government. Lines 50-54 indicate that the shoguns believed that city merchants had acquired most of the country's wealth. Because of that belief, they deemed it "reasonable" to turn to the city merchants. Thus, choice B is the best answer.

9. According to the passage, the actions of the Tokugawa shoguns in their search for solvency for the government were regrettable because those actions

   (A) raised the cost of living by pushing up prices
   (B) resulted in the exhaustion of the most easily worked deposits of silver and gold
   (C) were far lower in yield than had originally been anticipated
   (D) did not succeed in reducing government spending
   (E) acted as a deterrent to trade

The best answer is A. To answer this question, you must determine why the author of the passage judges the actions of the shoguns as "regrettable," a judgment rendered in the conclusion of the passage. The passage indicates that the forced loans demanded of city merchants by the shoguns (lines 54-60) had the ultimate effect of driving up prices. The next sentence discusses the effects of the rise in prices on the cost of living, an effect that the author finds unfortunate ("Thus, regrettably," line 60). Therefore, choice A is the best answer.

10. Which of the following would be the most appropriate title for the passage?

    (A) Botticelli's Contribution to Florentine Art
    (B) Botticelli and the Traditions of Classical Art
    (C) Sandro Botticelli: From Denigration to Appreciation
    (D) Botticelli and Michelangelo: A Study in Contrasts
    (E) Standards of Taste: Botticelli's Critical Reputation up to the Nineteenth Century

The best answer is C because it is the only title that states the central theme of the passage, which is the history of the change in the response to the work of Botticelli, from unpopularity to approbation. This theme is made particularly clear in lines 1-4, 8-10, and 66-67. There are also repeated references to this theme throughout the body of the passage.

11. It can be inferred that the author of the passage would be likely to find most beneficial a study of an artist that

    (A) avoided placing the artist in an evolutionary scheme of the history of art
    (B) analyzed the artist's work in relation to the artist's personality
    (C) analyzed the artist's relationship to the style and subject matter of classical art
    (D) analyzed the artist's work in terms of both traditional characteristics and unique achievement
    (E) sanctioned and extended the evaluation of the artist's work made by the artist's contemporaries

The best answer is D. In lines 63-65 the author states that "Horne's emphasis on the way a talented artist reflects a tradition yet moves beyond that tradition" is "an emphasis crucial to any study of art." The word "crucial" indicates that the author would be likely to find a study that "analyzed the artist's work in terms of both traditional characteristics and unique achievement" (choice D) to be most beneficial.

12. The passage suggests that Vasari would most probably have been more enthusiastic about Botticelli's work if that artist's work

    (A) had not revealed Botticelli's inability to depict a story clearly
    (B) had not evolved so straightforwardly from the Florentine art of the fourteenth century
    (C) had not seemed to Vasari to be so similar to classical art
    (D) could have been appreciated by amateur viewers as well as by connoisseurs
    (E) could have been included more easily in Vasari's discussion of art history

The best answer is E. Vasari's views are described in lines 4-8, which imply that Vasari was uneasy about Botticelli's work because it did not fit Vasari's evolutionary scheme of the history of art. Thus, it can be inferred that, had Botticelli's work been easier to include in Vasari's discussion of art history, Vasari would probably have been more enthusiastic about Botticelli's work.

13. The author most likely mentions the fact that many of Botticelli's best paintings were "hidden away in obscure churches and private homes" (lines 17-18) in order to

    (A) indicate the difficulty of trying to determine what an artist's best work is
    (B) persuade the reader that an artist's work should be available for general public viewing
    (C) prove that academic art historians had succeeded in keeping Botticelli's work from general public view
    (D) call into question the assertion that antiacademic art historians disagreed with their predecessors
    (E) suggest a reason why, for a period of time, Botticelli's work was not generally appreciated

The best answer is E. The sentence in lines 16-18 appears in parentheses, suggesting that the author is commenting on or qualifying what immediately precedes this sentence. Thus, the purpose of the parenthetical statement is determined by the sentence preceding it. In lines 11-15, the author asserts that Botticelli's work remained "outside of accepted taste." The author then offers the comment in parentheses: in lines 16-18, using "however" as a qualifier, the author mentions the obscure location of many of Botticelli's best paintings, implying that much of the best of Botticelli's work was not available for viewing. Thus, the author suggests "a reason why, for a period of time, Botticelli's work was not generally appreciated."

14. The passage suggests that most seventeenth- and eighteenth-century academic art historians and most early-nineteenth-century antiacademic art historians would have disagreed significantly about which of the following?

   I. The artistic value of Botticelli's work
  II. The criteria by which art should be judged
 III. The features that characterized fifteenth-century Florentine art

   (A) I only
   (B) II only
   (C) III only
   (D) II and III only
   (E) I, II, and III

The best answer is B (II only). I is incorrect because lines 8-16 indicate that most seventeenth-, eighteenth-, and early-nineteenth-century art historians agreed on the artistic value of Botticelli's work — they all denigrated it. Choice III is wrong because the lines that discuss the features that characterized fifteenth-century Florentine art (lines 20-28) do not suggest that most seventeenth- and eighteenth-century academic art historians would have disagreed with most early-nineteenth-century antiacademic art historians about these features. Choice II is correct because lines 11-14 state that "antiacademic art historians of the early nineteenth century rejected many of the standards of evaluation espoused by their predecessors."

15. According to the passage, which of the following is an accurate statement about Botticelli's relation to classical art?

   (A) Botticelli more often made use of classical subject matter than classical style.
   (B) Botticelli's interest in perspective led him to study classical art.
   (C) Botticelli's style does not share any similarities with the style of classical art.
   (D) Because he saw little classical art, Botticelli did not exhibit much interest in imitating such art.
   (E) Although Botticelli sometimes borrowed his subject matter from classical art, he did not create large-scale paintings of these subjects.

The best answer is A. Lines 32-37 describe Botticelli's use of classical style and subject matter. They state that large-scale classical subjects were the focus of Botticelli's painting and that he borrowed little from the classical style. Thus it can be inferred that Botticelli used classical subject matter more often than he used classical style.

16. According to the passage, Horne believed which of the following about the relation of the Sistine frescoes to the tradition of fifteenth-century Florentine art?

   (A) The frescoes do not exhibit characteristics of such art.
   (B) The frescoes exhibit more characteristics of such art than do the paintings of Michelangelo.
   (C) The frescoes exhibit some characteristics of such art, but these qualities are not the dominant features of the frescoes.
   (D) Some of the frescoes exhibit characteristics of such art, but most do not.
   (E) More of the frescoes exhibit skillful representation of anatomical proportions than skillful representation of the human figure in motion.

The best answer is C. Lines 53-62 describe Horne's views about Botticelli's Sistine frescoes. According to lines 53-55, "the frescoes shared important features with paintings by other fifteenth-century Florentines"; thus, the frescoes exhibit some characteristics of fifteenth-century Florentine art. Lines 57-62 point out that "Botticelli did not treat these qualities as ends in themselves" and that, in his work, "the traditional Florentine qualities [were] less central"; thus, these qualities are not the dominant features of the frescoes.

17. The passage suggests that, before Horne began to study Botticelli's work in 1908, there had been

   (A) little appreciation of Botticelli in the English-speaking world
   (B) an overemphasis on Botticelli's transformation, in the Sistine frescoes, of the principles of classical art
   (C) no attempt to compare Botticelli's work to that of Michelangelo
   (D) no thorough investigation of Botticelli's Sistine frescoes
   (E) little agreement among connoisseurs and amateurs about the merits of Botticelli's work.

The best answer is D. According to lines 48-52, "Botticelli's work, especially the Sistine frescoes, did not generate world-wide attention until it was finally subjected to a comprehensive and scrupulous analysis by Horne in 1908." The word "finally" suggests that Horne's study of the frescoes was the first thorough investigation of them.

18. The author is primarily concerned with

(A) proving that immunological reactions do not involve antibodies
(B) establishing that most immunological reactions involve antigens
(C) criticizing scientists who will not change their theories regarding immunology
(D) analyzing the importance of cells in fighting disease
(E) explaining two different kinds of immunological reactions

The best answer is E. This question asks for the author's primary interest or concern in writing this passage, or the central idea of the passage as a whole. To answer this question, carefully evaluate the first words in the five choices. Choice A begins with "proving"; choice B begins with "establishing." Both of these words may fit the procedure of the passage, but the statements are false. Choice C can be rejected because, although the author states that reluctance to abandon a hypothesis made new research difficult (lines 22-27), the author does not directly criticize scientists. Paragraphs one and three are almost entirely descriptive; therefore, the author's purpose must not be to analyze immunological reactions (choice D), but to explain them (choice E).

19. The author argues that the antigen-antibody explanation of immunity "had to be seriously qualified" (line 37) because

(A) antibodies were found to activate unstable components in the blood
(B) antigens are not exactly complementary to antibodies
(C) lymphocytes have the ability to bind to the surface of antigens
(D) antibodies are synthesized from protein whereas antigens are made from nucleic acid
(E) antigens have no apparent mechanism to direct the formation of an antibody

The best answer is E. First, examine each of the choices to determine which makes an accurate statement, based on evidence in the passage, about the reasons that scientists had to qualify the antigen-antibody theory. The question refers to line 37, which is part of a sentence that says, in combination with the preceding sentence, that scientists qualified the antigen-antibody theory when they could not explain "how an antigen is recognized" (lines 29-30) and "how a structure exactly complementary to it is then synthesized" (lines 30-31). From this, scientists realized that the mechanism for directing the synthesis of the antibody did not operate in the way they had thought. The other choices are plausible statements, but they are not relevant to the cause-and-effect relationship asked about in the question.

20. The author most probably believes that the antigen-antibody theory of immunological reaction

(A) is wrong
(B) was accepted without evidence
(C) is unverifiable
(D) is a partial explanation
(E) has been a divisive issue among scientists

The best answer is D. The author mentions "difficulties" with the theory but does not call it "wrong." Therefore, A is incorrect. The author refers to two important manifestations of the antigen-antibody reactions in the first paragraph, and so does not believe, as B states, that the theory "was accepted without evidence," or, as C states, "is unverifiable." Nowhere does the author suggest, as E states, that the theory "has been a divisive issue among scientists." Lines 37-43 do state that research "led scientists to realize that a second immunological reaction" also takes place in the body. Thus, scientists realized that the antigen-antibody theory was, as choice D states, "a partial explanation."

21. The author mentions all of the following as being involved in antigen-antibody immunological reactions EXCEPT the

(A) synthesis of a protein
(B) activation of *complement* in the bloodstream
(C) destruction of antibodies
(D) entrapment of antigens by macrophages
(E) formation of a substance with a structure complementary to that of an antigen

The best answer is C. This question asks you to gather from the first two paragraphs the processes the author attributes to antigen-antibody reactions, and then to recognize which of the choices is not mentioned in the passage. Choice A, synthesis of a protein, is mentioned in lines 3-6. Choice B, activation of *complement* in the bloodstream, is mentioned in lines 15-18. Choice D, entrapment of antigens by macrophages, is explained as phagocytosis in lines 12-14. Choice E, formation of a substance with a structure complementary to that of an antigen, is discussed in paragraph two, lines 28-31, as part of the "primary difficulty" of the antigen-antibody theory. The only choice not mentioned in the passage is the destruction of antibodies. Therefore, the best answer is choice C.

22. The passage contains information that would answer which of the following questions about cell-mediated immunological reactions?

    I. Do lymphocytes form antibodies during cell-mediated immunological reactions?

   II. Why are lymphocytes more hostile to antigens during cell-mediated immunological reactions than are other cell groups?

 III. Are cell-mediated reactions more pronounced after transplants than they are after parasites have invaded the organism?

    (A) I only
    (B) I and II only
    (C) I and III only
    (D) II and III only
    (E) I, II, and III

The best answer is A. The format of this question requires you to evaluate each of the questions designated with Roman numerals separately and carefully. Question I is answered by paragraph three, which indicates that, in cell-mediated immunological reactions, lymphocytes do not produce antibodies but destroy foreign tissue cells by themselves. Nowhere does the passage answer question II; it does not discuss why lymphocytes are more hostile to antigens during cell-mediated reactions than are other cell groups. Nor does the passage answer question III; it does not compare the cell-mediated reaction involved in transplants to the cell-mediated reaction involved in parasite invasion; instead, the passage simply states that the reaction occurs in both cases. Therefore, the passage answers question I only.

23. The passage suggests that scientists might not have developed the theory of cell-mediated immunological reactions if

    (A) proteins existed in specific group types
    (B) proteins could have been shown to direct the synthesis of other proteins
    (C) antigens were always destroyed by proteins
    (D) antibodies were composed only of protein
    (E) antibodies were the body's primary means of resisting disease

The best answer is B. According to the passage, scientists arrived at the theory of cell-mediated immunological reactions because the theory of antigen-antibody immunological reaction could not explain how an antibody, which is made of protein, could recognize and synthesize another protein (lines 27-37). It can be inferred that scientists might *not* have developed the theory of cell-mediated immunological reactions if they had discovered the reverse — that proteins could direct the synthesis of other proteins.

24. According to the passage, antibody-antigen and cell-mediated immunological reactions both involve which of the following processes?

    I. The destruction of antigens
   II. The creation of antibodies
  III. The destruction of intracellular parasites

    (A) I only
    (B) II only
    (C) III only
    (D) I and II only
    (E) II and III only

The best answer is A. The question requires you to compare the information given in the passage about antigen-antibody responses to the information given in the passage about cell-mediated responses, and to decide which of the Roman numeral choices the two reactions have in common. Choice I, the destruction of antigens, is discussed in paragraph one and paragraph two in connection with both types of immunological reaction. Choice II, the creation of antibodies, is discussed in paragraph one in connection with antigen-antibody reactions only. Choice III, the destruction of intracellular parasites, is discussed in paragraph three in connection with cell-mediated reactions only. Therefore, the answer is A: the two reactions have in common choice I only.

25. The author supports the theory of cell-mediated reactions primarily by

    (A) pointing out a contradiction in the assumption leading to the antigen-antibody theory
    (B) explaining how cell mediation accounts for phenomena that the antigen-antibody theory cannot account for
    (C) revealing new data that scientists arguing for the antigen-antibody theory have continued to ignore
    (D) showing that the antigen-antibody theory fails to account for the breakup of antigens
    (E) demonstrating that cell mediation explains lysis and phagocytosis more fully than the antigen-antibody theory does

The best answer is B. This question requires you to recognize the structure of the passage as a whole. Paragraph one describes the way the antigen-antibody reaction works. Paragraph two discusses the difficulties with the antigen-antibody theory, which are, in this case, that the antigen-antibody theory cannot account for certain phenomena. Paragraph two also claims that accounting for these phenomena led scientists to the theory of cell-mediated reactions. Paragraph three describes the way the cell-mediated reaction works. The discussion is thus structured to support the theory of cell-mediated reactions by explaining how cell mediation accounts for phenomena not explained by the antigen-antibody theory.

30 Minutes
25 Questions

Directions: Each passage in this group is followed by questions based on its content. After reading a passage, choose the best answer to each question and fill in the corresponding oval on the answer sheet. Answer all questions following a passage on the basis of what is stated or implied in that passage.

Those examples of poetic justice that occur in medieval and Elizabethan literature, and that seem so satisfying, have encouraged a whole school of twentieth-century scholars to "find"
(5) further examples. In fact, these scholars have merely forced victimized characters into a moral framework by which the injustices inflicted on them are, somehow or other, justified. Such scholars deny that the sufferers in a tragedy are
(10) innocent; they blame the victims themselves for their tragic fates. Any misdoing is enough to subject a character to critical whips. Thus, there are long essays about the misdemeanors of Webster's Duchess of Malfi, who defied her brothers, and
(15) the behavior of Shakespeare's Desdemona, who disobeyed her father.
Yet it should be remembered that the Renaissance writer Matteo Bandello strongly protests the injustice of the severe penalties issued to
(20) women for acts of disobedience that men could, and did, commit with virtual impunity. And Shakespeare, Chaucer, and Webster often enlist their readers on the side of their tragic heroines by describing injustices so cruel that readers
(25) cannot but join in protest. By portraying Griselda, in The Clerk's Tale, as a meek, gentle victim who does not criticize, much less rebel against the persecutor, her husband Walter, Chaucer incites readers to espouse Griselda's
(30) cause against Walter's oppression. Thus, efforts to supply historical and theological rationalizations for Walter's persecutions tend to turn Chaucer's fable upside down, to deny its most obvious effect on readers' sympathies. Similarly,
(35) to assert that Webster's Duchess deserved torture and death because she chose to marry the man she loved and to bear their children is, in effect, to join forces with her tyrannical brothers, and so to confound the operation of poetic
(40) justice, of which readers should approve, with precisely those examples of social injustice that Webster does everything in his power to make readers condemn. Indeed, Webster has his heroine so heroically lead the resistance to tyranny
(45) that she may well inspire members of the audience to imaginatively join forces with her against the cruelty and hypocritical morality of her brothers.
Thus Chaucer and Webster, in their different

(50) ways, attack injustice, argue on behalf of the victims, and prosecute the persecutors. Their readers serve them as a court of appeal that remains free to rule, as the evidence requires, and as common humanity requires, in favor of
(55) the innocent and injured parties. For, to paraphrase the noted eighteenth-century scholar, Samuel Johnson, despite all the refinements of subtlety and the dogmatism of learning, it is by the common sense and compassion of readers
(60) who are uncorrupted by the prejudices of some opinionated scholars that the characters and situations in medieval and Elizabethan literature, as in any other literature, can best be judged.

1. According to the passage, some twentieth-century scholars have written at length about

(A) Walter's persecution of his wife in Chaucer's The Clerk's Tale
(B) the Duchess of Malfi's love for her husband
(C) the tyrannical behavior of the Duchess of Malfi's brothers
(D) the actions taken by Shakespeare's Desdemona
(E) the injustices suffered by Chaucer's Griselda

2. The primary purpose of the passage is to

(A) describe the role of the tragic heroine in medieval and Elizabethan literature
(B) resolve a controversy over the meaning of "poetic justice" as it is discussed in certain medieval and Elizabethan literary treatises
(C) present evidence to support the view that characters in medieval and Elizabethan tragedies are to blame for their fates
(D) assert that it is impossible for twentieth-century readers to fully comprehend the characters and situations in medieval and Elizabethan literary works
(E) argue that some twentieth-century scholars have misapplied the concept of "poetic justice" in analyzing certain medieval and Elizabethan literary works

GO ON TO THE NEXT PAGE.

3. It can be inferred from the passage that the author considers Chaucer's Griselda to be

   (A) an innocent victim
   (B) a sympathetic judge
   (C) an imprudent person
   (D) a strong individual
   (E) a rebellious daughter

4. The author's tone in her discussion of the conclusions reached by the "school of twentieth-century scholars" (line 4) is best described as

   (A) plaintive
   (B) philosophical
   (C) disparaging
   (D) apologetic
   (E) enthusiastic

5. It can be inferred from the passage that the author believes that most people respond to intended instances of poetic justice in medieval and Elizabethan literature with

   (A) annoyance
   (B) disapproval
   (C) indifference
   (D) amusement
   (E) gratification

6. As described in the passage, the process by which some twentieth-century scholars have reached their conclusions about the blameworthiness of victims in medieval and Elizabethan literary works is most similar to which of the following?

   (A) Derivation of logically sound conclusions from well-founded premises
   (B) Accurate observation of data, inaccurate calculation of statistics, and drawing of incorrect conclusions from the faulty statistics
   (C) Establishment of a theory, application of the theory to ill-fitting data, and drawing of unwarranted conclusions from the data
   (D) Development of two schools of thought about a factual situation, debate between the two schools, and rendering of a balanced judgment by an objective observer
   (E) Consideration of a factual situation by a group, discussion of various possible explanatory hypotheses, and agreement by consensus on the most plausible explanation

7. The author's paraphrase of a statement by Samuel Johnson (lines 55-63) serves which of the following functions in the passage?

   (A) It furnishes a specific example.
   (B) It articulates a general conclusion.
   (C) It introduces a new topic.
   (D) It provides a contrasting perspective.
   (E) It clarifies an ambiguous assertion.

8. The author of the passage is primarily concerned with

   (A) reconciling opposing viewpoints
   (B) encouraging innovative approaches
   (C) defending an accepted explanation
   (D) advocating an alternative interpretation
   (E) analyzing an unresolved question

GO ON TO THE NEXT PAGE.

Woodrow Wilson was referring to the liberal idea of the economic market when he said that the free enterprise system is the most efficient economic system. Maximum freedom means
(5) maximum productiveness; our "openness" is to be the measure of our stability. Fascination with this ideal has made Americans defy the "Old World" categories of settled possessiveness *versus* unsettling deprivation, the cupidity of retention
(10) *versus* the cupidity of seizure, a "status quo" defended or attacked. The United States, it was believed, had no *status quo ante*. Our only "station" was the turning of a stationary wheel, spinning faster and faster. We did not base our
(15) system on property but opportunity—which meant we based it not on stability but on mobility. The more things changed, that is, the more rapidly the wheel turned, the steadier we would be. The conventional picture of class politics is
(20) composed of the Haves, who want a stability to keep what they have, and the Have-Nots, who want a touch of instability and change in which to scramble for the things they have not. But Americans imagined a condition in which spec-
(25) ulators, self-makers, runners are always using the new opportunities given by our land. These economic leaders (front-runners) would thus be mainly agents of change. The nonstarters were considered the ones who wanted stability, a
(30) strong referee to give them some position in the race, a regulative hand to calm manic speculation; an authority that can call things to a halt, begin things again from compensatorily staggered "starting lines."
(35) "Reform" in America has been sterile because it can imagine no change except through the extension of this metaphor of a race, wider inclusion of competitors, "a piece of the action," as it were, for the disenfranchised. There is no
(40) attempt to call off the race. Since our only stability is change, America seems not to honor the quiet work that achieves social interdependence and stability. There is, in our legends, no heroism of the office clerk, no stable industrial work
(45) force of the people who actually make the system work. There is no pride in being an employee (Wilson asked for a return to the time when everyone was an employer). There has been no boasting about our social workers—they are
(50) merely signs of the system's failure, of opportunity denied or not taken, of things to be eliminated. We have no pride in our growing interdependence, in the fact that our system can serve others, that we are able to help those in
(55) need; empty boasts from the past make us ashamed of our present achievements, make us try to forget or deny them, move away from them. There is no honor but in the Wonderland race we must all run, all trying to win, none
(60) winning in the end (for there is no end).

9. The primary purpose of the passage is to

(A) criticize the inflexibility of American economic mythology
(B) contrast "Old World" and "New World" economic ideologies
(C) challenge the integrity of traditional political leaders
(D) champion those Americans whom the author deems to be neglected
(E) suggest a substitute for the traditional metaphor of a race

10. According to the passage, "Old World" values were based on

(A) ability
(B) property
(C) family connections
(D) guild hierarchies
(E) education

11. In the context of the author's discussion of regulating change, which of the following could be most probably regarded as a "strong referee" (line 30) in the United States?

(A) A school principal
(B) A political theorist
(C) A federal court judge
(D) A social worker
(E) A government inspector

12. The author sets off the word " 'Reform' " (line 35) with quotation marks in order to

(A) emphasize its departure from the concept of settled possessiveness
(B) show his support for a systematic program of change
(C) underscore the flexibility and even amorphousness of United States society
(D) indicate that the term was one of Wilson's favorites
(E) assert that reform in the United States has not been fundamental

GO ON TO THE NEXT PAGE.

13. It can be inferred from the passage that the author most probably thinks that giving the disenfranchised "'a piece of the action'" (line 38) is

   (A) a compassionate, if misdirected, legislative measure
   (B) an example of Americans' resistance to profound social change
   (C) an innovative program for genuine social reform
   (D) a monument to the efforts of industrial reformers
   (E) a surprisingly "Old World" remedy for social ills

14. Which of the following metaphors could the author most appropriately use to summarize his own assessment of the American economic system (lines 35-60)?

   (A) A windmill
   (B) A waterfall
   (C) A treadmill
   (D) A gyroscope
   (E) A bellows

15. It can be inferred from the passage that Woodrow Wilson's ideas about the economic market

   (A) encouraged those who "make the system work" (lines 45-46)
   (B) perpetuated traditional legends about America
   (C) revealed the prejudices of a man born wealthy
   (D) foreshadowed the stock market crash of 1929
   (E) began a tradition of presidential proclamations on economics

16. The passage contains information that would answer which of the following questions?

   I. What techniques have industrialists used to manipulate a free market?
   II. In what ways are "New World" and "Old World" economic policies similar?
   III. Has economic policy in the United States tended to reward independent action?

   (A) I only
   (B) II only
   (C) III only
   (D) I and II only
   (E) II and III only

17. Which of the following best expresses the author's main point?

   (A) Americans' pride in their jobs continues to give them stamina today.
   (B) The absence of a *status quo ante* has undermined United States economic structure.
   (C) The free enterprise system has been only a useless concept in the United States.
   (D) The myth of the American free enterprise system is seriously flawed.
   (E) Fascination with the ideal of "openness" has made Americans a progressive people.

GO ON TO THE NEXT PAGE.

No very satisfactory account of the mechanism that caused the formation of the ocean basins has yet been given. The traditional view supposes that the upper mantle of the earth behaves as a
(5) liquid when it is subjected to small forces for long periods and that differences in temperature under oceans and continents are sufficient to produce convection in the mantle of the earth with rising convection currents under the mid-
(10) ocean ridges and sinking currents under the continents. Theoretically, this convection would carry the continental plates along as though they were on a conveyor belt and would provide the forces needed to produce the split that occurs
(15) along the ridge. This view may be correct; it has the advantage that the currents are driven by temperature differences that themselves depend on the position of the continents. Such a back-coupling, in which the position of the moving
(20) plate has an impact on the forces that move it, could produce complicated and varying motions.
On the other hand, the theory is implausible because convection does not normally occur along lines, and it certainly does not occur along
(25) lines broken by frequent offsets or changes in direction, as the ridge is. Also it is difficult to see how the theory applies to the plate between the Mid-Atlantic Ridge and the ridge in the Indian Ocean. This plate is growing on both sides, and
(30) since there is no intermediate trench, the two ridges must be moving apart. It would be odd if the rising convection currents kept exact pace with them. An alternative theory is that the sinking part of the plate, which is denser than the
(35) hotter surrounding mantle, pulls the rest of the plate after it. Again it is difficult to see how this applies to the ridge in the South Atlantic, where neither the African nor the American plate has a sinking part.
(40) Another possibility is that the sinking plate cools the neighboring mantle and produces convection currents that move the plates. This last theory is attractive because it gives some hope of explaining the enclosed seas, such as the Sea of
(45) Japan. These seas have a typical oceanic floor, except that the floor is overlaid by several kilometers of sediment. Their floors have probably been sinking for long periods. It seems possible that a sinking current of cooled mantle material
(50) on the upper side of the plate might be the cause of such deep basins. The enclosed seas are an important feature of the earth's surface and seriously require explanation because, in addition to the enclosed seas that are developing at
(55) present behind island arcs, there are a number of older ones of possibly similar origin, such as the Gulf of Mexico, the Black Sea, and perhaps the North Sea.

18. According to the traditional view of the origin of the ocean basins, which of the following is sufficient to move the continental plates?

(A) Increases in sedimentation on ocean floors
(B) Spreading of ocean trenches
(C) Movement of mid-ocean ridges
(D) Sinking of ocean basins
(E) Differences in temperature under oceans and continents

19. It can be inferred from the passage that, of the following, the deepest sediments would be found in the

(A) Indian Ocean
(B) Black Sea
(C) Mid-Atlantic
(D) South Atlantic
(E) Pacific

20. The author refers to a "conveyor belt" in line 13 in order to

(A) illustrate the effects of convection in the mantle
(B) show how temperature differences depend on the positions of the continents
(C) demonstrate the linear nature of the Mid-Atlantic Ridge
(D) describe the complicated motions made possible by back-coupling
(E) account for the rising currents under certain mid-ocean ridges

21. The author regards the traditional view of the origin of the oceans with

(A) slight apprehension
(B) absolute indifference
(C) indignant anger
(D) complete disbelief
(E) guarded skepticism

GO ON TO THE NEXT PAGE.

22. According to the passage, which of the following are separated by a plate that is growing on both sides?

(A) The Pacific Ocean and the Sea of Japan
(B) The South Atlantic Ridge and the North Sea Ridge
(C) The Gulf of Mexico and the South Atlantic Ridge
(D) The Mid-Atlantic Ridge and the Indian Ocean Ridge
(E) The Black Sea and the Sea of Japan

23. Which of the following, if it could be demonstrated, would most support the traditional view of ocean formation?

(A) Convection usually occurs along lines.
(B) The upper mantle behaves as a dense solid.
(C) Sedimentation occurs at a constant rate.
(D) Sinking plates cool the mantle.
(E) Island arcs surround enclosed seas.

24. According to the passage, the floor of the Black Sea can best be compared to a

(A) rapidly moving conveyor belt
(B) slowly settling foundation
(C) rapidly expanding balloon
(D) violently erupting volcano
(E) slowly eroding mountain

25. Which of the following titles would best describe the content of the passage?

(A) A Description of the Oceans of the World
(B) Several Theories of Ocean Basin Formation
(C) The Traditional View of the Oceans
(D) Convection and Ocean Currents
(E) Temperature Differences Among the Oceans of the World

S T O P

IF YOU FINISH BEFORE TIME IS CALLED, YOU MAY CHECK YOUR WORK ON THIS SECTION ONLY.
DO NOT TURN TO ANY OTHER SECTION IN THE TEST.

Answer Key for Sample Test Section 4

READING COMPREHENSION

1.	D	14.	C
2.	E	15.	B
3.	A	16.	C
4.	C	17.	D
5.	E	18.	E
6.	C	19.	B
7.	B	20.	A
8.	D	21.	E
9.	A	22.	D
10.	B	23.	A
11.	C	24.	B
12.	E	25.	B
13.	B		

Explanatory Material: Reading Comprehension Sample Test Section 4

1. **According to the passage, some twentieth-century scholars have written at length about**

   (A) Walter's persecution of his wife in Chaucer's *The Clerk's Tale*
   (B) the Duchess of Malfi's love for her husband
   (C) the tyrannical behavior of the Duchess of Malfi's brothers
   (D) the actions taken by Shakespeare's Desdemona
   (E) the injustices suffered by Chaucer's Griselda

   The best answer is D because lines 12-16 state that "long essays" have been written by scholars about the "behavior of Shakespeare's Desdemona."

2. **The primary purpose of the passage is to**

   (A) describe the role of the tragic heroine in medieval and Elizabethan literature
   (B) resolve a controversy over the meaning of "poetic justice" as it is discussed in certain medieval and Elizabethan literary treatises
   (C) present evidence to support the view that characters in medieval and Elizabethan tragedies are to blame for their fates
   (D) assert that it is impossible for twentieth-century readers to fully comprehend the characters and situations in medieval and Elizabethan literary works
   (E) argue that some twentieth-century scholars have misapplied the concept of "poetic justice" in analyzing certain medieval and Elizabethan literary works

   The best answer is E. The author argues in the passage that a school of twentieth-century scholars has inappropriately applied the concept of poetic justice to a number of medieval

and Elizabethan literary figures, including the Duchess of Malfi, Desdemona, and Griselda. Thus the first paragraph describes these scholars as having "merely forced victimized characters" (line 6) into the framework of poetic justice, the second paragraph presents specific examples of the misapplication of poetic justice, and the third paragraph argues that it is readers "uncorrupted by the prejudices of some opinionated scholars" (lines 60-61) who can best judge medieval and Elizabethan literature.

3. **It can be inferred from the passage that the author considers Chaucer's Griselda to be**

   (A) an innocent victim
   (B) a sympathetic judge
   (C) an imprudent person
   (D) a strong individual
   (E) a rebellious daughter

   The best answer is A, because lines 25-30 indicate that the author considers Griselda to be "a meek, gentle victim" who does not even criticize her husband, and thus is an innocent victim of his "oppression."

4. **The author's tone in her discussion of the conclusions reached by the "school of twentieth-century scholars" (line 4) is best described as**

   (A) plaintive
   (B) philosophical
   (C) disparaging
   (D) apologetic
   (E) enthusiastic

   The best answer is C. The whole thrust of the author's argument is that the "school of twentieth-century scholars" referred to in line 4 has come to the wrong conclusions about a number of medieval and Elizabethan works. Thus she describes these scholars as having "merely forced victimized characters" into a framework (lines 6-7), "somehow or other" justified injustices (lines 7-8), subjected characters to "critical whips" (line 12), confounded poetic justice with social injustice (lines 39-41), and been corrupted by prejudices (line 60). In all these ways the author establishes a tone of disparagement toward these scholars and their work.

5. **It can be inferred from the passage that the author believes that most people respond to intended instances of poetic justice in medieval and Elizabethan literature with**

   (A) annoyance
   (B) disapproval
   (C) indifference
   (D) amusement
   (E) gratification

   The best answer is E, because lines 1-3 indicate that the examples of poetic justice that do occur in medieval and Elizabethan literature are very "satisfying" to the readers of that literature.

6. As described in the passage, the process by which some twentieth-century scholars have reached their conclusions about the blameworthiness of victims in medieval and Elizabethan literary works is most similar to which of the following?

(A) Derivation of logically sound conclusions from well-founded premises
(B) Accurate observation of data, inaccurate calculation of statistics, and drawing of incorrect conclusions from the faulty statistics
(C) Establishment of a theory, application of the theory to ill-fitting data, and drawing of unwarranted conclusions from the data
(D) Development of two schools of thought about a factual situation, debate between the two schools, and rendering of a balanced judgment by an objective observer
(E) Consideration of a factual situation by a group, discussion of various possible explanatory hypotheses, and agreement by consensus on the most plausible explanation

The best answer is C. The author describes the twentieth-century scholars as using a few clear examples of poetic justice as models for analyzing other literary works (lines 1-5). Their "discoveries," the author implies, were cases that fit the model poorly, for she describes the scholars as having "to 'find' further examples" (lines 4-5), and as forcing characters into a moral framework (lines 6-7). The results of these activities, the author points out, are that these scholars deny obvious effects (lines 33-34), and "confound the cooperation of poetic justice" (lines 39-40). Thus the author portrays these twentieth-century scholars as establishing a theory, applying it to ill-fitting data, and then drawing from this data unwarranted conclusions.

7. The author's paraphrase of a statement by Samuel Johnson (lines 55-63) serves which of the following functions in the passage?

(A) It furnishes a specific example.
(B) It articulates a general conclusion.
(C) It introduces a new topic.
(D) It provides a contrasting perspective.
(E) It clarifies an ambiguous assertion.

The best answer is B. The author's point is that a group of scholars has misjudged a body of literature by holding too tenaciously to their preconceived theory about the prevalence of poetic justice in medieval and Elizabethan literature. In so doing they are unable to act as the authors of this literature intended their readers to act, and it is left to the average reader to serve "as a court of appeal that remains free to rule, as the evidence requires, in favor of the innocent and injured parties" (lines 52-55). The quote from Samuel Johnson serves to articulate this conclusion with precision, for it contrasts "opinionated scholars" (line 61) with "the common sense and compassion" (line 59) of average readers.

8. The author of the passage is primarily concerned with

(A) reconciling opposing viewpoints
(B) encouraging innovative approaches
(C) defending an accepted explanation
(D) advocating an alternative interpretation
(E) analyzing an unresolved question

The best answer is D. The author begins by criticizing the use of the theory of "poetic justice" by a group of twentieth-century scholars, in particular condemning them for having to "blame the victims themselves for their tragic fates" (lines 10-11). In contrast, the author offers an alternative explanation, best expressed in lines 49-51: "Thus, Chaucer and Webster, in their different ways, attack injustice, argue on behalf of the victims, and prosecute the persecutors." She analyzes two specific cases, Chaucer's Griselda and Webster's Duchess of Malfi, to substantiate this claim. She concludes with a paraphrase of Samuel Johnson that she uses to chastise the twentieth-century scholars and to reiterate her own alternative interpretation.

9. The primary purpose of the passage is to

(A) criticize the inflexibility of American economic mythology
(B) contrast "Old World" and "New World" economic ideologies
(C) challenge the integrity of traditional political leaders
(D) champion those Americans whom the author deems to be neglected
(E) suggest a substitute for the traditional metaphor of a race

The best answer is A. The passage is structured so that the first paragraph sets out the basic issue to be explored—the nature of the dominant economic mythology in America—and the second paragraph provides the actual purpose of the passage—the presentation of a sharp critique of this mythology. In particular, lines 35-60 describe this mythology as resulting in sterile reform, not permitting change in the race metaphor, not honoring quiet work or social work or interdependence, and not valuing present achievements. Choice B is incorrect because the passage focuses mainly on the "New World" ideologies; C is incorrect because no one's integrity is challenged; D is only a supporting point; and E does not appear in the passage.

10. According to the passage, "Old World" values were based on

(A) ability
(B) property
(C) family connections
(D) guild hierarchies
(E) education

The best answer is B. In lines 6-11, "the 'Old World' categories of settled possessiveness" and "the cupidity of retention" are contrasted with the American categories of "unsettling deprivation" and "the cupidity of seizure." This contrast is continued in lines 14-17: "We did not base our system on property but opportunity." All of these references state or imply that property was the basis for "Old World" values.

11. In the context of the author's discussion of regulating change, which of the following could be most probably regarded as a "strong referee" (line 30) in the United States?

   (A) A school principal
   (B) A political theorist
   (C) A federal court judge
   (D) A social worker
   (E) A government inspector

The best answer is C. Lines 31-34 describe the "strong referee" mentioned in the question as "a regulative hand to calm manic speculation; an authority that can call things to a halt, begin things again from compensatorily staggered 'starting lines.'" Of the choices, only C has sufficient and appropriate authority to satisfy this description.

12. The author sets off the word " 'Reform' " (line 35) with quotation marks in order to

   (A) emphasize its departure from the concept of settled possessiveness
   (B) show his support for a systematic program of change
   (C) underscore the flexibility and even amorphousness of United States society
   (D) indicate that the term was one of Wilson's favorites
   (E) assert that reform in the United States has not been fundamental

The best answer is E. Lines 35-39 assert that "reform" has been "sterile because it can imagine no change" except in the terms already described by the passage. Since it is the entire thrust of the second paragraph that the race metaphor is the problem, "reform" that accepts this metaphor can in no way solve the underlying problem. The author signals this point by setting the word "reform" off with quotation marks.

13. It can be inferred from the passage that the author most probably thinks that giving the disenfranchised " 'a piece of the action' " (line 38) is

   (A) a compassionate, if misdirected, legislative measure
   (B) an example of Americans' resistance to profound social change
   (C) an innovative program for genuine social reform
   (D) a monument to the efforts of industrial reformers
   (E) a surprisingly "Old World" remedy for social ills

The best answer is B. The author implies, in lines 35-39, that Americans will not permit fundamental reform (i.e., social change); they will permit only sterile "reform," such as giving the disenfranchised "a piece of the action." Thus, giving

the disenfranchised "a piece of the action" is, for the author, an example of Americans' resistance to profound social change.

14. Which of the following metaphors could the author most appropriately use to summarize his own assessment of the American economic system (lines 35-60)?

   (A) A windmill
   (B) A waterfall
   (C) A treadmill
   (D) A gyroscope
   (E) A bellows

The best answer is C. The author states in lines 58-60 that "There is no honor but in the Wonderland race we must all run, all trying to win, none winning in the end (for there is no end)." Of the choices given, only a treadmill fits this description of people running without end.

15. It can be inferred from the passage that Woodrow Wilson's ideas about the economic market

   (A) encouraged those who "make the system work" (lines 45-46)
   (B) perpetuated traditional legends about America
   (C) revealed the prejudices of a man born wealthy
   (D) foreshadowed the stock market crash of 1929
   (E) began a tradition of presidential proclamations on economics

The best answer is B. Woodrow Wilson's ideas about the economic market are mentioned in lines 1-4 and lines 47-48. Both appear in contexts that imply that Wilson's ideas are consistent with the "legends" (line 43) that Americans have traditionally held about their economic system. This is especially evident in lines 46-48, where it is noted that Wilson called specifically for "a return to the time when everyone was an employer," which corresponds to the legend that "There is no pride in being an employee." In articulating ideas such as these, Wilson was perpetuating traditional legends about America.

16. The passage contains information that would answer which of the following questions?

   I. What techniques have industrialists used to manipulate a free market?
   II. In what ways are "New World" and "Old World" economic policies similar?
   III. Has economic policy in the United States tended to reward independent action?

   (A) I only
   (B) II only
   (C) III only
   (D) I and II only
   (E) II and III only

The best answer is C. Question I can be eliminated because the passage never mentions specific techniques of manipulation. Question II can be eliminated because the passage discusses only differences between the "Old World" and the American economic systems, not similarities. Question III can be answered on the basis of information contained in the passage. Lines 40-43 indicate that America is a land of change where "work that achieves social interdependence and stability" is not honored. What is honored is that which promotes constant change, the work of speculators, self-makers, and runners who consistently respond to new opportunities (lines 24-28). Thus those who are rewarded by the American economic system, according to the passage, are those who act independently.

17. **Which of the following best expresses the author's main point?**

(A) Americans' pride in their jobs continues to give them stamina today.
(B) The absence of a *status quo ante* has undermined United States economic structure.
(C) The free enterprise system has been only a useless concept in the United States.
(D) The myth of the American free enterprise system is seriously flawed.
(E) Fascination with the ideal of "openness" has made Americans a progressive people.

The best answer is D. The first paragraph compares Americans' ideas concerning their own economic system with "Old World" beliefs and provides a basis for criticism of the American view in the second paragraph. Thus, the main point of the passage is that the "myth" described in the first paragraph is "seriously flawed," as shown in the second paragraph. Choice A does not describe a point made in the passage. Choice B inaccurately states a point made in the passage. Choice C is an overstatement and does not articulate the idea of "myth" as it is developed in the first paragraph. Choice E does not convey the criticism that is the concern of the second paragraph.

18. **According to the traditional view of the origin of the ocean basins, which of the following is sufficient to move the continental plates?**

(A) Increases in sedimentation on ocean floors
(B) Spreading of ocean trenches
(C) Movement of mid-ocean ridges
(D) Sinking of ocean basins
(E) Differences in temperature under oceans and continents

The best answer is E. The traditional view of the origin of the ocean basins is described in lines 3-21. Lines 6-7 state that, according to the traditional view, "differences in temperature under oceans and continents are sufficient to produce convection in the mantle of the earth." Lines 11-13 state that, according to the traditional view, "this convection would carry the continental plates along as though they were

on a conveyor belt." Thus, it can be inferred that the temperature differences are sufficient to move the continental plates, according to the traditional view.

19. **It can be inferred from the passage that, of the following, the deepest sediments would be found in the**

(A) Indian Ocean
(B) Black Sea
(C) Mid-Atlantic
(D) South Atlantic
(E) Pacific

The best answer is B. Lines 42-58 discuss the enclosed seas, describing them in lines 45-47 as having "a typical oceanic floor, except that the floor is overlaid by several kilometers of sediment." From this it can be inferred that seas that are not enclosed do not have deep sediments on their floors. Of the choices, only the Black Sea is mentioned in the passage as an enclosed sea (lines 51-57). Therefore, it can be inferred that, of the five choices, the Black Sea has the deepest sediments.

20. **The author refers to a "conveyor belt" in line 13 in order to**

(A) illustrate the effects of convection in the mantle
(B) show how temperature differences depend on the positions of the continents
(C) demonstrate the linear nature of the Mid-Atlantic Ridge
(D) describe the complicated motions made possible by back-coupling
(E) account for the rising currents under certain mid-ocean ridges

The best answer is A because "as though they were on a conveyor belt" in lines 12-13 refers to the manner in which convection in the mantle carries the continental plates along. The "conveyor belt" image enables the author to illustrate the effects of convection.

21. **The author regards the traditional view of the origin of the oceans with**

(A) slight apprehension
(B) absolute indifference
(C) indignant anger
(D) complete disbelief
(E) guarded skepticism

The best answer is E. Throughout the passage, the author refers to the traditional view of the origin of the oceans in terms that indicate a cautious and doubtful but not totally disbelieving attitude. Lines 1-3 state, "'No very satisfactory account of the mechanism that caused the formation of the ocean basins has yet been given." Line 15 says, "This view may be correct." Lines 22-23 say, "On the other hand, the theory is implausible because. . . ." Lines 26-27 add, "Also it is difficult to see how. . . ." Line 31 says, "It would be odd if. . . ." Taken together, these references convey an attitude of guarded skepticism, though not complete disbelief, toward the traditional view.

22. According to the passage, which of the following are separated by a plate that is growing on both sides?

    (A) The Pacific Ocean and the Sea of Japan
    (B) The South Atlantic Ridge and the North Sea Ridge
    (C) The Gulf of Mexico and the South Atlantic Ridge
    (D) The Mid-Atlantic Ridge and the Indian Ocean Ridge
    (E) The Black Sea and the Sea of Japan

The best answer is D because lines 27-29 mention "the plate between the Mid-Atlantic Ridge and the ridge in the Indian Ocean," and line 29 then refers to it, stating, "This plate is growing on both sides."

23. Which of the following, if it could be demonstrated, would most support the traditional view of ocean formation?

    (A) Convection usually occurs along lines.
    (B) The upper mantle behaves as a dense solid.
    (C) Sedimentation occurs at a constant rate.
    (D) Sinking plates cool the mantle.
    (E) Island arcs surround enclosed seas.

The best answer is A. If it could be demonstrated that convection usually occurs along lines, the objection to the traditional view that is stated in lines 22-24 would be removed, and the traditional view's assumptions about the way in which convection occurs would be supported. The other choices either contradict the traditional view (and thus would weaken it) or are irrelevant to it.

24. According to the passage, the floor of the Black Sea can best be compared to a

    (A) rapidly moving conveyor belt
    (B) slowly settling foundation
    (C) rapidly expanding balloon
    (D) violently erupting volcano
    (E) slowly eroding mountain

The best answer is B. Lines 53-57 indicate that the Black Sea is an enclosed sea, and lines 47-48 state that the floors of enclosed seas "have probably been sinking for long periods." Thus it can be inferred that the floor of the Black Sea has been slowly settling. Since the floor of an ocean supports water in the same general way that the foundation of a building supports a building, the floor of the Black Sea can be compared to a slowly settling foundation. The passage provides no support for the comparisons in the other choices.

25. Which of the following titles would best describe the content of the passage?

    (A) A Description of the Oceans of the World
    (B) Several Theories of Ocean Basin Formation
    (C) The Traditional View of the Oceans
    (D) Convection and Ocean Currents
    (E) Temperature Differences Among the Oceans of the World

The best answer is B. The passage discusses three theories of ocean basin formation—the "traditional view" in lines 1-33, an "alternative theory" in lines 33-39, and a third theory in lines 42-58. These theories are the focus of the passage and constitute its entire content. Therefore, B is an excellent description of the content of the passage. Choice A is incorrect because the passage describes only a few oceans of the world and then only peripherally. Choice C is too narrow, leaving out two of the theories. Choices D and E refer to only small portions of the passage's content.

READING COMPREHENSION SAMPLE TEST SECTION 5

30 Minutes
24 Questions

Directions: Each passage in this group is followed by questions based on its content. After reading a passage, choose the best answer to each question and fill in the corresponding oval on the answer sheet. Answer all questions following a passage on the basis of what is stated or implied in that passage.

The fossil remains of the first flying vertebrates, the pterosaurs, have intrigued paleontologists for more than two centuries. How such large creatures, which weighed in some cases as much as a piloted hang-glider and had wingspans from 8 to 12 meters, solved the problems of powered flight, and exactly what these creatures were—reptiles or birds—are among the questions scientists have puzzled over.

Perhaps the least controversial assertion about the pterosaurs is that they were reptiles. Their skulls, pelvises, and hind feet are reptilian. The anatomy of their wings suggests that they did not evolve into the class of birds. In pterosaurs a greatly elongated fourth finger of each forelimb supported a winglike membrane. The other fingers were short and reptilian, with sharp claws. In birds the second finger is the principal strut of the wing, which consists primarily of feathers. If the pterosaurs walked on all fours, the three short fingers may have been employed for grasping. When a pterosaur walked or remained stationary, the fourth finger, and with it the wing, could only turn upward in an extended inverted V-shape along each side of the animal's body.

The pterosaurs resembled both birds and bats in their overall structure and proportions. This is not surprising because the design of any flying vertebrate is subject to aerodynamic constraints. Both the pterosaurs and the birds have hollow bones, a feature that represents a savings in weight. In the birds, however, these bones are reinforced more massively by internal struts.

Although scales typically cover reptiles, the pterosaurs probably had hairy coats. T.H. Huxley reasoned that flying vertebrates must have been warm-blooded because flying implies a high rate of metabolism, which in turn implies a high internal temperature. Huxley speculated that a coat of hair would insulate against loss of body heat and might streamline the body to reduce drag in flight. The recent discovery of a pterosaur specimen covered in long, dense, and relatively thick hairlike fossil material was the first clear evidence that his reasoning was correct.

Efforts to explain how the pterosaurs became airborne have led to suggestions that they launched themselves by jumping from cliffs, by dropping from trees, or even by rising into light winds from the crests of waves. Each hypothesis has its difficulties. The first wrongly assumes that the pterosaurs' hind feet resembled a bat's and could serve as hooks by which the animal could hang in preparation for flight. The second hypothesis seems unlikely because large pterosaurs could not have landed in trees without damaging their wings. The third calls for high waves to channel updrafts. The wind that made such waves however, might have been too strong for the pterosaurs to control their flight once airborne.

1. It can be inferred from the passage that scientists now generally agree that the

    (A) enormous wingspan of the pterosaurs enabled them to fly great distances
    (B) structure of the skeleton of the pterosaurs suggests a close evolutionary relationship to bats
    (C) fossil remains of the pterosaurs reveal how they solved the problem of powered flight
    (D) pterosaurs were reptiles
    (E) pterosaurs walked on all fours

2. The author views the idea that the pterosaurs became airborne by rising into light winds created by waves as

    (A) revolutionary
    (B) unlikely
    (C) unassailable
    (D) probable
    (E) outdated

3. According to the passage, the skeleton of a pterosaur can be distinguished from that of a bird by the

    (A) size of its wingspan
    (B) presence of hollow spaces in its bones
    (C) anatomic origin of its wing strut
    (D) presence of hooklike projections on its hind feet
    (E) location of the shoulder joint joining the wing to its body

GO ON TO THE NEXT PAGE.

4. The ideas attributed to T.H. Huxley in the passage suggest that he would most likely agree with which of the following statements?

   (A) An animal's brain size has little bearing on its ability to master complex behaviors.
   (B) An animal's appearance is often influenced by environmental requirements and physical capabilities.
   (C) Animals within a given family group are unlikely to change their appearance dramatically over a period of time.
   (D) The origin of flight in vertebrates was an accidental development rather than the outcome of specialization or adaptation.
   (E) The pterosaurs should be classified as birds, not reptiles.

5. It can be inferred from the passage that which of the following is characteristic of the pterosaurs?

   (A) They were unable to fold their wings when not in use.
   (B) They hung upside down from branches as bats do before flight.
   (C) They flew in order to capture prey.
   (D) They were an early stage in the evolution of the birds.
   (E) They lived primarily in a forestlike habitat.

6. Which of the following best describes the organization of the last paragraph of the passage?

   (A) New evidence is introduced to support a traditional point of view.
   (B) Three explanations for a phenomenon are presented, and each is disputed by means of specific information.
   (C) Three hypotheses are outlined, and evidence supporting each is given.
   (D) Recent discoveries are described, and their implications for future study are projected.
   (E) A summary of the material in the preceding paragraphs is presented, and conclusions are drawn.

7. It can be inferred from the passage that some scientists believe that pterosaurs

   (A) lived near large bodies of water
   (B) had sharp teeth for tearing food
   (C) were attacked and eaten by larger reptiles
   (D) had longer tails than many birds
   (E) consumed twice their weight daily to maintain their body temperature

GO ON TO THE NEXT PAGE.

How many really suffer as a result of labor market problems? This is one of the most critical yet contentious social policy questions. In many ways, our social statistics exaggerate the degree of hard-
(5) ship. Unemployment does not have the same dire consequences today as it did in the 1930's when most of the unemployed were primary breadwinners, when income and earnings were usually much closer to the margin of subsistence, and when there
(10) were no countervailing social programs for those failing in the labor market. Increasing affluence, the rise of families with more than one wage earner, the growing predominance of secondary earners among the unemployed, and improved social welfare pro-
(15) tection have unquestionably mitigated the consequences of joblessness. Earnings and income data also overstate the dimensions of hardship. Among the millions with hourly earnings at or below the minimum wage level, the overwhelming majority
(20) are from multiple-earner, relatively affluent families. Most of those counted by the poverty statistics are elderly or handicapped or have family responsibilities which keep them out of the labor force, so the poverty statistics are by no means an
(25) accurate indicator of labor market pathologies.

Yet there are also many ways our social statistics underestimate the degree of labor-market-related hardship. The unemployment counts exclude the millions of fully employed workers whose wages are
(30) so low that their families remain in poverty. Low wages and repeated or prolonged unemployment frequently interact to undermine the capacity for self-support. Since the number experiencing joblessness at some time during the year is several times
(35) the number unemployed in any month, those who suffer as a result of forced idleness can equal or exceed average annual unemployment, even though only a minority of the jobless in any month really suffer. For every person counted in the monthly
(40) unemployment tallies, there is another working part-time because of the inability to find full-time work, or else outside the labor force but wanting a job. Finally, income transfers in our country have always focused on the elderly, disabled, and depen-
(45) dent, neglecting the needs of the working poor, so that the dramatic expansion of cash and in-kind transfers does not necessarily mean that those failing in the labor market are adequately protected.

As a result of such contradictory evidence, it is
(50) uncertain whether those suffering seriously as a result of labor market problems number in the hundreds of thousands or the tens of millions, and, hence, whether high levels of joblessness can be tolerated or must be countered by job creation and

(55) economic stimulus. There is only one area of agreement in this debate—that the existing poverty, employment, and earnings statistics are inadequate for one of their primary applications, measuring the consequences of labor market problems.

8. Which of the following is the principal topic of the passage?

(A) What causes labor market pathologies that result in suffering
(B) Why income measures are imprecise in measuring degrees of poverty
(C) Which of the currently used statistical procedures are the best for estimating the incidence of hardship that is due to unemployment
(D) Where the areas of agreement are among poverty, employment, and earnings figures
(E) How social statistics give an unclear picture of the degree of hardship caused by low wages and insufficient employment opportunities

9. The author uses "labor market problems" in lines 1-2 to refer to which of the following?

(A) The overall causes of poverty
(B) Deficiencies in the training of the work force
(C) Trade relationships among producers of goods
(D) Shortages of jobs providing adequate income
(E) Strikes and inadequate supplies of labor

10. The author contrasts the 1930's with the present in order to show that

(A) more people were unemployed in the 1930's
(B) unemployment now has less severe effects
(C) social programs are more needed now
(D) there now is a greater proportion of elderly and handicapped people among those in poverty
(E) poverty has increased since the 1930's

GO ON TO THE NEXT PAGE.

11. Which of the following proposals best responds to the issues raised by the author?

   (A) Innovative programs using multiple approaches should be set up to reduce the level of unemployment.
   (B) A compromise should be found between the positions of those who view joblessness as an evil greater than economic control and those who hold the opposite view.
   (C) New statistical indices should be developed to measure the degree to which unemployment and inadequately paid employment cause suffering.
   (D) Consideration should be given to the ways in which statistics can act as partial causes of the phenomena that they purport to measure.
   (E) The labor force should be restructured so that it corresponds to the range of job vacancies.

12. The author's purpose in citing those who are repeatedly unemployed during a twelve-month period is most probably to show that

   (A) there are several factors that cause the payment of low wages to some members of the labor force
   (B) unemployment statistics can underestimate the hardship resulting from joblessness
   (C) recurrent inadequacies in the labor market can exist and can cause hardships for individual workers
   (D) a majority of those who are jobless at any one time do not suffer severe hardship
   (E) there are fewer individuals who are without jobs at some time during a year than would be expected on the basis of monthly unemployment figures

13. The author states that the mitigating effect of social programs involving income transfers on the income level of low-income people is often not felt by

   (A) the employed poor
   (B) dependent children in single-earner families
   (C) workers who become disabled
   (D) retired workers
   (E) full-time workers who become unemployed

14. According to the passage, one factor that causes unemployment and earnings figures to overpredict the amount of economic hardship is the

   (A) recurrence of periods of unemployment for a group of low-wage workers
   (B) possibility that earnings may be received from more than one job per worker
   (C) fact that unemployment counts do not include those who work for low wages and remain poor
   (D) establishment of a system of record-keeping that makes it possible to compile poverty statistics
   (E) prevalence, among low-wage workers and the unemployed, of members of families in which others are employed

15. The conclusion stated in lines 33-39 about the number of people who suffer as a result of forced idleness depends primarily on the point that

   (A) in times of high unemployment, there are some people who do not remain unemployed for long
   (B) the capacity for self-support depends on receiving moderate-to-high wages
   (C) those in forced idleness include, besides the unemployed, both underemployed part-time workers and those not actively seeking work
   (D) at different times during the year, different people are unemployed
   (E) many of those who are affected by unemployment are dependents of unemployed workers

16. Which of the following, if true, is the best criticism of the author's argument concerning why poverty statistics cannot properly be used to show the effects of problems in the labor market?

   (A) A short-term increase in the number of those in poverty can indicate a shortage of jobs, because the basic number of those unable to accept employment remains approximately constant.
   (B) For those who are in poverty as a result of joblessness, there are social programs available that provide a minimum standard of living.
   (C) Poverty statistics do not consistently agree with earnings statistics, when each is taken as a measure of hardship resulting from unemployment.
   (D) The elderly and handicapped categories include many who previously were employed in the labor market.
   (E) Since the labor market is global in nature, poor workers in one country are competing with poor workers in another with respect to the level of wages and the existence of jobs.

GO ON TO THE NEXT PAGE.

(The following passage was adapted from a work published in 1978.)

The conventional spark-ignition (Otto) automobile engine has inherent virtues that become more apparent when alternative engines are considered. These virtues include a respectable efficiency (especially under partial load), light weight, ease of starting, acceptable emissions (with control devices), and a negligible requirement for expensive fabrication materials (and hence a low manufacturing cost). Nonetheless, concern about air pollution has focused attention on alternative engines that are potentially more promising with respect to achieving minimal emission levels—the compression-ignition (Diesel) engine, the steam or vapor-cycle (Rankine) engine, the gas turbine (Brayton engine), and the Stirling engine.

The conventional automobile engine is indeed at a disadvantage with respect to exhaust emissions because many pollutants are formed as a consequence of the intermittent combustion process, with its rapid chilling of the combustion products. The engine has been substantially cleaned up but, with one or two exceptions, this task has called for catalytic emission-control devices that tend to degenerate rapidly. All the continuous-combustion engines emit far smaller quantities of pollutants than the spark-ignition engine emits in the absence of emission-control devices; in fact, experimental models of vapor-cycle engines, gas turbines, and Stirling engines have surpassed the most stringent emission requirements yet established. Although the Diesel engine is an intermittent-combustion engine, it has the advantage of operating with excess air, so that its carbon monoxide emission is negligible. Moreover, hydrocarbons are normally only a small constituent of Diesel exhaust. However, because oxides of nitrogen are formed in hot flames and are retained as a result of rapid chilling, the Diesel engine would not be able to meet stringent oxides-of-nitrogen standards. There are also unsubstantiated suspicions that Diesel-engine exhaust particulates carry carcinogens.

If emission standards were to necessitate the replacement of the Otto engine, the Stirling engine would be the most promising candidate. The part-load efficiency of some experimental Stirling engines (40 percent) is the highest of any of the alternative engines. The engine has the further advantage, shared by steam engines and gas turbines, of being able to operate on almost any fuel. It is very quiet, is the easiest of all alternative engines to start, and operates satisfactorily in freezing temperatures. Since the Stirling engine works on a gas cycle, it has the potential of operating at still higher temperatures and pressures than it does at present, which would make it even more efficient and lighter. Unfortunately, because present experimental models need a substantial amount of metal capable of withstanding high temperatures, they would be expensive to manufacture, but there is hope that alternative ceramic components can be developed.

In conclusion, at present the venerable spark-ignition engine remains largely unsurpassed except with respect to emissions. But if an alternative engine must be developed, automobile makers would be wise to invest in the Stirling.

17. According to the passage, the carcinogenicity of Diesel-engine exhaust particulates is

(A) an insoluble problem
(B) a known fact
(C) a common belief
(D) an unsupported hypothesis
(E) an unacceptable risk

18. The passage suggests that the major disadvantage of the spark-ignition engine would be greatly reduced if which of the following were to occur?

(A) A starter that makes the engine much easier to start is invented.
(B) A method of removing oxides of nitrogen from the engine's exhaust emissions is devised.
(C) An emissions-control device that maintains its effectiveness is designed for the engine.
(D) Materials that make the engine much less expensive to manufacture are developed.
(E) Manufacturing materials that make the engine much lighter in weight are developed.

GO ON TO THE NEXT PAGE.

19. According to the passage, the Rankine, Brayton, and Stirling engines are similar in which of the following respects?

      I.   They are continuous-combustion engines.
     II.   They can operate on almost any fuel.
   III.   They meet very strict antipollution standards.

(A) I only
(B) I and II only
(C) I and III only
(D) II and III only
(E) I, II, and III

20. It can be inferred from the passage that the major purpose of developing ceramic parts for the Stirling engine would be to replace some current metal components with parts that are

(A) less expensive
(B) lighter in weight
(C) easier to manufacture
(D) more capable of withstanding freezing temperatures
(E) more capable of withstanding high temperatures

21. The passage implies that which of the following is currently a disadvantage of at least one of the alternative automobile engines?

(A) Rapid degeneration
(B) High manufacturing cost
(C) High cost of fuel
(D) Excessive carbon monoxide emissions
(E) Excessive hydrocarbon emissions

22. The author's attitude toward the potential of the Stirling engine can best be described as

(A) ironic
(B) derogatory
(C) confused
(D) cautiously optimistic
(E) completely neutral

23. It can be inferred from the passage that which of the following events, if it were to occur, would immediately cause the most difficulties for manufacturers of automobiles that have Diesel engines?

(A) Emission requirements for carbon monoxide are made more rigid.
(B) Emission requirements for oxides of nitrogen are made very strict.
(C) A study is undertaken to determine whether Diesel-engine exhaust particulates are carcinogenic.
(D) Researchers find that catalytic emission control devices create a by-product that is harmful to health.
(E) Researchers find that all continuous-combustion engines have a serious, previously undiscovered drawback when used as automobile engines.

24. Which of the following best summarizes the author's main point?

(A) Except in the area of oxides-of-nitrogen emissions, the Diesel engine is nonpolluting; of the other alternative engines, the Stirling engine is the most promising.
(B) Except in the area of exhaust emissions, the conventional automobile engine is currently better overall than alternative engines; of these, the Stirling engine most warrants further development.
(C) Although the conventional automobile engine has many advantages, its failure to meet stringent emission standards makes development of the Stirling engine essential.
(D) Although concern about air pollution has focused attention on the emissions of alternative automobile engines, it has not led to full development of any of them.
(E) Once automobile makers become fully aware of the advantages offered by the spark-ignition engine, they will realize that even the very efficient Stirling engine is not worth developing.

S T O P

IF YOU FINISH BEFORE TIME IS CALLED, YOU MAY CHECK YOUR WORK ON THIS SECTION ONLY.
DO NOT TURN TO ANY OTHER SECTION IN THE TEST.

Answer Key for Sample Test Section 5

READING COMPREHENSION

1.	D	13.	A
2.	B	14.	E
3.	C	15.	D
4.	B	16.	A
5.	A	17.	D
6.	B	18.	C
7.	A	19.	E
8.	E	20.	A
9.	D	21.	B
10.	B	22.	D
11.	C	23.	B
12.	B	24.	B

Explanatory Material: Reading Comprehension Sample Test Section 5

1. It can be inferred from the passage that scientists now generally agree that the

   (A) enormous wingspan of the pterosaurs enabled them to fly great distances
   (B) structure of the skeleton of the pterosaurs suggests a close evolutionary relationship to bats
   (C) fossil remains of the pterosaurs reveal how they solved the problem of powered flight
   (D) pterosaurs were reptiles
   (E) pterosaurs walked on all fours

The best answer is D. In the first paragraph, the author observes that for more than two centuries paleontologists have been puzzled by the question of whether pterosaurs are birds or reptiles. Lines 9-10 state that the assertion that the pterosaurs were reptiles is "perhaps the least controversial" of those that paleontologists have made about them. The author then cites evidence to support the classification of the pterosaurs as reptiles. In lines 11-13, the author observes that the skulls, pelvises, and feet of the pterosaurs are "reptilian," and that the "anatomy of their wings suggests that they did not evolve into the class of birds." Lines 13-16 elaborate on this difference in wing structure, noting that in pterosaurs it is the "greatly elongated fourth finger of each forelimb"—and in birds "the second finger"—that provides principle support for the wing. It can thus be inferred that at present scientists generally agree that pterosaurs were reptiles.

2. The author views the idea that the pterosaurs became airborne by rising into light winds created by waves as

   (A) revolutionary
   (B) unlikely
   (C) unassailable
   (D) probable
   (E) outdated

The best answer is B. In the last paragraph of the passage, the author observes that each of three hypotheses concerning how pterosaurs became airborne "has its difficulties." In relation to the third hypothesis—the suggestion that pterosaurs became airborne "by rising into light winds from the crests of waves"—the author further observes that such waves would have to be high in order to "channel updrafts" and that wind that made waves as high as these "might have been too strong for the pterosaurs to control their flight once airborne."

3. According to the passage, the skeleton of a pterosaur can be distinguished from that of a bird by the

   (A) size of its wingspan
   (B) presence of hollow spaces in its bones
   (C) anatomic origin of its wing strut
   (D) presence of hooklike projections on its hind feet
   (E) location of the shoulder joint joining the wing to its body

The best answer is C. Choices A and E are incorrect because the passage states that the "pterosaurs resembled both birds and bats in their overall structure and proportions" (lines 24-25). Choice D can be eliminated because, in the last paragraph of the passage, the author notes that it is wrongly assumed that the "pterosaurs' hind feet. . .could serve as hooks by which the animal could hang in preparation for flight" (lines 47-49). Lines 27-28 state that the bones of both pterosaurs and birds are hollow, making B an incorrect choice. Choice C is correct because, in lines 13-17, the author observes that the anatomical structure of the pterosaur differs from that of birds in that the fourth, rather than the second, finger of each forelimb provided the major support for the pterosaur's "winglike membrane."

4. The ideas attributed to T. H. Huxley in the passage suggest that he would most likely agree with which of the following statements?

    (A) An animal's brain size has little bearing on its ability to master complex behaviors.

    (B) An animal's appearance is often influenced by environmental requirements and physical capabilities.

    (C) Animals within a given family group are unlikely to change their appearance dramatically over a period of time.

    (D) The origin of flight in vertebrates was an accidental development rather than the outcome of specialization or adaptation.

    (E) The pterosaurs should be classified as birds, not reptiles.

The best answer is B. According to the second paragraph of the passage, Huxley theorized that the pterosaurs had to have been warm-blooded in order to maintain the high rate of metabolism and high internal temperature necessitated by their flight, and that an external coat of hair would have helped the pterosaurs to maintain their relatively high internal body temperature in addition to streamlining the body "to reduce drag in flight." It can thus be concluded that Huxley would agree with the assertion that "An animal's appearance is often influenced by environmental requirements and physical capabilities."

5. It can be inferred from the passage that which of the following is characteristic of the pterosaurs?

    (A) They were unable to fold their wings when not in use.

    (B) They hung upside down from branches as bats do before flight.

    (C) They flew in order to capture prey.

    (D) They were an early stage in the evolution of the birds.

    (E) They lived primarily in a forestlike habitat.

The best answer is A. Lines 19-23 state that when it was walking or remaining stationary, the pterosaur could only turn its wings "upward in an extended inverted V-shape" along the sides of its body. Since most winged creatures' wings fold horizontally close to the body, it can therefore be inferred that pterosaurs could not fold their wings when they were not being used.

6. Which of the following best describes the organization of the last paragraph of the passage?

    (A) New evidence is introduced to support a traditional point of view.

    (B) Three explanations for a phenomenon are presented, and each is disputed by means of specific information.

    (C) Three hypotheses are outlined, and evidence supporting each is given.

    (D) Recent discoveries are described, and their implications for future study are projected.

    (E) A summary of the material in the preceding paragraphs is presented, and conclusions are drawn.

The best answer is B. The question requires you to examine the organization of the last paragraph as a whole. Choice B is the best answer because, in the last paragraph, the author presents three explanations of how pterosaurs became airborne and provides specific information that undermines each of them. The author disputes the first explanation—that pterosaurs "launched themselves by jumping from cliffs"—by noting that pterosaurs could not use their hind feet to "hang in preparation for flight." The author disputes the second explanation—that pterosaurs became airborne "by dropping from trees"—with the assertion that "pterosaurs could not have landed in trees without damaging their wings." The author undermines the third explanation—that pterosaurs launched themselves "by rising into light winds from the crests of waves"—by observing that the winds that generated such waves "might have been too strong for the pterosaurs to control their flight once airborne."

7. It can be inferred from the passage that some scientists believe that pterosaurs

    (A) lived near large bodies of water

    (B) had sharp teeth for tearing food

    (C) were attacked and eaten by larger reptiles

    (D) had longer tails than many birds

    (E) consumed twice their weight daily to maintain their body temperature

The best answer is A. In the last paragraph, the author observes that some scientists have argued that pterosaurs launched themselves "by rising into light winds from the crests of waves." If this explanation of how pterosaurs became airborne were true, it would be reasonable to conclude that pterosaurs must have lived in the vicinity of bodies of water large enough to create such waves; otherwise, according to this theory, pterosaurs would never have been able to use their capacity to fly. Thus, it is reasonable to infer that at least some scientists believe that pterosaurs "lived near large bodies of water."

8. Which of the following is the principal topic of the passage?

    (A) What causes labor market pathologies that result in suffering

    (B) Why income measures are imprecise in measuring degrees of poverty

    (C) Which of the currently used statistical procedures are the best for estimating the incidence of hardship that is due to unemployment

    (D) Where the areas of agreement are among poverty, employment, and earnings figures

    (E) How social statistics give an unclear picture of the degree of hardship caused by low wages and insufficient employment opportunities

The best answer is E. The author begins the passage with a question about the degree of hardship caused by labor market problems. The first paragraph is devoted to an exploration of the ways in which social statistics may exaggerate such hardship. Paragraph two explores the ways in which the same social statistics may underestimate such hardship. The final paragraph acknowledges the contradictory nature of the evidence available from social statistics that report the degree of hardship caused by labor market problems. None of the topics mentioned in A, B, C, and D are examined in the passage.

9. The author uses "labor market problems" in lines 1-2 to refer to which of the following?

    (A) The overall causes of poverty
    (B) Deficiencies in the training of the work force
    (C) Trade relationships among producers of goods
    (D) Shortages of jobs providing adequate income
    (E) Strikes and inadequate supplies of labor

The best answer is D. This question asks you to determine what the author means by a particular phrase used in the opening sentence of the passage. To answer the question, you must connect that opening sentence with the rest of the passage. The first paragraph discusses the labor market problems connected with unemployment and earnings; the second paragraph also discusses unemployment and earnings. The concluding paragraph mentions "poverty, employment, and earnings statistics" (lines 56-57) in connection with "labor market problems" (line 59). Thus, the author uses the phrase cited in the question to refer to "shortages of jobs providing adequate income," the topic mentioned in D. In its discussion of "labor market problems," the passage does not refer to the topics mentioned in the other choices.

10. The author contrasts the 1930's with the present in order to show that

    (A) more people were unemployed in the 1930's
    (B) unemployment now has less severe effects
    (C) social programs are more needed now
    (D) there now is a greater proportion of elderly and handicapped people among those in poverty
    (E) poverty has increased since the 1930's

The best answer is B. To answer this question, you must first find the author's statement contrasting the 1930's with the present. This contrast is contained in the sentence in lines 5-11: "Unemployment does not have the same dire consequences today as it did in the 1930's. . . ." The rest of the sentence supports this opening assertion with specific contrasting details. None of the topics mentioned in the other options are mentioned in the passage in connection with the 1930's.

11. Which of the following proposals best responds to the issues raised by the author?

    (A) Innovative programs using multiple approaches should be set up to reduce the level of unemployment.
    (B) A compromise should be found between the positions of those who view joblessness as an evil greater than economic control and those who hold the opposite view.
    (C) New statistical indices should be developed to measure the degree to which unemployment and inadequately paid employment cause suffering.
    (D) Consideration should be given to the ways in which statistics can act as partial causes of the phenomena that they purport to measure.
    (E) The labor force should be restructured so that it corresponds to the range of job vacancies.

The best answer is C. This question requires you to evaluate the choices in light of the passage as a whole. Thus, in choosing the answer, you must keep in mind what issues are central to the passage. The passage begins with a question that raises the issue of the accuracy of the statistical information available. In the first paragraph, the author details the ways in which social statistics exaggerate the hardship created by labor market problems. Then, in the second paragraph, the author discusses the ways in which these same statistics underestimate these hardships. In the last sentence of the passage, the author says, ". . .existing poverty, employment, and earnings statistics are inadequate for one of their primary applications. . . ." Thus, the issues raised by the passage are all connected with the adequacy of the social statistics used to measure the hardship caused by labor market problems. Only the proposal mentioned in C suggests the need for the improvement of social statistics.

12. The author's purpose in citing those who are repeatedly unemployed during a twelve-month period is most probably to show that

    (A) there are several factors that cause the payment of low wages to some members of the labor force
    (B) unemployment statistics can underestimate the hardship resulting from joblessness
    (C) recurrent inadequacies in the labor market can exist and can cause hardships for individual workers
    (D) a majority of those who are jobless at any one time do not suffer severe hardship
    (E) there are fewer individuals who are without jobs at some time during a year than would be expected on the basis of monthly unemployment figures

The best answer is B. This question asks you to identify the purpose of a particular statement in the passage. First, you must locate the statement mentioned in the question. In lines 30-32, the author mentions "Low wages and repeated or prolonged unemployment. . . ." To determine the purpose of this citation, you must look at the context in which it appears, the paragraph as a whole. The paragraph begins by asserting that "social statistics underestimate the degree of labor-market-related hardship" (lines 26-28). The first piece of evidence cited to support this assertion is the mention of "millions of fully employed workers whose wages are so low that their families remain in poverty" (lines 29-30). The second piece of evidence is the mention, in the next sentence, of those workers who experience repeated unemployment.

13. The author states that the mitigating effect of social programs involving income transfers on the income level of low-income people is often <u>not</u> felt by

   (A) the employed poor
   (B) dependent children in single-earner families
   (C) workers who become disabled
   (D) retired workers
   (E) full-time workers who become unemployed

The best answer is A. This question asks you to choose the option that would, in combination with the given statement, restate a point the author makes in the passage. To answer the question, you must locate in the passage the author's statements about the subject mentioned in the question, "the mitigating effect of social programs involving income transfers on the income level of low-income people. . . ." Income transfers are mentioned only once in the passage, in lines 43-48, and in that sentence the author clearly states that such transfers have ". . .neglect[ed] the needs of the working poor. . ." (line 45). Those individuals mentioned in B, C, and D are specifically cited in this sentence as beneficiaries of income transfers, while those individuals mentioned in E are not included in the author's discussion of income transfers.

14. According to the passage, one factor that causes unemployment and earnings figures to overpredict the amount of economic hardship is the

   (A) recurrence of periods of unemployment for a group of low-wage workers
   (B) possibility that earnings may be received from more than one job per worker
   (C) fact that unemployment counts do not include those who work for low wages and remain poor
   (D) establishment of a system of record-keeping that makes it possible to compile poverty statistics
   (E) prevalence, among low-wage workers and the unemployed, of members of families in which others are employed

The best answer is E. This question asks you to identify one factor mentioned in the passage as a cause for overprediction of economic hardship. The first paragraph of the pas-

sage asserts, in lines 3-5, that the degree of economic hardship reflected in social statistics is exaggerated in many ways. The rest of the first paragraph supports this assertion by citing various factors that lead to the exaggeration, or overprediction. Only choice E restates one of the factors mentioned in the first paragraph. Choices A and C mention factors cited in the second paragraph of the passage as support for the assertion that social statistics *underpredict* economic hardship. Choices B and D state factors not mentioned in the passage.

15. The conclusion stated in lines 33-39 about the number of people who suffer as a result of forced idleness depends primarily on the point that

   (A) in times of high unemployment, there are some people who do not remain unemployed for long
   (B) the capacity for self-support depends on receiving moderate-to-high wages
   (C) those in forced idleness include, besides the unemployed, both underemployed part-time workers and those not actively seeking work
   (D) at different times during the year, different people are unemployed
   (E) many of those who are affected by unemployment are dependents of unemployed workers

The best answer is D. To answer the question, you must first look at the conclusion cited in the question (lines 33-39 of the passage). This conclusion is stated in the context of the second paragraph, which begins by asserting that "social statistics underestimate the degree of labor-market-related hardship" (lines 26-28). In lines 33-39, the author suggests that the average annual unemployment rate, which is presented as one example of potentially problematic social statistics, does not measure the total number of people who are unemployed at some time during the year. The total number of people unemployed at some time is much larger than the average annual unemployment rate would indicate. The author uses this fact to draw a conclusion—"those who suffer as a result of forced idleness can equal or exceed average annual unemployment" (lines 35-37)—that supports the assertion at the beginning of the second paragraph. This conclusion depends on the point stated in choice D.

16. Which of the following, if true, is the best criticism of the author's argument concerning why poverty statistics cannot properly be used to show the effects of problems in the labor market?

(A) A short-term increase in the number of those in poverty can indicate a shortage of jobs, because the basic number of those unable to accept employment remains approximately constant.

(B) For those who are in poverty as a result of joblessness, there are social programs available that provide a minimum standard of living.

(C) Poverty statistics do not consistently agree with earnings statistics, when each is taken as a measure of hardship resulting from unemployment.

(D) The elderly and handicapped categories include many who previously were employed in the labor market.

(E) Since the labor market is global in nature, poor workers in one country are competing with poor workers in another with respect to the level of wages and the existence of jobs.

The best answer is A. To answer this question, you must first identify the author's argument concerning poverty statistics. Such statistics are mentioned in lines 21-25, where the author argues that they include people who are kept out of the labor force for reasons other than fluctuations in the labor market itself. Thus, according to the author, poverty statistics do not accurately reflect labor market problems. The best criticism of such an argument would be to show that poverty statistics do, in fact, reflect fluctuations in the labor market. Choice A provides such a criticism, by pointing out that the author's account of poverty statistics could still leave room for change in the statistics that does reflect labor market problems. None of the points mentioned in the other choices address the author's argument about the inadequacies of poverty statistics.

17. According to the passage, the carcinogenicity of Diesel-engine exhaust particulates is

(A) an insoluble problem
(B) a known fact
(C) a common belief
(D) an unsupported hypothesis
(E) an unacceptable risk

The best answer is D. The answer to the question is directly stated in the last sentence of the second paragraph. The carcinogenicity of Diesel-engine exhaust particulates is referred to as an unsubstantiated suspicion. Choice D is a paraphrase of that phrase.

18. The passage suggests that the major disadvantage of the spark-ignition engine would be greatly reduced if which of the following were to occur?

(A) A starter that makes the engine much easier to start is invented.

(B) A method of removing oxides of nitrogen from the engine's exhaust emissions is devised.

(C) An emissions-control device that maintains its effectiveness is designed for the engine.

(D) Materials that make the engine much less expensive to manufacture are developed.

(E) Manufacturing materials that make the engine much lighter in weight are developed.

The best answer is C. It is established in the second paragraph that a major drawback of the conventional engine is its relatively high emissions. Lines 19-22 state that catalytic emission-control devices have been used to reduce emissions, but these devices degenerate rapidly. Thus, a device that did not degenerate rapidly would solve a major problem associated with the conventional spark-ignition engines.

19. According to the passage, the Rankine, Brayton, and Stirling engines are similar in which of the following respects?

I. They are continuous-combustion engines.
II. They can operate on almost any fuel.
III. They meet very strict antipollution standards.

(A) I only
(B) I and II only
(C) I and III only
(D) II and III only
(E) I, II, and III

The best answer is E. In order to answer this question, you must examine each of the statements numbered I, II, and III and decide which can be accurately applied to the Rankine, Brayton, and Stirling engines. Lines 22-28 establish that all three engines are continuous-combustion engines; thus, statement I is part of the answer. In the same lines, it is also stated that all three engines surpass the most stringent emission standards to date (1978). Thus, statement III must also be part of the answer. Lines 43-45 establish that all three engines can operate on almost any fuel; thus, the best answer to the question is I, II, and III.

20. It can be inferred from the passage that the major purpose of developing ceramic parts for the Stirling engine would be to replace some current metal components with parts that are

(A) less expensive
(B) lighter in weight
(C) easier to manufacture
(D) more capable of withstanding freezing temperatures
(E) more capable of withstanding high temperatures

The best answer is A. Lines 51-56 indicate that a disadvantage of the Stirling engine is the high cost of metal components of the engine. Ceramic components are mentioned as a possible, less expensive alternative to the metal components.

21. The passage implies that which of the following is currently a disadvantage of at least one of the alternative automobile engines?

(A) Rapid degeneration
(B) High manufacturing cost
(C) High cost of fuel
(D) Excessive carbon monoxide emissions
(E) Excessive hydrocarbon emissions

The best answer is B. The high cost of metal components is mentioned as a disadvantage of the Stirling engine. None of the other choices is mentioned as a disadvantage of any of the alternative engines.

22. The author's attitude toward the potential of the Stirling engine can best be described as

(A) ironic
(B) derogatory
(C) confused
(D) cautiously optimistic
(E) completely neutral

The best answer is D. In the third paragraph, the author states that the Stirling engine is the most promising of the alternative engines, providing that the price of manufacturing it can be lowered. In addition, in lines 59-61 the author claims that it would be "wise to invest in the Stirling." Thus, "cautiously optimistic" is an accurate representation of the author's attitude toward the Stirling engine.

23. It can be inferred from the passage that which of the following events, if it were to occur, would immediately cause the most difficulties for manufacturers of automobiles that have Diesel engines?

(A) Emission requirements for carbon monoxide are made more rigid.
(B) Emission requirements for oxides of nitrogen are made very strict.
(C) A study is undertaken to determine whether Diesel-engine exhaust particulates are carcinogenic.
(D) Researchers find that catalytic emission control devices create a by-product that is harmful to health.
(E) Researchers find that all continuous-combustion engines have a serious, previously undiscovered drawback when used as automobile engines.

The best answer is B. In lines 33-36, it is stated that the Diesel engine cannot meet stringent oxides-of-nitrogen standards. Thus, if very stringent standards were set, manufacturers of Diesel engines would be presented with great difficulties. The passage states that Diesel engines can meet stringent standards for emissions of carbon dioxide; so the possibility presented in A would not be problematic for manufacturers of Diesel engines. The study mentioned in C would not cause difficulties unless the results indicated that Diesel emissions are carcinogenic; thus, the study itself does not present a difficulty and could even prove beneficial. The possibilities presented in D and E would, if anything, prove beneficial to manufacturers of Diesel engines, since both present what would be major drawbacks in the other types of engines discussed in the passage.

24. Which of the following best summarizes the author's main point?

(A) Except in the areas of oxides-of-nitrogen emissions, the Diesel engine is nonpolluting; of the other alternative engines, the Stirling engine is the most promising.
(B) Except in the area of exhaust emissions, the conventional automobile engine is currently better overall than alternative engines; of these, the Stirling engine most warrants further development.
(C) Although the conventional automobile engine has many advantages, its failure to meet stringent emission standards makes development of the Stirling engine essential.
(D) Although concern about air pollution has focused attention on the emissions of alternative automobile engines, it has not led to full development of any of them.
(E) Once automobile makers become fully aware of the advantages offered by the spark-ignition engine, they will realize that even the very efficient Stirling engine is not worth developing.

The best answer is B. The passage briefly discusses the advantages and disadvantages of the widely used conventional spark-ignition engine and those of several alternatives to the conventional engine. In the last paragraph of the passage, the author presents in summary an evaluation of the engines; choice B is essentially a paraphrase of the author's conclusion.

6 Critical Reasoning

In these questions, you are to analyze the situation on which each question is based, and then select the answer choice that is the most appropriate response to the question. No specialized knowledge of any particular field is required for answering the questions, and no knowledge of the terminology and of the conventions of formal logic is presupposed. The sample Critical Reasoning test sections that begin on page 247 provide good illustrations of the variety of topics that may be covered, of the kinds of questions that may be asked, and of the level of analysis that will generally be required.

Test-Taking Strategies for Critical Reasoning

1. The set of statements on which a question is based should be read very carefully with close attention to such matters as (1) what is put forward as factual information, (2) what is not said but necessarily follows from what is said, (3) what is claimed to follow from facts that have been put forward, and (4) how well substantiated are any claims to the effect that a particular conclusion follows from the facts that have been put forward. In reading arguments, it is important to attend to the soundness of the reasoning employed; it is not necessary to make a judgment of the actual truth of anything that is put forward as factual information.

2. If a question is based on an argument, be careful to identify clearly which part of the argument is its conclusion. The conclusion does not necessarily come at the end of the text of the argument; it may come somewhere in the middle, or it may even come at the beginning. Be alert to clues in the text that one of the statements made is not simply asserted but is said to follow logically from another statement or other statements in the text.

3. It is important to determine exactly what the question is asking; in fact, you might find it helpful to read the question first, before reading the material on which it is based. For example, an argument may appear to have an obvious flaw, and you may expect to be asked to detect that flaw; but the question may actually ask you to recognize the one among the answer choices that does NOT describe a weakness of the argument.

4. Read all the answer choices carefully. You should not assume that a given answer is the best answer without first reading all the choices.

When you take the sample test sections, use the answer spaces on page 245 to mark your answers.

Answer Spaces for Critical Reasoning Sample Test Sections

Sample Test Section 1

1 Ⓐ Ⓑ Ⓒ Ⓓ Ⓔ	6 Ⓐ Ⓑ Ⓒ Ⓓ Ⓔ	11 Ⓐ Ⓑ Ⓒ Ⓓ Ⓔ	16 Ⓐ Ⓑ Ⓒ Ⓓ Ⓔ
2 Ⓐ Ⓑ Ⓒ Ⓓ Ⓔ	7 Ⓐ Ⓑ Ⓒ Ⓓ Ⓔ	12 Ⓐ Ⓑ Ⓒ Ⓓ Ⓔ	17 Ⓐ Ⓑ Ⓒ Ⓓ Ⓔ
3 Ⓐ Ⓑ Ⓒ Ⓓ Ⓔ	8 Ⓐ Ⓑ Ⓒ Ⓓ Ⓔ	13 Ⓐ Ⓑ Ⓒ Ⓓ Ⓔ	18 Ⓐ Ⓑ Ⓒ Ⓓ Ⓔ
4 Ⓐ Ⓑ Ⓒ Ⓓ Ⓔ	9 Ⓐ Ⓑ Ⓒ Ⓓ Ⓔ	14 Ⓐ Ⓑ Ⓒ Ⓓ Ⓔ	19 Ⓐ Ⓑ Ⓒ Ⓓ Ⓔ
5 Ⓐ Ⓑ Ⓒ Ⓓ Ⓔ	10 Ⓐ Ⓑ Ⓒ Ⓓ Ⓔ	15 Ⓐ Ⓑ Ⓒ Ⓓ Ⓔ	20 Ⓐ Ⓑ Ⓒ Ⓓ Ⓔ

Sample Test Section 2

1 Ⓐ Ⓑ Ⓒ Ⓓ Ⓔ	6 Ⓐ Ⓑ Ⓒ Ⓓ Ⓔ	11 Ⓐ Ⓑ Ⓒ Ⓓ Ⓔ	16 Ⓐ Ⓑ Ⓒ Ⓓ Ⓔ
2 Ⓐ Ⓑ Ⓒ Ⓓ Ⓔ	7 Ⓐ Ⓑ Ⓒ Ⓓ Ⓔ	12 Ⓐ Ⓑ Ⓒ Ⓓ Ⓔ	17 Ⓐ Ⓑ Ⓒ Ⓓ Ⓔ
3 Ⓐ Ⓑ Ⓒ Ⓓ Ⓔ	8 Ⓐ Ⓑ Ⓒ Ⓓ Ⓔ	13 Ⓐ Ⓑ Ⓒ Ⓓ Ⓔ	18 Ⓐ Ⓑ Ⓒ Ⓓ Ⓔ
4 Ⓐ Ⓑ Ⓒ Ⓓ Ⓔ	9 Ⓐ Ⓑ Ⓒ Ⓓ Ⓔ	14 Ⓐ Ⓑ Ⓒ Ⓓ Ⓔ	19 Ⓐ Ⓑ Ⓒ Ⓓ Ⓔ
5 Ⓐ Ⓑ Ⓒ Ⓓ Ⓔ	10 Ⓐ Ⓑ Ⓒ Ⓓ Ⓔ	15 Ⓐ Ⓑ Ⓒ Ⓓ Ⓔ	20 Ⓐ Ⓑ Ⓒ Ⓓ Ⓔ

CRITICAL REASONING SAMPLE TEST SECTION 1

30 Minutes
20 Questions

Directions: For each question in this section, select the best of the answer choices given.

1. Nearly one in three subscribers to *Financial Forecaster* is a millionaire, and over half are in top management. Shouldn't you subscribe to *Financial Forecaster* now?

   A reader who is neither a millionaire nor in top management would be most likely to act in accordance with the advertisement's suggestion if he or she drew which of the following questionable conclusions invited by the advertisement?

   (A) Among finance-related periodicals, *Financial Forecaster* provides the most detailed financial information.
   (B) Top managers cannot do their jobs properly without reading *Financial Forecaster*.
   (C) The advertisement is placed where those who will be likely to read it are millionaires.
   (D) The subscribers mentioned were helped to become millionaires or join top management by reading *Financial Forecaster*.
   (E) Only those who will in fact become millionaires, or at least top managers, will read the advertisement.

Questions 2-3 are based on the following.

Contrary to the charges made by some of its opponents, the provisions of the new deficit-reduction law for indiscriminate cuts in the federal budget are justified. Opponents should remember that the New Deal pulled this country out of great economic troubles even though some of its programs were later found to be unconstitutional.

2. The author's method of attacking the charges of certain opponents of the new deficit-reduction law is to

   (A) attack the character of the opponents rather than their claim
   (B) imply an analogy between the law and some New Deal programs
   (C) point out that the opponents' claims imply a dilemma
   (D) show that the opponents' reasoning leads to an absurd conclusion
   (E) show that the New Deal also called for indiscriminate cuts in the federal budget

3. The opponents could effectively defend their position against the author's strategy by pointing out that

   (A) the expertise of those opposing the law is outstanding
   (B) the lack of justification for the new law does not imply that those who drew it up were either inept or immoral
   (C) the practical application of the new law will not entail indiscriminate budget cuts
   (D) economic troubles present at the time of the New Deal were equal in severity to those that have led to the present law
   (E) the fact that certain flawed programs or laws have improved the economy does not prove that every such program can do so

4. In Millington, a city of 50,000 people, Mercedes Pedrosa, a realtor, calculated that a family with Millington's median family income, $28,000 a year, could afford to buy Millington's median-priced $77,000 house. This calculation was based on an 11.2 percent mortgage interest rate and on the realtor's assumption that a family could only afford to pay up to 25 percent of its income for housing.

   Which of the following corrections of a figure appearing in the passage above, if it were the only correction that needed to be made, would yield a new calculation showing that even incomes below the median family income would enable families in Millington to afford Millington's median-priced house?

   (A) Millington's total population was 45,000 people.
   (B) Millington's median annual family income was $27,000.
   (C) Millington's median-priced house cost $80,000.
   (D) The rate at which people in Millington had to pay mortgage interest was only 10 percent.
   (E) Families in Millington could only afford to pay up to 22 percent of their annual income for housing.

5. Psychological research indicates that college hockey and football players are more quickly moved to hostility and aggression than are college athletes in noncontact sports such as swimming. But the researchers' conclusion—that contact sports encourage and teach participants to be hostile and aggressive—is untenable. The football and hockey players were probably more hostile and aggressive to start with than the swimmers.

Which of the following, if true, would most strengthen the conclusion drawn by the psychological researchers?

(A) The football and hockey players became more hostile and aggressive during the season and remained so during the off-season, whereas there was no increase in aggressiveness among the swimmers.
(B) The football and hockey players, but not the swimmers, were aware at the start of the experiment that they were being tested for aggressiveness.
(C) The same psychological research indicated that the football and hockey players had a great respect for cooperation and team play, whereas the swimmers were most concerned with excelling as individual competitors.
(D) The research studies were designed to include no college athletes who participated in both contact and noncontact sports.
(E) Throughout the United States, more incidents of fan violence occur at baseball games than occur at hockey or football games.

6. Ross: The profitability of Company X, restored to private ownership five years ago, is clear evidence that businesses will always fare better under private than under public ownership.

   Julia: Wrong. A close look at the records shows that X has been profitable since the appointment of a first-class manager, which happened while X was still in the public sector.

Which of the following best describes the weak point in Ross's claim on which Julia's response focuses?

(A) The evidence Ross cites comes from only a single observed case, that of Company X.
(B) The profitability of Company X might be only temporary.
(C) Ross's statement leaves open the possibility that the cause he cites came after the effect he attributes to it.
(D) No mention is made of companies that are partly government owned and partly privately owned.
(E) No exact figures are given for the current profits of Company X.

7. Stronger patent laws are needed to protect inventions from being pirated. With that protection, manufacturers would be encouraged to invest in the development of new products and technologies. Such investment frequently results in an increase in a manufacturer's productivity.

Which of the following conclusions can most properly be drawn from the information above?

(A) Stronger patent laws tend to benefit financial institutions as well as manufacturers.
(B) Increased productivity in manufacturing is likely to be accompanied by the creation of more manufacturing jobs.
(C) Manufacturers will decrease investment in the development of new products and technologies unless there are stronger patent laws.
(D) The weakness of current patent laws has been a cause of economic recession.
(E) Stronger patent laws would stimulate improvements in productivity for many manufacturers.

8. Which of the following best completes the passage below?

At large amusement parks, live shows are used very deliberately to influence crowd movements. Lunchtime performances relieve the pressure on a park's restaurants. Evening performances have a rather different purpose: to encourage visitors to stay for supper. Behind this surface divergence in immediate purpose there is the unified underlying goal of _ _ _ _ _ _ _.

(A) keeping the lines at the various rides short by drawing off part of the crowd
(B) enhancing revenue by attracting people who come only for the live shows and then leave the park
(C) avoiding as far as possible traffic jams caused by visitors entering or leaving the park
(D) encouraging as many people as possible to come to the park in order to eat at the restaurants
(E) utilizing the restaurants at optimal levels for as much of the day as possible

9. James weighs more than Kelly.
   Luis weighs more than Mark.
   Mark weighs less than Ned.
   Kelly and Ned are exactly the same weight.

If the information above is true, which of the following must also be true?

(A) Luis weighs more than Ned.
(B) Luis weighs more than James.
(C) Kelly weighs less than Luis.
(D) James weighs more than Mark.
(E) Kelly weighs less than Mark.

Partly because of bad weather, but also partly because some major pepper growers have switched to high-priced cocoa, world production of pepper has been running well below worldwide sales for three years. Pepper is consequently in relatively short supply. The price of pepper has soared in response: it now equals that of cocoa.

10. Which of the following can be inferred from the passage?

    (A) Pepper is a profitable crop only if it is grown on a large scale.
    (B) World consumption of pepper has been unusually high for three years.
    (C) World production of pepper will return to previous levels once normal weather returns.
    (D) Surplus stocks of pepper have been reduced in the past three years.
    (E) The profits that the growers of pepper have made in the past three years have been unprecedented.

11. Some observers have concluded that the rise in the price of pepper means that the switch by some growers from pepper to cocoa left those growers no better off than if none of them had switched; this conclusion, however, is unwarranted because it can be inferred to be likely that

    (A) those growers could not have foreseen how high the price of pepper would go
    (B) the initial cost involved in switching from pepper to cocoa is substantial
    (C) supplies of pepper would not be as low as they are if those growers had not switched crops
    (D) cocoa crops are as susceptible to being reduced by bad weather as are pepper crops
    (E) as more growers turn to growing cocoa, cocoa supplies will increase and the price of cocoa will fall precipitously

12. Using computer techniques, researchers analyze layers of paint that lie buried beneath the surface layers of old paintings. They claim, for example, that additional mountainous scenery once appeared in Leonardo da Vinci's *Mona Lisa*, which was later painted over. Skeptics reply to these claims, however, that X-ray examinations of the *Mona Lisa* do not show hidden mountains.

Which of the following, if true, would tend most to weaken the force of the skeptics' objections?

    (A) There is no written or anecdotal record that Leonardo da Vinci ever painted over major areas of his *Mona Lisa*.
    (B) Painters of da Vinci's time commonly created images of mountainous scenery in the backgrounds of portraits like the *Mona Lisa*.
    (C) No one knows for certain what parts of the *Mona Lisa* may have been painted by da Vinci's assistants rather than by da Vinci himself.
    (D) Infrared photography of the *Mona Lisa* has revealed no trace of hidden mountainous scenery.
    (E) Analysis relying on X-rays only has the capacity to detect lead-based white pigments in layers of paint beneath a painting's surface layers.

13. While Governor Verdant has been in office, the state's budget has increased by an average of 6 percent each year. While the previous governor was in office, the state's budget increased by an average of 11 ½ percent each year. Obviously, the austere budgets during Governor Verdant's term have caused the slowdown in the growth in state spending.

Which of the following, if true, would most seriously weaken the conclusion drawn above?

    (A) The rate of inflation in the state averaged 10 percent each year during the previous governor's term in office and 3 percent each year during Verdant's term.
    (B) Both federal and state income tax rates have been lowered considerably during Verdant's term in office.
    (C) In each year of Verdant's term in office, the state's budget has shown some increase in spending over the previous year.
    (D) During Verdant's term in office, the state has either discontinued or begun to charge private citizens for numerous services that the state offered free to citizens during the previous governor's term.
    (E) During the previous governor's term in office, the state introduced several so-called "austerity" budgets intended to reduce the growth in state spending.

14. Federal agricultural programs aimed at benefiting one group whose livelihood depends on farming often end up harming another such group.

Which of the following statements provides support for the claim above?

  I. An effort to help feed-grain producers resulted in higher prices for their crops, but the higher prices decreased the profits of livestock producers.

  II. In order to reduce crop surpluses and increase prices, growers of certain crops were paid to leave a portion of their land idle, but the reduction was not achieved because improvements in efficiency resulted in higher production on the land in use.

  III. Many farm workers were put out of work when a program meant to raise the price of grain provided grain growers with an incentive to reduce production by giving them surplus grain from government reserves.

  (A) I, but not II and not III
  (B) II, but not I and not III
  (C) I and III, but not II
  (D) II and III, but not I
  (E) I, II, and III

15. Technological education is worsening. People between eighteen and twenty-four, who are just emerging from their formal education, are more likely to be technologically illiterate than somewhat older adults. And yet, issues for public referenda will increasingly involve aspects of technology.

Which of the following conclusions can be properly drawn from the statements above?

  (A) If all young people are to make informed decisions on public referenda, many of them must learn more about technology.
  (B) Thorough studies of technological issues and innovations should be made a required part of the public and private school curriculum.
  (C) It should be suggested that prospective voters attend applied science courses in order to acquire a minimal competency in technical matters.
  (D) If young people are not to be overly influenced by famous technocrats, they must increase their knowledge of pure science.
  (E) On public referenda issues, young people tend to confuse real or probable technologies with impossible ideals.

16. In a political system with only two major parties, the entrance of a third-party candidate into an election race damages the chances of only one of the two major candidates. The third-party candidate always attracts some of the voters who might otherwise have voted for one of the two major candidates, but not voters who support the other candidate. Since a third-party candidacy affects the two major candidates unequally, for reasons neither of them has any control over, the practice is unfair and should not be allowed.

If the factual information in the passage above is true, which of the following can be most reliably inferred from it?

  (A) If the political platform of the third party is a compromise position between that of the two major parties, the third party will draw its voters equally from the two major parties.
  (B) If, before the emergence of a third party, voters were divided equally between the two major parties, neither of the major parties is likely to capture much more than one-half of the vote.
  (C) A third-party candidate will not capture the votes of new voters who have never voted for candidates of either of the two major parties.
  (D) The political stance of a third party will be more radical than that of either of the two major parties.
  (E) The founders of a third party are likely to be a coalition consisting of former leaders of the two major parties.

17. Companies considering new cost-cutting manufacturing processes often compare the projected results of making the investment against the alternative of not making the investment with costs, selling prices, and share of market remaining constant.

Which of the following, assuming that each is a realistic possibility, constitutes the most serious disadvantage for companies of using the method above for evaluating the financial benefit of new manufacturing processes?

  (A) The costs of materials required by the new process might not be known with certainty.
  (B) In several years interest rates might go down, reducing the interest costs of borrowing money to pay for the investment.
  (C) Some cost-cutting processes might require such expensive investments that there would be no net gain for many years, until the investment was paid for by savings in the manufacturing process.
  (D) Competitors that do invest in a new process might reduce their selling prices and thus take market share away from companies that do not.
  (E) The period of year chosen for averaging out the cost of the investment might be somewhat longer or shorter, thus affecting the result.

18. There are far fewer children available for adoption than there are people who want to adopt. Two million couples are currently waiting to adopt, but in 1982, the last year for which figures exist, there were only some 50,000 adoptions.

Which of the following statements, if true, most strengthens the author's claim that there are far fewer children available for adoption than there are people who want to adopt?

(A) The number of couples waiting to adopt has increased significantly in the last decade.
(B) The number of adoptions in the current year is greater than the number of adoptions in any preceding year.
(C) The number of adoptions in a year is approximately equal to the number of children available for adoption in that period.
(D) People who seek to adopt children often go through a long process of interviews and investigation by adoption agencies.
(E) People who seek to adopt children generally make very good parents.

Questions 19-20 are based on the following.

Archaeologists seeking the location of a legendary siege and destruction of a city are excavating in several possible places, including a middle and a lower layer of a large mound. The bottom of the middle layer contains some pieces of pottery of type 3, known to be from a later period than the time of the destruction of the city, but the lower layer does not.

19. Which of the following hypotheses is best supported by the evidence above?

(A) The lower layer contains the remains of the city where the siege took place.
(B) The legend confuses stories from two different historical periods.
(C) The middle layer does not represent the period of the siege.
(D) The siege lasted for a long time before the city was destroyed.
(E) The pottery of type 3 was imported to the city by traders.

20. The force of the evidence cited above is most seriously weakened if which of the following is true?

(A) Gerbils, small animals long native to the area, dig large burrows into which objects can fall when the burrows collapse.
(B) Pottery of types 1 and 2, found in the lower level, was used in the cities from which, according to the legend, the besieging forces came.
(C) Several pieces of stone from a lower-layer wall have been found incorporated into the remains of a building in the middle layer.
(D) Both the middle and the lower layer show evidence of large-scale destruction of habitations by fire.
(E) Bronze axheads of a type used at the time of the siege were found in the lower level of excavation.

S T O P

IF YOU FINISH BEFORE TIME IS CALLED, YOU MAY CHECK YOUR WORK ON THIS SECTION ONLY.
DO NOT TURN TO ANY OTHER SECTION IN THE TEST.

Answer Key for Sample Test Section 1

CRITICAL REASONING

1. D	11. C
2. B	12. E
3. E	13. A
4. D	14. C
5. A	15. A
6. C	16. B
7. E	17. D
8. E	18. C
9. D	19. C
10. D	20. A

Explanatory Material: Critical Reasoning Sample Test Section 1

The following discussion of Critical Reasoning is intended to illustrate the variety of ways Critical Reasoning questions may be approached, and to give you an indication of the degree of precision and depth of reasoning that solving these problems will typically require. The particular questions in the sample test section in this chapter are generally representative of the kinds of questions you will encounter in this section of the GMAT. Remember that the subject matter of a particular question is less important than the reasoning task you are asked to perform.

1. Nearly one in three subscribers to *Financial Forecaster* is a millionaire, and over half are in top management. Shouldn't you subscribe to *Financial Forecaster* now?

   A reader who is neither a millionaire nor in top management would be most likely to act in accordance with the advertisement's suggestion if he or she drew which of the following questionable conclusions invited by the advertisement?

   (A) Among finance-related periodicals, *Financial Forecaster* provides the most detailed financial information.
   (B) Top managers cannot do their jobs properly without reading *Financial Forecaster*.
   (C) The advertisement is placed where those who will be likely to read it are millionaires.
   (D) The subscribers mentioned were helped to become millionaires or join top management by reading *Financial Forecaster*.
   (E) Only those who will in fact become millionaires, or at least top managers, will read the advertisement.

The advertisement presents statistics about the representation of millionaires and top managers among *Financial Forecaster's* subscribers and suggests that these statistics might induce the reader to subscribe. A nonsubscriber who is neither a millionaire nor in top management would have a good reason to subscribe if that nonsubscriber thought that D was true and further thought, "If it worked for them, why not for me?" Therefore, D is the best answer.

Choice A is inappropriate because the advertisement does not touch on the contents of the magazine. For the nonsubscriber who is not in top management, B is not a reason to subscribe now. Someone who concluded C would probably feel that the advertisement was not addressed to nonmillionaires. The advertisement associates being a millionaire or top manager with being a subscriber, but not with being a reader of the advertisement, as E suggests.

Questions 2-3 are based on the following.

Contrary to the charges made by some of its opponents, the provisions of the new deficit-reduction law for indiscriminate cuts in the federal budget are justified. Opponents should remember that the New Deal pulled this country out of great economic troubles even though some of its programs were later found to be unconstitutional.

2. The author's method of attacking the charges of certain opponents of the new deficit-reduction law is to

   (A) attack the character of the opponents rather than their claim
   (B) imply an analogy between the law and some New Deal programs
   (C) point out that the opponents' claims imply a dilemma
   (D) show that the opponents' reasoning leads to an absurd conclusion
   (E) show that the New Deal also called for indiscriminate cuts in the federal budget

The author cites certain New Deal programs as a relevant precedent for certain highly desirable ends justifying the use of controversial means. The New Deal programs and the new deficit-reduction law are treated as analogous inasmuch as they are the controversial means in the two situations. Therefore, B is the best answer.

Choice A is inappropriate because the author takes issue with what the opponents say, not with their character. The author claims that the opponents are wrong, not that their position leads to a choice between two equally unsatisfactory alternatives, as C implies. The author attempts to show that the opponents' position is wrong, not, as D states, that it is absurd. Choice E adds information not given by the author, who does not indicate what was found unconstitutional in the New Deal programs.

3. The opponents could effectively defend their position against the author's strategy by pointing out that

  (A) the expertise of those opposing the law is outstanding
  (B) the lack of justification for the new law does not imply that those who drew it up were either inept or immoral
  (C) the practical application of the new law will not entail indiscriminate budget cuts
  (D) economic troubles present at the time of the New Deal were equal in severity to those that have led to the present law
  (E) the fact that certain flawed programs or laws have improved the economy does not prove that every such program can do so

Choice E is an instance of a basic defense against any loose argument by analogy: the mere fact that two situations share one set of characteristics—here, an economic goal and the use of controversial means to achieve that goal—does not mean that they will automatically share other characteristics—here, effectiveness in reaching the objective. Therefore, E is the best answer.

Choices A and B suggest that the disagreement between author and opponents deserves to be taken seriously, but neither addresses the specific merits of the author's argument. Both C and D seem to favor the author's, not the opponents', side of the argument—C by suggesting judicious implemetation of the new law and D by suggesting that the circumstances that engendered New Deal programs are analogous and thus New Deal programs are an appropriate precedent.

4. In Millington, a city of 50,000 people, Mercedes Pedrosa, a realtor, calculated that a family with Millington's median family income, $28,000 a year, could afford to buy Millington's median-priced $77,000 house. This calculation was based on an 11.2 percent mortgage interest rate and on the realtor's assumption that a family could only afford to pay up to 25 percent of its income for housing.

Which of the following corrections of a figure appearing in the passage above, if it were the only correction that needed to be made, would yield a new calculation showing that even incomes below the median family income would enable families in Millington to afford Millington's median-priced house?

  (A) Millington's total population was 45,000 people.
  (B) Millington's median annual family income was $27,000.
  (C) Millington's median-priced house cost $80,000.
  (D) The rate at which people in Millington had to pay mortgage interest was only 10 percent.
  (E) Families in Millington could only afford to pay up to 22 percent of their annual income for housing.

A given monthly mortgage payment can pay off a higher mortgage if the rate of mortgage interest is lower. Thus, if correction D were made, a family with the median family income could afford a more expensive house than the median-priced house, and median-priced houses would come within the reach of lower-than-median family incomes. Therefore, D is the best answer.

If A is the only correction, none of the figures entering into Pedrosa's calculations change. Both B and E imply a reduced ability to pay on the part of the median-income family, which would put the median-priced house out of its reach. Choice C implies large mortgage payments without any improvement in ability to pay.

5. Psychological research indicates that college hockey and football players are more quickly moved to hostility and aggression than are college athletes in noncontact sports such as swimming. But the researchers' conclusion—that contact sports encourage and teach participants to be hostile and aggressive—is untenable. The football and hockey players were probably more hostile and aggressive to start with than the swimmers.

Which of the following, if true, would most strengthen the conclusion drawn by the psychological researchers?

  (A) The football and hockey players became more hostile and aggressive during the season and remained so during the off-season, whereas there was no increase in aggressiveness among the swimmers.
  (B) The football and hockey players, but not the swimmers, were aware at the start of the experiment that they were being tested for aggressiveness.
  (C) The same psychological research indicated that the football and hockey players had a great respect for cooperation and team play, whereas the swimmers were most concerned with excelling as individual competitors.
  (D) The research studies were designed to include no college athletes who participated in both contact and noncontact sports.
  (E) Throughout the United States, more incidents of fan violence occur at baseball games than occur at hockey or football games.

Choice A strengthens the psychologists' conclusion by citing facts that their conclusion can help account for while the opposing view cannot. Therefore, A is the best answer.

The differential awareness among experimental subjects suggested in B is a serious design flaw that tends to invalidate the experimental results and any conclusions drawn from them. Based on the available information, C has no bearing on the conclusion being examined. Choice D is an element of good experimental design that increases the likelihood that the experimental data were sound but not the likelihood that the correct conclusion was drawn from them. Choice E makes a statement about spectators that has no direct relevance to the psychological states of athletes participating in the games.

6. Ross: The profitability of Company X, restored to private ownership five years ago, is clear evidence that businesses will always fare better under private than under public ownership.

   Julia: Wrong. A close look at the records shows that X has been profitable since the appointment of a first-class manager, which happened while X was still in the public sector.

Which of the following best describes the weak point in Ross's claim on which Julia's response focuses?

(A) The evidence Ross cites comes from only a single observed case, that of Company X.
(B) The profitability of Company X might be only temporary.
(C) Ross's statement leaves open the possibility that the cause he cites came after the effect he attributes to it.
(D) No mention is made of companies that are partly government owned and partly privately owned.
(E) No exact figures are given for the current profits of Company X.

Ross cites the fact that X is profitable under the current private ownership as evidence that this type of ownership is causally related to a company's ability to show a profit. But Ross neglects to establish specifically that X had failed to be profitable under its previous, public ownership. Julia's response focuses on this omission on Ross's part. Therefore, C is the best answer.

Ross overgeneralizes, as A says, but Julia does not react to that. The condition cited by Ross as evidence might not be stable, as B suggests, but Julia does not take up this point. Those companies with mixed ownership mentioned in D would not clearly bear on Ross's conclusion. Julia's response ignores the size of current profits, the issue mentioned in E; it concentrates on when the return to profitability occurred.

7. Stronger patent laws are needed to protect inventions from being pirated. With that protection, manufacturers would be encouraged to invest in the development of new products and technologies. Such investment frequently results in an increase in a manufacturer's productivity.

Which of the following conclusions can most properly be drawn from the information above?

(A) Stronger patent laws tend to benefit financial institutions as well as manufacturers.
(B) Increased productivity in manufacturing is likely to be accompanied by the creation of more manufacturing jobs.
(C) Manufacturers will decrease investment in the development of new products and technologies unless there are stronger patent laws.
(D) The weakness of current patent laws has been a cause of economic recession.
(E) Stronger patent laws would stimulate improvements in productivity for many manufacturers.

Stronger patent laws increase protection; protection encourages investment; investment often raises productivity. Thus, stronger patent laws initiate a chain of events that often culminates in improved productivity. Choice E expresses that and is, therefore, the best answer.

Choice A is inappropriate because the role, if any, that financial institutions would play in investments is left open. The increased productivity mentioned in B may mean fewer hours of labor for a given level of output, and may thus threaten jobs. Investments of the sort described in C may already be at the lowest possible level. The passage gives no indication that there has been an economic recession as D suggests; hence, there is no attempt to isolate the causes of economic recessions.

8. Which of the following best completes the passage below?

At large amusement parks, live shows are used very deliberately to influence crowd movements. Lunchtime performances relieve the pressure on a park's restaurants. Evening performances have a rather different purpose: to encourage visitors to stay for supper. Behind this surface divergence in immediate purpose there is the unified underlying goal of ____ ____ ____ ____ ____ ____.

(A) keeping the lines at the various rides short by drawing off part of the crowd
(B) enhancing revenue by attracting people who come only for the live shows and then leave the park
(C) avoiding as far as possible traffic jams caused by visitors entering or leaving the park
(D) encouraging as many people as possible to come to the park in order to eat at the restaurants
(E) utilizing the restaurants at optimal levels for as much of the day as possible

Lunchtime performances keep people away from the restaurants at the restaurants' busiest time, presumably causing restaurant patrons to have lunch either early or late, when they can be accommodated better. Evening performances can be inferred to bring customers to the restaurants at a time when business there is slack. The effect is to spread out business in the restaurants and bring the level of business more in line with capacity. Therefore, E is the best answer.

Choice A is inappropriate because the lines at rides are not mentioned as a consideration. Live shows are said to be aimed at people already in the park, making B inaccurate. Choice C is inadequate: evening performances might actually create traffic jams if everyone leaves at their conclusion. Choice D is incompatible with the stated purpose of lunchtime performances.

9. James weighs more than Kelly.
   Luis weighs more than Mark.
   Mark weighs less than Ned.
   Kelly and Ned are exactly the same weight.

   If the information above is true, which of the following must also be true?

   (A) Luis weighs more than Ned.
   (B) Luis weighs more than James.
   (C) Kelly weighs less than Luis.
   (D) James weighs more than Mark.
   (E) Kelly weighs less than Mark.

Since Mark weighs less than Ned, and since Ned weighs the same as Kelly, Mark also weighs less than Kelly. Since James weighs more than Kelly, James must also weigh more than Mark. Therefore, D is the best answer.

A, B, and C might be true, but none of them can be inferred to be true, since not enough information is given about Luis's weight in relation to the weight of the others. Choice E can be inferred to be false from the information given.

Questions 10-11 are based on the following.

Partly because of bad weather, but also partly because some major pepper growers have switched to high-priced cocoa, world production of pepper has been running well below worldwide sales for three years. Pepper is consequently in relatively short supply. The price of pepper has soared in response: it now equals that of cocoa.

10. Which of the following can be inferred from the passage?

   (A) Pepper is a profitable crop only if it is grown on a large scale.
   (B) World consumption of pepper has been unusually high for three years.
   (C) World production of pepper will return to previous levels once normal weather returns.
   (D) Surplus stocks of pepper have been reduced in the past three years.
   (E) The profits that the growers of pepper have made in the past three years have been unprecedented.

If more pepper was sold than was produced, some sales must have come from surplus stocks, and those stocks must have dropped during the three-year period in question. Therefore, D is the best answer.

Choice A is inappropriate because the information in the passage is consistent with pepper being a profitable crop if grown on a modest scale. The passage provides no figures on which to base estimates of the world consumption of pepper, such as those made in B. Choice C is inconsistent with the information in the passage that states that world production will not return to previous levels unless either the pepper acreage lost to cocoa is replaced or the reduced remaining acreage is made more productive. No clear inferences can be made about growers' profits in the last three, or any earlier, years; consequently, E is inappropriate.

11. Some observers have concluded that the rise in the price of pepper means that the switch by some growers from pepper to cocoa left those growers no better off than if none of them had switched; this conclusion, however, is unwarranted because it can be inferred to be likely that

   (A) those growers could not have foreseen how high the price of pepper would go
   (B) the initial cost involved in switching from pepper to cocoa is substantial
   (C) supplies of pepper would not be as low as they are if those growers had not switched crops
   (D) cocoa crops are as susceptible to being reduced by bad weather as are pepper crops
   (E) as more growers turn to growing cocoa, cocoa supplies will increase and the price of cocoa will fall precipitously

Choice C can be inferred to be likely: it requires only the assumption that those growers, if they had not switched crops, would have continued to grow pepper. But if supplies of pepper were not as low as they are, the price of pepper would not have risen enough to equal the price of cocoa, and the growers in question would not have done as well, financially, as they actually did as a result of switching to cocoa. Therefore, C is the best answer.

The better foresight mentioned in A might have kept the growers from doing what they did, but it is irrelevant to the outcome of what they did do. Choices B, D, and E are not inferrable and do not bear on the role of the rise in the price of pepper in affecting the financial consequences of the switch in crops.

12. Using computer techniques, researchers analyze layers of paint that lie buried beneath the surface layers of old paintings. They claim, for example, that additional mountainous scenery once appeared in Leonardo da Vinci's *Mona Lisa,* which was later painted over. Skeptics reply to these claims, however, that X-ray examinations of the *Mona Lisa* do not show hidden mountains.

   Which of the following, if true, would tend most to weaken the force of the skeptics' objections?

   (A) There is no written or anecdotal record that Leonardo da Vinci ever painted over major areas of his *Mona Lisa.*
   (B) Painters of da Vinci's time commonly created images of mountainous scenery in the backgrounds of portraits like the *Mona Lisa.*
   (C) No one knows for certain what parts of the *Mona Lisa* may have been painted by da Vinci's assistants rather than by da Vinci himself.
   (D) Infrared photography of the *Mona Lisa* has revealed no trace of hidden mountainous scenery.
   (E) Analysis relying on X-rays only has the capacity to detect lead-based white pigments in layers of paint beneath a painting's surface layers.

Even assuming that lead-based white pigments were in fact used in painting the *Mona Lisa,* it is not clear, without further argument, that mountainous scenery, if it had been painted, would contain white pigments in such a configuration that the presence of mountainous scenery could be deduced. Thus, the skeptics' evidence might have no force. Therefore, E is the best answer.

The fact cited in A does not bear on whether mountainous scenery was ever present; it merely suggests that, if someone painted over any mountainous scenery, it was not da Vinci. The skeptics base their case on a physical examination of the *Mona Lisa.* Unless it is shown that their method yields inconclusive results, counterevidence derived from general artistic conventions, such as that mentioned in B, has no force. The information in C does not help determine what was in the painting. The statement in D strengthens the skeptics' case, or is irrelevant if infrared photography does not reveal deeper layers of paint.

13. While Governor Verdant has been in office, the state's budget has increased by an average of 6 percent each year. While the previous governor was in office, the state's budget increased by an average of 11½ percent each year. Obviously, the austere budgets during Governor Verdant's term have caused the slowdown in the growth in state spending.

    Which of the following, if true, would most seriously weaken the conclusion drawn above?

    (A) The rate of inflation in the state averaged 10 percent each year during the previous governor's term in office and 3 percent each year during Verdant's term.
    (B) Both federal and state income tax rates have been lowered considerably during Verdant's term in office.
    (C) In each year of Verdant's term in office, the state's budget has shown some increase in spending over the previous year.
    (D) During Verdant's term in office, the state has either discontinued or begun to charge private citizens for numerous services that the state offered free to citizens during the previous governor's term.
    (E) During the previous governor's term in office, the state introduced several so-called "austerity" budgets intended to reduce the growth in state spending.

If inflation is, say 5 percent, then an amount of $105 at the end of a year has the same "real value" (purchasing power) as an amount of $100 at the beginning of that year. Given this, the figures in A show that "real" spending has increased by more under Verdant than under Verdant's predecessor. Therefore, A is the best answer.

Choice B deals with the sources of government income, not with government spending. The accuracy of the 6-percent figure given in the argument and on which the argument rests is not called into question, so C does not weaken the conclusion. Choice D tends to strengthen, rather than weaken, the position that Verdant's budgets have been austere. Choice E is inappropriate because the conclusion is based on actual figures, not descriptive phrases and avowed goals.

14. Federal agricultural programs aimed at benefiting one group whose livelihood depends on farming often end up harming another such group.

    Which of the following statements provides support for the claim above?

    I. An effort to help feed-grain producers resulted in higher prices for their crops, but the higher prices decreased the profits of livestock producers.
    II. In order to reduce crop surpluses and increase prices, growers of certain crops were paid to leave a portion of their land idle, but the reduction was not achieved because improvements in efficiency resulted in higher production on the land in use.
    III. Many farm workers were put out of work when a program meant to raise the price of grain provided grain growers with an incentive to reduce production by giving them surplus grain from government reserves.

    (A) I, but not II and not III
    (B) II, but not I and not III
    (C) I and III, but not II
    (D) II and III, but not I
    (E) I, II, and III

Any specific agricultural program that is designed to benefit one group whose livelihood depends on farming but also harms another such group provides support for the claim made here. Statement I describes such a case: feed-grain producers were intended to benefit, but livestock producers' interests were hurt. Statement III also describes such a case: grain growers were meant to benefit, but farm workers were adversely affected. Statement II does not describe a relevantly similar case: growers of certain crops were meant to benefit, but the hoped-for benefit did not materialize; yet there is no indication of any harm coming to another group making its living from farming. Therefore, C is the best answer.

15. Technological education is worsening. People between eighteen and twenty-four, who are just emerging from their formal education, are more likely to be technologically illiterate than somewhat older adults. And yet, issues for public referenda will increasingly involve aspects of technology.

Which of the following conclusions can be properly drawn from the statements above?

(A) If all young people are to make informed decisions on public referenda, many of them must learn more about technology.
(B) Thorough studies of technological issues and innovations should be made a required part of the public and private school curriculum.
(C) It should be suggested that prospective voters attend applied science courses in order to acquire a minimal competency in technical matters.
(D) If young people are not to be overly influenced by famous technocrats, they must increase their knowledge of pure science.
(E) On public referenda issues, young people tend to confuse real or probable technologies with impossible ideals.

The technologically illiterate among the young people cannot make informed decisions about technological issues that are increasingly a part of referenda. Informed decisions require knowledge. Therefore, choice A can be inferred and is the best answer.

Choices B, C, and D are inappropriate because while the passage presents a problem and allows the general outlines of a solution to be inferred, specific solutions such as those presented in B and C go beyond what can be inferred, as do recommendations like D that address potential problems that are not touched on in the passage. Choice E is too specific: the passage supports the conclusion that some young people will be unable to make informed decisions, but it suggests nothing about the kinds of errors young people might make.

16. In a political system with only two major parties, the entrance of a third-party candidate into an election race damages the chances of only one of the two major candidates. The third-party candidate always attracts some of the voters who might otherwise have voted for one of the two major candidates, but not voters who support the other candidate. Since a third-party candidacy affects the two major candidates unequally, for reasons neither of them has any control over, the practice is unfair and should not be allowed.

If the factual information in the passage above is true, which of the following can be most reliably inferred from it?

(A) If the political platform of the third party is a compromise position between that of the two major parties, the third party will draw its voters equally from the two major parties.
(B) If, before the emergence of a third party, voters were divided equally between the two major parties, neither of the major parties is likely to capture much more than one-half of the vote.
(C) A third-party candidate will not capture the votes of new voters who have never voted for candidates of either of the two major parties.
(D) The political stance of a third party will be more radical than that of either of the two major parties.
(E) The founders of a third party are likely to be a coalition consisting of former leaders of the two major parties.

If, as B hypothesizes, the electorate is split evenly between two parties, and if then a third-party candidate attracts votes from only one of the two parties, even the party that loses no votes to the third party is unlikely to capture more than one-half of the votes. Therefore, B is the best answer. best answer.

Choice A is inappropriate because it contradicts information given in the passage, while C goes beyond the passage, which does not exclude new voters from those "who might otherwise have voted for one of the two major candidates." The information given in the passage is not specific enough to make the inferences about the politics, or the founding, of the third party, as suggested in D and E.

17. Companies considering new cost-cutting manufacturing processes often compare the projected results of making the investment against the alternative of not making the investment with costs, selling prices, and share of market remaining constant.

Which of the following, assuming that each is a realistic possibility, constitutes the most serious disadvantage for companies of using the method above for evaluating the financial benefit of new manufacturing processes?

(A) The costs of materials required by the new process might not be known with certainty.

(B) In several years interest rates might go down, reducing the interest costs of borrowing money to pay for the investment.

(C) Some cost-cutting processes might require such expensive investments that there would be no net gain for many years, until the investment was paid for by savings in the manufacturing process.

(D) Competitors that do invest in a new process might reduce their selling prices and thus take market share away from companies that do not.

(E) The period of year chosen for averaging out the cost of the investment might be somewhat longer or shorter, thus affecting the result.

The method of evaluation described assumes that D will not happen. If D did happen, the method would systematically tend to value the noninvestment option too highly. Since D is said to be entirely possible, it represents a disadvantage of the method described. Therefore, D is the best answer.

Since the cost mentioned in A has to be estimated no matter what method of evaluation is chosen, A cannot be a disadvantage of one method relative to another. The factor mentioned in B may affect the timing of the investment, but the method described can accommodate alternative investment dates. The payback of the investment is a feature that the method described can presumably accommodate, and thus C is not appropriate. Evaluating the investment option inevitably involves uncertainty, but this is not a function of the method used, as E suggests it is.

18. There are far fewer children available for adoption than there are people who want to adopt. Two million couples are currently waiting to adopt, but in 1982, the last year for which figures exist, there were only some 50,000 adoptions.

Which of the following statements, if true, most strengthens the author's claim that there are far fewer children available for adoption than there are people who want to adopt?

(A) The number of couples waiting to adopt has increased significantly in the last decade.

(B) The number of adoptions in the current year is greater than the number of adoptions in any preceding year.

(C) The number of adoptions in a year is approximately equal to the number of children available for adoption in that period.

(D) People who seek to adopt children often go through a long process of interviews and investigation by adoption agencies.

(E) People who seek to adopt children generally make very good parents.

The evidence the author presents is weak because it is unclear how the number of adoptions in a year is related to the number of children available for adoption. Choice C settles that question in a way that strengthens the author's claim. The only remaining point of uncertainty is whether the 1982 figures are representative. Choices A, B, and D are all compatible with a situation in which there are as many children available for adoption as there are people wanting to adopt, but only a small fraction of the children available get adopted in any given year. The quality of parenting mentioned in E is irrelevant to any of the numbers cited. Thus, C is the only choice that clearly strengthens the author's claim and is, therefore, the best answer.

Questions 19-20 are based on the following.

Archaeologists seeking the location of a legendary siege and destruction of a city are excavating in several possible places, including a middle and a lower layer of a large mound. The bottom of the middle layer contains some pieces of pottery of type 3, known to be from a later period than the time of the destruction of the city, but the lower layer does not.

19. Which of the following hypotheses is best supported by the evidence above?

   (A) The lower layer contains the remains of the city where the siege took place.
   (B) The legend confuses stories from two different historical periods.
   (C) The middle layer does not represent the period of the siege.
   (D) The siege lasted for a long time before the city was destroyed.
   (E) The pottery of type 3 was imported to the city by traders.

If the city was destroyed before any pottery of type 3 was made, the hypothesis that the middle layer represents a period later than that of the siege is strongly supported. The major assumptions on which this hypothesis rests are only that lower layers represent earlier time periods and that objects from a later period did not become embedded in some unusual way in layers representing earlier periods. Hypothesis A is not strongly supported since the large mound may just be the wrong place to look. The evidence as described reveals nothing about any particular siege or episode of destruction; so neither hypothesis B nor D is supported. Hypothesis E is unsupported because the city of the legend is known to have been destroyed before type-3 pottery was first made. On balance, then, the best answer is C.

20. The force of the evidence cited above is most seriously weakened if which of the following is true?

   (A) Gerbils, small animals long native to the area, dig large burrows into which objects can fall when the burrows collapse.
   (B) Pottery of types 1 and 2, found in the lower level, was used in the cities from which, according to the legend, the besieging forces came.
   (C) Several pieces of stone from a lower-layer wall have been found incorporated into the remains of a building in the middle layer.
   (D) Both the middle and the lower layer show evidence of large-scale destruction of habitations by fire.
   (E) Bronze axheads of a type used at the time of the siege were found in the lower level of excavation.

Choice A provides a way for an object from a higher, thus more recent, layer to get into a lower, older layer. If the lower layer is dated by such an object, that layer's age will be underestimated. Choice A suggests that it is possible that the type-3 pottery ended up in an older layer than is chronologically appropriate. The evidence cited leaves open what B and E suggest: that the lower layer represents the period of the siege. B and E are thus not contrary to the evidence cited. Choice C shows that materials from an earlier period may be reused in a later period. The question raised by the evidence cited, however, is whether materials from a later period can end up in a layer that dates from an earlier period. D is additional evidence of a neutral kind. Therefore, A is the best answer.

CRITICAL REASONING SAMPLE TEST SECTION 2

30 Minutes
20 Questions

Directions: For each question in this section, select the best of the answer choices given.

1. After the national speed limit of 55 miles per hour was imposed in 1974, the number of deaths per mile driven on a highway fell abruptly as a result. Since then, however, the average speed of vehicles on highways has risen, but the number of deaths per mile driven on a highway has continued to fall.

Which of the following conclusions can be properly drawn from the statements above?

(A) The speed limit alone is probably not responsible for the continued reduction in highway deaths in the years after 1974.
(B) People have been driving less since 1974.
(C) Driver-education courses have been more effective since 1974 in teaching drivers to drive safely.
(D) In recent years highway patrols have been less effective in catching drivers who speed.
(E) The change in the speed limit cannot be responsible for the abrupt decline in highway deaths in 1974.

2. Neighboring landholders: Air pollution from the giant aluminum refinery that has been built next to our land is killing our plants.

Company spokesperson: The refinery is not to blame, since our study shows that the damage is due to insects and fungi.

Which of the following, if true, most seriously weakens the conclusion drawn by the company spokesperson?

(A) The study did not measure the quantity of pollutants emitted into the surrounding air by the aluminum refinery.
(B) The neighboring landholders have made no change in the way they take care of their plants.
(C) Air pollution from the refinery has changed the chemical balance in the plants' environment, allowing the harmful insects and fungi to thrive.
(D) Pollutants that are invisible and odorless are emitted into the surrounding air by the refinery.
(E) The various species of insects and fungi mentioned in the study have been occasionally found in the locality during the past hundred years.

3. Sales taxes tend to be regressive, affecting poor people more severely than wealthy people. When all purchases of consumer goods are taxed at a fixed percentage of the purchase price, poor people pay a larger proportion of their income in sales taxes than wealthy people do.

It can be correctly inferred on the basis of the statements above that which of the following is true?

(A) Poor people constitute a larger proportion of the taxpaying population than wealthy people do.
(B) Poor people spend a larger proportion of their income on purchases of consumer goods than wealthy people do.
(C) Wealthy people pay, on average, a larger amount of sales taxes than poor people do.
(D) The total amount spent by all poor people on purchases of consumer goods exceeds the total amount spent by all wealthy people on consumer goods.
(E) The average purchase price of consumer goods bought by wealthy people is higher than that of consumer goods bought by poor people.

GO ON TO THE NEXT PAGE.

4. Reviewing historical data, medical researchers in California found that counties with the largest number of television sets per capita have had the lowest incidence of a serious brain disease, mosquito-borne encephalitis. The researchers have concluded that people in these counties stay indoors more and thus avoid exposure to the disease.

The researchers' conclusion would be most strengthened if which of the following were true?

(A) Programs designed to control the size of disease-bearing mosquito populations have not affected the incidence of mosquito-borne encephalitis.

(B) The occupations of county residents affect their risk of exposure to mosquito-borne encephalitis more than does television-watching.

(C) The incidence of mosquito-borne encephalitis in counties with the largest number of television sets per capita is likely to decrease even further.

(D) The more time people in a county spend outdoors, the greater their awareness of the dangers of mosquito-borne encephalitis.

(E) The more television sets there are per capita in a county, the more time the average county resident spends watching television.

5. The city's public transportation system should be removed from the jurisdiction of the municipal government, which finds it politically impossible either to raise fares or to institute cost-saving reductions in service. If public transportation were handled by a private firm, profits would be vigorously pursued, thereby eliminating the necessity for covering operating costs with government funds.

The statements above best support the conclusion that

(A) the private firms that would handle public transportation would have experience in the transportation industry

(B) political considerations would not prevent private firms from ensuring that revenues cover operating costs

(C) private firms would receive government funding if it were needed to cover operating costs

(D) the public would approve the cost-cutting actions taken by the private firm

(E) the municipal government would not be resigned to accumulating merely enough income to cover costs

6. To entice customers away from competitors, Red Label supermarkets have begun offering discounts on home appliances to customers who spend $50 or more on any shopping trip to Red Label. Red Label executives claim that the discount program has been a huge success, since cash register receipts of $50 or more are up thirty percent since the beginning of the program.

Which of the following, if true, most seriously weakens the claim of the Red Label executives?

(A) Most people who switched to Red Label after the program began spend more than $50 each time they shop at Red Label.

(B) Most people whose average grocery bill is less than $50 would not be persuaded to spend more by any discount program.

(C) Most people who received discounts on home appliances through Red Label's program will shop at Red Label after the program ends.

(D) Since the beginning of the discount program, most of the people who spend $50 or more at Red Label are people who have never before shopped there and whose average grocery bill has always been higher than $50.

(E) Almost all of the people who have begun spending $50 or more at Red Label since the discount program began are longtime customers who have increased the avarage amount of their shopping bills by making fewer trips.

7. Throughout the 1950's, there were increases in the numbers of dead birds found in agricultural areas after pesticide sprayings. Pesticide manufacturers claimed that the publicity given to bird deaths stimulated volunteers to look for dead birds, and that the increase in numbers reported was attributable to the increase in the number of people looking.

Which of the following statements, if true, would help to refute the claim of the pesticide manufacturers?

(A) The publicity given to bird deaths was largely regional and never reached national proportions.

(B) Pesticide sprayings were timed to coincide with various phases of the life cycles of the insects they destroyed.

(C) No provision was made to ensure that a dead bird would not be reported by more than one observer.

(D) Initial increases in bird deaths had been noticed by agricultural workers long before any publicity had been given to the matter.

(E) Dead birds of the same species as those found in agricultural areas had been found along coastal areas where no farming took place.

GO ON TO THE NEXT PAGE.

8. Teenagers are often priced out of the labor market by the government-mandated minimum-wage level because employers cannot afford to pay that much for extra help. Therefore, if Congress institutes a subminimum wage, a new lower legal wage for teenagers, the teenage unemployment rate, which has been rising since 1960, will no longer increase.

Which of the following, if true, would most weaken the argument above?

(A) Since 1960 the teenage unemployment rate has risen when the minimum wage has risen.
(B) Since 1960 the teenage unemployment rate has risen even when the minimum wage remained constant.
(C) Employers often hire extra help during holiday and warm weather seasons.
(D) The teenage unemployment rate rose more quickly in the 1970's than it did in the 1960's.
(E) The teenage unemployment rate has occasionally declined in the years since 1960.

9. Which of the following best completes the passage below?

The computer industry's estimate that it loses millions of dollars when users illegally copy programs without paying for them is greatly exaggerated. Most of the illegal copying is done by people with no serious interest in the programs. Thus, the loss to the industry is much smaller than estimated because

(A) many users who illegally copy programs never find any use for them
(B) most of the illegally copied programs would not be purchased even if purchasing them were the only way to obtain them
(C) even if the computer industry received all the revenue it claims to be losing, it would still be experiencing financial difficulties
(D) the total market value of all illegal copies is low in comparison to the total revenue of the computer industry
(E) the number of programs that are frequently copied illegally is low in comparison to the number of programs available for sale

10. This year the New Hampshire Division of Company X set a new record for annual sales by that division. This record is especially surprising since the New Hampshire Division has the smallest potential market and the lowest sales of any of Company X's divisions.

Which of the following identifies a flaw in the logical coherence of the statement above?

(A) If overall sales for Company X were sharply reduced, the New Hampshire Division's new sales record is irrelevant to the company's prosperity.
(B) Since the division is competing against its own record, the comparison of its sales record with that of other divisions is irrelevant.
(C) If this is the first year that the New Hampshire Division has been last in sales among Company X's divisions, the new record is not surprising at all.
(D) If overall sales for Company X were greater than usual, it is not surprising that the New Hampshire Division was last in sales.
(E) Since the New Hampshire Division has the smallest potential market, it is not surprising that it had the lowest sales.

11. Statement of a United States copper mining company: Import quotas should be imposed on the less expensive copper mined outside the country to maintain the price of copper in this country; otherwise, our companies will not be able to stay in business.

Response of a United States copper wire manufacturer: United States wire and cable manufacturers purchase about 70 percent of the copper mined in the United States. If the copper prices we pay are not at the international level, our sales will drop, and then the demand for United States copper will go down.

If the factual information presented by both companies is accurate, the best assessment of the logical relationship between the two arguments is that the wire manufacturer's argument

(A) is self-serving and irrelevant to the proposal of the mining company
(B) is circular, presupposing what it seeks to prove about the proposal of the mining company
(C) shows that the proposal of the mining company would have a negative effect on the mining company's own business
(D) fails to give a reason why the proposal of the mining company should not be put into effect to alleviate the concern of the mining company for staying in business
(E) establishes that even the mining company's business will prosper if the mining company's proposal is rejected

GO ON TO THE NEXT PAGE.

12. Y has been believed to cause Z. A new report, noting that Y and Z are often observed to be preceded by X, suggests that X, not Y, may be the cause of Z.

Which of the following further observations would best support the new report's suggestion?

(A) In cases where X occurs but Y does not, X is usually followed by Z.
(B) In cases where X occurs, followed by Y, Y is usually followed by Z.
(C) In cases where Y occurs but X does not, Y is usually followed by Z.
(D) In cases where Y occurs but Z does not, Y is usually preceded by X.
(E) In cases where Z occurs, it is usually preceded by X and Y.

13. Mr. Primm: If hospitals were private enterprises, dependent on profits for their survival, there would be no teaching hospitals, because of the intrinsically high cost of running such hospitals.

Ms. Nakai: I disagree. The medical challenges provided by teaching hospitals attract the very best physicians. This, in turn, enables those hospitals to concentrate on nonroutine cases.

Which of the following, if true, would most strengthen Ms. Nakai's attempt to refute Mr. Primm's claim?

(A) Doctors at teaching hospitals command high salaries.
(B) Sophisticated, nonroutine medical care commands a high price.
(C) Existing teaching hospitals derive some revenue from public subsidies.
(D) The patient mortality rate at teaching hospitals is high.
(E) The modern trend among physicians is to become highly specialized.

14. A recent survey of all auto accident victims in Dole County found that, of the severely injured drivers and front-seat passengers, 80 percent were not wearing seat belts at the time of their accidents. This indicates that, by wearing seat belts, drivers and front-seat passengers can greatly reduce their risk of being severely injured if they are in an auto accident.

The conclusion above is not properly drawn unless which of the following is true?

(A) Of all the drivers and front-seat passengers in the survey, more than 20 percent were wearing seat belts at the time of their accidents.
(B) Considerably more than 20 percent of drivers and front-seat passengers in Dole County always wear seat belts when traveling by car.
(C) More drivers and front-seat passengers in the survey than rear-seat passengers were very severely injured.
(D) More than half of the drivers and front-seat passengers in the survey were not wearing seat belts at the time of their accidents.
(E) Most of the auto accidents reported to police in Dole County do not involve any serious injury.

5. Six months or so after getting a video recorder, many early buyers apparently lost interest in obtaining videos to watch on it. The trade of businesses selling and renting videos is still buoyant, because the number of homes with video recorders is still growing. But clearly, once the market for video recorders is saturated, businesses distributing videos face hard times.

Which of the following, if true, would most seriously weaken the conclusion above?

(A) The market for video recorders would not be considered saturated until there was one in 80 percent of homes.
(B) Among the items handled by video distributors are many films specifically produced as video features.
(C) Few of the early buyers of video recorders raised any complaints about performance aspects of the new product.
(D) The early buyers of a novel product are always people who are quick to acquire novelties, but also often as quick to tire of them.
(E) In a shrinking market, competition always intensifies and marginal businesses fail.

GO ON TO THE NEXT PAGE.

16. Advertiser: The revenue that newspapers and magazines earn by publishing advertisements allows publishers to keep the prices per copy of their publications much lower than would otherwise be possible. Therefore, consumers benefit economically from advertising.

Consumer: But who pays for the advertising that pays for low-priced newspapers and magazines? We consumers do, because advertisers pass along advertising costs to us through the higher prices they charge for their products.

Which of the following best describes how the consumer counters the advertiser's argument?

(A) By alleging something that, if true, would weaken the plausibility of the advertiser's conclusion
(B) By questioning the truth of the purportedly factual statement on which the advertiser's conclusion is based
(C) By offering an interpretation of the advertiser's opening statement that, if accurate, shows that there is an implicit contradiction in it
(D) By pointing out that the advertiser's point of view is biased
(E) By arguing that the advertiser too narrowly restricts the discussion to the effects of advertising that are economic

17. Mr. Lawson: We should adopt a national family policy that includes legislation requiring employers to provide paid parental leave and establishing government-sponsored day care. Such laws would decrease the stress levels of employees who have responsibility for small children. Thus, such laws would lead to happier, better-adjusted families.

Which of the following, if true, would most strengthen the conclusion above?

(A) An employee's high stress level can be a cause of unhappiness and poor adjustment for his or her family.
(B) People who have responsibility for small children and who work outside the home have higher stress levels than those who do not.
(C) The goal of a national family policy is to lower the stress levels of parents.
(D) Any national family policy that is adopted would include legislation requiring employers to provide paid parental leave and establishing government-sponsored day care.
(E) Most children who have been cared for in day-care centers are happy and well adjusted.

18. Lark Manufacturing Company initiated a voluntary Quality Circles program for machine operators. Independent surveys of employee attitudes indicated that the machine operators participating in the program were less satisfied with their work situations after two years of the program's existence than they were at the program's start. Obviously, any workers who participate in a Quality Circles program will, as a result, become less satisfied with their jobs.

Each of the following, if true, would weaken the conclusion drawn above EXCEPT:

(A) The second survey occurred during a period of recession when rumors of cutbacks and layoffs at Lark Manufacturing were plentiful.
(B) The surveys also showed that those Lark machine operators who neither participated in Quality Circles nor knew anyone who did so reported the same degree of lessened satisfaction with their work situations as did the Lark machine operators who participated in Quality Circles.
(C) While participating in Quality Circles at Lark Manufacturing, machine operators exhibited two of the primary indicators of improved job satisfaction: increased productivity and decreased absenteeism.
(D) Several workers at Lark Manufacturing who had participated in Quality Circles while employed at other companies reported that, while participating in Quality Circles in their previous companies, their work satisfaction had increased.
(E) The machine operators who participated in Quality Circles reported that, when the program started, they felt that participation might improve their work situations.

GO ON TO THE NEXT PAGE.

Questions 19-20 are based on the following.

Blood banks will shortly start to screen all donors for NANB hepatitis. Although the new screening tests are estimated to disqualify up to 5 percent of all prospective blood donors, they will still miss two-thirds of donors carrying NANB hepatitis. Therefore, about 10 percent of actual donors will still supply NANB-contaminated blood.

19. The argument above depends on which of the following assumptions?

   (A) Donors carrying NANB hepatitis do not, in a large percentage of cases, carry other infections for which reliable screening tests are routinely performed.
   (B) Donors carrying NANB hepatitis do not, in a large percentage of cases, develop the disease themselves at any point.
   (C) The estimate of the number of donors who would be disqualified by tests for NANB hepatitis is an underestimate.
   (D) The incidence of NANB hepatitis is lower among the potential blood donors than it is in the population at large.
   (E) The donors who will still supply NANB-contaminated blood will donate blood at the average frequency for all donors.

20. Which of the following inferences about the consequences of instituting the new tests is best supported by the passage above?

   (A) The incidence of new cases of NANB hepatitis is likely to go up by 10 percent.
   (B) Donations made by patients specifically for their own use are likely to become less frequent.
   (C) The demand for blood from blood banks is likely to fluctuate more strongly.
   (D) The blood supplies available from blood banks are likely to go down.
   (E) The number of prospective first-time donors is likely to go up by 5 percent.

STOP

IF YOU FINISH BEFORE TIME IS CALLED, YOU MAY CHECK YOUR WORK ON THIS SECTION ONLY.
DO NOT TURN TO ANY OTHER SECTION IN THE TEST.

Answer Key for Sample Test Section 2

CRITICAL REASONING

1. A	11. C
2. C	12. A
3. B	13. B
4. E	14. A
5. B	15. D
6. E	16. A
7. D	17. A
8. B	18. E
9. B	19. A
10. B	20. D

Explanatory Material: Critical Reasoning Sample Test Section 2

1. After the national speed limit of 55 miles per hour was imposed in 1974, the number of deaths per mile driven on a highway fell abruptly as a result. Since then, however, the average speed of vehicles on highways has risen, but the number of deaths per mile driven on a highway has continued to fall.

   Which of the following conclusions can be properly drawn from the statements above?

   (A) The speed limit alone is probably not responsible for the continued reduction in highway deaths in the years after 1974.
   (B) People have been driving less since 1974.
   (C) Driver-education courses have been more effective since 1974 in teaching drivers to drive safely.
   (D) In recent years highway patrols have been less effective in catching drivers who speed.
   (E) The change in the speed limit cannot be responsible for the abrupt decline in highway deaths in 1974.

Choices B and C cannot be inferred, because the denial of each is compatible with the given statements. Similarly with D—the rise in average speeds might occur despite relatively greater success by patrols in catching speeders—and with E—the possibility is left open that the abrupt decline *was* due to the new speed limit.

Any effect the speed limit may have had on the fatality rate probably came about through the effect that imposing the speed limit had on average highway speeds. These, however, have since risen even though the speed limit is unchanged. It is thus highly unlikely that the continuing decrease in the fatality rate stems from the speed limit alone. Therefore, A, which expresses this inference, is the best answer.

2. Neighboring landholders: Air pollution from the giant aluminum refinery that has been built next to our land is killing our plants.

   Company spokesperson: The refinery is not to blame, since our study shows that the damage is due to insects and fungi.

   Which of the following, if true, most seriously weakens the conclusion drawn by the company spokesperson?

   (A) The study did not measure the quantity of pollutants emitted into the surrounding air by the aluminum refinery.
   (B) The neighboring landholders have made no change in the way they take care of their plants.
   (C) Air pollution from the refinery has changed the chemical balance in the plants' environment, allowing the harmful insects and fungi to thrive.
   (D) Pollutants that are invisible and odorless are emitted into the surrounding air by the refinery.
   (E) The various species of insects and fungi mentioned in the study have been occasionally found in the locality during the past hundred years.

The company spokesperson's defense is essentially that pollution does not directly kill the plants. Choice C, however, establishes that the immediate causes—insects and fungi—are abundant *because* of the pollution. Since blame can properly attach to the initial link in a causal chain, C strongly suggests that the refinery can be blamed, contrary to the spokesperson's conclusion. Therefore, C is the best answer.

Neither A nor D weakens the spokesperson's conclusion, since quantity and specific characteristics of the pollution are irrelevant unless a connection between pollution and damaged vegetation can be established. Choices B and E each eliminate potential causes—changed plant-care practices and newly imported harmful organisms not yet subject to natural controls—but neither specifically points to pollution as the culprit.

3. Sales taxes tend to be regressive, affecting poor people more severely than wealthy people. When all purchases of consumer goods are taxed at a fixed percentage of the purchase price, poor people pay a larger proportion of their income in sales taxes than wealthy people do.

It can be correctly inferred on the basis of the statements above that which of the following is true?

(A) Poor people constitute a larger proportion of the tax-paying population than wealthy people do.
(B) Poor people spend a larger proportion of their income on purchases of consumer goods than wealthy people do.
(C) Wealthy people pay, on average, a larger amount of sales taxes than poor people do.
(D) The total amount spent by all poor people on purchases of consumer goods exceeds the total amount spent by all wealthy people on consumer goods.
(E) The average purchase price of consumer goods bought by wealthy people is higher than that of consumer goods bought by poor people.

If sales tax is a higher proportion of poor people's income than of rich people's, then the total of taxable purchases must be too, because, with the tax rate equal for everyone, taxes are directly proportional to purchase totals. Therefore, B is the best answer.

Choice A cannot be inferred: none of the information given bears on group size. Choices C and E cannot be inferred because it is not inconsistent with the passage that wealthy people's purchases of consumer goods, as well as price paid per consumer product, should be on average no higher than poor people's. Since the total amount mentioned in D is the product of average amount times number of people in each group, and since it cannot be inferred that one group exceeds the other either in size or in average amount, D is not inferable.

4. Reviewing historical data, medical researchers in California found that counties with the largest number of television sets per capita have had the lowest incidence of a serious brain disease, mosquito-borne encephalitis. The researchers have concluded that people in these counties stay indoors more and thus avoid exposure to the disease.

The researchers' conclusion would be most strengthened if which of the following were true?

(A) Programs designed to control the size of disease-bearing mosquito populations have not affected the incidence of mosquito-borne encephalitis.
(B) The occupations of county residents affect their risk of exposure to mosquito-borne encephalitis more than does television-watching.
(C) The incidence of mosquito-borne encephalitis in counties with the largest number of television sets per capita is likely to decrease even further.
(D) The more time people in a county spend outdoors, the greater their awareness of the dangers of mosquito-borne encephalitis.
(E) The more television sets there are per capita in a county, the more time the average county resident spends watching television.

The researchers' conclusion is particularly vulnerable to the objection that unwatched television sets, no matter how numerous they are, do not keep people indoors. Choice E addresses this potential objection in a way favorable to the researchers' position: the more sets per capita, the more time spent watching and thus spent, most likely, indoors. Therefore, E is the best answer.

Neither A nor B strengthens appreciably: A does not, because ineffective control programs do not bear on different counties differently, and B does not, because nothing is said about how low-risk occupations are distributed across counties. C and D most probably weaken the conclusion: C by suggesting some unidentified cause possibly unrelated to television sets, and D because greater awareness might help compensate for greater exposure.

5. The city's public transportation system should be removed from the jurisdiction of the municipal government, which finds it politically impossible either to raise fares or to institute cost-saving reductions in service. If public transportation were handled by a private firm, profits would be vigorously pursued, thereby eliminating the necessity for covering operating costs with government funds.

The statements above best support the conclusion that

(A) the private firms that would handle public transportation would have experience in the transportation industry
(B) political considerations would not prevent private firms from ensuring that revenues cover operating costs
(C) private firms would receive government funding if it were needed to cover operating costs
(D) the public would approve the cost-cutting actions taken by the private firm
(E) the municipal government would not be resigned to accumulating merely enough income to cover costs

Since the necessity for covering operating costs with government funds is said to be eliminable through a transfer of the system to a private operator, that operator must be able to make enough profit to stay in business. Choice B is well supported because it attributes to private firms a level of freedom from political considerations that must be reached for profits to be made. Therefore, B is the best answer.

Choice A is unsupported: the private firm may not even exist yet. Because the basic point is to eliminate government subsidies, C is not supported, since it contemplates continuing subsidies; neither is E supported, since breaking even would in fact do away with the need for subsidies. The public's reaction is not raised as a concern, so D is unsupported.

6. To entice customers away from competitors, Red Label supermarkets have begun offering discounts on home appliances to customers who spend $50 or more on any shopping trip to Red Label. Red Label executives claim that the discount program has been a huge success, since cash register receipts of $50 or more are up thirty percent since the beginning of the program.

Which of the following, if true, most seriously weakens the claim of the Red Label executives?

(A) Most people who switched to Red Label after the program began spend more than $50 each time they shop at Red Label.
(B) Most people whose average grocery bill is less than $50 would not be persuaded to spend more by any discount program.
(C) Most people who received discounts on home appliances through Red Label's program will shop at Red Label after the program ends.
(D) Since the beginning of the discount program, most of the people who spend $50 or more at Red Label are people who have never before shopped there and whose average grocery bill has always been higher than $50.
(E) Almost all of the people who have begun spending $50 or more at Red Label since the discount program began are longtime customers who have increased the average amount of their shopping bills by making fewer trips.

The discount program is not a success unless people who would otherwise do their shopping elsewhere shop at Red Label, thanks to the program. Red Label's executives claim success because of the increase in certain receipts they cite. Choice E, however, establishes that this increase comes almost entirely from longtime Red Label customers. The executives' claim of success is thereby seriously weakened. Therefore, E is the best answer.

Choices A and D strengthen the executives' claim, since each suggests that the program actually brought Red Label new customers. The people mentioned in B—not particularly addressed by the program—are essentially irrelevant to its success. What C describes is as compatible with success as with failure of the program.

7. Throughout the 1950's, there were increases in the numbers of dead birds found in agricultural areas after pesticide sprayings. Pesticide manufacturers claimed that the publicity given to bird deaths stimulated volunteers to look for dead birds, and that the increase in numbers reported was attributable to the increase in the number of people looking.

Which of the following statements, if true, would help to refute the claim of the pesticide manufacturers?

(A) The publicity given to bird deaths was largely regional and never reached national proportions.

(B) Pesticide sprayings were timed to coincide with various phases of the life cycles of the insects they destroyed.

(C) No provision was made to ensure that a dead bird would not be reported by more than one observer.

(D) Initial increases in bird deaths had been noticed by agricultural workers long before any publicity had been given to the matter.

(E) Dead birds of the same species as those found in agricultural areas had been found along coastal areas where no farming took place.

Choice D establishes that some increases in bird deaths preceded the publicity given to bird deaths, and thus raises the presumption, contrary to the pesticide manufacturers' claim, that there were genuine increases in the number of bird deaths. Therefore, D is the best answer.

Since the manufacturers' claim might be about the consequences of regional publicity, A does nothing to refute it. Choice B is entirely compatible with the manufacturers' claim. Choice C suggests a way that relatively few volunteers could generate reports of misleadingly large numbers of dead birds. This is, on balance, favorable to the manufacturers' case. Concerning E, it cannot be determined whether the information it provides is even relevant.

8. Teenagers are often priced out of the labor market by the government-mandated minimum-wage level because employers cannot afford to pay that much for extra help. Therefore, if Congress institutes a subminimum wage, a new lower legal wage for teenagers, the teenage unemployment rate, which has been rising since 1960, will no longer increase.

Which of the following, if true, would most weaken the argument above?

(A) Since 1960 the teenage unemployment rate has risen when the minimum wage has risen.

(B) Since 1960 the teenage unemployment rate has risen even when the minimum wage remained constant.

(C) Employers often hire extra help during holiday and warm weather seasons.

(D) The teenage unemployment rate rose more quickly in the 1970's than it did in the 1960's.

(E) The teenage unemployment rate has occasionally declined in the years since 1960.

Choice B suggests that there are economic forces pushing up the teenage unemployment rate that are not directly related to the minimum-wage level. This casts doubt on any prediction, such as the one in the passage, that appears to treat wage level as the sole determinant of the unemployment rate. Therefore, B is the best answer.

Choice A relates wage level and unemployment rate in the same way as the passage, thus strengthening the conclusion. Choice C suggests that care must be taken to distinguish seasonal fluctuations from general trends, but there is no indication that the argument neglects this distinction. Since neither D nor E relates changes in unemployment rate to prevailing wage levels, it cannot be determined how either bears on the argument.

9. Which of the following best completes the passage below?

The computer industry's estimate that it loses millions of dollars when users illegally copy programs without paying for them is greatly exaggerated. Most of the illegal copying is done by people with no serious interest in the programs. Thus, the loss to the industry is much smaller than estimated because

(A) many users who illegally copy programs never find any use for them

(B) most of the illegally copied programs would not be purchased even if purchasing them were the only way to obtain them

(C) even if the computer industry received all the revenue it claims to be losing, it would still be experiencing financial difficulties

(D) the total market value of the illegal copies is low in comparison to the total revenue of the computer industry

(E) the number of programs that are frequently copied illegally is low in comparison to the number of programs available for sale

The computer industry is presented in the passage as basing its loss estimate on the estimated number of illegal copies made of programs, and on the difference between the profit the industry derives from illegal copies (zero dollars) and the profit it would have realized from program sales if programs could not have been illegally copied. If this loss estimate is too high, the reason might be that the number of illegal copies was overestimated, and/or that the assumption is false that each illegal copy represents a program that would have been sold if there were no copying, and/or that the profit per extra program imagined sold was overestimated. Only B expresses one of these possible reasons, and is thus the best answer.

10. This year the New Hampshire Division of Company X set a new record for annual sales by that division. This record is especially surprising since the New Hampshire Division has the smallest potential market and the lowest sales of any of Company X's divisions.

Which of the following identifies a flaw in the logical coherence of the statement above?

(A) If overall sales for Company X were sharply reduced, the New Hampshire Division's new sales record is irrelevant to the company's prosperity.
(B) Since the division is competing against its own record, the comparison of its sales record with that of other divisions is irrelevant.
(C) If this is the first year that the New Hampshire Division has been last in sales among Company X's divisions, the new record is not surprising at all.
(D) If overall sales for Company X were greater than usual, it is not surprising that the New Hampshire Division was last in sales.
(E) Since the New Hampshire Division has the smallest potential market, it is not surprising that it had the lowest sales.

Surprise is appropriate when something happens that one had reasonably expected would not happen. It is not reasonable to expect that a division of a company cannot have higher sales than it ever had before if the only basis for that expectation is the fact that the division is relatively small. Thus, the passage fails to cohere because it posits surprise where there should be none, and B best expresses why there should be none.

The other choices range from statements that seem quite accurate (e.g., E) to statements that seem highly dubious (e.g., C), but they all fail to address the flaw in the logical coherence of the passage.

11. Statement of a United States copper mining company: Import quotas should be imposed on the less expensive copper mined outside the country to maintain the price of copper in this country; otherwise, our companies will not be able to stay in business.

Response of a United States copper wire manufacturer: United States wire and cable manufacturers purchase about 70 percent of the copper mined in the United States. If the copper prices we pay are not at the international level, our sales will drop, and then the demand for United States copper will go down.

If the factual information presented by both companies is accurate, the best assessment of the logical relationship between the two arguments is that the wire manufacturer's argument

(A) is self-serving and irrelevant to the proposal of the mining company
(B) is circular, presupposing what it seeks to prove about the proposal of the mining company
(C) shows that the proposal of the mining company would have a negative effect on the mining company's own business
(D) fails to give a reason why the proposal of the mining company should not be put into effect to alleviate the concern of the mining company for staying in business
(E) establishes that even the mining company's business will prosper if the mining company's proposal is rejected

If demand for United States copper goes down, as the wire manufacturer predicts, then a given copper mining company may either cut prices, trying to maintain sales, or lose sales, trying to maintain prices, or cut prices *and* lose sales. In each case, there is a negative effect on the mining company's business as a foreseeable consequence of implementing its own proposal. Therefore, C is the best answer.

The assessment given in C shows that the wire manufacturer's argument is relevant—contrary to A—and that the manufacturer does give reasons against the mining company's proposal—contrary to D. There is no evidence here of circularity—contrary to B—and nothing to suggest that the mining company has misanalyzed the implications of current business conditions—contrary to E.

12. Y has been believed to cause Z. A new report, noting that Y and Z are often observed to be preceded by X, suggests that X, not Y, may be the cause of Z.

Which of the following further observations would best support the new report's suggestion?

(A) In cases where X occurs but Y does not, X is usually followed by Z.
(B) In cases where X occurs, followed by Y, Y is usually followed by Z.
(C) In cases where Y occurs but X does not, Y is usually followed by Z.
(D) In cases where Y occurs but Z does not, Y is usually preceded by X.
(E) In cases where Z occurs, it is usually preceded by X and Y.

The speculation that X rather than Y may be the cause of Z would be considerably strengthened if one or both of two circumstances were discovered to prevail: in cases where Y occurs but X does not, Z generally does not occur (or, better still, never occurs), and in cases where X occurs but Y does not, Z generally (or, better still, always) occurs after X has occurred. Choice A states the second of these circumstances and is, therefore, the best answer.

Choices B and E offer no information that would help one choose between the original belief and the current speculation. Choice C supports the original belief. Choice D casts some doubt on both the original belief and the current speculation.

13. Mr. Primm: If hospitals were private enterprises, dependent on profits for their survival, there would be no teaching hospitals, because of the intrinsically high cost of running such hospitals.

Ms. Nakai: I disagree. The medical challenges provided by teaching hospitals attract the very best physicians. This, in turn, enables those hospitals to concentrate on nonroutine cases.

Which of the following, if true, would most strengthen Ms. Nakai's attempt to refute Mr. Primm's claim?

(A) Doctors at teaching hospitals command high salaries.
(B) Sophisticated, nonroutine medical care commands a high price.
(C) Existing teaching hospitals derive some revenue from public subsidies.
(D) The patient mortality rate at teaching hospitals is high.
(E) The modern trend among physicians is to become highly specialized.

Ms. Nakai's attempted rebuttal seems to confirm Mr. Primm's point that teaching hospitals are expensive to run since "the very best physicians" and "nonroutine cases" both sound costly. But if B is true, high charges to patients might compensate for the high expenses. Choice B makes Ms. Nakai's challenge more effective, and it is thus the best answer.

Choice A supports Mr. Primm's position concerning high costs. Public subsidies, mentioned in C, suggest that Mr. Primm is correct in his doubts about the profitability of private teaching hospitals. Since high mortality rates are not plausibly related to greater profitability, D does not strengthen Ms. Nakai's case. The impact of E, if any, on Ms. Nakai's position cannot be gauged on the basis of the information given.

14. A recent survey of all auto accident victims in Dole County found that, of the severely injured drivers and front-seat passengers, 80 percent were not wearing seat belts at the time of their accidents. This indicates that, by wearing seat belts, drivers and front-seat passengers can greatly reduce their risk of being severely injured if they are in an auto accident.

The conclusion above is not properly drawn unless which of the following is true?

(A) Of all the drivers and front-seat passengers in the survey, more than 20 percent were wearing seat belts at the time of their accidents.
(B) Considerably more than 20 percent of drivers and front-seat passengers in Dole County always wear seat belts when traveling by car.
(C) More drivers and front-seat passengers in the survey than rear-seat passengers were very severely injured.
(D) More than half of the drivers and front-seat passengers in the survey were not wearing seat belts at the time of their accidents.
(E) Most of the auto accidents reported to police in Dole County do not involve any serious injury.

The survey results support the conclusion drawn only if those wearing seat belts are a smaller proportion of the severely injured than they are of all those covered by the survey. Choice A expresses this precondition and is thus the best answer.

Since the conclusion might be properly drawn even if it were true that no one in Dole County wears seat belts 100 percent of the time, B can be eliminated. Choice C draws a comparison with rear-seat passengers that is irrelevant to the conclusion. Choice D can be ruled out because the smaller the proportion of those not wearing seat belts among the total survey population, the better the conclusion is supported. Since the conclusion might be properly drawn even if most of the accidents referred to in E did involve serious injuries, E can also be ruled out.

15. Six months or so after getting a video recorder, many early buyers apparently lost interest in obtaining videos to watch on it. The trade of businesses selling and renting videos is still buoyant, because the number of homes with video recorders is still growing. But clearly, once the market for video recorders is saturated, businesses distributing videos face hard times.

Which of the following, if true, would most seriously weaken the conclusion above?

(A) The market for video recorders would not be considered saturated until there was one in 80 percent of homes.

(B) Among the items handled by video distributors are many films specifically produced as video features.

(C) Few of the early buyers of video recorders raised any complaints about performance aspects of the new product.

(D) The early buyers of a novel product are always people who are quick to acquire novelties, but also often as quick to tire of them.

(E) In a shrinking market, competition always intensifies and marginal businesses fail.

The argument treats early buyers as typical. If they are, it can reasonably be predicted that the demand for videos will sharply decline soon after the market for video recorders has become saturated. But D raises the distinct possibility that early buyers may be unusual in precisely the respect on which the prediction depends: rapid loss of interest in videos. Therefore, D is the best answer.

Choice A is not a good answer since nothing rules out saturation so defined. Choices B and C, on balance, make the early buyers' loss of interest seem surprising, but give no hint that it is not a real phenomenon. Choice E points out an unfortunate consequence of the conclusion but raises no doubt about its truth.

16. Advertiser: The revenue that newspapers and magazines earn by publishing advertisements allows publishers to keep the prices per copy of their publications much lower than would otherwise be possible. Therefore, consumers benefit economically from advertising.

Consumer: But who pays for the advertising that pays for low-priced newspapers and magazines? We consumers do, because advertisers pass along advertising costs to us through the higher prices they charge for their products.

Which of the following best describes how the consumer counters the advertiser's argument?

(A) By alleging something that, if true, would weaken the plausibility of the advertiser's conclusion

(B) By questioning the truth of the purportedly factual statement on which the advertiser's conclusion is based

(C) By offering an interpretation of the advertiser's opening statement that, if accurate, shows that there is an implicit contradiction in it

(D) By pointing out that the advertiser's point of view is biased

(E) By arguing that the advertiser too narrowly restricts the discussion to the effects of advertising that are economic

The advertiser says that consumers benefit because of the low prices for newspapers and magazines that advertising makes possible. The consumer counters that advertising hurts consumers by driving up the prices of products being advertised. The consumer's claim, if true, means that quite possibly consumers will not enjoy any financial net benefit from advertising. Choice A accurately describes this and is, therefore, the best answer.

The consumer does question the advertiser's conclusion, but neither disputes the claim it is based on nor offers to reinterpret it; thus, B and C are incorrect. Although the consumer argues that the advertiser overlooked an important fact, there is no allegation of bias or of the excessive narrowness of purely economic concerns, contrary to D and E, respectively.

17. Mr. Lawson: We should adopt a national family policy that includes legislation requiring employers to provide paid parental leave and establishing government-sponsored day care. Such laws would decrease the stress levels of employees who have responsibility for small children. Thus, such laws would lead to happier, better-adjusted families.

Which of the following, if true, would most strengthen the conclusion above?

(A) An employee's high stress level can be a cause of unhappiness and poor adjustment for his or her family.

(B) People who have responsiblity for small children and who work outside the home have higher stress levels than those who do not.

(C) The goal of a national family policy is to lower the stress levels of parents.

(D) Any national family policy that is adopted would include legislation requiring employers to provide paid parental leave and establishing government-sponsored day care.

(E) Most children who have been cared for in day care centers are happy and well adjusted.

Mr. Lawson bases his case on the claim that certain laws would lead to happier, better-adjusted families. He fails to substantiate that claim, however, since he does not relate stress reduction causally to families' greater happiness. Choice A suggests such a causal connection. It thereby strengthens the basis for Mr. Lawson's conclusion, and is, therefore, the best answer.

Choice B establishes instances of relatively high levels of stress but in no way suggests that families would be happier or better adjusted without those stress levels. Choices C and D suggest that Mr. Lawson knows what a family policy aims to accomplish and how, but not that it would be good to have one. Choice E does not comment on whether parental stress levels were significant in influencing the situation.

18. Lark Manufacturing Company initiated a voluntary Quality Circles program for machine operators. Independent surveys of employee attitudes indicated that the machine operators participating in the program were less satisfied with their work situations after two years of the program's existence than they were at the program's start. Obviously, any workers who participate in a Quality Circles program will, as a result, become less satisfied with their jobs.

Each of the following, if true, would weaken the conclusion draw above EXCEPT:

(A) The second survey occurred during a period of recession when rumors of cutbacks and layoffs at Lark Manufacturing were plentiful.

(B) The surveys also showed that those Lark machine operators who neither participated in Quality Circles nor knew anyone who did so reported the same degree of lessened satisfaction with their work situations as did the Lark machine operators who participated in Quality Circles.

(C) While participating in Quality Circles at Lark Manufacturing, machine operators exhibited two of the primary indicators of improved job satisfaction: increased productivity and decreased absenteeism.

(D) Several workers at Lark Manufacturing who had participated in Quality Circles while employed at other companies reported that, while participating in Quality Circles in their previous companies, their work satisfaction had increased.

(E) The machine operators who participated in Quality Circles reported that, when the program started, they felt that participation might improve their work situations.

The task is to find the answer choice that would *not* weaken the stated conclusion. Choices A and B both weaken the conclusion, since each describes a situation in which it is likely that the reduced level of satisfaction stems from causes other than participation in the Quality Circles program. Choice C weakens because it indicates that there are objective measures of job satisfaction that contradict the workers' self-reports. Choice D weakens by providing relevant hearsay evidence that directly contradicts the conclusion.

Choice E, however, does not weaken the conclusion: the workers seem to have had neither overly high expectations that were bound to be disappointed nor any self-fulfilling expectations of failure. Therefore, E is the best answer.

Blood banks will shortly start to screen all donors for NANB hepatitis. Although the new screening tests are estimated to disqualify up to 5 percent of all prospective blood donors, they will still miss two-thirds of donors carrying NANB hepatitis. Therefore, about 10 percent of actual donors will still supply NANB-contaminated blood.

19. The argument above depends on which of the following assumptions?

   (A) Donors carrying NANB hepatitis do not, in a large percentage of cases, carry other infections for which reliable screening tests are routinely performed.
   (B) Donors carrying NANB hepatitis do not, in a large perentage of cases, develop the disease themselves at any point.
   (C) The estimate of the number of donors who would be disqualified by tests for NANB hepatitis is an underestimate.
   (D) The incidence of NANB hepatitis is lower among the potential blood donors than it is in the population at large.
   (E) The donors who will still supply NANB-contaminated blood will donate blood at the average frequency for all donors.

Contrary to C, the argument proceeds as if the figures used were essentially accurate. Choice D is irrelevant because the argument is concerned only with the threat of NANB contamination posed by donors, and ignores the population at large. Choice E is incorrect because the argument focuses on quantitative information about donors, not donations, so nothing is assumed about relative frequencies of donations. Choice B is also incorrect: the argument may hold even if B is false, provided there is a rough balance between carriers developing the disease and newly infected carriers.

However, if a large proportion of carriers of NANB hepatitis were eliminated by other screening tests, the 10 percent figure would be significantly too high, and the conclusion incorrect. Choice A is thus assumed.

20. Which of the following inferences about the consequences of instituting the new tests is best supported by the passage above?

   (A) The incidence of new cases of NANB hepatitis is likely to go up by 10 percent.
   (B) Donations made by patients specifically for their own use are likely to become less frequent.
   (C) The demand for blood from blood banks is likely to fluctuate more strongly.
   (D) The blood supplies available from blood banks are likely to go down.
   (E) The number of prospective first-time donors is likely to go up by 5 percent.

The passage claims that there are new screening tests that will eliminate up to 5 percent of prospective donors. The most likely consequence is that there will be less blood donated overall, and thus less blood going to blood banks. Therefore, D is the best answer.

Choice A is unsupported: the incidence of any new cases of NANB hepatitis from contaminated blood should go down, not up. Since nothing is said about donations for the donors' own use, no inferences about such donations receive any support; this rules out B. Choice C can also be eliminated, since the argument is not concerned with the demand for donated blood. The argument does not consider the issue of first-time donors separately; thus E remains unsupported.

7 Sentence Correction

Sample Sentence Correction test sections begin on page 279; answers to the questions follow the test sections. After the answers are explanations for all of the questions. These explanations address types of grammatical and syntactical problems you are likely to encounter in the Sentence Correction section of the GMAT.

Study Suggestions

1. One way to gain familiarity with the basic conventions of standard written English is to read material that reflects standard usage. Suitable material will usually be found in good magazines and nonfiction books, editorials in outstanding newspapers, and the collections of essays used by many college and university writing courses.

2. A general review of basic rules of grammar and practice with writing exercises are also ways of studying for the Sentence Correction section. If you have papers that have been carefully evaluated for grammatical errors, it may be helpful to review the comments and corrections.

Test-Taking Strategies for Sentence Correction

1. Read the entire sentence carefully. Try to understand the specific idea or relationship that the sentence should express.

2. Since the part of the sentence that *may* be incorrect is underlined, concentrate on evaluating the underlined part for errors and possible corrections before reading the answer choices.

3. Read each answer choice carefully. Choice A always repeats the underlined portion of the original sentence. Choose A if you think that the sentence is best as it stands, but only after examining all of the other choices.

4. Try to determine how well each choice corrects whatever you consider wrong with the original sentence.

5. Make sure that you evaluate the sentence and the choices in terms of general clarity, grammatical and idiomatic usage, economy and precision of language, and appropriateness of diction.

6. Read the whole sentence, substituting the choice that you prefer for the underlined part. A choice may be wrong because it does not fit grammatically or structurally with the rest of the sentence. Remember that some sentences will require no corrections. The answer to such sentences should be A.

When you take the sample test sections, use the answer spaces on pages 277 and 278 to mark your answers.

Answer Spaces for Sentence Correction Sample Test Sections

Sample Test Section 1

1 (A) (B) (C) (D) (E)	8 (A) (B) (C) (D) (E)	15 (A) (B) (C) (D) (E)	22 (A) (B) (C) (D) (E)
2 (A) (B) (C) (D) (E)	9 (A) (B) (C) (D) (E)	16 (A) (B) (C) (D) (E)	23 (A) (B) (C) (D) (E)
3 (A) (B) (C) (D) (E)	10 (A) (B) (C) (D) (E)	17 (A) (B) (C) (D) (E)	24 (A) (B) (C) (D) (E)
4 (A) (B) (C) (D) (E)	11 (A) (B) (C) (D) (E)	18 (A) (B) (C) (D) (E)	25 (A) (B) (C) (D) (E)
5 (A) (B) (C) (D) (E)	12 (A) (B) (C) (D) (E)	19 (A) (B) (C) (D) (E)	
6 (A) (B) (C) (D) (E)	13 (A) (B) (C) (D) (E)	20 (A) (B) (C) (D) (E)	
7 (A) (B) (C) (D) (E)	14 (A) (B) (C) (D) (E)	21 (A) (B) (C) (D) (E)	

Sample Test Section 2

1 (A) (B) (C) (D) (E)	8 (A) (B) (C) (D) (E)	15 (A) (B) (C) (D) (E)	22 (A) (B) (C) (D) (E)
2 (A) (B) (C) (D) (E)	9 (A) (B) (C) (D) (E)	16 (A) (B) (C) (D) (E)	23 (A) (B) (C) (D) (E)
3 (A) (B) (C) (D) (E)	10 (A) (B) (C) (D) (E)	17 (A) (B) (C) (D) (E)	24 (A) (B) (C) (D) (E)
4 (A) (B) (C) (D) (E)	11 (A) (B) (C) (D) (E)	18 (A) (B) (C) (D) (E)	25 (A) (B) (C) (D) (E)
5 (A) (B) (C) (D) (E)	12 (A) (B) (C) (D) (E)	19 (A) (B) (C) (D) (E)	
6 (A) (B) (C) (D) (E)	13 (A) (B) (C) (D) (E)	20 (A) (B) (C) (D) (E)	
7 (A) (B) (C) (D) (E)	14 (A) (B) (C) (D) (E)	21 (A) (B) (C) (D) (E)	

Sample Test Section 3

1 (A) (B) (C) (D) (E)	8 (A) (B) (C) (D) (E)	15 (A) (B) (C) (D) (E)	22 (A) (B) (C) (D) (E)
2 (A) (B) (C) (D) (E)	9 (A) (B) (C) (D) (E)	16 (A) (B) (C) (D) (E)	23 (A) (B) (C) (D) (E)
3 (A) (B) (C) (D) (E)	10 (A) (B) (C) (D) (E)	17 (A) (B) (C) (D) (E)	24 (A) (B) (C) (D) (E)
4 (A) (B) (C) (D) (E)	11 (A) (B) (C) (D) (E)	18 (A) (B) (C) (D) (E)	25 (A) (B) (C) (D) (E)
5 (A) (B) (C) (D) (E)	12 (A) (B) (C) (D) (E)	19 (A) (B) (C) (D) (E)	
6 (A) (B) (C) (D) (E)	13 (A) (B) (C) (D) (E)	20 (A) (B) (C) (D) (E)	
7 (A) (B) (C) (D) (E)	14 (A) (B) (C) (D) (E)	21 (A) (B) (C) (D) (E)	

Sample Test Section 4

1 (A) (B) (C) (D) (E)	8 (A) (B) (C) (D) (E)	15 (A) (B) (C) (D) (E)	22 (A) (B) (C) (D) (E)
2 (A) (B) (C) (D) (E)	9 (A) (B) (C) (D) (E)	16 (A) (B) (C) (D) (E)	23 (A) (B) (C) (D) (E)
3 (A) (B) (C) (D) (E)	10 (A) (B) (C) (D) (E)	17 (A) (B) (C) (D) (E)	24 (A) (B) (C) (D) (E)
4 (A) (B) (C) (D) (E)	11 (A) (B) (C) (D) (E)	18 (A) (B) (C) (D) (E)	25 (A) (B) (C) (D) (E)
5 (A) (B) (C) (D) (E)	12 (A) (B) (C) (D) (E)	19 (A) (B) (C) (D) (E)	
6 (A) (B) (C) (D) (E)	13 (A) (B) (C) (D) (E)	20 (A) (B) (C) (D) (E)	
7 (A) (B) (C) (D) (E)	14 (A) (B) (C) (D) (E)	21 (A) (B) (C) (D) (E)	

Sample Test Section 5

1 (A) (B) (C) (D) (E)   8 (A) (B) (C) (D) (E)   15 (A) (B) (C) (D) (E)   22 (A) (B) (C) (D) (E)
2 (A) (B) (C) (D) (E)   9 (A) (B) (C) (D) (E)   16 (A) (B) (C) (D) (E)   23 (A) (B) (C) (D) (E)
3 (A) (B) (C) (D) (E)   10 (A) (B) (C) (D) (E)   17 (A) (B) (C) (D) (E)   24 (A) (B) (C) (D) (E)
4 (A) (B) (C) (D) (E)   11 (A) (B) (C) (D) (E)   18 (A) (B) (C) (D) (E)   25 (A) (B) (C) (D) (E)
5 (A) (B) (C) (D) (E)   12 (A) (B) (C) (D) (E)   19 (A) (B) (C) (D) (E)
6 (A) (B) (C) (D) (E)   13 (A) (B) (C) (D) (E)   20 (A) (B) (C) (D) (E)
7 (A) (B) (C) (D) (E)   14 (A) (B) (C) (D) (E)   21 (A) (B) (C) (D) (E)

SENTENCE CORRECTION SAMPLE TEST SECTION 1

30 Minutes
25 Questions

<u>Directions:</u> In each of the following sentences, some part of the sentence or the entire sentence is underlined. Beneath each sentence you will find five ways of phrasing the underlined part. The first of these repeats the original; the other four are different. If you think the original is better than any of the alternatives, choose answer A; otherwise choose one of the others. Select the best version and fill in the corresponding oval on your answer sheet.

This is a test of correctness and effectiveness of expression. In choosing answers, follow the requirements of standard written English; that is, pay attention to grammar, choice of words, and sentence construction. Choose the answer that expresses most effectively what is presented in the original sentence; this answer should be clear and exact, without awkwardness, ambiguity, or redundancy.

1. After the Civil War Harriet Tubman, herself an escaped slave, continued her efforts in behalf of former slaves, helping to educate freedmen, supporting children, and <u>she was assisting impoverished old people</u>.

   (A) she was assisting impoverished old people
   (B) impoverished old people were assisted
   (C) to assist impoverished old people
   (D) assisting impoverished old people
   (E) also in assisting impoverished old people

2. The percentage of the labor force that is unemployed has dropped sharply this month, <u>even though it may be only temporarily</u>.

   (A) even though it may be only temporarily
   (B) but it may be temporary only
   (C) but the drop may be only temporary
   (D) even though the drop may only be temporary
   (E) but such a drop may only be a temporary one

3. As more and more subjects take the Rorschach test, the body of information tying styles of response <u>with specific problems or tendencies grow, and the predictive power of the test increases</u>.

   (A) with specific problems or tendencies grow, and the predictive power of the test increases
   (B) with specific problems or tendencies grow, and the predictive powers increase in the test
   (C) to specific problems or tendencies grow, and the predictive power of the test increases
   (D) to specific problems or tendencies grows, and the predictive power of the test increases
   (E) and specific problems and tendencies grow, increasing the predictive power of the test

4. Unlike the <u>Second World War, when long voyages home aboard troopships gave soldiers</u> a chance to talk out their experiences and begin to absorb them, Vietnam returnees often came home by jet, singly or in small groups.

   (A) Second World War, when long voyages home aboard troopships gave soldiers
   (B) soldier coming home after the Second World War on long voyages aboard troopships who had
   (C) soldiers of the Second World War, whose long voyage home aboard a troopship gave him
   (D) troopships on long voyages home after the Second World War which gave the soldier
   (E) soldiers of the Second World War, whose long voyages home aboard troopships gave them

5. Contestants in many sports <u>prepare for competition by eating pasta as</u> part of a "carbohydrate-loading" regimen that is supposed to provide quick energy.

   (A) prepare for competition by eating pasta as
   (B) prepare for competition and eat pasta, which is
   (C) prepare for competition by eating pasta because this is
   (D) eat pasta to prepare for competing, which is
   (E) eat pasta to prepare for competing as

GO ON TO THE NEXT PAGE.

6. In August 1883, Krakatoa erupted and sent clouds of dust, ash, and sulphate to a height of 50 miles, blotted out the sun for more than two days within a 50-mile radius and for nearly a day at an observation post 130 miles away.

   (A) blotted out the sun for more than two days within
   (B) blotting out the sun for more than two days within
   (C) the sun being blotted out for more than two days in
   (D) having blotted out the sun for more than two days in
   (E) for more than two days blotting out the sun within

7. Added to the increase in hourly wages requested last July, the railroad employees are now seeking an expanded program of retirement benefits.

   (A) Added to the increase in hourly wages requested last July, the railroad employees are now seeking an expanded program of retirement benefits.
   (B) Added to the increase in hourly wages which had been requested last July, the employees of the railroad are now seeking an expanded program of retirement benefits.
   (C) The railroad employees are now seeking an expanded program of retirement benefits added to the increase in hourly wages that were requested last July.
   (D) In addition to the increase in hourly wages that were requested last July, the railroad employees are now seeking an expanded program of retirement benefits.
   (E) In addition to the increase in hourly wages requested last July, the employees of the railroad are now seeking an expanded program of retirement benefits.

8. Child prodigies are marked not so much by their skills but instead by the fact that these skills are fully developed at a very early age.

   (A) but instead
   (B) rather than
   (C) than
   (D) as
   (E) so much as

9. The department defines a private passenger vehicle as one registered to an individual with a gross weight of less than 8,000 pounds.

   (A) as one registered to an individual with a gross weight of less than 8,000 pounds
   (B) to be one that is registered to an individual with a gross weight of less than 8,000 pounds
   (C) as one that is registered to an individual and that has a gross weight of less than 8,000 pounds
   (D) to have a gross weight less than 8,000 pounds and being registered to an individual
   (E) as having a gross weight of less than 8,000 pounds and registered to an individual

10. Urban officials want the census to be as accurate and complete as possible for the reason that the amount of low-income people in a given area affect the distribution of about fifty billion dollars a year in federal funds.

    (A) for the reason that the amount of low-income people in a given area affect
    (B) for the reason because the amount of low-income people in a given area effects
    (C) in that the amount of low-income people in given areas effect
    (D) because the number of low-income people in a given area affects
    (E) because the numbers of low-income people in given areas effects

GO ON TO THE NEXT PAGE.

11. After the Arab conquest of Egypt in A. D. 640, Arabic became the dominant language of the Egyptians, replacing older languages and writing systems.

   (A) became the dominant language of the Egyptians, replacing older languages
   (B) became the dominant language of the Egyptians, replacing languages that were older
   (C) becomes the dominant language of the Egyptians and it replaced older languages
   (D) becomes the dominant language of the Egyptians and it replaced languages that were older
   (E) becomes the dominant language of the Egyptians, having replaced languages that were older

12. The use of gravity waves, which do not interact with matter in the way electromagnetic waves do, hopefully will enable astronomers to study the actual formation of black holes and neutron stars.

   (A) in the way electromagnetic waves do, hopefully will enable
   (B) in the way electromagnetic waves do, will, it is hoped, enable
   (C) like electromagnetic waves, hopefully will enable
   (D) like electromagnetic waves, would enable, hopefully
   (E) such as electromagnetic waves do, will, it is hoped, enable

13. If a single strain of plant is used for a given crop over a wide area, a practice fostered by modern seed-marketing methods, it increases the likelihood that the impact of a single crop disease or pest will be disastrous.

   (A) If a single strain of plant is used for a given crop over a wide area, a practice fostered by modern seed-marketing methods, it
   (B) If a single strain of plant is used for a given crop over a wide area, as is fostered by modern seed-marketing methods, it
   (C) A practice fostered by modern seed-marketing methods, a single strain of plant used for a given crop over a wide area
   (D) A single strain of plant used for a given crop over a wide area, a practice fostered by modern seed-marketing methods,
   (E) The use of a single strain of plant for a given crop over a wide area, a practice fostered by modern seed-marketing methods,

14. A majority of the international journalists surveyed view nuclear power stations as unsafe at present but that they will, or could, be made sufficiently safe in the future.

   (A) that they will, or could,
   (B) that they would, or could,
   (C) they will be or could
   (D) think that they will be or could
   (E) think the power stations would or could

15. A controversial figure throughout most of his public life, the Black leader Marcus Garvey advocated that some Blacks return to Africa, the land that, to him, symbolized the possibility of freedom.

   (A) that some Blacks return to Africa, the land that, to him, symbolized the possibility of freedom
   (B) that some Blacks return to the African land symbolizing the possibility of freedom to him
   (C) that some Blacks return to Africa which was the land which symbolized the possibility of freedom to him
   (D) some Black's returning to Africa which was the land that to him symbolized the possibility of freedom
   (E) some Black's return to the land symbolizing the possibility of freedom to him, Africa

GO ON TO THE NEXT PAGE.

-281-

16. The fear of rabies is well founded; few people are known to recover from the disease after the appearance of the clinical symptoms.

   (A) few people are known to recover from the disease after the appearance of the clinical symptoms

   (B) few people are known to have recovered from the disease once the clinical symptoms have appeared

   (C) there are few known people who have recovered from the disease once the clinical symptoms have appeared

   (D) after the clinical symptoms appear, there are few known people who have recovered from the disease

   (E) recovery from the disease is known for only a few people after the clinical symptoms appear

17. The growth of the railroads led to the abolition of local times, which was determined by when the sun reached the observer's meridian and differing from city to city, and to the establishment of regional times.

   (A) which was determined by when the sun reached the observer's meridian and differing

   (B) which was determined by when the sun reached the observer's meridian and which differed

   (C) which were determined by when the sun reached the observer's meridian and differing

   (D) determined by when the sun reached the observer's meridian and differed

   (E) determined by when the sun reached the observer's meridian and differing

18. Although partially destroyed, the archaeologists were able to infer from what remained of the inscription that the priest Zonainos was buried in the crypt.

   (A) Although partially destroyed, the archaeologists were able to infer

   (B) Although partially destroyed, the archaeologists had inferred

   (C) Although it had been partially destroyed, the archaeologists were able to infer

   (D) Partially destroyed though it had been, the archaeologists had been able to infer

   (E) Destroyed partially, the archaeologists were able to infer

19. For all his professed disdain of such activities, Auden was an inveterate literary gossip.

   (A) For all his professed disdain of such activities,

   (B) Having always professed disdain for such activities,

   (C) All such activities were, he professed, disdained, and

   (D) Professing that all such activities were disdained,

   (E) In spite of professions of disdaining all such activities,

20. The earnings of women are well below that of men in spite of educational differences that are diminishing between the sexes.

   (A) well below that of men in spite of educational differences that are diminishing

   (B) much below that of men's despite educational differences diminishing

   (C) much below men in spite of diminishing educational differences

   (D) well below those of men in spite of diminishing educational differences

   (E) below men's despite their educational differences that are diminishing

GO ON TO THE NEXT PAGE.

21. Acid rain and snow result from the chemical reactions between industrial emissions of sulfur dioxide and nitrogen oxides with atmospheric water vapor to produce highly corrosive sulfuric and nitric acids.

(A) with atmospheric water vapor to produce highly corrosive sulfuric and nitric acids
(B) with atmospheric water vapor producing highly corrosive sulfuric and nitric acids
(C) and atmospheric water vapor which has produced highly corrosive sulfuric and nitric acids
(D) and atmospheric water vapor which have produced sulfuric and nitric acids which are highly corrosive
(E) and atmospheric water vapor to produce highly corrosive sulfuric and nitric acids

22. It is characteristic of the Metropolitan Museum of Art, as of virtually every great American museum, the taste of local collectors has played at least as large a part in the formation of their collections as has the judgments of the art historian.

(A) of virtually every great American museum, the taste of local collectors has played at least as large a part in the formation of their collections as has
(B) of virtually every great American museum, that the taste of local collectors has played at least as large a part in the formation of their collections as has
(C) it is of virtually every great American museum, that the taste of local collectors has played at least as large a part in the formation of its collections as have
(D) it is of virtually every great American museum, that the taste of local collectors have played at least as large a part in the formation of its collections as have
(E) it is of virtually every great American museum, the taste of local collectors has played at least as large a part in the formation of its collections as has

23. There has been a 30- to 40-fold increase in the incidence of malaria caused by increasing mosquito resistance against pesticides.

(A) increase in the incidence of malaria caused by increasing mosquito resistance against
(B) increase in the incidence of malaria because of increasing resistance of mosquitoes to
(C) increasing malaria incidence because of increasing resistance of mosquitoes to
(D) incidence of malaria increase caused by increasing mosquito resistance against
(E) incidence of malaria increase because of increased mosquito resistance to

24. Aging is a property of all animals that reach a fixed size at maturity, and the variations in life spans among different species are far greater as that among individuals from the same species: a fruit fly is ancient at 40 days, a mouse at 3 years, a horse at 30, a man at 100, and some tortoises at 150.

(A) among different species are far greater as that among individuals from
(B) among different species are far greater than that among individuals from
(C) among different species are far greater than those among individuals of
(D) between different species are far more than that between individuals of
(E) between different species are greater by far than is that between individuals from

25. The herbicide Oryzalin was still being produced in 1979, three years after the wives of workers producing the chemical in Rensselaer, New York, were found to have borne children with heart defects or miscarriages, and none of their pregnancies was normal.

(A) to have borne children with heart defects or miscarriages, and none of their pregnancies was
(B) to have had children born with heart defects or miscarriages, and none of the pregnancies was
(C) either to have had children with heart defects or miscarriages, without any of their pregnancies being
(D) either to have had miscarriages or to have borne children with heart defects; none of the pregnancies was
(E) either to have had miscarriages or children born with heart defects, without any of their pregnancies being

S T O P

IF YOU FINISH BEFORE TIME IS CALLED, YOU MAY CHECK YOUR WORK ON THIS SECTION ONLY.
DO NOT TURN TO ANY OTHER SECTION IN THE TEST.

Answer Key for Sample Test Section 1

SENTENCE CORRECTION

1. D	14. D
2. C	15. A
3. D	16. B
4. E	17. E
5. A	18. C
6. B	19. A
7. E	20. D
8. D	21. E
9. C	22. C
10. D	23. B
11. A	24. C
12. B	25. D
13. E	

Explanatory Material: Sentence Correction

The following discussion of Sentence Correction is intended to familiarize you with the most efficient and effective approaches to Sentence Correction. The particular questions on the sample test sections in this chapter are generally representative of the kinds of questions you will encounter in this section of the GMAT. Remember that it is the problem-solving strategy that is important, not the specific details of a particular question.

Sample Test Section 1

1. After the Civil War Harriet Tubman, herself an escaped slave, continued her efforts in behalf of former slaves, helping to educate freedmen, supporting children, and she was assisting impoverished old people.

   (A) she was assisting impoverished old people
   (B) impoverished old people were assisted
   (C) to assist impoverished old people
   (D) assisting impoverished old people
   (E) also in assisting impoverished old people

The corrected sentence must conclude with a verb phrase that is parallel with the two preceding verb phrases, *helping to educate freedmen* and *supporting children*; in other words, the final phrase should begin with another present participle, or "-ing" verb form. Choice A breaks the parallel by adding *she was* and thus making another independent clause. Choice B, also an independent clause, employs a passive verb (*were assisted*) instead of a present participle, and C uses an infinitive (*to assist*) instead of a present participle. In E, *in* produces a prepositional rather than a participial phrase. Choice D, the best answer, supplies the parallel verb form.

2. The percentage of the labor force that is unemployed has dropped sharply this month, even though it may be only temporarily.

   (A) even though it may be only temporarily
   (B) but it may be temporary only
   (C) but the drop may be only temporary
   (D) even though the drop may only be temporary
   (E) but such a drop may only be a temporary one

In choices A and B, the pronoun *it* has no noun referent and must be replaced by a noun such as *drop*. That noun should be modified by an adjective (*temporary*), not an adverb (*temporarily*), as in A. In choices A and D, *even though* misstates the relationship between ideas by suggesting that unemployment dropped sharply despite the possibility that the drop is temporary; the word *but* suggests nothing more than a contrast between a recent drop and possible future reversal. In choices B, D, and E *only* is separated from the adjective it modifies; in the correct answer *only* should (or must) immediately precede *temporary*. The phrase *such a drop* in E wrongly implies that this drop is but one example of a whole class of similar events being discussed. C is the best answer.

3. As more and more subjects take the Rorschach test, the body of information tying styles of response with specific problems or tendencies grow, and the predictive power of the test increases.

   (A) with specific problems or tendencies grow, and the predictive power of the test increases
   (B) with specific problems or tendencies grow, and the predictive powers increase in the test
   (C) to specific problems or tendencies grow, and the predictive power of the test increases
   (D) to specific problems or tendencies grows, and the predictive power of the test increases
   (E) and specific problems and tendencies grow, increasing the predictive power of the test

The grammatical subject of this sentence is *body,* and so the correct verb form is *grows*; hence choices A, B, C, and E are incorrect because they use *grow.* Also, the best answer will start with *to* because the correct form of expression is *tying X to Y.* The wording of B illogically suggests that predictive powers are growing within the test, not that the predictive power of the test increases. D is the best choice.

4. Unlike the Second World War, when long voyages home aboard troopships gave soldiers a chance to talk out their experiences and begin to absorb them, Vietnam returnees often came home by jet, singly or in small groups.

(A) Second World War, when long voyages home aboard troopships gave soldiers

(B) soldier coming home after the Second Word War on long voyages aboard troopships who had

(C) soldiers of the Second World War, whose long voyage home aboard a troopship gave him

(D) troopships on long voyages home after the Second World War which gave the soldier

(E) soldiers of the Second World War, whose long voyages home aboard troopships gave them

The sentence with choice A wrongly compares *Vietnam returnees* with *the Second World War.* In choice B, the singular *soldier* does not agree in number with the plural *returnees*; also, B is awkward because the pronoun *who* is so far from its noun referent, *soldier,* that it seems to modify *troopships,* the nearest noun. Choice C correctly compares *soldiers* with *returnees,* but the singular *him* does not agree with the plural *soldiers.* In choice D, *returnees* are compared with *troopships, which* illogically refers to *the Second World War,* and *soldier* is singular rather than plural. Choice E is the best answer: the comparison is logical, the nouns and pronouns agree in number, and the pronoun references are clear.

5. Contestants in many sports prepare for competition by eating pasta as part of a "carbohydrate-loading" regimen that is supposed to provide quick energy.

(A) prepare for competition by eating pasta as

(B) prepare for competition and eat pasta, which is

(C) prepare for competition by eating pasta because this is

(D) eat pasta to prepare for competing, which is

(E) eat pasta to prepare for competing as

Choice A is best. In choice B, *which* is ambiguous: it is not clear whether *which* refers only to *pasta,* the nearest noun, or to the whole preceding clause. Moreover, *and* incorrectly suggests that contestants eat pasta in addition to preparing for competition, not that they eat pasta as a means of preparation. Choice C wrongly states that contestants eat pasta not to become prepared but simply because pasta is part of a regimen. Also, *this* may refer either to *pasta* or to *eating pasta.* In D, *which* is ambiguous, and *for competition* would be more idiomatic. Choice E says that those who eat pasta are competing not as athletes but as *part of a "carbohydrate-loading" regimen.*

6. In August 1883, Krakatoa erupted and sent clouds of dust, ash, and sulphate to a height of 50 miles, blotted out the sun for more than two days within a 50-mile radius and for nearly a day at an observation post 130 miles away.

(A) blotted out the sun for more than two days within

(B) blotting out the sun for more than two days within

(C) the sun being blotted out for more than two days in

(D) having blotted out the sun for more than two days in

(E) for more than two days blotting out the sun within

In choice A, *blotted* is incorrect; the present participial *blotting . . .* is needed to described an event that is simultaneous with the action of the main clause. Choice B presents the correctly formed modifier. The passive construction of choice C does not indicate that Krakatoa was responsible for blotting out the sun; also, *within* would be preferable to *in* here. The verb form as well as the preposition can be faulted in D; *having blotted* states that Krakatoa had blotted out the sun before it erupted. Choice E produces a sentence that is ungrammatical and lacks parallelism: *blotting out the sun* must precede *for more . . .* and *for nearly . . .* if it is to be modified by both phrases.

7. Added to the increase in hourly wages requested last July, the railroad employees are now seeking an expanded program of retirement benefits.

(A) Added to the increase in hourly wages requested last July, the railroad employees are now seeking an expanded program of retirement benefits.

(B) Added to the increase in hourly wages which had been requested last July, the employees of the railroad are now seeking an expanded program of retirement benefits.

(C) The railroad employees are now seeking an expanded program of retirement benefits added to the increase in hourly wages that were requested last July.

(D) In addition to the increase in hourly wages that were requested last July, the railroad employees are now seeking an expanded program of retirement benefits.

(E) In addition to the increase in hourly wages requested last July, the employees of the railroad are now seeking an expanded program of retirement benefits.

Choice A presents a dangling modifier. The phrase beginning the sentence can fit nowhere in the sentence and make logical sense. Coming first, it modifies *employees,* the nearest free noun in the main clause; i.e., choice A says that the employees were added to the increase in hourly wages. Choice B also begins with a dangling modifier; moreover, the simple past tense *requested* is needed to place an action before the present action *are . . . seeking.* In choice C, *were* does not agree in number with the subject of the clause, *increase,* and it is not clear whether *added to the increase* is supposed to modify *program* or *benefits.* Choice D also lacks agreement (*increase . . . were*). Choice E is best.

8. Child prodigies are marked not so much by their skills <u>but instead</u> by the fact that these skills are fully developed at a very early age.

 (A) but instead
 (B) rather than
 (C) than
 (D) as
 (E) so much as

The idiomatic form for this kind of statement is *not so much by X as by Y.* Hence, D is the best answer. Each of the other options produces an unidiomatic statement.

9. The department defines a private passenger vehicle <u>as one registered to an individual with a gross weight of less than 8,000 pounds.</u>

 (A) as one registered to an individual with a gross weight of less than 8,000 pounds
 (B) to be one that is registered to an individual with a gross weight of less than 8,000 pounds
 (C) as one that is registered to an individual and that has a gross weight of less than 8,000 pounds
 (D) to have a gross weight less than 8,000 pounds and being registered to an individual
 (E) as having a gross weight of less than 8,000 pounds and registered to an individual

Choices A and B say that the *individual,* not the *vehicle,* has a gross weight of less than 8,000 pounds, and *defines . . . to be* in B is incorrect. Choice C, the best answer, produces the correct phrase (*defines . . . as*) and clarifies the statement with a parallel construction (*one that is . . . and that has . . .*). In choice D, *defines . . . to have* is faulty, *of* is missing between *weight* and *less,* and *being* is not parallel with *to have.* In choice E, the verb forms *having* and *registered* are not parallel.

10. Urban officials want the census to be as accurate and complete as possible <u>for the reason that the amount of low-income people in a given area affect</u> the distribution of about fifty billion dollars a year in federal funds.

 (A) for the reason that the amount of low-income people in a given area affect
 (B) for the reason because the amount of low-income people in a given area effects
 (C) in that the amount of low-income people in given areas effect
 (D) because the number of low-income people in a given area affects
 (E) because the numbers of low-income people in given areas effects

The best answer will start with *because.* The initial phrase of A is wordy, that of B is unidiomatic, and that of C does not precisely establish causal relationship. Also, *amount* is incorrect; *number* refers to a group of countable members, whereas *amount* is for undifferentiated masses such as *sand* or *water.* There is no subject-verb agreement in A (*amount . . . affect*), C (*amount . . . effect*), or E (*numbers . . . effects*); moreover, the proper verb here is *affects,* not *effects.* In E, *numbers* and *areas* should be singular, not only to agree with the verb but also to refer precisely to the sum total of low-income people in each region where the census is conducted. Choice D is the best answer.

11. After the Arab conquest of Egypt in A.D. 640, Arabic <u>became the dominant language of the Egyptians, replacing older languages</u> and writing systems.

 (A) became the dominant language of the Egyptians, replacing older languages
 (B) became the dominant language of the Egyptians, replacing languages that were older
 (C) becomes the dominant language of the Egyptians and it replaced older languages
 (D) becomes the dominant language of the Egyptians and it replaced languages that were older
 (E) becomes the dominant language of the Egyptians, having replaced languages that were older

In choice A, the best answer, *older* is placed so that it modifies both *languages* and *writing systems.* Choice B is incorrect because the wording suggests that Arabic replaced all writing systems, not just older ones. The present tense *becomes* in choice C is inconsistent with *replaced.* Also, *and* implies that two separate events are being discussed: that Arabic became the dominant language and then that it replaced older languages. Choice D combines the erroneous wording of choice B, the tense problem of choice C, and the imprecise use of *and.* Choice E includes wording and tense mistakes, and, contrary to the sense of the sentence, *having replaced* states that Arabic replaced older languages before the Arab conquest of Egypt.

12. The use of gravity waves, which do not interact with matter in the way electromagnetic waves do, hopefully will enable astronomers to study the actual formation of black holes and neutron stars.

(A) in the way electromagnetic waves do, hopefully will enable
(B) in the way electromagnetic waves do, will, it is hoped, enable
(C) like electromagnetic waves, hopefully will enable
(D) like electromagnetic waves, would enable, hopefully
(E) such as electromagnetic waves do, will, it is hoped, enable

Choices A, C, and D use *hopefully* to mean "it is hoped" rather than "in a hopeful manner"; such usage still meets with strong and widespread opposition from editors, lexicographers, and authors of usage handbooks. In addition, because they misuse *like*, choices C and D are potentially ambiguous. As a comparative preposition, "like" relates noun to noun, not verb to verb; i.e., C and D seem to say that gravity waves do not interact with matter that is like electromagnetic waves. Choice E is incorrect because *such as*, like *like*, connects *matter* and *waves*, not *interact* and *do*. Choice B is the best answer.

13. If a single strain of plant is used for a given crop over a wide area, a practice fostered by modern seed-marketing methods, it increases the likelihood that the impact of a single crop disease or pest will be disastrous.

(A) If a single strain of plant is used for a given crop over a wide area, a practice fostered by modern seed-marketing methods, it
(B) If a single strain of plant is used for a given crop over a wide area, as is fostered by modern seed-marketing methods, it
(C) A practice fostered by modern seed-marketing methods, a single strain of plant used for a given crop over a wide area
(D) A single strain of plant used for a given crop over a wide area, a practice fostered by modern seed-marketing methods,
(E) The use of a single strain of plant for a given crop over a wide area, a practice fostered by modern seed-marketing methods,

Choice A is faulty because the pronoun *it* and the appositive *a practice* each lack a noun referent. Nor are there logical referents in choice B for *as is* and *it*. Choice C entails a false appositive: the sentence now says that the *single strain of plant* is itself a practice fostered by modern seed-marketing methods, not that the use of a single strain is such a practice. Choice D reverses the order of the constructions, but the appositive remains illogical. Choice E is the best answer: *use* is the proper subject for the verb *increases* and a logical governing noun for the appositive *practice*.

14. A majority of the international journalists surveyed view nuclear power stations as unsafe at present but that they will, or could, be made sufficiently safe in the future.

(A) that they will, or could,
(B) that they would, or could,
(C) they will be or could
(D) think that they will be or could
(E) think the power stations would or could

The corrected sentence must have a compound main verb *view . . . but* (verb); that is, the best answer above must begin with a verb that can be linked with *view* to complete the construction. Consequently, choices A, B, and C are incorrect. In choice E, *would* is faulty because it suggests without warrant that the stations would be made safe if some unnamed conditions were met. Choice D is best: *that*, although not essential, is preferable here; *they* is better than the needless repetition of *power stations* in choice E; and the verb forms are correct.

15. A controversial figure throughout most of his public life, the Black leader Marcus Garvey advocated that some Blacks return to Africa, the land that, to him, symbolized the possibility of freedom.

(A) that some Blacks return to Africa, the land that, to him, symbolized the possibility of freedom
(B) that some Blacks return to the African land symbolizing the possibility of freedom to him
(C) that some Blacks return to Africa which was the land which symbolized the possibility of freedom to him
(D) some Black's returning to Africa which was the land that to him symbolized the possibility of freedom
(E) some Black's return to the land symbolizing the possibility of freedom to him, Africa

Choice A is best. In choice B, the phrase *the African land symbolizing the possibility of freedom to him* suggests without reason that only one of the various African lands symbolized the possibility of freedom to Garvey. The double use of *which* to create needless clauses within clauses makes C very wordy and awkward. The *which* clause is awkward in D also, and the singular possessive *Black's* is erroneous. *Black's* is again wrong in E, and the noun *Africa* is clumsily placed as an appositive coming after the lengthy phrase that describes it.

16. The fear of rabies is well founded; few people are known to recover from the disease after the appearance of the clinical symptoms.

   (A) few people are known to recover from the disease after the appearance of the clinical symptoms
   (B) few people are known to have recovered from the disease once the clinical symptoms have appeared
   (C) there are few known people who have recovered from the disease once the clinical symptoms have appeared
   (D) after the clinical symptoms appear, there are few known people who have recovered from the disease
   (E) recovery from the disease is known for only a few people after the clinical symptoms appear

Choice A does not clarify the timing of events but rather suggests that a few people continue to recover indefinitely. In B, the best choice, *have recovered* and *have appeared* indicate that the action of recovery is completed rather than ongoing. In choice C, the impersonal construction (*there are*) is needlessly wordy; moreover, the placement of *known* wrongly implies that the issue is whether the people rather than the instances of recovery are known. Choice D further confuses matters by placing the *after* phrase well before *recovered*, the verb it modifies. Choice E is indirect and unidiomatic.

17. The growth of the railroads led to the abolition of local times, which was determined by when the sun reached the observer's meridian and differing from city to city, and to the establishment of regional times.

   (A) which was determined by when the sun reached the observer's meridian and differing
   (B) which was determined by when the sun reached the observer's meridian and which differed
   (C) which were determined by when the sun reached the observer's meridian and differing
   (D) determined by when the sun reached the observer's meridian and differed
   (E) determined by when the sun reached the observer's meridian and differing

In choice A, *was* is incorrect; the verb must be *were* to agree with *times*. Also, *which* becomes the subject of a compound verb that lacks parallelism: *was determined . . . and differing*. In choice B, *was* is again incorrect, and the use of two *which* clauses is awkward. In choice C, *which were determined . . . and differing* is another faulty compound verb. Choice D presents a false compound: *determined* is an adjective modifying *local times* and *differed* is the simple past tense of *to differ*. Because they serve different grammatical functions, these words cannot be treated as parallel elements joined by *and*. Choice E is best: without *which*, *determined* and *differing* function not as verb elements but as parallel modifiers of *local times*.

18. Although partially destroyed, the archaeologists were able to infer from what remained of the inscription that the priest Zonainos was buried in the crypt.

   (A) Although partially destroyed, the archaeologists were able to infer
   (B) Although partially destroyed, the archaeologists had inferred
   (C) Although it had been partially destroyed, the archaeologists were able to infer
   (D) Partially destroyed though it had been, the archaeologists had been able to infer
   (E) Destroyed partially, the archaeologists were able to infer

In choice A, the phrase *Although partially destroyed* modifies *archaeologists,* the nearest noun and the subject of the sentence; in other words, choice A says that the archaeologists were partially destroyed. They fare no better in choice B, where the change in verb form alone cannot save them. Choice C is best: *partially destroyed* describes *it,* which refers to *the inscription*. The opening phrase of choice D is needlessly wordy and awkward, and *had been able to infer* fails to indicate that the archaeologists made their inference after the inscription had been partially destroyed. In choice E, *were able to infer* establishes the sequence of events, but the archaeologists are now *destroyed partially*.

19. For all his professed disdain of such activities, Auden was an inveterate literary gossip.

   (A) For all his professed disdain of such activities,
   (B) Having always professed disdain for such activities,
   (C) All such activities were, he professed, disdained, and
   (D) Professing that all such activities were disdained,
   (E) In spite of professions of disdaining all such activities,

Choice A is the best answer and is idiomatically phrased. Choice B fails to express the sense that Auden indulged in literary gossip despite professing disdain for it. Choices C, D, and E do not establish precisely that Auden was the one professing disdain for literary gossip. The *and* in C makes the disembodied professions of disdain and the indulgence in gossip seem like wholly separate matters, and E is especially awkward.

20. The earnings of women are <u>well below that of men in spite of educational differences that are diminishing</u> between the sexes.

  (A) well below that of men in spite of educational differences that are diminishing
  (B) much below that of men's despite educational differences diminishing
  (C) much below men in spite of diminishing educational differences
  (D) well below those of men in spite of diminishing educational differences
  (E) below men's despite their educational differences that are diminishing

In choice A, the pronoun *that* does not agree in number with its noun, *earnings*; the phrasing is wordy and does not convey the sense that diminishing the educational differences between the sexes would be expected to narrow the gap in earnings. In choice B, *that* and the possessive *men's* are faulty, and *much below* is less idiomatic than *well below*; furthermore, the sentence with B is awkward. Choice C illogically compares *the earnings of women* to *men* rather than to *the earnings of men*. In choice E, *their* seems to refer to *earnings, men's* is not parallel with *of women*, and the phrasing is unclear. Choice D is best.

21. Acid rain and snow result from the chemical reactions between industrial emissions of sulfur dioxide and nitrogen oxides <u>with atmospheric water vapor to produce highly corrosive sulfuric and nitric acids.</u>

  (A) with atmospheric water vapor to produce highly corrosive sulfuric and nitric acids
  (B) with atmospheric water vapor producing highly corrosive sulfuric and nitric acids
  (C) and atmospheric water vapor which has produced highly corrosive sulfuric and nitric acids
  (D) and atmospheric water vapor which have produced sulfuric and nitric acids which are highly corrosive
  (E) and atmospheric water vapor to produce highly corrosive sulfuric and nitric acids

Choices A and B are faulty because the idiomatic form of expression is *between X and Y,* not *between X with Y.* Also, in choice B *producing* . . . modifies the nearest noun, *water vapor,* rather than *chemical reactions* and thereby seems to say that the water vapor alone produced the corrosive acids. Choices C and D are clumsy, and both misuse *which:* in C *which has* . . . illogically modifies *water vapor,* and in D it is unclear whether *which have* modifies *reactions* or *sulfur dioxide, nitrogen oxides,* and *water vapor* taken together. E is the best choice.

22. It is characteristic of the Metropolitan Museum of Art, as <u>of virtually every great American museum, the taste of local collectors has played at least as large a part in the formation of their collections as has</u> the judgments of the art historian.

  (A) of virtually every great American museum, the taste of local collectors has played at least as large a part in the formation of their collections as has
  (B) of virtually every great American museum, that the taste of local collectors has played at least as large a part in the formation of their collections as has
  (C) it is of virtually every great American museum, that the taste of local collectors has played at least as large a part in the formation of its collections as have
  (D) it is of virtually every great American museum, that the taste of local collectors have played at least as large a part in the formation of its collections as have
  (E) it is of virtually every great American museum, the taste of local collectors has played at least as large a part in the formation of its collections as has

In the corrected sentence, *It is characteristic of* should be paralleled by *as it is of,* and this parallel construction should be completed by *that* before *the taste.* . . . Choice A lacks these elements as well as noun-pronoun agreement (*Museum* . . . *their*) and noun-verb agreement (*judgments* . . . *has*). Choice B rectifies only the missing *that.* Lack of agreement (*taste* . . . *have*) makes choice D wrong. Choice E needs *that* before *the taste* and *as have* in place of *as has.* C is the best answer.

23. There has been a 30- to 40-fold <u>increase in the incidence of malaria caused by increasing mosquito resistance against</u> pesticides.

    (A) increase in the incidence of malaria caused by increasing mosquito resistance against
    (B) increase in the incidence of malaria because of increasing resistance of mosquitoes to
    (C) increasing malaria incidence because of increasing resistance of mosquitoes to
    (D) incidence of malaria increase caused by increasing mosquito resistance against
    (E) incidence of malaria increase because of increased mosquito resistance to

Choice A can be faulted because it is not at first clear whether *caused by* modifies *increase* or *malaria*. Also, the proper expression here and in choice D is not *resistance against* but *resistance to*. Choices C, D, and E are wrong because the completed sentence must read *30- to 40-fold increase*. In these choices, *30- to 40-fold* illogically modifies *incidence*; furthermore, *incidence of . . . increase* in D and E is illogical. Choice B is best.

24. Aging is a property of all animals that reach a fixed size at maturity, and the variations in life spans <u>among different species are far greater as that among individuals from</u> the same species: a fruit fly is ancient at 40 days, a mouse at 3 years, a horse at 30, a man at 100, and some tortoises at 150.

    (A) among different species are far greater as that among individuals from
    (B) among different species are far greater than that among individuals from
    (C) among different species are far greater than those among individuals of
    (D) between different species are far more than that between individuals of
    (E) between different species are greater by far than is that between individuals from

Choice A is incorrect on several grounds: *greater as* should be *greater than*, *that* should be *those* to agree in number with its referent, *variations*, and *from* should be *of*. Choice B amends only the first error. Choice C is the best answer. In D, *between* is faulty because many more than two species are being considered, *more* illogically refers to the quantity rather than the size of variations in life span, and *that* does not agree with *variations*. Besides including *between*, *that*, and *from*, choice E is needlessly wordy and lacks agreement in verb number.

25. The herbicide Oryzalin was still being produced in 1979, three years after the wives of workers producing the chemical in Rensselaer, New York, were found <u>to have borne children with heart defects or miscarriages, and none of their pregnancies was</u> normal.

    (A) to have borne children with heart defects or miscarriages, and none of their pregnancies was
    (B) to have had children born with heart defects or miscarriages, and none of the pregnancies was
    (C) either to have had children with heart defects or miscarriages, without any of their pregnancies being
    (D) either to have had miscarriages or to have borne children with heart defects; none of the pregnancies was
    (E) either to have had miscarriages or children born with heart defects, without any of their pregnancies being

Choices A and B are incorrect because *with* governs both *heart defects* and *miscarriages*; in other words, choice A says that the children and not the women suffered the miscarriages. For the sentence to make sense, *miscarriages* must be the object of a verb that has *wives* as its subject. Also, *their* in choices A, C, and E is ambiguous because it is far from its referent, *wives*. Choices C and E lack parallel construction: a verb form like the one after *either* should appear after *or*. Choice D, both logical and parallel, is the best answer.

30 Minutes
25 Questions

Directions: In each of the following sentences, some part of the sentence or the entire sentence is underlined. Beneath each sentence you will find five ways of phrasing the underlined part. The first of these repeats the original; the other four are different. If you think the original is better than any of the alternatives, choose answer A; otherwise choose one of the others. Select the best version and fill in the corresponding oval on your answer sheet.

This is a test of correctness and effectiveness of expression. In choosing answers, follow the requirements of standard written English; that is, pay attention to grammar, choice of words, and sentence construction. Choose the answer that expresses most effectively what is presented in the original sentence; this answer should be clear and exact, without awkwardness, ambiguity, or redundancy.

1. Never before in the history of music have musical superstars been able to command so extraordinary fees of the kind they do today.

   (A) so extraordinary fees of the kind they do today
   (B) so extraordinary fees as they are today
   (C) such extraordinary fees as they do today
   (D) such extraordinary fees of the kind today's have
   (E) so extraordinary a fee of the kind they can today

2. As it becomes more frequent to have spouses who both work outside the home, companies are beginning to help in finding new employment for the spouses of transferred employees.

   (A) it becomes more frequent to have spouses who both work outside the home
   (B) it becomes more frequent to have couples both working outside the home
   (C) it becomes more common that both husband and wife should be working outside the home
   (D) it becomes more common for both husband and wife to work outside the home
   (E) couples in which both of the spouses working outside the home become more common

3. Like the one reputed to live in Loch Ness, also an inland lake connected to the ocean by a river, inhabitants of the area around Lake Champlain claim sightings of a long and narrow "sea monster."

   (A) Like the one reputed to live in Loch Ness, also an inland lake connected to the ocean by a river, inhabitants of the area around Lake Champlain claim sightings of a long and narrow "sea monster."
   (B) Inhabitants of the area around Lake Champlain claim sightings of a long and narrow "sea monster" similar to the one reputed to live in Loch Ness, which, like Lake Champlain, is an inland lake connected to the ocean by a river.
   (C) Inhabitants of the area around Lake Champlain claim sightings of a long and narrow "sea monster" similar to Loch Ness's, which, like Lake Champlain, is an inland lake connected to the ocean by a river.
   (D) Like Loch Ness's reputed monster, inhabitants of the area around Lake Champlain, also an inland lake connected to the ocean by a river, claim sightings of a long and narrow "sea monster."
   (E) Similar to that reputed to live in Loch Ness, inhabitants of the area around Lake Champlain, also an inland lake connected to the ocean by a river, claim sightings of a long and narrow "sea monster."

GO ON TO THE NEXT PAGE.

4. Since 1965 there are four times as many Black college students enrolled, and the one million Black people in college today represent 11 percent of all college students.

   (A) Since 1965 there are four times as many Black college students enrolled
   (B) The enrollment of Black college students was only one-fourth in 1965
   (C) The enrollment of Black college students has increased four times from 1965 on
   (D) Quadrupling since 1965, there are now four times as many Black college students enrolled
   (E) The enrollment of Black college students has quadrupled since 1965

5. A common disability in test pilots is hearing impairment, a consequence of sitting too close to large jet engines for long periods of time.

   (A) a consequence of sitting too close to large jet engines for long periods of time
   (B) a consequence from sitting for long periods of time too near to large jet engines
   (C) a consequence which resulted from sitting too close to large jet engines for long periods of time
   (D) damaged from sitting too near to large jet engines for long periods of time
   (E) damaged because they sat too close to large jet engines for long periods of time

6. Europe's travel industry is suffering as a result of a sluggish economy, a stretch of bad weather, as well as the chilling effects of terrorist activity that is persistent.

   (A) as well as the chilling effects of terrorist activity that is persistent
   (B) and the chilling effect of terrorist activity that is persistent
   (C) but persistent terrorist activity has had a chilling effect too
   (D) and the chilling effects of persistent terrorist activity
   (E) as well as the chilling effects of terrorist activity that persists

7. Opening with tributes to jazz-age divas like Bessie Smith and closing with Koko Taylor's electrified gravel-and-thunder songs, the program will trace the blues' vigorous matriarchal line over more than 50 years.

   (A) the program will trace
   (B) the program shall trace
   (C) there will be a program tracing
   (D) it is a program that traces
   (E) it will be a program tracing

8. In 1929 relatively small declines in the market ruined many speculators having bought on margin; they had to sell, and their selling pushed other investors to the brink.

   (A) speculators having bought on margin; they had to sell, and
   (B) speculators who had bought on margin; having had to sell,
   (C) speculators who had bought on margin; they had to sell, and
   (D) speculators, those who had bought on margin; these speculators had to sell, and
   (E) speculators, who, having bought on margin and having to sell,

9. The mistakes children make in learning to speak tell linguists more about how they learn language than the correct forms they use.

   (A) how they learn language than
   (B) how one learns language than
   (C) how children learn language than do
   (D) learning language than
   (E) their language learning than do

10. Building large new hospitals in the bistate area would constitute a wasteful use of resources, on the basis of avoidance of duplicated facilities alone.

   (A) on the basis of avoidance of duplicated facilities alone
   (B) on the grounds of avoiding duplicated facilities alone
   (C) solely in that duplicated facilities should be avoided
   (D) while the duplication of facilities should be avoided
   (E) if only because the duplication of facilities should be avoided

GO ON TO THE NEXT PAGE.

11. Freedman's survey showed that people living in small towns and rural areas consider themselves no happier than do people living in big cities.

(A) no happier than do people living
(B) not any happier than do people living
(C) not any happier than do people who live
(D) no happier than are people who are living
(E) not as happy as are people who live

12. It may someday be worthwhile to try to recover uranium from seawater, but at present this process is prohibitively expensive.

(A) It may someday be worthwhile to try to recover uranium from seawater
(B) Someday, it may be worthwhile to try and recover uranium from seawater
(C) Trying to recover uranium out of seawater may someday be worthwhile
(D) To try for the recovery of uranium out of seawater may someday be worthwhile
(E) Recovering uranium from seawater may be worthwhile to try to do someday

13. The underlying physical principles that control the midair gyrations of divers and gymnasts are the same as the body orientation controlling astronauts in a weightless environment.

(A) as the body orientation controlling
(B) as the body orientation which controls
(C) as those controlling the body orientation of
(D) ones to control the body orientation of
(E) ones used in controlling the body orientation of

14. The spraying of pesticides can be carefully planned, but accidents, weather conditions that could not be foreseen, and pilot errors often cause much larger deposits of spray than they had anticipated.

(A) weather conditions that could not be foreseen, and pilot errors often cause much larger deposits of spray than they had
(B) weather conditions that cannot be foreseen, and pilot errors often cause much larger deposits of spray than
(C) unforeseeable weather conditions, and pilot errors are the cause of much larger deposits of spray than they had
(D) weather conditions that are not foreseeable, and pilot errors often cause much larger deposits of spray than
(E) unforeseeable weather conditions, and pilot errors often cause much larger deposits of spray than they had

15. To read of Abigail Adams' lengthy separation from her family, her difficult travels, and her constant battles with illness is to feel intensely how harsh life was even for the so-called aristocracy of Revolutionary times.

(A) To read of
(B) Reading about
(C) Having read about
(D) Once one reads of
(E) To have read of

16. A star will compress itself into a white dwarf, a neutron star, or a black hole after it passes through a red giant stage, depending on mass.

(A) A star will compress itself into a white dwarf, a neutron star, or a black hole after it passes through a red giant stage, depending on mass.
(B) After passing through a red giant stage, depending on its mass, a star will compress itself into a white dwarf, a neutron star, or a black hole.
(C) After passing through a red giant stage, a star's mass will determine if it compresses itself into a white dwarf, a neutron star, or a black hole.
(D) Mass determines whether a star, after passing through the red giant stage, will compress itself into a white dwarf, a neutron star, or a black hole.
(E) The mass of a star, after passing through the red giant stage, will determine whether it compresses itself into a white dwarf, a neutron star, or a black hole.

GO ON TO THE NEXT PAGE.

17. In the main, incidents of breakdowns in nuclear reactors have not resulted from lapses of high technology but commonplace inadequacies in plumbing and wiring.

(A) not resulted from lapses of high technology but
(B) resulted not from lapses of high technology but from
(C) resulted from lapses not of high technology but
(D) resulted from lapses not of high technology but have stemmed from
(E) resulted not from lapses of high technology but have stemmed from

18. Seeming to be the only organization fighting for the rights of poor people in the South, Hosea Hudson, a laborer in Alabama, joined the Communist party in 1931.

(A) Seeming to be
(B) As
(C) In that they seemed
(D) Since it seemed
(E) Because it seemed to be

19. Although many art patrons can readily differentiate a good debenture from an undesirable one, they are much less expert in distinguishing good paintings and poor ones, authentic art and fakes.

(A) much less expert in distinguishing good paintings and poor ones, authentic art and
(B) far less expert in distinguishing good paintings from poor ones, authentic art from
(C) much less expert when it comes to distinguishing good paintings and poor ones, authentic art from
(D) far less expert in distinguishing good paintings and poor ones, authentic art and
(E) far less the expert when it comes to distinguishing between good painting, poor ones, authentic art, and

20. Rules banning cancer-causing substances from food apply to new food additives and not to natural constituents of food because their use as additives is entirely avoidable.

(A) their use as additives is
(B) as additives, their use is
(C) the use of such additives is
(D) the use of such additives are
(E) the use of them as additives is

21. The average weekly wage nearly doubled in the 1970's, rising from $114 to $220, yet the average worker ended the decade with a decrease in what their pay may buy.

(A) with a decrease in what their pay may buy
(B) with what was a decrease in what they were able to buy
(C) having decreased that which they could buy
(D) decreasing in purchasing power
(E) with a decrease in purchasing power

22. Since chromosome damage may be caused by viral infections, medical x-rays, and exposure to sunlight, it is important that the chromosomes of a population to be tested for chemically induced damage be compared with those of a control population.

(A) to be tested for chemically induced damage be compared with
(B) being tested for damage induced chemically are compared with
(C) being tested for chemically induced damage should be compared to
(D) being tested for chemically induced damage are to be compared to
(E) that is to be tested for chemically induced damage are to be comparable with

23. The suspect in the burglary was advised of his right to remain silent, told he could not leave, and was interrogated in a detention room.

(A) of his right to remain silent, told he could not leave, and was
(B) of his right to remain silent, told he could not leave, and
(C) of his right to remain silent and that he could not leave and
(D) that he had a right to remain silent, could not leave, and was
(E) that he had a right to remain silent, that he could not leave, and was

GO ON TO THE NEXT PAGE.

24. The United States petroleum industry's cost to meet environmental regulations is projected at ten percent of the price per barrel of refined petroleum by the end of the decade.

(A) The United States petroleum industry's cost to meet environmental regulations is projected at ten percent of the price per barrel of refined petroleum by the end of the decade.

(B) The United States petroleum industry's cost by the end of the decade to meet environmental regulations is estimated at ten percent of the price per barrel of refined petroleum.

(C) By the end of the decade, the United States petroleum industry's cost of meeting environmental regulations is projected at ten percent of the price per barrel of refined petroleum.

(D) To meet environmental regulations, the cost to the United States petroleum industry is estimated at ten percent of the price per barrel of refined petroleum by the end of the decade.

(E) It is estimated that by the end of the decade the cost to the United States petroleum industry of meeting environmental regulations will be ten percent of the price per barrel of refined petroleum.

25. The relationship between corpulence and disease remain controversial, although statistics clearly associate a reduced life expectancy with chronic obesity.

(A) remain controversial, although statistics clearly associate a reduced life expectancy with

(B) remain controversial, although statistics clearly associates a reduced life expectancy with

(C) remain controversial, although statistics clearly associates reduced life expectancy to

(D) remains controversial, although statistics clearly associate a reduced life expectancy with

(E) remains controversial, although statistics clearly associates reduced life expectancy to

S T O P

IF YOU FINISH BEFORE TIME IS CALLED, YOU MAY CHECK YOUR WORK ON THIS SECTION ONLY.
DO NOT TURN TO ANY OTHER SECTION IN THE TEST.

Answer Key for Sample Test Section 2

SENTENCE CORRECTION

1. C	14. B
2. D	15. A
3. B	16. D
4. E	17. B
5. A	18. E
6. D	19. B
7. A	20. C
8. C	21. E
9. C	22. A
10. E	23. B
11. A	24. E
12. A	25. D
13. C	

Explanatory Material: Sentence Correction Sample Test Section 2

1. Never before in the history of music have musical superstars been able to command <u>so extraordinary fees of the kind they do today</u>.

   (A) so extraordinary fees of the kind they do today
   (B) so extraordinary fees as they are today
   (C) such extraordinary fees as they do today
   (D) such extraordinary fees of the kind today's have
   (E) so extraordinary a fee of the kind they can today

The correct form of expression will include the phrase *such extraordinary fees as*. In A, B, and E, *so* in place of *such* produces the ungrammatical phrase *so. . .fees* where *such. . .fees* is required. Also, *do* is needed to complete the verb *command*: *are* in B and *have* in D produce the ungrammatical verb forms *are command* and *have command*. Finally, *as*, not *of the kind*, correctly completes the construction begun by *such*. C, with the correct forms "such . . . as" and "do," is the best answer.

2. <u>As it becomes more frequent to have spouses who both work outside the home</u>, companies are beginning to help in finding new employment for the spouses of transferred employees.

   (A) it becomes more frequent to have spouses who both work outside the home
   (B) it becomes more frequent to have couples both working outside the home
   (C) it becomes more common that both husband and wife should be working outside the home
   (D) it becomes more common for both husband and wife to work outside the home
   (E) couples in which both of the spouses working outside the home become more common

The phrasing of A and B is imprecise: *frequent* describes an event that recurs often; *common* is needed here to describe a general condition. Also, it is not clear who is *to have* the spouses. In B, *couples* creates an additional problem; the intended meaning is that both *spouses* (two people) work outside the home, not that both *couples* (four people) do. C is wordy and potentially ambiguous in that *should be working* could be read as *ought to work*. E, wordy and garbled, does not clearly indicate what it is that is becoming more common—*couples, spouses,* or households in which both husband and wife work outside the home. D is the best answer.

3. <u>Like the one reputed to live in Loch Ness, also an inland lake connected to the ocean by a river, inhabitants of the area around Lake Champlain claim sightings of a long and narrow "sea monster."</u>

   (A) Like the one reputed to live in Loch Ness, also an inland lake connected to the ocean by a river, inhabitants of the area around Lake Champlain claim sightings of a long and narrow "sea monster."
   (B) Inhabitants of the area around Lake Champlain claim sightings of a long and narrow "sea monster" similar to the one reputed to live in Loch Ness, which, like Lake Champlain, is an inland lake connected to the ocean by a river.
   (C) Inhabitants of the area around Lake Champlain claim sightings of a long and narrow "sea monster" similar to Loch Ness's, which, like Lake Champlain, is an inland lake connected to the ocean by a river.
   (D) Like Loch Ness's reputed monster, inhabitants of the area around Lake Champlain, also an inland lake connected to the ocean by a river, claim sightings of a long and narrow "sea monster."
   (E) Similar to that reputed to live in Loch Ness, inhabitants of the area around Lake Champlain, also an inland lake connected to the ocean by a river, claim sightings of a long and narrow "sea monster."

Choices A, D, and E illogically compare the monster reputed to live in Loch Ness to the inhabitants of the area around Lake Champlain, not to the monster that some local inhabitants claim to have sighted. Furthermore, in E the phrase *Similar to that reputed to live in Loch Ness* is needlessly wordy and indirect. C is faulty because the pronoun *which* would refer to *Loch Ness*, not to the *"sea monster" similar to Loch Ness's*. B, the best choice, uses *which* correctly and makes a logical comparison.

4. <u>Since 1965 there are four times as many Black college students enrolled</u>, and the one million Black people in college today represent 11 percent of all college students.

   (A) Since 1965 there are four times as many Black college students enrolled
   (B) The enrollment of Black college students was only one-fourth in 1965
   (C) The enrollment of Black college students has increased four times from 1965 on
   (D) Quadrupling since 1965, there are now four times as many Black college students enrolled
   (E) The enrollment of Black college students has quadrupled since 1965

The comparison in A is incomplete: the reader may be left wondering, *four times as many* as what? B, also incomplete, would have to say something like "one-fourth of the present enrollment" to make clear sense. Taken out of context, the meaning of C is uncertain: C could be read as saying that *the enrollment of Black college students has increased* fourfold or that it has increased four different times. D presents a dangling modifier because there is no noun in the main clause that *Quadrupling since 1965* can modify: Black college students have not quadrupled since 1965; their enrollment has. E states the idea clearly and correctly and is the best answer.

5. A common disability in test pilots is hearing impairment, <u>a consequence of sitting too close to large jet engines for long periods of time</u>.

   (A) a consequence of sitting too close to large jet engines for long periods of time
   (B) a consequence from sitting for long periods of time too near to large jet engines
   (C) a consequence which resulted from sitting too close to large jet engines for long periods of time
   (D) damaged from sitting too near to large jet engines for long periods of time
   (E) damaged because they sat too close to large jet engines for long periods of time

Choice A is best. Choice B is faulty because *a consequence from* is unidiomatic and because the modifying phrases are awkwardly placed. In C, *a consequence which resulted* is redundant in that *consequence* expresses the idea of *result*. D and E both present dangling modifiers in that nothing

named in the main clause can be said to be *damaged*; i.e., the pilots' *hearing* has been damaged, but their *hearing impairment* has not.

6. Europe's travel industry is suffering as a result of a sluggish economy, a stretch of bad weather, <u>as well as the chilling effects of terrorist activity that is persistent</u>.

   (A) as well as the chilling effects of terrorist activity that is persistent
   (B) and the chilling effect of terrorist activity that is persistent
   (C) but persistent terrorist activity has had a chilling effect too
   (D) and the chilling effects of persistent terrorist activity
   (E) as well as the chilling effects of terrorist activity that persists

The best answer for this question will begin with *and* because the phrase *the chilling effects* is the last of three parallel elements in a list, which should follow the form "X, Y, and Z." A and E are incorrect because *as well as* cannot replace *and* in such a list. Moreover, these answer choices are wordy and suggest without warrant that there is terrorist activity that does *not* affect Europe's travel industry because it is not persistent. B emends only the first fault. C is incorrect because *and*, not *but*, should precede the last element in an inclusive series; in this case, *but* introduces an independent clause that deviates from the structure of parallel noun phrases. D is the best answer.

7. Opening with tributes to jazz-age divas like Bessie Smith and closing with Koko Taylor's electrified gravel-and-thunder songs, <u>the program will trace</u> the blues' vigorous matriarchal line over more than 50 years.

   (A) the program will trace
   (B) the program shall trace
   (C) there will be a program tracing
   (D) it is a program that traces
   (E) it will be a program tracing

Choice A is best because *will* is appropriate for simple future tense. In B, *shall* implies intent or determination on the part of the *program*. In addition to being needlessly wordy, C, D, and E create problems in modification because the verb phrase *Opening . . .* seems to describe *there* or *it* rather than *program*; for the modification to be clear and logical, *program* must be the first noun and grammatical subject of the main clause.

8. In 1929 relatively small declines in the market ruined many <u>speculators having bought on margin; they had to sell, and</u> their selling pushed other investors to the brink.

    (A) speculators having bought on margin; they had to sell, and

    (B) speculators who had bought on margin; having had to sell,

    (C) speculators who had bought on margin; they had to sell, and

    (D) speculators, those who had bought on margin; these speculators had to sell, and

    (E) speculators, who, having bought on margin and having to sell,

Choice A can be faulted because *having bought on margin* does not precisely establish a sequence of events; *who had bought on margin* is needed to indicate that the speculators made their purchases before there were declines in the market and before they were forced to sell. B supplies the needed phrasing but introduces another problem: the phrase *having had to sell* dangles for lack of an appropriate noun to modify, and the sentence illogically states that *their selling,* not the *speculators,* had to sell. Choice C is the best answer. D is needlessly wordy, awkward, and repetitious. E is ungrammatical because *who* is presented as the subject of a clause with no completing verb.

9. The mistakes children make in learning to speak tell linguists more about <u>how they learn language than</u> the correct forms they use.

    (A) how they learn language than

    (B) how one learns language than

    (C) how children learn language than do

    (D) learning language than

    (E) their language learning than do

In choice A, the pronoun reference is awkward and potentially ambiguous because a plural noun, *linguists,* comes between *they* and its noun referent, *children.* In addition, *do* is needed after *than* in A, B, and D to prevent the misreading that mistakes tell linguists more about how children learn language than about correct forms. B also entails a shift in voice and number between *one* and *they.* In E, the grammar of the sentence does not clearly specify whether *their language learning* refers to the accomplishments of children or linguists. C is the best choice.

10. Building large new hospitals in the bistate area would constitute a wasteful use of resources, <u>on the basis of avoidance of duplicated facilities alone</u>.

    (A) on the basis of avoidance of duplicated facilities alone

    (B) on the grounds of avoiding duplicated facilities alone

    (C) solely in that duplicated facilities should be avoided

    (D) while the duplication of facilities should be avoided

    (E) if only because the duplication of facilities should be avoided

Choices A and B are unclear and imprecise: *on the basis of avoidance. . .* and *on the grounds of avoiding. . .* do not present reasons that support the statement in the main clause, and *alone* seems illogically to modify *duplicated facilities.* Also, *duplicated facilities* in A, B, and C identifies the problem with the facilities that have been duplicated, not with the act of duplicating facilities; for example, C apparently advises people to avoid facilities that have been duplicated. In D, *while* establishes no logical relation between the main clause and the rest of the sentence. E is best: *if only because* introduces a reason for the preceding statement, and the remainder of the answer choice is logically worded.

11. Freedman's survey showed that people living in small towns and rural areas consider themselves <u>no happier than do people living</u> in big cities.

    (A) no happier than do people living

    (B) not any happier than do people living

    (C) not any happier than do people who live

    (D) no happier than are people who are living

    (E) not as happy as are people who live

Choice A is best. In B, C, and E, the phrases beginning with *not* in place of *no* are wordy and unidiomatic. In D and E, the use of *are* presents a verb substitution problem: *are* cannot take the place of the verb *consider,* as *do* can in A, because *consider* is something that people *do,* not something that they *are.* D and E thus fail to compare the attitudes of the two groups of people, referring instead only to how those in small towns and rural areas consider themselves. E also distorts the intended meaning by saying that people living in small towns and rural areas consider themselves less happy than people living in big cities.

12. It may someday be worthwhile to try to recover uranium from seawater, but at present this process is prohibitively expensive.

    (A) It may someday be worthwhile to try to recover uranium from seawater
    (B) Someday, it may be worthwhile to try and recover uranium from seawater
    (C) Trying to recover uranium out of seawater may someday be worthwhile
    (D) To try for the recovery of uranium out of seawater may someday be worthwhile
    (E) Recovering uranium from seawater may be worthwhile to try to do someday

Choice A is best. In choice B, *Someday* is misplaced. Coming first and set off with a comma, it refers loosely to the whole clause; the placement of *someday* in A allows the word to modify the verb precisely. Also, *try to* in A is preferable to *try and* in B. Although *try and* is acceptable in informal contexts, many editors and usage handbooks prefer *try to* in formal writing. In C, *recover. . .out of* is unidiomatic. D is needlessly wordy and contains *recovery . . . out of*. E awkwardly inverts logical word order by placing *to try to do* well after *recovering*.

13. The underlying physical principles that control the midair gyrations of divers and gymnasts are the same as the body orientation controlling astronauts in a weightless environment.

    (A) as the body orientation controlling
    (B) as the body orientation which controls
    (C) as those controlling the body orientation of
    (D) ones to control the body orientation of
    (E) ones used in controlling the body orientation of

Choice A illogically identifies the *physical principles* of line 1 as *body orientation*, not as principles; moreover, the original sentence confusedly states that body orientation controls the astronauts, not that physical principles control their body orientation. B changes *controlling* to *which controls,* but the logical problems remain. C, the best answer, correctly uses the plural pronoun *those* to identify principles as principles. By substituting *to control* for *that control* (line 1), D violates parallel construction. E, wordy and imprecise, seems to imply that some external agency is using physical principles to control the body orientation of astronauts.

14. The spraying of pesticides can be carefully planned, but accidents, weather conditions that could not be foreseen, and pilot errors often cause much larger deposits of spray than they had anticipated.

    (A) weather conditions that could not be foreseen, and pilot errors often cause much larger deposits of spray than they had
    (B) weather conditions that cannot be foreseen, and pilot errors often cause much larger deposits of spray than
    (C) unforeseeable weather conditions, and pilot errors are the cause of much larger deposits of spray than they had
    (D) weather conditions that are not foreseeable, and pilot errors often cause much larger deposits of spray than
    (E) unforeseeable weather conditions, and pilot errors often cause much larger deposits of spray than they had

Choices A, C, and E are faulty because the pronoun *they* has no logical noun to which it can refer; also *could not be foreseen* in A seems to describe specific weather conditions in the past, not ones that are still unforeseeable and so continue to affect spraying. B, the best answer, corrects both problems. C contains the unattached *they* and inflates *cause* to *are the cause of;* moreover, by changing *cause* from a verb to a noun, C states that all three factors acting together constitute the one and only cause of excessive deposits. The initial phrase of D is less compact and idiomatic than that of B.

15. To read of Abigail Adams' lengthy separation from her family, her difficult travels, and her constant battles with illness is to feel intensely how harsh life was even for the so-called aristocracy of Revolutionary times.

    (A) To read of
    (B) Reading about
    (C) Having read about
    (D) Once one reads of
    (E) To have read of

Choice A is best because the sentence must begin with a verb form that completes the construction *To. . . is to feel.* Each of the other choices breaks the parallelism in some way, and B and C substitute *about* for *of,* the preferred preposition here. E begins with *To,* but *have read* creates a disjunction of tense by placing the action of reading in the past while *to feel* is still in the present.

16. <u>A star will compress itself into a white dwarf, a neutron star, or a black hole after it passes through a red giant stage, depending on mass.</u>

    (A) A star will compress itself into a white dwarf, a neutron star, or a black hole after it passes through a red giant stage, depending on mass.
    (B) After passing through a red giant stage, depending on its mass, a star will compress itself into a white dwarf, a neutron star, or a black hole.
    (C) After passing through a red giant stage, a star's mass will determine if it compresses itself into a white dwarf, a neutron star, or a black hole.
    (D) Mass determines whether a star, after passing through the red giant stage, will compress itself into a white dwarf, a neutron star, or a black hole.
    (E) The mass of a star, after passing through the red giant stage, will determine whether it compresses itself into a white dwarf, a neutron star, or a black hole.

Choice A is ambiguous because the grammatical function of *depending on mass* is uncertain: the phrase could modify either the whole preceding statement or only the words *after it passes through a red giant stage*. In the latter case, choice A states in effect that a star depends on its mass as it passes through this phase, not that the fate of the star depends on the star's mass. Choice B suffers from the same ambiguity. Choices C and E illogically maintain that the star's mass, not the star itself, passes through the red giant state to assume another form. Choice D is the best answer.

17. In the main, incidents of breakdowns in nuclear reactors have <u>not resulted from lapses of high technology but</u> commonplace inadequacies in plumbing and wiring.

    (A) not resulted from lapses of high technology but
    (B) resulted not from lapses of high technology but from
    (C) resulted from lapses not of high technology but
    (D) resulted from lapses not of high technology but have stemmed from
    (E) resulted not from lapses of high technology but have stemmed from

Parallelism requires that in a *not. . .but. . .*construction, the words after *not* and *but* have the same grammatical form and function. Choice A breaks the parallel because *not resulted. . .but commonplace* erroneously links a verb and an adjective. Choice B is best. The wording in C creates a false parallel between *lapses. . .of high technology* and *lapses. . .of commonplace inadequacies* because *lapses* precedes and governs both elements in the *not. . .but. . .*construction. D and E lack grammatical parallelism and would be needlessly wordy even if *not* had been appropriately placed before *resulted*.

18. <u>Seeming to be</u> the only organization fighting for the rights of poor people in the South, Hosea Hudson, a laborer in Alabama, joined the Communist party in 1931.

    (A) Seeming to be
    (B) As
    (C) In that they seemed
    (D) Since it seemed
    (E) Because it seemed to be

Choices A and B wrongly identify Hosea Hudson, not the Communist party, as the organization under discussion. In choice C, the plural pronoun *they* does not agree in number with the singular noun *party*. *In that* in C and *Since* in D are less direct and idiomatic than *Because* in this context, and *to be* is needed to complete the predicate begun by *seemed*. E is the best answer.

19. Although many art patrons can readily differentiate a good debenture from an undesirable one, they are <u>much less expert in distinguishing good paintings and poor ones, authentic art and</u> fakes.

    (A) much less expert in distinguishing good paintings and poor ones, authentic art and
    (B) far less expert in distinguishing good paintings from poor ones, authentic art from
    (C) much less expert when it comes to distinguishing good paintings and poor ones, authentic art from
    (D) far less expert in distinguishing good paintings and poor ones, authentic art and
    (E) far less the expert when it comes to distinguishing between good painting, poor ones, authentic art, and

The best answer will follow the idiomatic form *distinguishing X from Y*. The substitution of *and* for *from* makes choices A, C, D, and E faulty. Moreover, *far* is a better modifier of *less expert* than *much* is in A and C, *when it comes to distinguishing* is wordy in C and E, and E fails to acknowledge that two distinctions are being considered—one between good and poor paintings, another between authentic art and fakes. B is the best answer.

20. Rules banning cancer-causing substances from food apply to new food additives and not to natural constituents of food because <u>their use as additives is</u> entirely avoidable.

    (A) their use as additives is
    (B) as additives, their use is
    (C) the use of such additives is
    (D) the use of such additives are
    (E) the use of them as additives is

Choices A, B, and E are incorrect because the pronouns *their* and *them* could refer to any of several plural nouns. B and E are also awkwardly constructed. In choice D, the plural verb *are* does not agree in number with the singular noun *use*. Choice C is the best answer for this question.

21. The average weekly wage nearly doubled in the 1970's, rising from $114 to $220, yet the average worker ended the decade <u>with a decrease in what their pay may buy</u>.

    (A) with a decrease in what their pay may buy
    (B) with what was a decrease in what they were able to buy
    (C) having decreased that which they could buy
    (D) decreasing in purchasing power
    (E) with a decrease in purchasing power

Choices A, B, and C incorrectly use a plural pronoun, *their* or *they,* to refer to a singular noun, *worker.* Moreover, A and B are wordy and awkwardly constructed, and C wrongly asserts that the *average worker* decreased the amount or value of what could be bought. D misrepresents the intended meaning by saying that at the end of the decade, the *average worker* —not the money—was *decreasing in purchasing power.* E is the best answer.

22. Since chromosome damage may be caused by viral infections, medical x-rays, and exposure to sunlight, it is important that the chromosomes of a population <u>to be tested for chemically induced damage be compared with</u> those of a control population.

    (A) to be tested for chemically induced damage be compared with
    (B) being tested for damage induced chemically are compared with
    (C) being tested for chemically induced damage should be compared to
    (D) being tested for chemically induced damage are to be compared to
    (E) that is to be tested for chemically induced damage are to be comparable with

Choice A is best because the infinitive *to be tested* and the subjunctive *be compared* are correct for describing a hypothetical course of action. Also, *compared with* rather than *compared to* is preferred when a comparison is intended, as here with *chromosomes,* to reveal differences among things of the same order. Choice B lacks the infinitive and subjunctive forms, and *damage induced chemically* is more awkward than the comparable phrase in A. C and D have *being* instead of *to be* and *to* instead of *with;* also *should* and *are to* do not belong in the subjunctive. E is wordy, *are to* again intrudes, and *comparable* changes the meaning of the statement.

23. The suspect in the burglary was advised <u>of his right to remain silent, told he could not leave, and was</u> interrogated in a detention room.

    (A) of his right to remain silent, told he could not leave, and was
    (B) of his right to remain silent, told he could not leave, and
    (C) of his right to remain silent and that he could not leave and
    (D) that he had a right to remain silent, could not leave, and was
    (E) that he had a right to remain silent, that he could not leave, and was

The best answer will exhibit parallelism. Choice B is the best because it correctly forms a parallel structure: *was advised. . ., told. . ., and interrogated. . . .* Because all three verbs are governed by the *was* in line 1, the *was* after *and* in choice A is not merely unnecessary but actually wrong because it disrupts the parallel. Choice C is wordy and ungrammatical: the syntax forces *was advised* rather than *was* to govern all three elements, a construction that becomes impossible with *was advised. . .interrogated.* A similar misconstruction in D produces the misstatement that the suspect *was advised that he. . .was interrogated.* E forms a list of nonparallel elements; placing *and* after *silent* and dropping the commas would make E grammatical but no less wordy.

24. The United States petroleum industry's cost to meet environmental regulations is projected at ten percent of the price per barrel of refined petroleum by the end of the decade.

   (A) The United States petroleum industry's cost to meet environmental regulations is projected at ten percent of the price per barrel of refined petroleum by the end of the decade.

   (B) The United States petroleum industry's cost by the end of the decade to meet environmental regulations is estimated at ten percent of the price per barrel of refined petroleum.

   (C) By the end of the decade, the United States petroleum industry's cost of meeting environmental regulations is projected at ten percent of the price per barrel of refined petroleum.

   (D) To meet environmental regulations, the cost to the United States petroleum industry is estimated at ten percent of the price per barrel of refined petroleum by the end of the decade.

   (E) It is estimated that by the end of the decade the cost to the United States petroleum industry of meeting environmental regulations will be ten percent of the price per barrel of refined petroleum.

Choices A, B, C, and D are awkward and confusing. In A, for example, the issue is not the *industry's cost* but the cost to the industry; also, *to meet* should be *of meeting* here, *projected at* is unidiomatic, and *by the end of the decade* is placed so that its meaning is unclear. B and C suffer from many of the same problems. The wording of D implies that *cost. . .is estimated* in order *to meet environmental regulations.* E alone makes a logical statement and varies verb tense to indicate that the issue is present estimates of future costs. It is the best answer.

25. The relationship between corpulence and disease remain controversial, although statistics clearly associate a reduced life expectancy with chronic obesity.

   (A) remain controversial, although statistics clearly associate a reduced life expectancy with

   (B) remain controversial, although statistics clearly associates a reduced life expectancy with

   (C) remain controversial, although statistics clearly associates reduced life expectancy to

   (D) remains controversial, although statistics clearly associate a reduced life expectancy with

   (E) remains controversial, although statistics clearly associates reduced life expectancy to

Choice A is incorrect because *remain* should be *remains;* the subject of the verb is *relationship,* not *corpulence and disease,* which are hardly controversial. Choices B and C are similarly flawed, and *associates* in B, C, and E should be *associate* to agree with the intended number of *statistics.* Finally, *associate(s). . .to* is unidiomatic in C and E. D is the best answer.

SENTENCE CORRECTION SAMPLE TEST SECTION 3

30 Minutes
25 Questions

1. Researchers at Cornell University have demonstrated that homing pigeons can sense changes in the earth's magnetic field, see light waves that people cannot see, detect low-frequency sounds from miles away, sense changes in air pressure, and can identify familiar odors.

   (A) sense changes in air pressure, and can identify familiar odors
   (B) can sense changes in air pressure, and can identify familiar odors
   (C) sense changes in air pressure, and identify familiar odors
   (D) air pressure changes can be sensed, and familiar odors identified
   (E) air pressure changes are sensed, and familiar odors identified

2. In ancient times, Nubia was the principal corridor where there were cultural influences transmitted between Black Africa and the Mediterranean basin.

   (A) where there were cultural influences transmitted
   (B) through which cultural influences were transmitted
   (C) where there was a transmission of cultural influences
   (D) for the transmitting of cultural influences
   (E) which was transmitting cultural influences

3. It is a special feature of cell aggregation in the developing nervous system that in most regions of the brain the cells not only adhere to one another and also adopt some preferential orientation.

   (A) to one another and also adopt
   (B) one to the other, and also they adopt
   (C) one to the other, but also adopting
   (D) to one another but also adopt
   (E) to each other, also adopting

4. Among the reasons for the decline of New England agriculture in the last three decades were the high cost of land, the pressure of housing and commercial development, and basing a marketing and distribution system on importing produce from Florida and California.

   (A) basing a marketing and distribution system on importing produce from Florida and California
   (B) basing a marketing and distribution system on the imported produce of Florida and California
   (C) basing a system of marketing and distribution on the import of produce from Florida and California
   (D) a marketing and distribution system based on importing produce from Florida and California
   (E) a marketing and distribution system importing produce from Florida and California as its base

GO ON TO THE NEXT PAGE.

5. Like Byron at Missolonghi, Jack London was slowly killed by the mistakes of the medical men who treated him.

    (A) Like Byron
    (B) Like Byron's death
    (C) Just as Byron died
    (D) Similar to Byron
    (E) As did Byron

6. One of every two new businesses fail within two years.

    (A) fail
    (B) fails
    (C) should fail
    (D) may have failed
    (E) has failed

7. Even today, a century after Pasteur developed the first vaccine, rabies almost always kills its victims unless inoculated in the earliest stages of the disease.

    (A) its victims unless inoculated
    (B) its victims unless they are inoculated
    (C) its victims unless inoculation is done
    (D) the victims unless there is an inoculation
    (E) the victims unless inoculated

8. In a period of time when women typically have had a narrow range of choices, Mary Baker Eddy became a distinguished writer and the founder, architect, and builder of a growing church.

    (A) In a period of time when women typically have
    (B) During a time in which typically women have
    (C) Typically, during a time when women
    (D) At a time when women typically
    (E) Typically in a time in which women

9. As the price of gasoline rises, which makes substituting alcohol distilled from cereal grain attractive, the prices of bread and livestock feed are sure to increase.

    (A) which makes substituting alcohol distilled from cereal grain attractive
    (B) which makes substituting the distillation of alcohol from cereal grain attractive
    (C) which makes distilling alcohol from cereal grain an attractive substitute
    (D) making an attractive substitution of alcohol distilled from cereal grain
    (E) making alcohol distilled from cereal grain an attractive substitute

10. Climatic shifts are so gradual as to be indistinguishable at first from ordinary fluctuations in the weather.

    (A) so gradual as to be indistinguishable
    (B) so gradual they can be indistinguishable
    (C) so gradual that they are unable to be distinguished
    (D) gradual enough not to be distinguishable
    (E) gradual enough so that one cannot distinguish them

11. Although the lesser cornstalk borer is widely distributed, control of them is necessary only in the South.

    (A) the lesser cornstalk borer is widely distributed, control of them is
    (B) widely distributed, measures to control the lesser cornstalk borer are
    (C) widely distributed, lesser cornstalk borer control is
    (D) the lesser cornstalk borer is widely distributed, measures to control it are
    (E) it is widely distributed, control of the lesser cornstalk borer is

GO ON TO THE NEXT PAGE.

12. Traveling the back roads of Hungary, in 1905 Béla Bartók and Zoltán Kodály began their pioneering work in ethnomusicology, and they were armed only with an Edison phonograph and insatiable curiosity.

(A) Traveling the back roads of Hungary, in 1905 Béla Bartók and Zoltán Kodály began their pioneering work in ethnomusicology, and they were armed only

(B) In 1905, Béla Bartók and Zoltán Kodály, traveling the back roads of Hungary, began their pioneering work in ethnomusicology, and they were only armed

(C) In 1905 Béla Bartók and Zoltán Kodály began their pioneering work in ethnomusicology, traveling the back roads of Hungary armed only

(D) Having traveled the back roads of Hungary, in 1905 Béla Bartók and Zoltán Kodály began their pioneering work in ethnomusicology; they were only armed

(E) Béla Bartók and Zoltán Kodály, in 1905 began their pioneering work in ethnomusicology, traveling the back roads of Hungary, arming themselves only

13. It is as difficult to prevent crimes against property as those that are against a person.

(A) those that are against a
(B) those against a
(C) it is against a
(D) preventing those against a
(E) it is to prevent those against a

14. Unlike the acid smoke of cigarettes, pipe tobacco, cured by age-old methods, yields an alkaline smoke too irritating to be drawn into the lungs.

(A) Unlike the acid smoke of cigarettes, pipe tobacco, cured by age-old methods, yields an alkaline smoke

(B) Unlike the acid smoke of cigarettes, pipe tobacco is cured by age-old methods, yielding an alkaline smoke

(C) Unlike cigarette tobacco, which yields an acid smoke, pipe tobacco, cured by age-old methods, yields an alkaline smoke

(D) Differing from cigarettes' acid smoke, pipe tobacco's alkaline smoke, cured by age-old methods, is

(E) The alkaline smoke of pipe tobacco differs from cigarettes' acid smoke in that it is cured by age-old methods and is

15. Joplin's faith in his opera "Tremonisha" was unshakeable; in 1911 he published the score at his own expense and decided on staging it himself.

(A) on staging it himself
(B) that he himself would do the staging
(C) to do the staging of the work by himself
(D) that he himself would stage it
(E) to stage the work himself

16. Los Angeles has a higher number of family dwellings per capita than any large city.

(A) a higher number of family dwellings per capita than any large city

(B) higher numbers of family dwellings per capita than any other large city

(C) a higher number of family dwellings per capita than does any other large city

(D) higher numbers of family dwellings per capita than do other large cities

(E) a high per capita number of family dwellings, more than does any other large city

GO ON TO THE NEXT PAGE.

17. During the nineteenth century Emily Eden and Fanny Parks journeyed throughout India, sketching and keeping journals forming the basis of news reports about the princely states where they had visited.

(A) forming the basis of news reports about the princely states where they had
(B) that were forming the basis of news reports about the princely states
(C) to form the basis of news reports about the princely states which they have
(D) which had formed the basis of news reports about the princely states where they had
(E) that formed the basis of news reports about the princely states they

18. School integration plans that involve busing between suburban and central-city areas have contributed, according to a recent study, to significant increases in housing integration, which, in turn, reduces any future need for busing.

(A) significant increases in housing integration, which, in turn, reduces
(B) significant integration increases in housing, which, in turn, reduces
(C) increase housing integration significantly, which, in turn, reduces
(D) increase housing integration significantly, in turn reducing
(E) significantly increase housing integration, which, in turn, reduce

19. The commission acknowledged that no amount of money or staff members can ensure the safety of people who live in the vicinity of a nuclear plant, but it approved the installation because it believed that all reasonable precautions had been taken.

(A) no amount of money or staff members
(B) neither vast amounts of money nor staff members
(C) neither vast amounts of money nor numbers of staff members
(D) neither vast amounts of money nor a large staff
(E) no matter how large the staff or how vast the amount of money

20. Sartre believed each individual is responsible to choose one course of action over another one, that it is the choice that gives value to the act, and that nothing that is not acted upon has value.

(A) each individual is responsible to choose one course of action over another one
(B) that each individual is responsible for choosing one course of action over another
(C) that each individual is responsible, choosing one course of action over another
(D) that each individual is responsible to choose one course of action over the other
(E) each individual is responsible for choosing one course of action over other ones

21. While the owner of a condominium apartment has free and clear title to the dwelling, owners of cooperative apartments have shares in a corporation that owns a building and leases apartments to them.

(A) While the owner of a condominium apartment has free and clear title to the dwelling,
(B) The owner of a condominium apartment has free and clear title to the dwelling, but
(C) Whereas owners of condominium apartments have free and clear title to their dwellings,
(D) An owner of a condominium apartment has free and clear title to the dwelling, whereas
(E) Condominium apartment owners have a title to their dwelling that is free and clear, while

GO ON TO THE NEXT PAGE.

22. Although <u>films about the American West depict coyotes as solitary animals howling mournfully on the tops of distant hills</u>, in reality these gregarious creatures live in stable groups that occupy the same territory for long periods.

    (A) films about the American West depict coyotes as solitary animals howling mournfully on the tops of distant hills

    (B) in films about the American West coyotes are depicted to be solitary animals that howl mournfully on the tops of distant hills

    (C) coyotes are depicted as solitary animals howling mournfully on the tops of distant hills in films about the American West

    (D) films about the American West depict coyotes as if they were solitary, mournfully howling animals on the tops of distant hills

    (E) films about the American West depict coyotes to be solitary and mournfully howling animals on the tops of distant hills

23. In 1980 the United States exported <u>twice as much of its national output of goods as they had</u> in 1970.

    (A) twice as much of its national output of goods as they had

    (B) double the amount of their national output of goods as they did

    (C) twice as much of its national output of goods as it did

    (D) double the amount of its national output of goods as it has

    (E) twice as much of their national output of goods as they had

24. <u>Even though its per capita food supply hardly increased during</u> two decades, stringent rationing and planned distribution have allowed the People's Republic of China to ensure nutritional levels of 2,000 calories per person per day for its population.

    (A) Even though its per capita food supply hardly increased during

    (B) Even though its per capita food supply has hardly increased in

    (C) Despite its per capita food supply hardly increasing over

    (D) Despite there being hardly any increase in its per capita food supply during

    (E) Although there is hardly any increase in per capita food supply for

25. Few people realize that the chance of accidental injury or death <u>may be as great or greater in the "safety" of their own homes than</u> in a plane or on the road.

    (A) may be as great or greater in the "safety" of their own homes than

    (B) is at least as great or greater in the "safety" of their own homes than

    (C) might be so great or greater in the "safety" of their own home as

    (D) may be at least as great in the "safety" of their own homes as

    (E) can be at least so great in the "safety" of their own home as

S T O P

IF YOU FINISH BEFORE TIME IS CALLED, YOU MAY CHECK YOUR WORK ON THIS SECTION ONLY.
DO NOT TURN TO ANY OTHER SECTION IN THE TEST.

Answer Key for Sample Test Section 3

SENTENCE CORRECTION

1. C	14. C
2. B	15. E
3. D	16. C
4. D	17. E
5. A	18. A
6. B	19. D
7. B	20. B
8. D	21. C
9. E	22. A
10. A	23. C
11. D	24. B
12. C	25. D
13. E	

Explanatory Material: Sentence Correction Sample Test Section 3

1. Researchers at Cornell University have demonstrated that homing pigeons can sense changes in the earth's magnetic field, see light waves that people cannot see, detect low-frequency sounds from miles away, sense changes in air pressure, and can identify familiar odors.

   (A) sense changes in air pressure, and can identify familiar odors
   (B) can sense changes in air pressure, and can identify familiar odors
   (C) sense changes in air pressure, and identify familiar odors
   (D) air pressure changes can be sensed, and familiar odors identified
   (E) air pressure changes are sensed, and familiar odors identified

This question requires you to choose an answer that completes a series of parallel verbs. Choice A is incorrect because the *can* before *identify* breaks a parallel sequence of verbs that complete the *can* in line 2: A states, *homing pigeons can sense, . . . see, . . . detect, . . . sense, . . . and can identify*. Choice B makes the problem worse by adding *can* before two verbs so that both are nonparallel. Choice C is best. Choices D and E wrongly substitute independent clauses for the verb phrases in C that continue the parallel construction.

2. In ancient times, Nubia was the principal corridor where there were cultural influences transmitted between Black Africa and the Mediterranean basin.

   (A) where there were cultural influences transmitted
   (B) through which cultural influences were transmitted
   (C) where there was a transmission of cultural influences
   (D) for the transmitting of cultural influences
   (E) which was transmitting cultural influences

Choice A is imprecise and unidiomatic. In choice B, the best answer, *through which* suggests the movement or passage of cultural influences between the ends of the corridor and so provides a clearer description of Nubia's role in the ancient world. Choice C, like A, is unidiomatic and needlessly indirect; D is awkward and imprecise. In choice E, *which* refers to *corridor*, thereby suggesting somewhat imprecisely that the corridor itself, not the civilizations it connected, *was transmitting cultural influences*. Also, *transmitted* is preferable to *transmitting* in a description of past events.

3. It is a special feature of cell aggregation in the developing nervous system that in most regions of the brain the cells not only adhere to one another and also adopt some preferential orientation.

   (A) to one another and also adopt
   (B) one to the other, and also they adopt
   (C) one to the other, but also adopting
   (D) to one another but also adopt
   (E) to each other, also adopting

Choices A and B are incorrect because *and* should be *but* to conform to the idiomatic construction *not only but also*. Choice B can be faulted for including *they* where there should be only *adopt* to form a parallel with *adhere*. Moreover, *the other* in B is inappropriate because many more than two brain cells are being discussed. Choice C contains *the other* and has *adopting* in place of *adopt,* the verb form parallel to *adhere*. Choice D is best. In choice E, *adopting* is again wrong and *each other* is less appropriate than *one another* for referring to a multitude of cells.

4. Among the reasons for the decline of New England agriculture in the last three decades were the high cost of land, the pressure of housing and commercial development, and basing a marketing and distribution system on importing produce from Florida and California.

   (A) basing a marketing and distribution system on importing produce from Florida and California
   (B) basing a marketing and distribution system on the imported produce of Florida and California
   (C) basing a system of marketing and distribution on the import of produce from Florida and California
   (D) a marketing and distribution system based on importing produce from Florida and California
   (E) a marketing and distribution system importing produce from Florida and California as its base

Choices A, B, and C can be faulted for putting a verb phrase, *basing . . .*, where a noun phrase is needed to continue the list of parallel elements that begins with *the high cost of land, the pressure of housing. . . .* Also, *the imported produce* in B suggests that the system is based on the produce itself rather than on the practice of importing produce. In C, *the import of produce* is unidiomatic. D, the best choice, presents a noun phrase (*. . . a marketing and distribution system*) that completes the list of parallel elements and refers to the act of *importing produce*. E also supplies the noun phrase but states illogically that the system imports produce *as its base*.

5. <u>Like Byron</u> at Missolonghi, Jack London was slowly killed by the mistakes of the medical men who treated him.

   (A) Like Byron
   (B) Like Byron's death
   (C) Just as Byron died
   (D) Similar to Byron
   (E) As did Byron

Choice A, the best answer, correctly compares two persons, Byron and Jack London. Choice B illogically compares Byron's death to London. Choice C does not compare one person to another and could be read as saying *Just at the time that Byron died.* Choice D misstates the idea: the point is not that London was *similar to Byron* but that he was like Byron in the manner of his death. In choice E, *did* cannot grammatically be substituted for *was* in the phrase *was slowly killed.*

6. One of every two new businesses <u>fail</u> within two years.

   (A) fail
   (B) fails
   (C) should fail
   (D) may have failed
   (E) has failed

Choice A is wrong because the verb *fail* does not agree in number with *One,* the subject of the sentence; *businesses* is not the subject of the sentence but the object of the preposition *of.* In choice C, *should fail* is inappropriate for a statement of fact and carries the unintended suggestion of *ought to fail.* In choices D and E, *may have failed* and *has failed* wrongly refer to a completed action rather than an ongoing condition. Choice B is best.

7. Even today, a century after Pasteur developed the first vaccine, rabies almost always kills <u>its victims unless inoculated</u> in the earliest stages of the disease.

   (A) its victims unless inoculated
   (B) its victims unless they are inoculated
   (C) its victims unless inoculation is done
   (D) the victims unless there is an inoculation
   (E) the victims unless inoculated

Choices A and E illogically suggest that rabies rather than the victims of rabies should be inoculated in the earliest stages of the disease. Choice B is best: it is logical, clear, and more precise than C and D, which do not specify who or what is being inoculated.

8. <u>In a period of time when women typically have</u> had a narrow range of choices, Mary Baker Eddy became a distinguished writer and the founder, architect, and builder of a growing church.

   (A) In a period of time when women typically have
   (B) During a time in which typically women have
   (C) Typically, during a time when women
   (D) At a time when women typically
   (E) Typically in a time in which women

Choices A and B are wrong because *have had* in the resulting sentence does not correspond to *became;* a simple *had* is needed to match *became* in referring to past events. Choice C drops the erroneous *have,* but *Typically* is misplaced so that it modifies the main clause; in other words, C says that it was typical for Mary Baker Eddy to become distinguished, not that it was typical for women to have a narrow range of choices. Choice E suffers from the same confusion. D is the best answer.

9. As the price of gasoline rises, <u>which makes substituting alcohol distilled from cereal grain attractive,</u> the prices of bread and livestock feed are sure to increase.

   (A) which makes substituting alcohol distilled from cereal grain attractive
   (B) which makes substituting the distillation of alcohol from cereal grain attractive
   (C) which makes distilling alcohol from cereal grain an attractive substitute
   (D) making an attractive substitution of alcohol distilled from cereal grain
   (E) making alcohol distilled from cereal grain an attractive substitute

Choices A, B, and C are faulty because the pronoun *which* refers loosely to the whole clause rather than to some noun. The original sentence is intended to say that alcohol is an attractive substitute for gasoline, but the understood phrase *for gasoline* cannot be inserted anywhere in A without producing an awkward construction. Both B and C are illogically worded: the *distillation of alcohol,* not the alcohol itself, is substituted for gasoline in B, as the act of *distilling alcohol* is in C. Choice D is unidiomatic and suggests that the rising price of gasoline is what makes the substitution. Choice E is the best for this question.

10. Climatic shifts are <u>so gradual as to be indistinguishable</u> at first from ordinary fluctuations in the weather.

  (A) so gradual as to be indistinguishable
  (B) so gradual they can be indistinguishable
  (C) so gradual that they are unable to be distinguished
  (D) gradual enough not to be distinguishable
  (E) gradual enough so that one cannot distinguish them

Choice A, the best answer, presents the idiomatic form (*some things) are so X as to be Y.* Choices B, C, D, and E can be faulted for not using this form. In addition, C confusedly refers to the climatic shifts themselves as being *unable* when it is really people who are unable at first to distinguish climatic shifts.

11. Although <u>the lesser cornstalk borer is widely distributed, control of them is</u> necessary only in the South.

  (A) the lesser cornstalk borer is widely distributed, control of them is
  (B) widely distributed, measures to control the lesser cornstalk borer are
  (C) widely distributed, lesser cornstalk borer control is
  (D) the lesser cornstalk borer is widely distributed, measures to control it are
  (E) it is widely distributed, control of the lesser cornstalk borer is

Choice A is incorrect because the plural pronoun *them* does not agree in number with its singular noun referent, *the lesser cornstalk borer.* Choice B wrongly states that *measures* are widely distributed, not that *the cornstalk borer* is. Similarly, C and E assert that *control* is widely distributed. Choice D is the best answer.

12. <u>Traveling the back roads of Hungary, in 1905 Béla Bartók and Zoltán Kodály began their pioneering work in ethnomusicology, and they were armed only</u> with an Edison phonograph and insatiable curiosity.

  (A) Traveling the back roads of Hungary, in 1905 Béla Bartók and Zoltán Kodály began their pioneering work in ethnomusicology, and they were armed only
  (B) In 1905, Béla Bartók and Zoltán Kodály, traveling the back roads of Hungary, began their pioneering work in ethnomusicology, and they were only armed
  (C) In 1905 Béla Bartók and Zoltán Kodály began their pioneering work in ethnomusicology, traveling the back roads of Hungary armed only
  (D) Having traveled the back roads of Hungary, in 1905 Béla Bartók and Zoltán Kodály began their pioneering work in ethnomusicology; they were only armed
  (E) Béla Bartók and Zoltán Kodály, in 1905 began their pioneering work in ethnomusicology, traveling the back roads of Hungary, arming themselves only

Choices A and B are wordy and imprecise: the phrasing suggests that Bartók and Kodály were already *traveling the back roads of Hungary* when they began their pioneering work, not that they traveled the back roads in order to conduct such work. Moreover, *and* suggests in both cases that they were armed with a phonograph *in addition* to being on the road, rather than *while* they were on the road, and *only* in B is misplaced before the verb *armed*. In choice D, *Having traveled* ... suggests that the two had finished traveling before they began their work in ethnomusicology, and *only* is again misplaced. Choice E is wordy and awkwardly constructed. Choice C is best.

13. It is as difficult to prevent crimes against property as <u>those that are against a</u> person.

  (A) those that are against a
  (B) those against a
  (C) it is against a
  (D) preventing those against a
  (E) it is to prevent those against a

This sentence compares two actions, preventing *crimes against property* and preventing *crimes against a person,* in terms of difficulty. These actions should be described in grammatically parallel structures. Consequently, choices A, B, and D are faulty because they fail to parallel the first clause, which has *it* as a subject and *is* as a verb. Choice C contains *it is* but lacks *to prevent those,* words needed to complete the required clause and identify the other action in the comparison. Choice E is best: all of the elements necessary to describe the second action are presented in a form that is both idiomatic and grammatically parallel to the description of the first action.

14. Unlike the acid smoke of cigarettes, pipe tobacco, cured by age-old methods, yields an alkaline smoke too irritating to be drawn into the lungs.

   (A) Unlike the acid smoke of cigarettes, pipe tobacco, cured by age-old methods, yields an alkaline smoke
   (B) Unlike the acid smoke of cigarettes, pipe tobacco is cured by age-old methods, yielding an alkaline smoke
   (C) Unlike cigarette tobacco, which yields an acid smoke, pipe tobacco, cured by age-old methods, yields an alkaline smoke
   (D) Differing from cigarettes' acid smoke, pipe tobacco's alkaline smoke, cured by age-old methods, is
   (E) The alkaline smoke of pipe tobacco differs from cigarettes' acid smoke in that it is cured by age-old methods and is

Choices A and B illogically compare *the acid smoke of cigarettes* with *pipe tobacco,* not with the *smoke* from pipe tobacco. B is also faulty for making the curing methods rather than the nature of the smoke the basis of comparison. Choice C is best, for it compares cigarette tobacco with pipe tobacco in terms of the type of smoke each produces. Choices D and E garble the intended meaning by saying that the *smoke* of pipe tobacco is *cured by age-old methods.* Moreover, the phrasing is less compact and idiomatic than *Unlike* is for expressing a contrast.

15. Joplin's faith in his opera "Tremonisha" was unshakeable; in 1911 he published the score at his own expense and decided on staging it himself.

   (A) on staging it himself
   (B) that he himself would do the staging
   (C) to do the staging of the work by himself
   (D) that he himself would stage it
   (E) to stage the work himself

Choice A is poorly worded: *it* refers to *the score,* not to the opera itself, and *decided on staging it* is unidiomatic. Choice B does not specify what it was that Joplin decided to stage. Choice C is unidiomatic and needlessly wordy. Because the pronoun reference of *it* is faulty, choice D, like choice A, confuses staging the score with staging the work. Choice E is best.

16. Los Angeles has a higher number of family dwellings per capita than any large city.

   (A) a higher number of family dwellings per capita than any large city
   (B) higher numbers of family dwellings per capita than any other large city
   (C) a higher number of family dwellings per capita than does any other large city
   (D) higher numbers of family dwellings per capita than do other large cities
   (E) a high per capita number of family dwellings, more than does any other large city

Choice A is illogical because it implies that Los Angeles is not a large city. Choice B emends this problem by specifying *any other large city,* but the plural *numbers* is incorrect in that there is only a single number of such dwellings. Choice C is best. The plural *numbers* is again wrong in choice D, which in addition fails to establish that Los Angeles exceeds *all* other large cities in family dwellings per capita. Choice E is wordy and very awkward.

17. During the nineteenth century Emily Eden and Fanny Parks journeyed throughout India, sketching and keeping journals forming the basis of news reports about the princely states where they had visited.

   (A) forming the basis of news reports about the princely states where they had
   (B) that were forming the basis of news reports about the princely states
   (C) to form the basis of news reports about the princely states which they have
   (D) which had formed the basis of news reports about the princely states where they had
   (E) that formed the basis of news reports about the princely states they

In choice A it is not immediately clear whether *forming* modifies *journals* or parallels *sketching* and *keeping.* Also, *where they had visited* is wordy and inappropriate for a simple reference to past events. Choice B does not establish who visited the *princely states,* and *that were forming* should be *that formed.* Choice C is unclear because *to form* could be read as either *in order to form* or *so as to form,* and the present perfect *have visited* does not agree with the past tense *journeyed.* In choice D, as in choice A, *where they had* is faulty, and *had formed* suggests that the journals and news reports existed before the journey. E is best for this question.

18. School integration plans that involve busing between suburban and central-city areas have contributed, according to a recent study, to significant increases in housing integration, which, in turn, reduces any future need for busing.

(A) significant increases in housing integration, which, in turn, reduces
(B) significant integration increases in housing, which, in turn, reduces
(C) increase housing integration significantly, which, in turn, reduces
(D) increase housing integration significantly, in turn reducing
(E) significantly increase housing integration, which, in turn, reduce

Choice A is best. In choice B, the phrase *integration increases in housing* is unidiomatic and imprecise: *integration* cannot modify *increases,* and the increases are not in *housing* but rather in *housing integration.* Choices C, D, and E entail the ungrammatical construction *have contributed. . .to increase.* Moreover, it is not clear whether *which* in C and *reducing* in D refer to *housing integration* or the *increase* in housing integration. In choice E, *which* clearly refers to *housing integration,* making the plural verb *reduce* incorrect.

19. The commission acknowledged that no amount of money or staff members can ensure the safety of people who live in the vicinity of a nuclear plant, but it approved the installation because it believed that all reasonable precautions had been taken.

(A) no amount of money or staff members
(B) neither vast amounts of money nor staff members
(C) neither vast amounts of money nor numbers of staff members
(D) neither vast amounts of money nor a large staff
(E) no matter how large the staff or how vast the amount of money

In choice A, *amount of. . .staff members* is incorrect; *amount* properly refers to an undifferentiated mass, as in the case of *money.* Choice B does not make clear whether *vast amounts* is supposed to describe *money* only or *money* and *staff members,* and in choice C it is not certain whether *vast* modifies *amounts* only or *amounts* and *numbers.* Choice D is best. Choice E cannot fit grammatically into the original sentence because it supplies no noun that can function as a subject for the verb *can.*

20. Sartre believed each individual is responsible to choose one course of action over another one, that it is the choice that gives value to the act, and that nothing that is not acted upon has value.

(A) each individual is responsible to choose one course of action over another one
(B) that each individual is responsible for choosing one course of action over another
(C) that each individual is responsible, choosing one course of action over another
(D) that each individual is responsible to choose one course of action over the other
(E) each individual is responsible for choosing one course of action over other ones

Choice A is faulty because *that* is needed after *believed* to make the clause parallel with the two *that. . .* clauses following it. Also, the idiomatic expression is *responsible for choosing* rather than *responsible to choose,* and *one* is superfluous. Choice B is best. Choice C distorts the intended meaning because it says, in effect, only that individuals are responsible and that they choose a course of action, not that they are *responsible for choosing* such a course. In choice D, *responsible to choose* is unidiomatic and *the other* wrongly suggests that there is some particular alternative under discussion. Choice E lacks the necessary *that,* and *other ones* is less precise than *another.*

21. While the owner of a condominium apartment has free and clear title to the dwelling, owners of cooperative apartments have shares in a corporation that owns a building and leases apartments to them.

(A) While the owner of a condominium apartment has free and clear title to the dwelling,
(B) The owner of a condominium apartment has free and clear title to the dwelling, but
(C) Whereas owners of condominium apartments have free and clear title to their dwellings,
(D) An owner of a condominium apartment has free and clear title to the dwelling, whereas
(E) Condominium apartment owners have a title to their dwelling that is free and clear, while

Choices A, B, and D can be faulted for comparing a single *owner of a condominium* with *owners of cooperative apartments.* In choice C, the best answer, the nouns agree in number. Nouns also agree in choice E, but one cannot tell whether the *title* or the *dwelling* is said to be *free and clear.*

22. Although <u>films about the American West depict coyotes as solitary animals howling mournfully on the tops of distant hills</u>, in reality these gregarious creatures live in stable groups that occupy the same territory for long periods.

(A) films about the American West depict coyotes as solitary animals howling mournfully on the tops of distant hills

(B) in films about the American West coyotes are depicted to be solitary animals that howl mournfully on the tops of distant hills

(C) coyotes are depicted as solitary animals howling mournfully on the tops of distant hills in films about the American West

(D) films about the American West depict coyotes as if they were solitary, mournfully howling animals on the tops of distant hills

(E) films about the American West depict coyotes to be solitary and mournfully howling animals on the tops of distant hills

Choice A is best. In choice B, *depicted to be* is unidiomatic. The phrase *in films about the American West* is misplaced in choice C so that one cannot tell whether it indicates where the distant hills are, where the animals howl, or where coyotes are depicted as solitary creatures; the phrase should appear next to the word it is meant to modify. Choice D is wordy and awkward, and choice E contains the faulty *depict. . .to be*.

23. In 1980 the United States exported <u>twice as much of its national output of goods as they had</u> in 1970.

(A) twice as much of its national output of goods as they had

(B) double the amount of their national output of goods as they did

(C) twice as much of its national output of goods as it did

(D) double the amount of its national output of goods as it has

(E) twice as much of their national output of goods as they had

Choice A is incorrect because the plural pronoun *they* does not agree with its singular noun referent, *the United States,* and because *had* cannot substitute for *exported.* In choice B, *double the amount* is a less idiomatic form of comparison than *twice as much;* also, the plural pronouns *their* and *they* are incorrect. Choice C is best: the form of the comparison is idiomatic, the pronouns agree with the noun referent, and *did* — the simple past tense of *do* — can substitute for *exported.* Choice D contains *double the amount* as well as *has* for *exported,* and choice E is faulty because of *their* and *they had.*

24. <u>Even though its per capita food supply hardly increased during</u> two decades, stringent rationing and planned distribution have allowed the People's Republic of China to ensure nutritional levels of 2,000 calories per person per day for its population.

(A) Even though its per capita food supply hardly increased during

(B) Even though its per capita food supply has hardly increased in

(C) Despite its per capita food supply hardly increasing over

(D) Despite there being hardly any increase in its per capita food supply during

(E) Although there is hardly any increase in per capita food supply for

In choice A, the simple past tense *hardly increased* does not match the present perfect *have allowed;* consequently, it seems that two different time periods are being discussed. In B, the best choice, *has hardly increased* parallels *have allowed* to indicate that the events described took place at the same time. Also *in* is the best word here for making a comparison between the beginning and the end of the twenty-year period. Choices C and D are awkward and unidiomatic, and choice E fails to specify *where* there was no increase in per capita food supply.

25. Few people realize that the chance of accidental injury or death <u>may be as great or greater in the "safety" of their own homes than</u> in a plane or on the road.

(A) may be as great or greater in the "safety" of their own homes than

(B) is at least as great or greater in the "safety" of their own homes than

(C) might be so great or greater in the "safety" of their own home as

(D) may be at least as great in the "safety" of their own homes as

(E) can be at least so great in the "safety" of their own home as

In choices A and B, *as great or greater. . .than* is incorrect: *greater* takes *than,* but *as great* must be completed by *as.* The statement in B is also redundant in that the notion of *greater* is contained in *at least as great,* and *may be* would be better than *is* for expressing a distinct possibility. In choice C, *might* expresses too much doubt, *so* in place of *as* is unidiomatic, *home* should be *homes* to agree with *people,* and *greater. . .as* is erroneous. Choice D is best. In choice E, *so* and *home* are faulty.

SENTENCE CORRECTION SAMPLE TEST SECTION 4

30 Minutes
25 Questions

<u>Directions:</u> In each of the following sentences, some part of the sentence or the entire sentence is underlined. Beneath each sentence you will find five ways of phrasing the underlined part. The first of these repeats the original; the other four are different. If you think the original is better than any of the alternatives, choose answer A; otherwise choose one of the others. Select the best version and fill in the corresponding oval on your answer sheet.

This is a test of correctness and effectiveness of expression. In choosing answers, follow the requirements of standard written English; that is, pay attention to grammar, choice of words, and sentence construction. Choose the answer that expresses most effectively what is presented in the original sentence; this answer should be clear and exact, without awkwardness, ambiguity, or redundancy.

1. A fire in an enclosed space burns with the aid of reflected radiation that preheats the fuel, making ignition much easier and <u>flames spreading</u> more quickly.

   (A) flames spreading
   (B) flame spreads
   (C) flames are caused to spread
   (D) causing flames to spread
   (E) causing spreading of the flames

2. Roy Wilkins was among the last of a generation of civil rights activists who led the nation through decades of change <u>so profound many young Americans are not able to imagine, even less to remember</u>, what segregation was like.

   (A) so profound many young Americans are not able to imagine, even less to remember
   (B) so profound that many young Americans cannot imagine, much less remember
   (C) so profound many young Americans cannot imagine nor even less remember
   (D) of such profundity many young Americans cannot imagine, even less can they remember
   (E) of such profundity that many young Americans are not able to imagine, much less to remember

3. The residents' opposition to the spraying program has rekindled an old debate <u>among those who oppose the use of pesticides and</u> those who feel that the pesticides are necessary to save the trees.

   (A) among those who oppose the use of pesticides and
   (B) between those who oppose the use of pesticides and
   (C) among those opposing the use of pesticides with
   (D) between those who oppose the use of pesticides with
   (E) among those opposing the use of pesticides and

4. In cold-water habitats, certain invertebrates and fish convert starches into complex carbohydrates called glycerols, <u>in effect manufacturing its own antifreeze</u>.

   (A) in effect manufacturing its own antifreeze
   (B) effectively manufacturing antifreeze of its own
   (C) in effect manufacturing their own antifreeze
   (D) so that they manufacture their own antifreeze
   (E) thus the manufacture of its own antifreeze

5. Slips of the tongue do not necessarily reveal concealed beliefs or intentions <u>but rather are the result from</u> the competition between various processing mechanisms in the brain.

   (A) but rather are the result from
   (B) and instead are the result from
   (C) being rather the result of
   (D) and rather result from
   (E) but rather result from

6. The new contract <u>forbids a strike by the transportation union</u>.

   (A) forbids a strike by the transportation union
   (B) forbids the transportation union from striking
   (C) forbids that there be a strike by the transportation union
   (D) will forbid the transportation union from striking
   (E) will forbid that the transportation union strikes

GO ON TO THE NEXT PAGE.

7. Monitoring heart patients' exercise, as well as athletes exercising, is now done by small transmitters broadcasting physiological measurements to nearby recording machines.

   (A) Monitoring heart patients' exercise, as well as athletes exercising, is now done by small transmitters broadcasting physiological measurements to nearby recording machines.
   (B) Monitoring the exercise of heart patients, as well as athletes exercising, is now done by small transmitters broadcasting physiological measurements to nearby recording machines.
   (C) Small transmitters broadcasting physiological measurements to nearby recording machines are now used to monitor the exercise of both heart patients and athletes.
   (D) Broadcasting physiological measurements to nearby recording machines, small transmitters are now used to monitor heart patients' exercise, as well as athletes exercising.
   (E) Both athletes exercising and heart patients' exercise are now monitored by small transmitters broadcasting physiological measurements to nearby recording machines.

8. The commission has directed advertisers to restrict the use of the word "natural" to foods that do not contain color or flavor additives, chemical preservatives, or nothing that has been synthesized.

   (A) or nothing that has been
   (B) nor anything that was
   (C) and nothing that is
   (D) or anything that has been
   (E) and anything

9. Bringing the Ford Motor Company back from the verge of bankruptcy shortly after the Second World War was a special governmentally sanctioned price increase during a period of wage and price controls.

   (A) Bringing the Ford Motor Company back from the verge of bankruptcy shortly after the Second World War was a special governmentally sanctioned price increase during a period of wage and price controls.
   (B) What brought the Ford Motor Company back from the verge of bankruptcy shortly after the Second World War was a special price increase that the government sanctioned during a period of wage and price controls.
   (C) That which brought the Ford Motor Company back from the verge of bankruptcy shortly after the Second World War was a special governmentally sanctioned price increase during a period of wage and price controls.
   (D) What has brought the Ford Motor Company back from the verge of bankruptcy shortly after the Second World War was a special price increase that the government sanctioned during a period of wages and price controls.
   (E) To bring the Ford Motor Company back from the verge of bankruptcy shortly after the Second World War, there was a special price increase during a period of wages and price controls that government sanctioned.

10. Like Haydn, Schubert wrote a great deal for the stage, but he is remembered principally for his chamber and concert-hall music.

    (A) Like Haydn, Schubert
    (B) Like Haydn, Schubert also
    (C) As has Haydn, Schubert
    (D) As did Haydn, Schubert also
    (E) As Haydn did, Schubert also

GO ON TO THE NEXT PAGE.

11. Charlotte Perkins Gilman, a late nineteenth-century feminist, called for urban apartment houses including child-care facilities and clustered suburban houses including communal eating and social facilities.

    (A) including child-care facilities and clustered suburban houses including communal eating and social facilities
    (B) that included child-care facilities, and for clustered suburban houses to include communal eating and social facilities
    (C) with child-care facilities included and for clustered suburban houses to include communal eating and social facilities
    (D) that included child-care facilities and for clustered suburban houses with communal eating and social facilities
    (E) to include child-care facilities and for clustered suburban houses with communal eating and social facilities included

12. The odds are about 4 to 1 against surviving a takeover offer, and many business consultants therefore advise that a company's first line of defense in eluding offers like these be to even refuse to take calls from likely corporate raiders.

    (A) that a company's first line of defense in eluding offers like these be to even refuse
    (B) that a company's first line of defense in eluding such offers be to refuse even
    (C) a company defending itself against offers of this kind that, as a first line of defense, they should even refuse
    (D) companies which are defending themselves against such an offer that, as a first line of defense, they should even refuse
    (E) that the first line of defense for a company who is eluding offers like these is the refusal even

13. Japan received huge sums of capital from the United States after the Second World War, using it to help build a modern industrial system.

    (A) Japan received huge sums of capital from the United States after the Second World War, using it to help build
    (B) Japan received huge sums of capital from the United States after the Second World War and used it to help in building
    (C) Japan used the huge sums of capital it received from the United States after the Second World War to help build
    (D) Japan's huge sums of capital received from the United States after the Second World War were used to help it in building
    (E) Receiving huge sums of capital from the United States after the Second World War, Japan used it to help build

14. Although one link in the chain was demonstrated to be weak, but not sufficiently so to require the recall of the automobile.

    (A) demonstrated to be weak, but not sufficiently so to require
    (B) demonstrated as weak, but it was not sufficiently so that it required
    (C) demonstrably weak, but not sufficiently so to require
    (D) demonstrably weak, it was not so weak as to require
    (E) demonstrably weak, it was not weak enough that it required

15. Although the Supreme Court ruled as long ago as 1880 that Blacks could not be excluded outright from jury service, nearly a century of case-by-case adjudication has been necessary to develop and enforce the principle that all juries must be drawn from "a fair cross section of the community."

    (A) has been necessary to develop and enforce the principle that all juries must be
    (B) was necessary for developing and enforcing the principle of all juries being
    (C) was to be necessary in developing and enforcing the principle of all juries to be
    (D) is necessary to develop and enforce the principle that all juries must be
    (E) will be necessary for developing and enforcing the principle of all juries being

16. The modernization program for the steel mill will cost approximately 51 million dollars, which it is hoped can be completed in the late 1980's.

    (A) The modernization program for the steel mill will cost approximately 51 million dollars, which it is hoped can be completed in the late 1980's.
    (B) The modernization program for the steel mill, hopefully completed in the late 1980's, will cost approximately 51 million dollars.
    (C) Modernizing the steel mill, hopefully to be completed in the late 1980's, will cost approximately 51 million dollars.
    (D) The program for modernizing the steel mill, which can, it is hoped, be completed in the late 1980's and cost approximately 51 million dollars.
    (E) Modernizing the steel mill, a program that can, it is hoped, be completed in the late 1980's, will cost approximately 51 million dollars.

GO ON TO THE NEXT PAGE.

17. Camus broke with Sartre <u>in a bitter dispute over</u> the nature of Stalinism.

    (A) in a bitter dispute over
    (B) over bitterly disputing
    (C) after there was a bitter dispute over
    (D) after having bitterly disputed about
    (E) over a bitter dispute about

18. Nowhere in Prakta is the influence of modern European architecture <u>more apparent than their</u> government buildings.

    (A) more apparent than their
    (B) so apparent as their
    (C) more apparent than in its
    (D) so apparent than in their
    (E) as apparent as it is in its

19. Federal legislation establishing a fund for the cleanup of sites damaged by toxic chemicals permits <u>compensating state governments for damage to</u> their natural resources but does not allow claims for injury to people.

    (A) compensating state governments for damage to
    (B) compensating state governments for the damaging of
    (C) giving state governments compensation for damaging
    (D) giving compensation to state governments for the damage of
    (E) the giving of compensation to state governments for damaging

20. The lawyer for the defense charged that she suspected the police of having illegally taped her confidential conversations with her client and then <u>used the information obtained to find evidence supporting</u> their murder charges.

    (A) used the information obtained to find evidence supporting
    (B) used such information as they obtained to find evidence supporting
    (C) used the information they had obtained to find evidence that would support
    (D) of using the information they had obtained to find evidence that would support
    (E) of using such information as they obtained to find evidence that would be supportive of

21. According to surveys by the National Institute on Drug Abuse, about 20 percent of young adults used cocaine in 1979, <u>doubling those reported in the 1977 survey</u>.

    (A) doubling those reported in the 1977 survey
    (B) to double the number the 1977 survey reported
    (C) twice those the 1977 survey reported
    (D) twice as much as those reported in the 1977 survey
    (E) twice the number reported in the 1977 survey

GO ON TO THE NEXT PAGE.

22. Inflation has made many Americans reevaluate their assumptions about the future; they still expect to live better than their parents have, but not so well as they once thought they could.

    (A) they still expect to live better than their parents have
    (B) they still expect to live better than their parents did
    (C) they still expect to live better than their parents had
    (D) still expecting to live better than their parents had
    (E) still expecting to live better than did their parents

23. Europeans have long known that eating quail sometimes makes the eater ill, but only recently has it been established that the illness is caused by a toxin present in the quail's body only under certain conditions.

    (A) Europeans have long known that eating quail sometimes makes
    (B) Europeans have long known quail eating is sometimes able to make
    (C) Eating quail has long been known to Europeans to sometimes make
    (D) It has long been known to Europeans that quail eating will sometimes make
    (E) It has long been known to Europeans that quail, when it is eaten, has sometimes made

24. The caterpillar of the geometrid moth strikes when special tactile hairs on its body are disturbed, after capturing its prey, holds the victim so that it cannot escape.

    (A) strikes when special tactile hairs on its body are disturbed,
    (B) striking when special tactile hairs on its body are disturbed, but
    (C) which strikes when special tactile hairs on its body are disturbed,
    (D) which, striking when special tactile hairs on its body are disturbed,
    (E) strikes when special tactile hairs on its body are disturbed and,

25. In assessing the problems faced by rural migrant workers, the question of whether they are better off materially than the urban working poor is irrelevant.

    (A) In assessing the problems faced by rural migrant workers, the question of whether they are better off materially than the urban working poor is irrelevant.
    (B) The question of whether the rural migrant worker is better off materially than the urban working poor is irrelevant in assessing the problems that they face.
    (C) A question that is irrelevant in assessing the problems that rural migrant workers face is whether they are better off materially than the urban working poor.
    (D) In an assessment of the problems faced by rural migrant workers, the question of whether they are better off materially than the urban working poor is irrelevant.
    (E) The question of whether the rural migrant worker is better off materially than the urban working poor is irrelevant in an assessment of the problems that they face.

S T O P

IF YOU FINISH BEFORE TIME IS CALLED, YOU MAY CHECK YOUR WORK ON THIS SECTION ONLY.
DO NOT TURN TO ANY OTHER SECTION IN THE TEST.

Answer Key for Sample Test Section 4

SENTENCE CORRECTION

1. D	14. D
2. B	15. A
3. B	16. E
4. C	17. A
5. E	18. C
6. A	19. A
7. C	20. D
8. D	21. E
9. B	22. B
10. A	23. A
11. D	24. E
12. B	25. D
13. C	

Explanatory Material: Sentence Correction Sample Test Section 4

1. A fire in an enclosed space burns with the aid of reflected radiation that preheats the fuel, making ignition much easier and flames spreading more quickly.

   (A) flames spreading
   (B) flame spreads
   (C) flames caused to spread
   (D) causing flames to spread
   (E) causing spreading of the flames

Choices A, B, and C are incorrect because a present participial (or "—ing") verb must precede *flames* to form a structure parallel to the phrase *making ignition much easier.* . . . Choice D is best. Choice E is wordy, unidiomatic, and also awkward in that *spreading,* although used here as a noun, appears at first to be another present participle that could be modified by *more quickly.*

2. Roy Wilkins was among the last of a generation of civil rights activists who led the nation through decades of change so profound many young Americans are not able to imagine, even less to remember, what segregation was like.

   (A) so profound many young Americans are not able to imagine, even less to remember
   (B) so profound that many young Americans cannot imagine, much less remember
   (C) so profound many young Americans cannot imagine nor even less remember
   (D) of such profundity many young Americans cannot imagine, even less can they remember
   (E) of such profundity that many young Americans are not able to imagine, much less to remember

Choice A can be faulted for omitting *that* after *profound;* the idiomatic form of the expression is "*so X that Y.*" Also, *much less remember* is more idiomatic than *even less to remember,* and *cannot imagine* is more concise than *are not able to imagine.* Choice B is best. Choice C lacks *that* after *profound,* and *nor* is incorrectly used to join verbs modified by *cannot.* In choice D, *of such profundity* is wordy, *that* is missing, and *even less can they remember* is not an idiomatic way to complete *cannot imagine.* In choice E, *of such profundity* and *are not able to imagine* are wordy, and the *to* in *to remember* is unnecessary.

3. The residents' opposition to the spraying program has rekindled an old debate among those who oppose the use of pesticides and those who feel that the pesticides are necessary to save the trees.

   (A) among those who oppose the use of pesticides and
   (B) between those who oppose the use of pesticides and
   (C) among those opposing the use of pesticides with
   (D) between those who oppose the use of pesticides with
   (E) among those opposing the use of pesticides and

Choices A, C, and E can be faulted for using *among* in place of *between* to refer to two factions. Choices C and D incorrectly use *with* in place of *and.* Also, *those opposing* in choices C and E is not parallel with *those who feel.* Choice B is best.

4. In cold-water habitats, certain invertebrates and fish convert starches into complex carbohydrates called glycerols, in effect manufacturing its own antifreeze.

   (A) in effect manufacturing its own antifreeze
   (B) effectively manufacturing antifreeze of its own
   (C) in effect manufacturing their own antifreeze
   (D) so that they manufacture their own antifreeze
   (E) thus the manufacture of its own antifreeze

Choices A and B are incorrect because the pronoun *its* does not agree in number with *invertebrates and fish,* the noun referents. B also distorts the intended meaning of the sentence by making a statement about how effectively the invertebrates and fish manufacture their own antifreeze. Choice C is best. In D and E, *so that they manufacture* and *thus the manufacture* do not form logical connections with the rest of the sentence, and *its* in E is incorrect.

5. Slips of the tongue do not necessarily reveal concealed beliefs or intentions but rather are the result from the competition between various processing mechanisms in the brain.

   (A) but rather are the result from
   (B) and instead are the result from
   (C) being rather the result of
   (D) and rather result from
   (E) but rather result from

Choices A and B are incorrect because *are the result from* is unidiomatic; *result from* or *are the result of* are the idiomatic forms. Choices B, C, and D are faulty because *but* is needed to complete the construction *do not reveal but (verb)*. E is the best answer.

6. The new contract forbids a strike by the transportation union.

   (A) forbids a strike by the transportation union
   (B) forbids the transportation union from striking
   (C) forbids that there be a strike by the transportation union
   (D) will forbid the transportation union from striking
   (E) will forbid that the transportation union strikes

Choice A is best. B, C, D, and E are unidiomatic: a form of the verb *forbid* may be completed by a noun, as in *forbids a strike,* or by a noun and an infinitive, as in *forbids the union to strike.*

7. Monitoring heart patients' exercise, as well as athletes exercising, is now done by small transmitters broadcasting physiological measurements to nearby recording machines.

   (A) Monitoring heart patients' exercise, as well as athletes exercising, is now done by small transmitters broadcasting physiological measurements to nearby recording machines.
   (B) Monitoring the exercise of heart patients, as well as athletes exercising, is now done by small transmitters broadcasting physiological measurements to nearby recording machines.
   (C) Small transmitters broadcasting physiological measurements to nearby recording machines are now used to monitor the exercise of both heart patients and athletes.
   (D) Broadcasting physiological measurements to nearby recording machines, small transmitters are now used to monitor heart patients' exercise, as well as athletes exercising.
   (E) Both athletes exercising and heart patients' exercise are now monitored by small transmitters broadcasting physiological measurements to nearby recording machines.

Choices A, B, D, and E incorrectly compare *heart patients' exercise* and *athletes* who are *exercising*, not *patients' exercise* and *athletes' exercise*, a more logical pairing. Choice C, which clarifies the comparison, is best.

8. The commission has directed advertisers to restrict the use of the word "natural" to foods that do not contain color or flavor additives, chemical preservatives, or nothing that has been synthesized.

   (A) or nothing that has been
   (B) nor anything that was
   (C) and nothing that is
   (D) or anything that has been
   (E) and anything

Choices A, B, and C are faulty because the *not* in *do not contain* makes the negatives *nothing* and *nor* unidiomatic. Choice D is best. In E, *and* fails to indicate that *anything. . .* is an all-inclusive term, not another separate item in the list *additives, . . . preservatives. . . .*

9. Bringing the Ford Motor Company back from the verge of bankruptcy shortly after the Second World War was a special governmentally sanctioned price increase during a period of wage and price controls.

   (A) Bringing the Ford Motor Company back from the verge of bankruptcy shortly after the Second World War was a special governmentally sanctioned price increase during a period of wage and price controls.
   (B) What brought the Ford Motor Company back from the verge of bankruptcy shortly after the Second World War was a special price increase that the government sanctioned during a period of wage and price controls.
   (C) That which brought the Ford Motor Company back from the verge of bankruptcy shortly after the Second World War was a special governmentally sanctioned price increase during a period of wage and price controls.
   (D) What has brought the Ford Motor Company back from the verge of bankruptcy shortly after the Second World War was a special price increase that the government sanctioned during a period of wages and price controls.
   (E) To bring the Ford Motor Company back from the verge of bankruptcy shortly after the Second World War, there was a special price increase during a period of wages and price controls that government sanctioned.

Choice A, awkward and imprecise, leaves one confused about what it was that happened *during a period of wage and price controls*—the revitalization of the Ford Motor Company or the sanctioning of a price increase. B, the best answer, clarifies the matter by making *during. . .* modify *the government sanctioned*. Choice C, wordy and awkward, suffers from the same imprecision as choice A. The present perfect *has brought* in D is inappropriate for action completed well in the past, and *wages,* which should modify *control,* is not idiomatic. In choice E, *wages* is again wrong, and E, contrary to intent, suggests that the government sanctioned a *period of . . . controls* rather than *a special price increase.*

10. <u>Like Haydn, Schubert</u> wrote a great deal for the stage, but he is remembered principally for his chamber and concert-hall music.

   (A) Like Haydn, Schubert
   (B) Like Haydn, Schubert also
   (C) As has Haydn, Schubert
   (D) As did Haydn, Schubert also
   (E) As Haydn did, Schubert also

Choice A is best. In B, *also* is redundant after *Like,* which establishes the similarity between Haydn and Schubert. *As* in choices C, D, and E is not idiomatic in a comparison of persons; *has* in C wrongly suggests that the action was recently completed; and *also* in D and E is superfluous.

11. Charlotte Perkins Gilman, a late nineteenth-century feminist, called for urban apartment houses <u>including child-care facilities and clustered suburban houses including communal eating and social facilities.</u>

   (A) including child-care facilities and clustered suburban houses including communal eating and social facilities
   (B) that included child-care facilities, and for clustered suburban houses to include communal eating and social facilities
   (C) with child-care facilities included and for clustered suburban houses to include communal eating and social facilities
   (D) that included child-care facilities and for clustered suburban houses with communal eating and social facilities
   (E) to include child-care facilities and for clustered suburban houses with communal eating and social facilities included

The function and meaning of the *including . . .* phrases are unclear in choice A: for example, it is hard to tell whether Gilman called for urban apartment houses that included child-care facilities or whether such facilities represent one variety of the urban apartment houses she wanted built. Choice B resolves the ambiguity concerning *child-care facilities,* but *called for . . . houses to include . . . facilities* is unidiomatic in B and C. Choice D is best. In E, *to include* is again faulty.

12. The odds are about 4 to 1 against surviving a takeover offer, and many business consultants therefore advise <u>that a company's first line of defense in eluding offers like these be to even refuse</u> to take calls from likely corporate raiders.

   (A) that a company's first line of defense in eluding offers like these be to even refuse
   (B) that a company's first line of defense in eluding such offers be to refuse even
   (C) a company defending itself against offers of this kind that, as a first line of defense, they should even refuse
   (D) companies which are defending themselves against such an offer that, as a first line of defense, they should even refuse
   (E) that the first line of defense for a company who is eluding offers like these is the refusal even

Choice A is awkward and poorly phrased: *these* has no plural noun to which it can refer, and *even* should be placed immediately before *to take calls,* the phrase it modifies. Choice B is best. In C, the plural *they* does not agree with the singular *company, even* is misplaced, and *advise . . . that . . . they should* is unidiomatic. D has the plural *companies* but retains the other flaws of C. In E, *who* in place of *that* is an inappropriate pronoun for *company, these* does not agree with the singular *offer,* and *is the refusal* should be *be to refuse.*

13. <u>Japan received huge sums of capital from the United States after the Second World War, using it to help build</u> a modern industrial system.

   (A) Japan received huge sums of capital from the United States after the Second World War, using it to help build
   (B) Japan received huge sums of capital from the United States after the Second World War and used it to help in building
   (C) Japan used the huge sums of capital it received from the United States after the Second World War to help build
   (D) Japan's huge sums of capital received from the United States after the Second World War were used to help it in building
   (E) Receiving huge sums of capital from the United States after the Second World War, Japan used it to help build

Choice A can be faulted because *it,* a singular pronoun, does not agree with *sums of capital*; also, *using* does not establish a logical time sequence in which Japan first received and then used the capital from the United States. In B, *it* is again wrong, and *to help in building* is less compact and idiomatic than *to help build.* Choice C is best. In D, *to help it in building* is flawed, and *it* has no free noun as its referent since *Japan's* is a possessive modifier of *sums.* In E, *it* is again without a singular noun referent, and *Receiving huge sums . . ., Japan used . . .* does not make clear the sequence of events.

14. Although one link in the chain was <u>demonstrated to be weak, but not sufficiently so to require</u> the recall of the automobile.

    (A) demonstrated to be weak, but not sufficiently so to require
    (B) demonstrated as weak, but it was not sufficiently so that it required
    (C) demonstrably weak, but not sufficiently so to require
    (D) demonstrably weak, it was not so weak as to require
    (E) demonstrably weak, it was not weak enough that it required

Choices A and C entail ungrammatical constructions because they do not produce a sentence that has a main clause with a subject and a verb. In choice B, *demonstrated as weak* is un-idiomatic; also in choices B and C *Although* and *but* should not be used together because only one is needed to express the relationship between the ideas. Choice D is best. Choice E is less concise and idiomatic than D; moreover, it is impre-cise to say that *one link in the chain* (the referent of *it*) actu-ally *required the recall*.

15. Although the Supreme Court ruled as long ago as 1880 that Blacks could not be excluded outright from jury service, nearly a century of case-by-case adjudi-cation <u>has been necessary to develop and enforce the principle that all juries must be</u> drawn from "a fair cross section of the community."

    (A) has been necessary to develop and enforce the principle that all juries must be
    (B) was necessary for developing and enforcing the principle of all juries being
    (C) was to be necessary in developing and enforcing the principle of all juries to be
    (D) is necessary to develop and enforce the principle that juries must be
    (E) will be necessary for developing and enforcing the principle of all juries being

Choice A is best: *has been* appropriately refers to recently completed action. In B, *was* does not indicate that the action is recent. Also, *necessary for developing . . .* is less idiom-atic than *necessary to develop . . .*, and *principle of all juries being* is less direct than *principle that all juries must be*. The *to be* infinitives make choice C incorrect. The present tense *is* in D and the future tense *will be* in E make these choices faulty.

16. <u>The modernization program for the steel mill will cost approximately 51 million dollars, which it is hoped can be completed in the late 1980's.</u>

    (A) The modernization program for the steel mill will cost approximately 51 million dollars, which it is hoped can be completed in the late 1980's.
    (B) The modernization program for the steel mill, hopefully completed in the late 1980's will cost approximately 51 million dollars.
    (C) Modernizing the steel mill, hopefully to be com-pleted in the late 1980's will cost approximately 51 million dollars.
    (D) The program for modernizing the steel mill, which can, it is hoped, be completed in the late 1980's and cost approximately 51 million dollars.
    (E) Modernizing the steel mill, a program that can, it is hoped, be completed in the late 1980's, will cost approximately 51 million dollars.

Choice A can be faulted because *which* grammatically refers to *51 million dollars,* the nearest noun phrase. At any rate, it is not clear in choices A, B, C, or D whether the moderniza-tion program or the steel mill is supposed to be completed in the late 1980's. In B and C, the use of *hopefully* for *it is hoped* still meets with strong and widespread objection from many editors, lexicographers, and authors of usage hand-books. Aside from having an ambiguous *which*, D contains no independent clause and so cannot stand as a sentence. Choice E is the best answer.

17. Camus broke with Sartre <u>in a bitter dispute over</u> the nature of Stalinism.

    (A) in a bitter dispute over
    (B) over bitterly disputing
    (C) after there was a bitter dispute over
    (D) after having bitterly disputed about
    (E) over a bitter dispute about

Choice A is best. In B, *over* is misused: it should appear immediately before the issue in dispute (i.e., *the nature of Stalinism*). Choice C, wordy and imprecise, does not specify who was involved in the dispute. In D and E, *dispute(d) about* is less direct and idiomatic than *dispute(d) over*. Also, D is needlessly wordy and *over* is misused in E.

18. Nowhere in Prakta is the influence of modern European architecture <u>more apparent than their</u> government buildings.

    (A) more apparent than their
    (B) so apparent as their
    (C) more apparent than in its
    (D) so apparent than in their
    (E) as apparent as it is in its

Choice A is incorrect because *in* must appear after *than* and because the plural pronoun *their* does not agree in number with the singular noun *Prakta*. B also lacks *in* and misuses *their*. Choice C is best. In D, *so. . .than* in place of *more. . . than* is unidiomatic, and *their* is again wrong. Choice E is confusing because *it* refers to *architecture* whereas *its* refers to *Prakta*.

19. Federal legislation establishing a fund for the cleanup of sites damaged by toxic chemicals permits <u>compensating state governments for damage to</u> their natural resources but does not allow claims for injury to people.

    (A) compensating state governments for damage to
    (B) compensating state governments for the damaging of
    (C) giving state governments compensation for damaging
    (D) giving compensation to state governments for the damage of
    (E) the giving of compensation to state governments for damaging

Choice A is best. Choices B, C, and E could be read as saying that state governments can be compensated for damaging their own natural resources. The phrasing in C, D, and E is needlessly wordy, and *for the damage of* in D is unidiomatic.

20. The lawyer for the defense charged that she suspected the police of having illegally taped her confidential conversations with her client and then <u>used the information obtained to find evidence supporting</u> their murder charges.

    (A) used the information obtained to find evidence supporting
    (B) used such information as they obtained to find evidence supporting
    (C) used the information they had obtained to find evidence that would support
    (D) of using the information they had obtained to find evidence that would support
    (E) of using such information as they obtained to find evidence that would be supportive of

Choices A, B, and C are incorrect because *then* must be followed by a construction that parallels *of having* in line 2 — that is, by *of* and a present participial, or "-ing," verb form. Choice D is best. Choice E is very wordy, awkward, and indirect.

21. According to surveys by the National Institute on Drug Abuse, about 20 percent of young adults used cocaine in 1979, <u>doubling those reported in the 1977 survey.</u>

    (A) doubling those reported in the 1977 survey
    (B) to double the number the 1977 survey reported
    (C) twice those the 1977 survey reported
    (D) twice as much as those reported in the 1977 survey
    (E) twice the number reported in the 1977 survey

Choice A is phrased illogically in that it says the young adults in the 1979 survey somehow doubled the people in the 1977 survey, not that the *number* of young adults using cocaine doubled. The infinitive *to double*, used unidiomatically in B, carries the sense of *in order to double*. Again in choice C, *twice the number* would be preferable to *twice those (people)*. It is not clear in choice D whether *twice as much . . .* refers to the number of young adults using cocaine in 1979 or the amount of cocaine they used. Choice E is best.

22. Inflation has made many Americans reevaluate their assumptions about the future; <u>they still expect to live better than their parents have</u>, but not so well as they once thought they could.

    (A) they still expect to live better than their parents have
    (B) they still expect to live better than their parents did
    (C) they still expect to live better than their parents had
    (D) still expecting to live better than their parents had
    (E) still expecting to live better than did their parents

Choice A is incorrect because *have* cannot function as the auxiliary of *live*; i.e., *have live* is ungrammatical. Choice B, which substitutes *did* for *have*, is correct and logically places the parents' action in the past. In C and D, *had* places the parents' action in the past but is wrong as an auxiliary, just as *have* is in A. Choices D and E are faulty because neither is the independent clause that is needed to complete a grammatical sentence.

23. Europeans have long known that eating quail sometimes makes the eater ill, but only recently has it been
established that the illness is caused by a toxin present
in the quail's body only under certain conditions.

(A) Europeans have long known that eating quail
    sometimes makes
(B) Europeans have long known quail eating is some-
    times able to make
(C) Eating quail has long been known to Europeans
    to sometimes make
(D) It has long been known to Europeans that quail
    eating will sometimes make
(E) It has long been known to Europeans that quail,
    when it is eaten, has sometimes made

Choice A is best. Choice B is awkward: *that* is preferable
after *known* to introduce the clause describing what
Europeans have long known, and *quail eating is . . . able* is
unidiomatic. Choices C, D, and E are also awkward; moreover, *will. . .make* in D and *has. . .made* in E are inappropriate to describe a condition that holds true in the present as
well as in the future or the past.

24. The caterpillar of the geometrid moth strikes when
    special tactile hairs on its body are disturbed, after
    capturing its prey, holds the victim so that it cannot
    escape.

(A) strikes when special tactile hairs on its body are
    disturbed,
(B) striking when special tactile hairs on its body are
    disturbed, but
(C) which strikes when special tactile hairs on its
    body are disturbed,
(D) which, striking when special tactile hairs on its
    body are disturbed,
(E) strikes when special tactile hairs on its body are
    disturbed and,

Choice A is incorrect because it provides no word or construction that can form a grammatical link with the remainder of the sentence. By substituting *striking* for *strikes,*
choice B improperly removes the verb form that is needed with *caterpillar,* the grammatical subject, to make a complete sentence.
C is awkward and also ambiguous because it is not immediately clear whether *which* is meant to refer to *caterpillar* or
moth. In D, *which* is again ambiguous, and with *striking* in
place of *strikes, which* takes *holds* as its verb, leaving no verb
for the subject of the sentence. Choice E is best: *and* links the
verbs *strikes* and *holds* to form a compound verb for the subject, *caterpillar.*

25. In assessing the problems faced by rural migrant
    workers, the question of whether they are better off
    materially than the urban working poor is irrelevant.

(A) In assessing the problems faced by rural migrant
    workers, the question of whether they are better
    off materially than the urban working poor is
    irrelevant.
(B) The question of whether the rural migrant
    worker is better off materially than the urban
    working poor is irrelevant in assessing the prob-
    lems that they face.
(C) A question that is irrelevant in assessing the
    problems that rural migrant workers face is
    whether they are better off materially than the
    urban working poor.
(D) In an assessment of the problems faced by rural
    migrant workers, the question of whether they
    are better off materially than the urban working
    poor is irrelevant.
(E) The question of whether the rural migrant
    worker is better off materially than the urban
    working poor is irrelevant in an assessment of the
    problems that they face.

Choice A presents a dangling modifier because nothing mentioned in the sentence can perform the action of *assessing the
problems faced by rural migrant workers.* Choice A states
illogically that *the question* is assessing these problems. In B,
the plural pronoun *they* cannot refer as intended to the singular *rural migrant worker.* C is awkward and ambiguous:
again, the *question* is not *assessing the problems,* and *irrelevant in assessing* could be taken to mean either that the act
of assessing the problems is irrelevant or that the question
described is irrelevant in an assessment of the problems.
Choice D is best. Lack of agreement between *worker* and
they makes E wrong.

SENTENCE CORRECTION SAMPLE TEST 5

30 Minutes
25 Questions

<u>Directions:</u> In each of the following sentences, some part of the sentence or the entire sentence is underlined. Beneath each sentence you will find five ways of phrasing the underlined part. The first of these repeats the original; the other four are different. If you think the original is better than any of the alternatives, choose answer A; otherwise choose one of the others. Select the best version and fill in the corresponding oval on your answer sheet.

This is a test of correctness and effectiveness of expression. In choosing answers, follow the requirements of standard written English; that is, pay attention to grammar, choice of words, and sentence construction. Choose the answer that expresses most effectively what is presented in the original sentence; this answer should be clear and exact, without awkwardness, ambiguity, or redundancy.

1. The sale of government surplus machinery <u>will begin at 9 a.m. and continue until the supply lasts.</u>

   (A) will begin at 9 a.m. and continue until the supply lasts
   (B) begins at 9 a.m., continuing until the supply lasts
   (C) will begin at 9 a.m. and, until the supply lasts, will continue
   (D) begins at 9 a.m. and, as long as the supply may last, it continues
   (E) will begin at 9 a.m. and continue as long as the supply lasts

2. In England the well-dressed <u>gentleman of the eighteenth century protected their clothing while having their wig powdered by poking their head</u> through a device that resembled the stocks.

   (A) gentleman of the eighteenth century protected their clothing while having their wig powdered by poking their head
   (B) gentleman of the eighteenth century protected his clothing while having his wig powdered by poking his head
   (C) gentleman of the eighteenth century protected their clothing while having their wigs powdered by poking their heads
   (D) gentlemen of the eighteenth century protected his clothing while having his wig powdered by poking his head
   (E) gentlemen of the eighteenth century protected their clothing while having his wig powdered by poking his head

3. <u>Reared apart from each other, a recent United States study showed striking similarities in identical twins, including many idiosyncrasies of behavior.</u>

   (A) Reared apart from each other, a recent United States study showed striking similarities in identical twins, including many idiosyncrasies of behavior.
   (B) Reared apart from each other, striking similarities between identical twins that include many idiosyncrasies of behavior were shown in a recent United States study.
   (C) A recent United States study showed striking similarities in identical twins reared apart from each other that include many idiosyncrasies of behavior.
   (D) According to a recent United States study, identical twins reared apart from each other showed striking similarities, including many idiosyncrasies of behavior.
   (E) According to a recent United States study, identical twins showed striking similarities reared apart from each other, including many idiosyncrasies of behavior.

GO ON TO THE NEXT PAGE.

4. Developing nations in various parts of the world have amassed $700 billion in debts; at stake, <u>should a significant number of these debts be repudiated, is</u> the solvency of some of the world's largest multinational banks.

   (A) should a significant number of these debts be repudiated, is
   (B) should a significant number of these debts be repudiated, are
   (C) should they repudiate a significant number of these debts, are
   (D) if there is a repudiation of a significant number of these debts, would be
   (E) if a significant number of these debts will be repudiated, is

5. South Korea has witnessed the world's most dramatic growth of Christian congregations; church membership is expanding by 6.6 percent a year, fully two-thirds of the growth <u>coming from conversions rather than the population increasing</u>.

   (A) coming from conversions rather than the population increasing
   (B) coming from conversions rather than increases in the population
   (C) coming from conversions instead of the population's increasing
   (D) is from conversions instead of population increases
   (E) is from conversions rather than increasing the population

6. There is ample evidence, derived from the lore of traditional folk medicine, that naturally occurring antibiotics <u>are usually able to be modified to make them a more effective drug.</u>

   (A) are usually able to be modified to make them a more effective drug
   (B) are usually able to be modified to make them more effective drugs
   (C) are usually able to be modified, which makes them more effective drugs
   (D) can usually be modified to make them a more effective drug
   (E) can usually be modified to make them more effective drugs

7. Many investors base their choice <u>between bonds and stocks on comparing bond yields to</u> the dividends available on common stocks.

   (A) between bonds and stocks on comparing bond yields to
   (B) among bonds and stocks on comparisons of bond yields to
   (C) between bonds and stocks on comparisons of bond yields with
   (D) among bonds and stocks on comparing bond yields and
   (E) between bonds and stocks on comparing bond yields with

GO ON TO THE NEXT PAGE.

8. Some of the tenth-century stave churches of Norway are still standing, demonstrating that with sound design and maintenance, wooden buildings can last indefinitely.

   (A) standing, demonstrating that with sound design and maintenance, wooden buildings can last indefinitely
   (B) standing, demonstrating how wooden buildings, when they have sound design and maintenance, can last indefinitely
   (C) standing; they demonstrate if a wooden building has sound design and maintenance it can last indefinitely
   (D) standing, and they demonstrate wooden buildings can last indefinitely when there is sound design and maintenance
   (E) standing, and they demonstrate how a wooden building can last indefinitely when it has sound design and maintenance

9. In the United States, trade unions encountered far more intense opposition against their struggle for social legitimacy than the organized labor movements of most other democratic nations.

   (A) against their struggle for social legitimacy than
   (B) in their struggle for social legitimacy than did
   (C) against their struggle for social legitimacy as
   (D) in their struggle for social legitimacy as did
   (E) when they struggled for social legitimacy than has

10. For many people, household labor remains demanding even if able to afford household appliances their grandparents would find a miracle.

    (A) even if able to afford household appliances their grandparents would find a miracle
    (B) despite being able to afford household appliances their grandparents would find a miracle
    (C) even if they can afford household appliances their grandparents would have found miraculous
    (D) although they could afford household appliances their grandparents would find miraculous
    (E) even if they are able to afford household appliances which would have been a miracle to their grandparents

11. In the most common procedure for harvesting forage crops such as alfalfa, as much as 20 percent of the leaf and small-stem material, which is the most nutritious of all the parts of the plant, shattered and fell to the ground.

    (A) which is the most nutritious of all the parts of the plant, shattered and fell
    (B) the most nutritious of all parts of the plant, shatter and fall
    (C) the parts of the plant which were most nutritious, will shatter and fall
    (D) the most nutritious parts of the plant, shatters and falls
    (E) parts of the plant which are the most nutritious, have shattered and fallen

GO ON TO THE NEXT PAGE.

12. To ensure consistently high quality in its merchandise, the chain of retail stores became involved in every aspect of their suppliers' operations, dictating not only the number of stitches and the width of the hem in every garment as well as the profit margins of those suppliers.

    (A) their suppliers' operations, dictating not only the number of stitches and the width of the hem in every garment as well as
    (B) its suppliers' operations, dictating not only the number of stitches and the width of the hem in every garment as well as
    (C) their suppliers' operations, dictating not only the number of stitches and the width of the hem in every garment but also
    (D) its suppliers' operations, dictating not only the number of stitches and the width of the hem in every garment but also
    (E) their suppliers' operations, dictating the number of stitches, the width of the hem in every garment, and

13. The medieval scholar made almost no attempt to investigate the anatomy of plants, their mechanisms of growth, nor the ways where each was related to the other.

    (A) nor the ways where each was related to the other
    (B) nor how each was related to some other
    (C) or the way where one is related to the next
    (D) or the ways in which they are related to one another
    (E) or the ways that each related to some other

14. Originally published in 1950, *Some Tame Gazelle* was Barbara Pym's first novel, but it does not read like an apprentice work.

    (A) does not read like an apprentice work
    (B) seems not to read as an apprentice work
    (C) does not seem to read as an apprentice work would
    (D) does not read like an apprentice work does
    (E) reads unlike an apprentice work

15. By installing special electric pumps, farmers' houses could be heated by the warmth from cows' milk, according to one agricultural engineer.

    (A) farmers' houses could be heated by the warmth from cows' milk, according to one agricultural engineer
    (B) the warmth from cows' milk could be used by farmers to heat their houses, according to one agricultural engineer
    (C) one agricultural engineer reports that farmers could use the warmth from cows' milk to heat their houses
    (D) farmers, according to one agricultural engineer, could use the warmth from cows' milk to heat their houses
    (E) one agricultural engineer reports that farmers' houses could be heated by the warmth from cows' milk

16. In the traditional Japanese household, most clothing could be packed flatly, and so it was not necessary to have elaborate closet facilities.

    (A) flatly, and so it was not necessary to have elaborate closet facilities
    (B) flat, and so elaborate closet facilities were unnecessary
    (C) flatly, and so there was no necessity for elaborate closet facilities
    (D) flat, there being no necessity for elaborate closet facilities
    (E) flatly, as no elaborate closet facilities were necessary

GO ON TO THE NEXT PAGE.

17. The unskilled workers at the Allenby plant realized that their hourly rate of $4.11 to $4.75 was better than many nearby factory wages.

    (A) many nearby factory wages
    (B) many wages in nearby factories
    (C) what are offered by many nearby factories
    (D) it is in many nearby factories
    (E) that offered by many nearby factories

18. Since 1970 the number of Blacks elected to state and federal offices in the United States has multiplied nearly four times.

    (A) has multiplied nearly four times
    (B) has almost quadrupled
    (C) has almost multiplied by four
    (D) is almost four times as great
    (E) is nearly fourfold what it was

19. India is a country with at least fifty major regional languages, of whom fourteen have official recognition.

    (A) of whom fourteen have official recognition
    (B) fourteen that have official recognition
    (C) fourteen of which are officially recognized
    (D) fourteen that are officially recognized
    (E) among whom fourteen have official recognition

20. Wind resistance created by opening windows while driving results in a fuel penalty as great or greater than is incurred by using air conditioning.

    (A) as great or greater than is incurred by using air conditioning
    (B) that is as great or greater than is incurred using air conditioning
    (C) as great as or greater than that of using air conditioning
    (D) at least as great as air conditioning's
    (E) at least as great as that incurred by using air conditioning

21. At the time of the Mexican agrarian revolution, the most radical faction, that of Zapata and his followers, proposed a return to communal ownership of land, to what had been a pre-Columbian form of ownership respected by the Spaniards.

    (A) land, to what had been a pre-Columbian form of ownership respected by the Spaniards
    (B) land, a form of ownership of the pre-Columbians and respected by the Spaniards
    (C) land, respected by the Spaniards and a pre-Columbian form of ownership
    (D) land in which a pre-Columbian form of ownership was respected by the Spaniards
    (E) land that had been a pre-Columbian form of ownership respected by the Spaniards

GO ON TO THE NEXT PAGE.

-329-

22. Even though Béla Bartók's music has proved less popular than Igor Stravinsky's and less influential than Arnold Schönberg's, it is no less important.

    (A) Stravinsky's and less influential than Arnold Schönberg's, it
    (B) Stravinsky's and less influential than Arnold Schönberg's, he
    (C) Stravinsky's is and less influential than Arnold Schönberg's is, it
    (D) Stravinsky and not as influential as Arnold Schönberg, he
    (E) Stravinsky and not as influential as Arnold Schönberg, it

23. According to United States Air Force officials, a cannon shooting dead chickens at airplanes has proved helpful to demonstrate what kind of damage can result when jets fly into a flock of large birds.

    (A) shooting dead chickens at airplanes has proved helpful to demonstrate
    (B) shooting dead chickens at airplanes has proved itself helpful as a demonstration of
    (C) shooting dead chickens at airplanes proves itself helpful as demonstrating
    (D) that shoots dead chickens at airplanes proves itself helpful to demonstrate
    (E) that shoots dead chickens at airplanes has proved helpful in demonstrating

24. In his eagerness to find a city worthy of Priam, the German archaeologist Schliemann cut through Troy and uncovered a civilization a thousand years older as was the city Homer's heroes knew.

    (A) older as was the city Homer's heroes knew
    (B) more ancient than the city known to Homer's heroes
    (C) older than was the city known to Homer's heroes
    (D) more ancient of a city than Homer's heroes knew
    (E) older of a city than was the one known to Homer's heroes

25. To speak habitually of the "truly needy" is gradually instilling the notion that many of those who are just called "needy" actually have adequate resources; such a conclusion is unwarranted.

    (A) To speak habitually of the "truly needy" is gradually instilling the notion
    (B) To speak habitually of the "truly needy" is instilling the notion gradually
    (C) To speak habitually of the "truly needy" is gradually to instill the notion
    (D) Speaking habitually of the "truly needy" is to instill the gradual notion
    (E) Speaking habitually of the "truly needy" is instilling the gradual notion

S T O P

IF YOU FINISH BEFORE TIME IS CALLED, YOU MAY CHECK YOUR WORK ON THIS SECTION ONLY.
DO NOT TURN TO ANY OTHER SECTION IN THE TEST.

Answer Key for Sample Test Section 5

SENTENCE CORRECTION

1. E	14. A
2. B	15. D
3. D	16. B
4. A	17. E
5. B	18. B
6. E	19. C
7. C	20. E
8. A	21. A
9. B	22. A
10. C	23. E
11. D	24. B
12. D	25. C
13. D	

Explanatory Material: Sentence Correction Sample Test Section 5

1. The sale of government surplus machinery <u>will begin at 9 a.m. and continue until the supply lasts</u>.

   (A) will begin at 9 a.m. and continue until the supply lasts
   (B) begins at 9 a.m., continuing until the supply lasts
   (C) will begin at 9 a.m. and, until the supply lasts, will continue
   (D) begins at 9 a.m. and, as long as the supply may last, it continues
   (E) will begin at 9 a.m. and continue as long as the supply lasts

In A, B, and C, the phrase *until the supply lasts* is illogical. *Until* means "up to but not beyond a certain time"; it could indicate the time at which the sale will end, but not the condition (*the supply lasts*) that allows it to continue. Choices D and E correctly use *as long as* rather than *until,* but, in addition to being awkward, D contains errors in its verb forms. The use of *may last* to suggest a possibility is inappropriate, since the supply will last for a certain period of time. Also, the present tense *continues* fails to indicate that the sale will continue beyond 9 a.m. In E, the best choice, *will* refers both to *begin* and *continue.*

2. In England the well-dressed <u>gentleman of the eighteenth century protected their clothing while having their wig powdered by poking their head</u> through a device that resembled the stocks.

   (A) gentleman of the eighteenth century protected their clothing while having their wig powdered by poking their head
   (B) gentleman of the eighteenth century protected his clothing while having his wig powdered by poking his head
   (C) gentleman of the eighteenth century protected their clothing while having their wigs powdered by poking their heads
   (D) gentlemen of the eighteenth century protected his clothing while having his wig powdered by poking his head
   (E) gentlemen of the eighteenth century protected their clothing while having his wig powdered by poking his head

In A, C, D, and E, pronouns do not agree with the nouns to which they refer. In A and C, the plural *their* refers incorrectly to the singular *gentleman,* while in D and E, the singular *his* refers incorrectly to the plural *gentlemen.* Only in B do all the pronouns agree with all the nouns. Choice B is the best answer.

3. <u>Reared apart from each other, a recent United States study showed striking similarities in identical twins, including many idiosyncrasies of behavior.</u>

   (A) Reared apart from each other, a recent United States study showed striking similarities in identical twins, including many idiosyncrasies of behavior.
   (B) Reared apart from each other, striking similarities between identical twins that include many idiosyncrasies of behavior were shown in a recent United States study.
   (C) A recent United States study showed striking similarities in identical twins reared apart from each other that include many idiosyncrasies of behavior.
   (D) According to a recent United States study, identical twins reared apart from each other showed striking similarities, including many idiosyncrasies of behavior.
   (E) According to a recent United States study, identical twins showed striking similarities reared apart from each other, including many idiosyncrasies of behavior.

Choices A, B, C, and E all contain errors of modification. The phrase *reared apart from each other* is intended to describe the twins, but grammatically it modifies the nearest noun phrase. Thus, in A, it illogically describes *a recent study,* and, in B and E, it illogically describes *striking similarities.* In C, the adjective clause *that include many idiosyncrasies of behavior* is awkwardly and confusingly separated from its antecedent, *similarities.* Only D, the best choice, presents a logical and clear statement.

4. Developing nations in various parts of the world have amassed $700 billion in debts; at stake, <u>should a significant number of these debts be repudiated, is</u> the solvency of some of the world's largest multinational banks.

   (A) should a significant number of these debts be repudiated, is
   (B) should a significant number of these debts be repudiated, are
   (C) should they repudiate a significant number of these debts, are
   (D) if there is a repudiation of a significant number of these debts, would be
   (E) if a significant number of these debts will be repudiated, is

Choice A correctly presents both the singular verb (*is*) for the singular subject (*solvency*) and the subjunctive verb form for a situation that might happen but has not yet happened (*should a significant number. . .be repudiated*). Choices B and C mistakenly pair the plural verb (*are*) with the singular subject (*solvency*), and the pronoun reference in C is awkward because other plural nouns intrude between *they* and its antecedent, *nations*. In D, the use of the conditional (*if there is. . .would be*) is incorrect: since the solvency of the banks *is* at stake, it is incorrect to state that the solvency *would be* at stake. Choice E wrongly uses the future tense (*will be repudiated*) to indicate what is, in the context of the sentence, merely a possibility.

5. South Korea has witnessed the world's most dramatic growth of Christian congregations; church membership is expanding by 6.6 percent a year, fully two-thirds of the growth <u>coming from conversions rather than the population increasing</u>.

   (A) coming from conversions rather than the population increasing
   (B) coming from conversions rather than increases in the population
   (C) coming from conversions instead of the population's increasing
   (D) is from conversions instead of population increases
   (E) is from conversions rather than increasing the population

The terms of the contrast established by the underlined portion of the sentence (from x rather than y) are equivalent in kind and importance, and should therefore be presented in parallel grammatical form. In this sentence, the object of the preposition *from* is a simple noun, *conversions*. To maintain parallelism, *conversions* should be matched with another simple noun rather than the participle (*increasing*) that appears in A, C, and E. The presence of the verb *is* in D and E results in comma splices, and therefore run-on sentences, because the comma after *year* is not alone sufficient to join two independent clauses. Choice B, the best choice, correctly uses a participle, *coming,* in a subordinate construction, and also matches *conversions* with the noun *increases*.

6. There is ample evidence, derived from the lore of traditional folk medicine, that naturally occurring antibiotics <u>are usually able to be modified to make them a more effective drug</u>.

   (A) are usually able to be modified to make them a more effective drug
   (B) are usually able to be modified to make them more effective drugs
   (C) are usually able to be modified, which makes them more effective drugs
   (D) can usually be modified to make them a more effective drug
   (E) can usually be modified to make them more effective drugs

Choices A, B, and C unidiomatically describe the antibiotics as having abilities; in A, moreover, *a. . .drug* does not agree in number with *them* (meaning *antibiotics*). In C, the word *which* refers awkwardly and imprecisely to the action denoted by an entire clause. Choice D correctly states that the antibiotics *can. . .be modified,* but *drug* does not agree in number with *antibiotics* and *them*. Choice E is the best answer for this question.

7. Many investors base their choice <u>between bonds and stocks on comparing bond yields to</u> the dividends available on common stocks.

   (A) between bonds and stocks on comparing bond yields to
   (B) among bonds and stocks on comparisons of bond yields to
   (C) between bonds and stocks on comparisons of bond yields with
   (D) among bonds and stocks on comparing bond yields and
   (E) between bonds and stocks on comparing bond yields with

Choice C is the best answer. Choosing A, D, or E produces the phrase *base their choice. . .on comparing*, which is unidiomatic and imprecise; *on comparisons* correctly completes the construction begun by *base their choice*. The use of *among* in B and D is also incorrect; *among* is used with three or more things, but the investors have only two options—bonds and stocks. Choice C uses the appropriate preposition, *between,* to refer to the investors' options, and also uses the appropriate preposition, *with,* to describe the comparison the investors make: "to compare x *to* y" is to stress the similarities of x and y, but "to compare x *with* y" is to stress their differences.

8. Some of the tenth-century stave churches of Norway are still <u>standing, demonstrating that with sound design and maintenance, wooden buildings can last indefinitely</u>.

   (A) standing, demonstrating that with sound design and maintenance, wooden buildings can last indefinitely
   (B) standing, demonstrating how wooden buildings, when they have sound design and maintenance, can last indefinitely
   (C) standing; they demonstrate if a wooden building has sound design and maintenance it can last indefinitely
   (D) standing, and they demonstrate wooden buildings can last indefinitely when there is sound design and maintenance
   (E) standing, and they demonstrate how a wooden building can last indefinitely when it has sound design and maintenance

Choice A is best. In B and E, the use of *how* is unidiomatic: the fact that the churches are standing demonstrates *that* such buildings can last, not *how* they can last. Choices B, C, and E state awkwardly that buildings can "have" *maintenance*. In D, the wording of the clause *when there is sound design and maintenance* is especially vague. In C and E, the shift from the plural *churches* and *they* to the singular *building* and *it* is distracting and unnecessary.

9. In the United States, trade unions encountered far more intense opposition <u>against their struggle for social legitimacy than</u> the organized labor movements of most other democratic nations.

   (A) against their struggle for social legitimacy than
   (B) in their struggle for social legitimacy than did
   (C) against their struggle for social legitimacy as
   (D) in their struggle for social legitimacy as did
   (E) when they struggled for social legitimacy than has

In A and C, *against* is awkward and redundant because the idea of the resistance met by the trade unions is already established by the phrase *encountered. . .opposition*. Additionally, the failure in A and C to include *did* makes the comparisons in those choices incomplete, allowing the misreading that trade unions in the United States encountered the organized labor movements of other nations. Choices C and D both incorrectly use *more. . .as* to make a comparison; the idiomatic form of this expression is "more x than y." Choice B is best, both idiomatic and unambiguous. Choice E is awkward, and the singular verb *has* does not agree with the plural subject of the clause, *labor movements*.

10. For many people, household labor remains demanding <u>even if able to afford household appliances their grandparents would find a miracle</u>.

    (A) even if able to afford household appliances their grandparents would find a miracle
    (B) despite being able to afford household appliances their grandparents would find a miracle
    (C) even if they can afford household appliances their grandparents would have found miraculous
    (D) although they could afford household appliances their grandparents would find miraculous
    (E) even if they are able to afford household appliances which would have been a miracle to their grandparents

Choices A and B are imprecise because they do not say who is able to afford appliances. In fact, the wording of B suggests that it is *household labor* that can afford them. In D, *although* is less precise than *even if* in stating the relationship between the ideas that household labor is demanding and that people can afford household appliances. Also, in A, B, and D, the verb used with *grandparents* must show past action for the sentence to make sense: *would find* is therefore incorrect. The wordy and awkward choice E needlessly switches noun number from the plural *appliances* to the singular *a miracle*. Choice C is the best answer.

11. In the most common procedure for harvesting forage crops such as alfalfa, as much as 20 percent of the leaf and small-stem material, <u>which is the most nutritious of all the parts of the plant, shattered and fell</u> to the ground.

    (A) which is the most nutritious of all the parts of the plant, shattered and fell
    (B) the most nutritious of all parts of the plant, shatter and fall
    (C) the parts of the plant which were most nutritious, will shatter and fall
    (D) the most nutritious parts of the plant, shatters and falls
    (E) parts of the plant which are the most nutritious, have shattered and fallen

Making a factual statement about a regularly repeated occurrence—in this case, the harvesting of crops—requires conjugated verbs in the simple present tense. Choice A uses the past (*shattered and fell*), C the future (*will shatter and fall*), and E the past perfect (*have shattered and fallen*). Choice B uses the present, but the verbs *shatter and fall* do not agree in number with the singular subject, *20 percent*. Choice A contains an additional error of agreement (*the leaf and small-stem material. . .is*), and C contains an additional error of tense (*were most nutritious*). Only D, the best answer, matches the subject with verbs appropriate in tense and number: *as much as 20 percent. . .shatters and falls*. D is also the most concise choice.

12. To ensure consistently high quality in its merchandise, the chain of retail stores became involved in every aspect of their suppliers' operations, dictating not only the number of stitches and the width of the hem in every garment as well as the profit margins of those suppliers.

    (A) their suppliers' operations, dictating not only the number of stitches and the width of the hem in every garment as well as
    (B) its suppliers' operations, dictating not only the number of stitches and the width of the hem in every garment as well as
    (C) their suppliers' operations, dictating not only the number of stitches and the width of the hem in every garment but also
    (D) its suppliers' operations, dictating not only the number of stitches and the width of the hem in every garment but also
    (E) their suppliers' operations, dictating the number of stitches, the width of the hem in every garment, and

In A, C, and E, the pronoun (*their*) does not agree in number with the noun (*chain*) to which it refers. Choices A and B do not properly complete the construction beginning with *not only:* the correct version of the sentence should contain the phrase *not only. . .but also.* The best choice for this question is D.

13. The medieval scholar made almost no attempt to investigate the anatomy of plants, their mechanisms of growth, nor the ways where each was related to the other.

    (A) nor the ways where each was related to the other
    (B) nor how each was related to some other
    (C) or the way where one is related to the next
    (D) or the ways in which they are related to one another
    (E) or the ways that each related to some other

Choice D is the best answer. Choices A and B incorrectly use the conjunction *nor* to connect elements in an expression that begins with *no*. Since *no* negates all of the activities listed, the correct form in this sentence is "no attempt to investigate x, y, *or* z." Choices A, B, and E inappropriately use the past tense; although the scholar's studies were conducted in the past, the relatedness of the plants is a condition that continues into the present and should be described in the present tense. Finally, all the choices except D are awkward and unidiomatic, and they shift unnecessarily from a plural noun (*plants*) to a singular pronoun (*each* in A, B, and E, and *one* in C).

14. Originally published in 1950, *Some Tame Gazelle* was Barbara Pym's first novel, but it does not read like an apprentice work.

    (A) does not read like an apprentice work
    (B) seems not to read as an apprentice work
    (C) does not seem to read as an apprentice work would
    (D) does not read like an apprentice work does
    (E) reads unlike an apprentice work

Choice A is best, for it uses the comparative preposition *like* properly in stating a comparison between *it* (Pym's first novel) and *an apprentice work*. In B, *as* inappropriately suggests the meaning, "in the capacity of an apprentice work." Choices C and D wrongly attribute the act of reading to the book itself rather than to the reader. The use of *unlike* in E is unidiomatic: *unlike* can negate only the noun phrase *apprentice work*, but *not* is needed to negate the condition expressed by the verb phrase *read like an apprentice work*.

15. By installing special electric pumps, farmers' houses could be heated by the warmth from cows' milk, according to one agricultural engineer.

    (A) farmers' houses could be heated by the warmth from cows' milk, according to one agricultural engineer
    (B) the warmth from cows' milk could be used by farmers to heat their houses, according to one agricultural engineer
    (C) one agricultural engineer reports that farmers could use the warmth from cows' milk to heat their houses
    (D) farmers, according to one agricultural engineer, could use the warmth from cows' milk to heat their houses
    (E) one agricultural engineer reports that farmers' houses could be heated by the warmth from cows' milk

The introductory phrase *By installing special electric pumps* modifies the subject of the sentence—who or what installs the pumps. For clarity, this subject should be the noun closest to the modifier. None of the subjects in A, B, C, or E is the intended subject of the modifier: A illogically suggests that *farmers' houses* install the pumps; B suggests that *the warmth from cows milk* installs the pumps; C and E falsely attribute this action to the agricultural engineer. Logically, the farmers would install the pumps. Only D, the best answer, makes this clear by using *farmers* as the subject of the sentence and positioning it immediately after the modifier.

16. In the traditional Japanese household, most clothing could be packed flatly, and so it was not necessary to have elaborate closet facilities.

    (A) flatly, and so it was not necessary to have elaborate closet facilities
    (B) flat, and so elaborate closet facilities were unnecessary
    (C) flatly, and so there was no necessity for elaborate closet facilities
    (D) flat, there being no necessity for elaborate closet facilities
    (E) flatly, as no elaborate closet facilities were necessary

The best answer will begin with an adjective (*flat*) to describe the noun (*clothing*); A, C, and E begin with an adverb (*flatly*) that describes the act of packing rather than the arrangement of the clothing. Choices D and E do not correctly state the cause-and-effect relationship between the way in which clothes are packed and the need for closet facilities, suggesting instead that clothes are packed flat because closets are not necessary. Choice B, which contains both the adjective *flat* and the appropriate statement of cause-and-effect, *and so,* is the best answer.

17. The unskilled workers at the Allenby plant realized that their hourly rate of $4.11 to $4.75 was better than many nearby factory wages.

   (A) many nearby factory wages
   (B) many wages in nearby factories
   (C) what are offered by many nearby factories
   (D) it is in many nearby factories
   (E) that offered by many nearby factories

To be clear and logical, comparisons should be made between like items. Choices A and B, however, compare an hourly rate of pay not with another rate, but with actual *wages*. These choices are also imprecise in that *many* modifies *wages* rather than *factories*. In C, *what* is imprecise as a substitute for *hourly rate,* and in D *it* refers illogically to the Allenby workers' rate, which cannot be said to be in. . .nearby *factories*. Both choices illogically shift from the past tense in one part of the comparison to the present tense in the other part; C compounds this error by using a plural rather than a singular verb. Choice E is best because it uses the correct pronoun, *that,* and does not introduce inconsistencies of tense.

18. Since 1970 the number of Blacks elected to state and federal offices in the United States has multiplied nearly four times.

   (A) has multiplied nearly four times
   (B) has almost quadrupled
   (C) has almost multiplied by four
   (D) is almost four times as great
   (E) is nearly fourfold what it was

The best choice for this sentence will be the one that most accurately and idiomatically conveys the information that a number is now nearly four times greater than it was in 1970. Choice A inaccurately speaks of the number as having *multiplied nearly four times*; this phrase does not express the intended meaning, that the number has been multiplied by a factor of nearly four. Choice C speaks of the number as having *almost multiplied*. D does not complete the comparison by specifying what the number is *almost four times as great* as. In E, the present tense *is* cannot describe action that has occurred over a period of years; also, *what it was* is redundant because the starting point for the comparison is established by the phrase *Since 1970*. Choice B is the best answer for this question.

19. India is a country with at least fifty major regional languages, of whom fourteen have official recognition.

   (A) of whom fourteen have official recognition
   (B) fourteen that have official recognition
   (C) fourteen of which are officially recognized
   (D) fourteen that are officially recognized
   (E) among whom fourteen have official recognition

The use of *whom* in A and E is incorrect; *whom* refers to people, but the referent of the pronoun in this sentence is *languages*. The pronoun *which* refers to things and is idiomatic as the object of the preposition *of*; *of* helps to indicate that the fourteen officially recognized languages are part of the larger group of the fifty regional languages, and so should be retained. D wrongly uses *that* rather than *of which*. The phrase *have official recognition* in A, B, and E makes those choices unidiomatic: languages are described not as having recognition but rather as being recognized. Choice C, the best answer, is grammatically and idiomatically correct.

20. Wind resistance created by opening windows while driving results in a fuel penalty as great or greater than is incurred by using air conditioning.

   (A) as great or greater than is incurred by using air conditioning
   (B) that is as great or greater than is incurred using air conditioning
   (C) as great as or greater than that of using air conditioning
   (D) at least as great as air conditioning's
   (E) at least as great as that incurred by using air conditioning

The corrected sentence should compare the fuel penalty incurred by opening windows while driving with the fuel penalty incurred by using air conditioning. Choices A and B are grammatically incomplete: *as great* must be *as great as*. Also, the noun phrase *fuel penalty* must be compared to a noun or pronoun; changing *is incurred* to *that incurred* would supply the missing element. Although C sets up the comparison correctly, *as great as or greater than* is needlessly wordy, and *of using air conditioning* is imprecise. In choices D and E, *at least as great as* expresses the comparison between fuel penalties succinctly. In D, however, *air conditioning's* does not indicate that a fuel penalty results from the *use* of air conditioning. Choice E is best.

21. At the time of the Mexican agrarian revolution, the most radical faction, that of Zapata and his followers, proposed a return to communal ownership of land, to what had been a pre-Columbian form of ownership respected by the Spaniards.

   (A) land, to what had been a pre-Columbian form of ownership respected by the Spaniards
   (B) land, a form of ownership of the pre-Columbians and respected by the Spaniards
   (C) land, respected by the Spaniards and a pre-Columbian form of ownership
   (D) land in which a pre-Columbian form of ownership was respected by the Spaniards
   (E) land that had been a pre-Columbian form of ownership respected by the Spaniards

Choice A is the best answer. In A, the meaning of *communal ownership of land* is clearly and logically amplified by a parallel noun phrase also introduced by *to*. Choice B contains an ambiguous construction that leaves it unclear whether *form of ownership of the pre-Columbians* means "*form. . .of ownership associated with*" or "*form of owning the pre-Columbians*"; B can also be faulted for an illogical *and* before *respected*. Choices C, D, and E all follow *land* with phra…s that can be read either as inappropriately referring to *land* or as awkwardly referring to *ownership*.

22. Even though Béla Bartók's music has proved less popular than Igor <u>Stravinsky's and less influential than Arnold Schönberg's, it</u> is no less important.

    (A) Stravinsky's and less influential than Arnold Schönberg's, it
    (B) Stravinsky's and less influential than Arnold Schönberg's, he
    (C) Stravinsky's is and less influential than Arnold Schönberg's is, it
    (D) Stravinsky and not as influential as Arnold Schönberg, he
    (E) Stravinsky and not as influential as Arnold Schönberg, it

Choice A correctly compares the music of the three composers mentioned. In D and E, the music of Bartók is illogically compared to the other two composers themselves. The pronoun *he* in B and D is incorrect because the subject of the sentence the pronoun refers to is Bartók's music, not Bartók. Choice C is wordy and awkward.

23. According to United States Air Force officials, a cannon <u>shooting dead chickens at airplanes has proved helpful to demonstrate</u> what kind of damage can result when jets fly into a flock of large birds.

    (A) shooting dead chickens at airplanes has proved helpful to demonstrate
    (B) shooting dead chickens at airplanes has proved itself helpful as a demonstration of
    (C) shooting dead chickens at airplanes proves itself helpful as demonstrating
    (D) that shoots dead chickens at airplanes proves itself helpful to demonstrate
    (E) that shoots dead chickens at airplanes has proved helpful in demonstrating

Choice A is incorrect because *a cannon shooting* imprecisely suggests either an event, the shooting of dead chickens at airplanes, or what appears to be intended, a description of the cannon that specifies its use. Choices B and C also include this error. In addition, choices A, C, and D use unidiomatic constructions, *to demonstrate* and *as demonstrating*, after *helpful*, rather than the correct *in demonstrating*. The phrase *as a demonstration of* in choice B is idiomatic but inappropriate because it suggests a single event rather than a

purpose. Choices B, C, and D all introduce an unnecessary *itself* as well, and C and D wrongly use the present tense *proves* rather than *has proved* to indicate recently completed action. The best answer is choice E.

24. In his eagerness to find a city worthy of Priam, the German archaeologist Schliemann cut through Troy and uncovered a civilization a thousand years <u>older as was the city Homer's heroes knew</u>.

    (A) older as was the city Homer's heroes knew
    (B) more ancient than the city known to Homer's heroes
    (C) older than was the city known to Homer's heroes
    (D) more ancient of a city than Homer's heroes knew
    (E) older of a city than was the one known to Homer's heroes

Choice A is incorrect. The correct word following the comparative form of an adjective such as *older* is *than*, not *as*. Because the more ancient civilization continues to be a thousand years more ancient than Troy, it is incorrect to use the past tense *was* as choices A, C, and E do. Choices D and E also include an ungrammatical structure that follows the comparative form of an adjective with *of*. The best answer is B.

25. <u>To speak habitually of the "truly needy" is gradually instilling the notion</u> that many of those who are just called "needy" actually have adequate resources; such a conclusion is unwarranted.

    (A) To speak habitually of the "truly needy" is gradually instilling the notion
    (B) To speak habitually of the "truly needy" is instilling the notion gradually
    (C) To speak habitually of the "truly needy" is gradually to instill the notion
    (D) Speaking habitually of the "truly needy" is to instill the gradual notion
    (E) Speaking habitually of the "truly needy" is instilling the gradual notion

The correct form of the sentence requires parallel infinitive phrases in the form "to x is to y." Choices A, B, and D fail to provide one or the other of the *to* structures. Choice E abandons the infinitive parallelism entirely and substitutes a construction that awkwardly and unidiomatically makes *speaking. . ."needy"* the grammatical subject of *instilling*. Both choices D and E use *gradual* instead of *gradually* and position it before *notion* so that it appears that the notion itself, rather than the instilling of the notion, is what is gradual. The best answer is choice C.

8 An Authentic Graduate Management Admission Test

The test that follows is a Graduate Management Admission test that has been slightly modified. This specific test was administered in October 1988. The actual test book contained seven sections, one of which consisted of trial questions that were not counted in the scoring. Those trial questions have been omitted from the test. Also, the total testing time for the test reproduced here is three hours; the actual test took about three and a half hours. All actual GMAT tests contain seven sections, and the total test time is three and a half hours.

Taking this test will help you become acquainted with testing procedures and requirements and thereby approach the real test with more assurance. Therefore, you should try to take this test under conditions similar to those in an actual test administration, observing the time limitations, and thinking about each question seriously.

The facsimile of the response portion of a GMAT answer sheet on page 339 may be used for marking your answers to the test. After you have taken the test, compare your answers with the correct ones on page 379 and determine your scores using the information that follows the answer key.

Answer Sheet

Section 1

1 Ⓐ Ⓑ Ⓒ Ⓓ Ⓔ
2 Ⓐ Ⓑ Ⓒ Ⓓ Ⓔ
3 Ⓐ Ⓑ Ⓒ Ⓓ Ⓔ
4 Ⓐ Ⓑ Ⓒ Ⓓ Ⓔ
5 Ⓐ Ⓑ Ⓒ Ⓓ Ⓔ
6 Ⓐ Ⓑ Ⓒ Ⓓ Ⓔ
7 Ⓐ Ⓑ Ⓒ Ⓓ Ⓔ
8 Ⓐ Ⓑ Ⓒ Ⓓ Ⓔ
9 Ⓐ Ⓑ Ⓒ Ⓓ Ⓔ
10 Ⓐ Ⓑ Ⓒ Ⓓ Ⓔ
11 Ⓐ Ⓑ Ⓒ Ⓓ Ⓔ
12 Ⓐ Ⓑ Ⓒ Ⓓ Ⓔ
13 Ⓐ Ⓑ Ⓒ Ⓓ Ⓔ
14 Ⓐ Ⓑ Ⓒ Ⓓ Ⓔ
15 Ⓐ Ⓑ Ⓒ Ⓓ Ⓔ
16 Ⓐ Ⓑ Ⓒ Ⓓ Ⓔ
17 Ⓐ Ⓑ Ⓒ Ⓓ Ⓔ
18 Ⓐ Ⓑ Ⓒ Ⓓ Ⓔ
19 Ⓐ Ⓑ Ⓒ Ⓓ Ⓔ
20 Ⓐ Ⓑ Ⓒ Ⓓ Ⓔ
21 Ⓐ Ⓑ Ⓒ Ⓓ Ⓔ
22 Ⓐ Ⓑ Ⓒ Ⓓ Ⓔ
23 Ⓐ Ⓑ Ⓒ Ⓓ Ⓔ
24 Ⓐ Ⓑ Ⓒ Ⓓ Ⓔ
25 Ⓐ Ⓑ Ⓒ Ⓓ Ⓔ

Section 2

1 Ⓐ Ⓑ Ⓒ Ⓓ Ⓔ
2 Ⓐ Ⓑ Ⓒ Ⓓ Ⓔ
3 Ⓐ Ⓑ Ⓒ Ⓓ Ⓔ
4 Ⓐ Ⓑ Ⓒ Ⓓ Ⓔ
5 Ⓐ Ⓑ Ⓒ Ⓓ Ⓔ
6 Ⓐ Ⓑ Ⓒ Ⓓ Ⓔ
7 Ⓐ Ⓑ Ⓒ Ⓓ Ⓔ
8 Ⓐ Ⓑ Ⓒ Ⓓ Ⓔ
9 Ⓐ Ⓑ Ⓒ Ⓓ Ⓔ
10 Ⓐ Ⓑ Ⓒ Ⓓ Ⓔ
11 Ⓐ Ⓑ Ⓒ Ⓓ Ⓔ
12 Ⓐ Ⓑ Ⓒ Ⓓ Ⓔ
13 Ⓐ Ⓑ Ⓒ Ⓓ Ⓔ
14 Ⓐ Ⓑ Ⓒ Ⓓ Ⓔ
15 Ⓐ Ⓑ Ⓒ Ⓓ Ⓔ
16 Ⓐ Ⓑ Ⓒ Ⓓ Ⓔ
17 Ⓐ Ⓑ Ⓒ Ⓓ Ⓔ
18 Ⓐ Ⓑ Ⓒ Ⓓ Ⓔ
19 Ⓐ Ⓑ Ⓒ Ⓓ Ⓔ
20 Ⓐ Ⓑ Ⓒ Ⓓ Ⓔ
21 Ⓐ Ⓑ Ⓒ Ⓓ Ⓔ
22 Ⓐ Ⓑ Ⓒ Ⓓ Ⓔ
23 Ⓐ Ⓑ Ⓒ Ⓓ Ⓔ
24 Ⓐ Ⓑ Ⓒ Ⓓ Ⓔ
25 Ⓐ Ⓑ Ⓒ Ⓓ Ⓔ

Section 3

1 Ⓐ Ⓑ Ⓒ Ⓓ Ⓔ
2 Ⓐ Ⓑ Ⓒ Ⓓ Ⓔ
3 Ⓐ Ⓑ Ⓒ Ⓓ Ⓔ
4 Ⓐ Ⓑ Ⓒ Ⓓ Ⓔ
5 Ⓐ Ⓑ Ⓒ Ⓓ Ⓔ
6 Ⓐ Ⓑ Ⓒ Ⓓ Ⓔ
7 Ⓐ Ⓑ Ⓒ Ⓓ Ⓔ
8 Ⓐ Ⓑ Ⓒ Ⓓ Ⓔ
9 Ⓐ Ⓑ Ⓒ Ⓓ Ⓔ
10 Ⓐ Ⓑ Ⓒ Ⓓ Ⓔ
11 Ⓐ Ⓑ Ⓒ Ⓓ Ⓔ
12 Ⓐ Ⓑ Ⓒ Ⓓ Ⓔ
13 Ⓐ Ⓑ Ⓒ Ⓓ Ⓔ
14 Ⓐ Ⓑ Ⓒ Ⓓ Ⓔ
15 Ⓐ Ⓑ Ⓒ Ⓓ Ⓔ
16 Ⓐ Ⓑ Ⓒ Ⓓ Ⓔ
17 Ⓐ Ⓑ Ⓒ Ⓓ Ⓔ
18 Ⓐ Ⓑ Ⓒ Ⓓ Ⓔ
19 Ⓐ Ⓑ Ⓒ Ⓓ Ⓔ
20 Ⓐ Ⓑ Ⓒ Ⓓ Ⓔ
21 Ⓐ Ⓑ Ⓒ Ⓓ Ⓔ
22 Ⓐ Ⓑ Ⓒ Ⓓ Ⓔ
23 Ⓐ Ⓑ Ⓒ Ⓓ Ⓔ
24 Ⓐ Ⓑ Ⓒ Ⓓ Ⓔ
25 Ⓐ Ⓑ Ⓒ Ⓓ Ⓔ

Section 4

1 Ⓐ Ⓑ Ⓒ Ⓓ Ⓔ
2 Ⓐ Ⓑ Ⓒ Ⓓ Ⓔ
3 Ⓐ Ⓑ Ⓒ Ⓓ Ⓔ
4 Ⓐ Ⓑ Ⓒ Ⓓ Ⓔ
5 Ⓐ Ⓑ Ⓒ Ⓓ Ⓔ
6 Ⓐ Ⓑ Ⓒ Ⓓ Ⓔ
7 Ⓐ Ⓑ Ⓒ Ⓓ Ⓔ
8 Ⓐ Ⓑ Ⓒ Ⓓ Ⓔ
9 Ⓐ Ⓑ Ⓒ Ⓓ Ⓔ
10 Ⓐ Ⓑ Ⓒ Ⓓ Ⓔ
11 Ⓐ Ⓑ Ⓒ Ⓓ Ⓔ
12 Ⓐ Ⓑ Ⓒ Ⓓ Ⓔ
13 Ⓐ Ⓑ Ⓒ Ⓓ Ⓔ
14 Ⓐ Ⓑ Ⓒ Ⓓ Ⓔ
15 Ⓐ Ⓑ Ⓒ Ⓓ Ⓔ
16 Ⓐ Ⓑ Ⓒ Ⓓ Ⓔ
17 Ⓐ Ⓑ Ⓒ Ⓓ Ⓔ
18 Ⓐ Ⓑ Ⓒ Ⓓ Ⓔ
19 Ⓐ Ⓑ Ⓒ Ⓓ Ⓔ
20 Ⓐ Ⓑ Ⓒ Ⓓ Ⓔ
21 Ⓐ Ⓑ Ⓒ Ⓓ Ⓔ
22 Ⓐ Ⓑ Ⓒ Ⓓ Ⓔ
23 Ⓐ Ⓑ Ⓒ Ⓓ Ⓔ
24 Ⓐ Ⓑ Ⓒ Ⓓ Ⓔ
25 Ⓐ Ⓑ Ⓒ Ⓓ Ⓔ

Section 5

1 Ⓐ Ⓑ Ⓒ Ⓓ Ⓔ
2 Ⓐ Ⓑ Ⓒ Ⓓ Ⓔ
3 Ⓐ Ⓑ Ⓒ Ⓓ Ⓔ
4 Ⓐ Ⓑ Ⓒ Ⓓ Ⓔ
5 Ⓐ Ⓑ Ⓒ Ⓓ Ⓔ
6 Ⓐ Ⓑ Ⓒ Ⓓ Ⓔ
7 Ⓐ Ⓑ Ⓒ Ⓓ Ⓔ
8 Ⓐ Ⓑ Ⓒ Ⓓ Ⓔ
9 Ⓐ Ⓑ Ⓒ Ⓓ Ⓔ
10 Ⓐ Ⓑ Ⓒ Ⓓ Ⓔ
11 Ⓐ Ⓑ Ⓒ Ⓓ Ⓔ
12 Ⓐ Ⓑ Ⓒ Ⓓ Ⓔ
13 Ⓐ Ⓑ Ⓒ Ⓓ Ⓔ
14 Ⓐ Ⓑ Ⓒ Ⓓ Ⓔ
15 Ⓐ Ⓑ Ⓒ Ⓓ Ⓔ
16 Ⓐ Ⓑ Ⓒ Ⓓ Ⓔ
17 Ⓐ Ⓑ Ⓒ Ⓓ Ⓔ
18 Ⓐ Ⓑ Ⓒ Ⓓ Ⓔ
19 Ⓐ Ⓑ Ⓒ Ⓓ Ⓔ
20 Ⓐ Ⓑ Ⓒ Ⓓ Ⓔ
21 Ⓐ Ⓑ Ⓒ Ⓓ Ⓔ
22 Ⓐ Ⓑ Ⓒ Ⓓ Ⓔ
23 Ⓐ Ⓑ Ⓒ Ⓓ Ⓔ
24 Ⓐ Ⓑ Ⓒ Ⓓ Ⓔ
25 Ⓐ Ⓑ Ⓒ Ⓓ Ⓔ

Section 6

1 Ⓐ Ⓑ Ⓒ Ⓓ Ⓔ
2 Ⓐ Ⓑ Ⓒ Ⓓ Ⓔ
3 Ⓐ Ⓑ Ⓒ Ⓓ Ⓔ
4 Ⓐ Ⓑ Ⓒ Ⓓ Ⓔ
5 Ⓐ Ⓑ Ⓒ Ⓓ Ⓔ
6 Ⓐ Ⓑ Ⓒ Ⓓ Ⓔ
7 Ⓐ Ⓑ Ⓒ Ⓓ Ⓔ
8 Ⓐ Ⓑ Ⓒ Ⓓ Ⓔ
9 Ⓐ Ⓑ Ⓒ Ⓓ Ⓔ
10 Ⓐ Ⓑ Ⓒ Ⓓ Ⓔ
11 Ⓐ Ⓑ Ⓒ Ⓓ Ⓔ
12 Ⓐ Ⓑ Ⓒ Ⓓ Ⓔ
13 Ⓐ Ⓑ Ⓒ Ⓓ Ⓔ
14 Ⓐ Ⓑ Ⓒ Ⓓ Ⓔ
15 Ⓐ Ⓑ Ⓒ Ⓓ Ⓔ
16 Ⓐ Ⓑ Ⓒ Ⓓ Ⓔ
17 Ⓐ Ⓑ Ⓒ Ⓓ Ⓔ
18 Ⓐ Ⓑ Ⓒ Ⓓ Ⓔ
19 Ⓐ Ⓑ Ⓒ Ⓓ Ⓔ
20 Ⓐ Ⓑ Ⓒ Ⓓ Ⓔ
21 Ⓐ Ⓑ Ⓒ Ⓓ Ⓔ
22 Ⓐ Ⓑ Ⓒ Ⓓ Ⓔ
23 Ⓐ Ⓑ Ⓒ Ⓓ Ⓔ
24 Ⓐ Ⓑ Ⓒ Ⓓ Ⓔ
25 Ⓐ Ⓑ Ⓒ Ⓓ Ⓔ

Print your full name here:_____

(last)   (first)   (middle)

Graduate Management
Admission Test

SECTION 1

Time—30 minutes

25 Questions

Directions: Each passage in this group is followed by questions based on its content. After reading a passage, choose the best answer to each question and fill in the corresponding oval on the answer sheet. Answer all questions following a passage on the basis of what is stated or implied in that passage.

Between the eighth and eleventh centuries A.D., the Byzantine Empire staged an almost unparalleled economic and cultural revival, a recovery that is all the
Line more striking because it followed a long period of severe
(5) internal decline. By the early eighth century, the empire had lost roughly two-thirds of the territory it had possessed in the year 600, and its remaining area was being raided by Arabs and Bulgarians, who at times threatened to take Constantinople and extinguish the
(10) empire altogether. The wealth of the state and its subjects was greatly diminished, and artistic and literary production had virtually ceased. By the early eleventh century, however, the empire had regained almost half of its lost possessions, its new frontiers were secure, and its
(15) influence extended far beyond its borders. The economy had recovered, the treasury was full, and art and scholarship had advanced.

To consider the Byzantine military, cultural, and economic advances as differentiated aspects of a single
(20) phenomenon is reasonable. After all, these three forms of progress have gone together in a number of states and civilizations. Rome under Augustus and fifth-century Athens provide the most obvious examples in antiquity. Moreover, an examination of the apparent sequential
(25) connections among military, economic, and cultural forms of progress might help explain the dynamics of historical change.

The common explanation of these apparent connections in the case of Byzantium would run like this:
(30) when the empire had turned back enemy raids on its own territory and had begun to raid and conquer enemy territory, Byzantine resources naturally expanded and more money became available to patronize art and literature. Therefore, Byzantine military achievements led to
(35) economic advances, which in turn led to cultural revival.

No doubt this hypothetical pattern did apply at times during the course of the recovery. Yet it is not clear that military advances invariably came first, economic advances second, and intellectual advances third. In the
(40) 860's the Byzantine Empire began to recover from Arab incursions so that by 872 the military balance with the Abbasid Caliphate had been permanently altered in the empire's favor. The beginning of the empire's economic revival, however, can be placed between 810 and 830.
(45) Finally, the Byzantine revival of learning appears to have begun even earlier. A number of notable scholars and writers appeared by 788 and, by the last decade of the eighth century, a cultural revival was in full bloom, a revival that lasted until the fall of Constantinople in
(50) 1453. Thus the commonly expected order of military

revival followed by economic and then by cultural recovery was reversed in Byzantium. In fact, the revival of Byzantine learning may itself have influenced the subsequent economic and military expansion.

1. Which of the following best states the central idea of the passage?

    (A) The Byzantine Empire was a unique case in which the usual order of military and economic revival preceding cultural revival was reversed.

    (B) The economic, cultural, and military revival in the Byzantine Empire between the eighth and eleventh centuries was similar in its order to the sequence of revivals in Augustan Rome and fifth-century Athens.

    (C) After 810 Byzantine economic recovery spurred a military and, later, cultural expansion that lasted until 1453.

    (D) The eighth-century revival of Byzantine learning is an inexplicable phenomenon, and its economic and military precursors have yet to be discovered.

    (E) The revival of the Byzantine Empire between the eighth and eleventh centuries shows cultural rebirth preceding economic and military revival, the reverse of the commonly accepted order of progress.

2. The primary purpose of the second paragraph is which of the following?

    (A) To establish the uniqueness of the Byzantine revival

    (B) To show that Augustan Rome and fifth-century Athens are examples of cultural, economic, and military expansion against which all subsequent cases must be measured

    (C) To suggest that cultural, economic, and military advances have tended to be closely interrelated in different societies

    (D) To argue that, while the revivals of Augustan Rome and fifth-century Athens were similar, they are unrelated to other historical examples

    (E) To indicate that, wherever possible, historians should seek to make comparisons with the earliest chronological examples of revival

GO ON TO THE NEXT PAGE.

3. It can be inferred from the passage that by the eleventh century the Byzantine military forces

(A) had reached their peak and begun to decline
(B) had eliminated the Bulgarian army
(C) were comparable in size to the army of Rome under Augustus
(D) were strong enough to withstand the Abbasid Caliphate's military forces
(E) had achieved control of Byzantine governmental structures

4. It can be inferred from the passage that the Byzantine Empire sustained significant territorial losses

(A) in 600
(B) during the seventh century
(C) a century after the cultural achievements of the Byzantine Empire had been lost
(D) soon after the revival of Byzantine learning
(E) in the century after 873

5. In the third paragraph, the author most probably provides an explanation of the apparent connections among economic, military, and cultural development in order to

(A) suggest that the process of revival in Byzantium accords with this model
(B) set up an order of events that is then shown to be not generally applicable to the case of Byzantium
(C) cast aspersions on traditional historical scholarship about Byzantium
(D) suggest that Byzantium represents a case for which no historical precedent exists
(E) argue that military conquest is the paramount element in the growth of empires

6. Which of the following does the author mention as crucial evidence concerning the manner in which the Byzantine revival began?

(A) The Byzantine military revival of the 860's led to economic and cultural advances.
(B) The Byzantine cultural revival lasted until 1453.
(C) The Byzantine economic recovery began in the 900's.
(D) The revival of Byzantine learning began toward the end of the eighth century.
(E) By the early eleventh century the Byzantine Empire had regained much of its lost territory.

7. According to the author, "The common explanation" (line 28) of connections between economic, military, and cultural development is

(A) revolutionary and too new to have been applied to the history of the Byzantine Empire
(B) reasonable, but an antiquated theory of the nature of progress
(C) not applicable to the Byzantine revival as a whole, but does perhaps accurately describe limited periods during the revival
(D) equally applicable to the Byzantine case as a whole and to the history of military, economic, and cultural advances in ancient Greece and Rome
(E) essentially not helpful, because military, economic, and cultural advances are part of a single phenomenon

GO ON TO THE NEXT PAGE.

Virtually everything astronomers know about objects outside the solar system is based on the detection of photons—quanta of electromagnetic radiation. Yet there
Line
(5) is another form of radiation that permeates the universe: neutrinos. With (as its name implies) no electric charge, and negligible mass, the neutrino interacts with other particles so rarely that a neutrino can cross the entire universe, even traversing substantial aggregations of matter, without being absorbed or even deflected. Neu-
(10) trinos can thus escape from regions of space where light and other kinds of electromagnetic radiation are blocked by matter. Furthermore, neutrinos carry with them information about the site and circumstances of their production; therefore, the detection of cosmic neutrinos
(15) could provide new information about a wide variety of cosmic phenomena and about the history of the universe.

But how can scientists detect a particle that interacts so infrequently with other matter? Twenty-five years
(20) passed between Pauli's hypothesis that the neutrino existed and its actual detection; since then virtually all research with neutrinos has been with neutrinos created artificially in large particle accelerators and studied under neutrino microscopes. But a neutrino telescope,
(25) capable of detecting cosmic neutrinos, is difficult to construct. No apparatus can detect neutrinos unless it is extremely massive, because great mass is synonymous with huge numbers of nucleons (neutrons and protons), and the more massive the detector, the greater the prob-
(30) ability of one of its nucleon's reacting with a neutrino. In addition, the apparatus must be sufficiently shielded from the interfering effects of other particles.

Fortunately, a group of astrophysicists has proposed a means of detecting cosmic neutrinos by harnessing the
(35) mass of the ocean. Named DUMAND, for Deep Underwater Muon and Neutrino Detector, the project calls for placing an array of light sensors at a depth of five kilometers under the ocean surface. The detecting medium is the seawater itself: when a neutrino interacts with a
(40) particle in an atom of seawater, the result is a cascade of electrically charged particles and a flash of light that can be detected by the sensors. The five kilometers of seawater above the sensors will shield them from the interfering effects of other high-energy particles raining down
(45) through the atmosphere.

The strongest motivation for the DUMAND project is that it will exploit an important source of information about the universe. The extension of astronomy from visible light to radio waves to x-rays and gamma rays
(50) never failed to lead to the discovery of unusual objects such as radio galaxies, quasars, and pulsars. Each of these discoveries came as a surprise. Neutrino astronomy will doubtless bring its own share of surprises.

8. Which of the following titles best summarizes the passage as a whole?

(A) At the Threshold of Neutrino Astronomy
(B) Neutrinos and the History of the Universe
(C) The Creation and Study of Neutrinos
(D) The DUMAND System and How It Works
(E) The Properties of the Neutrino

9. With which of the following statements regarding neutrino astronomy would the author be most likely to agree?

(A) Neutrino astronomy will supersede all present forms of astronomy.
(B) Neutrino astronomy will be abandoned if the DUMAND project fails.
(C) Neutrino astronomy can be expected to lead to major breakthroughs in astronomy.
(D) Neutrino astronomy will disclose phenomena that will be more surprising than past discoveries.
(E) Neutrino astronomy will always be characterized by a large time lag between hypothesis and experimental confirmation.

10. In the last paragraph, the author describes the development of astronomy in order to

(A) suggest that the potential findings of neutrino astronomy can be seen as part of a series of astronomical successes
(B) illustrate the role of surprise in scientific discovery
(C) demonstrate the effectiveness of the DUMAND apparatus in detecting neutrinos
(D) name some cosmic phenomena that neutrino astronomy will illuminate
(E) contrast the motivation of earlier astronomers with that of the astrophysicists working on the DUMAND project

11. According to the passage, one advantage that neutrinos have for studies in astronomy is that they

(A) have been detected for the last twenty-five years
(B) possess a variable electric charge
(C) are usually extremely massive
(D) carry information about their history with them
(E) are very similar to other electromagnetic particles

GO ON TO THE NEXT PAGE.

12. According to the passage, the primary use of the apparatus mentioned in lines 24-32 would be to

(A) increase the mass of a neutrino
(B) interpret the information neutrinos carry with them
(C) study the internal structure of a neutrino
(D) see neutrinos in distant regions of space
(E) detect the presence of cosmic neutrinos

13. The passage states that interactions between neutrinos and other matter are

(A) rare
(B) artificial
(C) undetectable
(D) unpredictable
(E) hazardous

14. The passage mentions which of the following as a reason that neutrinos are hard to detect?

(A) Their pervasiveness in the universe
(B) Their ability to escape from different regions of space
(C) Their inability to penetrate dense matter
(D) The similarity of their structure to that of nucleons
(E) The infrequency of their interaction with other matter

15. According to the passage, the interaction of a neutrino with other matter can produce

(A) particles that are neutral and massive
(B) a form of radiation that permeates the universe
(C) inaccurate information about the site and circumstances of the neutrino's production
(D) charged particles and light
(E) a situation in which light and other forms of electromagnetic radiation are blocked

16. According to the passage, one of the methods used to establish the properties of neutrinos was

(A) detection of photons
(B) observation of the interaction of neutrinos with gamma rays
(C) observation of neutrinos that were artificially created
(D) measurement of neutrinos that interacted with particles of seawater
(E) experiments with electromagnetic radiation

GO ON TO THE NEXT PAGE.

Barbara Strozzi was a singer and composer of madrigals, arias, and cantatas published in Venice between 1644 and 1664. Her use of these vocal forms places her directly within the cantata tradition of the mid-seventeenth century, along with such major figures as Rossi, Carissimi, and Cesti. With the notable exception of Francesca Caccini (1587-c.1640), she is the only known woman among the many aria and cantata composers of seventeenth-century Italy, and is, presumably, among the very few women of the period to have pursued a career as a composer and to have achieved some measure of public recognition.

This historical distinction attracted attention to her works early in the present century, even when the music of most of her male contemporaries, and, indeed, most women composers of any era, remained relatively ignored. But appreciation of her style was limited by prevailing convention to an isolation of its supposedly feminine qualities: "great spontaneity, exquisite grace, marvelously fine taste." Such an appreciation now appears irrelevant as well as polemical in its incompleteness because we are in a better position—with regard to both historical knowledge and social awareness—to attempt a more precise evaluation of a somewhat anomalous figure like Barbara Strozzi.

Born in 1619 in Venice, she grew up in the home of Giulio Strozzi, a renowned poet and leading figure among Venetian intellectuals. Barbara's presence in Giulio's household guaranteed her an early and full exposure to Venetian musical and literary society. Indeed, she was able to enter a world that was, apparently, closed to other members of her sex. Similarly, Francesca Caccini, the most prominent and successful Italian woman composer of the period, was the daughter of professional musicians and therefore exposed to music from infancy. This parallel suggests that such an environment may have been essential for the development of a female composer.

But though Strozzi's music certainly shares fully the aesthetic aim of her contemporaries, and of the baroque in general—to move the passions—her life and her work distinguish her from these contemporaries in various ways. Whereas other composers sought (and found) a public forum for their affective expression in the theater and the Church, her world remained more private. Strozzi was a singer in Venice, surrounded by opera librettists and impresarios at a time when opera was the main cultural interest of a large segment of Venetian society, yet she apparently never sang in opera, nor did she write an opera. She is not a composer of dramatic works; her songs are addressed to a more intimate audience, expressing less the feeling of fictive characters than her own: "These harmonic notes," she writes, "are the language of the soul, and instruments of the heart."

17. According to the passage, Barbara Strozzi's music attracted attention early in the twentieth century because of

(A) its uniquely private character
(B) its influence on Francesca Caccini
(C) the scarcity of seventeenth-century women composers
(D) the unconventionality of its forms
(E) the historical importance of Giulio Strozzi

18. The author's use of the word "supposedly" in line 18 implies which of the following?

(A) The author doubts the historical authenticity of the quotation that follows.
(B) The author doubts the accuracy of the facts she is reporting.
(C) The author disagrees with the judgment she is discussing.
(D) The author does not believe that Strozzi's music has the qualities cited in the quotation.
(E) The author is not sure of the significance of the quotation.

19. With which of the following statements would the author of the passage be most likely to agree?

(A) The music of seventeenth-century Italy is less frequently performed today than it was 50 years ago.
(B) Contemporary music historians no longer discuss the music of a given composer in terms of its particular individual style.
(C) The cantata tradition of seventeenth-century Italy is much better understood today than it ever has been.
(D) Late-twentieth-century music historians have more accurate historical information than their early-twentieth-century counterparts.
(E) Music historians of the early twentieth century were uninterested in the details of social life in seventeenth-century Venetian musical circles.

GO ON TO THE NEXT PAGE.

20. The author of the passage bases her assertion that Strozzi is one of the very few seventeenth-century Italian women composers (lines 7-12) on which of the following assumptions?

    (A) Public recognition is an indispensable part of a career as a composer.
    (B) Strozzi and Caccini were influenced by the same composers.
    (C) The music of any woman composer whom her seventeenth-century contemporaries regarded as noteworthy would be known to modern scholars.
    (D) The cantata tradition of the mid-seventeenth century includes composers and performers of madrigals and arias as well as cantatas.
    (E) More women pursued careers as composers in seventeenth-century Italy than is evident from music published in the seventeenth century.

21. The author of the passage implies that which of the following was most essential to the success of both Francesca Caccini and Barbara Strozzi?

    (A) Their presence in Venice at a time when vocal music flourished
    (B) Their early firsthand exposure to music and musicians
    (C) The lack of competition from other composers
    (D) The popularity of madrigals and cantatas in seventeenth-century Italy
    (E) The uniqueness of the musical forms they created

22. It can be inferred from the passage that all of the following made Barbara Strozzi "a somewhat anomalous figure" (lines 24-25) EXCEPT:

    (A) She was a woman composer during the seventeenth century.
    (B) She was intimately involved in Venetian literary and musical society.
    (C) She did not write dramatic works for voice.
    (D) She did not perform operatic works.
    (E) She wrote moving baroque vocal works.

23. The author of the passage implies that composers of Italian baroque music typically

    (A) composed more operas than cantatas
    (B) preferred sacred to secular musical forms
    (C) aspired to reach large segments of the public with their works
    (D) avoided emotional expression in their works
    (E) wrote music for solo voices rather than for choral ensembles

24. The author of the passage quotes Barbara Strozzi in lines 53-54 most probably in order to

    (A) support the claim that Strozzi's works are self-revealing
    (B) qualify the point concerning Strozzi's dramatic works
    (C) illustrate Strozzi's confident approach to her art
    (D) show why Strozzi avoided opera as both composer and performer
    (E) suggest that Strozzi's viewpoint was typical of baroque musicians

25. The passage provides information to answer which of the following questions?

    (A) What was the exact family relationship between Giulio Strozzi and Barbara Strozzi?
    (B) What is the evidence that indicates that Barbara Strozzi never sang in an opera?
    (C) Were Barbara Strozzi's compositions known to her contemporaries?
    (D) Did Barbara Strozzi know Francesca Caccini?
    (E) What instruments provided the accompaniment for Barbara Strozzi's vocal works?

STOP

IF YOU FINISH BEFORE TIME IS CALLED, YOU MAY CHECK YOUR WORK ON THIS SECTION ONLY. DO NOT TURN TO ANY OTHER SECTION IN THE TEST.

SECTION 2

Time—30 minutes

25 Questions

Directions: Each of the data sufficiency problems below consists of a question and two statements, labeled (1) and (2), in which certain data are given. You have to decide whether the data given in the statements are <u>sufficient</u> for answering the question. Using the data given in the statements <u>plus</u> your knowledge of mathematics and everyday facts (such as the number of days in July or the meaning of <u>counterclockwise</u>), you are to fill in oval

- A   if statement (1) ALONE is sufficient, but statement (2) alone is not sufficient to answer the question asked;
- B   if statement (2) ALONE is sufficient, but statement (1) alone is not sufficient to answer the question asked;
- C   if BOTH statements (1) and (2) TOGETHER are sufficient to answer the question asked, but NEITHER statement ALONE is sufficient;
- D   if EACH statement ALONE is sufficient to answer the question asked;
- E   if statements (1) and (2) TOGETHER are NOT sufficient to answer the question asked, and additional data specific to the problem are needed.

Numbers: All numbers used are real numbers.

Figures: A figure in a data sufficiency problem will conform to the information given in the question, but will not necessarily conform to the additional information given in statements (1) and (2).

        You may assume that lines shown as straight are straight and that angle measures are greater than zero.

        You may assume that the positions of points, angles, regions, etc., exist in the order shown.

        All figures lie in a plane unless otherwise indicated.

Example:

In $\triangle PQR$, what is the value of x?

(1) $PQ = PR$

(2) $y = 40$

Explanation: According to statement (1), $PQ = PR$; therefore, $\triangle PQR$ is isosceles and $y = z$. Since $x + y + z = 180$, $x + 2y = 180$. Since statement (1) does not give a value for y, you cannot answer the question using statement (1) by itself. According to statement (2), $y = 40$; therefore, $x + z = 140$. Since statement (2) does not give a value for z, you cannot answer the question using statement (2) by itself. Using both statements together, you can find y and z; therefore, you can find x, and the answer to the problem is C.

GO ON TO THE NEXT PAGE.

-348-

A Statement (1) ALONE is sufficient, but statement (2) alone is not sufficient.
B Statement (2) ALONE is sufficient, but statement (1) alone is not sufficient.
C BOTH statements TOGETHER are sufficient, but NEITHER statement ALONE is sufficient.
D EACH statement ALONE is sufficient.
E Statements (1) and (2) TOGETHER are NOT sufficient.

1. What is the value of x?

 (1) x is negative.
 (2) $2x = -4$

2. Did United States carriers use more than 10 billion gallons of jet fuel during 1983?

 (1) United States carriers paid a total of $9.4 billion for the jet fuel used in 1983.
 (2) United States carriers paid an average (arithmetic mean) of $0.90 per gallon for the jet fuel used in 1983.

3. In Country S, if 60 percent of the women aged 18 and over are in the labor force, how many million women are in the labor force?
 (1) In Country S, women comprise 45 percent of the labor force.
 (2) In Country S, there are no women under 18 years of age in the labor force.

4. If x and y are different positive numbers, is z between x and y?

 (1) $z > 0$
 (2) $z < y$

5. What percent of 16 is m?

 (1) m is 5 percent of 10.
 (2) 400 percent of m is 2.

6. Kay put 12 cards on a table, some faceup and the rest facedown. How many were put facedown?

 (1) Kay put an even number of the cards faceup.
 (2) Kay put twice as many of the cards faceup as she put facedown.

7. Is $\triangle RST$ a right triangle?

 (1) The degree measure of $\angle R$ is twice the degree measure of $\angle T$.
 (2) The degree measure of $\angle T$ is 30.

8. If x is a positive number, is x greater than 1?

 (1) $1 > \dfrac{1}{x}$
 (2) $-\dfrac{1}{x} > -1$

GO ON TO THE NEXT PAGE.

A   Statement (1) ALONE is sufficient, but statement (2) alone is not sufficient.
B   Statement (2) ALONE is sufficient, but statement (1) alone is not sufficient.
C   BOTH statements TOGETHER are sufficient, but NEITHER statement ALONE is sufficient.
D   EACH statement ALONE is sufficient.
E   Statements (1) and (2) TOGETHER are NOT sufficient.

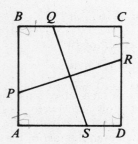

9. The figure above shows four pieces of tile that have been glued together to form a square tile $ABCD$. Is $PR = QS$?

(1) $BQ = CR = DS = AP$

(2) The perimeter of $ABCD$ is 16.

10. How old is Jim?

(1) Eight years ago Jim was half as old as he is now.

(2) Four years from now Jim will be twice as old as he was six years ago.

11. What is the value of x?

(1) When x is multiplied by 8, the result is between 50 and 60.

(2) When x is doubled, the result is between 10 and 15.

12. At a certain state university last term, there were p students each of whom paid either the full tuition of x dollars or half the full tuition. What percent of the tuition paid by the p students last term was tuition from students who paid the full tuition?

(1) Of the p students, 20 percent paid the full tuition.

(2) The p students paid a total of $91.2 million for tuition last term.

GO ON TO THE NEXT PAGE.

A Statement (1) ALONE is sufficient, but statement (2) alone is not sufficient.
B Statement (2) ALONE is sufficient, but statement (1) alone is not sufficient.
C BOTH statements TOGETHER are sufficient, but NEITHER statement ALONE is sufficient.
D EACH statement ALONE is sufficient.
E Statements (1) and (2) TOGETHER are NOT sufficient.

13. If a bottle is to be selected at random from a certain collection of bottles, what is the probability that the bottle will be defective?

(1) The ratio of the number of bottles in the collection that are defective to the number that are not defective is $3:500$.

(2) The collection contains 3,521 bottles.

14. If a grocery shopper received \$0.25 off the original price of a certain product by using a coupon, what was the original price of the product?

(1) The shopper received a 20 percent discount by using the coupon.

(2) The original price was 25 percent higher than the price the shopper paid by using the coupon.

15. What was Casey's total score for eighteen holes of golf?

(1) Casey's score for the first nine holes was 13 less than his score for the last nine holes.

(2) Twice Casey's score for the last nine holes was 58 more than his score for the first nine holes.

16. What is the rate, in cubic feet per minute, at which water is flowing into a certain rectangular tank?

(1) The height of the water in the tank is increasing at the rate of 2 feet per minute.

(2) The capacity of the tank is 216 cubic feet.

17. Is the positive integer n equal to the square of an integer?

(1) For every prime number p, if p is a divisor of n, then so is p^2.

(2) $\sqrt{n}$ is an integer.

18. What is the volume of a certain cube?

(1) The sum of the areas of the faces of the cube is 54.

(2) The greatest possible distance between two points on the cube is $3\sqrt{3}$.

19. What is the value of $k^2 - k$?

(1) The value of $k - \dfrac{1}{k}$ is 1.

(2) The value of $2k - 1$ is $\sqrt{5}$.

GO ON TO THE NEXT PAGE.

A   Statement (1) ALONE is sufficient, but statement (2) alone is not sufficient.
B   Statement (2) ALONE is sufficient, but statement (1) alone is not sufficient.
C   BOTH statements TOGETHER are sufficient, but NEITHER statement ALONE is sufficient.
D   EACH statement ALONE is sufficient.
E   Statements (1) and (2) TOGETHER are NOT sufficient.

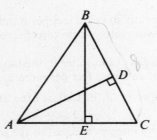

20. In the figure above, what is the product of the lengths of AD and BC ?

(1) The product of the lengths of AC and BE is 60.

(2) The length of BC is 8.

21. At a business association conference, the registration fee for members of the association was $20 and the registration fee for nonmembers was $25. If the total receipts from registration were $5,500, did more members than nonmembers pay the registration fee?

(1) Registration receipts from members were $500 greater than receipts from nonmembers.

(2) A total of 250 people paid the registration fee.

22. If x and y are positive integers and x is a multiple of y, is $y = 2$?

(1) $y \neq 1$

(2) $x + 2$ is a multiple of y.

23. What is the value of n ?

(1) $n(n - 1)(n - 2) = 0$

(2) $n^2 + n - 6 = 0$

GO ON TO THE NEXT PAGE.

A   Statement (1) ALONE is sufficient, but statement (2) alone is not sufficient.
B   Statement (2) ALONE is sufficient, but statement (1) alone is not sufficient.
C   BOTH statements TOGETHER are sufficient, but NEITHER statement ALONE is sufficient.
D   EACH statement ALONE is sufficient.
E   Statements (1) and (2) TOGETHER are NOT sufficient.

24. If x and y are integers between 10 and 99, inclusive, is $\dfrac{x - y}{9}$ an integer?

(1) x and y have the same two digits, but in reverse order.

(2) The tens' digit of x is 2 more than the units' digit, and the tens' digit of y is 2 less than the units' digit.

25. Pam and Ed are in a line to purchase tickets. How many people are in the line?

(1) There are 20 people behind Pam and 20 people in front of Ed.

(2) There are 5 people between Pam and Ed.

STOP

**IF YOU FINISH BEFORE TIME IS CALLED, YOU MAY CHECK YOUR WORK ON THIS SECTION ONLY.
DO NOT TURN TO ANY OTHER SECTION IN THE TEST.**

SECTION 3

Time—30 minutes

25 Questions

Directions: In each of the following sentences, some part of the sentence or the entire sentence is underlined. Beneath each sentence you will find five ways of phrasing the underlined part. The first of these repeats the original; the other four are different. If you think the original is better than any of the alternatives, choose answer A; otherwise choose one of the others. Select the best version and fill in the corresponding oval on your answer sheet.

This is a test of correctness and effectiveness of expression. In choosing answers, follow the requirements of standard written English; that is, pay attention to grammar, choice of words, and sentence construction. Choose the answer that expresses most effectively what is presented in the original sentence; this answer should be clear and exact, without awkwardness, ambiguity, or redundancy.

1. During the first one hundred fifty years of the existence of this republic, no one expected the press was fair; newspapers were mostly shrill, scurrilous, and partisan.

   (A) was
   (B) to be
   (C) of being
   (D) should be
   (E) had to be

2. Most victims of infectious mononucleosis recover after a few weeks of listlessness, but an unlucky few may suffer for years.

   (A) but an unlucky few may suffer
   (B) and an unlucky few have suffered
   (C) that an unlucky few might suffer
   (D) that a few being unlucky may suffer
   (E) but a few who, being unlucky, suffered

3. It was the loss of revenue from declines in tourism that in 1935 led the Saudi authorities' granting a concession for oil exploration to the company that would later be known by the name of Aramco.

   (A) authorities' granting a concession for oil exploration to the company that would later be known by the name of
   (B) authorities' granting a concession for oil exploration to the company later to be known as named
   (C) authorities granting a concession for oil exploration to the company that would later be known by the name of
   (D) authorities to grant a concession for oil exploration to the company that later will be known as being
   (E) authorities to grant a concession for oil exploration to the company later to be known as

4. Framed by traitorous colleagues, Alfred Dreyfus was imprisoned for twelve years before there was exoneration and his freedom.

   (A) there was exoneration and his freedom
   (B) he was to be exonerated with freedom
   (C) being exonerated and freed
   (D) exoneration and his freedom
   (E) being freed, having been exonerated

GO ON TO THE NEXT PAGE.

-355-

5. By studying the primitive visual systems of single-cell aquatic organisms, <u>biophysicists have discovered a striking similarity between algae and cows</u>, a similarity that indicates the common evolutionary origin of plants and animals: both algae and cows produce a light-sensitive protein called rhodopsin.

   (A) biophysicists have discovered a striking similarity between algae and cows
   (B) a striking similarity between algae and cows has been discovered by biophysicists
   (C) there is a striking similarity that biophysicists have discovered between algae and cows
   (D) the discovery of a striking similarity between algae and cows was made by biophysicists
   (E) algae and cows have a striking similarity that was discovered by biophysicists

6. Because young children do not organize their attention or perceptions systematically, <u>like adults</u>, they may notice and remember details that their elders ignore.

   (A) like adults
   (B) unlike an adult
   (C) as adults
   (D) as adults do
   (E) as an adult

7. As many as 300 of <u>the 720 paintings attributed to Rembrandt may</u> actually be the works of his students or other admirers.

   (A) the 720 paintings attributed to Rembrandt may
   (B) the 720 paintings attributed to be Rembrandt's might
   (C) the 720 paintings that were attributed to be by Rembrandt may
   (D) the 720 Rembrandt paintings that were once attributed to him might
   (E) Rembrandt's paintings, although 720 were once attributed to him, may

8. Studies of the human "sleep-wake cycle" have practical relevance for matters ranging from duty assignments in nuclear submarines and air-traffic control towers <u>to the staff of</u> shifts in 24-hour factories.

   (A) to the staff of
   (B) to those who staff
   (C) to the staffing of
   (D) and staffing
   (E) and the staff of

9. Many psychologists and sociologists now contend that the deliberate and even brutal aggression integral to some forms of competitive athletics <u>increase the likelihood of imitative violence that erupts</u> among crowds of spectators dominated by young adult males.

   (A) increase the likelihood of imitative violence that erupts
   (B) increase the likelihood that there will be an eruption of imitative violence
   (C) increase the likelihood of imitative violence erupting
   (D) increases the likelihood for imitative violence to erupt
   (E) increases the likelihood that imitative violence will erupt

10. More than five thousand years ago, Chinese scholars accurately described the flow of blood as a continuous circle controlled by the heart, <u>but it went</u> unnoticed in the West.

   (A) but it went
   (B) but it was
   (C) although it was
   (D) but the discovery went
   (E) although the discovery was

GO ON TO THE NEXT PAGE.

11. Several studies have found that the coronary patients who exercise most actively <u>have half or less than half the chance of dying of a heart attack as those who are sedentary</u>.

   (A) have half or less than half the chance of dying of a heart attack as those who are sedentary
   (B) have half the chance, or less, of dying of a heart attack than those who are sedentary do
   (C) have half the chance that they will die of a heart attack, or less, than those who are sedentary do
   (D) are at least fifty percent less likely to die of a heart attack as those who are sedentary
   (E) are at least fifty percent less likely than those who are sedentary to die of a heart attack

12. Most nations regard their airspace <u>as extending</u> upward as high as an aircraft can fly; no specific altitude, however, has been officially recognized as a boundary.

   (A) as extending
   (B) as the extent
   (C) to be an extent
   (D) to be an extension
   (E) to extend

13. According to scientists at the University of California, the pattern of changes that have occurred in human DNA over the millennia <u>indicate the possibility that everyone alive today might be descended from a single female ancestor who</u> lived in Africa sometime between 140,000 and 280,000 years ago.

   (A) indicate the possibility that everyone alive today might be descended from a single female ancestor who
   (B) indicate that everyone alive today might possibly be a descendant of a single female ancestor who had
   (C) may indicate that everyone alive today has descended from a single female ancestor who had
   (D) indicates that everyone alive today may be a descendant of a single female ancestor who
   (E) indicates that everyone alive today might be a descendant from a single female ancestor who

14. Several senior officials spoke to the press on condition <u>that they not be named</u> in the story.

   (A) that they not be named
   (B) that their names will not be used
   (C) that their names are not used
   (D) of not being named
   (E) they will not be named

15. According to his own account, Frédéric-Auguste Bartholdi, the sculptor of the Statue of Liberty, <u>modeled the face of the statue like his mother's and the body like his wife's</u>.

   (A) modeled the face of the statue like his mother's and the body like his wife's
   (B) modeled the face of the statue after that of his mother and the body after that of his wife
   (C) modeled the face of the statue like his mother and the body like his wife
   (D) made the face of the statue after his mother and the body after his wife
   (E) made the face of the statue look like his mother and the body look like his wife

16. One of Ronald Reagan's first acts as President was to rescind President Carter's directive <u>that any chemical banned on medical grounds in the United States be prohibited from sale to other countries</u>.

   (A) that any chemical banned on medical grounds in the United States be prohibited from sale to other countries
   (B) that any chemical be prohibited from sale to other countries that was banned on medical grounds in the United States
   (C) prohibiting the sale to other countries of any chemical banned on medical grounds in the United States
   (D) prohibiting that any chemical banned on medical grounds in the United States is sold to other countries
   (E) that any chemical banned in the United States on medical grounds is prohibited from being sold to other countries

17. <u>Although just inside the orbit of</u> Jupiter, amateur astronomers with good telescopes should be able to see the comet within the next few weeks.

   (A) Although just inside the orbit of
   (B) Although it is just inside the orbit of
   (C) Just inside the orbit of
   (D) Orbiting just inside
   (E) Having orbited just inside

GO ON TO THE NEXT PAGE.

18. Under Napoleon the French were not able to organize an adequate supply system, and it was a major cause of the failure of their invasion of Russia.

   (A) Under Napoleon the French were not able to organize an adequate supply system, and it
   (B) The French being unable to organize an adequate supply system under Napoleon
   (C) For the French under Napoleon, to be unable to organize an adequate supply system
   (D) The inability of the French under Napoleon to organize an adequate supply system
   (E) The French inability under Napoleon of organizing an adequate supply system

19. To help preserve ancient Egyptian monuments threatened by high water tables, a Swedish engineering firm has proposed installing pumps, perhaps solar powered, to lower the underground water level and dig trenches around the bases of the stone walls.

   (A) to lower the underground water level and dig trenches
   (B) to lower the underground water level and to dig trenches
   (C) to lower the underground water level and digging trenches
   (D) that lower the underground water level and that trenches be dug
   (E) that lower the underground water level and trench digging

20. When rates were raised in 1985, postal service officials predicted they would make further rate increases unnecessary for at least three years.

   (A) they would make further rate increases unnecessary
   (B) they would mean that further rate increases would not be needed
   (C) that it would not be necessary for further rate increases
   (D) that the increase would make further rate increases unnecessary
   (E) further rate increases will not be needed

21. With its plan to develop seven and a half acres of shore land, Cleveland is but one of a large number of communities on the Great Lakes that is looking to its waterfront as a way to improve the quality of urban life and attract new businesses.

   (A) is looking to its waterfront as a way to improve the quality of urban life and attract
   (B) is looking at its waterfront to improve the quality of urban life and attract
   (C) are looking to their waterfronts to improve the quality of urban life and attract
   (D) are looking to its waterfront as a way of improving the quality of urban life and attracting
   (E) are looking at their waterfronts as a way they can improve the quality of urban life and attract

22. A collection of 38 poems by Phillis Wheatley, a slave, was published in the 1770's, the first book by a Black woman and it was only the second published by an American woman.

   (A) it was only the second published by an American woman
   (B) it was only the second that an American woman published
   (C) the second one only published by an American woman
   (D) the second one only that an American woman published
   (E) only the second published by an American woman

23. A huge flying reptile that died out with the dinosaurs some 65 million years ago, the Quetzalcoatlus had a wingspan of 36 feet, believed to be the largest flying creature the world has ever seen.

   (A) believed to be
   (B) and that is believed to be
   (C) and it is believed to have been
   (D) which was, it is believed,
   (E) which is believed to be

GO ON TO THE NEXT PAGE.

24. A "calendar stick" carved centuries ago by the Winnebago tribe may provide the first evidence <u>that the North American Indians have developed advanced full-year calendars basing them</u> on systematic astronomical observation.

(A) that the North American Indians have developed advanced full-year calendars basing them

(B) of the North American Indians who have developed advanced full-year calendars and based them

(C) of the development of advanced full-year calendars by North American Indians, basing them

(D) of the North American Indians and their development of advanced full-year calendars based

(E) that the North American Indians developed advanced full-year calendars based

25. Federal incentives now encourage <u>investing capital in commercial office buildings despite vacancy rates in existing structures that are exceptionally high and</u> no demand for new construction.

(A) investing capital in commercial office buildings despite vacancy rates in existing structures that are exceptionally high and

(B) capital investment in commercial office buildings even though vacancy rates in existing structures are exceptionally high and there is

(C) capital to be invested in commercial office buildings even though there are exceptionally high vacancy rates in existing structures with

(D) investing capital in commercial office buildings even though the vacancy rates are exceptionally high in existing structures with

(E) capital investment in commercial office buildings despite vacancy rates in existing structures that are exceptionally high, and although there is

STOP

IF YOU FINISH BEFORE TIME IS CALLED, YOU MAY CHECK YOUR WORK ON THIS SECTION ONLY. DO NOT TURN TO ANY OTHER SECTION IN THE TEST.

SECTION 4

Time — 30 minutes

20 Questions

Directions: In this section solve each problem, using any available space on the page for scratchwork. Then indicate the best of the answer choices given.

Numbers: All numbers used are real numbers.

Figures: Figures that accompany problems in this section are intended to provide information useful in solving the problems. They are drawn as accurately as possible EXCEPT when it is stated in a specific problem that its figure is not drawn to scale. All figures lie in a plane unless otherwise indicated.

1. The 180 students in a group are to be seated in rows so that there is an equal number of students in each row. Each of the following could be the number of rows EXCEPT

(A) 4
(B) 20
(C) 30
(D) 40
(E) 90

2. A parking garage rents parking spaces for $10 per week or $30 per month. How much does a person save in a year by renting by the month rather than by the week?

(A) $140   (B) $160   (C) $220
(D) $240   (E) $260

3. If $y = 5x^2 - 2x$ and $x = 3$, then $y =$

(A) 24   (B) 27   (C) 39   (D) 51   (E) 219

4. Of the following, which is the best approximation to $\sqrt{0.0026}$?

(A) 0.05   (B) 0.06   (C) 0.16   (D) 0.5   (E) 0.6

5. At a certain diner, a hamburger and coleslaw cost $3.95, and a hamburger and french fries cost $4.40. If french fries cost twice as much as coleslaw, how much do french fries cost?

(A) $0.30
(B) $0.45
(C) $0.60
(D) $0.75
(E) $0.90

GO ON TO THE NEXT PAGE.

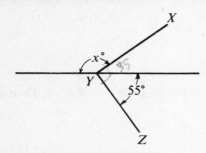

6. If $\angle XYZ$ in the figure above is a right angle, what is the value of x ?

(A) 155   (B) 145   (C) 135   (D) 125   (E) 110

7.
$$\frac{\left(\dfrac{a}{b}\right)}{c}$$

In the expression above, a, b, and c are different numbers and each is one of the numbers 2, 3, or 5. What is the least possible value of the expression?

(A) $\dfrac{1}{30}$ (B) $\dfrac{2}{15}$ (C) $\dfrac{1}{6}$ (D) $\dfrac{3}{10}$ (E) $\dfrac{5}{6}$

8. A certain culture of bacteria quadruples every hour. If a container with these bacteria was half full at 10:00 a.m., at what time was it one-eighth full?

(A) 9:00 a.m.
(B) 7:00 a.m.
(C) 6:00 a.m.
(D) 4:00 a.m.
(E) 2:00 a.m.

9. Al, Lew, and Karen pooled their funds to buy a gift for a friend. Al contributed \$2 less than $\dfrac{1}{3}$ of the cost of the gift and Lew contributed \$2 more than $\dfrac{1}{4}$ of the cost. If Karen contributed the remaining \$15, what was the cost of the gift?

(A) \$24
(B) \$33
(C) \$36
(D) \$43
(E) \$45

GO ON TO THE NEXT PAGE.

10. What is the total number of integers between 100 and 200 that are divisible by 3 ?

   (A) 33   (B) 32   (C) 31   (D) 30   (E) 29

11. Which of the following inequalities is equivalent to $10 - 2x > 18$?

   (A) $x > -14$
   (B) $x > -4$
   (C) $x > 4$
   (D) $x < 4$
   (E) $x < -4$

12. In 1979 approximately $\frac{1}{3}$ of the 37.3 million airline passengers traveling to or from the United States used Kennedy Airport. If the number of such passengers that used Miami Airport was $\frac{1}{2}$ the number that used Kennedy Airport and 4 times the number that used Logan Airport, approximately how many millions of these passengers used Logan Airport that year?

   (A) 18.6
   (B) 9.3
   (C) 6.2
   (D) 3.1
   (E) 1.6

13. A certain basketball team that has played $\frac{2}{3}$ of its games has a record of 17 wins and 3 losses. What is the greatest number of the remaining games that the team can lose and still win at least $\frac{3}{4}$ of all of its games?

   (A) 7
   (B) 6
   (C) 5
   (D) 4
   (E) 3

14. Dan and Karen, who live 10 miles apart, meet at a café that is directly north of Dan's house and directly east of Karen's house. If the café is 2 miles closer to Dan's house than to Karen's house, how many miles is the café from Karen's house?

   (A) 6
   (B) 7
   (C) 8
   (D) 9
   (E) 10

GO ON TO THE NEXT PAGE.

4 4 4 4 4 4 4 4 4 4 4

15. If n is an integer and $n = \dfrac{2 \cdot 3 \cdot 5 \cdot 7 \cdot 11 \cdot 13}{77k}$,

    then which of the following could be the value

    of k?

    (A) 22   (B) 26   (C) 35   (D) 54   (E) 60

16. There were 36,000 hardback copies of a certain
    novel sold before the paperback version was issued.
    From the time the first paperback copy was sold
    until the last copy of the novel was sold, 9 times as
    many paperback copies as hardback copies were
    sold. If a total of 441,000 copies of the novel were
    sold in all, how many paperback copies were sold?

    (A)   45,000
    (B) 360,000
    (C) 364,500
    (D) 392,000
    (E) 396,900

17. In the formula $w = \dfrac{p}{\sqrt[t]{v}}$, integers p and t are

    positive constants. If $w = 2$ when $v = 1$ and if

    $w = \dfrac{1}{2}$ when $v = 64$, then $t =$

    (A)   1
    (B)   2
    (C)   3
    (D)   4
    (E)   16

18. Last year Mrs. Long received $160 in dividends
    on her shares of Company X stock, all of which she
    had held for the entire year. If she had had 12 more
    shares of the stock last year, she would have
    received $15 more in total annual dividends. How
    many shares of the stock did she have last year?

    (A) 128
    (B) 140
    (C) 172
    (D) 175
    (E) 200

GO ON TO THE NEXT PAGE.

Month	Average Price per Dozen
April	$1.26
May	$1.20
June	$1.08

19. The table above shows the average (arithmetic mean) price per dozen of the large grade A eggs sold in a certain store during three successive months. If $\frac{2}{3}$ as many dozen were sold in April as in May, and twice as many were sold in June as in April, what was the average price per dozen of the eggs sold over the three-month period?

(A) $1.08
(B) $1.10
(C) $1.14
(D) $1.16
(E) $1.18

20. If $y \neq 3$ and $\frac{3x}{y}$ is a prime integer greater than 2, which of the following must be true?

   I. $x = y$
  II. $y = 1$
 III. x and y are prime integers.

(A) None
(B) I only
(C) II only
(D) III only
(E) I and III

STOP

IF YOU FINISH BEFORE TIME IS CALLED, YOU MAY CHECK YOUR WORK ON THIS SECTION ONLY. DO NOT TURN TO ANY OTHER SECTION IN THE TEST.

SECTION 5
Time—30 minutes
20 Questions

Directions: For each question in this section, select the best of the answer choices given.

1. Child's World, a chain of toy stores, has relied on a "supermarket concept" of computerized inventory control and customer self-service to eliminate the category of sales clerks from its force of employees. It now plans to employ the same concept in selling children's clothes.

   The plan of Child's World assumes that

   (A) supermarkets will not also be selling children's clothes in the same manner
   (B) personal service by sales personnel is not required for selling children's clothes successfully
   (C) the same kind of computers will be used in inventory control for both clothes and toys at Child's World
   (D) a self-service plan cannot be employed without computerized inventory control
   (E) sales clerks are the only employees of Child's World who could be assigned tasks related to inventory control

2. Continuous indoor fluorescent light benefits the health of hamsters with inherited heart disease. A group of them exposed to continuous fluorescent light survived twenty-five percent longer than a similar group exposed instead to equal periods of indoor fluorescent light and of darkness.

   The method of the research described above is most likely to be applicable in addressing which of the following questions?

   (A) Can industrial workers who need to see their work do so better by sunlight or by fluorescent light?
   (B) Can hospital lighting be improved to promote the recovery of patients?
   (C) How do deep-sea fish survive in total darkness?
   (D) What are the inherited illnesses to which hamsters are subject?
   (E) Are there plants that require specific periods of darkness in order to bloom?

3. Millions of identical copies of a plant can be produced using new tissue-culture and cloning techniques.

   If plant propagation by such methods in laboratories proves economical, each of the following, if true, represents a benefit of the new techniques to farmers EXCEPT:

   (A) The techniques allow the development of superior strains to take place more rapidly, requiring fewer generations of plants grown to maturity.
   (B) It is less difficult to care for plants that will grow at rates that do not vary widely.
   (C) Plant diseases and pests, once they take hold, spread more rapidly among genetically uniform plants than among those with genetic variations.
   (D) Mechanical harvesting of crops is less difficult if plants are more uniform in size.
   (E) Special genetic traits can more easily be introduced into plant strains with the use of the new techniques.

4. Which of the following best completes the passage below?

   Sales campaigns aimed at the faltering personal computer market have strongly emphasized ease of use, called user-friendliness. This emphasis is oddly premature and irrelevant in the eyes of most potential buyers, who are trying to address the logically prior issue of whether -------.

   (A) user-friendliness also implies that owners can service their own computers
   (B) personal computers cost more the more user-friendly they are
   (C) currently available models are user-friendly enough to suit them
   (D) the people promoting personal computers use them in their own homes
   (E) they have enough sensible uses for a personal computer to justify the expense of buying one

GO ON TO THE NEXT PAGE.

5. A weapons-smuggling incident recently took place in country Y. We all know that Y is a closed society. So Y's government must have known about the weapons.

Which of the following is an assumption that would make the conclusion above logically correct?

(A) If a government knows about a particular weapons-smuggling incident, it must have intended to use the weapons for its own purposes.
(B) If a government claims that it knew nothing about a particular weapons-smuggling incident, it must have known everything about it.
(C) If a government does not permit weapons to enter a country, it is a closed society.
(D) If a country is a closed society, its government has a large contingent of armed guards patrolling its borders.
(E) If a country is a closed society, its government has knowledge about everything that occurs in the country.

6. Banning cigarette advertisements in the mass media will not reduce the number of young people who smoke. They know that cigarettes exist and they know how to get them. They do not need the advertisements to supply that information.

The above argument would be most weakened if which of the following were true?

(A) Seeing or hearing an advertisement for a product tends to increase people's desire for that product.
(B) Banning cigarette advertisements in the mass media will cause an increase in advertisements in places where cigarettes are sold.
(C) Advertisements in the mass media have been an exceedingly large part of the expenditures of the tobacco companies.
(D) Those who oppose cigarette use have advertised against it in the mass media ever since cigarettes were found to be harmful.
(E) Older people tend to be less influenced by mass-media advertisements than younger people tend to be.

7. People tend to estimate the likelihood of an event's occurrence according to its salience; that is, according to how strongly and how often it comes to their attention.

By placement and headlines, newspapers emphasize stories about local crime over stories about crime elsewhere and about many other major events.

It can be concluded on the basis of the statements above that, if they are true, which of the following is most probably also true?

(A) The language used in newspaper headlines about local crime is inflammatory and fails to respect the rights of suspects.
(B) The coverage of international events in newspapers is neglected in favor of the coverage of local events.
(C) Readers of local news in newspapers tend to overestimate the amount of crime in their own localities relative to the amount of crime in other places.
(D) None of the events concerning other people that are reported in newspapers is so salient in people's minds as their own personal experiences.
(E) The press is the news medium that focuses people's attention most strongly on local crimes.

8. By analyzing the garbage of a large number of average-sized households, a group of modern urban anthropologists has found that a household discards less food the more standardized—made up of canned and prepackaged foods—its diet is. The more standardized a household's diet is, however, the greater the quantities of fresh produce the household throws away.

Which of the following can be properly inferred from the passage?

(A) An increasing number of households rely on a highly standardized diet.
(B) The less standardized a household's diet is, the more nonfood waste the household discards.
(C) The less standardized a household's diet is, the smaller is the proportion of fresh produce in the household's food waste.
(D) The less standardized a household's diet is, the more canned and prepackaged foods the household discards as waste.
(E) The more fresh produce a household buys, the more fresh produce it throws away.

GO ON TO THE NEXT PAGE.

Questions 9-10 are based on the following.

In the past, teachers, bank tellers, and secretaries were predominantly men; these occupations slipped in pay and status when they became largely occupied by women. Therefore, if women become the majority in currently male-dominated professions like accounting, law, and medicine, the income and prestige of these professions will also drop.

9. The argument above is based on

   (A) another argument that contains circular reasoning
   (B) an attempt to refute a generalization by means of an exceptional case
   (C) an analogy between the past and the future
   (D) an appeal to popular beliefs and values
   (E) an attack on the character of the opposition

10. Which of the following, if true, would most likely be part of the evidence used to refute the conclusion above?

   (A) Accountants, lawyers, and physicians attained their current relatively high levels of income and prestige at about the same time that the pay and status of teachers, bank tellers, and secretaries slipped.
   (B) When large numbers of men join a female-dominated occupation, such as airline flight attendant, the status and pay of the occupation tend to increase.
   (C) The demand for teachers and secretaries has increased significantly in recent years, while the demand for bank tellers has remained relatively stable.
   (D) If present trends in the awarding of law degrees to women continue, it will be at least two decades before the majority of lawyers are women.
   (E) The pay and status of female accountants, lawyers, and physicians today are governed by significantly different economic and sociological forces than were the pay and status of female teachers, bank tellers, and secretaries in the past.

11. An electric-power company gained greater profits and provided electricity to consumers at lower rates per unit of electricity by building larger-capacity, more efficient plants and by stimulating greater use of electricity within its area. To continue these financial trends, the company planned to replace an old plant by a plant with triple the capacity of its largest plant.

The company's plan as described above assumed each of the following EXCEPT:

   (A) Demand for electricity within the company's area of service would increase in the future.
   (B) Expenses would not rise beyond the level that could be compensated for by efficiency or volume of operation, or both.
   (C) The planned plant would be sufficiently reliable in service to contribute a net financial benefit to the company as a whole.
   (D) Safety measures to be instituted for the new plant would be the same as those for the plant it would replace.
   (E) The tripling of capacity would not result in insuperable technological obstacles to efficiency.

GO ON TO THE NEXT PAGE.

Questions 12-13 are based on the following.

Meteorologists say that if only they could design an accurate mathematical model of the atmosphere with all its complexities, they could forecast the weather with real precision. But this is an idle boast, immune to any evaluation, for any inadequate weather forecast would obviously be blamed on imperfections in the model.

12. Which of the following, if true, could best be used as a basis for arguing against the author's position that the meteorologists' claim cannot be evaluated?

(A) Certain unusual configurations of data can serve as the basis for precise weather forecasts even though the exact causal mechanisms are not understood.
(B) Most significant gains in the accuracy of the relevant mathematical models are accompanied by clear gains in the precision of weather forecasts.
(C) Mathematical models of the meteorological aftermath of such catastrophic events as volcanic eruptions are beginning to be constructed.
(D) Modern weather forecasts for as much as a full day ahead are broadly correct about 80 percent of the time.
(E) Meteorologists readily concede that the accurate mathematical model they are talking about is not now in their power to construct.

13. Which of the following, if true, would cast the most serious doubt on the meteorologists' boast, aside from the doubt expressed in the passage above?

(A) The amount of energy that the Earth receives from the Sun is monitored closely and is known not to be constant.
(B) Volcanic eruptions, the combustion of fossil fuels, and several other processes that also cannot be quantified with any accuracy are known to have a significant and continuing impact on the constitution of the atmosphere.
(C) As current models of the atmosphere are improved, even small increments in complexity will mean large increases in the number of computers required for the representation of the models.
(D) Frequent and accurate data about the atmosphere collected at a large number of points both on and above the ground are a prerequisite for the construction of a good model of the atmosphere.
(E) With existing models of the atmosphere, large-scale weather patterns can be predicted with greater accuracy than can relatively local weather patterns.

14. Of the countries that were the world's twenty largest exporters in 1953, four had the same share of total world exports in 1984 as in 1953. These countries can therefore serve as models for those countries that wish to keep their share of the global export trade stable over the years.

Which of the following, if true, casts the most serious doubt on the suitability of those four countries as models in the sense described?

(A) Many countries wish to increase their share of world export trade, not just keep it stable.
(B) Many countries are less concerned with exports alone than with the balance between exports and imports.
(C) With respect to the mix of products each exports, the four countries are very different from each other.
(D) Of the four countries, two had a much larger, and two had a much smaller, share of total world exports in 1970 than in 1984.
(E) The exports of the four countries range from 15 percent to 75 percent of the total national output.

GO ON TO THE NEXT PAGE.

Questions 15-16 are based on the following.

In the United States, the Postal Service has a monopoly on first-class mail, but much of what is sent first class could be transmitted electronically. Electronic transmittal operators argue that if the Postal Service were to offer electronic transmission, it would have an unfair advantage, since its electronic transmission service could be subsidized from the profits of the monopoly.

15. Which of the following, if each is true, would allay the electronic transmittal operators' fears of unfair competition?

(A) If the Postal Service were to offer electronic transmission, it could not make a profit on first-class mail.
(B) If the Postal Service were to offer electronic transmission, it would have a monopoly on that kind of service.
(C) Much of the material that is now sent by first-class mail could be delivered much faster by special package couriers, but is not sent that way because of cost.
(D) There is no economy of scale in electronic transmission—that is, the cost per transaction does not go down as more pieces of information are transmitted.
(E) Electronic transmission will never be cost-effective for material not sent by first-class mail such as newspapers and bulk mail.

16. Which of the following questions can be answered on the basis of the information in the passage above?

(A) Is the Postal Service as efficient as privately owned electric transmission services?
(B) If private operators were allowed to operate first-class mail services, would they choose to do so?
(C) Do the electronic transmittal operators believe that the Postal Service makes a profit on first-class mail?
(D) Is the Postal Service prohibited from offering electronic transmission services?
(E) Is the Postal Service expected to have a monopoly on electronic transmission?

17. Lists of hospitals have been compiled showing which hospitals have patient death rates exceeding the national average. The data have been adjusted to allow for differences in the ages of patients.

Each of the following, if true, provides a good logical ground for hospitals to object to interpreting rank on these lists as one of the indices of the quality of hospital care EXCEPT:

(A) Rank order might indicate insignificant differences, rather than large differences, in numbers of patient deaths.
(B) Hospitals that keep patients longer are likely to have higher death rates than those that discharge patients earlier but do not record deaths of patients at home after discharge.
(C) Patients who are very old on admission to a hospital are less likely than younger patients to survive the same types of illnesses or surgical procedures.
(D) Some hospitals serve a larger proportion of low-income patients, who tend to be more seriously ill when admitted to a hospital.
(E) For-profit hospitals sometimes do not provide intensive-care units and other expensive services for very sick patients but refer or transfer such patients to other hospitals.

18. Teresa: Manned spaceflight does not have a future, since it cannot compete economically with other means of accomplishing the objectives of spaceflight.

Edward: No mode of human transportation has a better record of reliability: two accidents in twenty-five years. Thus manned spaceflight definitely has a positive future.

Which of the following is the best logical evaluation of Edward's argument as a response to Teresa's argument?

(A) It cites evidence that, if true, tends to disprove the evidence cited by Teresa in drawing her conclusion.
(B) It indicates a logical gap in the support that Teresa offers for her conclusion.
(C) It raises a consideration that outweighs the argument Teresa makes.
(D) It does not meet Teresa's point because it assumes that there is no serious impediment to transporting people into space, but this was the issue raised by Teresa.
(E) It fails to respond to Teresa's argument because it does not address the fundamental issue of whether space activities should have priority over other claims on the national budget.

GO ON TO THE NEXT PAGE.

19. Black Americans are, on the whole, about twice as likely as White Americans to develop high blood pressure. This likelihood also holds for westernized Black Africans when compared to White Africans. Researchers have hypothesized that this predisposition in westernized Blacks may reflect an interaction between western high-salt diets and genes that adapted to an environmental scarcity of salt.

Which of the following statements about present-day, westernized Black Africans, if true, would most tend to confirm the researchers' hypothesis?

(A) The blood pressures of those descended from peoples situated throughout their history in Senegal and Gambia, where salt was always available, are low.
(B) The unusually high salt consumption in certain areas of Africa represents a serious health problem.
(C) Because of their blood pressure levels, most White Africans have markedly decreased their salt consumption.
(D) Blood pressures are low among the Yoruba, who, throughout their history, have been situated far inland from sources of sea salt and far south of Saharan salt mines.
(E) No significant differences in salt metabolism have been found between those peoples who have had salt available throughout their history and those who have not.

20. The following proposal to amend the bylaws of an organization was circulated to its members for comment.

When more than one nominee is to be named for an office, prospective nominees must consent to nomination and before giving such consent must be told who the other nominees will be.

Which of the following comments concerning the logic of the proposal is accurate if it cannot be known who the actual nominees are until prospective nominees have given their consent to be nominated?

(A) The proposal would make it possible for each of several nominees for an office to be aware of who all of the other nominees are.
(B) The proposal would widen the choice available to those choosing among the nominees.
(C) If there are several prospective nominees, the proposal would deny the last nominee equal treatment with the first.
(D) The proposal would enable a prospective nominee to withdraw from competition with a specific person without making that withdrawal known.
(E) If there is more than one prospective nominee, the proposal would make it impossible for anyone to become a nominee.

STOP

IF YOU FINISH BEFORE TIME IS CALLED, YOU MAY CHECK YOUR WORK ON THIS SECTION ONLY. DO NOT TURN TO ANY OTHER SECTION IN THE TEST.

SECTION 6
Time—30 minutes
20 Questions

Directions: In this section solve each problem, using any available space on the page for scratchwork. Then indicate the best of the answer choices given.

Numbers: All numbers used are real numbers.

Figures: Figures that accompany problems in this section are intended to provide information useful in solving the problems. They are drawn as accurately as possible EXCEPT when it is stated in a specific problem that its figure is not drawn to scale. All figures lie in a plane unless otherwise indicated.

1. The market value of a certain machine decreased by 30 percent of its purchase price each year. If the machine was purchased in 1982 for its market value of $8,000, what was its market value two years later?

   (A) $8,000
   (B) $5,600
   (C) $3,200
   (D) $2,400
   (E) $800

2. What percent of 50 is 15 ?

   (A) 30%   (B) 35%   (C) 70%

   (D) 300%   (E) $333\frac{1}{3}\%$

3. In a certain diving competition, 5 judges score each dive on a scale from 1 to 10. The point value of the dive is obtained by dropping the highest score and the lowest score and multiplying the sum of the remaining scores by the degree of difficulty. If a dive with a degree of difficulty of 3.2 received scores of 7.5, 8.0, 9.0, 6.0, and 8.5, what was the point value of the dive?

   (A) 68.8   (B) 73.6   (C) 75.2

   (D) 76.8   (E) 81.6

4. If $2x = 3y = 10$, then $12xy =$

   (A) 1,200   (B) 200   (C) 120   (D) 40   (E) 20

GO ON TO THE NEXT PAGE.

5. If Jack walked 5 miles in 1 hour and 15 minutes, what was his rate of walking in miles per hour?

   (A) 4   (B) 4.5   (C) 6   (D) 6.25   (E) 15

6. Of a certain high school graduating class, 75 percent of the students continued their formal education, and 80 percent of those who continued their formal education went to four-year colleges. If 300 students in the class went to four-year colleges, how many students were in the graduating class?

   (A) 500   (B) 375   (C) 240   (D) 225   (E) 180

7. What is the least integer greater than $-2 + 0.5$?

   (A) -2 (B) -1 (C) 0   (D) 1   (E) 2

8. Which of the following is equivalent to $\dfrac{2x + 4}{2x^2 + 8x + 8}$ for all values of x for which both expressions are defined?

   (A) $\dfrac{1}{2x^2 + 6}$

   (B) $\dfrac{1}{9x + 2}$

   (C) $\dfrac{2}{x + 6}$

   (D) $\dfrac{1}{x + 4}$

   (E) $\dfrac{1}{x + 2}$

GO ON TO THE NEXT PAGE.

9. A certain business printer can print 40 characters per second, which is 4 times as fast as an average printer. If an average printer can print 5 times as fast as an electric typewriter, how many characters per <u>minute</u> can an electric typewriter print?

(A) 2   (B) 32   (C) 50   (D) 120   (E) 600

10. When ticket sales began, Pat was the nth customer in line for a ticket, and customers purchased their tickets at the rate of x customers per minute. Of the following, which best approximates the time, in minutes, that Pat had to wait in line from the moment ticket sales began?

(A) $(n - 1)x$

(B) $n + x - 1$

(C) $\dfrac{n - 1}{x}$

(D) $\dfrac{x}{n - 1}$

(E) $\dfrac{n}{x - 1}$

11. If 6 gallons of gasoline are added to a tank that is already filled to $\dfrac{3}{4}$ of its capacity, the tank is then filled to $\dfrac{9}{10}$ of its capacity. How many gallons does the tank hold?

(A) 20   (B) 24   (C) 36   (D) 40   (E) 60

12. A bus trip of 450 miles would have taken 1 hour less if the average speed S for the trip had been greater by 5 miles per hour. What was the average speed S, in miles per hour, for the trip?

(A) 10   (B) 40   (C) 45   (D) 50   (E) 55

13. 10^3 is how many times $(0.01)^3$?

(A) 10^6 (B) 10^8 (C) 10^9 (D) 10^{12} (E) 10^{18}

GO ON TO THE NEXT PAGE.

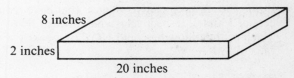

6 6 6 6 6 6 6 6 6 6 6

14. Which of the following groups of numbers could be the lengths of the sides of a right triangle?

    I. $1, 4, \sqrt{17}$

    II. $4, 7, \sqrt{11}$

    III. $4, 9, 6$

(A) I only
(B) I and II only
(C) I and III only
(D) II and III only
(E) I, II, and III

15. When the stock market opened yesterday, the price of a share of stock X was $10\frac{1}{2}$. When the market closed, the price was $11\frac{1}{4}$. Of the following, which is closest to the percent increase in the price of stock X ?

(A) 0.5%   (B) 1.0%   (C) 6.7%

(D) 7.1%   (E) 7.5%

16. If x and y are integers and xy^2 is a positive odd integer, which of the following must be true?

    I. xy is positive.

    II. xy is odd.

    III. $x + y$ is even.

(A) I only
(B) II only
(C) III only
(D) I and II
(E) II and III

8 inches

2 inches

20 inches

17. The figure above shows the dimensions of a rectangular box that is to be completely wrapped with paper. If a single sheet of paper is to be used without patching, then the dimensions of the paper could be

(A) 17 in by 25 in
(B) 21 in by 24 in
(C) 24 in by 12 in
(D) 24 in by 14 in
(E) 26 in by 14 in

GO ON TO THE NEXT PAGE.

18.
$$x - y = 3$$
$$2x = 2y + 6$$

The system of equations above has how many solutions?

(A) None
(B) Exactly one
(C) Exactly two
(D) Exactly three
(E) Infinitely many

19. If M and N are positive integers that have remainders of 1 and 3, respectively, when divided by 6, which of the following could NOT be a possible value of $M + N$?

(A) 86 (B) 52 (C) 34 (D) 28 (E) 10

20. The R students in a class agree to contribute equally to buy their teacher a birthday present that costs y dollars. If x of the students later fail to contribute their share, which of the following represents the additional number of dollars that each of the remaining students must contribute in order to pay for the present?

(A) $\dfrac{y}{R}$

(B) $\dfrac{y}{R - x}$

(C) $\dfrac{xy}{R - x}$

(D) $\dfrac{xy}{R(R - x)}$

(E) $\dfrac{y}{R(R - x)}$

STOP

IF YOU FINISH BEFORE TIME IS CALLED, YOU MAY CHECK YOUR WORK ON THIS SECTION ONLY.
DO NOT TURN TO ANY OTHER SECTION IN THE TEST.

Answer Key
And Explanatory Material

Section 1

1	E
2	C
3	D
4	B
5	B
6	D
7	C
8	A
9	C
10	A
11	D
12	E
13	A
14	E
15	D
16	C
17	C
18	D
19	D
20	C
21	B
22	E
23	D
24	A
25	C

Section 2

1	B
2	B
3	E
4	E
5	D
6	B
7	D
8	C
9	A
10	D
11	E
12	A
13	B
14	C
15	C
16	E
17	B
18	D
19	D
20	A
21	B
22	B
23	C
24	A
25	E

Section 3

1	B
2	A
3	E
4	C
5	A
6	D
7	A
8	B
9	C
10	D
11	E
12	A
13	D
14	A
15	B
16	C
17	B
18	D
19	C
20	E
21	C
22	D
23	B
24	E
25	B

Section 4

1	D
2	B
3	C
4	A
5	E
6	B
7	C
8	A
9	C
10	A
11	E
12	E
13	D
14	C
15	B
16	D
17	D
18	A
19	D
20	A
21	
22	
23	
24	
25	

Section 5

1	B
2	B
3	C
4	E
5	D
6	B
7	C
8	B
9	C
10	E
11	D
12	B
13	B
14	B
15	A
16	E
17	C
18	E
19	A
20	E
21	
22	
23	
24	
25	

Section 6

1	C
2	A
3	D
4	B
5	A
6	A
7	C
8	A
9	
10	C
11	C
12	C
13	
14	A
15	D
16	E
17	
18	E
19	A
20	D
21	
22	
23	
24	
25	

Explanatory Material:
Reading Comprehension, Section 1

1. Which of the following best states the central idea of the passage?

   (A) The Byzantine Empire was a unique case in which the usual order of military and economic revival preceding cultural revival was reversed.

   (B) The economic, cultural, and military revival in the Byzantine Empire between the eighth and eleventh centuries was similar in its order to the sequence of revivals in Augustan Rome and fifth-century Athens.

   (C) After 810 Byzantine economic recovery spurred a military and, later, cultural expansion that lasted until 1453.

   (D) The eight-century revival of Byzantine learning is an inexplicable phenomenon, and its economic and military precursors have yet to be discovered.

   (E) The revival of the Byzantine Empire between the eighth and eleventh centuries shows cultural rebirth preceding economic and military revival, the reverse of the commonly accepted order of progress.

The best answer is E. The passage examines the revival of the Byzantine Empire between the eighth and eleventh centuries A.D., and evidence suggesting how the revival occurred is discussed. The author acknowledges in the second paragraph that "sequential connections among military, economic, and cultural forms of progress" have in the past helped to explain historical changes. It is further granted, in the third paragraph, that one usually expects military revival first, leading to economic revival, which, in turn, leads to cultural revival. The last paragraph points out, however, that in the Byzantine Empire a cultural revival preceded both economic revival and military revival. Choice E summarizes these points. There is no evidence that the Byzantine Empire is a "unique case"; thus, choice A is not correct. Choices B, C, and D are not statements supported by information in the passage.

2. The primary purpose of the second paragraph is which of the following?

   (A) To establish the uniqueness of the Byzantine revival

   (B) To show that Augustan Rome and fifth-century Athens are examples of cultural, economic, and military expansion against which all subsequent cases must be measured

   (C) To suggest that cultural, economic, and military advances have tended to be closely interrelated in different societies

   (D) To argue that, while the revivals of Augustan Rome and fifth-century Athens were similar, they are unrelated to other historical examples

   (E) To indicate that, wherever possible, historians should seek to make comparisons with the earliest chronological examples of revival

The best answer is C. In the second paragraph, the author suggests a way to analyze the Byzantine revival—i.e., by suggesting factors that have explained "the dynamics of historical change" in other societies. The passage indicates that these factors—cultural, military, and economic advances—have "gone together in a number of states and civilizations." The other answer choices do not accurately reflect either the purpose or the content of the second paragraph.

3. It can be inferred from the passage that by the eleventh century the Byzantine military forces

   (A) had reached their peak and begun to decline

   (B) had eliminated the Bulgarian army

   (C) were comparable in size to the army of Rome under Augustus

   (D) were strong enough to withstand the Abbasid Caliphate's military forces

   (E) had achieved control of Byzantine governmental structures

The best answer is D. This question requires you to select a statement that must be true given the information in the passage. According to the passage, by the eleventh century, the Byzantine Empire was militarily secure (lines 12-14). In lines 41-43, it is stated that "by 872 the military balance with the Abbasid Caliphate had been permanently altered in the empire's favor." This information allows the conclusion stated in Choice D. There is no information in the passage that supports the other choices.

4. It can be inferred from the passage that the Byzantine Empire sustained significant territorial losses

   (A) in 600

   (B) during the seventh century

   (C) a century after the cultural achievements of the Byzantine Empire had been lost

   (D) soon after the revival of Byzantine learning

   (E) in the century after 873

The best answer is B. The passage indicates that "By the early eighth century, the empire had lost roughly two-thirds of the territory it had possessed in the year 600" (lines 5-7). Thus, it can be inferred that territorial losses occurred between 600 and the early 700's, i.e., during the seventh century, as is stated in choice B.

5. In the third paragraph, the author most probably provides an explanation of the apparent connections among economic, military, and cultural development in order to

   (A) suggest that the process of revival in Byzantium accords with this model

   (B) set up an order of events that is then shown to be not generally applicable to the case of Byzantium

   (C) cast aspersions on traditional historical scholarship about Byzantium

   (D) suggest that Byzantium represents a case for which no historical precedent exists

   (E) argue that military conquest is the paramount element in the growth of empires

The best answer is B. The main purpose of the passage is to establish and explain the sequence in which the Byzantine revival occurred. The author examines an order of events that might be used to explain the growth of the Byzantine Empire. The author then shows that the Byzantine revival did not actually adhere to this pattern.

6. Which of the following does the author mention as crucial evidence concerning the manner in which the Byzantine revival began?

   (A) The Byzantine military revival of the 860's led to economic and cultural advances.

   (B) The Byzantine cultural revival lasted until 1453.

   (C) The Byzantine economic recovery began in the 900's.

   (D) The revival of Byzantine learning began toward the end of the eighth century.

   (E) By the early eleventh century the Byzantine Empire had regained much of its lost territory.

The best answer is D. An important point made by the author is that the sequence of events that led to the recovery of the Byzantine Empire did not begin with military achievements, but with a cultural revival (lines 45-48). An important piece of evidence supporting this assertion is the revival of learning, which began before 788. Choice D restates this evidence.

7. According to the author, "The common explanation" (line 28) of connections between economic, military, and cultural development is

   (A) revolutionary and too new to have been applied to the history of the Byzantine Empire

   (B) reasonable, but an antiquated theory of the nature of progress

   (C) not applicable to the Byzantine revival as a whole, but does perhaps accurately describe limited periods during the revival

   (D) equally applicable to the Byzantine case as a whole and to the history of military, economic, and cultural advances in ancient Greece and Rome

   (E) essentially not helpful, because military, economic, and cultural advances are part of a single phenomenon

The best answer is C. The author states that the "common explanation," which is referred to as a "hypothetical pattern" in line 36, did probably "apply at times during the course of the recovery." But the paragraph then indicates that another sequence of events characterized the Byzantine revival as a whole.

8. Which of the following titles best summarizes the passage as a whole?

   (A) At the Threshold of Neutrino Astronomy

   (B) Neutrinos and the History of the Universe

   (C) The Creation and Study of Neutrinos

   (D) The DUMAND System and How It Works

   (E) The Properties of the Neutrino

The best answer is A. The passage describes how the study of neutrinos could be useful (lines 12-17) and discusses efforts that are being made to detect neutrinos. These are developments that have led astronomy to a point at which knowledge about the universe can be increased by detecting neutrinos, that is, to the threshold of neutrino astronomy. In the last sentence, the author suggests that neutrino astronomy will become a reality.

   The titles given in C, D, and E summarize only portions of the passage. The title given in B describes a topic too broad to be a summary of the passage.

9. With which of the following statements regarding neutrino astronomy would the author be most likely to agree?

   (A) Neutrino astronomy will supersede all present forms of astronomy.
   (B) Neutrino astronomy will be abandoned if the DUMAND project fails.
   (C) Neutrino astronomy can be expected to lead to major breakthroughs in astronomy.
   (D) Neutrino astronomy will disclose phenomena that will be more surprising than past discoveries.
   (E) Neutrino astronomy will always be characterized by a large time lag between hypothesis and experimental confirmation.

The best answer is C. In lines 14-17, the author mentions new information about a wide variety of cosmic phenomena and about the history of the universe as advances in knowledge that could be derived from the detection of cosmic neutrinos. There is no evidence in the passage to indicate that the author would agree with the statements in choice A, B, D, or E.

10. In the last paragraph, the author describes the development of astronomy in order to

   (A) suggest that the potential findings of neutrino astronomy can be seen as part of a series of astronomical successes
   (B) illustrate the role of surprise in scientific discovery
   (C) demonstrate the effectiveness of the DUMAND apparatus in detecting neutrinos
   (D) name some cosmic phenomena that neutrino astronomy will illuminate
   (E) contrast the motivation of earlier astronomers with that of the astrophysicists working on the DUMAND project

The best answer is A. In the last paragraph, the author mentions that each of several extensions of astronomy led to important and surprising discoveries or successes. The statement that "Neutrino astronomy will doubtless bring its own share of surprises" (lines 52-53) ties neutrino astronomy to this series of successes.

11. According to the passage, one advantage that neutrinos have for studies in astronomy is that they

   (A) have been detected for the last twenty-five years
   (B) possess a variable electric charge
   (C) are usually extremely massive
   (D) carry information about their history with them
   (E) are very similar to other electromagnetic particles

The best answer is D. The answer to this question can be found in lines 12-17 of the passage, which state that "neutrinos carry with them information about the site and circumstances of their production" (that is, about their history) and so "could provide new information about a wide variety of cosmic phenomena and about the history of the universe."

12. According to the passage, the primary use of the apparatus mentioned in lines 24-32 would be to

   (A) increase the mass of a neutrino
   (B) interpret the information neutrinos carry with them
   (C) study the internal structure of a neutrino
   (D) see neutrinos in distant regions of space
   (E) detect the presence of cosmic neutrinos

The best answer is E, since the apparatus mentioned in lines 24-32 is "capable of detecting cosmic neutrinos" (line 25). D is not correct because, in order to be detected, the cosmic neutrinos must encounter the apparatus; therefore, the purpose of the apparatus is not to simply "see neutrinos in distant regions of space." There is no indication in the passage that the apparatus would analyze or operate on neutrinos as suggested in choices A, B, and C.

13. The passage states that interactions between neutrinos and other matter are

   (A) rare
   (B) artificial
   (C) undetectable
   (D) unpredictable
   (E) hazardous

The best answer is A. Lines 6-9 state that neutrinos can cross the entire universe without interacting with other particles of matter. Thus, these interactions can correctly be described as "rare."

   B is not the best answer because, although neutrinos can be artificially created, their interactions with other matter are not artificial. Although interactions between neutrinos and other matter are difficult to detect, they are not undetectable, as stated in C. The passage does not state that interactions between neutrinos and other matter are unpredictable or hazardous (D and E).

14. The passage mentions which of the following as a reason that neutrinos are hard to detect?

   (A) Their pervasiveness in the universe
   (B) Their ability to escape from different regions of space
   (C) Their inability to penetrate dense matter
   (D) The similarity of their structure to that of nucleons
   (E) The infrequency of their interaction with other matter

The best answer is E. Lines 5-9 describe the infrequency of the interactions of neutrinos with other matter. The question in lines 18-19, "how can scientists detect a particle that interacts so infrequently with other matter?" implies that the infrequent interaction of neutrinos with other matter makes detection of the neutrinos difficult.

15. According to the passage, the interaction of a neutrino with other matter can produce

(A) particles that are neutral and massive
(B) a form of radiation that permeates the universe
(C) inaccurate information about the site and circumstances of the neutrino's production
(D) charged particles and light
(E) a situation in which light and other forms of electromagnetic radiation are blocked

The best answer is D. Lines 39-42 describe the result of an interaction of a neutrino with other matter (a particle in an atom of seawater) as "a cascade of electrically charged particles and a flash of light."

16. According to the passage, one of the methods used to establish the properties of neutrinos was

(A) detection of photons
(B) observation of the interaction of neutrinos with gamma rays
(C) observation of neutrinos that were artifically created
(D) measurement of neutrinos that interacted with particles of seawater
(E) experiments with electromagnetic radiation

The best answer is C. According to the second paragraph of the passage, since neutrinos were first detected, most neutrino research has been done with artifically created neutrinos.

17. According to the passage, Barbara Strozzi's music attracted attention early in the twentieth century because of

(A) its uniquely private character
(B) its influence on Francesca Caccini
(C) the scarcity of seventeenth-century women composers
(D) the unconventionality of its forms
(E) the historical importance of Giulio Strozzi

The best answer is C. The reference for this answer can be found in lines 7-12, which state that Barbara Strozzi was one of the very few women composers in Italy during the seventeenth century. That this particular distinction was what attracted attention to her music early in the twentieth century is affirmed in lines 13-14.

18. The author's use of the word "supposedly" in line 18 implies which of the following?

(A) The author doubts the historical authenticity of the quotation that follows.
(B) The author doubts the accuracy of the facts she is reporting.
(C) The author disagrees with the judgment she is discussing.
(D) The author does not believe that Strozzi's music has the qualities cited in the quotation.
(E) The author is not sure of the significance of the quotation.

The best answer is C. The author states that early-twentieth-century appreciation of Strozzi's style was limited to qualities that were "supposedly feminine." This appreciation "now appears irrelevant as well as polemical." The author goes on to state (lines 22-24) that we are now in "a better position . . . to attempt a more precise evaluation." Choice D is not correct; although the author believes the appreciation itself was limited to certain of the qualities of Strozzi's work, there is no indication whether the author believes that spontaneity, grace, and taste actually characterized Strozzi's work. Choices A, B, and E are not supported by the information in the passage.

19. With which of the following statements would the author of the passage be most likely to agree?

(A) The music of seventeenth-century Italy is less frequently performed today than it was 50 years ago.
(B) Contemporary music historians no longer discuss the music of a given composer in terms of its particular individual style.
(C) The cantata tradition of seventeenth-century Italy is much better understood today than it ever has been.
(D) Late-twentieth-century music historians have more accurate historical information than their early-twentieth-century counterparts.
(E) Music historians of the early twentieth century were uninterested in the details of social life in seventeenth-century Venetian musical circles.

The best answer is D. In the second paragraph, the author states that early-twentieth-century appreciation of Strozzi's work was limited. The passage states that modern historians are in a better position with regard to historical knowledge. From this it can be inferred that the author would agree that late-twentieth-century historians have more accurate historical information.

20. The author of the passage bases her assertion that Strozzi is one of the very few seventeenth-century Italian women composers (lines 7-12) on which of the following assumptions?

(A) Public recognition is an indispensable part of a career as a composer.

(B) Strozzi and Caccini were influenced by the same composers.

(C) The music of any woman composer whom her seventeenth-century contemporaries regarded as noteworthy would be known to modern scholars.

(D) The cantata tradition of the mid-seventeenth century includes composers and performers of madrigals and arias as well as cantatas.

(E) More women pursued careers as composers in seventeenth-century Italy than is evident from music published in the seventeenth century.

In lines 7-9, the author establishes that Strozzi and Francesca Caccini are the only known women "among the many aria and cantata composers of seventeenth-century Italy." The author goes on to claim that Strozzi "is, presumably, among the very few women of the period to have pursued a career as a composer." In order to make this connection between the number of women composers known to modern scholars and the scarcity of women composers, the author must make an assumption. The assumption stated in C suggests the logical connection the author makes: if there had been other women composers known in their time, modern scholars would be likely to have encountered evidence of their presence. Since modern scholars do not know of other women composers from the seventeenth century, there were probably very few of them. None of the other choices is logically connected to the claim made in lines 7-12.

21. The author of the passage implies that which of the following was most essential to the success of both Francesca Caccini and Barbara Strozzi?

(A) Their presence in Venice at a time when vocal music flourished

(B) Their early firsthand exposure to music and musicians

(C) The lack of competition from other composers

(D) The popularity of madrigals and cantatas in seventeenth-century Italy

(E) The uniqueness of the musical forms they created

The best answer is B. According to the third paragraph, both Strozzi and Caccini grew up in musical families. In lines 36-38, the author states that "such an environment may have been essential" for their musical development. Although it is stated that Barbara Strozzi lived in Venice, the author does not mention where Francesca Caccini lived. Therefore, A is not the answer. Neither C nor D is supported by information in the passage. The passage does not indicate that Barbara Strozzi and Francesca Caccini created unique musical forms. Therefore, E is not the answer.

22. It can be inferred from the passage that all of the following made Barbara Strozzi "a somewhat anomalous figure" (lines 24-25) EXCEPT:

(A) She was a woman composer during the seventeenth century.

(B) She was intimately involved in Venetian literary and musical society.

(C) She did not write dramatic works for voice.

(D) She did not perform operatic works.

(E) She wrote moving baroque vocal works.

The best answer is E. The question indicates that all of the qualities except that indicated in E contribute to the conception of Barbara Strozzi as an anomalous or unusual figure among composers who were her contemporaries. The fact that she was one of very few women composers during the seventeenth century (lines 9-11) makes her unusual. The fact that she was able to enter a world "closed to other members of her sex" (line 32) also makes her anomalous. She neither wrote dramatic works for voice (choice C) nor performed in operas (choice D) while living in Venice, where opera was a main cultural interest, thus reinforcing her anomalousness. Barbara Strozzi was unlike other composers for all of the reasons above, but she was like her contemporaries because she wrote moving baroque works (lines 39-41). Therefore, E is the answer.

23. The author of the passage implies that composers of Italian baroque music typically

(A) composed more operas than cantatas

(B) preferred sacred to secular musical forms

(C) aspired to reach large segments of the public with their works

(D) avoided emotional expression in their works

(E) wrote music for solo voices rather than for choral ensembles

The best answer is C. In lines 43-45, the author states that Italian baroque music composers "sought . . . a public forum . . . in the theater and the Church." Since seventeenth-century Italian composers presented their works in both the theater and the Church, the implication that they preferred sacred to secular music is not supported, so B is not the answer. The author does not provide evidence for the implication that Italian baroque music composers composed more operas than cantatas, so A is not the answer. Neither D nor E can be inferred from the information in the passage.

24. The author of the passage quotes Barbara Strozzi in lines 53-54 most probably in order to

(A) support the claim that Strozzi's works are self-revealing
(B) qualify the point concerning Strozzi's dramatic works
(C) illustrate Strozzi's confident approach to her art
(D) show why Strozzi avoided opera as both composer and performer
(E) suggest that Strozzi's viewpoint was typical of baroque musicians

The best answer is A. The colon following the phrase "expressing less the feeling of fictive characters than her own" (lines 52-53) indicates that information to support this claim follows. What follows is the quote from Barbara Strozzi (lines 53-54), which supports the claim that her compositions expressed her innermost feelings and revealed her true self.

25. The passage provides information to answer which of the following questions?

(A) What was the exact family relationship between Giulio Strozzi and Barbara Strozzi?
(B) What is the evidence that indicates that Barbara Strozzi never sang in an opera?
(C) Were Barbara Strozzi's compositions known to her contemporaries?
(D) Did Barbara Strozzi know Francesca Caccini?
(E) What instruments provided the accompaniment for Barbara Strozzi's vocal works?

The best answer is C. In the first paragraph, the author states that Barbara Strozzi was one of the few women composers during the seventeenth century who "achieved some measure of public recognition." This statement implies that her compositions were known to her contemporaries; therefore, the answer to the question is C. The passage contains no information to answer any of the other questions.

Explanatory Material: Data Sufficiency, Section 2

1. What is the value of x?

(1) x is negative.
(2) $2x = -4$

Statement (1) alone is clearly not sufficient to determine the value of x, since there are infinitely many negative numbers. Thus, the answer must be B, C, or E. Statement (2) implies that $x = -2$, since $2(-2) = -4$. Therefore, the best answer is B.

2. Did United States carriers use more than 10 billion gallons of jet fuel during 1983?

(1) United States carriers paid a total of $9.4 billion for the jet fuel used in 1983.
(2) United States carriers paid an average (arithmetic mean) of $0.90 per gallon for the jet fuel used in 1983.

The total amount paid for the jet fuel used, t, is equal to the number of gallons used, n, multiplied by the average price per gallon, p. In order to calculate n, the values of both t and p must be known. Statement (1) says only that $t = 9.4$ and statement (2) says only that $p = \$0.90$. Thus, both (1) and (2) together, but neither alone, are sufficient to determine the value of n. The best answer is C.

3. In Country S, if 60 percent of the women aged 18 and over are in the labor force, how many million women are in the labor force?

(1) In Country S, women comprise 45 percent of the labor force.
(2) In Country S, there are no women under 18 years of age in the labor force.

Statement (1) is not sufficient, since the size of the labor force is not specified. Therefore, the answer must be B, C, or E. From statement (2), together with the fact given in the question, it follows only that the female labor force comprises 60 percent of the women aged 18 and over, and the answer must be C or E. Since statements (1) and (2) together do not provide any actual numbers to which the percents given could be applied, the best answer is E.

4. If x and y are different positive numbers, is z between x and y?

(1) $z > 0$
(2) $z < y$

From statement (1) it follows that z is positive but not that z is between x and y. Thus, the answer must be B, C, or E. Statement (2) alone is also not sufficient, because it is not known whether or not $x < z$. Thus, the answer must be C or E. Since $0 < x < z < y$ or $0 < z < x < y$ or $0 < z < y < x$ are all consistent with (1) and (2), the best answer is E.

5. What percent of 16 is m?

   (1) m is 5 percent of 10.
   (2) 400 percent of m is 2.

The question can be answered if the value of m is known. According to statement (1), $m = \frac{5}{100}(10) = 0.5$. Therefore, $m = \left(\frac{0.5}{16}\right) \times 100\%$ of 16, and the answer must be A or D. According to statement (2), $4m = 2$, or $m = \frac{1}{2}$, and again m as a percent of 16 can be determined. Thus, the best answer is D.

6. Kay put 12 cards on a table, some faceup and the rest facedown. How many were put facedown?

   (1) Kay put an even number of the cards faceup.
   (2) Kay put twice as many of the cards faceup as she put facedown.

If x denotes the number of cards that were put facedown, it follows from statement (1) that x could be 2, 4, 6, 8, 10, or 12. Thus statement (1) alone is not sufficient, and the answer must be B, C, or E. From statement (2) it can be determined that $2x + x = 3x = 12$, or $x = 4$. Therefore, statement (2) alone is sufficient, and the best answer is B.

7. Is $\triangle RST$ a right triangle?

   (1) The degree measure of $\angle R$ is twice the degree measure of $\angle T$.
   (2) The degree measure of $\angle T$ is 30.

Let r, s, and t denote the degree measures of angles R, S, and T, respectively. Then $r + s + t = 180$. From statement (1) it follows that $r = 2t$, and thus $3t + s = 180$. Since infinitely many values of t can satisfy this equation, and $s = 90$ only if $t = 30$, statement (1) alone is not sufficient. Therefore, the answer must be B, C, or E. Clearly, statement (2) alone is not sufficient, and the answer must be C or E. Since $3t + s = 180$ and $t = 30$ together imply that $s = 90$, the best response is C.

8. If x is a positive number, is x greater than 1?

   (1) $1 > \frac{1}{x}$
   (2) $-\frac{1}{x} > -1$

Multiplying both sides of an inequality by a positive number does not change the order of the inequality, whereas multiplying both sides by a negative number reverses its order. In statement (1), multiplying both sides of $1 > \frac{1}{x}$ by x, which is given to be positive, yields $x > 1$. Therefore, statement (1) is

sufficient, and the answer must be A or D. In statement (2), multiplying both sides of $-\frac{1}{x} > -1$ by -1 yields $\frac{1}{x} < 1$, which is the same as statement (1). Therefore, the best answer is D.

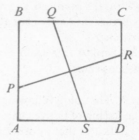

9. The figure above shows four pieces of tile that have been glued together to form a square tile $ABCD$. Is $PR = QS$?

   (1) $BQ = CR = DS = AP$
   (2) The perimeter of $ABCD$ is 16.

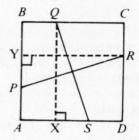

In the figure above, $QX \perp AD$ and $RY \perp AB$. Therefore, $AX = BQ$ and $BY = CR$. From statement (1) and the fact that $AB = AD$, it follows that $XS = YP$. Since $QX = YR$, it follows by the Pythagorean Theorem that $PR = QS$. Thus, statement (1) is sufficient, and the answer must be A or D. Note that the reasoning above assumes that neither points S and X nor points P and Y coincide. However, if both pairs of points do coincide, then $PR = QS =$ the length of a side of the square, and (1) alone is sufficient in this case also. Since statement (2) is clearly not sufficient, the best answer is A.

   Another solution is to observe that from statement (1) it follows that quadrilateral $BQSA$ is congruent to quadrilateral $CRPB$. Thus, since corresponding parts of congruent figures are equal, it follows that $PR = QS$.

10. How old is Jim?

   (1) Eight years ago Jim was half as old as he is now.
   (2) Four years from now Jim will be twice as old as he was six years ago.

Let j denote Jim's age. It follows from statement (1) that $j - 8 = \frac{j}{2}$, or $j = 16$. Thus, statement (1) alone is sufficient, and the answer must be A or D. From statement (2) it follows that $j + 4 = 2(j - 6)$, which has the solution $j = 16$. (Note that it is not necessary to actually solve the equation for the value of j.) Therefore, the best answer is D.

11. **What is the value of x?**

    (1) **When x is multiplied by 8, the result is between 50 and 60.**
    (2) **When x is doubled, the result is between 10 and 15.**

Statement (1) implies that $50 < 8x < 60$, or $6\frac{1}{4} < x < 7\frac{1}{2}$. Since it is not specified that x is an integer, x can be any real number in this interval and not just 7. Thus, statement (1) is not sufficient, and the answer must be B, C, or E. Statement (2) implies that $10 < 2x < 15$, or $5 < x < 7\frac{1}{2}$, which again determines a range of possible values. Therefore, the answer must be C or E. Since statements (1) and (2) together imply only that $6\frac{1}{4} < x < 7\frac{1}{2}$, the best answer is E.

12. **At a certain state university last term, there were p students each of whom paid either the full tuition of x dollars or half the full tuition. What percent of the tuition paid by the p students last term was tuition from students who paid the full tuition?**

    (1) **Of the p students, 20 percent paid the full tuition.**
    (2) **The p students paid a total of \$91.2 million for tuition last term.**

From statement (1) it follows that the tuition from students who paid the full tuition, F, was $0.2px$ dollars and the tuition from students who paid half the full tuition, H, was $0.8p\left(\dfrac{x}{2}\right) = 0.4px$ dollars. Thus,

$$\frac{F}{F + H} = \frac{0.2px}{0.2px + 0.4px} = \frac{1}{3}, \text{ or } 33\frac{1}{3}\%,$$ and the answer

must be A or D. Clearly, statement (2) alone is not sufficient, since the amount of tuition paid by students who paid the full tuition would also need to be known. Therefore, the best answer is A.

13. **If a bottle is to be selected at random from a certain collection of bottles, what is the probability that the bottle will be defective?**

    (1) **The ratio of the number of bottles in the collection that are defective to the number that are not defective is 3 : 500.**
    (2) **The collection contains 3,521 bottles.**

The probability that the bottle will be defective is the ratio of the number of defective bottles to the total number of bottles in the collection. From statement (1) it follows that, for some integer k, the number of defective bottles is $3k$ and the number of bottles that are not defective is $500k$. Thus, the probability in question is $\dfrac{3k}{503k} = \dfrac{3}{503}$. Statement (1) is sufficient, and the answer must be A or D. However, statement (2) alone is not sufficient, since the number of defective bottles or the number of nondefective bottles would also need to be known. Therefore, the best answer is A.

14. **If a grocery shopper received \$0.25 off the original price of a certain product by using a coupon, what was the original price of the product?**

    (1) **The shopper received a 20 percent discount by using the coupon.**
    (2) **The original price was 25 percent higher than the price the shopper paid by using the coupon.**

From statement (1) it follows that the discount of \$0.25 was 20 percent, or $\dfrac{1}{5}$, of the original price. Thus, the original price was $5(\$0.25) = \$1.25$. Statement (1) is sufficient, and the answer must be A or D. From statement (2) it follows that the original price was 125 percent, or $\dfrac{5}{4}$, of the discounted price; in other words, the discounted price was $\dfrac{4}{5}$, or 80 percent, of the original price. Since this is a discount of 20 percent, it again follows that the original price was \$1.25. Therefore, statement (2) is also sufficient and the best answer is D.

15. **What was Casey's total score for eighteen holes of golf?**

    (1) **Casey's score for the first nine holes was 13 less than his score for the last nine holes.**
    (2) **Twice Casey's score for the last nine holes was 58 more than his score for the first nine holes.**

If f and g denote Casey's score for the first nine holes and for the last nine holes, respectively, then the question asks for the value of $f + g$. Statement (1) implies that $f = g - 13$, or $f + g = 2g - 13$. Since the value of g is unknown, statement (1) is not sufficient, and the answer must be B, C, or E. Statement (2) implies that $2g = f + 58$, or $f + g = 3g - 58$. Again, the total score $f + g$ cannot be determined, and the answer must be C or E. From (1) and (2) together, it follows that the values of f and g, and thus the value of $f + g$, can be determined. Therefore, the best answer is C.

16. What is the rate, in cubic feet per minute, at which water is flowing into a certain rectangular tank?

   (1) The height of the water in the tank is increasing at the rate of 2 feet per minute.
   (2) The capacity of the tank is 216 cubic feet.

The desired rate can be calculated by multiplying the rate at which the height of the water increases, in feet per minute, by the surface area of the water in square feet. Statement (1) is, therefore, not sufficient, since the surface area of the water is not specified. Thus, the answer is B, C, or E. Clearly statement (2) is not sufficient, since it gives no information about either the flow of water into the tank or the surface area of the water in the tank. For example, the tank could have height 6 feet and water surface area 36 square feet, or height 3 feet and water surface area 72 square feet. Since neither statement (1) nor statement (2) gives any information about the surface area of the water in the tank, the best answer is E.

17. Is the positive integer n equal to the square of an integer?

   (1) For every prime number p, if p is a divisor of n, then so is p^2.
   (2) $\sqrt{n}$ is an integer.

Statement (1) is not sufficient since, for example, both $n = 2^2 = 4$, which is the square of an integer, and $n = 2^3 = 8$, which is not, satisfy the given conditions. Thus, the answer must be B, C, or E. From statement (2) it follows that $\sqrt{n} = r$, for some positive integer r, or that $n = r^2$. Therefore, statement (2) is sufficient and the best answer is B.

18. What is the volume of a certain cube?

   (1) The sum of the areas of the faces of the cube is 54.
   (2) The greatest possible distance between two points on the cube is $3\sqrt{3}$.

Since the volume of a cube is determined by the length of an edge, if the length of an edge can be determined, the question can be answered. If the surface area of the cube is known, the area of one face, and thus the length of an edge, can be determined. Furthermore, if the greatest possible distance between two points on the cube (i.e., the "space" diagonal) is known, the length of an edge of the cube can be found. Therefore, both statements (1) and (2) alone are sufficient, and the best answer is D.

19. What is the value of $k^2 - k$?

   (1) The value of $k - \dfrac{1}{k}$ is 1.
   (2) The value of $2k - 1$ is $\sqrt{5}$.

Statement (1) implies that $k - \dfrac{1}{k} = 1$. If both sides of the equation are multiplied by k, the result is $k^2 - 1 = k$, or $k^2 - k = 1$. Thus, statement (1) is sufficient, and the answer must be A or D. Statement (2) implies that $2k - 1 = \sqrt{5}$, from which the value of k, and thus the value of $k^2 - k$, can be determined. Therefore, statement (2) alone is also sufficient, and the best answer is D.

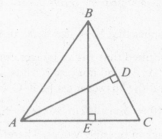

20. In the figure above, what is the product of the lengths of AD and BC?

   (1) The product of the lengths of AC and BE is 60.
   (2) The length of BC is 8.

The area of a triangle equals half the product of the length of a side and the length of the altitude to that side. Thus, in the figure $\dfrac{1}{2}(AC)(BE) = \dfrac{1}{2}(AD)(BC)$, or $(AC)(BE) = (AD)(BC)$. Statement (1) yields $(AC)(BE) = 60$, and the answer must be A or D. Statement (2) is clearly not sufficient, since the length of AD is not specified. Therefore, the best answer is A.

21. At a business association conference, the registration fee for members of the association was $20 and the registration fee for nonmembers was $25. If the total receipts from registration were $5,500, did more members than nonmembers pay the registration fee?

   (1) Registration receipts from members were $500 greater than receipts from nonmembers.
   (2) A total of 250 people paid the registration fee.

If m and n denote the number of members and nonmembers, respectively, the information given in the question can be expressed by the equation $20m + 25n = 5,500$. Since the information in statement (1) is given by $20m = 25n + 500$, the two equations can be solved for m and n. ($m = 150$ and $n = 100$, but it is not necessary to actually determine these values.) Thus, statement (1) is sufficient, and the answer must be A or D. Statement (2) yields $m + n = 250$. Again, this equation together with the equation $20m + 25n = 5,500$ can be solved for m and n. Thus, it can also be determined from statement (2) whether or not $m > n$. Therefore, the best answer is D.

22. If x and y are positive integers and x is a multiple of y, is $y = 2$?

    (1) $y \neq 1$
    (2) $x + 2$ is a multiple of y.

Since x is a multiple of y, there is an integer n such that $x = ny$. Statement (1) is clearly not sufficient. For example, $x = 4$, $y = 2$ and $x = 9$, $y = 3$ both satisfy the information given in the question. Thus, the answer must be B, C, or E. From statement (2) it follows that $x + 2 = my$ for some integer m. Since $x = ny$, $ny + 2 = my$ or $2 = (m - n)y$. Since y is positive, it follows that $y = 1$ or 2. Note that two values for y are determined, and not a unique value. Thus, statement (2) is not sufficient, and the answer must be C or E. From (1) and (2) together it can be concluded that $y = 2$. Therefore, the best answer is C.

23. What is the value of n?

    (1) $n(n - 1)(n - 2) = 0$
    (2) $n^2 + n - 6 = 0$

From statement (1) it follows that $n = 0, 1$, or 2. Since a unique value of n is not determined, statement (1) is not sufficient, and the answer must be B, C, or E. In statement (2), since $n^2 + n - 6 = (n + 3)(n - 2)$, it follows that $n = -3$ or 2, and statement (2) also is not sufficient. The only value of n that satisfies both statements (1) and (2) is $n = 2$. Therefore, the best answer is C.

24. If x and y are integers between 10 and 99, inclusive, is $\dfrac{x - y}{9}$ an integer?

    (1) x and y have the same two digits, but in reverse order.
    (2) The tens' digit of x is 2 more than the units' digit, and the tens' digit of y is 2 less than the units' digit.

From statement (1) it follows that
$$x = (M)(10) + N$$
$$y = (N)(10) + M,$$
where M and N are each digits from 1 to 9, inclusive. Subtracting the bottom equation from the top equation, it follows that $x - y = (M - N)10 + (N - M)$, or $x - y = (M - N)10 - (M - N)$. Thus, $x - y = (10 - 1)(M - N) = 9(M - N)$, and $\dfrac{x - y}{9} = M - N$, which is an integer. Thus, statement (1) is sufficient, and the answer must be A or D. Statement (2) is not sufficient. For example, if $x = 53$ and $y = 35$, then $x - y = 18$, which is divisible by 9; however, if $x = 53$ and $y = 46$, then $x - y = 7$, which is not divisible by 9. Therefore, the best answer is A.

25. Pam and Ed are in a line to purchase tickets. How many people are in the line?

    (1) There are 20 people behind Pam and 20 people in front of Ed.
    (2) There are 5 people between Pam and Ed.

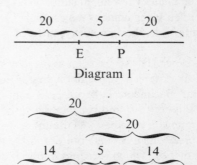

Note that either Pam is behind Ed in the line (see Diagram 1 above), or Ed is behind Pam (see Diagram 2 above). Clearly, neither statement alone is sufficient, and the answer must be C or E. As the diagrams indicate, statements (1) and (2) together are sufficient to determine the number of people in the line only if it is specified whether Pam is behind or ahead of Ed in the line. In the first case, there must be 47 people in the line, including Pam and Ed; in the second case, there must be 35 people in the line. Therefore, the best answer is E.

Explanatory Material: Sentence Correction, Section 3

1. During the first one hundred fifty years of the existence of this republic, no one expected the press <u>was</u> fair; newspapers were mostly shrill, scurrilous, and partisan.

    (A) was
    (B) to be
    (C) of being
    (D) should be
    (E) had to be

The idiomatic form of expression is either *expected that X would be Y* or *expected X to be Y*. Thus B, which follows the latter form, is the best answer. Each of the other options produces an unidiomatic statement.

2. Most victims of infectious mononucleosis recover after a few weeks of listlessness, but an unlucky few may suffer for years.

   (A) but an unlucky few may suffer
   (B) and an unlucky few have suffered
   (C) that an unlucky few might suffer
   (D) that a few being unlucky may suffer
   (E) but a few who, being unlucky, suffered

A is the best choice. The second clause presents a possible exception to the statement made in the first, a contrast that *but* makes clear. B is incorrect because the conjunction *and* fails to show this contrast and because the verb *have suffered* mistakenly presents a possibility as though it were an actual occurrence. *That*, which begins both C and D, is not a coordinating conjunction, which is required to join two independent clauses. D additionally is awkward. Although E begins with *but*, it is not an independent clause; the verb *suffered* takes the relative pronoun *who* as its subject, leaving no verb for the subject *few*. Moreover, E is awkward and, like B, mistakenly presents a possibility as though it were an actual occurrence.

3. It was the loss of revenue from declines in tourism that in 1935 led the Saudi authorities' granting a concession for oil exploration to the company that would later be known by the name of Aramco.

   (A) authorities' granting a concession for oil exploration to the company that would later be known by the name of
   (B) authorities' granting a concession for oil exploration to the compnay later to be known as named
   (C) authorities granting a concession for oil exploration to the company that would later be known by the name of
   (D) authorities to grant a concession for oil exploration to the company that later will be known as being
   (E) authorities to grant a concession for oil exploration to the company later to be known as

In this sentence, the verb *led* requires that a person or persons perform an action indicated by the infinitive, or "to ____ " form, of the verb, and so choices A, B, and C can be faulted because *led* is completed by *granting*. Choice B is also faulty because the phrase *known as* here requires a noun, and *named* is a past participle. Choice D has *to grant* but inappropriately uses *will* rather than *would* and employs *being* unidiomatically. The best choice is E because it supplies *authorities* for *led*, the infinitive *to grant*, and an idiomatic use of *known as*.

4. Framed by traitorous colleagues, Alfred Dreyfus was imprisoned for twelve years before there was exoneration and his freedom.

   (A) there was exoneration and his freedom
   (B) he was to be exonerated with freedom
   (C) being exonerated and freed
   (D) exoneration and his freedom
   (E) being freed, having been exonerated

This sentence is to be completed with two ideas—exoneration and freedom. Choices A, C, and D connect them with *and* and therefore need parallel words or phrases. In choices A and D, the phrases are not exactly parallel: *freedom* is modified by *his* but *exonerated* is not. Also, choice A uses the wordy and imprecise *there was*. Choice C, the best answer, supplies the parallelism in the past participles *exonerated* and *freed*. Choice B is confusing because the phrase *to be* could imply that the original intention when Dreyfus was imprisoned was to exonerate him in twelve years, and *with* could imply that *freedom* was an attribute of his exoneration. In addition to being awkward, the inappropriate tense shift in E makes it sound as if Dreyfus had been exonerated some period of time before being freed.

5. By studying the primitive visual systems of single-cell aquatic organisms, biophysicists have discovered a striking similarity between algae and cows, a similarity that indicates the common evolutionary origin of plants and animals: both algae and cows produce a light-sensitive protein called rhodopsin.

   (A) biophysicists have discovered a striking similarity between algae and cows
   (B) a striking similarity between algae and cows has been discovered by biophysicists
   (C) there is a striking similarity that biophysicists have discovered between algae and cows
   (D) the discovery of a striking similarity between algae and cows was made by biophysicists
   (E) algae and cows have a striking similarity that was discovered by biophysicists

This question requires that the opening participial phrase modify the subject of the sentence, *biophysicists*. The subject should therefore be placed as close to the phrase as possible. Choice A places the subject next to the phrase and is the best choice. In choice B a *similarity* is doing the studying, in choice D *the discovery* is, and in choice E the *algae and cows* are. By placing *there is* next to the phrase, choice C leaves the participle with nothing to modify.

6. Because young children do not organize their attention or perceptions systematically, <u>like adults</u>, they may notice and remember details that their elders ignore.

   (A) like adults
   (B) unlike an adult
   (C) as adults
   (D) as adults do
   (E) as an adult

The problem in this question concerns like/as. If the underline modified *children*, then *like* would be appropriate; however, if it parallels the clause *children do not organize*, then *as* is appropriate. To modify *children*, the underline should be next to the word, so choices A and B are not correct. Also, choice A states that *children* and *adults* are similar, whereas the rest of the sentence contrasts them. Choice B attempts to contrast them, but it uses the singular *adult*, which does not parallel the plural *children*. Choices C, D, and E use the correct connector, *as*, but choice E, like choice B, uses the singular *adult*, and choice C gives only part of the clause, the subject. Choice D provides the complete parallel clause.

7. As many as 300 of <u>the 720 paintings attributed to Rembrandt may</u> actually be the works of his students or other admirers.

   (A) the 720 paintings attributed to Rembrandt may
   (B) the 720 paintings attributed to be Rembrandt's might
   (C) the 720 paintings that were attributed to be by Rembrandt may
   (D) the 720 Rembrandt paintings that were once attributed to him might
   (E) Rembrandt's paintings, although 720 were once attributed to him, may

Both choices B and C can be faulted for the unidiomatic use of *to be* with *attributed*. Choice D seems contradictory by first calling all 720 paintings Rembrandt's (not just attributing them to the painter) and then saying that 300 of them might not be his. Choice E repeats the seeming contradiction in D and then creates further confusion by the awkward placement of the *although* clause. Choice A uses the correct phrase, *attributed to*, and is the best choice.

8. Studies of the human "sleep-wake cycle" have practical relevance for matters ranging from duty assignments in nuclear submarines and air-traffic control towers <u>to the staff of</u> shifts in 24-hour factories.

   (A) to the staff of
   (B) to those who staff
   (C) to the staffing of
   (D) and staffing
   (E) and the staff of

The best answer for this question must have a phrase parallel to *from duty assignments* — that is, a phrase with the preposition *to* and a word that indicates a thing or an activity. Choices D and E can be faulted for having *and* in place of *to*. Choices A, B, and C supply the proper preposition, but A and B attempt to parallel *duty assignments* with *staff* — that is, with people. Only choice C combines the proper preposition with *the staffing*, a correct parallel to *duty assignments*.

9. Many psychologists and sociologists now contend that the deliberate and even brutal aggression integral to some forms of competitive athletics <u>increase the likelihood of imitative violence that erupts</u> among crowds of spectators dominated by young adult males.

   (A) increase the likelihood of imitative violence that erupts
   (B) increase the likelihood that there will be an eruption of imitative violence
   (C) increase the likelihood of imitative violence erupting
   (D) increases the likelihood for imitative violence to erupt
   (E) increases the likelihood that imitative violence will erupt

Choices A, B, and C are incorrect because they supply a plural form of the verb *increase* for the singular subject *aggression*. Choices D and E supply the correct singular form of the verb, but in D *the likelihood for imitative violence to erupt* is unidiomatic. Choice E is the best choice for this question.

10. More than five thousand years ago, Chinese scholars accurately described the flow of blood as a continuous circle controlled by the heart, <u>but it went</u> unnoticed in the West.

   (A) but it went
   (B) but it was
   (C) although it was
   (D) but the discovery went
   (E) although the discovery was

Choices A, B, and C can be faulted for the lack of any clear antecedent for the pronoun *it*. The nouns that are present — *flow*, *circle*, and *heart* — do not make any sense if substituted for the pronoun. What *it* attempts to refer to is the entire event, and choices D and E, rather than use a pronoun, give that event a name, *the discovery*. In choice E the conjunction *although* implies illogically that the discovery was made in spite of the fact that the West did not notice it. Choice D supplies the correct conjunction, *but*, and is the best choice.

11. Several studies have found that the coronary patients who exercise most actively <u>have half or less than half the chance of dying of a heart attack as those who are sedentary</u>.

   (A) have half or less than half the chance of dying of a heart attack as those who are sedentary

   (B) have half the chance, or less, of dying of a heart attack than those who are sedentary do

   (C) have half the chance that they will die of a heart attack, or less, than those who are sedentary do

   (D) are at least fifty percent less likely to die of a heart attack as those who are sedentary

   (E) are at least fifty percent less likely than those who are sedentary to die of a heart attack

Choice A incorrectly uses *as those who are sedentary* for *that those who are sedentary have* in comparing the chances for survival that active patients have with the chances that sedentary patients have; *that*, a pronoun, is needed to refer to *chance*. Choice B incorrectly substitutes *than* for *that* and is awkward. In choice C, *that they will die* is more wordy and awkward than *of dying*, and the placement of *less* confuses the meaning of the sentence. Choice D incorrectly uses *as* for *than* and separates the elements being compared. Choice E is best.

12. Most nations regard their airspace <u>as extending</u> upward as high as an aircraft can fly; no specific altitude, however, has been offficially recognized as a boundary.

   (A) as extending

   (B) as the extent

   (C) to be an extent

   (D) to be an extension

   (E) to extend

Choice A is best because it is idiomatically correct; *regard*, when its meaning indicates seeing, looking at, or conceiving of something in a particular way, is paired with *as* in the idiomatic construction *regard X as Y*. Choices C, D, and E violate the *regard . . . as* construction. In choices B, C, and D, the nouns *extent* and *extension* cannot be modified by the adverbial phrase that follows: a verb form such as *extending* is needed.

13. According to scientists at the University of California, the pattern of changes that have occurred in human DNA over the millennia <u>indicate the possibility that everyone alive today might be descended from a single female ancestor who</u> lived in Africa sometime between 140,000 and 280,000 years ago.

   (A) indicate the possibility that everyone alive today might be descended from a single female ancestor who

   (B) indicate that everyone alive today might possibly be a descendant of a single female ancestor who had

   (C) may indicate that everyone alive today has descended from a single female ancestor who had

   (D) indicates that everyone alive today may be a descendant of a single female ancestor who

   (E) indicates that everyone alive today might be a descendant from a single female ancestor who

Choices A, B, and C are incorrect because the plural verb *indicate* does not agree with the singular subject *pattern*. Choices A, B, and E contain *might*, which expresses too much doubt; *may*, which expresses a distinct possibility, is preferable. Given *might*, *possibility* in A and *possibly* in B are redundant. In choices B and C, *had*, the auxiliary of *lived*, should be deleted because the simple past tense is correct; the past perfect is used to refer to action that precedes some other action occurring in the past. In choice C, *may* is misplaced before *indicate*. Also, *descended* would more appropriately take some form of the verb *to be* in place of *has*. Choice D is best. In choice E, *from* should be *of*.

14. Several senior officials spoke to the press on condition <u>that they not be named</u> in the story.

   (A) that they not be named

   (B) that their names will not be used

   (C) that their names are not used

   (D) of not being named

   (E) they will not be named

Choice A is best; it is the only choice that uses the subjunctive form of the verb, as is appropriate in referring to a conditional circumstance that has not yet been realized as fact. Also, *on condition that* is idiomatic. In addition to failing to use the subjunctive form, choices B and C are wordy. Choices D and E are unidiomatic and, like B and C, fail to use the subjunctive.

15. According to his own account, Frédéric-Auguste Bartholdi, the sculptor of the Statue of Liberty, modeled the face of the statue like his mother's and the body like his wife's.

(A) modeled the face of the statue like his mother's and the body like his wife's
(B) modeled the face of the statue after that of his mother and the body after that of his wife
(C) modeled the face of the statue like his mother and the body like his wife
(D) made the face of the statue after his mother and the body after his wife
(E) made the face of the statue look like his mother and the body look like his wife

In choices A and C, *like* is used inappropriately; as a preposition, it should compare one noun to another, but instead it is used to modify the verb *modeled*. Also, *modeled . . . like* is unidiomatic and awkward. Choice C is also unidiomatic and imprecise. The phrase should indicate that the sculptor modeled the face of the statue after the *face* of his mother and not the entire person; so too, the body of the statue was modeled after only the body of his wife. Choices D and E, like A and C, are imprecise and unidiomatic. Choice B is best; *modeled . . . after* is idiomatic, the prepositional phrases have objects, and each pronoun *that* has an antecedent, *face* and *body*, respectively.

16. One of Ronald Reagan's first acts as President was to rescind President Carter's directive that any chemical banned on medical grounds in the United States be prohibited from sale to other countries.

(A) that any chemical banned on medical grounds in the United States be prohibited from sale to other countries
(B) that any chemical be prohibited from sale to other countries that was banned on medical grounds in the United States
(C) prohibiting the sale to other countries of any chemical banned on medical grounds in the United States
(D) prohibiting that any chemical banned on medical grounds in the United States is sold to other countries
(E) that any chemical banned in the United States on medical grounds is prohibited from being sold to other countries

In choices A, B, and E, *prohibited from sale* and *prohibited from being sold* cannot properly modify *any chemical*: the chemicals are banned, and the *sale* of the chemicals is prohibited. Moreover, in A and B *prohibited from* must be completed by a present participial ("-ing") form, not by a noun such as *sale*. In addition, B clumsily separates modifying phrases, such as *banned on medical grounds*, from the words they modify. Choices D and E, aside from being very awkward, use *is* incorrectly in referring to a situation that did not exist but that President Carter tried to bring about through his directive. Choice C is the best answer.

17. Although just inside the orbit of Jupiter, amateur astronomers with good telescopes should be able to see the comet within the next few weeks.

(A) Although just inside the orbit of
(B) Although it is just inside the orbit of
(C) Just inside the orbit of
(D) Orbiting just inside
(E) Having orbited just inside

Initial phrases, which lack a subject and its conjugated verb, attach to the subject of the main clause and modify it. Consequently, the initial phrases represented by choices A and C state absurdly that amateur astronomers with good telescopes are just inside the orbit of Jupiter. D and E worsen their predicament by having them orbit just inside the planet itself. Choice B, the best answer, conveys the intended meaning clearly: the pronoun *it* refers to *the comet* and functions as the subject of a subordinate clause that is grammatically joined to the main clause by *Although*.

18. Under Napoleon the French were not able to organize an adequate supply system, and it was a major cause of the failure of their invasion of Russia.

(A) Under Napoleon the French were not able to organize an adequate supply system, and it
(B) The French being unable to organize an adequate supply system under Napoleon
(C) For the French under Napoleon, to be unable to organize an adequate supply system
(D) The inability of the French under Napoleon to organize an adequate supply system
(E) The French inability under Napoleon of organizing an adequate supply system

In choice A, *it* has no logical noun referent; to make complete sense, a noun phrase such as *this inability* would have to replace *it* as the subject of *was*. B also lacks a noun or construction that can be a subject for *was*. The infinitive *to be unable* in C wrongly suggests a permanent or general condition rather than a specific instance of failure. In choice E, *French inability . . . of organizing* is badly worded: *inability* requires *to organize*, and the inability itself was not *French* —it was in this historical circumstance a characteristic *of* the French. Choice D, the best answer, provides idiomatic phrasing and a proper grammatical subject for *was*.

19. To help preserve ancient Egyptian monuments threatened by high water tables, a Swedish engineering firm has proposed installing pumps, perhaps solar powered, <u>to lower the underground water level and dig trenches</u> around the bases of the stone walls.

    (A) to lower the underground water level and dig trenches
    (B) to lower the underground water level and to dig trenches
    (C) to lower the underground water level and digging trenches
    (D) that lower the underground water level and that trenches be dug
    (E) that lower the underground water level and trench digging

Choice C, the best answer, is the only one that achieves parallel verb form by producing the construction *has proposed installing pumps . . . and digging trenches*: *dig trenches* in A, *to dig trenches* in B, *that trenches be dug* in D, and *trench digging* in E do not follow the same grammatical form as *installing pumps*. The false parallels with *to lower* in A and B make it sound as if the pumps were installed in order to dig trenches, and *that lower the underground water level* in D and E seems imprecisely to describe a characteristic of the pumps rather than to identify the purpose for which pumps would be installed.

20. When rates were raised in 1985, postal service officials predicted <u>they would make further rate increases unnecessary</u> for at least three years.

    (A) they would make further rate increases unnecessary
    (B) they would mean that further rate increases would not be needed
    (C) that it would not be necessary for further rate increases
    (D) that the increase would make further rate increases unnecessary
    (E) further rate increases will not be needed

The pronoun *they* is confusing in choices A and B because it seems to refer to *officials*, the nearest plural noun, rather than to *rates*. Choice C is grammatically incomplete: *it would not be necessary* must be completed by an infinitive, such as *to increase rates further*, rather than by the prepositional phrase *for further rate increases*. In choice E, the *will* should be *would* to indicate that what was predicted was only a prediction and not an accomplished fact. Choice D is best.

21. With its plan to develop seven and a half acres of shore land, Cleveland is but one of a large number of communities on the Great Lakes that <u>is looking to its waterfront as a way to improve the quality of urban life and attract</u> new businesses.

    (A) is looking to its waterfront as a way to improve the quality of urban life and attract
    (B) is looking at its waterfront to improve the quality of urban life and attract
    (C) are looking to their waterfronts to improve the quality of urban life and attract
    (D) are looking to its waterfront as a way of improving the quality of urban life and attracting
    (E) are looking at their waterfronts as a way they can improve the quality of urban life and attract

In choices A and B, the singular *is* does not agree in number with its subject, *that*; *that* is plural here because it refers to the plural noun *communities*, not to *one*. The phrase *looking to* describes not only Cleveland but all of the communities it is grouped with, and so the plural *that are looking to* is required. B and E can be faulted because *looking at* is less idiomatic here than *looking to*: people look *to* something, not *at* something, for a solution. In D, *its* does not agree with the plural subject, the *communities*, and the phrasing is wordy. Choice C, the best answer, is concise and grammatical.

22. A collection of 38 poems by Phillis Wheatley, a slave, was published in the 1770's, the first book by a Black woman and <u>it was only the second published by an American woman</u>.

    (A) it was only the second published by an American woman
    (B) it was only the second that an American woman published
    (C) the second one only published by an American woman
    (D) the second one only that an American woman published
    (E) only the second published by an American woman

In this question, the phrase that completes the sentence should be grammatically parallel to *the first book by a Black woman*, the phrase it is linked to by *and*. A and B are not parallel because they introduce a new grammatical subject and verb, *it was*, thus producing a clause rather than a parallel phrase. In C and D, *only* is misplaced, and *that an American woman published* in B and D does not parallel *by a Black woman*. Choice E, the best answer, supplies the needed parallel phrase, with the word *book* omitted as being understood.

-394-

23. A huge flying reptile that died out with the dinosaurs some 65 million years ago, the Quetzalcoatlus had a wingspan of 36 feet, believed to be the largest flying creature the world has ever seen.

   (A) believed to be
   (B) and that is believed to be
   (C) and it is believed to have been
   (D) which was, it is believed,
   (E) which is believed to be

In choice A, *believed to be* incorrectly modifies *wingspan*, producing the illogical statement that the wingspan, and not the Quetzalcoatlus, is considered the largest flying creature the world has ever seen. The pronouns *that* and *which* cause the same confusion in B, D, and E by referring grammatically to the noun *wingspan*. Also, the use of *to be* in A, B, and E suggests wrongly that the flying reptile still exists. In choice C, the best answer, *it* refers to the Quetzalcoatlus, and the verb form *is believed to have been* indicates that the belief is current but the creature extinct.

24. A "calendar stick" carved centuries ago by the Winnebago tribe may provide the first evidence that the North American Indians have developed advanced full-year calendars basing them on systematic astronomical observation.

   (A) that the North American Indians have developed advanced full-year calendars basing them
   (B) of the North American Indians who have developed advanced full-year calendars and based them
   (C) of the development of advanced full-year calendars by North American Indians, basing them
   (D) of the North American Indians and their development of advanced full-year calendars based
   (E) that the North American Indians developed advanced full-year calendars based

Choices A and B contain incorrect verb forms: the present perfect *have developed*, which wrongly suggests a recent accomplishment, should be the simple past form *developed* in order to indicate action that occurred "centuries ago." In A and C, *basing* seems again to describe present action and in C lacks a noun that it can modify grammatically; *based* is needed to describe calendars that were developed in the distant past. In B and D, *(evidence) of the North American Indians* confuses the meaning of the sentence: the issue is not evidence of the Indians' existence, but evidence of their achievement. Concisely and logically phrased, choice E is best.

25. Federal incentives now encourage investing capital in commercial office buildings despite vacancy rates in existing structures that are exceptionally high and no demand for new construction.

   (A) investing capital in commercial office buildings despite vacancy rates in existing structures that are exceptionally high and
   (B) capital investment in commercial office buildings even though vacancy rates in existing structures are exceptionally high and there is
   (C) capital to be invested in commercial office buildings even though there are exceptionally high vacancy rates in existing structures with
   (D) investing capital in commercial office buildings even though the vacancy rates are exceptionally high in existing structures with
   (E) capital investment in commercial office buildings despite vacancy rates in existing structures that are exceptionally high, and although there is

In choices A, C, and D, *investing capital* and *capital to be invested* are awkward and imprecise; the verb *encourage* more appropriately takes a noun such as *investment* for its object. Moreover, these choices and choice E contain ambiguous wording: *that are exceptionally high* in A and E, and *with (no demand)* in C and D, illogically seem to modify *existing structures*. In A and E, *despite vacancy rates* does not allow for a grammatically complete sentence with parallel construction. Choice B is best: *capital investment* is the proper object for *encourage*, modifying phrases are placed so as to avoid ambiguity, and the construction *even though vacancy rates . . . are . . . high and there is (no demand)* is grammatically parallel.

Explanatory Material: Problem Solving I, Section 4

1. The 180 students in a group are to be seated in rows so that there is an equal number of students in each row. Each of the following could be the number of rows EXCEPT

   (A) 4
   (B) 20
   (C) 30
   (D) 40
   (E) 90

Since there is an equal number of students in each row, it follows that the total number of students, or 180, is a multiple of the number of rows. 180 is a multiple of all of the options except 40. Thus, the best answer is D.

2. A parking garage rents parking spaces for $10 per week or $30 per month. How much does a person save in a year by renting by the month rather than by the week?

(A) $140   (B) $160   (C) $220
(D) $240   (E) $260

The yearly cost of renting a parking space on a weekly basis is $10 × 52, or $520.

The yearly cost of renting a parking space on a monthly basis is $30 × 12, or $360.

The amount saved by renting a parking space by the month rather than by the week equals the difference between the two costs, which is ($520 − $360) or $160. Therefore, the best answer is B.

3. If $y = 5x^2 - 2x$ and $x = 3$, then $y =$

(A) 24   (B) 27   (C) 39   (D) 51   (E) 219

Substituting $x = 3$ in the equation $y = 5x^2 - 2x$ yields $y = 5(3)^2 - 2(3) = 45 - 6 = 39$. Thus, the best answer is C.

4. Of the following, which is the best approximation to $\sqrt{0.0026}$?

(A) 0.05   (B) 0.06   (C) 0.16   (D) 0.5   (E) 0.6

One way to approximate $\sqrt{.0026}$ is to notice that $.0026 = \dfrac{26}{10^4}$ and 25 (or 5^2) is the perfect square closest to 26.

So $\sqrt{.0026} = \sqrt{\dfrac{26}{10^4}} = \dfrac{\sqrt{26}}{\sqrt{10^4}} = \dfrac{\sqrt{26}}{10^2}$, which is approximately $\dfrac{5}{10^2}$ or 0.05. Thus, the best answer is A.

5. At a certain diner, a hamburger and coleslaw cost $3.95, and a hamburger and french fries cost $4.40. If french fries cost twice as much as coleslaw, how much do french fries cost?

(A) $0.30
(B) $0.45
(C) $0.60
(D) $0.75
(E) $0.90

Let h, c, and f denote the cost of a hamburger, coleslaw, and french fries, respectively.
Then,
$$(1)\ h + c = \$3.95$$
$$(2)\ h + f = \$4.40$$
$$(2) - (1)\ f - c = \$0.45$$
Since $f = 2c$, $c = \dfrac{f}{2}$; therefore,

$f - c = f - \dfrac{f}{2} = \dfrac{f}{2} = \$0.45$, and $f = \$0.90$. Thus, the best answer is E.

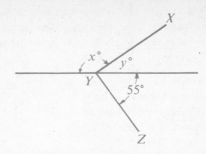

6. If $\angle XYZ$ in the figure above is a right angle, what is the value of x?

(A) 155   (B) 145   (C) 135   (D) 125   (E) 110

Since $\angle XYZ$ is a right angle, it follows that $y + 55 = 90$, and $y = 35$. Since x and y are the degree measures of supplementary angles, it follows that $x + y = 180$. Therefore, $x = 180 - y = 180 - 35 = 145$. Thus, the best answer is B.

7.
$$\dfrac{\left(\dfrac{a}{b}\right)}{c}$$

In the expression above, a, b, and c are different numbers and each is one of the numbers 2, 3, or 5. What is the least possible value of the expression?

(A) $\dfrac{1}{30}$ (B) $\dfrac{2}{15}$ (C) $\dfrac{1}{6}$ (D) $\dfrac{3}{10}$ (E) $\dfrac{5}{6}$

Note that $\dfrac{\left(\dfrac{a}{b}\right)}{c} = \dfrac{a}{bc}$.

The expression will be least when its numerator is as small as possible and its denominator is as large as possible. Setting $a = 2$, $b = 3$, and $c = 5$ yields $\dfrac{a}{bc} = \dfrac{2}{3(5)} = \dfrac{2}{15}$. Thus, the best answer is B.

8. A certain culture of bacteria quadruples every hour. If a container with these bacteria was half full at 10:00 a.m., at what time was it one-eighth full?

(A) 9:00 a.m.
(B) 7:00 a.m.
(C) 6:00 a.m.
(D) 4:00 a.m.
(E) 2:00 a.m.

Since the culture quadruples every hour, it follows that one hour prior to any given time the container was $\dfrac{1}{4}$ as full as it was at the given time. Therefore, if the container was $\dfrac{1}{2}$ full at 10:00 a.m., it was $\dfrac{1}{4}\left(\dfrac{1}{2}\right) = \dfrac{1}{8}$ full at 9:00 a.m. Thus, the best answer is A.

9. Al, Lew, and Karen pooled their funds to buy a gift for a friend. Al contributed $2 less than $\frac{1}{3}$ of the cost of the gift and Lew contributed $2 more than $\frac{1}{4}$ of the cost. If Karen contributed the remaining $15, what was the cost of the gift?

(A) $24
(B) $33
(C) $36
(D) $43
(E) $45

Let C = the cost of the gift.

Al's contribution = $\frac{1}{3} C - 2$.

Lew's contribution = $\frac{1}{4} C + 2$.

Karen's contribution = 15.

Total cost of gift = $C = \left(\frac{1}{3} C - 2 \right) + \left(\frac{1}{4} C + 2 \right) + 15$.

Thus, $C = \frac{7}{12} C + 15$

or $\frac{5}{12} C = 15$

or $C = 36$.

Therefore, the best answer is C.

10. What is the total number of integers between 100 and 200 that are divisible by 3?

(A) 33   (B) 32   (C) 31   (D) 30   (E) 29

The integers between 100 and 200 that are divisible by 3 are 102 (= 3(34)), 105, . . . , 198(= 3(66)). Thus, the number of integers between 100 and 200 that are divisible by 3 is equal to the number of integers between 34 and 66, inclusive. That is, 66 − 33 or 33 integers. Thus, the best answer is A.

11. Which of the following inequalities is equivalent to $10 - 2x > 18$?

(A) $x > -14$
(B) $x > -4$
(C) $x > 4$
(D) $x < 4$
(E) $x < -4$

$10 - 2x > 18$
$-8 > 2x$
$-4 > x$ or $x < -4$

Thus, E is the best answer.

12. In 1979 approximately $\frac{1}{3}$ of the 37.3 million airline passengers traveling to or from the United States used Kennedy Airport. If the number of such passengers that used Miami Airport was $\frac{1}{2}$ the number that used Kennedy Airport and 4 times the number that used Logan Airport, approximately how many millions of these passengers used Logan Airport that year?

(A) 18.6
(B) 9.3
(C) 6.2
(D) 3.1
(E) 1.6

The number of millions of passengers that used Kennedy Airport was approximately $\frac{1}{3}$ (37.3) $\approx$ 12.4 million. Thus, the number of millions of passengers that used Miami Airport was approximately $\frac{1}{2}$ (12.4) $\approx$ 6.2 million. This was 4 times the number of millions of passengers that used Logan Airport, so approximately $\frac{1}{4}$ (6.2) $\approx$ 1.6 million passengers used Logan Airport. Thus, the best answer is E.

13. A certain basketball team that has played $\frac{2}{3}$ of its games has a record of 17 wins and 3 losses. What is the greatest number of the remaining games that the team can lose and still win at least $\frac{3}{4}$ of all of its games?

(A) 7
(B) 6
(C) 5
(D) 4
(E) 3

The total number of games to be played by the team is 30, since 20 games is $\frac{2}{3}$ of the total number to be played. To win at least $\frac{3}{4}$ of all its games, the team must win a whole number of games greater than $\frac{3}{4}$ (30) = $22\frac{1}{2}$. Thus, the least number of games the team must win is 23. This implies that no more than 30 − 23 = 7 games can be lost. Since 3 games have already been lost, it follows that no more than 4 of the remaining games can be lost. Thus, the best answer is D.

14. Dan and Karen, who live 10 miles apart, meet at a café that is directly north of Dan's house and directly east of Karen's house. If the café is 2 miles closer to Dan's house than to Karen's house, how many miles is the café from Karen's house?

   (A) 6
   (B) 7
   (C) 8
   (D) 9
   (E) 10

Let a = the distance to the café from Karen's house. Then $a - 2$ = the distance to the café from Dan's house. Since the café is north of Dan's house and east of Karen's house, the following figure represents the information given:

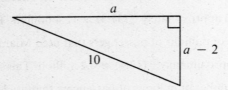

Using the Pythagorean Theorem yields
$$a^2 + (a - 2)^2 = 10^2$$
$$a^2 + a^2 - 4a + 4 = 100$$
$$2a^2 - 4a - 96 = 0$$
$$2(a^2 - 2a - 48) = 0$$
$$2(a - 8)(a + 6) = 0$$
$$a = 8 \text{ or } a = -6.$$
Since a represents the distance to the café from Karen's house, it follows that $a = 8$. Thus, the best answer is C.

15. If n is an integer and $n = \dfrac{2 \cdot 3 \cdot 5 \cdot 7 \cdot 11 \cdot 13}{77k}$, then which of the following could be the value of k?

   (A) 22   (B) 26   (C) 35   (D) 54   (E) 60

$$n = \frac{2 \cdot 3 \cdot 5 \cdot 7 \cdot 11 \cdot 13}{77k} = \frac{2 \cdot 3 \cdot 5 \cdot 13}{k}$$

Since n is an integer, k must be a factor of the numerator $2 \cdot 3 \cdot 5 \cdot 13$. Note that $22 = 2 \cdot 11$, $26 = 2 \cdot 13$, $35 = 5 \cdot 7$, $54 = 2 \cdot 3 \cdot 3 \cdot 3$, and $60 = 2 \cdot 2 \cdot 3 \cdot 5$. Therefore, only 26 is a factor of $2 \cdot 3 \cdot 5 \cdot 13$. Thus, the best answer is B.

16. There were 36,000 hardback copies of a certain novel sold before the paperback version was issued. From the time the first paperback copy was sold until the last copy of the novel was sold, 9 times as many paperback copies as hardback copies were sold. If a total of 441,000 copies of the novel were sold in all, how many paperback copies were sold?

   (A) 45,000
   (B) 360,000
   (C) 364,500
   (D) 392,000
   (E) 396,900

After the paperback version was issued, $441,000 - 36,000 = 405,000$ copies of the book were sold, 9 out of 10, or $\dfrac{9}{10}$, of which were paperback. Thus,

$\dfrac{9}{10}(405,000) = 364,500$ paperback copies were sold, and C is the best answer.

17. In the formula $w = \dfrac{p}{\sqrt[t]{v}}$, integers p and t are positive constants. If $w = 2$ when $v = 1$ and if $w = \dfrac{1}{2}$ when $v = 64$, then $t =$

   (A) 1
   (B) 2
   (C) 3
   (D) 4
   (E) 16

When $w = 2$ and $v = 1$, the formula yields
$2 = \dfrac{p}{\sqrt[t]{1}}$. Since $\sqrt[t]{1} = 1$ for any t,
this implies that $p = 2$. Thus, when $w = \dfrac{1}{2}$ and $v = 64$, the
formula yields $\dfrac{1}{2} = \dfrac{2}{\sqrt[t]{64}}$.
$$\sqrt[t]{64} = 4$$
$$64 = 4^t$$
$$t = 3$$
Thus, the best answer is C.

18. Last year Mrs. Long received $160 in dividends on her shares of Company X stock, all of which she had held for the entire year. If she had had 12 more shares of the stock last year, she would have received $15 more in total annual dividends. How many shares of the stock did she have last year?

   (A) 128
   (B) 140
   (C) 172
   (D) 175
   (E) 200

Since 12 shares of stock earned $15 in dividends, it follows that each share of stock earned $1.25 in dividends. To receive $160 in dividends, Mrs. Long must have owned

$\dfrac{160}{1.25} = 128$ shares of stock. Thus, A is the best answer.

Month	Average Price per Dozen
April	$1.26
May	$1.20
June	$1.08

19. The table above shows the average (arithmetic mean) price per dozen of the large grade A eggs sold in a certain store during three successive months. If $\frac{2}{3}$ as many dozen were sold in April as in May, and twice as many were sold in June as in April, what was the average price per dozen of the eggs sold over the three-month period?

(A) $1.08
(B) $1.10
(C) $1.14
(D) $1.16
(E) $1.18

To solve this problem it is convenient to let $A =$ the number of dozens of eggs sold in May and organize the information in a table as shown below:

Month	Number of Dozens of Eggs Sold	Price Paid for Eggs
April	$\frac{2}{3}A$	$1.26\left(\frac{2}{3}A\right)$
May	A	$1.20A$
June	$2\left(\frac{2}{3}A\right)$	$1.08\left[2\left(\frac{2}{3}A\right)\right]$

The average price per dozen of the eggs over the three-month period is thus

$$\frac{\$1.26\left(\frac{2}{3}A\right) + \$1.20A + \$1.08\left(2\left(\frac{2}{3}A\right)\right)}{\frac{2}{3}A + A + 2\left(\frac{2}{3}A\right)}$$

$$= \frac{\$3.48A}{3A}$$

$$= \$1.16.$$

The best answer is D.

20. If $y \neq 3$ and $\frac{3x}{y}$ is a prime integer greater than 2, which of the following must be true?

  I. $x = y$
  II. $y = 1$
  III. x and y are prime integers.

(A) None
(B) I only
(C) II only
(D) III only
(E) I and III

One way to approach this problem is to determine whether each of conditions I, II, and III could be false. I is false if $x \neq y$. If $x \neq y$, it follows that $\frac{3x}{y}$ would be a prime integer greater than 3, say, 5. $x = 15$ and $y = 9$ satisfy the desired conditions. When $x = 15$ and $y = 9$ it is also true that $y \neq 1$ and x and y are not prime integers. Thus, none of conditions I, II, and III must necessarily be true. Therefore, A is the best answer.

Explanatory Material: Critical Reasoning, Section 5

1. Child's World, a chain of toy stores, has relied on a "supermarket concept" of computerized inventory control and customer self-service to eliminate the category of sales clerks from its force of employees. It now plans to employ the same concept in selling children's clothes.

   The plan of Child's World assumes that

   (A) supermarkets will not also be selling children's clothes in the same manner
   (B) personal service by sales personnel is not required for selling children's clothes successfully
   (C) the same kind of computers will be used in inventory control for both clothes and toys at Child's World
   (D) a self-service plan cannot be employed without computerized inventory control
   (E) sales clerks are the only employees of Child's World who could be assigned tasks related to inventory control

If B were false, eliminating the sales personnel for children's clothes would be an economic mistake. Since the plan is presumably regarded as laying out an economically desirable course of action, the truth of B must be assumed.

If A were false, Child's World might nevertheless be successful in competition with supermarkets; thus A is not assumed. Neither is C: if inventory control for children's clothes really was more sensibly computerized using a different kind of computer, the plan itself would remain unaffected. Choice D is also not assumed: Child's World may plan to combine self-service and computerized inventory control because it is cost-effective, not because there are no alternatives. Finally, E is not assumed, especially not for computerized inventory control.

2. Continuous indoor fluorescent light benefits the health of hamsters with inherited heart disease. A group of them exposed to continuous fluorescent light survived twenty-five percent longer than a similar group exposed instead to equal periods of indoor fluorescent light and of darkness.

The method of the research described above is most likely to be applicable in addressing which of the following questions?

(A) Can industrial workers who need to see their work do so better by sunlight or by fluorescent light?
(B) Can hospital lighting be improved to promote the recovery of patients?
(C) How do deep-sea fish survive in total darkness?
(D) What are the inherited illnesses to which hamsters are subject?
(E) Are there plants that require specific periods of darkness in order to bloom?

The variable controlled in the research is the length of exposure to artificial light. This aspect of the research also applies to patients in a hospital. The statistical aspect of the method—the collection of quantitative results about the entire group of subjects—is likewise applicable. Therefore, B is the best of the choices.

Choice A involves exposure to different kinds of light, not different lengths of exposure. The method of differential exposure to light is unpromising in the case of C, where total darkness is a given, and the method is not germane in the case of D. Choice E can be eliminated because the statistical aspect of the method is inapplicable: the only information of concern here is presence or absence of blooms.

3. Millions of identical copies of a plant can be produced using new tissue-culture and cloning techniques.

If plant propagation by such methods in laboratories proves economical, each of the following, if true, represents a benefit of the new techniques to farmers EXCEPT:

(A) The techniques allow the development of superior strains to take place more rapidly, requiring fewer generations of plants grown to maturity.
(B) It is less difficult to care for plants that will grow at rates that do not vary widely.
(C) Plant diseases and pests, once they take hold, spread more rapidly among genetically uniform plants than among those with genetic variations.
(D) Mechanical harvesting of crops is less difficult if plants are more uniform in size.
(E) Special genetic traits can more easily be introduced into plant strains with the use of the new techniques.

From the perspective of C, genetic variability is more highly valued than genetic uniformity. But the new techniques, while making it easy to achieve previously unattainable uniformity, are not described as providing any means of achieving variability. Therefore, C does not represent or imply a benefit to farmers, and is thus the best answer.

Because identical copies, given similar growing conditions, will not differ appreciably in either growth rate or size attained by harvest time, both B and D represent benefits to farmers. Choice A suggests the benefit of having superior strains available earlier than would otherwise be possible, and E suggests the benefit of being able to obtain strains that are superior in specific, predesignated ways.

4. Which of the following best completes the passage below?

Sales campaigns aimed at the faltering personal computer market have strongly emphasized ease of use, called user-friendliness. This emphasis is oddly premature and irrelevant in the eyes of most potential buyers, who are trying to address the logically prior issue of whether ------.

(A) user-friendliness also implies that owners can service their own computers
(B) personal computers cost more the more user-friendly they are
(C) currently available models are user-friendly enough to suit them
(D) the people promoting personal computers use them in their own homes
(E) they have enough sensible uses for a personal computer to justify the expense of buying one

The question raised in A is closely related to user-friendliness: it explores potential further implications of user-friendliness. The issue raised by B also concerns user-friendliness: is it an advantageous feature that buyers pay for? Choice C presupposes user-friendliness as a criterion for purchasing decisions. The issue mentioned in D is not logically prior to user-friendliness, though D may be a way of probing promotional claims, including claims about user-friendliness.

Choice E, however, depicts potential buyers as asking themselves whether buying a computer at all makes sense for them. As long as their answer might still be "no," questions of user-friendliness, which bear on the choice from among competing models, are indeed premature. Therefore, E is the best answer.

5. A weapons-smuggling incident recently took place in country Y. We all know that Y is a closed society. So Y's government must have known about the weapons.

Which of the following is an assumption that would make the conclusion above logically correct?

(A) If a government knows about a particular weapons-smuggling incident, it must have intended to use the weapons for its own purposes.
(B) If a government claims that it knew nothing about a particular weapons-smuggling incident, it must have known everything about it.
(C) If a government does not permit weapons to enter a country, it is a closed society.
(D) If a country is a closed society, its government has a large contingent of armed guards patrolling its borders.
(E) If a country is a closed society, its government has knowledge about everything that occurs in the country.

Choice E is the best answer. If E is true, country Y's government must have known about the weapons, even if they were coming into Y from abroad (rather than being smuggled out of Y), as soon as they had crossed Y's border.

Choice A draws out implications of the conclusion but leaves the conclusion itself inadequately supported. The assumption in B is insufficient to establish the conclusion as correctly drawn: no information about claims by Y's government is given. The prospect offered by C—being able to tell whether Y is closed—is of no consequence: Y is known to be closed. The patrols mentioned in D make it likely, but not deductively certain, that Y's government found out about the weapons.

6. Banning cigarette advertisements in the mass media will not reduce the number of young people who smoke. They know that cigarettes exist and they know how to get them. They do not need the advertisements to supply that information.

The above argument would be most weakened if which of the following were true?

(A) Seeing or hearing an advertisement for a product tends to increase people's desire for that product.
(B) Banning cigarette advertisements in the mass media will cause an increase in advertisements in places where cigarettes are sold.
(C) Advertisements in the mass media have been an exceedingly large part of the expenditures of the tobacco companies.
(D) Those who oppose cigarette use have advertised against it in the mass media ever since cigarettes were found to be harmful.
(E) Older people tend to be less influenced by mass-media advertisements than younger people tend to be.

The possibility that A raises is that, in the case of some young nonsmokers, cigarette advertising increases their desire for cigarettes just enough to make the difference between their continuing to be nonsmokers and their taking up smoking, thus affecting the numbers of young smokers. Therefore, A is the best answer.

Both B and C leave open the possibility that advertising affects only smokers' choice of cigarette brands, and not who smokes and who does not. Similarly, the relevance of D has not been established: the effects of anti-cigarette advertising are no more settled than are the effects of pro-cigarette advertising. Choice E presupposes that advertising does influence people but leaves unspecified the nature of this influence.

7. People tend to estimate the likelihood of an event's occurrence according to its salience; that is, according to how strongly and how often it comes to their attention.

By placement and headlines, newspapers emphasize stories about local crime over stories about crime elsewhere and about many other major events.

It can be concluded on the basis of the statements above that, if they are true, which of the following is most probably also true?

(A) The language used in newspaper headlines about local crime is inflammatory and fails to respect the rights of suspects.
(B) The coverage of international events in newspapers is neglected in favor of the coverage of local events.
(C) Readers of local news in newspapers tend to overestimate the amount of crime in their own localities relative to the amount of crime in other places.
(D) None of the events concerning other people that are reported in newspapers is so salient in people's minds as their own personal experiences.
(E) The press is the news medium that focuses people's attention most strongly on local crimes.

The fact that newspapers emphasize local crime coverage relative to coverage of crimes elsewhere means that readers will be more likely to be aware of local crime, or will be aware of it more strongly; in short, local crime will be more salient. Consequently, local crime will be judged to be relatively more likely to occur, though it may actually be no more frequent. The best answer, therefore, is C.

The information given neither suggests emphasis by questionable means—contrary to A—nor suggests special relative emphasis on *all* local events—contrary to B. Choices D and E can be eliminated: it is entirely possible that people's personal experiences are unremarkable, and that other news media highlight local crime even more than newspapers do.

8. By analyzing the garbage of a large number of average-sized households, a group of modern urban anthropologists has found that a household discards less food the more standardized—made up of canned and prepackaged foods—its diet is. The more standardized a household's diet is, however, the greater the quantities of fresh produce the household throws away.

Which of the following can be properly inferred from the passage?

(A) An increasing number of households rely on a highly standardized diet.

(B) The less standardized a household's diet is, the more nonfood waste the household discards.

(C) The less standardized a household's diet is, the smaller is the proportion of fresh produce in the household's food waste.

(D) The less standardized a household's diet is, the more canned and prepackaged foods the household discards as waste.

(E) The more fresh produce a household buys, the more fresh produce it throws away.

If households with more standardized diets discard less food overall, but more fresh produce, than do households with less standardized diets, then fresh produce will be a greater proportion of total food waste in households with more standardized diets, and a smaller proportion in those with less standardized diets. Choice C correctly reflects this relationship and is, therefore, the best answer.

Choices A and B can be ruled out because the passage makes no claims about numbers of households or nonfood waste. Since many foods are neither fresh produce nor canned or prepackaged, D cannot be inferred. The passage provides no basis for relating amount of produce purchased to amount discarded, because in different households different amounts may be consumed. Thus, E is incorrect.

Questions 9-10 are based on the following.

In the past, teachers, bank tellers, and secretaries were predominantly men; these occupations slipped in pay and status when they became largely occupied by women. Therefore, if women become the majority in currently male-dominated professions like accounting, law, and medicine, the income and prestige of these professions will also drop.

9. The argument above is based on

(A) another argument that contains circular reasoning

(B) an attempt to refute a generalization by means of an exceptional case

(C) an analogy between the past and the future

(D) an appeal to popular beliefs and values

(E) an attack on the character of the opposition

The argument assumes that, in relevant respects, the future will be like the past. Those relevant respects are the levels of pay and prestige associated with occupations that are occupied at one stage mostly by men and, at a later stage, mostly by women. Therefore, C is the best answer.

Choice A is incorrect because there is no indication that the argument is based on another argument. Neither is there any suggestion that the argument depends on a refutation, so B is also incorrect. The argument does not mention any popular beliefs or values, nor can one infer that it tacitly appeals to any; thus, D is unsupported. The argument is presented as though it had no opponents, so E cannot be correct.

10. Which of the following, if true, would most likely be part of the evidence used to refute the conclusion above?

(A) Accountants, lawyers, and physicians attained their current relatively high levels of income and prestige at about the same time that the pay and status of teachers, bank tellers, and secretaries slipped.

(B) When large numbers of men join a female-dominated occupation, such as airline flight attendant, the status and pay of the occupation tend to increase.

(C) The demand for teachers and secretaries has increased significantly in recent years, while the demand for bank tellers has remained relatively stable.

(D) If present trends in the awarding of law degrees to women continue, it will be at least two decades before the majority of lawyers are women.

(E) The pay and status of female accountants, lawyers, and physicians today are governed by significantly different economic and sociological forces than were the pay and status of female teachers, bank tellers, and secretaries in the past.

The argument relies on continuity between past and present with regard to the phenomena being considered. Choice E strongly suggests that such continuity cannot be relied on, and would thus be useful evidence in refuting the conclusion. Therefore, E is the best answer.

The argument says nothing about gains in pay or status; thus, it is unaffected by the coincidence described in A. Choice B is most probably evidence for, not against, the conclusion, since it associates higher pay and status with larger numbers of men employed. Choice C focuses on changes in total numbers employed rather than changes in the male/female ratio and is thus irrelevant. Choice D only bears on when the prediction may become testable, not on whether it is correct.

11. An electric-power company gained greater profits and provided electricity to consumers at lower rates per unit of electricity by building larger-capacity, more efficient plants and by stimulating greater use of electricity within its area. To continue these financial trends, the company planned to replace an old plant by a plant with triple the capacity of its largest plant.

The company's plan as described above assumed each of the following EXCEPT:

(A) Demand for electricity within the company's area of service would increase in the future.
(B) Expenses would not rise beyond the level that could be compensated for by efficiency or volume of operation, or both.
(C) The planned plant would be sufficiently reliable in service to contribute a net financial benefit to the company as a whole.
(D) Safety measures to be instituted for the new plant would be the same as those for the plant it would replace.
(E) The tripling of capacity would not result in insuperable technological obstacles to efficiency.

Choice A is assumed, because the added capacity is financially worthless unless there is a market for extra output. Choice B is assumed, because if expenses rose beyond the level described, it would not be possible to increase profits while reducing unit rates. Choice C is assumed, because a new investment will increase overall profits only if it contributes a net financial benefit. Finally, E is assumed, since rising profits combined with lower unit rates are impossible unless unit costs decrease, i.e., unless efficiency improves.

Choice D, however, is not assumed. There is no reason to think that changes in safety measures would be bound to jeopardize the company's plan.

Questions 12-13 are based on the following.

Meteorologists say that if only they could design an accurate mathematical model of the atmosphere with all its complexities, they could forecast the weather with real precision. But this is an idle boast, immune to any evaluation, for any inadequate weather forecast would obviously be blamed on imperfections in the model.

12. Which of the following, if true, could best be used as a basis for arguing against the author's position that the meteorologists' claim cannot be evaluated?

(A) Certain unusual configurations of data can serve as the basis for precise weather forecasts even though the exact causal mechanisms are not understood.
(B) Most significant gains in the accuracy of the relevant mathematical models are accompanied by clear gains in the precision of weather forecasts.
(C) Mathematical models of the meteorological aftermath of such catastrophic events as volcanic eruptions are beginning to be constructed.
(D) Modern weather forecasts for as much as a full day ahead are broadly correct about 80 percent of the time.
(E) Meteorologists readily concede that the accurate mathematical model they are talking about is not now in their power to construct.

The author does not presuppose that precise weather forecasts based on imperfect understanding cannot ever occur, so A cannot be used to argue against the author. Choice C, which says nothing about the quality of the models or their effect on the precision of the weather forecasts, also provides no material for a counterargument. The author's position is consistent with D. The concession described in E is already tacitly conveyed in the author's report of the meteorologists' claim.

However, B can be used to argue that the claim is not impossible to evaluate but actually somewhat plausible, because B indicates that there is a strong correlation between increasing perfection of the model and increasingly accurate forecasts. Therefore, B is the best answer.

13. Which of the following, if true, would cast the most serious doubt on the meteorologists' boast, aside from the doubt expressed in the passage above?

   (A) The amount of energy that the Earth receives from the Sun is monitored closely and is known not to be constant.

   (B) Volcanic eruptions, the combustion of fossil fuels, and several other processes that also cannot be quantified with any accuracy are known to have a significant and continuing impact on the constitution of the atmosphere.

   (C) As current models of the atmosphere are improved, even small increments in complexity will mean large increases in the number of computers required for the representation of the models.

   (D) Frequent and accurate data about the atmosphere collected at a large number of points both on and above the ground are a prerequisite for the construction of a good model of the atmosphere.

   (E) With existing models of the atmosphere, large-scale weather patterns can be predicted with greater accuracy than can relatively local weather patterns.

A mathematical model, a system of postulates, data, and inferences, cannot be accurate unless its components are accurate. Choice B strongly indicates that a model of the atmosphere will be inaccurate in at least one respect: the data. This source of inaccuracy known in advance means that meteorologists know that their claim is likely to remain unverifiable, and the characterization of their boast as idle is thus supported, in a way different from the way the author supports it. Therefore, B is the best choice.

   Choice A describes an activity and a piece of information that, on balance, favor accuracy in forecasting. Choices C and D both state prerequisites, but do not suggest that those cannot be met. Choice E only refers to the present state of affairs, with no obvious bearing on the meteorologists' claim.

14. Of the countries that were the world's twenty largest exporters in 1953, four had the same share of total world exports in 1984 as in 1953. These countries can therefore serve as models for those countries that wish to keep their share of the global export trade stable over the years.

   Which of the following, if true, casts the most serious doubt on the suitability of those four countries as models in the sense described?

   (A) Many countries wish to increase their share of world export trade, not just keep it stable.

   (B) Many countries are less concerned with exports alone than with the balance between exports and imports.

   (C) With respect to the mix of products each exports, the four countries are very different from each other.

   (D) Of the four countries, two had a much larger, and two had a much smaller, share of total world exports in 1970 than in 1984.

   (E) The exports of the four countries range from 15 percent to 75 percent of the total national output.

Choice D establishes that the four countries cannot have maintained a stable share of total world exports from 1953 through 1984. There is no reason to suppose that 1970 was an exceptional year, so D suggests that the four countries are not good models in the sense described. Therefore, D is the best answer.

   Choices A and B are concerned with countries that would not particularly wish for a constant share of world exports, and are thus irrelevant to the question posed. Choices C and E indicate that the proposed models are rather varied. Variety would be a desirable property of the models—countries could select the models most like themselves as the ones to emulate—and thus casts no doubt on their suitability.

Questions 15-16 are based on the following.

In the United States, the Postal Service has a monopoly on first-class mail, but much of what is sent first class could be transmitted electronically. Electronic transmittal operators argue that if the Postal Service were to offer electronic transmission, it would have an unfair advantage, since its electronic transmission service could be subsidized from the profits of the monopoly.

15. Which of the following, if each is true, would allay the electronic transmittal operators' fears of unfair competition?

   (A) If the Postal Service were to offer electronic transmission, it could not make a profit on first-class mail.
   (B) If the Postal Service were to offer electronic transmission, it would have a monopoly on that kind of service.
   (C) Much of the material that is now sent by first-class mail could be delivered much faster by special package couriers, but is not sent that way because of cost.
   (D) There is no economy of scale in electronic transmission—that is, the cost per transaction does not go down as more pieces of information are transmitted.
   (E) Electronic transmission will never be cost-effective for material not sent by first-class mail such as newspapers and bulk mail.

The fears of unfair competition are based on the speculation that the Postal Service could use profits from its monopoly on first-class mail to subsidize its electronic transmission service. Choice A states that there would be no such profit if the Postal Service had an electronic transmission service; thus, the fears are unfounded. Therefore, A is the best answer.

Choice B, rather than allaying fears, probably expresses the private operators' worst fears. The issues raised by C—the importance of relative cost—and by D—absence of economies of scale—are side issues. Choice E cannot allay private operators' fears, because what those operators fear is specifically unfair competition in the electronic transmission of materials otherwise sent by first-class mail.

16. Which of the following questions can be answered on the basis of the information in the passage above?

   (A) Is the Postal Service as efficient as privately owned electric transmission services?
   (B) If private operators were allowed to operate first-class mail services, would they choose to do so?
   (C) Do the electronic transmittal operators believe that the Postal Service makes a profit on first-class mail?
   (D) Is the Postal Service prohibited from offering electronic transmission services?
   (E) Is the Postal Service expected to have a monopoly on electronic transmission?

The answer to the question in C is yes, for the operators could not reasonably make their argument unless they believed that first-class mail was profitable. Therefore, C is the best of the choices.

Since private operators might worry about an unfair advantage regardless of how the Postal Service's efficiency compares to their own, the question in A cannot be answered. Neither can the question in B: the Postal Service, highly experienced with first-class mail, might enjoy advantages that prevent newcomers from competing effectively. Since the current unavailability of electronic transmissions through the Postal Service may be a matter either of choice or of law, D poses an unanswerable question, as does E, since a large enough unfair advantage might confer a monopoly.

17. Lists of hospitals have been compiled showing which hospitals have patient death rates exceeding the national average. The data have been adjusted to allow for differences in the ages of patients.

   Each of the following, if true, provides a good logical ground for hospitals to object to interpreting rank on these lists as one of the indices of the quality of hospital care EXCEPT:

   (A) Rank order might indicate insignificant differences, rather than large differences, in numbers of patient deaths.
   (B) Hospitals that keep patients longer are likely to have higher death rates than those that discharge patients earlier but do not record deaths of patients at home after discharge.
   (C) Patients who are very old on admission to a hospital are less likely than younger patients to survive the same types of illnesses or surgical procedures.
   (D) Some hospitals serve a larger proportion of low-income patients, who tend to be more seriously ill when admitted to a hospital.
   (E) For-profit hospitals sometimes do not provide intensive-care units and other expensive services for very sick patients but refer or transfer such patients to other hospitals.

Choice A supports an objection based on the possibility that even seemingly large differences in rank may have rather small differences in death rates associated with them. Choices B, D, and E all support objections because they describe circumstances not related to quality of hospital care that distort the death rates for some hospitals relative to those for others. These circumstances are hospitals' discharge policies, patients' economic circumstances, and the range of medical services offered, respectively.

On the other hand, C, as stated, supports no objection, because any substantial differences among hospitals with regard to the age profile of their patient populations will have been allowed for. That is the express purpose of the data adjustment mentioned. Therefore, C is the best answer.

18. Teresa: Manned spaceflight does not have a future, since it cannot compete economically with other means of accomplishing the objectives of spaceflight.

Edward: No mode of human transportation has a better record of reliability: two accidents in twenty-five years. Thus manned spaceflight definitely has a positive future.

Which of the following is the best logical evaluation of Edward's argument as a response to Teresa's argument?

(A) It cities evidence that, if true, tends to disprove the evidence cited by Teresa in drawing her conclusion.
(B) It indicates a logical gap in the support that Teresa offers for her conclusion.
(C) It raises a consideration that outweighs the argument Teresa makes.
(D) It does not meet Teresa's point because it assumes that there is no serious impediment to transporting people into space, but this was the issue raised by Teresa.
(E) It fails to respond to Teresa's argument because it does not address the fundamental issue of whether space activities should have priority over other claims on the national budget.

Teresa evaluates manned spaceflight as a means of accomplishing the objectives of spaceflight, finds it excessively costly, and predicts its demise. Edward makes the opposite prediction, on the basis of the safety record of manned spaceflight as a mode of human transportation. Edward ignores the issue Teresa raises: that manned spaceflight is an economically unjustifiable instance of human transportation. Therefore, D is the best answer.

Nothing in Edward's evidence suggests that Teresa's evidence is false or her conclusion ill-supported, so A and B are incorrect. Because Teresa evidently favors unmanned spaceflight, Edward's concern with human safety is irrelevant, and C can be eliminated. Regarding the "fundamental issue" described in E, neither Teresa nor Edward seems to question the availability of funds for space activities.

19. Black Americans are, on the whole, about twice as likely as White Americans to develop high blood pressure. This likelihood also holds for westernized Black Africans when compared to White Africans. Researchers have hypothesized that this predisposition in westernized Blacks may reflect an interaction between western high-salt diets and genes that adapted to an environmental scarcity of salt.

Which of the following statements about present-day, westernized Black Africans, if true, would most tend to confirm the researchers' hypothesis?

(A) The blood pressures of those descended from peoples situated throughout their history in Senegal and Gambia, where salt was always available, are low.
(B) The unusually high salt consumption in certain areas of Africa represents a serious health problem.
(C) Because of their blood pressure levels, most White Africans have markedly decreased their salt consumption.
(D) Blood pressures are low among the Yoruba, who, throughout their history, have been situated far inland from sources of sea salt and far south of Saharan salt mines.
(E) No significant differences in salt metabolism have been found between those peoples who have had salt available throughout their history and those who have not.

Choice A describes a situation in which one of the interacting factors is present, but the second—genes adapted to an environmental scarcity of salt—is not. If the result were nonetheless high blood pressure, then the second explanatory factor, and thus the hypothesis, would be called into question. In actual fact, low blood pressure is reported. The hypothesis has thus withstood potentially disconfirming evidence, and this circumstance tends to confirm it. The best answer, therefore, is A.

Both B and C are compatible with any explanation that relates high blood pressure to high salt intake, and thus have no special bearing on the current hypothesis. Both D and E are unexpected, given the hypothesis, and so tend to disconfirm rather than confirm it.

20. The following proposal to amend the bylaws of an organization was circulated to its members for comment.

> When more than one nominee is to be named for an office, prospective nominees must consent to nomination and before giving such consent must be told who the other nominees will be.

Which of the following comments concerning the logic of the proposal is accurate if it cannot be known who the actual nominees are until prospective nominees have given their consent to be nominated?

(A) The proposal would make it possible for each of several nominees for an office to be aware of who all of the other nominees are.

(B) The proposal would widen the choice available to those choosing among the nominees.

(C) If there are several prospective nominees, the proposal would deny the last nominee equal treatment with the first.

(D) The proposal would enable a prospective nominee to withdraw from competition with a specific person without making that withdrawal known.

(E) If there is more than one prospective nominee, the proposal would make it impossible for anyone to become a nominee.

Suppose that there were to be two nominees. Neither of them can consent to being nominated unless the other one has already so consented. But this, in effect, means that neither can consent to being nominated. Thus, neither can be nominated, and it is impossible to have two nominees. Analogous arguments would show that having more than two nominees is likewise impossible. Therefore, E is the best answer.

The impossibility of having two or more nominees means that A makes a false assumption, B makes a wrong prediction, and C describes an impossible scenario, so none of them accurately comments on the logic of the proposal. Nor does D: if the sort of withdrawal it describes were currently prohibited, the proposal would not change the situation.

Explanatory Material: Problem Solving II, Section 6

1. The market value of a certain machine decreased by 30 percent of its purchase price each year. If the machine was purchased in 1982 for its market value of $8,000, what was its market value two years later?

(A) $8,000
(B) $5,600
(C) $3,200
(D) $2,400
(E) $800

The market value of the machine decreased by $0.3(\$8,000) = \$2,400$ each year. At the end of two years its market value was $\$8,000 - 2(\$2,400) = \$3,200$. Thus, the best answer is C.

2. What percent of 50 is 15?

(A) 30%   (B) 35%   (C) 70%

(D) 300%   (E) $333\frac{1}{3}$%

Since $\frac{15}{50} = \frac{30}{100}$, 15 is 30% of 50. Therefore, the best answer is A.

3. In a certain diving competition, 5 judges score each dive on a scale from 1 to 10. The point value of the dive is obtained by dropping the highest score and the lowest score and multiplying the sum of the remaining scores by the degree of difficulty. If a dive with a degree of difficulty of 3.2 received scores of 7.5, 8.0, 9.0, 6.0, and 8.5, what was the point value of the dive?

(A) 68.8   (B) 73.6   (C) 75.2   (D) 76.8   (E) 81.6

The scores remaining after dropping the highest and lowest scores were 7.5, 8.0, and 8.5. Multiplying their sum, which is 24, by a degree of difficulty of 3.2 yields a point value of 76.8. Thus, the best answer is D.

4. If $2x = 3y = 10$, then $12xy =$

(A) 1,200   (B) 200   (C) 120   (D) 40   (E) 20

Solving $2x = 3y = 10$ for x and y yields

$x = 5$ and $y = \frac{10}{3}$. Thus, $12xy = 12(5)\left(\frac{10}{3}\right) = 200$. Therefore, the best answer is B.

An alternative method for solving this problem is:
$12xy = 2(2x)(3y) = 2(10)(10) = 200$. Therefore, the best answer is B.

5. If Jack walked 5 miles in 1 hour and 15 minutes, what was his rate of walking in miles per hour?

(A) 4   (B) 4.5   (C) 6   (D) 6.25   (E) 15

1 hour and 15 minutes = $\frac{5}{4}$ hours. Thus, Jack walked

$$\frac{5 \text{ miles}}{\frac{5}{4} \text{ hour}} = \frac{4 \text{ miles}}{1 \text{ hour}}.$$

Therefore, the best answer is A.

6. Of a certain high school graduating class, 75 percent of the students continued their formal education, and 80 percent of those who continued their formal education went to four-year colleges. If 300 students in the class went to four-year colleges, how many students were in the graduating class?

   (A) 500   (B) 375   (C) 240   (D) 225   (E) 180

If S is the number of students in the graduating class, it follows that $0.80(0.75S) = 300$. Solving for S yields $S = 500$. Thus, the best answer is A.

7. What is the least integer greater than $-2 + 0.5$?

   (A) -2 (B) -1 (C) 0   (D) 1   (E) 2

$-2 + 0.5 = -1.5$. The least integer greater than -1.5 is -1. Therefore, the best answer is B.

8. Which of the following is equivalent to $\dfrac{2x + 4}{2x^2 + 8x + 8}$ for all values of x for which both expressions are defined?

   (A) $\dfrac{1}{2x^2 + 6}$

   (B) $\dfrac{1}{9x + 2}$

   (C) $\dfrac{2}{x + 6}$

   (D) $\dfrac{1}{x + 4}$

   (E) $\dfrac{1}{x + 2}$

$$\frac{2x + 4}{2x^2 + 8x + 8} = \frac{2(x + 2)}{2(x^2 + 4x + 4)} = \frac{x + 2}{(x + 2)(x + 2)} = \frac{1}{x + 2}$$

Thus, E is the best answer.

9. A certain business printer can print 40 characters per second, which is 4 times as fast as an average printer. If an average printer can print 5 times as fast as an electric typewriter, how many characters per <u>minute</u> can an electric typewriter print?

   (A) 2   (B) 32   (C) 50   (D) 120   (E) 600

The business printer can print $40(60) = 2{,}400$ characters per minute. Thus, an average printer can print $\dfrac{2{,}400}{4} = 600$ characters per minute and an electric typewriter can print $\dfrac{600}{5} = 120$ characters per minute. The best answer is D.

10. When ticket sales began, Pat was the nth customer in line for a ticket, and customers purchased their tickets at the rate of x customers per minute. Of the following, which best approximates the time, in minutes, that Pat had to wait in line from the moment ticket sales began?

    (A) $(n - 1)x$
    (B) $n + x - 1$
    (C) $\dfrac{n - 1}{x}$
    (D) $\dfrac{x}{n - 1}$
    (E) $\dfrac{n}{x - 1}$

Since x customers purchased their tickets each minute, it follows that, on the average, it took each customer $\dfrac{1}{x}$ minutes to purchase tickets. Since Pat was the nth customer in line, $n - 1$ customers purchased tickets before Pat. Therefore, Pat waited approximately $(n - 1)\left(\dfrac{1}{x}\right) = \dfrac{n - 1}{x}$ minutes to purchase tickets. Thus, the best answer is C.

11. If 6 gallons of gasoline are added to a tank that is already filled to $\dfrac{3}{4}$ of its capacity, the tank is then filled to $\dfrac{9}{10}$ of its capacity. How many gallons does the tank hold?

    (A) 20   (B) 24   (C) 36   (D) 40   (E) 60

If G is the capacity, in gallons, of the tank, it follows that
$$\frac{3}{4}G + 6 = \frac{9}{10}G;$$
$$6 = \left(\frac{9}{10} - \frac{3}{4}\right)G;$$
$$6 = \frac{6}{40}G;$$
$$G = 40.$$
Thus, the best answer is D.

12. A bus trip of 450 miles would have taken 1 hour less if the average speed S for the trip had been greater by 5 miles per hour. What was the average speed S, in miles per hour, for the trip?

    (A) 10   (B) 40   (C) 45   (D) 50   (E) 55

If t is the time, in hours, taken for the trip, then $St = 450$ and $(S + 5)(t - 1) = 450$. Solving the first equation for t yields $t = \dfrac{450}{S}$. Substituting for t in the second equation yields

$$(S + 5)\left(\left(\frac{450}{S}\right) - 1\right) = 450;$$

$$450 + \frac{5(450)}{S} - S - 5 = 450;$$

$$\frac{2{,}250}{S} - S - 5 = 0;$$

$$2{,}250 - S^2 - 5S = 0;$$

$$S^2 + 5S - 2{,}250 = 0;$$

$$(S + 50)(S - 45) = 0;$$

$$S = 45.$$

Thus, the best answer is C.

13. 10^3 is how many times $(0.01)^3$?

(A) 10^6 (B) 10^8 (C) 10^9 (D) 10^{12} (E) 10^{18}

$$\frac{10^3}{(0.01)^3} = \left(\frac{10}{0.01}\right)^3 = (1{,}000)^3 = (10^3)^3 = 10^9$$

Therefore, the best answer is C.

14. Which of the following groups of numbers could be the lengths of the sides of a right triangle?

   I. $1, 4, \sqrt{17}$

   II. $4, 7, \sqrt{11}$

   III. $4, 9, 6$

(A) I only
(B) I and II only
(C) I and III only
(D) II and III only
(E) I, II, and III

If a, b, and c are the lengths of the sides of a right triangle, with c greater than a and b, then $a^2 + b^2 = c^2$. By squaring the numbers in each group (I, II, and III) and arranging them appropriately, it can be verified that only the group of numbers listed in I could be the lengths of the sides of a right triangle.

I. $1^2 + 4^2 = \left(\sqrt{17}\right)^2$

II. $4^2 + \left(\sqrt{11}\right)^2 \neq 7^2$

III. $4^2 + 6^2 \neq 9^2$

Thus, the best answer is A.

15. When the stock market opened yesterday, the price of a share of stock X was $10\frac{1}{2}$. When the market closed, the price was $11\frac{1}{4}$. Of the following, which is closest to the percent increase in the price of stock X?

(A) 0.5%   (B) 1.0%   (C) 6.7%

(D) 7.1%   (E) 7.5%

The price per share of stock X increased by $\frac{3}{4}$ over the opening price of $10\frac{1}{2}$. The percent increase is thus

$\dfrac{\frac{3}{4}}{10\frac{1}{2}} \times 100 = \dfrac{100}{14}$, which is equal to 7.1 (when rounded to the nearest tenth). Therefore, the best answer is D.

16. If x and y are integers and xy^2 is a positive odd integer, which of the following must be true?

   I. xy is positive.
   II. xy is odd.
   III. $x + y$ is even.

(A) I only
(B) II only
(C) III only
(D) I and II
(E) II and III

Since xy^2 is positive and y^2 must be positive, it follows that x must be positive. Since xy^2 is odd, it follows that both x and y, which are factors of xy^2, must be odd. Thus, x is a positive odd integer and y is an odd integer.

I need not be true, since xy is negative when x is positive and y is negative.

II must be true, since the product of two odd integers must be odd.

III must be true, since the sum of two odd integers must be even.

Therefore, the best answer is E.

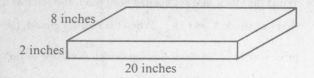

8 inches

2 inches

20 inches

17. The figure above shows the dimensions of a rectangular box that is to be completely wrapped with paper. If a single sheet of paper is to be used without patching, then the dimensions of the paper could be

(A) 17 in by 25 in
(B) 21 in by 24 in
(C) 24 in by 12 in
(D) 24 in by 14 in
(E) 26 in by 14 in

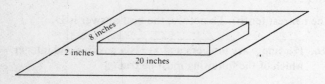

8 inches

2 inches

20 inches

Center the box on the sheet of paper, as shown in the figure above. To cover the box completely, the paper must be wide enough to span the 20-inch width and half of the 2-inch height on each side. Thus, the paper must be at least 22 inches wide. The paper must also be long enough to cover the 8-inch top and bottom and the 2-inch heights on each side. Thus, it must be at least 20 inches long. Therefore, the paper must be at least 20 inches by 22 inches. Note that of the options only 21 inches by 24 inches is bigger than 20 inches by 22 inches. Thus, the best answer is B.

18.
$$x - y = 3$$
$$2x = 2y + 6$$

The system of equations above has how many solutions?

(A) None
(B) Exactly one
(C) Exactly two
(D) Exactly three
(E) Infinitely many

$2x = 2y + 6$
$x = y + 3$ (divide by 2)

$x - y = 3$

Note that this equation is equivalent to the first equation. Therefore, any solution of the first equation is a solution of the second equation. $x - y = 3$ has infinitely many solutions. Therefore, the best answer is E.

19. If M and N are positive integers that have remainders of 1 and 3, respectively, when divided by 6, which of the following could NOT be a possible value of $M + N$?

(A) 86　(B) 52　(C) 34　(D) 28　(E) 10

M can be written as $6q + 1$ and N as $6r + 3$, where q and r are integers. Thus, $M + N = (6q + 1) + (6r + 3) = 6(q + r) + 4$, or $M + N$ has a remainder of 4 when divided by 6. The only option for which this is not true is 86. Thus, the best answer is A.

20. The R students in a class agree to contribute equally to buy their teacher a birthday present that costs y dollars. If x of the students later fail to contribute their share, which of the following represents the additional number of dollars that each of the remaining students must contribute in order to pay for the present?

(A) $\dfrac{y}{R}$

(B) $\dfrac{y}{R - x}$

(C) $\dfrac{xy}{R - x}$

(D) $\dfrac{xy}{R(R - x)}$

(E) $\dfrac{y}{R(R - x)}$

In order to contribute equally to the cost of the y dollar present, each of the R students must contribute $\dfrac{y}{R}$ dollars. The total contribution of the x students who failed to contribute is $x\left(\dfrac{y}{r}\right) = \dfrac{xy}{r}$ dollars, which is the additional amount the other $R - x$ students must contribute as a group. Thus, each of the remaining students must contribute an additional $\dfrac{\frac{xy}{R}}{R - x} = \dfrac{xy}{R(R - x)}$ dollars.

An alternative method for solving this problem is:

The additional amount each of the remaining $R - x$ students must contribute is equal to the difference between the amount they each need to contribute to share the y dollar cost of the present equally among themselves and the amount they each contributed, assuming that all R students would contribute, or

$$\dfrac{y}{R - x} - \dfrac{y}{R} = \dfrac{Ry - (R - x)y}{R(R - x)} = \dfrac{xy}{R(R - x)}.$$

Therefore, the best answer is D.

Scoring Information

How to Calculate Your Scores

Your Verbal Raw Score

Step 1:	Using the answer key, mark your answer sheet as follows: put a C next to each question that you answered correctly; put an I next to each question that you answered incorrectly. Cross out any questions that you did not answer or for which you marked more than one answer; these will not be counted in the scoring.	
Step 2:	Sections 1, 3, and 5 are used to determine your verbal score. In these sections only, count the number of correct answers (marked C) and enter this number here	_____
Step 3:	In these same sections (1, 3, and 5), count the number of questions that you answered incorrectly (marked I). Enter the number here	_____
Step 4:	Count the number of questions in sections 1, 3, and 5 that you crossed out because you did not answer them or marked more than one answer. Enter this number here.	_____
Step 5:	Add the numbers in Steps 2, 3, and 4. Enter the number here. . . . . (This number should be 70, the total number of verbal questions. If it is not, check your work for Steps 2, 3, and 4.)	_____
Step 6:	Enter the number from Step 2 here.	_____
Step 7:	Enter the number from Step 3 here $\dfrac{}{4}$; divide it by 4. (This is the correction for guessing.) Write the resulting number here	− _____
Step 8:	Subtract the number in Step 7 from the number in Step 6; enter the result here	_____
		+ _____.5_____
Step 9:	Add .5 to the number in Step 8. Enter the result here.	_____
Step 10:	Drop all the digits to the right of the decimal point and write the result here.	_____
This is your verbal raw score corrected for guessing. Instructions for converting this score to a scaled score are on page 414.		

Your Quantitative Raw Score

Step 1:	Sections 2, 4, and 6 are used to determine your quantitative score. In these sections only, count the number of correct answers (marked C) and enter this number here	_____
Step 2:	In these same sections (2, 4, and 6), count the number of questions that you answered incorrectly (marked I). Enter the number here	_____
Step 3:	Count the number of questions in sections 2, 4, and 6 that you crossed out because you did not answer them or marked more than one answer. Enter this number here.	_____
Step 4:	Add the numbers in Steps 1, 2, and 3. Enter the total here . . . . (This number should be 65, the total number of quantitative questions. If it is not, check your work for Steps 1, 2, and 3.)	_____
Step 5:	Enter the number from Step 1 here.	_____
Step 6:	Enter the number from Step 2 here _____ ; divide it by 4. (This is the correction for guessing.) Write the resulting number here	− _____
Step 7:	Subtract the number in Step 6 from the number in Step 5; enter the result here	_____
		+ _____.5
Step 8:	Add .5 to the number in Step 7. Enter the result here.	_____
Step 9:	Drop all the digits to the right of the decimal point and write the result here.	_____

This is your quantitative raw score corrected for guessing. Instructions for converting this score to a scaled score are on page 414.

Your Total Raw Score

Step 1:	Using all the sections of the test, count the number of correct answers (marked C) and enter this number here.	_____
Step 2:	Count the number of questions in all the sections that you answered incorrectly (marked I). Enter the number here.	_____
Step 3:	Count the number of questions in all sections that you crossed out because you did not answer them or marked more than one answer. Enter this number here.	_____
Step 4:	Add the numbers in Steps 1, 2, and 3. Enter the total here . . . . (This number should be 135, the total number of questions in the test. If it is not, check your work for Steps 1, 2, and 3.)	_____
Step 5:	Enter the number from Step 1 here.	_____
Step 6:	Enter the number from Step 2 here_____; divide it by 4. (This is the correction for guessing.) Write the resulting number here	− _____
Step 7:	Subtract the number in Step 6 from the number in Step 5; enter the result here	_____
Step 8:	Add .5 to the number in Step 7. Enter the result here.	+ _____.5_____
Step 9:	Drop all the digits to the right of the decimal point and write the result here.	_____
	This is your total raw score corrected for guessing. It is possible that the sum of your verbal and quantitative raw scores may be one point higher or lower than the total raw score due to the rounding procedures for each score. Instructions for converting this score—along with your verbal and quantitative raw scores corrected for guessing—to scaled scores follow.	

Converting Your Raw Scores to Scaled Scores

The raw scores corrected for guessing that you have obtained (last step in each worksheet) may be converted to scaled scores using the conversion tables on the following pages. Raw scores are converted to scaled scores to ensure that a score earned on any one form of the GMAT is directly comparable to the same scaled score earned (within a five-year period) on any other form of the test. Scaled scores are "standard scores" with understood and accepted meanings. The scores reported to schools when you take the actual GMAT will be scaled scores.

Using the conversion tables, find the GMAT scaled scores that correspond to your three raw scores (verbal, quantitative, total), corrected for guessing. For example, a verbal raw score of 44 would correspond to a scaled score of 34; a quantitative raw score of 44 would correspond to a scaled score of 39. A total raw score of 88 would correspond to a scaled score of 600.

When you take the GMAT at an actual administration, one or more of your scores will probably differ from the scaled scores you obtained on this representative GMAT test. Even the same student performs at different levels at different times—for a variety of reasons unrelated to the test itself. In addition, your test scores may differ because the conditions under which you took this test could not be exactly the same as those at an actual test administration.

After you have scored your test, analyze the results with a view to improving your performance when you take the actual GMAT.

■ Did the time you spent reading directions make serious inroads on the time you had available for answering questions? If you become thoroughly familiar with the directions given in this book (in Chapter 1, Chapters 3-7, and the representative test), you may need to spend less time reading directions in the actual test.

■ Did you run out of time before you reached the end of a section? If so, could you pace yourself better in the actual test? Remember, not everyone finishes all sections; accuracy is also important.

■ Look at the specific questions you missed. In which ones did you suffer from lack of knowledge? Faulty reasoning? Faulty reading of the questions? Being aware of the causes of your errors may enable you to avoid some errors when you actually take the GMAT.

What Your Scaled Scores Mean

The tables on page 417 contain information that will be of help in understanding your scaled scores. Each table consists of a column marked "Scaled Scores" and a column indicating the percentages of test takers in the time period specified who scored below the scores listed. For example, if you earned a total scaled score of about 600 on the representa-

tive test and you are able to achieve the same score on an actual GMAT, the 85 opposite 600 tells you that 85 percent of the 616,018 people taking the test in the 1985 to 1988 period earned scores lower than that; the remainder earned the same or a higher score. Also given in each table is the average score of the group tested in the 1985-1988 time period.

Graduate school admissions officers understand the statistical meaning of GMAT scores, but each institution uses and interprets the scores according to the needs of its own programs. You should, therefore, consult the schools to which you are applying to learn how they will interpret and use your scores.

Some Cautions about Score Interpretation

1. The GMAT is designed to yield only the reported verbal, quantitative, and total scaled scores. One should not calculate raw scores for individual test sections and infer specific strengths or weaknesses from a comparison of the raw score results by section. There are two reasons for this.

   First, different sections have different numbers of questions and, even if the numbers were the same or if percentages were used to make the numbers comparable, the sections might not be equally difficult. For illustrative purposes only, suppose that one section had 20 items and another had 25. Furthermore, suppose you received a corrected raw score of 10 on the first and 10 on the second. It would be inappropriate to conclude that you had equal ability in the two sections because the corrected raw scores were equal, as you really obtained 50 percent on the first section and only 40 percent on the second. It could be equally inappropriate, however, to conclude from the percentages that you were better on the first section than on the second. Suppose the first section was relatively easy for most candidates (say, an average corrected raw score percentage across candidates of 55 percent) and the second was relatively difficult (an average corrected raw score percentage of 35 percent). Now you might conclude that you were worse than average on the first section and better than average on the second.

   Differences in difficulty level between editions are accounted for in the procedure for converting the verbal, quantitative, and total corrected raw scores to scaled scores. Since the raw scores for individual sections are not converted to produce scaled scores by section, performance on individual sections of the test cannot be compared.

   Second, corrected raw scores by section are not converted to scaled scores by section because the GMAT is not designed to reliably measure specific strengths and weaknesses beyond the general verbal and quantitative abilities for which separate scaled scores are reported. Reliability is dependent, in part, on the number of questions in the test—the more questions, the higher the reliability. The relatively few questions in each section, taken alone, are not sufficient to produce a reliable result for each section. Only the reported verbal, quantitative, and total scaled scores (which include questions across several sections) have sufficient reliability to permit their use in counseling and predicting graduate school performance.

2. It is possible, if you repeat the test, that your second raw scores corrected for guessing could be higher than on the first test, but your scaled scores could be lower and vice versa. This is a result of the slight differences in difficulty level between editions of the test, which are taken into account when corrected raw scores are converted to the GMAT scaled scores. That is, for a given scaled score, a more difficult edition requires a lower corrected raw score and an easier edition requires a higher corrected raw score.

Conversion Table for Verbal and Quantitative Scores
Graduate Management Admission Test

Corrected Raw Score	Verbal	Quantitative	Corrected Raw Score	Verbal	Quantitative	Corrected Raw Score	Verbal	Quantitative
70	51		45	35	40	20	19	23
69	50		44	34	39	19	19	22
68	49		43	34	38	18	18	21
67	49		42	33	38	17	17	21
66	48		41	32	37	16	17	20
65	47	53	40	32	36	15	16	19
64	47	52	39	31	36	14	16	19
63	46	52	38	31	35	13	15	18
62	46	51	37	30	34	12	14	17
61	45	50	36	29	34	11	14	17
60	44	50	35	29	33	10	13	16
59	44	49	34	28	32	9	12	15
58	43	48	33	27	32	8	12	15
57	42	48	32	27	31	7	11	14
56	42	47	31	26	30	6	10	13
55	41	46	30	26	30	5	10	13
54	41	46	29	25	29	4	9	12
53	40	45	28	24	28	3	9	11
52	39	44	27	24	27	2	8	11
51	39	44	26	23	27	1	7	10
50	38	43	25	22	26	0	7	9
49	37	42	24	22	25			
48	37	42	23	21	25			
47	36	41	22	21	24			
46	36	40	21	20	23			

Corrected Raw Score	Total Scaled Score	Corrected Raw Score	Total Scaled Score	Corrected Raw Score	Total Scaled Score	Corrected Raw Score	Total Scaled Score	Corrected Raw Score	Total Scaled Score
		105	670	75	540	45	410	15	280
		104	670	74	540	44	410	14	280
133 and up	800	103	670	73	530	43	400	13	270
132	790	102	660	72	530	42	400	12	270
131	790	101	660	71	520	41	390	11	260
130	780	100	650	70	520	40	390	10	260
129	780	99	650	69	520	39	380	9	250
128	770	98	640	68	510	38	380	8	250
127	770	97	640	67	510	37	380	7	240
126	770	96	630	66	500	36	370	6	240
125	760	95	630	65	500	35	370	5	240
124	760	94	630	64	490	34	360	4	230
123	750	93	620	63	490	33	360	3	230
122	750	92	620	62	490	32	350	2	220
121	740	91	610	61	480	31	350	1	210
120	740	90	610	60	480	30	350	0	200
119	740	89	600	59	470	29	340		
118	730	88	600	58	470	28	340		
117	730	87	600	57	460	27	330		
116	720	86	590	56	460	26	330		
115	720	85	590	55	450	25	320		
114	710	84	580	54	450	24	320		
113	710	83	580	53	450	23	310		
112	700	82	570	52	440	22	310		
111	700	81	570	51	440	21	310		
110	700	80	560	50	430	20	300		
109	690	79	560	49	430	19	300		
108	690	78	560	48	420	18	290		
107	680	77	550	47	420	17	290		
106	680	76	550	46	420	16	280		

Test Content

If you have questions about specific items in the representative test or in any of the sample test sections included in Chapters 3-7, please write to School and Higher Education Test Development, Educational Testing Service, P.O. Box 6656, Princeton, NJ 08541-6656. Please include in your letter the page number on which the item appears and the number of the question, along with specifics of your inquiry or comment. If you have a question about a particular item or items in an actual GMAT, please write to the same address and include in your letter your name, address, sex, date of birth, the date on which you took the test, the test center name, the section number(s) and number(s) of the questions involved. This information is necessary for ETS to retrieve your answer sheet and determine the particular form of the GMAT you took.

Percentages of Examinees Tested from June 1985 through March 1988 (Including Repeaters) Who Scored Below Selected Total Scores	
Scaled Scores	**Percentage Below**
740	>99
720	99
700	98
680	97
660	95
640	92
620	89
600	85
580	80
560	73
540	67
520	60
500	52
480	45
460	38
440	31
420	25
400	20
380	15
360	11
340	8
320	5
300	4
280	2
260	1
240	1
220	0
Number of Examinees	616,018*
Mean	486
Standard Deviation	104

*Self-selected sample

Percentages of Examinees Tested from June 1985 through March 1988 (Including Repeaters) Who Scored Below Selected Verbal and Quantitative Scores			
		Percentages Below	
Scaled Scores		**Verbal**	**Quantitative**
50		>99	>99
48		>99	99
46		99	97
44		98	94
42		95	91
40		92	86
38		87	81
36		81	74
34		74	67
32		67	59
30		58	50
28		50	42
26		42	33
24		33	26
22		26	19
20		20	13
18		14	9
16		10	5
14		7	3
12		4	1
10		2	1
8		1	0
6		0	0
Number of Examinees		616,018*	616,018*
Mean		27	29
Standard Deviation		9	9

*Self-selected sample

Guidelines for Use of Graduate Management Admission Test Scores

Introduction

These guidelines have been prepared to provide information about appropriate score use for those who interpret scores and set criteria for admission and to protect students from unfair decisions based on inappropriate use of scores.

The guidelines are based on several policy and psychometric considerations.

- The Graduate Management Admission Council has an obligation to inform users of the scores' strengths and limitations and the users have a concomitant obligation to use the scores in an appropriate, rather than the most convenient, manner.

- The purpose of any testing instrument, including the Graduate Management Admission Test, is to provide information to *assist* in making decisions; the test alone should not be presumed to be a decision maker.

- GMAT test scores are but one of a number of sources of information and should be used, whenever possible, in combination with other information and, in every case, with full recognition of what the test can and cannot do.

The primary asset of the GMAT is that it provides a common measure, administered under standard conditions, with known reliability, validity, and other psychometric qualities, for evaluating the academic skills of many individuals. The GMAT has two primary limitations: (1) it cannot and does not measure all the qualities important for graduate study in management and other pursuits, whether in education, career, or other areas of experience; (2) there are psychometric limitations to the test —for example, only score differences of certain magnitudes are reliable indicators of real differences in performance. Such limits should be taken into consideration as GMAT scores are used.

These guidelines consist of general standards and recommended appropriate uses of GMAT scores as well as a listing of inappropriate uses.

Specific Guidelines

1. **In recognition of the test's limitations, use multiple criteria.** Multiple sources of information should be used when evaluating an applicant for graduate management study. The GMAT itself does not measure every discipline-related skill necessary for academic work, nor does it measure subjective factors important to academic and career success, such as motivation, creativity, and interpersonal skills. Therefore, all available pertinent information about an applicant must be considered before a selection decision is made, with GMAT scores being *only one* of these several criteria. The test's limitations are discussed clearly in the GMAT *Bulletin of Information* and in the *GMAT Technical Report*.

2. **Establish the relationship between GMAT scores and performance in your graduate management school.** It is incumbent on any institution using GMAT scores in the admissions process that it demonstrate empirically the relationship between test scores and measures of performance in its academic program. Data should be collected and analyzed to provide information about the predictive validity of GMAT scores and their appropriateness for the particular use and in the particular circumstances at the score-using school. In addition, any formula used in the admissions process that combines test scores with other criteria should be validated to determine whether the weights attached to the particular measures are appropriate for optimizing the prediction of performance in the program. Once set, these weights should be reviewed regularly through the considered deliberation of qualified experts.

3. **Avoid the use of cutoff scores.** The use of arbitrary cutoff scores (below which no applicant will be considered for admission) is strongly discouraged, primarily for the reasons cited in the introduction to these guidelines. Distinctions based on score differences not substantial enough to be reliable should be avoided. (For information about reliability, see the GMAT *Examinee Score Interpretation Guide*.) Cutoff scores should be used only if there is clear empirical evidence that a large proportion of the applicants scoring below the cutoff scores have substantial difficulty doing satisfactory graduate work. In addition, it is incumbent on the school to demonstrate that the use of cutoff scores does not result in the systematic exclusion of members of either sex, of any age or ethnic groups, or of any other relevant groups in the face of other evidence that would indicate their competence or predict their success.

4. **Do not compare GMAT scores with those on other tests.** GMAT scores cannot be derived from scores on other tests. While minor differences among different editions of the GMAT that have been constructed to be parallel can be compensated for by the statistical process of score equating, the GMAT is not intended to be parallel to graduate admission tests offered by other testing programs.

5. **Interpret the scores of disabled persons cautiously.** The GMAT is offered with special arrangements to accommodate the needs of candidates with visual, physical, and learning disabilities. However, no studies have been performed to validate GMAT scores earned under nonstandard conditions. Therefore, test scores earned under nonstandard conditions are reported with a special notice that disabled persons may be at a disadvantage when taking standardized tests such as the GMAT, even when the test is administered in a manner chosen by the candidate to minimize any adverse effect of his or her disability on test performance. In using these scores, admissions officers should note the usual caution that GMAT scores be considered as only one part of an applicant's record.

Normally Appropriate Uses of GMAT Scores

1. **For selection of applicants for graduate study in management.** A person's GMAT scores tell how the person performed on a test designed to measure general verbal and quantitative abilities that are associated with success in the first year of study at graduate schools of management and that have been developed over a long period of time. The scores can be used in conjunction with other information to help estimate performance in a graduate management program.

2. **For selection of applicants for financial aid based on academic potential.**

3. **For counseling and guidance.** Undergraduate counselors, if they maintain appropriate records, such as the test scores and undergraduate grade-point averages of their students accepted by various graduate management programs, may be able to help students estimate their chances of acceptance at given graduate management schools.

Normally Inappropriate Uses of GMAT Scores

1. **As a requisite for awarding a degree.** The GMAT is designed to measure broadly defined verbal and quantitative skills and is primarily useful for predicting success in graduate management schools. The use of the test for anything other than selection for graduate management study, financial aid awards, or counseling and guidance is to be avoided.

2. **As a requirement for employment, for licensing or certification to perform a job, or for job-related rewards (raises, promotions, etc.).** For the reasons listed in #1 above, the use of the GMAT for these purposes is inappropriate. Further, approved score-receiving institutions are not permitted to make score reports available for any of these purposes.

3. **As an achievement test.** The GMAT is not designed to assess an applicant's achievement or knowledge in specific subject areas.

4. **As a diagnostic test.** Beyond general statements about verbal and quantitative ability, the GMAT does not provide diagnostic information about relative strengths of a person's academic abilities.

Order Form for Official GMAC Publications

My payment is enclosed for (check appropriate box):

		U.S. Delivery*	Foreign Delivery**
The Official Guide for GMAT Review	#238405	☐ $ 9.95	☐ $21.95
The Official Guide to MBA Programs	#238324	☐ $12.95	☐ $24.95
Both Guides	#238406	☐ $18.00	☐ $34.00
The Official Software for GMAT Review† (including The Official Guide for GMAT Review)	#299603	☐ $59.95	☐ $75.00
The Official Software for GMAT Review† (including The Official Guide for GMAT Review) with The Official Guide to MBA Programs	#299622	☐ $68.00	☐ $88.00

*Priority delivery to United States, Guam, Puerto Rico, U.S. Virgin Islands, and U.S. territories
**Airmail delivery to Canada and all countries and areas other than those named above

Reminder: If you order any of the above *Guides* when registering for the GMAT, be sure to enter the amount of your payment in item 32 of the registration form.

†*IMPORTANT: See hardware requirements on reverse side.*

This is your mailing label. Type or print clearly.

TO

GRADUATE MANAGEMENT ADMISSION TEST
EDUCATIONAL TESTING SERVICE
P.O. BOX 6108
PRINCETON, NJ 08541-6108

692-38
GMAC
GUIDES
G-96

Order Form for Official GMAC Publications

My payment is enclosed for (check appropriate box):

		U.S. Delivery*	Foreign Delivery**
The Official Guide for GMAT Review	#238405	☐ $ 9.95	☐ $21.95
The Official Guide to MBA Programs	#238324	☐ $12.95	☐ $24.95
Both Guides	#238406	☐ $18.00	☐ $34.00
The Official Software for GMAT Review† (including The Official Guide for GMAT Review)	#299603	☐ $59.95	☐ $75.00
The Official Software for GMAT Review† (including The Official Guide for GMAT Review) with The Official Guide to MBA Programs	#299622	☐ $68.00	☐ $88.00

*Priority delivery to United States, Guam, Puerto Rico, U.S. Virgin Islands, and U.S. territories
**Airmail delivery to Canada and all countries and areas other than those named above

Reminder: If you order any of the above *Guides* when registering for the GMAT, be sure to enter the amount of your payment in item 32 of the registration form.

†*IMPORTANT: See hardware requirements on reverse side.*

This is your mailing label. Type or print clearly.

TO

GRADUATE MANAGEMENT ADMISSION TEST
EDUCATIONAL TESTING SERVICE
P.O. BOX 6108
PRINCETON, NJ 08541-6108

692-38
GMAC
GUIDES
G-96

Order Form for Official GMAC Publications

My payment is enclosed for (check appropriate box):

		U.S. Delivery*	Foreign Delivery**
The Official Guide for GMAT Review	#238405	☐ $ 9.95	☐ $21.95
The Official Guide to MBA Programs	#238324	☐ $12.95	☐ $24.95
Both Guides	#238406	☐ $18.00	☐ $34.00
The Official Software for GMAT Review† (including The Official Guide for GMAT Review)	#299603	☐ $59.95	☐ $75.00
The Official Software for GMAT Review† (including The Official Guide for GMAT Review) with The Official Guide to MBA Programs	#299622	☐ $68.00	☐ $88.00

*Priority delivery to United States, Guam, Puerto Rico, U.S. Virgin Islands, and U.S. territories
**Airmail delivery to Canada and all countries and areas other than those named above

Reminder: If you order any of the above *Guides* when registering for the GMAT, be sure to enter the amount of your payment in item 32 of the registration form.

†*IMPORTANT: See hardware requirements on reverse side.*

This is your mailing label. Type or print clearly.

TO

GRADUATE MANAGEMENT ADMISSION TEST
EDUCATIONAL TESTING SERVICE
P.O. BOX 6108
PRINCETON, NJ 08541-6108

692-38
GMAC
GUIDES
G-96

Three Publications from the Graduate Management Admission Council...

The Official Guide for GMAT Review, 1990-92 Edition, features:

- more than 700 test questions with answers and explanations and test-taking strategies
- a comprehensive math review chapter
- an authentic GMAT test with answer key and scoring instructions

The Official Software for GMAT Review, 1990-92 Edition, offers:

- an automated version of the questions and answers in the *GMAT Review* book with on-screen timer and automatic scoring
- a copy of *The Official Guide for GMAT Review*, a user's manual, and two sets of software disks (3½" and 5¼")
- Hardware requirements are:
  IBM PC, XT, AT, PS/2, or 100% compatible computer with two disk drives (3½" or 5¼") or one disk drive and a hard disk with at least 2.0 megabytes of free space; 256K; DOS 2.0 through 4.0; CGA, EGA, VGA, Hercules Graphics or 100% compatible adapter card and monitor. A printer is optional.

The Official Guide to MBA Programs, 1990-92 Edition, includes:

- descriptions of more than 550 graduate management programs prepared by the schools themselves
- an introductory section discussing management programs, the application process, financial aid, and career opportunities
- information request cards to send to schools of your choice

How to Order

Both *The Official Guide for GMAT Review* and *The Official Guide to MBA Programs* are sold in many bookstores or can be ordered by mail from ETS. *The Official Software for GMAT Review* is available only through mail order. Fill out the order form and mailing label on the reverse side and send it with the appropriate payment to ETS, either with your GMAT registration form or in a separate envelope addressed to Graduate Management Admission Test, Educational Testing Service, P.O. Box 6108, Princeton, NJ 08541-6108.

All book orders to be sent to addresses in the United States or U.S. territories will be shipped by priority mail (first class) at no additional charge. Because software packages are sent via UPS, a *street address* is required. UPS will *not* deliver to a P.O. box number. Please allow three to four weeks from order receipt for delivery to U.S. addresses. For delivery to other countries, please allow six to eight weeks from time of order receipt.

Three Publications from the Graduate Management Admission Council...

The Official Guide for GMAT Review, 1990-92 Edition, features:

- more than 700 test questions with answers and explanations and test-taking strategies
- a comprehensive math review chapter
- an authentic GMAT test with answer key and scoring instructions

The Official Software for GMAT Review, 1990-92 Edition, offers:

- an automated version of the questions and answers in the *GMAT Review* book with on-screen timer and automatic scoring
- a copy of *The Official Guide for GMAT Review*, a user's manual, and two sets of software disks (3½" and 5¼")
- Hardware requirements are:
  IBM PC, XT, AT, PS/2, or 100% compatible computer with two disk drives (3½" or 5¼") or one disk drive and a hard disk with at least 2.0 megabytes of free space; 256K; DOS 2.0 through 4.0; CGA, EGA, VGA, Hercules Graphics or 100% compatible adapter card and monitor. A printer is optional.

The Official Guide to MBA Programs, 1990-92 Edition, includes:

- descriptions of more than 550 graduate management programs prepared by the schools themselves
- an introductory section discussing management programs, the application process, financial aid, and career opportunities
- information request cards to send to schools of your choice

How to Order

Both *The Official Guide for GMAT Review* and *The Official Guide to MBA Programs* are sold in many bookstores or can be ordered by mail from ETS. *The Official Software for GMAT Review* is available only through mail order. Fill out the order form and mailing label on the reverse side and send it with the appropriate payment to ETS, either with your GMAT registration form or in a separate envelope addressed to Graduate Management Admission Test, Educational Testing Service, P.O. Box 6108, Princeton, NJ 08541-6108.

All book orders to be sent to addresses in the United States or U.S. territories will be shipped by priority mail (first class) at no additional charge. Because software packages are sent via UPS, a *street address* is required. UPS will *not* deliver to a P.O. box number. Please allow three to four weeks from order receipt for delivery to U.S. addresses. For delivery to other countries, please allow six to eight weeks from time of order receipt.

Three Publications from the Graduate Management Admission Council...

The Official Guide for GMAT Review, 1990-92 Edition, features:

- more than 700 test questions with answers and explanations and test-taking strategies
- a comprehensive math review chapter
- an authentic GMAT test with answer key and scoring instructions

The Official Software for GMAT Review, 1990-92 Edition, offers:

- an automated version of the questions and answers in the *GMAT Review* book with on-screen timer and automatic scoring
- a copy of *The Official Guide for GMAT Review*, a user's manual, and two sets of software disks (3½" and 5¼")
- Hardware requirements are:
  IBM PC, XT, AT, PS/2, or 100% compatible computer with two disk drives (3½" or 5¼") or one disk drive and a hard disk with at least 2.0 megabytes of free space; 256K; DOS 2.0 through 4.0; CGA, EGA, VGA, Hercules Graphics or 100% compatible adapter card and monitor. A printer is optional.

The Official Guide to MBA Programs, 1990-92 Edition, includes:

- descriptions of more than 550 graduate management programs prepared by the schools themselves
- an introductory section discussing management programs, the application process, financial aid, and career opportunities
- information request cards to send to schools of your choice

How to Order

Both *The Official Guide for GMAT Review* and *The Official Guide to MBA Programs* are sold in many bookstores or can be ordered by mail from ETS. *The Official Software for GMAT Review* is available only through mail order. Fill out the order form and mailing label on the reverse side and send it with the appropriate payment to ETS, either with your GMAT registration form or in a separate envelope addressed to Graduate Management Admission Test, Educational Testing Service, P.O. Box 6108, Princeton, NJ 08541-6108.

All book orders to be sent to addresses in the United States or U.S. territories will be shipped by priority mail (first class) at no additional charge. Because software packages are sent via UPS, a *street address* is required. UPS will *not* deliver to a P.O. box number. Please allow three to four weeks from order receipt for delivery to U.S. addresses. For delivery to other countries, please allow six to eight weeks from time of order receipt.